Dreamweaver 4:
The Complete Reference

About the Author

Jennifer Kettell has contributed to six books on Web design theory and applications, including *Special Edition Using HTML* 4, 5th and 6th Editions, by Molly E. Holzschlag. Jennifer first got online in 1984 on BITNET while earning her B.A. in Psychology at Boston University. She has over 11 years of experience building online communities, working for such online services as Genie, Delphi, and MSN in both community manager and product management roles. She has also designed dozens of Web sites for various commercial and non-profit entities.

Jenn lives with her husband, two children, a dog, a cat, and two dwarf hamsters in Arizona. She spends most of her free time trying to keep cool. You can visit her Web site at http://www.pendragn.com.

Dreamweaver 4:
The Complete Reference

Jennifer Ackerman Kettell

Osborne/**McGraw-Hill**
New York Chicago San Francisco
Lisbon London Madrid Mexico City
Milan New Delhi San Juan
Seoul Singapore Sydney Toronto

Osborne/**McGraw-Hill**
2600 Tenth Street
Berkeley, California 94710
U.S.A.

To arrange bulk purchase discounts for sales promotions, premiums, or fund-raisers, please contact Osborne/**McGraw-Hill** at the above address. For information on translations or book distributors outside the U.S.A., please see the International Contact Information page immediately following the index of this book.

Dreamweaver 4: The Complete Reference

1234567890 CUS CUS 01987654321

ISBN 0-07-213171-3

Publisher
Brandon A. Nordin

Vice President & Associate Publisher
Scott Rogers

Acquisitions Editor
Megg Bonar

Project Editor
Monika Faltiss

Acquisitions Coordinator
Alissa Larson

Technical Editor
Michael Raucci

Copy Editor
Marcia Baker

Proofreader
John Gildersleeve

Indexer
Jack Lewis

Computer Designers
Kelly Stanton-Scott, Carie Abrew, Elizabeth Jang

Illustrators
Beth E. Young, Michael Mueller, Lyssa Sieben-Wald

Series Design
Peter F. Hancik

This book was composed with Corel VENTURA™ Publisher.

In memory of my father, Leon Ackerman,
the philosopher/poet/electrician
who believed even when I doubted. I miss you.

And to my children, Amanda and Zachary, for everything.

Contents at a Glance

Contents

Part II

Building Your Web Site

Part III

Building Your Site's Pages

Beyond the Basics

Part V

Advanced Web Programming

21 JavaScript 481

22 Applets, Plug-ins, and Other Embedded Programs ... 501

Part VI

Enhancing Pages With Multimedia

Part VII

Dreamweaver Tools

Part VIII

Customizing Dreamweaver

Part IX

Dreamweaver into the Next Generation

Part X

Dreamweaver and Fireworks

Part XI

Appendixes

Acknowledgments

I am grateful and honored to have had the help and support of so many people. The Macromedia team—particularly Eric Ott, Heidi Bauer, John Dowdell, and Joe Marini—provided technical expertise and the answers to numerous questions at all hours of the day and night.

My editor, Megg Bonar, kept the faith through hardships great and small. Alissa Larson kept things on track. Monika Faltiss made sure I laughed my way through copy edits and proofs. Marcia Baker caught all the undotted i's and uncrossed t's. And Michael Raucci helped find the technical glitches.

My agent, David Fugate, offered support, wisdom, and humor throughout this project.

Joyce Evans wrote the chapters on images and Fireworks. Greg Kettell and Kacey Pickens also lent their writing and research talents. They can't be thanked enough.

Laura Phillips and Malia Martin graciously let me show off their work.

Molly Holzschlag is a true friend, mentor, and voice of reason in times of chaos. Jody McFadden is able to pick up a conversation exactly where we left off—even if it's three months later.

The RMLAC team—especially Jenn Naranjo, Robin Robinson, Leana Villarreal, Annette Esclavon, Heydi Peralta, and Nancy Arjara—asked dozens of questions about Dreamweaver that helped make this a better book. I am also grateful to them, the

Goalies, and Julie Hurwitz for their friendship, support, and all the little things that get taken for granted.

Finally, and most importantly, thanks to my children, Amanda and Zachary. They have made numerous sacrifices so I could write this book, and I couldn't have done it without them. And to my mother, Roberta Ackerman, for going above and beyond the roles of mom and grandmother.

My love to you all.
Jenn

Introduction

There are almost as many approaches to Web design and development as there are sites. The early Web "pioneers" did their coding in a text editor. Many still do today. But as HTML has evolved, so have the tools that are available to help Web developers create eye-popping sites in a fraction of the time. Dreamweaver 4 is the latest version of one of the most powerful of these tools. Providing a unique mix of time-saving visual tools and ready access to the underlying code, Dreamweaver appeals to developers of all skill levels. Its integration with Fireworks, a powerful graphics application, creates a sort of one-stop-shopping environment.

Of course, as is the way with software, any application this powerful certainly reaches beyond the scope of the manual provided with it. *Dreamweaver 4: The Complete Reference* attempts to bridge this gap between the bare bones of the manual and the full potential of the application.

About This Book

Dreamweaver 4: The Complete Reference is a guide to both the novice and advanced features of Dreamweaver and Fireworks. You'll become familiar with the application's interface, then move on to planning, creating, and maintaining a site. Because so many

Web designers are seeking introductory or continuing insight into site planning and the workflow of a project, some of that material is also included, for good measure. After you've mastered the basics, you'll learn about how to incorporate non-HTML elements such as JavaScripts, multimedia, databases, and e-commerce solutions into your sites.

How This Book Is Organized

Dreamweaver 4: The Complete Reference takes you through the stages of learning the application and developing a Web site. First, you'll learn about the Dreamweaver interface and how to set your work environment preferences. Then you'll explore how to plan and create a site. You'll learn how to add basic text, images, and layout features to the site's pages. Once you've mastered the basics, you'll be ready to add image maps, dynamic HTML, multimedia, JavaScripts, and other advanced features. You'll finish up with a look at how to customize Dreamweaver to meet your specific needs and how to use Dreamweaver with XML, databases, and e-commerce solutions. Finally, the Fireworks chapters will provide the basics on how to use that powerful graphics tool and integrate it with Dreamweaver.

Conventions Used In This Book

The following conventions are used in *Dreamweaver 4: The Complete Reference* in order to make it easier for you to follow the text and instructions:

Italic type signifies a new term or phrase.

SMALL CAPITAL LETTERS are used for keys to press on the keyboard, such as CTRL-F5. In this example, you would press the F5 key while holding down the CTRL (CONTROL) key. Where differences exist between key presses for the PC and Mac versions of Dreamweaver, these differences are noted.

`Courier` type is used for HTML code examples, whether entered manually or generated by Dreamweaver.

Menu selections are separated with a pipe (|) symbol, such as Text | List | Properties. In this example, click on the Text menu in Dreamweaver, then choose List from that menu, then choose Properties from the List sub-menu.

The Complete Reference

Part I

Dreamweaver Basics

The
Complete
Reference

Chapter 1

Introducing Dreamweaver

Dreamweaver is truly a Web developer's dream, which makes the mundane and repetitive tasks of hand-coding easier, while still allowing complete control over the code. It takes advantage of the latest Web technology and HTML standards while providing backward-compatibility for older browsers. Most importantly, because Dreamweaver was designed by professional Web developers, it accommodates a designer's work flow. Whether you are making updates to a single page or designing an entire Web site from scratch, Dreamweaver can help you speedily see your project to completion.

Even if you are new to the world of Web design, Dreamweaver enables you to add rollovers, JavaScript code, and forms with ease, adding immediate sophistication to your site. Experienced developers appreciate Dreamweaver's respect for their coding skills; Dreamweaver's Roundtrip HTML ensures that any code you provide by hand or import from another source remains intact—unless you ask the software to validate that code. Finally, Dreamweaver is customizable, enabling developers of all experience levels to add custom-designed or prepackaged objects, commands, and menus to create a unique work environment suited to your own unique style.

The best way to get started with Dreamweaver—whether you are a novice or an expert—is to install it and jump right into an exploration of its features. This chapter can help you install the software and point out some of the key features you'll want to discover.

Getting Started

Dreamweaver 4: The Complete Reference is intended to be read while sitting at your computer, so you can use the tricks and tips within the book firsthand. Using the software and working through the examples can help you become familiar with the tools in a way that reading alone cannot offer.

To this end, you need a copy of Dreamweaver 4 to get the full value of this book. If you don't already own a copy of Dreamweaver 4, a 30-day trial is available on the Macromedia Web site at **http://www.macromedia.com**.

Installing Dreamweaver

Dreamweaver 4 runs on both the Windows and Macintosh platforms. You need the following hardware to install Dreamweaver 4 on your computer:

Microsoft Windows installation requirements

- Intel Pentium processor, 150 MHz or equivalent
- Windows 95/98/2000, Windows ME, or Windows NT version 4.0 or later (with Service Pack 5 or later)
- 32MB of RAM
- 30MB available hard disk space

- Color monitor capable of 800 × 600 resolution
- CD-ROM drive

Macintosh installation requirements

- Power Macintosh running Mac OS 8.6 or later
- QuickTime 3.0 or later
- MRJ 2.2 (Mac OS Run time for Java)
- 32MB of RAM
- 30MB available hard disk space
- Color monitor capable of 800 × 600 resolution
- CD-ROM drive

You also need to have a Web browser. To test advanced Web features, you should have the most current version of your preferred browser installed on your computer. At a minimum, you should have the 4.0 version of either Microsoft Internet Explorer or Netscape Navigator.

Note *These are the minimum requirements for installing and using Dreamweaver 4. A faster processor and additional RAM increases performance considerably and enables you to run both Dreamweaver and your browser concurrently, which facilitates easier testing of your pages. A high-end graphics card allows better screen resolution, giving you more real estate for the document window and various panels. Current versions of Web browsers use more of the latest HTML standards.*

To install Dreamweaver from the CD:

1. Insert the Dreamweaver CD into the CD-ROM drive.
2. Depending on your computer platform:

   - In Windows, choose Start | Run. Click Browse and choose the Setup.exe file on the Dreamweaver CD. Click OK in the Run dialog box to begin the installation.
   - On the Macintosh, double-click the Dreamweaver Installer icon.
3. Follow the onscreen instructions, which includes entering your serial number (found on the registration cards that came with your software) when prompted.

If you downloaded the Dreamweaver 30-day trial from the Web site:

1. Locate the downloaded file on your hard disk.
2. Double-click the file to begin the installation process.
3. Follow the onscreen instructions.

During the installation process, Dreamweaver prompts you to decide if you want to establish the program as your default HTML, JavaScript, and Cascading Style Sheet editor. If you're committed to using Dreamweaver as your primary Web development tool, making Dreamweaver your default editor enables you to launch a file in Dreamweaver directly from a folder or your desktop. If you use various development tools to edit your HTML, JavaScript, and style sheets, you can opt out of giving Dreamweaver this control.

Dreamweaver Features

If this is your first time using Dreamweaver, you can look forward to several features not found in other development environments. Each of these features is explained in depth throughout this book. If you're already familiar with previous versions of Dreamweaver, you may want to skip to the section, "New in Dreamweaver 4."

Dreamweaver's Key Features

Web developers generally come in two forms: coders and designers. Coders are used to handling code and like to stay in control of how their sites are developed. Designers work visually and are concerned with the integrity of their site to their initial vision. Dreamweaver meets the needs of both developers, combining an HTML text editor and a visual editor into one interface (see Figure 1-1).

The WYSIWYG visual editor, known in Dreamweaver as *Design view*, enables designers to add such initially daunting elements as frames and tables without having to know one line of HTML code. The WYSIWYG view also enables even the best hand-coders to add tables and layers quickly.

WYSIWYG stands for *What You See Is What You Get*. While this is a lofty ideal, most visual HTML editors fall short of this claim. In some cases, this is true even of Dreamweaver. Where Dreamweaver has the advantage, however, is its Roundtrip HTML.

Roundtrip HTML

Dreamweaver has won critical acclaim and become the professional Web designer's tool of choice, primarily because of roundtrip HTML. *Roundtrip HTML* keeps intact any code you write yourself or import from another source. If you ever tried to import code into other WYSIWYG editors, you've seen how much the resulting code can differ from what you imported. These changes usually show up in the way of extra returns, extraneous <font> tags and nonbreaking spaces, and reformatting code into uppercase tags and removing indents. Sometimes, the code changes can even corrupt the integrity of your design by adding attributes, such as table-width constraints that cause the scalable table you envisioned to become fixed in width. In short, it's a mess.

Dreamweaver respects your prowess as a Web developer by leaving your code alone. Not only can you move your code among Dreamweaver and other editors, but

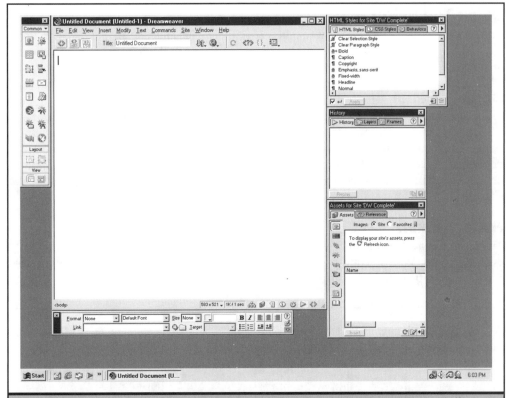

Figure 1-1.   *The Dreamweaver interface combines an HTML text editor and a visual design editor into a common work environment*

you can also edit the code generated by Dreamweaver itself. Once you've used Dreamweaver's Design view to create a table, you can either continue to modify it in the visual environment or change the code itself to your exact specifications using the HTML source editor, known as *Code view.* You can add custom tags to your source, secure in the knowledge that they'll remain in your source.

Of course, Dreamweaver also understands that not all code gets the job done, so it offers several tools to help you polish your code, if you want to use them. The *Clean Up HTML* command does just that, removing empty tags and combining redundant nested tags. The *Apply Source Formatting* command formats your source code for tag consistency (uppercase or lowercase tags) and indentation. If you import your HTML files from Microsoft Word using the Import feature, Dreamweaver automatically launches a tool to clean up the extraneous tags Word requires to format and display its documents. See Chapter 4 for more information about these tools.

Quick Tag Editor

The *Quick Tag Editor* enables you to edit a specific HTML tag without leaving Design View. This tool enables you to insert new tags, edit existing tags, or wrap new tags around a selection. Chapter 4 explains how to make full use of the Quick Tag Editor.

Objects Panel

The *Objects panel* (see Figure 1-2) puts design elements at your fingertips. A click of a button adds images, framesets, rollovers, special characters, and more. The Objects panel is also customizable. You can move the objects into different categories and add new ones to accommodate your personal work style. You can find more information about how to use the Objects panel in Chapter 2 and how to customize the panel in Chapter 24.

History Panel

The *History panel* (see the following illustration) records every action you take in designing your Web site and provides a visual history of your movements. You can use the panel to repeat or undo actions even after saving the file. The History panel is also

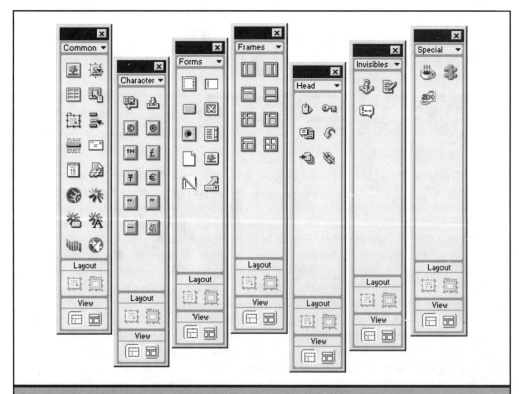

Figure 1-2. *The Objects panel puts the most common design elements within easy reach*

useful to create new commands for the actions you use most often. For more about the History panel, see Chapter 2.

Global Find and Replace

Dreamweaver's powerful *Find and Replace* works on a page, folder, or site level, giving you complete control over the changes in your site. As you move and rename files in your site, Dreamweaver automatically updates links to those files. You can also store Find and Replace queries for later use. Details about how to use these tools are in Chapter 4.

Site Maintenance

Dreamweaver understands you aren't simply creating a Web page—you're creating an entire Web site. And Web development doesn't end when the site goes live. Dreamweaver's site management tools assist with the often cumbersome task of maintaining your sites. The site map (see Figure 1-3) provides you with a visual overview of your entire site and gives you access to any file on the map at the click of your mouse. Dreamweaver also lets you create templates that can be modified to change the entire look of your site. Couple templates with Cascading Style Sheets, and site maintenance has never been easier.

Customization

As mentioned earlier, no two Web developers are the same. Dreamweaver not only understands this fact, it embraces it. The panels and inspectors can be moved or hidden independently from each other. The inspectors are dynamic, showing only the properties pertinent to the selection in the document window. Best of all, the menus

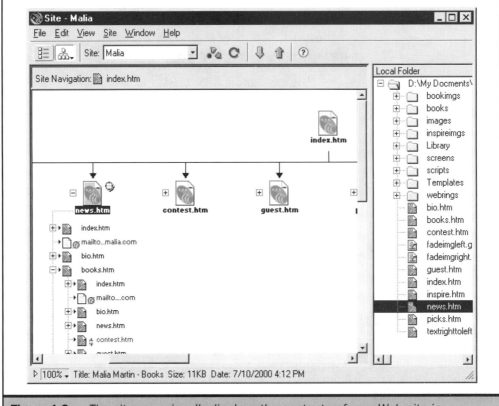

Figure 1-3. *The site map visually displays the contents of your Web site in hierarchical form*

and panels are customizable. The Extension Manager, covered in Chapter 31, enables you to personalize your work environment completely. Hundreds of extensions are available free on the Web, most of them accessible from the Macromedia Web site.

Cascading Style Sheets

Dreamweaver's *Cascading Style Sheet* (*CSS*) tools give you design control over the elements of your Web site. CSS enables you to set style attributes on a page-wide or even a site-wide basis, resulting in a consistent appearance and facilitating faster redesigns. Dreamweaver's CSS tools completely support the *World Wide Web Consortium*'s (*W3C*) specifications for Cascading Style Sheets. CSS is covered in Chapter 17.

Dynamic HTML

Dreamweaver has been an innovator in creating tools for use with Dynamic HTML. The *Timeline Inspector* (see Figure 1-4) gives you complete control over the placement and movement of layers. Layers can also be converted to tables to provide backward-compatibility for older browsers.

Latest Web Technologies

Dreamweaver supports all the current Web technologies. The text editor enables you to send files by JavaScript and XML directly in Dreamweaver. The JavaScript Debugger lets you debug your code, and the Reference feature on the Help menu provides JavaScript information. And, because Dreamweaver doesn't modify your code, you can import new technologies as they become available. More information about JavaScript and other technologies can be found in Part V.

Figure 1-4.   *The Timeline Inspector enables you to animate objects without the use of JavaScript or Flash*

New in Dreamweaver 4

Dreamweaver 4 offers something new for everybody. Macromedia has grouped the new features into three areas: Code, Design, and Collaboration.

Code

Because Dreamweaver is a professional tool, most users appreciate its handling of code most of all. This version of Dreamweaver adds several enhancements to its already strong arsenal of coding tools.

Split View   Previous versions of Dreamweaver have used a separate source window, which made for a sometimes awkward use of screen real estate for developers who go back and forth between WYSIWYG and HTML source coding. Dreamweaver 4 enables you to view your HTML source directly in the document window. You can either toggle between the two views or, even better, split the window to edit in the WYSIWYG and HTML source views at the same time. This feature provides a full-bodied instructional tool for novice coders. Add an element in Design view and immediately see the resulting code in the HTML source. The new document window is explained in detail in Chapter 2, "The Dreamweaver Environment."

Enhanced Toolbar   The new Dreamweaver toolbar (see the following illustration) adds commonly used options, such as Preview in Browser and the page title, eliminating repetitive menu navigation and saving time navigating menus for commonly used functions. For a complete list of features on the toolbar, see Chapter 2, "The Dreamweaver Environment."

Integrated Text Editor   Even if you never intend to hand-code, sooner or later, you're bound to find yourself knee-deep in tags and attributes. If you're a long-time hand-coder, you already know how much time can be lost searching for a stray table element in an unformatted list of HTML source code. For both types of developers, the new text editor (Figure 1-5) is a welcome enhancement. The editor auto-indents your code and lets you select multiple lines to indent them together. Live syntax coloring makes distinguishing tags from content easier and the colors can be customized.

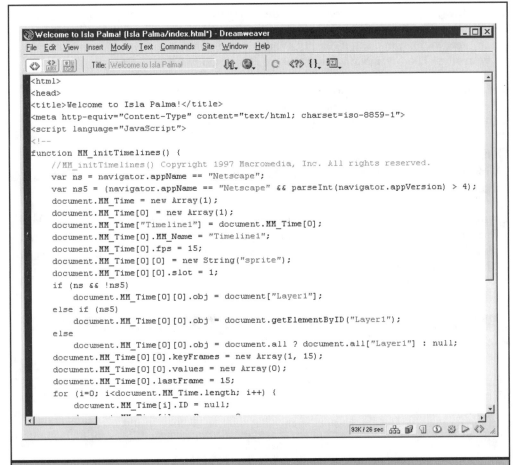

```
Welcome to Isla Palma! (Isla Palma/index.html*) - Dreamweaver
File  Edit  View  Insert  Modify  Text  Commands  Site  Window  Help

Title: Welcome to Isla Palma!

<html>
<head>
<title>Welcome to Isla Palma!</title>
<meta http-equiv="Content-Type" content="text/html; charset=iso-8859-1">
<script language="JavaScript">
<!--
function MM_initTimelines() {
    //MM_initTimelines() Copyright 1997 Macromedia, Inc. All rights reserved.
    var ns = navigator.appName == "Netscape";
    var ns5 = (navigator.appName == "Netscape" && parseInt(navigator.appVersion) > 4);
    document.MM_Time = new Array(1);
    document.MM_Time[0] = new Array(1);
    document.MM_Time["Timeline1"] = document.MM_Time[0];
    document.MM_Time[0].MM_Name = "Timeline1";
    document.MM_Time[0].fps = 15;
    document.MM_Time[0][0] = new String("sprite");
    document.MM_Time[0][0].slot = 1;
    if (ns && !ns5)
        document.MM_Time[0][0].obj = document["Layer1"];
    else if (ns5)
        document.MM_Time[0][0].obj = document.getElementByID("Layer1");
    else
        document.MM_Time[0][0].obj = document.all ? document.all["Layer1"] : null;
    document.MM_Time[0][0].keyFrames = new Array(1, 15);
    document.MM_Time[0][0].values = new Array(0);
    document.MM_Time[0].lastFrame = 15;
    for (i=0; i<document.MM_Time.length; i++) {
        document.MM_Time[i].ID = null;
```

93K / 26 sec

Figure 1-5.   *The new integrated text editor formats HTML source code into an easily navigated document*

Edit Non-HTML Documents   The new text editor also enables you to edit JavaScript, XML, and other text files directly in Dreamweaver. Dreamweaver detects these files and automatically opens them in Code view. For more about using JavaScript and other technologies in Dreamweaver, see Part V.

JavaScript Debugger   The new JavaScript Debugger enables you to debug your code directly in your Netscape or Internet Explorer browser. This feature is useful in determining how the two browsers implement JavaScript differently and how your code is implemented in various versions of each browser. You can learn more about the JavaScript Debugger in Chapter 21.

Code Navigation   Dreamweaver's Code Navigation feature enables you to move between JavaScript functions. This feature is accessible from a drop-down list in the Code View toolbar, making it readily available and a useful tool when using JavaScript on your sites. The Code Navigation feature is covered in Chapter 21.

Reference   Along with support for the application itself, Dreamweaver now offers a reference library for information about HTML, CSS, and JavaScript. This material is available from the Help menu or the Reference tab on the Assets panel.

Design

Those of us who think visually instead of in code haven't been forgotten in the feature enhancements to Dreamweaver 4.

Layout Mode   Layout view (see the following illustration) enables you to draw table cells directly in the document window, manipulate them, and group them into nested tables. This new view can also be used to create flexible layouts that conform to the size of the document window.

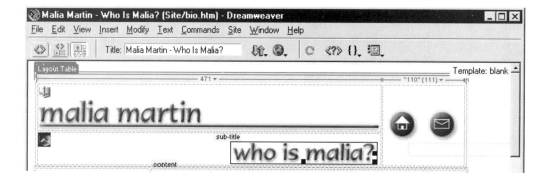

CSS and Template Enhancements   The CSS tools have been upgraded to make using external style sheets easier. Style sheets can be attached to a page from a button in the CSS Styles panel. Templates have been enhanced to make it easier to determine the editable regions of the template. The following illustration shows an example of editable regions within a template. Chapter 17 goes into detail about the new CSS tools. Chapter 29 explains how to use templates and define editable regions.

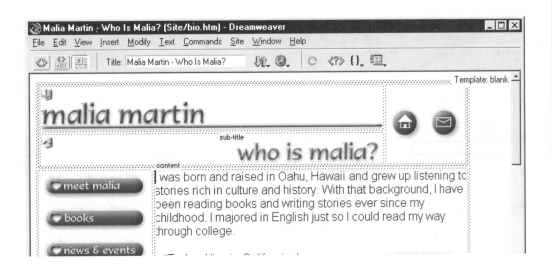

Flash Buttons and Text   Flash is now a Web standard and is no longer limited to high-end sites. The new Flash Buttons feature gives you the ability to integrate Flash from inside Dreamweaver. You can use predefined Flash styles or add custom styles. Flash Text enables you to create scalable, editable vector text in Dreamweaver. See Chapter 27 to learn how to take advantage of these features.

Roundtrip Graphics Editing   Current Fireworks and Dreamweaver users already enjoy the integration of these development tools to streamline their work flow. Dreamweaver 4 and Fireworks 4 are integrated more strongly than ever. A common interface makes for a smoother user experience. Images and tables imported from Fireworks now have their own Property Inspector to make shuffling between Fireworks and Dreamweaver easier, and Fireworks enables you to roundtrip back into Dreamweaver while updating your document to reflect your changes. To learn more about Fireworks and Dreamweaver-Fireworks integration, see Part X.

Collaboration

Dreamweaver's collaboration tools make it easy to design sites as a team. The Design Notes feature from previous versions has been enhanced, and several other tools have been added to facilitate team development.

Asset Management   The Asset panel makes it easy to manage the templates, images, color schemes, links, and other assets of a large site. These assets can be dragged directly into a document and can also be saved for use across sites.

Integrated E-mail Communication is critical to team development. To discuss a file that's been checked by someone else on your team, you can now click that person's name in the Site window to send a direct e-mail. Learn more about integrated e-mail in Chapter 6.

Design Notes Enhancements Design Notes can now be directly viewed in the site window. Members of your development team can now see each file's "Due By" date and status when they connect to the site. Information about this enhancement can be found in Chapter 6.

Site Testing Dreamweaver 4 offers several new reports to facilitate QA testing. Each report returns results to a display window that provides immediate access to documents that need editing. These reports are covered in detail in Chapter 6.

Visual SourceSafe Integration For Windows users who need the version control management of *Visual SourceSafe* (*VSS*), Dreamweaver is now integrated with that software. Microsoft Visual SourceSafe is used by large development houses to control updates and access to files. VSS integration is covered in Chapter 6.

Dreamweaver Resources

A program this vast is bound to spark hundreds of ideas for innovative uses of the software, extensions to customize the work environment, and tips on how to use all the bells and whistles. So it's no surprise dozens of resources exist for Dreamweaver users.

For questions about HTML, JavaScript, and Cascading Style Sheets, the Reference feature on the Help menu is a good place to start. These materials were professionally developed to provide information about the basics of Web development. The appendices to this book also contain lists of common HTML elements and CSS properties.

Other HTML Resources

Some other resources for learning HTML are

- *HTML: The Complete Reference*, Third Edition, by Thomas A. Powell (Osborne/McGraw-Hill, ISBN: 0072129514)
- *Special Edition Using HTML 4*, 6th Edition, by Molly E. Holzschlag (Que Publishing, ISBN: 0789722674)
- HTML Writers Guild—**http://www.hwg.org**
- Project Cool Developer Zone—**http://www.projectcool.com/developer**
- Webmonkey—**http://www.hotwired.com/webmonkey/index.html**

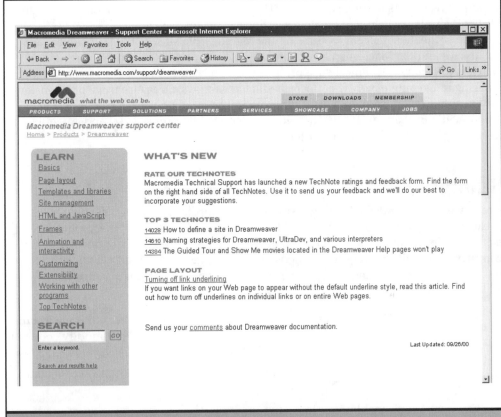

Figure 1-6. *The Macromedia Web site provides support, extensions, and access to the Dreamweaver user community*

The Dreamweaver software comes loaded with support resources. The printed manual is just the tip of the iceberg. For novices, the guided tour movies on the CD offer an animated overview of Dreamweaver's key features. The lessons found under the Help menu can also get you started. Dreamweaver's Help system is provided in HTML format, allowing for easy hyperlinking between entries. If you're interested in creating your own objects, commands, and behaviors, the *Extending Dreamweaver* manual, available from Macromedia, provides hundreds of pages of reference material.

One of the best sources for Dreamweaver support is the Macromedia Web site at **http://www.macromedia.com/support/dreamweaver** (see Figure 1-6). The Macromedia site offers current information about Dreamweaver 4. It also puts you in touch with other Dreamweaver users by way of newsgroups devoted to Dreamweaver. These newsgroups can be a tremendous source of information and ideas. While they're primarily populated by users, the Dreamweaver developers and support team monitor the groups and often step in with answers to tricky questions. They've even been known to look at individual files or Web sites to help find creative solutions to design problems.

Two of the most helpful features on the Macromedia site are the Dreamweaver TechNotes and the Macromedia Exchange. The TechNotes area of the site provides answers to common technical support questions and offers suggestions to facilitate working in Dreamweaver. The Macromedia Exchange is a treasure trove of extensions for Dreamweaver 4 (see Chapter 31 for more information about extensions and the Macromedia Exchange). These extensions are created by professional and amateur developers, and they're posted for the community's use.

Summary

Dreamweaver became the leading visual editor for professional Web developers because of its extensive feature set and Roundtrip HTML promise. The application has increasingly caught on with novice developers due to its ability to develop complex pages without requiring extensive knowledge of advanced HTML and JavaScript, while also generating lean, professional code. Macromedia appeals to all levels of Web designers.

- Roundtrip HTML means that you can import code from other editors without risk of Dreamweaver changing it. Also, Dreamweaver will not modify code you enter by hand even within the application.

- The new Code view and Code and Design view make it easier to access your HTML source.

- Layout view enables you to design complex tables to facilitate design.

- Professional developers can collaborate on large projects by using the Design Notes, Check Out/In feature, and VSS integration.

- The JavaScript debugger can be used to track down problems with scripts.

The next chapter introduces you to the Dreamweaver environment. Understanding the basic tools will make your development time more productive.

The
Complete
Reference

Chapter 2

The Dreamweaver Environment

I f you've never used a Macromedia product before, you'll find Dreamweaver's interface is rather unique. When you're developing a Web site, you want to save your brainpower for the design and coding of the site, not putting yourself into the mind of the software developer to figure out which menu contains the tool you want to use.

Dreamweaver uses panels and context menus to put the features you need within reach in an uncluttered, logical environment. Dreamweaver is also customizable to the way you work, with movable panels and inspectors to lay out your desktop so it's most comfortable for you. Right-handed people tend to look to the right of the screen, whereas lefties naturally veer to the left. Position your panels, inspectors, and the document window itself wherever you like, and you're bound to be more productive.

If you're new to Dreamweaver, terms like panels, inspectors, and the various editing views can be confusing. This chapter gives you a tour of Dreamweaver so you can get on to the nuts and bolts of building your site knowing what's what. Experienced Dreamweaver users might also find some useful information in this chapter because some of the tools and features have changed names and/or gained additional functionality in Dreamweaver 4.

The Document Window

The primary work environment for Dreamweaver is the *Document window*, shown in Figure 2-1. This is where you design and edit your Web page. Previous versions of Dreamweaver have required developers to open a separate window to view the source code, resulting in a lot of jockeying for precious screen real estate. Dreamweaver 4 provides several enhancements to the Document window, the most significant being that both design and HTML source code can be viewed and edited within the same window.

In Design view, Dreamweaver provides a visual representation of your site. Depending on your Preference settings (see Chapter 3), invisible elements of your page are hidden to provide you with a close approximation of how your page appears. Initially, the screen is empty—a daunting challenge to new designers. You quickly learn how to fill that empty space with text, images, tables, and other features.

In Code view, the Document window displays the code for your page. If you're familiar with earlier versions of Dreamweaver, this view is similar to the HTML Source Inspector, with the addition of color-coded HTML tags.

You can also split the Document window to show both Design and Code views simultaneously in the same window. For those of us who go back and forth between designing and hand-coding, this is one of the most welcome new features in Dreamweaver. If you're a new developer trying to learn how the code works, this feature enables you to position your cursor in various places within the Design view and to see the underlying code simultaneously in the Code view.

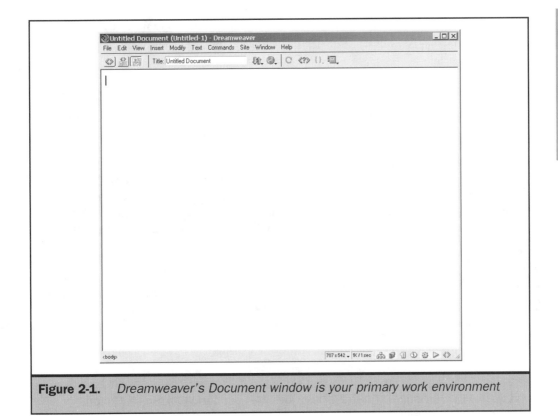

Figure 2-1.   *Dreamweaver's Document window is your primary work environment*

Changing views is as easy as clicking the new Dreamweaver toolbar, discussed later in this chapter.

The Document window is surrounded by all the tools you need to develop your site, including a title bar, menus, a toolbar, and a status bar. Let's look at each of these features:

Title Bar

The *title* bar provides just what its name implies, the title of your Web page. It also shows the filename for your page. Aside from being a reminder of the name of the page on which you're currently working, it can also serve as a reminder that you haven't yet given the page a title (covered in Chapter 8).

The title bar serves one other purpose. As you work, the filename listed in the title bar displays an asterisk after the filename signifying you have made changes to the document since you last saved your work. While you can try to save a document that's already been saved if you're not sure—or go to the trouble of looking under the *File* menu to see if the *Save* option is grayed out—it's much faster to look for the asterisk at the top of your screen.

Menus

Under the title bar is the menu bar. The *menu* bar contains nearly all the tools and features of Dreamweaver. Most of these tools are also accessible from panels and inspectors, as well as context menus that pop up when you right-click your mouse. How you use Dreamweaver is strictly a matter of personal preference. If you're used to working in a menu-driven environment, you might be more comfortable using Dreamweaver's menus at first. As you become more comfortable in the Dreamweaver environment, however, you'll probably rely more and more on the Launcher and panels. Even so, some commands, particularly File | Save, are only available through the menus or a keyboard shortcut. A list of keyboard shortcuts can be found in Appendix A.

Note   *Dreamweaver's menus may be modified by the user and by Extensions downloaded from the Macromedia Exchange. For this reason, your menus may vary from those that follow. The following tables are intended only as an overview of the default menu options.*

File

The File menu controls the creation and saving of documents, as well as the previewing and testing of your pages. Table 2-1 describes the commands on the File menu.

Command	Function(s)	Notes
New	Creates a new document in its own Document window.	
New from Template	Creates a new document based on an existing template.	See Chapter 29.
Open	Opens the file selection dialog box to open an existing document.	
Open in Frame	Opens an existing document in a selected frame.	See Chapter 15.
Close	Closes an open document.	
Save	Saves an open document. This prompts you for a filename the first time you save a new document.	

Table 2-1.   *The File Menu Enables You to Create and Save Web Pages, Frames, and Templates*

Command	Function(s)	Notes
Save As	Opens the file save dialog box to save an open document under a new name.	
Save as Template	Saves the open document as a template in the Templates folder of the open site.	See Chapter 29.
Save All Frames	Saves the open frames and frameset.	See Chapter 15.
Revert	Reloads the open document as it was last saved.	This command is handy if you make a major mistake while editing a page.
Import	Creates a new document by inserting an XML file into an open template. Imports an HTML file from Microsoft Word. Inserts a table into an open document using a file with delimited data.	Import Word HTML can also be set to clean up Word's HTML code. See Chapter 4.
Export	Saves a template's editable regions as an XML file. Creates an external style sheet using the CSS styles of the open document. Saves data in a table as a delimited text file for import into a spreadsheet or other file.	See Chapter 29 to learn how to export a template's editable regions. See Chapter 17 for information about Cascading Style Sheets. See Chapter 14 for more about table data.
Convert	Converts all layers to tables and creates a new Web page.	This feature allows for backward-compatibility with older browsers that don't support DHTML. For more about DHTML, see Chapter 19.
Preview in Browser	Enables you to choose a browser in which to view your page. You can also use this option to access the Preferences settings to set preview browsers.	
Debug in Browser	Enables you to debug client-side JavaScript in your preferred browser.	This is new for Dreamweaver 4. See Chapter 21 to learn how to use the debugger.
Check Links	Checks the integrity of all the links in the open document.	See Chapter 11.

Table 2-1. *The File Menu Enables You to Create and Save Web Pages, Frames, and Templates* (continued)

Command	Function(s)	Notes
Check Target Browsers	Enables you to validate an open document for compatibility with various browsers.	See Chapter 6.
Design Notes	Opens the Design Notes dialog box for the open document.	See Chapter 5.
Recent Files List	Lists the last four files you opened.	
Exit	Exits Dreamweaver, closing all open documents and prompting you to save any documents with changes since your last save.	On the Mac, this option is labeled Quit.

Table 2-1. *The File Menu Enables You to Create and Save Web Pages, Frames, and Templates* (continued)

 Some of the menus have slight differences between the Windows and Mac versions of the software. These differences are noted in the Notes column of each table.

Edit

The Edit menu offers standard commands, such as cut, copy, and paste. Dreamweaver's edit menu also provides other commands that let you quickly select and manipulate elements of your Web pages. Table 2-2 lists the commands available from the Edit menu.

Command	Function(s)	Notes
Undo	Removes the last change you made and reverts to the state of the document just prior to that change.	The number of layers of Undo available can be set in the Preferences setting. You can also undo multiple changes at once using the History panel.
Repeat	Repeats the last change you made to the document.	

Table 2-2. *The Edit Menu Offers Tools to Customize Dreamweaver, Cut and Paste, and Format HTML Code*

Command	Function(s)	Notes
Cut	Removes the selection from the document and places it in the clipboard.	
Copy	Copies selected image or text.	
Paste	Pastes selected image or text.	If you have used Copy HTML when making your selection, using this option to Paste in Design view pastes the HTML code itself onto your page.
Clear	Clears the selection from the file.	Unlike the Cut command, this option doesn't place the selection into the clipboard.
Copy HTML	In Design view, copies underlying HTML code.	
Paste HTML	In Design view, pastes selection with formatting.	
Select All	Selects all the elements in the open document or frame.	
Select Parent Tag	Highlights everything within the tag that surrounds the cursor position, including the tag itself.	
Select Child	Highlights the first tag completely contained inside a selection.	This item works in conjunction with Select Parent Tag. This option is only available in Design view.
Find and Replace	Brings up the Find and Replace dialog box.	This can be used to search and replace within the current document, the entire site, selected documents in the site, or a specified folder.
Find Next	Repeats the last Find command.	In the Mac version, this option is called Find Again.
Indent Code	In Code view or the Code Inspector, indents code for easier readability.	

Table 2-2.   *The Edit Menu Offers Tools to Customize Dreamweaver, Cut and Paste, and Format HTML Code* (continued)

Command	Function(s)	Notes
Outdent Code	In Code view or the Code Inspector, outdents code for easier readability.	
Balance Braces	In JavaScript, highlights everything within the first pair of braces surrounding the position of the cursor.	JavaScript is covered in Chapter 21.
Set Breakpoint	Sets a breakpoint in JavaScript code for testing purposes.	
Remove All Breakpoints	Removes all breakpoints you placed in a file.	
Edit with External Editor	Opens a third-party editor if you defined one in the Preferences settings.	Learn how to define an external editor in Chapter 3. Learn how to use an external editor in conjunction with Dreamweaver in Chapter 4. In the Mac version, this option is called Edit with BBEdit.
Preferences	Opens the Preferences dialog box.	Preferences are covered in Chapter 3.
Keyboard Shortcuts	Opens the Keyboard Shortcuts dialog box, which enables you to view and customize the keyboard shortcuts.	

Table 2-2. *The Edit Menu Offers Tools to Customize Dreamweaver, Cut and Paste, and Format HTML Code* (continued)

View

The View menu changes the way you look at Dreamweaver. This menu enables you to toggle your view of head elements, borders around tables, and features that are helpful in positioning layers. Table 2-3 lists the options contained in the View menu.

Command	Function(s)	Notes
Code	Sets the Document window to Code view.	
Design	Sets the Document window to Design view.	
Code and Design	Splits the Document window between Code and Design views.	You can edit your page in either view by clicking in the view to make it the focus.
Switch Views	Toggles between Design view and Code view.	
Refresh Design View	Refreshes the Design view when working in the split Code and Design view.	
Design View on Top	When in Split view, puts Design view at the top of the screen and Code view at the bottom.	This option can be toggled using the same menu option.
Head Content	Symbolically represents sections of the `<head>` contents, enabling you to modify those sections.	
Table View	Switches between Standard and Layout views.	Layout view is explained in Chapter 5 and Chapter 14.
Visual Aids	Shows display settings for borders and invisible elements.	
Code View Options	Shows display settings for Code view.	This option lets you automatically wrap your code to fit in the view window, color-key your code, and turn on line numbering.
Rulers	Sets and displays horizontal and vertical rulers in Design view.	

Table 2-3.   *The View Menu Controls the Layout of the Document Window*

Command	Function(s)	Notes
Grid	Sets and displays a background grid in Design view to assist in element positioning.	
Tracing Image	Sets and displays a tracing image to guide page layout according to a prepared design.	Tracing Images are discussed in Chapter 5.
Plugins	Controls the playback of selected plug-ins while editing a page.	
Hide Panels	Hides and restores all open panels at once.	
Toolbar	Toggles visibility of the Dreamweaver toolbar.	

Table 2-3. *The View Menu Controls the Layout of the Document Window* (continued)

Insert

The Insert menu duplicates the Objects panel, enabling you to place images, tables, layers, and other elements at the current cursor position. The objects contained in the Insert menu are listed in Table 2-4.

Command	Function(s)	Notes
Image	Prompts you to insert an image at the position of the cursor.	
Interactive Images	Prompts you through the addition of interactive images such as rollovers, navigation bars, and Flash buttons, as well as text.	Chapter 12 explains more about interactive images.
Media	Prompts you to insert Shockwave, Flash, and other media plug-ins.	Part VI details how to add audio and video to your pages.
Table	Prompts you to add a table at the insertion point.	Tables are covered in Chapter 14.

Table 2-4. *The Insert Menu Contains the Same Items as the Objects Panel*

Command	Function(s)	Notes
Layer	Adds a default layer to the page, which can then be manipulated.	See Chapter 19 to learn more about Layers.
Frames	Provides options for creating a frameset.	Chapter 15 explains frames and framesets.
Form	Adds form structure at the insertion point.	See Chapter 16 for information about forms.
Form Objects	Inserts form objects within the form structure.	
Server-Side Include	Prompts you to insert a server-side include.	
Email Link	Creates a mailto: link, prompting you to enter link text and the target e-mail address.	
Date	Prompts you through the creation of a date stamp on your page.	
Tabular Data	Inserts a new table generated from a delimited data file.	Importing tabular data is covered in Chapter 14.
Horizontal Rule	Adds a horizontal rule at the insertion point.	This option uses the `<hr>` tag and, therefore, doesn't let you set the color of the rule or use an image in place of the default rule.
Invisible Tags	Adds elements that aren't part of the visible page design, such as anchor tags and comments.	
Head Tags	Choosing one of the head tags from the submenu prompts you through adding tags to the `<head>` section of the page.	
Special Characters	Enables you to insert special characters, such as the copyright symbol and em-dashes.	
Get More Objects	Uses your Internet connection to connect you to the Macromedia Exchange.	The Macromedia Exchange is a vast resource for objects, behaviors, and extensions for Dreamweaver.

Table 2-4.   *The Insert Menu Contains the Same Items as the Objects Panel* (continued)

Modify

The Modify menu contains all the options to change the elements of your pages. Web developers rarely use the standard options for text, tables, and other elements. Once the basics are on the page, the real design work begins. Table 2-5 describes the features of the Modify menu.

Command	Function(s)	Notes
Page Properties	Displays the page properties.	
Selection Properties	Toggles the Property Inspector.	
Quick Tag Editor	Opens one of the three Quick Tag Editors for the selected element.	The three Quick Tag Editors are Insert HTML, Edit Tag, and Wrap Tag. These editors are explained in Chapter 4.
Make Link	Opens the Select File dialog box to let you turn the selection into a link.	This option can be used to create both internal and external links. See Chapter 11 to learn more about linking.
Remove Link	Removes the link from the selection without deleting the selection itself.	
Open Linked Page	Shows the linked page in Dreamweaver.	The linked page must exist on your local drive. You cannot use this feature to view external linked pages.
Link Target	Provides options to set a target for a link.	This menu option lets you direct a link to open in another window or within a specific frame.
Table	Provides options to edit an existing table.	This option is used for inserting and deleting cells, columns, and rows. Options also exist for merging and splitting cells. Finally, this option also enables you to convert table widths from percentages to pixels and vice versa.

Table 2-5.   *The Modify Menu Enables You to Adjust and Alter Elements of Your Web Pages*

Command	Function(s)	Notes
Frameset	Provides options to split a frameset and edit noframes content.	
Navigation Bar	Enables you to edit a navigation bar created using the Navigation Bar feature.	
Arrange	Sets the stacking order of layers.	This option also enables you to prevent layer overlaps.
Align	Sets the alignment of groups of layers or hotspots.	
Convert	Converts layers to tables or tables to layers.	
Library	Provides capability to modify the Library category of the Assets panel.	The Assets panel is discussed later in this chapter and in Chapter 28.
Templates	Enables the use and modification of a template.	This option enables you to link the current page to a template, break a link between the current page and an attached template, and edit a template. Templates are covered in detail in Chapter 29.
Timeline	Uses the Timeline Inspector to manage layers and behaviors.	See Chapter 20 for more about timelines.

Table 2-5. *The Modify Menu Enables You to Adjust and Alter Elements of Your Web Pages* (continued)

Text

Fancy images and innovative designs aside, the Internet is intended to convey information and connect communities. Unless your site is a virtual art gallery, this means you'll be using at least some text to convey your message. Table 2-6 lists the options on the Text menu.

By the way, even if your site *is* an art gallery, a descriptive word or two wouldn't hurt.

Command	Function(s)	Notes
Indent	Uses the `<blockquote>` tag to indent selected text.	
Outdent	Deletes a `<blockquote>` or `<div>` tag from an indented selection.	
Paragraph Format	Sets the paragraph format for the selection.	This option can be used to set heading and monospaced text formatting.
Align	Aligns the selection to the left, right, or center.	
List	Used to create lists and set list properties.	Lists are covered in Chapter 10.
Font	Sets the font for the selection.	The font options are displayed according to your font list, which can also be accessed and edited from this menu option.
Style	Sets the style of the selection.	This option enables you to set the appearance of text to bold, italics, and underline, as well as strikethrough, emphasis, and other styles.
HTML Styles	Applies and removes text formatting styles from the selection.	
CSS Styles	Applies styles defined in a Cascading Style Sheet and allows for the modification of style sheets.	See Chapter 17.
Size	Sets selected text to a chosen font size.	If no text is selected, this sets the font size for text typed after the insertion point.
Size Change	Changes the size of text relative to its current size.	If text is selected, this changes the size of that text. If no text is selected, this changes the size of text typed after the insertion point.

Table 2-6.   *The Text Menu Gives You Control Over the Appearance and Presentation of Your Textual Content*

Command	Function(s)	Notes
Color	Opens the Color dialog box to allow selection of a text color.	If text is selected, this option changes the color of the selected text. If no text is selected, choosing a color applies that color to text typed after the insertion point.
Check Spelling	Initiates a spelling check of the current page.	

Table 2-6. *The Text Menu Gives You Control Over the Appearance and Presentation of Your Textual Content* (continued)

Commands

Dreamweaver commands are useful automations of monotonous tasks. That's a short explanation, but commands actually go well beyond that summation. Commands can be used to modify everything from a single tag or attribute to an entire site. Best of all, commands are user-definable, meaning you can create your own commands using HTML and JavaScript or simply by using the Recording options available from the Commands menu.

Not every Web designer has a thorough understanding of JavaScript. And designers under a tight deadline don't necessarily have the time to develop their own commands. For this reason, Dreamweaver comes with its own set of commands. Using the included Macromedia Extension Manager, users can download hundreds of commands developed by others. Commands and extensions are covered in detail in Part VIII. Table 2-7 lists the options available from the Commands menu.

Note *As mentioned earlier, Dreamweaver's menu structure may be changed with the addition of user-generated and downloaded commands. Nowhere is this more evident than in the Commands menu, as any commands added to the Commands folder are automatically added to this menu. Therefore, the following default options might not mirror your own menu.*

Command	Function(s)	Notes
Start Recording	Starts recording command.	This option changes to Stop Recording once activated.
Play Recorded Command	Plays the most recently recorded command.	
Edit Command List	Allows modification of the Commands menu.	This feature allows for addition and deletion of user-created commands. To learn more about customization of the entire Dreamweaver menu structure, see Chapter 30.
Get More Commands	Launches an external browser and connects to the Macromedia Exchange for Dreamweaver.	You can also access the Macromedia Exchange manually by going to **http://www.macromedia.com/ exchange/dreamweaver**.
Manage Extensions	Launches the Macromedia Extension Manager to install, enable, and disable downloaded extensions.	See Chapter 31 for more information on using the Macromedia Extension Manager.
Apply Source Formatting	Applies the Source Format Profile to the open file. Useful for standardizing the indentation and appearance of the HTML code of imported pages.	The Source Format Profile can be customized. See Chapter 4 for details.
Clean Up HTML	Removes unnecessary tags from the open page.	
Clean Up Word HTML	Removes unnecessary tags and XML from pages created in Microsoft Word.	
Add/Remove Netscape Resize Fix	Fixes the Netscape 4 problem with layers and CSS positioning by adding a JavaScript routine to force a page reload after a user resizes her browser window.	This command can be toggled to add or delete this code fix. Netscape 6 fixes this problem without the need for this command.
Optimize Image in Fireworks	If Macromedia Fireworks is installed, optimizes the image in Fireworks and updates the image in Dreamweaver.	Learn more about Dreamweaver-Fireworks integration in Chapter 36.

Table 2-7. *The Commands Menu Offers Access to Dreamweaver's Extensibility Features, Including Commands, the Extension Manager, and Tools to Clean Up Imported HTML Code*

Command	Function(s)	Notes
Create Web Photo Album	Prompts for settings to create an automatic page of thumbnail images.	This feature requires you to have Macromedia Fireworks (versions 3 or 4) installed. See Chapter 13.
Set Color Scheme	Provides a selection of background, link, and text color schemes to facilitate quick design decisions.	This option provides a fail-safe method for establishing a site's color scheme. You can, of course, also create your own color scheme. Both options are covered in Chapter 7.
Format Table	Formats the selected table in one of the many predesigned table layouts.	The formatted table options let you quickly customize a table's alignment, text style, border width, and color scheme. See Chapter 14.
Sort Table	Sorts tabular data numerically or alphabetically.	This feature cannot be used in tables containing colspans or rowspans, but can be used on nested tables within these spans.

Table 2-7. *The Commands Menu Offers Access to Dreamweaver's Extensibility Features, Including Commands, the Extension Manager, and Tools to Clean Up Imported HTML Code* (continued)

Site

Dreamweaver urges Web developers to think of their projects at the site level. Even if a site consists of only one page, graphic elements and possibly Flash or other embedded objects are still on the page, all of which must be maintained in folders relative to the main page. To facilitate this site-level workflow, Dreamweaver has grouped the most commonly used site tools into one menu. These same options, plus additional ones, can also be found on the menus within the Site window on the Windows platform, one of Dreamweaver's many redundancies to accommodate itself to the various ways in which Web developers approach the software.

The Site menu is one of the few instances where the Windows and Mac screens are different. Because the menus for the Mac platform appear at the top of the screen rather than at the top of each window, the Site menu on the Mac platform contains all the site maintenance options within one menu. These same options are available for the Windows platform, but many of them are accessible only from the Site window rather than the Document window. For Windows users, the Site window and its options are covered in Chapter 6. To provide an easy reference, the Site menu for the Windows and Mac platforms are listed separately. Table 2-8 describes the Windows platform Site menu.

Command	Function(s)	Notes
Site Files	Opens the Site window.	The Site window is discussed in Chapter 6.
Site Map	Develops a Site map for the open site, which is displayed in the Site window.	You must have already defined the site in Dreamweaver to use this feature.
New Site	Prompts you through the creation of a new site.	
Open Site	Shows list of previously defined sites.	You can also use this option to Define Sites, a redundancy of the following option.
Define Sites	Enables you to create new sites or modify settings for previously defined sites.	
Get	Transfers files from the remote server to the local site.	The site, including the location of the remote server, must be defined before you can use this feature.
Check Out	Designates files as being in use.	You must activate this feature in the Site Definition if you want to use it. Check Out/Check In are useful when working on a development team because you can determine which files are being modified and by whom. When using these features, they take the place of Get and Put.
Put	Transfers files from the local site to the remote server.	
Check In	Transfers your modified file to the remote server and removes the Checked Out designation.	
Undo Check Out	Frees up a checked-out file without transferring modifications.	
Reports	Runs various reports at the page, folder, or site level.	The available reports include development team information and reports on common problems, such as missing <alt> tags and redundant or missing tags.

Table 2-8.   *The Windows Platform Site Menu Puts the Commonly Used Site Maintenance Commands Within Easy Reach*

Command	Function(s)	Notes
Check Links Sitewide	Performs link verification on the site.	This report lists broken internal links and orphaned pages. It also lists all external links, but doesn't verify them.
Locate in Local Site	Opens the Site window and selects the open page from the local file list.	
Locate in Remote Site	Opens the Site window and selects the open page from the remote server file list.	

Table 2-8. *The Windows Platform Site Menu Puts the Commonly Used Site Maintenance Commands Within Easy Reach* (continued)

Table 2-9 describes the Mac platform Site menu.

Command	Function(s)	Notes
New Site	Prompts you through the creation of a new site.	
Open Site	Shows list of previously defined sites.	You can also use this option to Define Sites, a redundancy of the following option.
Define Sites	Enables you to create new sites or modify settings for previously defined sites.	
Connect	Connects to the defined remote server.	
Refresh	Refreshes the file list.	This feature is useful to refresh the view of checked in/checked out files.
Site Files View	Contains options to create new files and folders, as well as to select existing files.	

Table 2-9. *The Mac Platform Site Menu Includes Features Found Elsewhere in the Windows Version*

Command	Function(s)	Notes
Site Map View	Contains options to display and modify a site map in the Site window.	
Get	Transfers files from the remote server to the local site.	The site, including the location of the remote server, must be defined before you can use this feature.
Check Out	Designates files as being in use.	You must activate this feature in the Site Definition if you want to use it. Check Out/Check In are useful when working on a development team because you can determine which files are being modified and by whom. When using these features, they take the place of Get and Put.
Put	Transfers files from the local site to the remote server.	
Check In	Transfers your modified file to the remote server and removes the Checked Out designation.	
Undo Check Out	Frees up a checked-out file without transferring modifications.	
Open	Opens a file.	
Rename	Renames a file.	
Unlock	Makes read-only files writable.	If you attempt to open a locked file, you are then also prompted to make the file writable. The Unlock command is useful for unlocking several files at a time to avoid this extra prompt.
Locate in Local Site	Opens the Site window and selects the open page from the local file list.	
Locate in Remote Site	Opens the Site window and selects the open page from the remote server file list.	

Table 2-9. *The Mac Platform Site Menu Includes Features Found Elsewhere in the Windows Version* (continued)

Command	Function(s)	Notes
Reports	Runs various reports at the page, folder, or site level.	The available reports include development team information and reports on common problems, such as missing \<alt\> tags and redundant or missing tags.
Check Links Sitewide	Performs link verification on the site.	This report lists broken internal links and orphaned pages. It also lists all external links, but won't verify them.
Change Link Sitewide	Modifies all occurrences of a link within a site to point to a new path.	
Synchronize	Synchronizes the files on both the remote server and local site.	
Recreate Site Cache	Rebuilds the site cache and updates the Assets panel.	
FTP Log	Displays the FTP log.	
Tool Tips	Displays the full filename or page title in the files list when moused over.	

Table 2-9.   *The Mac Platform Site Menu Includes Features Found Elsewhere in the Windows Version* (continued)

Window

The Window menu gives you control over your screen real estate by providing the options you need to open and hide panels and windows. The menu displays a check mark next to open panels. To display a panel, simply select the panel from the Window menu.

Many panels are docked within the same window by default. Therefore, when you choose an option from the Window menu, another panel may toggle to an inactive setting to bring the chosen panel to the forefront. Panels can also be separated into their own floating panel, as explained later in this chapter. Table 2-10 shows the options available from the Window menu.

Any open document windows are listed at the bottom of the Window menu. You can use this list to move quickly between pages.

Command	Function(s)	Notes
Objects	Displays the Objects panel.	
Properties	Opens the Property Inspector.	The Property Inspector is context sensitive and automatically displays the properties of the element surrounding the cursor position.
Launcher	Displays the Launcher panel.	The Launcher panel is a duplicate of the Mini-Launcher located at the bottom of the Document window, as described later in this chapter.
Site Files	Opens the Site window.	This option is the same as the one included in the Site menu.
Site Map	Displays a map of the current site within the Site window.	You must have previously defined the site using Dreamweaver's site tools to use this feature. See Chapter 5 to learn how to define sites.
Assets	Displays the Assets panel.	
Behaviors	Displays the Behaviors panel.	
Code Inspector	Opens the Code Inspector.	The Code Inspector has the same functionality as the Code view within the Document window, but is contained in a separate window. In previous versions of Dreamweaver, this was called the HTML Source Inspector.
CSS Styles	Displays the CSS Styles panel.	
Frames	Displays the Frames panel.	
History	Displays the History panel.	
HTML Styles	Displays the HTML Styles panel.	
Layers	Displays the Layers panel.	
Library	Opens the Library category of the Assets panel.	In previous versions, the Library category was its own panel (or palette, in old Dreamweaver parlance). Now it's one category within a powerful group of tools in the Assets panel.

Table 2-10.   *The Window Menu Gives You Control Over Your Screen Real Estate*

Command	Function(s)	Notes
Reference	Displays the Reference panel.	The Reference panel is new in Dreamweaver 4. It provides references on HTML, CSS, and JavaScript, written by O'Reilly Publications.
Templates	Opens the Templates category of the Assets panel.	
Timelines	Opens the Timelines Inspector.	
Arrange Panels	Returns all open panels to their default positions on the screen.	
Hide Panels	Toggles the visibility of all open panels.	This is the same as the Hide panels option on the View menu.
Minimize All	Minimizes all open Document windows and panels.	This option and Restore All (see the following) are only available on Windows versions of Dreamweaver.
Restore All	Restores all open Document windows and panels.	While this menu option and accompanying keyboard shortcut do exist, you must first open at least one window from the task bar before you can invoke the command.

Table 2-10.   *The Window Menu Gives You Control Over Your Screen Real Estate (continued)*

Help

The Help menu provides a plethora of resources for the Dreamweaver software. Contained on this menu is everything from standard help files to tutorials and lessons. With Dreamweaver 4, this menu also adds references for Web development in general. Table 2-11 lists the features available from the Help menu.

Command	Function(s)	Notes
Welcome	Displays a Welcome screen with links to help you get started with Dreamweaver.	

Table 2-11.   *The Help Menu Provides Access to Dreamweaver Help and Web Development Resources*

Command	Function(s)	Notes
Using Dreamweaver	Displays the Dreamweaver help files.	
Reference	Opens the Reference panel.	This panel is also accessible from the Window menu.
What's New	Lists the new features in Dreamweaver 4.	
Guided Tour	Guides for the basics of creating a Dreamweaver site.	
Lessons	Step-by-Step lessons for advanced design tasks.	
Dreamweaver Exchange	Access the Macromedia Exchange for Dreamweaver on the Internet.	You must connect to the Internet to access the Exchange.
Manage Extensions	Launches the Macromedia Extension Manager to install, enable, and disable downloaded extensions.	See Chapter 31 for more information on using the Macromedia Extension Manager.
Dreamweaver Support Center	Access the Macromedia Dreamweaver Support Center on the Internet.	The Support Center offers training, as well as hundreds of tips and tech notes.
Macromedia Online Forums	Access the list of Macromedia forums.	The forums are actually newsgroups located on the Macromedia server. The forums are monitored by Dreamweaver experts and the Dreamweaver support team.
Extending Dreamweaver	Displays the Extending Dreamweaver help files.	These help files guide you in customizing Dreamweaver by creating extensions.
Creating and Submitting Extensions	Explains how to submit new extensions to the Macromedia Exchange.	This option is only available on the Windows platform.
Register Dreamweaver	Registers Dreamweaver on Macromedia's Web site.	
About Dreamweaver	Displays the copyright and version information for Dreamweaver.	

Table 2-11.   *The Help Menu Provides Access to Dreamweaver Help and Web Development Resources* (continued)

Toolbar

The *toolbar* is found below the menu bar on the Windows platform and at the top of the Document window on the Mac platform. All the options available on the toolbar are also available elsewhere in the software, but this condenses the most commonly used document-specific tools into one place. Think of the toolbar as the middle ground between slogging through the menu structure in search of an option and memorizing the keyboard shortcut. Unfortunately, the toolbar is one of the few elements within Dreamweaver that isn't extensible, so you cannot add your own options to this feature. Each of the buttons on the toolbar is a graphic image, with a tool tip that displays after a moment. The following illustration shows the toolbar.

The tools available from the toolbar are as follows:

- **Code View**—sets the Document window into Code view.

- **Show Code and Design Views**—splits the Document window between Code and Design views.

- **Design View**—sets the Document window into the standard Design view.

- **Title**—enables you to set the page title. This is, perhaps, the most useful feature on the toolbar because it lets you immediately set the <title> tag without having to enter the Page Properties or to view the Head Content, both of which require several steps.

- **File Management**—drops down a menu for easy access to the site commands most commonly used on a per file basis, such as Get or Check Out.

- **Preview/Debug in Browser**—a shortcut to preview your page in the browser of your choice. If not haven't yet configured a browser, you can do so from this drop-down menu.

- **Refresh Design View**—used in the split Code and Design view to update the Design view after changing the code.

- **Reference**—opens the Reference panel, which contains resources on HTML, JavaScript, and *Cascading Style Sheets* (*CSS*).

- **Code Navigation**—enables you to navigate through JavaScript code in Code view, setting breakpoints and navigating to defined functions.

- **View Options**—drops down a view-sensitive menu of display options.

Status Bar

The *status bar*, which is located at the bottom of the Document window, provides useful information about the weight of your page and the dimensions of your design. The status bar also provides one-click access to tags and Dreamweaver panels. The following illustration highlights the features of the status bar.

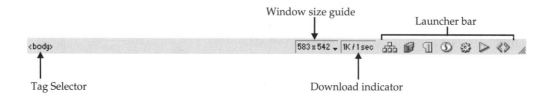

Tag Selector

The *Tag Selector* combines the best of working in Design view with the need to occasionally, and sometimes frequently, hand-tweak the underlying tags. The Tag Selector shows the HTML tags relative to the position of the cursor. Not only can you use this to see which tags are being applied to your work, you can also use it to select a specific tag for modification.

At first glance, it's easy to underestimate the power of this feature. After all, you can always switch to Code view and edit an element by hand. But when you're working with complex framesets or nested tables, you can easily get lost in the code. And switching views in the middle of a burst of creativity is also a hassle. Instead, you can simply click the appropriate tag in the Tag Selector. If you have the Property Inspector visible, it picks up the selection and displays the appropriate options for editing.

The Tag Selector also makes it easy to delete blocks of content. Choosing a <p> tag from the Tag Selector highlights the corresponding paragraph in the Design view. Then press DELETE to erase the paragraph. You can even use this to clear an entire page simply by selecting the <body> tag and deleting the selection. The <head> of the document remains, but the <body> tag reverts to a completely empty state.

If you look carefully at the Tag Selector when working on a complex document, you can see the hierarchy of listed tags from left to right, ranging from the most-encompassing tag that can define the cursor position (such as the <body> tag or an editable region of a template) to the most narrow (such as a bold tag).

The Tag Selector also has a context-sensitive menu available if you right-click a selected tag. You can use this context menu to open the Quick Tag Editor, apply a Class attribute, or set an ID.

Take the time to familiarize yourself with the Tag Selector now. This can save you from wasting a lot of time poking around your code later in search of an elusive tag.

Window Size Selector

As computers continue to evolve, the permutations of default screen resolution continue to increase. While more and more developers are designing based on an 800 × 600 screen size, plenty of Web surfers are still happy with their 640 × 480 displays. Also, some Internet surfers aren't even using dedicated computers, such as those accessing the Web via WebTV (which has a display size of only 560 × 384).

Dreamweaver understands the challenge of designing visually pleasing sites under a wide range of window sizes. To help ease that burden, the Window Size Selector enables you to test your page in a wide variety of dimensions. You can see if your nested tables resize properly as you increase and decrease the window size. Find out if that large image cuts off in an awkward spot at the bottom of the screen when it's resized. You can even set your own default screen dimensions and add them to the Selector list (see Chapter 6).

The Window Size Selector can also help you with your initial page design. If you want to design for a default of 800 × 600, you can select those dimensions in the Window Size Selector before beginning your layout (see Figure 2-2). Dreamweaver

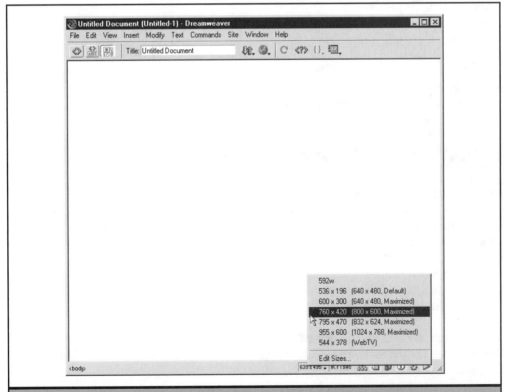

Figure 2-2.   *The Window Size Selector has several predefined window sizes and enables you to add your own dimensions to the list*

takes into account the margins of the window and the menu bar of the Netscape and Internet Explorer browsers, and sizes the window accordingly.

Download Indicator

With the increasing popularity of DSL and cable modems, developers might think they can build pages without a thought to download time and file size. In fact, as connect speeds increase, users' patience decreases. Web surfers want to see your site at the speed of light, while at the same time expecting a visually pleasing, compelling design.

The Download Indicator can keep you on the straight and narrow. The Download Indicator displays the size of your document including all the objects on the page. A general objective is to keep the size of your pages under 50K, although every rule was made to be broken by a knowledgeable designer. With the use of robust graphics optimization tools, such as those included in Macromedia Fireworks, you can create an elaborate page without going over the target page weight. To determine the size of a particular object in your document, open the Property Inspector and click the object. The Property Inspector displays the file size next to the thumbnail of the object on the left side of the Inspector.

Along with tracking your page's weight, the Download Indicator also tells you how much time it will take the average visitor to download your page. Remember, this is only an estimate based on the modem speed you set in Dreamweaver's Preferences (see Chapter 3 to learn how to change this setting). Factors such as traffic and server speed can greatly affect the download time of a page. Still, this information should give a good idea of how much patience you are expecting from your audience.

Launcher and Launcher Bar

The last element of the status bar is the Launcher bar. The Launcher bar and the Launcher (see the following illustration) are identical in functionality, so they are being presented together. The Launcher bar is located at the bottom of the Document window, to the right of the Download Indicator. The Launcher is a separate panel containing the same elements, and provides easy access to panels and inspectors.

The Launcher and the Launcher bar open, in order from left to right, the Site window, Assets panel, HTML Styles panel, CSS Styles panel, Behaviors panel, History panel, and

Code Inspector. Once one of these is selected, the choice remains highlighted in the Launcher and Launcher bar until the window is closed or another option is selected.

Note	*Both the Launcher and Launcher bar can open and close windows and panels. If the selected option is covered by another window or panel within its docking window, selecting that option brings it to the forefront. If the selected option is already open and at the top of its docking window, selecting that option closes the window entirely.*

Whether you use either, both, or neither of these features is up to you. The decision will probably be based on your screen real estate and work environment. If your screen real estate is limited because you have several Document windows and panels open simultaneously, you might find your screen is less cluttered by using the Launcher bar. If you prefer buttons with a textual reference along with the graphic, the Launcher is for you. Developers working on dual monitors also sometimes prefer the Launcher because they can move all their panels to one monitor while leaving the other monitor free for a full-screen Document window. Using the Launcher has the added bonus of freeing up more room in the status bar for the Tag Selector, which can be useful if you are working with numerous nested tables. Finally, if you choose to hide both Launchers, you can still access the same windows, panels, and inspectors using either the Window menu or keyboard shortcuts.

The Launcher and Launcher bar are customizable. This is covered in Chapter 3.

Displaying and Hiding Panels

As just discussed, the Launcher can display many of the panels, windows, and inspectors. Many other panels and inspectors aren't included in the default settings of the Launcher, however. You can access these panels in several ways:

1. All the panels are accessible from the Window menu.
2. The Launcher can be customized to provide options for additional panels.
3. The panels can be accessed by clicking their tab within an open docking window.

The third option deserves further consideration. By default, the panels are grouped within docking windows. These windows can be snapped into a fixed position around the perimeter of the Document window or moved freely around the screen. Each tabbed panel can be removed from its default docking window into either its own window or a different docking window simply by dragging the tab away from its current position into a new location. In fact, you can even dock all the panels together—including the Objects panel—as shown in the following illustration. Because the Objects panel isn't a tabbed window, you can only add new panels to the existing Objects panel, rather than moving the Objects panel into another docking window.

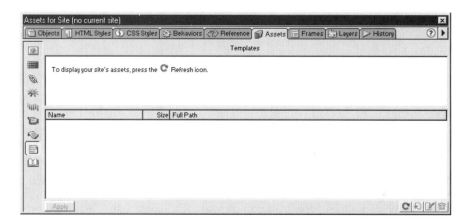

The Inspectors and Launcher cannot be docked. They can, however, be moved around the screen at your convenience. The Launcher can also be changed from a horizontal to a vertical orientation by toggling the button in the lower-right corner of the panel.

The following describes each of the panels and inspectors in general.

Site Window

The Site window, shown in Figure 2-3, facilitates all the key site management tasks. This window displays lists of files on both the local drive and the remote server, and conducts the transfer of files between the two. Site maps are built within the Site window, which provide a visual representation of your site's hierarchy and links.

The Property Inspector

The Property Inspector (see the following illustration) is arguably the most important tool in Dreamweaver. While other panels can be used to place objects on the page, the Property Inspector modifies the attributes of those objects. As you click text, images, tables, or even specific tags within the Tag Selector, the Property Inspector changes contextually to provide the options necessary to customize that element. If you select

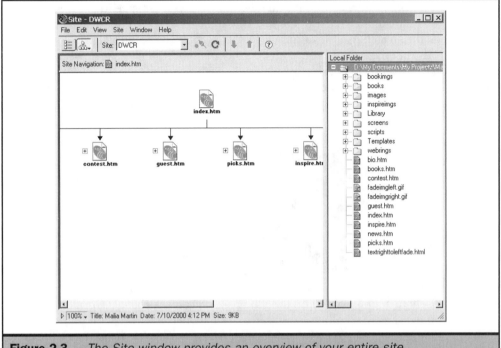

Figure 2-3.   *The Site window provides an overview of your entire site*

text, the Property Inspector enables you to change such attributes as the size, font, and color of the text, as well as the alignment of the paragraph.

As with all the panels in Dreamweaver, you can move the Property Inspector to suit your needs. If screen real estate isn't an issue, click the down arrow in the lower-right corner of the Property Inspector. This opens a second pane in the Inspector with still more options.

In addition to the usual drop-down options and text boxes, the Property Inspector has some unique interface characteristics.

The Color Picker   To set a color for an object, you can either type in the color's name or six-figure hexadecimal code into the text box adjacent to the color swatch box, or you can click the swatch itself to launch the color picker. The color picker, shown in the following illustration, presents you with an array of color swatches from which to choose. You can select one of these by clicking it with the eyedropper. To use the default color selection—to remove a previous color selection or if you change your mind about choosing a color—click the box with a red line through it.

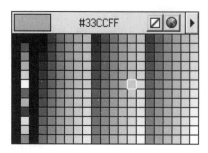

If none of the colors in the color picker catch your eye—or if you are trying to match a color precisely to another object on the screen—you can use the eyedropper to click anywhere on the screen, whether it's within an open Dreamweaver window, your desktop, or another application. To use the eyedropper tool, click your mouse button while you are still in the color picker, and then drag the mouse—while still holding down the mouse button—until you reach the color you want to choose. Release the mouse button to select a color.

Note   *The eyedropper still works, even if you forget to hold down the mouse button while you drag. If you drag the mouse outside the Dreamweaver application, however, the eyedropper then appears as a regular cursor and, when you click to select a color, you switch to the application (or the desktop) containing that color selection. Dreamweaver still registers your color selection, but you must switch back to Dreamweaver to continue your work. It's better to remember to hold down the mouse button whenever you use the eyedropper tool.*

If you prefer to choose a color using your system's color selector, click the color wheel at the top of the color picker. You can also click the arrow at the top-right corner of the color picker to change the palette. The following color selection options are available

- **Color Cubes**—this is the default setting, containing the Web-safe color palette grouped according to hexadecimal value.

- **Continuous Tone**—contains the Web-safe color palette grouped by hue.

- **Windows OS**—contains the Windows OS color palette. This palette is available on both the Windows and Mac versions of Dreamweaver. This isn't a Web-safe palette and, therefore, contains colors that might not display accurately on the user end.

■ **Mac OS**—contains the Mac OS color palette. This palette is available on both the Mac and Windows versions of Dreamweaver. This isn't a Web-safe palette.

■ **Grayscale**—displays a palette containing shades of gray, black, and white. This isn't a Web-safe palette.

■ **Snap to Web Safe**—if this option is selected, all the palettes, including the Windows OS, Mac OS, and Grayscale palettes, shows only Web-safe colors. Additionally, any colors you choose using the eyedropper tool map to their closest Web-safe color.

The Point to File Icon   You can establish a link in the Property Inspector in several ways. If you know the entire path, you can type it in the Link text box but, remember, if you later find a link is broken, the first thing you should do is check for typos. You can also cut-and-paste a URL from your browser into the text box. If the linked file is local, you can use the Point to File Icon to make the selection. Move the Site window so it's visible somewhere on the screen. Then click the Point to File Icon in the Property Inspector and drag it to the appropriate file in the file list in the Site window. Dreamweaver then enters the path into the link text box.

The Folder Icon   Yet another way to establish a link is to use the Folder Icon to open the Select File dialog box. This dialog box provides your standard system navigation to enable you to find the proper file on your local drive. The bottom of this dialog box shows the path for the file, relative to either the document or the site root.

Quick Tag Editor   While the Property Inspector provides a wide range of options for each element, you may sometimes need to add an attribute that isn't available directly within the Inspector. To add or modify these attributes manually, click the Quick Tag Editor button to open a pop-up window containing the tag. You can hand-code the attributes you need, and then click outside the Quick Tag Editor to record the changes and exit the window.

Assets Panel

The *Assets* panel is new in Dreamweaver 4. This resource can save you dozens of hours of repetitive coding and tracking down previously used elements. When you define a site, you are prompted to create a site cache with all the elements contained in the site root. These elements are sorted into categories. The Assets panel stores elements of the site which are likely to be repeated on multiple pages, such as the colors you use for your text, links, and backgrounds. As you develop your site and add images, links to external sites, and colors, these are added to the panel.

The Assets panel, shown in the following illustration, contains a row of buttons down the left side. Click these buttons to move from category to category within the panel. Each category has both a Site list and a Favorites list, with the exception of the templates and library categories. The Site list contains all the elements in the site root, whether or not they're used. The Favorites list contains elements you've explicitly chosen to mark as favorites using the Add to Favorites button at the bottom-right corner of the screen. If you know you'll be using certain images or external links repeatedly, add them to the Favorites list to make them easier to cull from the dozens of other items in each category.

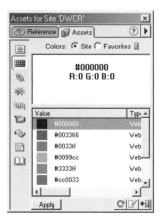

The Assets panel doesn't automatically pick up new assets until the cache is refreshed. For example, if you're creating new images in Fireworks while also working in Dreamweaver, the Assets panel won't list the new images immediately. Similarly, if you delete an external link, the URL won't immediately disappear from the Assets panel. To update the cache, click the Refresh button at the bottom of the Assets panel. This picks up any additions or deletions since the last refresh. To rebuild the site cache completely, CTRL-CLICK (CMD-CLICK on the Mac) the Refresh button. If you have a large site, be patient, as this can take a while.

As with all panels, the Assets panel can be resized. You can increase the overall size of the panel by dragging from the side of the panel (on the Mac, you must resize using the box in the lower-right corner of the window). The panel also contains a Splitter bar between the preview pane and the asset list, which can be dragged up or down to expand the viewing area of either panel. This is particularly helpful in viewing graphic assets.

The Assets panel categories are

- Every JPEG, GIF, or PNG image within the site is listed in the Images category. You can edit the images in this list by selecting them, and then choosing the Edit button to launch your external graphics editor.

- The Colors category contains a list of all the colors used in documents and style sheets within the site. Any time you apply a color to text, links, borders, or backgrounds, the color is added to the color category. You can apply these colors by highlighting a selection in either the Document window or Tag Selector, and then choosing a color from the Colors category and pressing the Apply button at the bottom of the panel.

- As you add external links to your documents, they are included in the URLs category. This category includes external sites, mailto (e-mail) links, FTP, gopher, JavaScript, and local files. The URL category doesn't list internal links because that's done within the Site window.

- Compressed Flash movies (SWF files) are listed in the Flash category. These files can be edited by clicking the edit icon to launch Flash.

- Movies in Macromedia's Shockwave format are listed in the Shockwave category.

- QuickTime or MPEG movies are listed in the Movies category.

- Independent JavaScript and VBScript files are listed in the Scripts category. Embedded scripts within a document aren't included in this list.

- If you've created templates for your site, they're listed in the Templates category. No Favorites list exists for templates because it's assumed all the templates you create for your site are integral to your project. The Templates category does, however, enable you to create a new template from within the Assets panel. Click the New Templates button to create a blank template asset, and then click the Edit button to open the new template document and create your template.

- The Library category contains any other snippets you choose to store. A library item can contain any element or series of elements in the <body> section of a document. A good example of a library item is a series of nested tables with backgrounds or formatting applied. You can create a library item containing these tables so you can apply the same table layout elsewhere. Perhaps one of the best uses of a library item is to update placeholders you created during the design process. Let's say you're working on a site with a logo that will appear on every page, but the logo isn't yet finished. Simply create a library item with the <img> tag and a placeholder for the image source. Apply the library item on your pages in the proper position. When the logo is complete, you can update the library item to point to the finished file, which will then automatically update that item throughout your site. The Library is covered in detail in Chapter 28.

Caution *While you can use the Library to store image references, the actual image isn't stored in the library item. If you apply the library item across various folders, the link may break because of an invalid path.*

Behaviors Panel

The *Behaviors* panel can help even a novice Web designer build advanced Web sites. *Behaviors* are JavaScripts that act when triggered by an event. An example is an image swapped with another image when the original is clicked by a user. This would be a *Swap Image* action triggered by an onClick event.

The Behaviors panel can be accessed either from the Launcher, through the Window menu, or by pressing SHIFT-F3 on your keyboard. The following illustration shows the Behaviors panel. The plus sign (+) button opens the panel menu. From this menu, you can access the list of available behaviors. At the bottom of the menu is an option called *Show Events For...*, which contains a list of common browsers. This option enables you to limit your choice of behaviors to those who'll work with the browsers you select.

Dreamweaver ships with 25 behaviors that can serve your immediate needs. Hundreds of other behaviors can be found at the Macromedia Exchange for Dreamweaver, commonly known as the Dreamweaver Exchange, on the Internet (**http://www.macromedia.com/exchange/dreamweaver/**). You can access this site directly through your browser or by using the Get More Behaviors option in the Behaviors panel menu. To learn how to use behaviors, see Chapter 23.

Code Inspector

The *Code Inspector* has undergone several changes since Dreamweaver 3. For one thing, the name has changed from HTML Source Inspector, which was quite a mouthful. The functionality of the Code Inspector is identical to that of the Code view in the Document window, with the notable exception that the Code Inspector launches its own window, as shown in Figure 2-4. The Code Inspector has also evolved from a quick tweak tool to a more full-bodied HTML editor with color-coded tags and attributes, custom indenting, and word wrap settings. The Code Inspector (and Code view) are covered in Chapter 4.

CSS Styles Panel

The *CSS Styles* panel facilitates the creation and use of Cascading Style Sheets. CSS is becoming the preferred way to control the appearance and even the positioning of

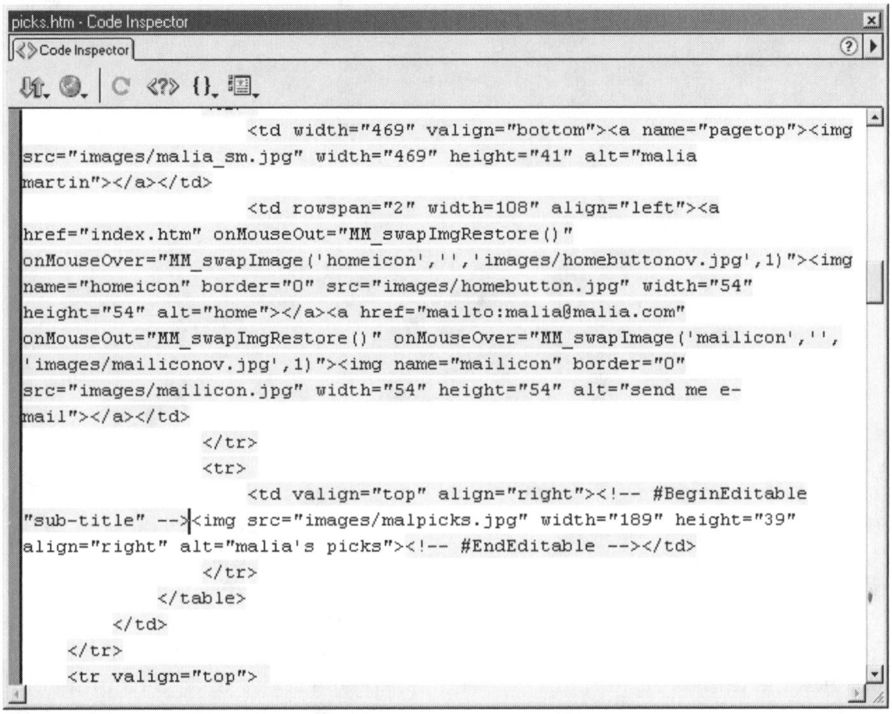

Figure 2-4. *The Code Inspector enables you to code by hand in a separate window, while keeping the Design view open in the full screen of the Document window*

elements in a document, although CSS has taken a while to catch on because of the lack of backward support for earlier browsers. As the majority of Internet users upgrade to version 4.0 and later browsers, this is becoming less of an issue. The ease of use, flexibility, and control offered by CSS is also attracting many developer converts. Finally, with XHTML making inroads into the developer community, <font> and other tags are being deprecated in favor of style sheets. This should provide considerable incentive to learn how to use this powerful tool. To learn how to use CSS and the CSS Styles panel, see Chapter 17.

Frames Panel

If your document contains frames, the *Frames* panel (see the following illustration) provides a simple diagram of your frameset. If your frameset consists of nested frames, keeping track of the frame hierarchy can be confusing. When you get lost, the Frames panel can help you get your bearings. The Frames panel also provides a shortcut to edit the frames properties in the Property Inspector—simply click a frame or the frameset border in the Frames panel and the Property Inspector picks up the context. For more on frames, see Chapter 15.

History Panel

Is there one Web developer who has never made a series of changes he wishes he hadn't made on an otherwise acceptable page? Not likely. A lot of repetitive processes are involved in designing a site, such as applying a style to every header. The *History* panel, shown in the following illustration, tracks your actions. If you make a mistake, you can undo several actions in one step. Likewise, if you want to repeat an action, you can click the Replay button. If you need to repeat a series of actions in several places, you can save a series of steps as a Command, which are then available from the Command menu.

The History panel has one notable limitation: it cannot track mouse movements. So, if you highlight text using the mouse or use the Point to File button to select a linked file, the History panel cannot track your actions.

HTML Styles Panel

While CSS is rapidly gaining in popularity, situations might still occur that require you to fall back on plain old HTML. If you're designing for an audience with older browsers, you'll either want to use HTML styles or redundantly code with both HTML and CSS styles. As mentioned earlier, as CSS becomes easier to use and more of a design standard, and as users upgrade their browsers to more current versions, the use of HTML styles will fade. To cover all the bases, though, the HTML Styles panel is covered in Chapter 9.

Layers Panel

Layers are used in *Dynamic HTML (DHTML)*. Each layer is almost a Web page itself, containing HTML elements, such as tables, graphics, and text. Whereas each page stands on its own, however, layers can do exactly what their name implies—be layered on a page. With the use of show/hide behaviors and timelines, layers can be used to make information appear and disappear in rollovers or even float across the page.

The *Layers* panel provides control over layers. Each new layer is added by default to the top of the layer stack. Using the Layers panel, you can change the stacking order of layers, as well as control their visibility and other attributes. For more about layers and how to use the Layers panel to its full effect, see Chapter 19, "Dynamic HTML."

Reference Panel

The Reference panel is new in Dreamweaver 4. In short, the *Reference* panel is a series of references to HTML, JavaScript, and CSS in general, as opposed to how to use them in Dreamweaver. The reference texts were written by O'Reilly Publications. These valuable resources are available by choosing Reference from the Window menu or by the keyboard shortcut CTRL-SHIFT-F1 (CMD-SHIFT-F1 for Mac users).

Timelines Panel

The *Timelines* panel, shown in the following illustration, controls the movement of layers and animations over time. It can also be used to cue in music and other background effects for a complete multimedia experience. To understand timelines, you first need to understand DHTML and behaviors. Chapter 20 explains the use of the Timelines panel in detail.

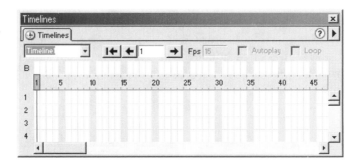

The Objects Panel

The last panel is the Objects panel, shown in the following illustration. The *Objects* panel is most likely the panel you'll use the most, especially as you familiarize yourself with the various elements of a Web page. More than just a single panel, the Objects panel is actually made up of seven categories of objects, all accessible from the category label at the top of the panel. Each item in the Objects panel is an item that can be added to a document. Rather than clicking Insert | Image from the menu, you can click the insert image button on the Common Objects panel—one click rather than a series of menu navigations.

The Objects panel is fully customizable, enabling you to add your own objects to each category. You can also move objects between categories to put your own favorite items on one panel. Because you'll be using this panel quite often, you'll probably want to keep it open at all times. Unless you are using a full-screen Document window, you can resize and reorient the Objects panel to fit somewhere around the perimeter of the Document window, thereby keeping your workspace clear.

Each of the items available from the Objects panel is described in the appropriate chapter of this book. The Objects panel itself, particularly the customization of this panel, is covered in Chapter 24.

Summary

In this chapter, you learned about all the basic features of the Dreamweaver workspace and the flexibility of this powerful tool.

Key points:

- The Document window is your main design and development workspace. The Document window is surrounded by menus, the Launcher bar, and the Status bar to put important information and accessibility in reach.

- The menus contain all the features of Dreamweaver. Most of the menu options are also available from the various panels and inspectors, as well as the keyboard shortcuts. The keyboard shortcuts for each option are listed in the menu as a reference.

- Dreamweaver 4 has added new panels, such as the powerful Assets panel and the informative Reference panel. The panels can be docked together or hidden easily.

- The Objects panel contains the most commonly used objects on a Web page. These objects can be rearranged and other objects can be added to each category.

In the next chapter, you learn how to set preferences for the Dreamweaver software and how it codes your documents.

The Complete Reference

Chapter 3

Setting Preferences

Now that you know the lay of the land, the next step is to customize Dreamweaver to your specific needs and work style. The best way to become comfortable with a new software tool is to put your own stamp on it. Looking at the settings and preferences available for a package can fire up your creativity, as well as give you an idea of the possibilities and limitations of the software.

One of the biggest assets of Dreamweaver is almost every panel, window, menu, and list of options is customizable, both in position and content. You don't learn about extensions and other advanced customization until later in this book, but this chapter can help you set the basic preferences so you can start using Dreamweaver.

Have it your way. Different people prefer different setups in their work environment. Dreamweaver enables you to change your preferences through the Preferences dialog box. You access the Preferences dialog box by selecting Edit | Preferences on the Menu bar. Or, you can use the keyboard shortcut CTRL-U (CMD-U on the Mac).

Each of the preference categories listed on the left side of the dialog box contain many options, which are listed on the right side of the box. Options with a check box toggle on and off as you check and uncheck the boxes. Other options enable you to choose a selection from a drop-down menu or type your own preference in a text box.

> **Note**   *If you've used previous versions of Dreamweaver, the Preferences dialog box has changed considerably. New categories exist to set preferences for Dreamweaver 4's new features. Other categories are renamed in keeping with changes in terminology, such as the change from HTML Source to Code. Within each category, some preferences have been added or rearranged into more logical groupings. If you're used to making changes to your preferences on the fly, familiarize yourself with the new layout of this dialog box before you inadvertently choose to open in the Site window when you intended to automatically add a file extension to your files.*

General Preferences

The first category of preferences is General. The General preferences control file and editing options. Even if you aren't yet ready to set the other preferences in Dreamweaver, the General preferences can help you customize your work environment enough to get started. The following illustration shows the General Preferences dialog box.

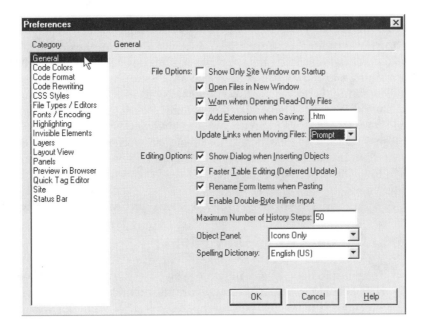

File Options

The first choices of General Preferences involve File options. These options control how files are saved and how link integrity between files is maintained. The following options can be selected or deselected.

Show Only Site Window on Startup

Some developers prefer to use the Site window, rather than the Document window, as their starting point, especially because Dreamweaver requires a defined site to make use of its Assets panel and other advanced features. Whereas most of the Preferences take effect immediately after clicking the OK box at the bottom of the dialog box, this option logically does not take effect until the next time you launch Dreamweaver.

If you select this option, you can still easily open a Document window by selecting File | New Window from the Site window menu bar or use the CTRL-N (CMD-N for Mac users) keyboard shortcut. You can also create a new file in the Site window by selecting File | New File (CTRL-SHIFT-N in Windows, CMD-SHIFT-N on the Mac), naming the new file added to the local file list, and then double-clicking the filename, just as you would to open any file from the Site window. See Chapter 5 to learn how to use the Site window effectively as a starting point in Dreamweaver.

Open Files in New Window (Windows Only)

If you're using the Windows platform, Dreamweaver gives you the option of opening files in a new window—cascading the windows on the screen space between your open panels—or opening each new document in the same window as previously opened documents. The former is preferable if you're making changes to multiple documents at once and have a large amount of system resources. The latter is useful if you're low on memory or you like to work in an uncluttered environment.

This option is selected by default, as most designers prefer to open each document in its own window. If you choose to deselect this option to have documents open in the same window, Dreamweaver prompts you to save your previous document before opening another.

On the Mac platform, Dreamweaver always opens documents in a new window.

Warn when Opening Read-Only Files

Read-only files are locked to prevent accidental overwrites. Selecting this option warns you when you attempt to open a read-only file. You have the option of proceeding to open the file while keeping it locked to changes or unlocking the file before you proceed to open it. If you choose the former, you can open the read-only file for viewing but, if you modify the document, you need to save the file using the File | Save As option to save it under a new filename.

Add Extension when Saving

The most common file extensions in Web design are .html and .htm. With the advent of new technologies, such as *Active Server Pages (ASP)*, you'll also find file extensions such as .asp becoming more prevalent. Dreamweaver enables you to set a default extension in your preferences. Thereafter, when you save a new file in Dreamweaver, it automatically adds the file extension. You can always bypass this feature by typing a complete filename with extension when you save the file. If you find a particular project is using ASP or requires a particular file extension, you can also change this option for the duration of the project.

Update Links when Moving Files

Web sites aren't static. Even after you open your virtual doors to the world, you'll invariably want to make changes to the site. As your site grows, chances are you'll eventually move a file or two in your site structure. You may find your images folder is becoming too cumbersome, for example, and decide to group your images by page. Moving folders changes the paths of your files and, unless you update your links to these files, those links will break. This option tells Dreamweaver how to handle link changes when you move, rename, or delete a file. Your choices for updating links are

■ **Always**—Dreamweaver automatically updates any links when you move a file.

- **Never**—Dreamweaver won't update any links when you move files. This option should be used with caution, as you must manually update your links. With large sites, this can be a time-consuming process that's prone to errors.
- **Prompt**—Dreamweaver warns you of the need to update links and asks you to select the Update button if you want to update the code.

Setting this option to Always and letting Dreamweaver maintain your links for you is usually easiest.

Dreamweaver can only maintain links if you make directory and file changes within the application itself. If you move folders and files outside of Dreamweaver, it cannot maintain link integrity any longer.

Editing Options

The General preferences category also enables you to set editing options. These options control how Dreamweaver handles objects you add to documents using the Objects panel or the Insert menu. You also use these options to configure the History panel, optimize table editing, and select a spell-check dictionary.

Show Dialog when Inserting Objects

By default, when you insert an object, Dreamweaver opens a related dialog box to select the specific object. If you insert an image, for example, Dreamweaver opens a Select Image Source dialog box to select an image file. If you insert a table, Dreamweaver displays a dialog box to set the number of columns and rows, the width of the table, and the border settings. Some developers prefer to use the Property Inspector to enter the specifics of an object. If you deselect the Show Dialog option, objects appear as placeholders or with default settings, which you then have to modify in the Property Inspector. An image displays an unformatted placeholder. A table appears with a default of three columns and two rows.

Some objects, such as the date object and rollover images, always display a dialog box, regardless of this preference setting.

Faster Table Editing (Deferred Update)

Tables can become complex, particularly when they're nested within other tables, and can take time to update in Dreamweaver. With this option selected, height and width adjustments in tables don't appear until you click outside the table. This can take some getting used to because what you see on the screen may not reflect the actual dimensions of the table. This option speeds up your work, however, so it can be a useful option.

If you want to update the table while you're still editing it, press CTRL-SPACE in Windows or CMD-SPACE on the Mac.

Rename Form Items when Pasting

Forms require each item to be uniquely named. If you're copying-and-pasting form items to set up a form quickly, such as a series of check boxes, forgetting to give the pasted items a new name is easy. This option automatically appends a number to the end of the form item name to ensure each item has a unique name. If you deselect this option, form items retain their original name and need to be renamed manually in the Property Inspector.

Enable Double-Byte Inline Input

Languages such as Chinese, Japanese, and Korean have large character sets. The maximum number of characters available in a single byte is 256, which isn't enough for these languages. Therefore, these languages require a double-byte character set. To enter double-byte characters directly into the Document window, you must enable this preference. If this preference is disabled, you can only enter double-byte characters using a text input window to convert the double-byte text.

Maximum Number of History Steps

The History panel is a visual list of the steps you took in creating or modifying your document. This option sets how many steps the History panel should track. When you exceed the maximum number of steps you set here, the oldest steps scroll out of the history as new ones are added.

Objects Panel

The Objects panel defaults to displaying its options as icons. For Dreamweaver newcomers, this can be less than intuitive. If you hover over an object long enough, you can view a tool tip with the name of the object, but all those extra seconds add up. Fortunately, this setting can be changed to display a combination of icons and text or only text.

Once you're familiar with the objects and icons, you may want to change this setting back to the default Icons Only view because this takes up the least amount of screen real estate.

Spelling Dictionary

This option enables you to select a spell-check dictionary from the drop-down list of available options. The English version of Dreamweaver ships with three English dictionaries, each for a different dialect or spelling conventions. Foreign language dictionaries are available from the Macromedia site at **http://www.macromedia.com/ support/dreamweaver/dictionary.html**. After downloading the file, unzip it into your Configuration/Dictionaries folder, found in your Dreamweaver application folder.

Code Preferences

The next three categories of preferences involve HTML coding preferences. Here, you can set many of the options for handling and displaying code.

Code Colors

Dreamweaver enables you set your preference of color for specific code items when they're displayed in Code view or the Code Inspector. These options don't change the functionality or content of the code at all. The colors simply provide easier readability when working your code. The following illustration shows the Code Color Preference box. You can set the color for the following items:

- **Background**—the background color of the Code view or Code Inspector.
- **Text**—the color of text content.
- **Comments**—the color of comment tags and their contents.
- **Tag Default**—the color of tags.
- **Reserved Keywords**—the color of reserved keywords in scripts.
- **Other Keywords**—the color of all other keywords.
- **Strings**—the color for strings.

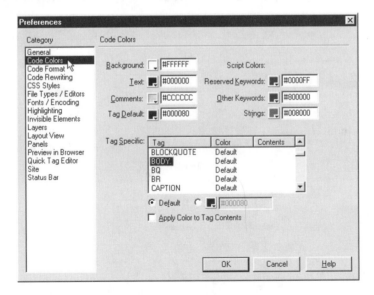

You can change the default color on any of these items by clicking the swatch next to any item and selecting a color from the color picker.

You can also select colors for a specific tag. You can use this option to make all your <table> tags, for example, stand out in a different color from other tags to make locating them on sight easier.

1. Scroll through the list of tags from the Tag Specific list.

2. Highlight the tag you want to change. You must highlight the entry in the Tag column of the list, not the Color or Contents columns.

3. Click the button next to the color swatch to change the color from the default.

4. Either type in a hexadecimal color value in the text field next to the color swatch or click the swatch to bring up the color picker box.

5. Select a color for the tag. If you want the tag to stand out, choose a different color from those set for other options.

6. If you want this color to be applied to text enclosed by the tag as well as the tag itself, select the Apply Color to Tag Contents option.

7. Choose other tag colors following the previous Steps 1-6. Click OK to exit the Preferences dialog box or click another category to choose other preferences.

Code Format

Dreamweaver also enables you to format your code to your liking. As with the color coding preferences, these options let you make your code more readable and, thus, easier to navigate. The following illustration shows the Code Format Preference. You can set the default format of many aspects of your code from the Preferences Dialog box.

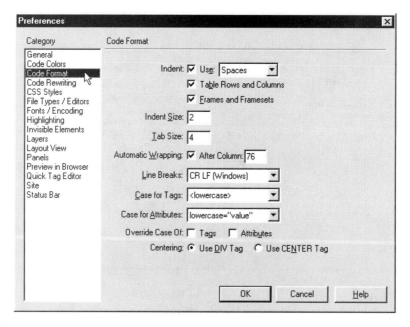

In addition to the customization options offered by these preference settings, you can also change the code format by editing the SourceFormat.txt file. This is covered in Chapter 4.

Indent

To make your code easier to read, Dreamweaver defaults to indenting most HTML tags by two spaces. This default setting can be changed to increase or decrease the indentation. You can choose to indent using spaces or tabs. You should choose this setting based on the nature of your code editing work. If you plan to do all your development in Dreamweaver or another dedicated Web design package, you should leave this at the default spaces setting. If, for some reason, you plan to edit your documents in a word processor, you may prefer to use the tabs setting to increase the size of the indentation. If you use the tab setting, you may also want to increase or decrease the tab size. If you worry about the added weight (and, therefore, download time) of extra spaces in your code, you can also turn off indentation entirely by deselecting the Indent options.

Tables and Frames are indented more than the default two spaces and are grouped according to the nesting structure of these elements. If you want to turn off the additional indenting of these, deselect the Table Rows and Columns option and the Frames and Framesets option. This additional indentation makes staying oriented in a complex page layout much easier.

Automatic Wrapping

When this option is selected, your code automatically wraps to fit within the Code view or Code Inspector window. You can select a specific column for the word wrap to take effect. The word wrap settings don't affect how your pages are viewed. The appearance of your pages on the Web are controlled strictly by the HTML tags themselves, not by line breaks in the code.

You can override the automatic wrapping settings on the fly using the View Options on the toolbar or by selecting View | Code View Options | Word Wrap. If you are doing this every time you work in Code view or the Code Inspector, consider modifying your preferences to suit your obvious work style.

Line Breaks

This option sets the type of line break that appears at the end of each line of your code. Windows uses a carriage return and line feed (CR-LF). Macintosh uses a carriage return (CR). UNIX uses a line feed (LF). Choose the correct option for the operating system of your remote server rather than your local computer system for the code to be viewed correctly on the server. Dreamweaver reads the code correctly regardless of this setting, but if you also use an external editor such as Notepad, you may need to change the setting in accordance with your local operating system order for the breaks to be recognized in these programs.

Case for Tags and Case for Attributes

While most browsers don't care if tags are in uppercase or lowercase, most Web developers have a decided preference for one or the other. Some developers prefer uppercase tag elements and lowercase attributes. Others prefer consistency and choose to keep their tags and attributes in either uppercase or lowercase. Personally, I prefer to use lowercase tags and attributes because this is more consistent with JavaScript.

Dreamweaver defaults to lowercase for tags and attributes, but the settings for each can be changed. Click the down arrow next to Case for Tags or Case for Attributes to change from lowercase to uppercase.

Override Case of Tags and Attributes

Setting the case preferences for tags and attributes only applies to coding done by Dreamweaver itself when you're working in Design view. Any code you enter by hand in the Code view or Code Inspector retains the case in which you enter that code. Also, Dreamweaver's Roundtrip HTML ensures Dreamweaver won't alter any existing code in a document—unless you tell the application to do so. If you want your tag and attribute preferences to prevail in all situations, you need to select the Override Case options. With these options, all tags and attributes in any open documents are converted to your case settings, and any documents you open thereafter are also converted.

Centering

Although the old `<center>` tag has been deprecated by the *World Wide Web Consortium* (*W3C*, the organization in charge of setting Web standards), some developers still use this method for centering images and text to preserve compatibility with older browsers. Dreamweaver uses the preferred centering method, `<div align="center">`, as its default. If you prefer to use the `<center>` tag, you can change your centering preference.

Code Rewriting

The options under Code Rewriting enable you to control what happens when you open a document in Dreamweaver. This is one situation where Dreamweaver breaks its promise of not modifying your code—unless you change the default settings of the Code Rewriting options to hold the application to that promise. When these options are selected, as they are by default, Dreamweaver automatically fixes improper tags. If you deselect these options, Dreamweaver highlights the improprieties for you without making any changes itself.

Note

Even with the Code Rewriting Options selected, Dreamweaver only modifies your code when opening a document. If you're working in Code view or the Code Inspector, Dreamweaver won't validate your code as you work. If you switch from Code view to Design view, Dreamweaver highlights invalid code, but won't make automatic modifications. Similarly, if you then switch back to Code view, invalid HTML is highlighted only if Highlight Invalid HTML is turned on (using either the View Options on the toolbar or View | Code View Options | Highlight Invalid HTML on the menu).

The following illustration shows the Code Rewriting Preferences dialog box.

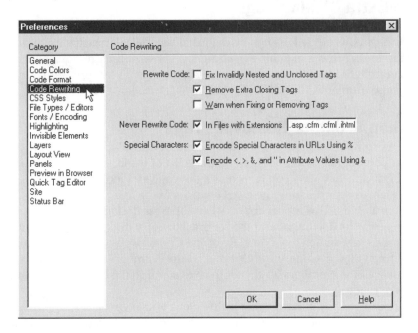

Fix Invalidly Nested and Unclosed Tags

In HTML, tags need to be closed in the reverse hierarchy from which they were opened, nesting each complete element within surrounding elements. If you open a document containing a table with text in italics, as follows,

```
<td><i>Caution: Coffee may be hot!</td></i>
```

Dreamweaver corrects the code to position the closing tag properly for the italics as follows:

```
<td><i>Caution: Coffee may be hot!</i></td>
```

With this setting, Dreamweaver also adds quotation marks around attribute values and the closing bracket (>) to a tag if the original code doesn't contain them, to close the tags properly.

If you deselect this option, Dreamweaver won't make any changes to invalid tags. It does, however, highlight the tags in yellow within both the Design and Code views (or the Code Inspector). If you're uncertain as to why your code has been marked as invalid, you can double-click the highlighted tag. The Property Inspector provides an explanation of the problem.

Remove Extra Closing Tags

When editing in the Code view or Code Inspector, it's easy to leave behind a stray closing tag. With this option selected, as it is by default, Dreamweaver strips extra closing tags when it doesn't find a matching opening tag. As with the previous nesting and unclosed tag preference, if this option is deselected, Dreamweaver highlights, but won't fix, these problems.

Warn when Fixing or Removing Tags

When editing complex documents created by another developer or using another application, you might want to view a complete list of the changes Dreamweaver makes to the code. That way, you can ensure the page still looks as intended. This option generates a report listing the exact changes made to a file, complete with line and column numbers. This report appears in a separate dialog box, enabling you to switch between your document and the report. To verify the changes in your code with your own eyes, switch to Code view or the Code Inspector, and then turn on line numbering (View | Code View Options | Line Numbers from the menu or View Options | Line Numbers on the toolbar) to scroll to the exact lines where changes were made.

Check Dreamweaver's changes carefully! Once you save the document again, the changes cannot be undone. If you don't want to accept the changes Dreamweaver has made, close the document without saving the file. You can then change your Code Rewriting preferences and open the document again to make changes manually.

Never Rewrite Code

ASP and database programs, such as Cold Fusion, embed their tags within HTML pages to add extra features and functionality to a Web site. These pages may look similar to a standard HTML page, but they have extensions, such as .asp or .cfm, to allow these pages to connect to the proper server applications. To prevent Dreamweaver from altering the codes the program may need to communicate with the server, you can turn off the rewriting of code on specified file types with the Never Rewrite Code option. By default, Dreamweaver won't rewrite code in the following types of files: Active Server Pages (.asp), Cold Fusion (.cfm and .cfml), Inline HTML (.ihtml), JavaScript source code (.js), Java Server Pages (.jsp), and PHP script (.php and .php3).

To add extensions to this list, simply add them in the text box. To delete extensions—thereby allowing Dreamweaver to modify those files—delete the extension from the list in the text box.

Note   *If you're making extensive use of databases and ASP, Dreamweaver UltraDev 4 may be better suited to your development needs. UltraDev has all the features of Dreamweaver 4 and adds database and server tools to help you create personalized, dynamic Web sites. For more information about UltraDev, visit the Macromedia site at http://www.macromedia.com.*

Special Characters

Certain characters—particularly spaces, tag brackets (< and >), quotation marks, ampersands, and other symbols—can cause trouble in HTML, particularly if you're on a UNIX server. When those characters are used in URLs, they can be interpreted differently by various servers, causing broken links. Some of these characters are also reserved in HTML for such things as the opening and closing of an attribute or tag, so if they appear elsewhere—especially in an attribute—this can cause the page to render differently than the developer intended. To prevent these problems, Dreamweaver is set by default to encode special characters to their decimal equivalents, preceded by a percent (%) symbol in URLs or ampersands (&) in tag attributes.

In most cases, this encoding does no harm and can ensure your code is readable on the widest variety of servers. If you're using certain third-party applications, however, this recoding can corrupt their tags. If you find this is the case for your projects, you can deselect these encoding options.

CSS Styles

As declared by the W3C, *Cascading Style Sheets* (CCS) are the preferred method for defining the appearance and layout of your pages, freeing up the actual HTML for structure. Chapter 17 covers this in greater detail. The current releases of the major Web browsers—Microsoft Internet Explorer, AOL Netscape, and Opera— not only support CSS, but also support the shorthand sometimes used to group related styles into one CSS declaration. Older versions of these browsers have limited support for CSS shorthand, if any. Dreamweaver enables you to set preferences relating to CSS shorthand. The next illustration shows the preferences for CCS Styles.

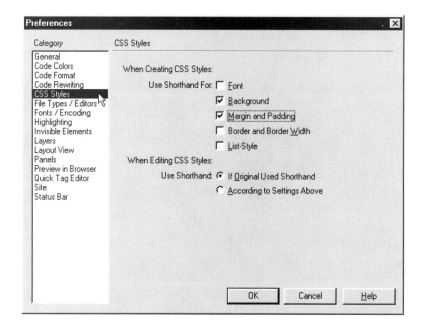

Selecting any of these preferences informs Dreamweaver to use CSS shorthand when creating style sheets. The difference in code can be considerable. Here is a declaration of a border in CSS:

```
p { border: #3366CC; border-style: solid; border-top-width: medium;
border-right-width: medium; border-bottom-width: medium;
border-left-width: medium; }
```

The following declaration has the same result in the browser, but is in CSS shorthand:

```
p { border: medium #3366CC solid; }
```

Note   *Although Dreamweaver provides options for a wide range of styles, it cannot display many of the advanced styles—such as the border styles used in the previous example— in the Document window. To test your style sheets fully, whether using the long form or shorthand form of CSS, you need to preview your pages in a browser.*

Along with setting preferences for new style sheets, Dreamweaver provides options for handling preexisting style sheets. You can elect to have Dreamweaver rewrite existing styles in shorthand according to your CSS settings or to leave any preexisting style sheets unchanged from their original state.

File Types/Editors

Because Dreamweaver takes a site-wide approach rather than a page-specific approach to Web development, the application acknowledges that not all aspects of a site can be created or maintained with the software itself. Images need to be created in a graphics editor; Java applets are generated in a Java development system; movies require video editing software; and so forth. While each of these objects require the use of different applications, however, all are brought together in your site by using Dreamweaver. This flow from external editor to Dreamweaver is maintained using the File Types/ Editors Preferences. When these preferences are configured for your applications, you can double-click a file in the Site window and launch the appropriate editor for that file type. The following illustration shows the options available for File Types/Editors.

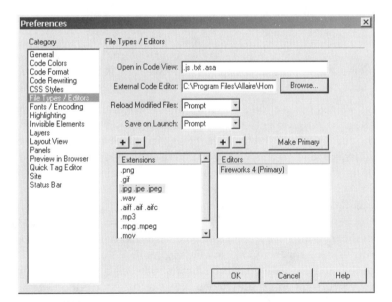

Open in Code View

Certain types of files are merely scripts or blocks of text rather than a visual Web page. When opening these files, it makes sense for them to appear in Code view rather than in Design view. By default, Dreamweaver opens .js, .txt, and .asa files in Code view. To add additional files types to this list, simply add their extension to the text box, leaving a space between each entry.

External Code Editor

If you've been developing in HTML for a while, chances are you have a favorite editor. You can certainly use Dreamweaver to handle all your HTML coding, especially with the improved Code view and Code Inspector but, at times, you want to revert to the tried and true. The full version of Dreamweaver 4 ships with either HomeSite 4.5 for Windows or an evaluation copy of BBEdit for the Mac (the Dreamweaver 4 upgrade ships with trial versions of these programs). Both these editors are integrated with Dreamweaver, enabling you to move easily between packages and update your code.

To set an external code editor, use the Browse button to locate the editor application file. To use the external code editor after it has been set, select Edit | Edit with... from the menu or CTRL-E (CMD-E on the Mac).

Reload Modified Files

Dreamweaver can handle files after they've been modified in an external editor in three ways:

- **Always**—automatically updates the modified file when it's reloaded in Dreamweaver.

- **Never**—doesn't update a file modified in an external editor. You have to repeat any modifications you made within Dreamweaver. Few situations exist in which you would choose this option.

- **Prompt**—gives you a choice of reloading the updated file in Dreamweaver or continuing to work on your original file. This option is helpful if you used the external editor to try out a modification you may or may not want to use on your finished page. In this way, you can use the external editor as a sort of test bed for new ideas without compromising your original file.

Save on Launch

Launching an external code editor from within Dreamweaver is similar to launching it from your desktop. Before it can edit a file, the external editor needs to open the file. When you launch the editor from Dreamweaver, the filename is passed to the external editor and opened automatically. But the editor still needs a saved file from which to work. If you saved your file in Dreamweaver, the external code editor opens this recent version. If you haven't saved, the external editor opens the most recently saved version, which may not contain any changes you just made in Dreamweaver. You can tell Dreamweaver how to handle the passing of the file to the external code editor through these options:

- **Always**—always saves the file before opening it in the external code editor. This is the safest option, as it ensures you have a saved copy of your current work before modifying it elsewhere.

- **Never**—always launches the most recently saved file without prompting you to save your current work, even if you've made changes to the file in Dreamweaver since your last save. If you created a new file that hasn't yet been saved, you are prompted to save the file first even if you choose this option. If you don't save the file, the external code editor won't launch because it doesn't have a saved file to open.

■ **Prompt**—prompts you to save your file before launching the external code editor. If you don't save the file at this time, the external code editor launches with the most recently saved version of the file. If you haven't saved the file at least once, the external editor won't launch because there's no available file to open.

Caution   *Choose your combination of Reload and Save on Launch Preferences carefully. If you set your Save on Launch preference to Never and your Reload preference to Always, you may find yourself in a situation where you haven't saved your most recent changes to a document before launching the external code editor, and then making changes you don't like and automatically overriding the document with those changes. If you choose this preference combination, be careful when moving between Dreamweaver and an external code editor.*

Other External Editors

You can easily launch an external program to modify many types of files. The bottom section of the File Types/Editors Preferences lets you associate file extensions with one or more external editors. If a file extension doesn't appear in Dreamweaver's default list, you can also add file extensions.

To associate a file extension with an external editor:

1. Scroll down the list of file types in the Extensions list.

2. Highlight a file extension.

3. Click the plus sign (+) button above the Editors list to add an editor for this file type.

4. A Select External Editor box then opens. Browse to the application you want to use to open that type of file.

5. Click Open.

6. If you want this program to be the primary editor of this file type, click the Make Primary button.

You can add another file type to the list of extensions by clicking the plus sign (+) button above the Extension box, and then typing in an extension in the blank entry created in the list. You can add variations to certain extensions—such as the list of JPEG extensions—by double-clicking one of the predefined extensions and adding the new extension to that entry.

Applications come and go as new products and upgrades are released. If you simply add the new application to the Editors list, you wind up with multiple editors associated with that file type extension. Unless you're doing this by design (see the following), you should delete the original association before adding a new one. To delete an association:

1. Select the file type extension in the Extensions list to bring up the list of associated editors for that file type.

2. Select the application name from the Editors list.

3. Click the minus sign (-) button above the Editors list to remove the editor.

You can then add a new editor for that file type using the earlier steps for associating a file extension with an external editor.

As just mentioned, times may occur when you want multiple editors listed for an extension. You may own Photoshop, Image Ready, and Fireworks, for example, and use each application for a specific aspect of image editing. If you have multiple editors for the same types of files, you can associate each of these editors to the same extensions. Simply follow the steps for associating a file extension with an external editor for each application. Each additional editor is listed in the Editors list for that file type extension. You can only designate one editor as the primary editor for each file type. If you double-click a file from the Site window, it automatically launches in the primary editor for that file type. If you right-click (in Windows) or control-click (on the Mac), however, the context menu displays a list of all associated editors for that type, enabling you to choose an editor.

Fonts/Encoding

The world is growing ever smaller as the Internet grows ever larger. Developers are more likely than ever before to need to code pages in multiple languages. Some of these languages have their own character sets, which are encoded differently from English. Additionally, not all fonts are available in each of these languages. The Fonts/Encoding category of the Preferences dialog box enables you to set the appropriate character and font sets for your work. The next illustration shows the Fonts/Encoding Preferences dialog box.

Default Encoding

The Fonts/Encoding Preferences control two different things: the character encoding for your Web pages and the font settings for your Dreamweaver environment. A page's character encoding tells the browser which character set to use to read the page. If your page is written in Japanese, which uses a Japanese character set, the encoding tells the browser to read the page using this character set. Without this information, the page would be a mass of gibberish in any other character set. Dreamweaver provides 20 font encoding options, including Western (Latin 1), which displays English and Western European languages, Japanese, Chinese, and Cyrillic, among others. Some of these languages have multiple options depending on the language and the computer platform. The encoding option inserts the appropriate <meta> tag at the top of the document to identify the character set. If a visitor doesn't have the appropriate character set loaded, the browser prompts them to download it.

Font Settings

The Font Settings have no relationship to the Font Encoding, although their placement in the same Preferences category can be confusing. The Font Settings enable you to specify a font family for the proportional and fixed fonts, as well as the default Code view font, for each of the listed languages. If you're only writing pages in Western languages, you needn't worry about the Font Settings for the other languages listed. If you're developing pages with other language encoding, you should be sure to install the appropriate fonts for each of those languages and look at the Font Settings for each of the languages in which you plan to work.

When you choose a language in the Font Settings list, notice the fonts listed in the Proportional Font, Fixed Font, and Code Inspector text boxes below change accordingly, providing you with the appropriate font options for each character set. These font settings specify the fonts Dreamweaver should use to display your text content when no font family is named in the HTML or linked style sheet.

Remember, these fonts have no bearing on how your page will be viewed by your site's visitors. If you set Arial as your proportional font, any text you type without a `<font>` tag or related font setting in a linked style sheet appears in the Design view in Arial. When your completed page is live on the Internet, however, each visitor to your site might have his own setting for proportional fonts. Most browsers default to Times Roman, but this can be changed by the user. You can test this for yourself:

1. In the Fonts/Encoding Preferences, set the Font Settings for Western (Latin 1).

2. Set the Proportional Font for Comic Sans (or some other noticeable font) by clicking the drop-down arrow, and then selecting a font.

3. Click OK to exit the Preferences.

4. Type a sentence in the Design view. The sentence appears in Comic Sans in the Document window.

5. Press F12 to Preview in Browser. The sentence appears with your default font in the browser.

Note *The only way to ensure a browser displays the font you want is to name that font in either a `<font>` tag or CSS. Otherwise, specific font options are left to the user.*

The Proportional Font setting controls the display of most text content. The Fixed Font setting controls the display of text in special situations, such as when using the `<pre>` and `<code>` tags. The Code Inspector Font strictly controls the appearance of the code listing in Code view or the Code Inspector, not the actual appearance of the document in either Dreamweaver or on the Web.

Highlighting

Dreamweaver enables you to use templates, libraries, third-party tags, and layout tools. When you're trying to modify a page that contains these features, keeping all these elements straight can be difficult. You can set Highlighting options to provide you with a visual clue. The following illustration shows the Highlighting Preferences.

DREAMWEAVER
BASICS

Preferences

Category   Highlighting

General
Code Colors
Code Format   Show
Code Rewriting   Editable Regions: [▾] [#CCFFFF]   ☑
CSS Styles
File Types / Editors   Locked Regions: [▾] [#FFFFCC]   ☑
Fonts / Encoding
Highlighting   Library Items: [▾] [#FFFFCC]   ☑
Invisible Elements
Layers   Third-Party Tags: [▾] [#CCFFFF]   ☑
Layout View
Panels
Preview in Browser
Quick Tag Editor
Site
Status Bar

                                        [OK]   [Cancel]   [Help]

Each of the options in the Highlighting Preferences provides both a color picker and a Show check box. If you want the object to be highlighted in your documents, check the Show box and choose a highlight color. If you don't want the object to be highlighted, make sure the Show check box for that item is empty.

When choosing highlight colors, keep your site design in mind. If you choose colors that blend in with your site colors, noticing them in Design view can be difficult, and distinguishing editable and locked regions of your template can be hard. Choosing colors that are too contrasting with your site colors can be distracting when you touch up your design. Remember, you can change these preferences at any time to accommodate your needs.

Editable and Locked Regions

Editable and locked regions refer to template settings. When you create a template, you mark certain areas to which content can be added for each page. These are *editable regions.* All the other regions of the page are marked as *locked* to prevent changes from being made to the overall design and <head> elements of the page. In the Code view or Code Inspector, these regions are highlighted according to the color you select in the Highlighting Preferences. In Design view, the regions are enclosed in boxes in the highlight color to designate each region.

Library Items

Library item highlighting marks any objects or snippets you add from your Library (found in the Assets panel).

Third-Party Tags

Third-party tags include ASP, PHP, and Cold Fusion elements. Highlighting these elements can be helpful because you'll most likely be generating the code in a third- party application or by hand.

Invisible Elements

Even when you're working in Design view, you might want to see your comments or other hidden elements at times. With the *Invisible Elements* Preferences, you can set various elements to display a representative icon in Design view. These icons don't appear on the page when viewed in a browser, but they can provide crucial landmarks in the design and development stages of your site. The next illustration shows the Invisible Elements Preferences.

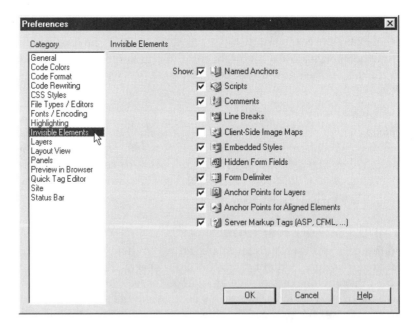

Place a check mark next to each element you want visible in Design view. Notice each of these elements has a unique icon, making it easy to determine which element is represented.

Named Anchors

Named anchors are used to designate specific portions of a page. If you click this icon in the Document window, you can change the name of the anchor in the Property Inspector or through the Name option of the context menu (right-click to bring up the context menu).

Scripts

If you select this option, Dreamweaver displays a script icon to show the location of JavaScript or VBScript. This option won't display scripts that appear in the <head> of the document, only in the <body>. If you click this icon in the Document window, you can edit the script in the Property Inspector. You can also change the link to an external script file through the Property Inspector.

Comments

You can use this option to display an icon for your comments. Clicking this icon displays the text of the comment in the Property Inspector. This is helpful when passing your documents along to others for final content if they aren't familiar with HTML, such as when working in a development group or handing off a completed project to a client. They can click the comment icon in the Design view for information about the layout without becoming disoriented in the Code view—or making a mess of your code.

Line Breaks

The *Line Break* icon doesn't note the end of each paragraph, only line breaks coded with the
tag. This icon can sometimes be more of a hindrance than a help because the icon itself can offset the appearance of your design in Design view, so it's deselected by default. You can toggle it on and off as needed through the Preferences settings.

Client-Side Image Maps

This icon marks client-side image maps. Click this icon to display the <map> tag in the Tag Selector to rename an image map.

Embedded Styles

If you embed your style sheets in the <body> of your document rather than the <head>, this icon marks their location. In most cases, you will embed your style sheets in the <head>, however, so this option may not be relevant to your work. This icon doesn't appear when you apply styles or class attributes; it only displays the location of the actual <style> tag within the <body> element.

Hidden Form Fields

When creating forms, you have the option of hiding certain fields. This icon marks the position of hidden form fields. Again, this icon offsets the layout of your document, so you want to deselect this option when lining up your form fields.

Form Delimiter

Rather than an icon, the *Form Delimiter* displays a border around forms. The border represents the beginning and end of the `<form>` tags. All form objects must be placed within this border to be included in the form, making this a useful option.

Anchor Points for Layers

While layers aren't invisible, the code that defines layers can be placed anywhere within the document. This icon marks the location of the defining code, not the layer itself. Knowing the location of this code can be particularly helpful when editing hidden layers. Clicking this icon makes the layer temporarily visible and enables you to change the layer's attributes in the Property Inspector.

Anchor Points for Aligned Elements

When you align an object, the placement of that object on the page can make telling where it was positioned within the code difficult. An example of this is an image object placed among text. This icon marks the position of the object's tag within the text. This is sometimes helpful when locating spacer images, but usually interferes with layout, so you may opt to deselect this option when fine-tuning your page design.

Server Markup Tags

While Dreamweaver can incorporate server markup into documents, it cannot display this markup in the Design view. Therefore, this icon can help you locate the position of server markup elements. To test these elements, you need to view your pages in a browser.

Even if you choose to make the default to show these elements on the document screen, you can quickly turn off the invisible elements at any time by selecting View | Visual Aids | Invisible Elements from the menu.

Layers

Layers are made possible through the use of CSS to control absolute positioning on a page. Once placed, layers can be designed independently of the rest of the page, including having their own backgrounds. Layers can be used to create fly-out and drop-down menus or to animate a page. Because you can add tables and other objects to a layer, you can essentially create a Web page within your Web page. The Layers Preferences enable you to set default values for many aspects of the layers you use on your Web site, as seen in the following illustration.

DREAMWEAVER
BASICS

Tag

The *Tag* setting determines how Dreamweaver codes new layers. The most common tags for layers are <div> and <span> because they comply with the W3C standard and are supported by the current versions of the popular browsers. The <layer> and <ilayer> tags are only supported by Netscape 4.x browsers and should only be used if you're developing solely for that browser. The latest version of Netscape no longer supports those tags.

Visibility

Layers can be visible or hidden, a useful feature when using layers for animation effects or creating drop-down menus. The Visibility option sets the default for new layers. Once you create a layer, you can change its visibility setting in the Property Inspector. If you set the visibility to inherit, new layers inherit their visibility or invisibility based on where they're nested. If one layer is created within another, the new layer inherits the visibility setting of its parent. If a layer is created independently, it's considered to be nested within the <body>, which is always visible.

Width and Height

By default, layers are created at a dimension of 200 pixels wide × 115 pixels high. You can change these default settings to whatever dimensions you prefer. You can also resize layers using the Property Inspector or by dragging the bounding box around the layer.

Background Color

Layers can have a background color independent of the page background color. To set the default background color, click the swatch and choose from the color picker. By default, layers are transparent.

Background Image

Just like a Web page, layers can contain background images. To set a default background image for all layers, enter the path of the image file in the Background Image setting. If the image is larger than the layer, it is cropped. If the image is smaller than the layer, it will tile, just as a background image tiles on a Web page or in a table.

Nesting

As mentioned earlier, layers can be nested. If you select the Nesting option, when you draw a layer within the boundary box of another layer, the new layer is nested. If this option is deselected—even if you draw a layer over another—it creates a new separate layer.

> **Note**   *Netscape 4.x browsers don't handle layers well, particularly nested layers. Even the current browsers still have idiosyncrasies in dealing with nested layers. Until browser support catches up with the full potential of layers and CSS positioning, you're better off using the z-index to control independent layers instead of nesting your layers.*

Netscape 4 Compatibility

Netscape 4.x has a problem displaying layers. If the user resizes her browser, the layers lose their position settings. The layers are usually left-aligned on the page after resizing, causing your carefully designed page to become a muddled mess. The only way to fix the mess is to reload the page. You can hardly force all your Netscape 4.x users to press Refresh every time they resize their browsers while visiting your site. Instead, select the Netscape 4 Compatibility option. This option places a JavaScript into your document that automatically reloads the page whenever the browser is resized. Unless you're absolutely sure you don't have any Netscape 4.x users visiting your site, you should select this option. It does no harm to other browsers, doesn't increase your file size by much, and will be appreciated by the remaining percentage of Netscape 4.x users.

Layout View

The *Layout* view, new in Dreamweaver 4, enables you to draw tables and cells in the Document window, and then position them as you want to create the underlying structure of your page. You can access this view from the Objects panel by selecting View | Table Views | Layout View from the menu or by using the CTRL-F6 (CMD-F6 on the Mac) keyboard shortcut. The Layout View options are shown in the next illustration.

Autoinsert Spacers

Spacer images are transparent images used to control layout. They are often used to prevent empty table cells from collapsing, such as when you want a colored margin along the right side of a page. Spacers are preferable to nonbreaking spaces because you can control the size of spacers more easily and they don't disappear when you add content to a cell. Dreamweaver automatically inserts spacers to autostretch tables if you select this option. If you deselect this option, you need to add your own space elements to ensure table layout integrity.

Spacer Image

Spacers are image files, therefore, they are inserted as links to the appropriate file. If you are using spacers, you need to establish the path to the spacer file for each new site you develop. If you don't have a spacer image already created, Dreamweaver can generate one for you. Dreamweaver's default name for this file is spacer.gif. Spacers are also commonly called *shims* or *single-pixel images,* so if you are inheriting a site from another developer, you may find a shim.gif or related file in the images folder. If you already have one of these spacers in your site folders, you can browse to the existing image rather than creating a new one.

Setting Colors

The color settings in the Layout View Preferences relate to how cells and tables created in Layout View are to be displayed in the Document window. The Cell Outline sets the outline color for cells. The Cell Highlight sets the color of the cell when you mouse over it, helping you identify individual cells. If you then click a cell, it reverts to the Cell Outline color with handles to enable you to move or resize the cell. The Table Outline sets the color for the outline of the entire table. The Table Background establishes the background color of the table in the Document window. Portions of the table that appear with the highlight color cannot hold any other elements unless you add a cell to that area. None of these color selections affect the actual appearance of the finished page. They're simply used for display purposes while you're working in Dreamweaver to make locating and manipulating each element easier. To change the default colors, either type a hex value into the text field or click the swatch and use the color picker.

Panels

Palettes have undergone a name change in Dreamweaver 4. They're now called *Panels,* and this preference category enables you to configure the Launcher bar and the visibility of panels when they overlap the Document window. The following illustration shows the Panels Preferences dialog box.

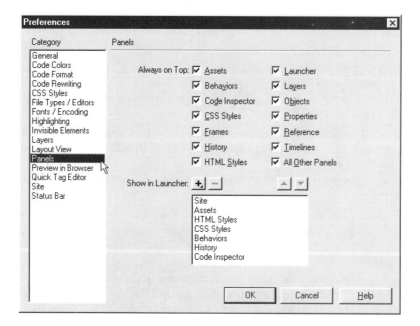

Always on Top

These options are straightforward. If you select a check box, that panel remains visible on top of the Document window, even while you're working in the window. If you deselect the check box, the panel can be covered by the Document window. If you populate the Launcher bar with your most commonly used panels, you can generally deselect most of the panels from the Always on Top settings knowing you can easily recall them. I always like to keep the Property Inspector on top, however, because I use it constantly.

Show in Launcher

The Launcher and Launcher bar are identical in functionality. Any panels you add to the Launcher also appear in the Launcher bar at the bottom of the Document window. As just mentioned, if you populate the Launcher with your most-used panels, you can access them with the touch of a button. The Show in Launcher Preferences enable you to add, remove, and change the order of the panels.

To add an item to the Launcher:

1. Press the plus sign (+) button.
2. Select an item to add from the pop-up menu of items.
3. Use the up and down arrows to adjust the placement of the new item.
4. Continue to add and reorder items as desired.
5. Click OK to exit the Preferences dialog box or continue to modify other preferences. The changes don't take place until you exit the Preferences dialog box.

To remove an item from the Launcher:

1. Highlight the item on the list.
2. Click the minus sign (-) button.
3. Continue to add, remove, or reorder items as desired.
4. Click OK to exit the Preferences dialog box or continue to modify other preferences. The changes don't take place until you exit the Preferences dialog box.

I rely heavily on the Launcher bar because I don't like to leave the Launcher open to steal valuable screen real estate. I also like to populate my Launcher bar with the Objects panel to make it easy to access that panel in the unlikely event that I ever close it. I recently removed the HTML Styles panel because I transitioned primarily to CSS and the Code Inspector because I prefer to use the Code view, or the split Design and Code view. Your preferences may vary.

Preview in Browser

Dreamweaver's Document window tries to present a fairly accurate view of your pages. Because each browser has different levels of support for HTML tags and CSS properties—coupled with Dreamweaver's need to facilitate easy editing of documents by using visual guides to various elements—there's no way Dreamweaver itself can ensure that your pages look good in every browser configuration. The only way to get a true picture of your page design is to test it in a variety of browsers. The next illustration shows the Preview in Browser Preferences dialog box.

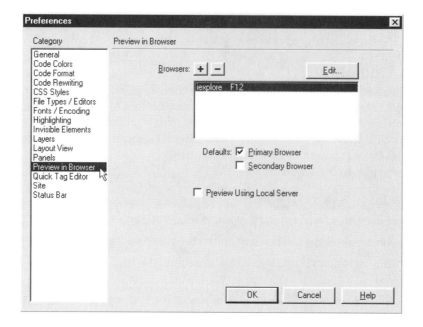

Browsers

When you install Dreamweaver, it generates a list of available browsers on your machine. To designate a primary browser:

1. Highlight one of the browsers in the list.

2. Check Primary Browser. This is the browser to be used as the default Web browser for previewing your work.

Once you choose a primary browser, you can use it to preview your work by using the F12 keyboard shortcut, selecting the Preview/Debug in Browser icon in the toolbar, or from the File | Preview in Browser menu. To select a secondary browser, follow the same steps, but check the Secondary Browser box. The secondary browser is available from the menu, the toolbar, or by using the CTRL-F12 (CMD-F12 on the Mac) keyboard shortcut.

If you install a new browser after you've already installed Dreamweaver, you need to add the browser to your list manually. To do this:

1. Select the plus (+) button. The Add Browser dialog box opens.

2. Give the browser a name. This name appears in the Preview in Browser menu.

3. Click the Browse button to locate the application file for the new browser.

4. If you want to make the browser either your primary or secondary browser, select the appropriate check box.

5. Click OK.

To remove a browser from the list, highlight the browser in the list and click the minus sign (-) button.

You may have up to 20 browsers installed, but Dreamweaver only applies keyboard shortcuts to the primary and secondary browsers you select. To preview your work in any other browsers, you need to select them from the File | Preview in Browser menu or the Preview/Debug in Browser icon on the toolbar.

Preview Using Local Server (Windows platform)

If you're on the Windows platform and are running local server software, you can use your computer as a test server. With the Preview Using Local Server option selected, you can test your pages with an actual URL (http://hostname/filename.htm) rather than a file path (file://path/filename.htm). The advantage of this option is you can test your root-relative paths for your links, something that cannot be handled correctly without a server.

Quick Tag Editor

The *Quick Tag Editor* enables you to make speedy code tweaks without leaving the Design view. When you launch the Quick Tag Editor—either by using the context menu in the Tag Selector or by clicking the Quick Tag Editor icon in the Property Inspector—a small window pops up with the appropriate tag and an editing window. This pop-up can be repositioned by dragging it across the screen. The Quick Tag Editor Preferences control the functionality of this tool, as shown in the following illustration.

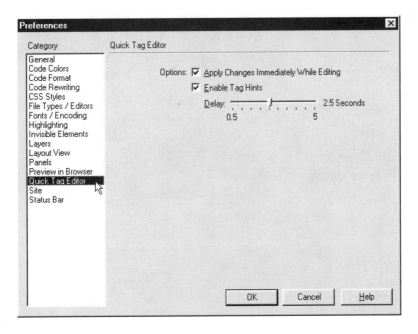

Apply Changes Immediately While Editing

If you want your changes to be applied immediately when you're editing, check the box beside the Apply Changes Immediately While Editing. The Quick Tag Editor has three modes, all of which are discussed in Chapter 4. This preference setting only applies to the Edit Tag mode. For the Insert HTML and Wrap Tag modes—and also the Edit Tag mode if you deselect this option—you need to press ENTER to apply your changes.

Enable Tag Hints

Tag Hints are a helpful list of tags that appear when you launch the Quick Tag Editor. You can scroll through the list to find the appropriate tag or type the initial letter of the tag to jump to that portion of the list. If you prefer to type in your own tags, you can deselect this option. You can also control the time delay between when you open the Quick Tag Editor and when the Tag Hints appear. At the minimum settings of .5 seconds, the Tag Hints appear almost immediately. At the maximum setting of 5 seconds, you have time to type the tag by hand, if you want, while still having the Tag Hints at hand if you get stuck.

Site

This preference was referred to as Site FTP in Dreamweaver 3. Not only does the *Site* window keep your files in order, it also facilitates transferring files between your local computer and the remote server by use of the file-transfer protocol. This option enables you to customize the connection and how the files are shown. The next illustration shows the Site Preferences.

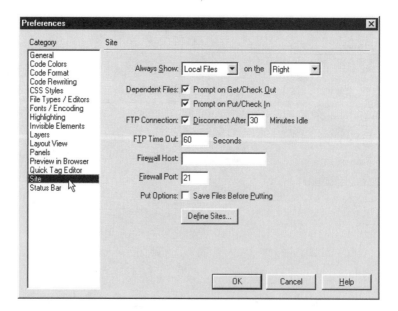

Always Show

Dreamweaver defaults to showing local files in the right pane on the Site window and remote files in the left pane. If you used WS-FTP in the past, this is the exact opposite of your familiar FTP layout. If you're used to seeing the local files on the left and remote files on the right, click the drop-down arrow next to the On The option and choose Left from the drop-down menu.

Dependent Files

A Web site is usually more than an individual page. A complete site can include dependent images, style sheets, and possibly even audio/video files. When you transfer files, Dreamweaver prompts you to transfer dependent files along with the HTML page(s). If you don't want to be prompted for this, you can deselect the Get/Check Out option (which downloads files from the remote server) and the Put/Check In option (which uploads files to the remote server).

FTP Connection and Time Out

Is easy to forget to disconnect from the remote server after transferring files. By default, Dreamweaver disconnects you if you haven't accessed the remote server in 30 minutes. You can change this time limit or disable this feature using the FTP Connection options.

At times, you might be unable to connect to the remote server because it's down or busy. Rather than tying you up with endless attempts to connect, Dreamweaver is set to warn you that your connection has timed out after 60 seconds without a response from the server. You can change this time limit using the FTP Time Out setting.

Firewall Host and Port

A *firewall* protects a network against unauthorized use. With the advent of DSL and cable modems, even home computer users are becoming more apt to use some sort of firewall to protect their personal data from malicious theft or hacking. If you use a firewall, you need to configure the firewall settings to allow Dreamweaver to connect to the remote server. If you use Dreamweaver at your office, you can obtain host and port information from your company's network administrator. If you use a firewall on your home network, you most likely have already configured your Web browser with your proxy server information. You can retrieve that information from your browser's preferences settings.

Put Options

Dreamweaver can automatically save an open document when you attempt to Put it on the remote server. To enable this feature, select Put Options.

Define Sites

If you click the Define Sites button, it brings up the Define Sites dialog box. From there, you can create a new site or edit an existing one.

Status Bar

As discussed in Chapter 2, the status bar appears at the bottom of the Document window. You can configure the layout of this bar using the Status Bar Preferences, as shown in the following illustration.

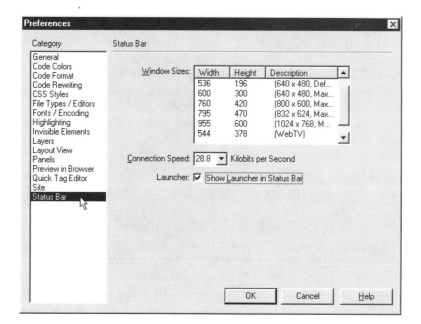

Window Sizes

While the Window Size feature contains the most common window defaults, you might want to add your own settings. To do this, select the Width column to add a width, and then tab to the height column to set the height of the window. You can add a description of the setting by tabbing to the Description column. Your new setting appears in the Window Size menu after you exit the Preferences dialog box.

Connection Speed

Just as a seemingly endless array of browsers and computer platforms exist, so do an equally wide array of connection speeds. Dreamweaver provides a page weight and

download time approximation, but you need to select a connection speed against
which the application can make this calculation.

Many companies now have T-1 or T-3 access, providing extremely fast connect
speeds for their employees, but not all companies encourage non-job-related Internet
use during office hours. Cable modems and DSL are bringing faster connect speeds to
the family computer, but they aren't yet available or affordable in all areas. This leaves
a large percentage of Web surfers at 56K or slower. While most Web users have tossed
aside their 28.8 modems in frustration at the slow speed, 56K modems don't usually
live up to their promise of a true 56K connection. Therefore, you probably want to set
your connection speed in Dreamweaver at 33.6K or 28.8K.

Show Launcher in Status Bar

By default, Dreamweaver displays the Launcher bar on the Status Bar. As mentioned
earlier, I prefer using the Launcher bar because it gives me ready access to important
panels. You may decide you prefer to have more space for the Tag Selector. If you want
to remove the Launcher bar, deselect this option.

Keyboard Shortcut Editor

Along with the Preferences dialog box, another option you want to set before beginning
your work in Dreamweaver is your keyboard shortcuts. *Keyboard shortcuts* are key presses that
take the place of navigating through the menus or panels of Dreamweaver. One common
keyboard shortcut is CTRL-S to save a document. This is much faster than using your mouse to
select File | Save from the menu, especially if your fingers are already on the keyboard.

If you're new to Dreamweaver, you'll probably rely initially on the panels and menus. As
you become more familiar with the application, you'll find keyboard shortcuts can save
you a lot of time. Note, these shortcuts must be easy for you to remember and access. If
you have small hands, it can be all but impossible to press CTRL-SHIFT-F6 gracefully to
switch from the Layout view to the Standard view. If you previously used Dreamweaver 3,
HomeSite, or BBEdit, you may already be used to the keyboard shortcuts available in those
applications. For those reasons, Dreamweaver enables you to edit your keyboard shortcuts.

The next illustration shows the Keyboard Shortcut Editor.

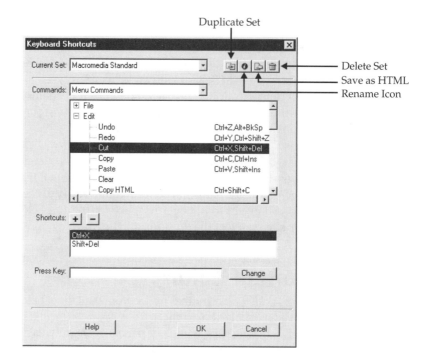

Duplicate Set

Delete Set
Save as HTML
Rename Icon

Current Set

To access the Keyboard Shortcut Editor, select Edit | Keyboard Shortcuts. Several options are available for editing your keyboard shortcuts. Dreamweaver offers three additional shortcut sets along with the default. Each of these other sets corresponds to one of the aforementioned development packages—Dreamweaver 3, HomeSite, and BBEdit. To change to one of these, simply choose the appropriate set from the Current Set drop-down menu.

If you change to a different keyboard shortcut set, the keyboard shortcuts for new Dreamweaver 4 features are still available. In cases where the keyboard shortcuts for these new features are the same as those for a different command in the other application, the Dreamweaver 4 shortcut takes precedence.

You cannot modify the default shortcut sets. If you want to modify your shortcuts, you first need to duplicate the set by clicking the Duplicate Set button. This opens a Duplicate Set dialog box that prompts you for a name for the new shortcut set. Be sure to give each shortcut set a unique name. If you change your mind about the name of a shortcut set, you can change it by selecting the Rename button.

Commands

Multiple command sets are in Dreamweaver: the menu commands appear on the Document window menus and the commands enable you to edit your document or code. The Site window has its own set of menus in Windows. To see a list of commands, you must first select a Commands category.

Command List

The Command List displays a list of commands related to the category you chose. In the case of menu commands, the list is organized according to the menu structure. In the case of editing commands, they're organized by command name.

Shortcuts Window

On selecting a command from the Command List, the current keyboard shortcut appears in the Shortcuts window. Each command can have up to two different keyboard shortcuts. To add a shortcut, select the plus sign (+) button, enter the new shortcut in the Press Key text field, and then press the Change button. To delete a shortcut, highlight the shortcut, and then select the minus sign (-) button. To modify an existing shortcut, select the shortcut you want to change, type the new shortcut in the Press Key field, and then click Change to complete the switch.

After you set your keyboard shortcuts to your liking, you can print a table listing all of your shortcuts. To do this, click the Save as HTML button at the top of the Keyboard Shortcuts Editor, open the resulting file in your browser, and print from there.

Summary

In this chapter, you learned how to set all of Dreamweaver's preferences to suit your work style. As you become more comfortable with the application, you may find your preferences change. You now understand:

- The Preferences dialog box controls both the display and functionality of the Dreamweaver application and some of the coding options.
- Some of the preferences have changed since previous versions of Dreamweaver.
- Preference settings exist for many of Dreamweaver's new features.
- The Keyboard Shortcuts Editor enables you to customize the keyboard shortcuts to your liking.

In Chapter 4, you learn how to code in Dreamweaver.

The Complete Reference

Chapter 4

Coding in Dreamweaver

The first time you open Dreamweaver, you're faced with a daunting white design screen, waiting for you to add text and images, plus all the bells and whistles. Experienced developers immediately want to learn how to access the underlying code to see how Dreamweaver sets up the basic HTML structure and to become familiar with the code editing tools. Even if you plan to let Dreamweaver handle the grunt work, old habits die hard, and you'll probably find yourself switching between the code and design features quite often.

Novice developers should do the same. Even if you intend to rely fully on Dreamweaver's design power, learning a bit about HTML can help you understand why and how things are going wrong when you have a design challenge. As you surf the Web, you constantly encounter intriguing user interfaces and new design techniques. If you understand HTML, you can analyze the source of these pages to understand how the designer achieved those results—and then use similar techniques to create your own original designs in Dreamweaver.

No matter how you create your Web sites, the end result is a file containing HTML code. This chapter explains how to access and manipulate that HTML using Dreamweaver's code tools. Knowing how Dreamweaver codes your documents and how you can modify your code directly can give you a better understanding of the objects and behaviors that comprise your sites when they're explained in later chapters. The brief overview of HTML can help you understand the structure of the code and explain some of the most common tags. You also learn how to modify the HTML you created or inherited from other sources.

Finding Your Code in Dreamweaver

Dreamweaver 4 provides several means of accessing HTML code. Previous versions of Dreamweaver had an HTML Source Inspector from which you could view the HTML code for your entire page. Although this option has been renamed to the Code Inspector, it remains and has improvements, such as syntax coloring and auto-indenting. If you want to hone in on a single tag, the Tag Selector and Quick Tag Editor enable you to make changes to the code on the fly without even having to leave the Design view.

Dreamweaver 4 has also added other code options that may better suit your needs, particularly if you are new to Web development. The standard Document window from previous versions of Dreamweaver has been enhanced to include not only the familiar Design view, but also a Code view to display your code. If you are using the toolbar, the Document window can be toggled from Design to Code view with the touch of a button (otherwise, views are accessible by selecting the desired option from the View menu or pressing CTRL-TAB (OPTION-TAB on the Mac). The following illustration shows the toolbar buttons for the new Document window settings.

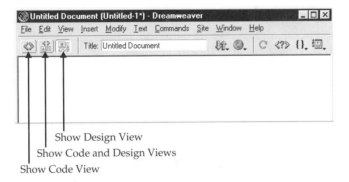

Show Design View

Show Code and Design Views

Show Code View

You can even split the Document window in half to display both the Code and Design views simultaneously. Splitting the Document window into Code and Design views, as seen in Figure 4-1, makes viewing the changes to the document as you change the code easy. As you create and modify the document in the Design view, the code is displayed in the Code View. If you're new to Web development, this can be a helpful way to learn HTML.

Figure 4-1.   *The new split Code and Design view gives you the best of both development worlds*

The split Code and Design view has one quirk. When you're adding and modifying objects in the Design pane, the Code pane automatically keeps up with your work. When you are typing in the Code pane, however, you need to refresh the Design pane by clicking inside the pane. Windows users can also select View | Refresh Design View or use the F5 keyboard shortcut. This quirk makes sense when you remember Dreamweaver cannot interpret your intentions while you're in the middle of typing a tag and attributes in Code view, so it's worth mentioning.

Basic Overview of HTML

Now you know where to look for your code, but before examining all the features of Dreamweaver's code tools, let's briefly look at HTML itself. This can give you a basic foundation on which to build your knowledge of Web development—and give you at least the gist of what to expect when you see a page full of HTML code.

When you view a Web page, the colored text, animated graphics, and photographic images appear to be a part of the page. In point of fact, HTML pages are simply text documents with commands that tell the browser where to locate images and other files, as well as how to display all the objects on the page. These commands are known as *tags* or *elements*.

Note *HTML commands are sometimes taken as mere suggestions by the end user's browser. While the* World Wide Web Consortium *(commonly known as the* W3C, *and found on the Web at* **http://www.w3.org***) has established standards for HTML, each browser has its own interpretation of how certain elements should be displayed. Even if you code your pages by hand, unavoidable variations still exist in how your site appears on every platform and browser.*

Tags and Attributes

Every HTML document contains a basic structure of tags. A tag is composed of a command surrounded by angle brackets, such as <body>. Most—although not all—tags have an accompanying end tag, which adds a forward slash before the command within the brackets, as in </body>. These tag pairs are sometimes called *containers* because they contain other tags and content between them.

Note *This section provides an overview of the basic HTML tags and document structure. If you want to learn more about HTML, I recommend* HTML: The Complete Reference, *3rd Edition by Thomas A. Powell (Osborne McGraw-Hill),* HTML: A Beginner's Guide, *by Wendy Willard (Osborne McGraw-Hill), and* Special Edition Using HTML 4, *6th Edition, by Molly E. Holzschlag (Que). For a quick reference of HTML tags, see Appendix B.*

Many tags can contain specific instructions about how to manipulate the tag's contents. These instructions are known as *attributes*. Attributes are placed within the brackets of the tag, and they contain the name of the attribute and a value, such as <body bgcolor="#FFFFFF">. This body tag has an attribute setting the background color of the page to the hex value #FFFFFF, which is white. Many tags can contain multiple attributes, such as <body bgcolor="#FFFFFF" text="#000000">. This tag sets the color of the page to white with black text. Attributes can only be contained in opening tags, never in end tags.

If you're just learning HTML, it's inevitable you'll make some mistakes. Dreamweaver can help catch them by highlighting invalid HTML code. This option is available from the View Options button on the toolbar or View | Code View Options | Highlight Invalid HTML on the menu. With this option selected, invalid HTML is highlighted in bright yellow in the Code view or Code Inspector. Even with this option deselected, invalid code is always highlighted in the Design view, which can be helpful if you're switching views while editing. An example of this highlighting—albeit in glorious grayscale rather than bright yellow—is seen in Figure 4-2.

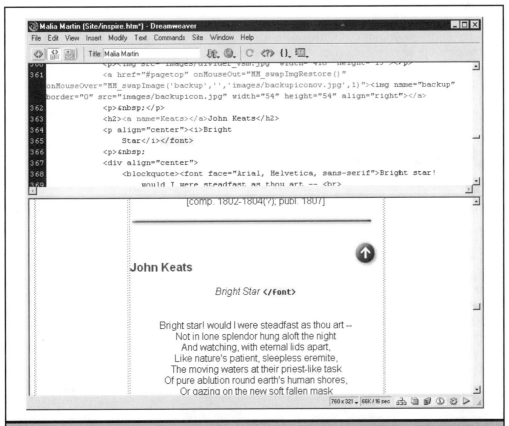

Figure 4-2. *Here's a </font> without an accompanying opening tag, obviously left behind when its companion <font> tag was deleted. Remembering to delete end tags when deleting the opening tag is important*

Required Tags

For a browser to know that a file contains HTML, the document has to declare itself. To do that, the document starts with an `<html>` tag (and is ended by a `</html>` tag). Other required tags are also in every HTML document. Every HTML document must contain a `<head>`, a `<body>`, and a `<title>`. These tags are generated automatically by Dreamweaver whenever you create a file.

The `<head>` of the document includes header information for the entire document. Any information relating to the page itself is contained in this section, including keywords, the title of the page, and character set encoding. Cascading Style Sheets and JavaScript routines are also enclosed in the `<head>` of the document, so they can be used throughout the document.

Included in the `<head>` of the document is a requisite `<title>` tag. This tag gives your page a name, which is then displayed in the title bar of the browser. If your page is lucky enough to find its way into someone's Favorites/Bookmarks, the title of the page will be the default reference name.

All HTML documents also contain a `<body>`. The body holds your site's content. All your text, images, and other features are placed in the `<body>`, each with its own tags to give the browser instructions on how to display and access those elements. The `<body>` tag itself can contain attributes to control the display of the page, such as setting a background color or setting an onLoad event.

Figure 4-3 shows the standard tags generated when you open a blank HTML document in Dreamweaver.

Other Common Tags

Now that the basic structure of the site is in place, you're ready to start building your site. HTML has hundreds of tags and attributes, but some are more common than others. Even if you choose not to learn HTML in depth, you should familiarize yourself with these common tags.

META Tags

If you examine Figure 4-3 closely, you'll notice a `<meta>` tag in the `<head>` of the document. *META* tags are contained tags (meaning they have no corresponding end tag), each with a single purpose. These tags can contain two types of information: `http-equiv` attributes to provide information to the browser or `name` attributes to provide information to search engines and Web spiders. Search engines interpret the keywords and descriptions contained in your `<meta>` tags to determine your site's ranking in their search results. In other words, if you make judicious use of your keywords and descriptions, you can ensure your site is listed on one of the first pages of search results under those keywords instead of 30 pages into the listing.

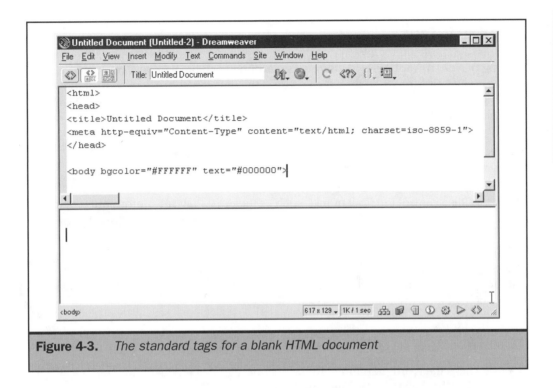

Figure 4-3. *The standard tags for a blank HTML document*

By default, Dreamweaver includes one `<meta>` tag in every new document:

```
<meta http-equiv="Content-Type" content="text/html; charset=iso-8859-1">
```

This tag contains font encoding information. In this case, the browser is told to use the Western (Latin 1) character set, which is used for English and most European languages.

Other `<meta>` tags can be added to the document, each containing its own attribute. When you plan your site, start thinking about a brief description and keywords for your pages. Before you turn your site live on the Web, these will be added to your documents as `<meta>` tags, such as:

```
<meta name="description" content="The Island is a virtual retreat, a place to
discuss and discover escapes from the stress of every day life.">
<meta name="keywords" content="island, retreat, relaxation, adventure, beach,
books, reading, music, travel">
```

Paragraph Tags

The most common tag for a Web document is the `<p>` tag to define paragraphs. The `<p>` tag places an empty line of white space around each block of text contained within the tag container. More than that, the `<p>` tag can contain attributes to control the alignment of the text and be used with style sheets to control the appearance of the text. A paragraph tag looks like this:

```
<p>Your island adventure awaits. Whether you like the beach, the rain forest, or
the relaxation of a day at the spa, we have it all.</p>
```

Other tags also control the flow of text, such as the `<pre>` tag for preformatted text and the `<code>` tag to display code listings. But you'll use the `<p>` tag most of all.

Anchor Tags

The beauty of the Internet is you can link to other pages and even other sites from within a page. The browser identifies these links through the use of anchor tags. Here's an example of an anchor tag:

```
<a href="rainforest.htm">Visit the rain forest!</a>
```

If a user clicks the words contained in the anchor tag, they are taken to the page referenced in the tag attribute. The same concept works for links to pages within the site and to other sites. The previous tag links to a page named **rainforest.htm** located in the same directory on the server. This is a relative link. A link to another site would contain an absolute link, that is, a complete URL, such as this:

```
<a href="http://www.pendragn.com">Say hi to Jenn at this site.</a>
```

The anchor tag is also used to link to other points within the same page. Intra-page links require the use of two anchor tags. The first tag sets the target or anchor point for the link. The target is given a name attribute rather than an href, as in:

```
<a name="pagetop">Welcome!</a>
```

Once a target has been set, it can be called using another anchor tag elsewhere in the document. This tag would look something like:

```
<a href="#pagetop">Back to Top</a>
```

To learn more about links, see Chapter 11, "Links."

Image Tags

When you hear the word "images" in a Web context, you probably first think about photographs and animated GIFs. *Images* are actually a whole lot more: logos, navigation bars, and buttons are also images. Every image you use in your Web site needs to be referenced with an image tag. Image tags use a source attribute to specify the location of the image file. The tag can also contain other attributes, such as the dimensions of the image, the border properties, and alternate text to make your pages accessible to sight-impaired users. Therefore, an image tag might look something like this:

```
<img src="images/sidehead.gif" width="90" height="40" border="0" alt="washed up">
```

In this example, the image file is called sidehead.gif, and is located in the images folder of the site. The image is 90 pixels wide × 40 pixels high. No border is around the image because this would detract from its appearance. This image is a stylized heading that reads, "see what washed up," so the alt text gives sight-impaired visitors a clue as to the contents of the image.

You can add images to a site in other ways. You can add a background image to the entire page by declaring it as an attribute of the <body> tag. You can also set an image file as the value of a CSS declaration. These possibilities are covered in greater detail in Chapter 13.

Comments

As your pages become more complex, you might want to leave notes within your code to guide you through the morass of tables and rollovers. These notes are particularly helpful when working in a Web development group, as there's often more than one way to approach a design challenge. A simple hint or two can save the other developers hours of second-guessing the intent of one contributor's code.

These notes are called *comments*, and they're coded in a special way:

```
<!-- This section is for text navigation. Remember to add links to both the
graphic and text navigation areas. -->
```

Anything placed within the <!-- and --> remains hidden in the code and won't show up in the browser window. Dreamweaver calls this an *invisible element*, and only displays it in the Code view. If you set your Invisibles preferences to show comments, the most you can see in the Design view is an icon representing the comment.

In the previous paragraph, notice I said *anything* placed within the comment delimiters is hidden. Comments can include multiple lines of text, including carriage returns and white space. They can even include portions of the code itself. One common use for comments is to hide style sheet declarations from older browsers. When an older browser encounters a style sheet, it doesn't recognize the <style> tag, so it ignores the tag. The browser sees the style declarations as regular text, however, and displays these declarations at the top of the page. To combat this, developers who worry about compatibility with older browsers put the declarations of their style sheet into a comment container, like this:

```
<style type="text/css"><!--
body {color: black;}
p {color: white;}
--></style>
```

The comment container doesn't prevent CSS-enabled browsers from interpreting the style declarations.

Although this chapter is about coding by hand, this is a good time to interject one handy Dreamweaver shortcut. While comments are straightforward once you get the hang of them, they're one of the most commonly mistyped tags in HTML. To get around this problem, you can add a comment tag by selecting the Comment button from the Invisibles category of the Objects panel or by selecting Insert | Invisible Tags | Comment from the menu. This opens a comment dialog box that enables you to enter the text of your comment.

A Word About Consistency

HTML is both forgiving and flexible in its formatting requirements. While few hard-and-fast rules exist about how you format your code, do give some thought to the process.

Case Sensitivity—HTML tags aren't case-sensitive. You can use a mix of uppercase and lowercase tags. You can even type your tags in uppercase and your attributes in lowercase. Decide how you want to code your tags, and then stick with it. You can set the Code Format preferences (Edit | Preferences or CTRL-U in Windows, CMD-U on the Mac) to instruct Dreamweaver to format its code according to your needs.

Code Organization—HTML documents ignore white space between tags. You can insert extra carriage returns between tags, indent tags, or group blocks of tags with carriage returns between. However you choose to organize your code, consistent formatting can greatly increase your ability to make quick modifications.

Optional End Tags—Some tags have an optional end tag, meaning most browsers can interpret the tag even without an accompanying end tag. A common example of this is the `<p>` tag. Some developers use an opening `<p>` tag at the *end* of a paragraph to insert a break, instead of marking the entire paragraph with opening and closing paragraph tags. Just because it works doesn't necessarily make it right, however. If you don't mark your paragraphs correctly, you cannot apply CSS styles to those paragraphs. Get in the habit of marking your elements properly now to save yourself trouble later when you decide to dress things up.

Unsupported HTML Tags

Dreamweaver supports an extensive array of HTML tags. Some tags aren't supported, however, either because they've been deprecated to the point where they're no longer commonly used or because they're so new or obscure they've not yet gained popular acceptance by the Web development community. Dreamweaver handles unsupported tags in one of two ways. Certain tags, such as the `<address>` tag, can only be added to a document by hand-coding it in either the Code view or the Quick Tag Editor, but they're displayed properly in the Design view. Other tags, such as the superscript tag (`<sup>`) can also be hand-coded, but cannot be displayed in the Design view.

Using the Quick Tag Editor

Now that you understand the barest essentials of HTML, let's put these skills to work. While you can certainly use Dreamweaver to code your entire page by hand, that defeats the purpose of using such a powerful visual editor. More than likely, you'll be doing a large part of your development in the Design view. When you want to make a simple change to a single tag, there's no reason to switch to the Code view. Instead, you can use the Tag Selector and Quick Tag Editor.

As its name implies, the Quick Tag Editor enables you to edit a single tag quickly. To open the Quick Tag Editor, press CTRL-T (CMD-T for Mac) or select Modify | Quick Tag Editor from the menu bar. You can also access the Quick Tag Editor from the context menu that appears when you RIGHT-CLICK (CMD-CLICK) on a tag in the Tag Selector. Finally, you can also access the Quick Tag Editor by clicking the Quick Tag Editor icon in the Property Inspector. The Quick Tag Editor appears in a small window, which can be repositioned by dragging on the title bar along the left side.

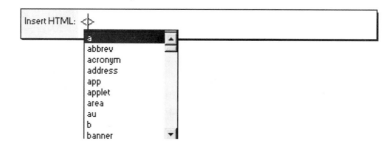

The preferences for the Quick Tag Editor are set from Edit | Preferences | Quick Tag Editor. You can control whether the changes you make with the Quick Tag Editor are automatically applied to the document. You can also enable and control Tag Hints. These preferences were discussed in Chapter 3.

The Quick Tag Editor has three different modes. The initial mode is determined by the context of your selection.

- **Insert HTML**—position your cursor at your desired insertion point without making a selection, and then press CTRL-T to enter Insert HTML mode.

- **Edit Tag**—select an element in the Tag Selector and press CTRL-T to enter in Edit Tag mode, as shown in Figure 4-4. You can also access the Quick Tag Editor from the Property Inspector to enter Edit Tag mode.

- **Wrap Tag**—select content without a surrounding tag, and then press CTRL-T to enter Wrap Tag mode.

Insert HTML

The Insert HTML mode enables you to enter tags. After positioning your cursor and launching the Quick Tag Editor, enter a tag—complete with attributes—content, and any required end tag. If your code is invalid, Dreamweaver attempts to fix it or

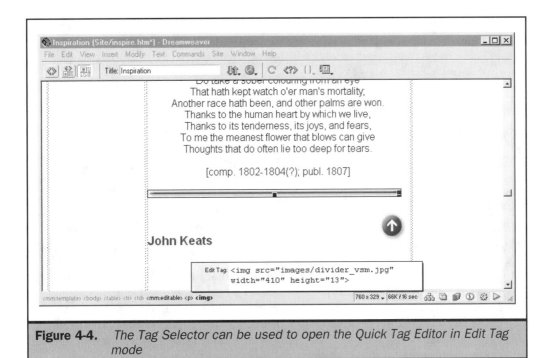

Figure 4-4. *The Tag Selector can be used to open the Quick Tag Editor in Edit Tag mode*

displays a warning message. After completing your tag, press ENTER to complete the process and return to the Design view. If you don't want to make the change, press ESC.

Edit Tag

The Edit Tag mode enables you to make changes to an existing tag. In this mode, the Quick Tag Editor displays the complete tag. You can edit the existing attributes or add new attributes. This feature is useful for adding attributes that don't appear in the Property Inspector. After you make your changes, press ENTER to complete the process and return to the Design view, or press ESC to exit the Quick Tag Editor without changing the document.

Wrap Tag

The *wrap tag* mode is used to wrap a new tag around your selection. This mode is helpful when trying to tag a selection of text within a <p> tag. You can, for example, select a few words of text, and then launch the Quick Tag Editor to wrap an anchor tag around the text to turn it into a link. You can also use this mode to wrap a selection in a tag that isn't supported in Dreamweaver, such as the subscript (<sub>) tag. Although the subscript won't appear in the Design view, you can test the tag by previewing your work in a browser. After you build your tag in the Quick Tag Editor, press ENTER to complete the process and return to the Design view. If you don't want the tag to become a part of your document, press ESC to exit the Quick Tag Editor without making changes.

Enabling and Using the Tag Hints

If you enabled the Tag Hints options in the Quick Tag Editor preferences, Dreamweaver can help you code in the Quick Tag Editor. *Tag Hints* are context-sensitive lists of tags, attributes, and values. If you enter the Quick Tag Editor in Insert HTML mode, you are initially faced with an empty pair of brackets. If you start typing immediately, you can enter a tag and attributes. If you get stuck, however, the list of Tag Hints opens after the time delay you set in the Quick Tag Editor preferences. You can use the Tag Hints by either scrolling through the list using the scroll bar or by typing the first letter or two of the tag to jump to the appropriate portion of the list. To insert a tag into the Quick Tag Editor, either double-click or select a tag and press ENTER.

Once you have a tag in the Quick Tag Editor—either by way of adding it using the Tag Hints or when you're in Edit HTML mode—the context of the Tag Hints changes. Now the Tag Hints provides a list of attributes related to the tag. Finally, if the attribute you chose has a limited set of values, such as the valign attribute of the <td> tag, the context of the Tag Hints changes once again to provide a list of those values. In cases where the values aren't limited, as when providing a width or height value for an <img> tag, the Quick Tag Editor positions the cursor between a set of quotation marks to enable you to type the value by hand.

To edit an existing attribute in the Edit Tag mode, press TAB to move to the attribute you want to edit. Press SHIFT-TAB to move backward. To add a new attribute, move the insertion point to where you want to insert the new attribute. Type an attribute or select one from the drop-down hints menu.

Modifying the Tag Hints

The TagAttributeList.txt file contains all the tags, attributes, and values shown on the hints menu. If you find you make frequent use of a tag that doesn't appear in the Tag Hints, you can add it by modifying this file. This is a good way to customize Dreamweaver to make unsupported HTML tags more accessible.

The TagAttributeList.txt file is in your Dreamweaver/Configuration folder. Before making modifications to this file, research the tag using the O'Reilly HTML Reference in the Reference panel to ascertain all the attributes and values, and to determine which options you want to make easily available from the Tag Hints. You can decide which attributes you want to enter, disregarding those you're certain you won't use, or you can take the thorough approach and enter all the possible attributes, just in case.

To edit the TagAttributeList.txt file, exit Dreamweaver and open the file in a text editor, such as Notepad. Be sure to save a copy of the file as a backup before you start to edit the file. After you save your changes, you can launch the Dreamweaver application, and your new additions will appear in the Tag Hints.

Using Dreamweaver's Reference Panel

Not only is the Reference panel useful for finding lists of tags and attributes to add to the Tag Hints, it's also a context-sensitive resource while you work. For a general reference, simply open the Reference panel from the Launcher by pressing CTRL-SHIFT-F1, or by choosing Window | Reference from the menu. Once the Reference panel is open, you can set the reference book you want to browse and the tag, object, or style (depending on the reference book) you seek. The description drop-down menu provides a general description of the object and lists any associated attributes. To learn more about an attribute, select it from the list.

The Reference panel is most handy when used in context with your work. If you press the Reference button on either the Code Inspector toolbar or the Document window toolbar, as shown in the following illustration, the Reference panel displays information about the current tag (see Figure 4-5). This feature works in both the Code and Design views.

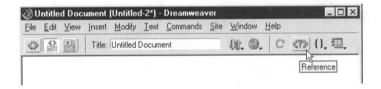

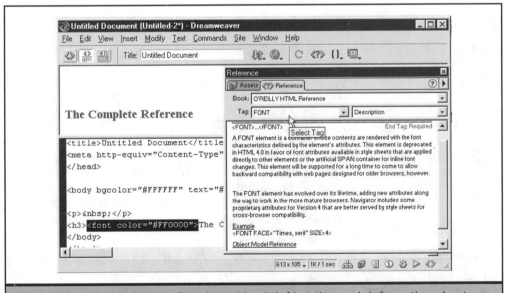

Figure 4-5. *The Reference Panel provides brief but thorough information about HTML, JavaScript, and Cascading Style Sheets*

Using the Code View and Code Inspector

Making quick changes to a single tag is useful but, at times, you'll want to look at the big picture. You can access your document's source code in its entirety in two ways: the Code view and the Code Inspector (formerly known as the HTML Source Inspector). These two features are identical in functionality, with one exception. *Code view* displays your code in the Document window, either using the whole window or splitting it with the Design view in a shared Code and Design view. The *Code Inspector* displays your code in its own window, which can be resized and repositioned on the screen. Using the Panels preferences, the Code Inspector can be set always to remain on top of the Document window when they overlap or it can be set to stay on top only when it's the active window.

You already learned how to access the Code view. To open the Code Inspector, select Window | Code Inspector from the menu, use the F10 keyboard shortcut, or click the Code Inspector button in the Launcher or Launcher bar.

Code Inspector and Code View Options

The options for the Code Inspector and Code View determine how code is shown in the Code View and in the Code Inspector.

To access the Code View options, press the View Options button on the Code Inspector panel or the Dreamweaver toolbar, as shown in Figure 4-6. If you're in Code view, these options are also accessible by selecting View | Code View Options from the menu.

The following options are available from either the Code Inspector or the Code View:

■ **Word Wrap**—Because carriage returns on a Web page are controlled by line breaks and paragraph tags, the HTML code itself can actually extend horizontally well beyond the range of a single screen. This option wraps the code within the confines of the window to make it easier to edit. Word Wrap doesn't insert any actual line breaks in the code, so it doesn't change the display of the code in a browser.

■ **Line Numbers**—Line numbers make tracking down bugs and problems with your code much easier. If you run a site report, as shown in Figure 4-7, or if you set your Code Rewriting preferences to be warned when invalid code is being corrected, the report or warning will contain line numbers for any questionable code. Viewing line numbers along the left side of the code can help you locate these problems much faster.

DREAMWEAVER
BASICS

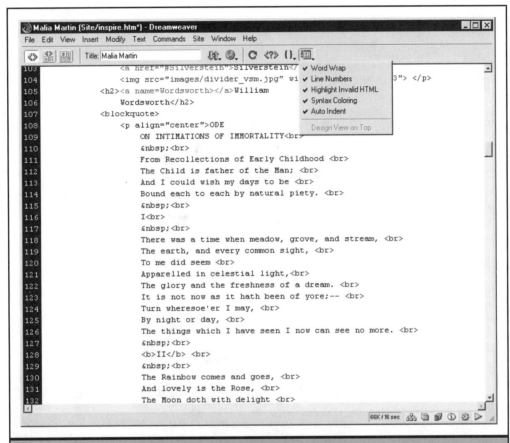

Figure 4-6. *The View Options are identical for both Code view and the Code Inspector*

- **Highlight Invalid HTML**—As discussed earlier in this chapter, this option marks invalid code, such as an end tag mistakenly left behind as a remnant of a deleted tag. While you can toggle this feature in the Code view and Code Inspector using this option, invalid HTML is always highlighted in the Design view. If you're unsure of the nature of the warning, you can click the highlighted tag to view a description of the problem in the Property Inspector.

- **Syntax Coloring**—Color coding various tags helps to distinguish tags from content. You can set your color choices in the Code Color preferences. The Syntax Coloring option toggles these color choices on and off. If this item is deselected, the entire page of code appears in black and white. Additionally, the Reference panel won't be able to distinguish between tags and, therefore, can't navigate automatically to the related tag page in its reference materials: Unless you have a good reason to deselect this option, leaving it selected is best.

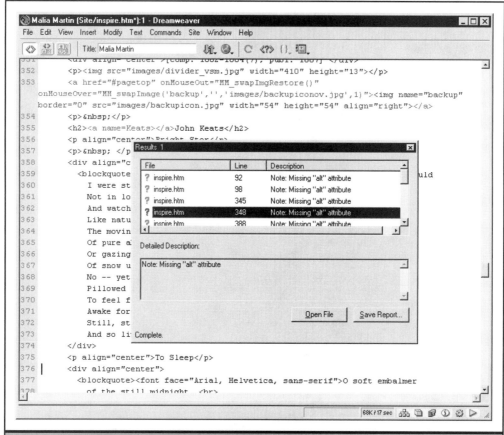

Figure 4-7. *This report has identified several image files without alt attributes. Each occurrence is identified by line number, which can be cross-referenced in the Code view or Code Inspector*

■ **Auto Indent**—Code that's left-aligned can be confusing to read, particularly in the case of nested tables. This option automatically indents code as you type it, based on your choices in the Code Format preferences. If you deselect this option, your Code Format preferences are ignored and all your code is left-aligned.

Adjusting Code and Design View

When you want to see the effects of changes to the code on your design, or vice versa, the split Code and Design view is handy. This view splits the Document window in half, so you can see both views at once. The splitter bar between the panes can be adjusted to favor one view or the other. You can also use the View | Design View on the Top menu option to toggle the position of the Design view, whether it remains on the bottom, as it is in the default, or at the top of the Document window, as shown in Figure 4-8.

You can achieve a similar effect with judicious placement of the Code Inspector and the Document window, but this new split view has some advantages. First, you can change your view options for both sections from one menu in the toolbar. The biggest advantage, however, is in maneuverability.

When using the Design view and the Code Inspector, one or the other window is constantly obscured. If you set the Code Inspector always to remain on top, it overlaps your Document window and can get in the way of your design work. If you set the Code Inspector to be overlapped, you have to root around for it after working in the Document window. If you're trying to see how changes in one window affect the other, you might find you're doing a lot of window swapping. To duplicate the split-view effect using the Design view and the Code Inspector, you would have to decrease the size of the Document window, so both windows are fully visible on the screen at the same time. This is fine if you intend to work in this manner consistently. But, suppose you then want to work solely in the Design view. To maximize your design space, you need to resize the Document window. Whew! Sounds like a lot of work to get the same effect as simply pressing one button to toggle the Code and Design view.

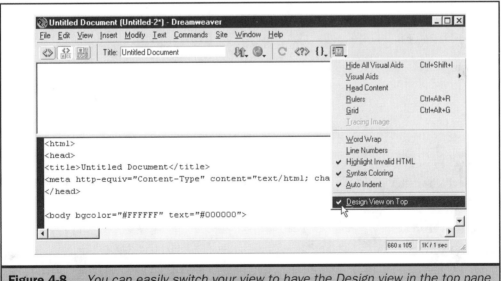

Figure 4-8. *You can easily switch your view to have the Design view in the top pane and the Code view in the bottom pane*

Navigating the Code

Unlike developing in the Design view, which often involves dragging objects from panels and switching to various panels and inspectors, *coding* is a keyboard-intensive operation. Instead of unnecessarily moving your hands from keyboard to mouse, it's easier to learn a few keyboard shortcuts to speed you through your document. Table 4-1 lists these shortcuts.

 These are the default keyboard shortcuts for Dreamweaver 4. If you made modifications to your keyboard shortcuts, your shortcuts may differ from those listed.

Function	Windows	Mac
Select Parent Tag (the tag surrounding the insertion point)	CTRL-SHIFT-<	CMD-SHIFT-<
Select Child Tag	CTRL-SHIFT->	CMD-SHIFT->
Indent Code	CTRL-]	CMD-]
Outdent Code	CTRL-[	CTRL-[
Select All	CTRL-A	CMD-A
Copy	CTRL-C	CMD-C
Cut	CTRL-X	CMD-X
Paste	CTRL-V	CMD-V
Redo	CTRL-Y	CMD-Y
Undo	CTRL-Z	CMD-Z
Select Line Up	SHIFT-UP ARROW	SHIFT-UP ARROW
Select Line Down	SHIFT-DOWN ARROW	SHIFT-DOWN ARROW
Select Character Left	SHIFT-LEFT ARROW	SHIFT-LEFT ARROW
Select Character Right	SHIFT-RIGHT ARROW	SHIFT-RIGHT ARROW
Select Word Left	CTRL-SHIFT-LEFT	CMD-SHIFT-LEFT
Select Word Right	CTRL-SHIFT-RIGHT	CMD-SHIFT-RIGHT

Table 4-1. *Keyboard Shortcuts for Code Editing*

Function	Windows	Mac
Select Page Up (selects from insertion point up one screen)	SHIFT-PAGE UP	SHIFT-PAGE UP
Select Page Down (selects from insertion point down one screen)	SHIFT-PAGE DOWN	SHIFT-PAGE DOWN
Select to Top of Document	CTRL-SHIFT-HOME	CMD-SHIFT-HOME
Select to Bottom of Document	CTRL-SHIFT-END	CMD-SHIFT-END
Move to Start of Line	HOME	HOME
Move to End of Line	END	END
Move to Top of Document	CTRL-HOME	CMD-HOME
Move to End of Document	CTRL-END	CMD-END

Table 4-1.   *Keyboard Shortcuts for Code Editing* (continued)

Using an External Code Editor

Experienced HTML coders probably already have a favorite coding environment. In some cases, it's as simple as a text editor, such as Notepad. For others, a full-featured code editor, such as HomeSite or BBEdit, provides all the wizards and tools a hand-coder can ever desire. Dreamweaver's own code editor is becoming more powerful with each new version of the application, but it still doesn't offer some of the advantages of a dedicated editor.

Fortunately, Dreamweaver acknowledges it can't be all things to all people. Not only can you set an external code editor of your choice in the Preferences dialog box, but Dreamweaver itself ships with a registered version of HomeSite 4.5 for Windows users and a trial version of BBEdit for Mac users. These applications integrate with Dreamweaver with a simple keystroke or button press, and add amazing functionality to your Web design toolbox.

Some of the features worth exploring in HomeSite or BBEdit include

- **Collapsible Code (Document Skeleton)**—the capability to hone in on container tags without viewing their contents.

- **Wizards**—helper applications to simplify tasks, such as adding tables, multimedia, or DHTML.

- **CSS Tools**—the capability to manage multiple style sheets and a full-featured style editor.

- **File Comparison**—the capability to compare the differences between multiple files.

- **Multiple Documents**—the capability to open multiple documents at once and easily tab between them.

Many HTML old-timers are just beginning to trust visual editors, such as Dreamweaver, with their code. The integration between Dreamweaver and external code editors makes this transition easier. I know several developers who continue to use HomeSite as their primary coding environment, but who turn to Dreamweaver for its layout and template capabilities. This truly provides developers with the best of all worlds.

Designating an External Code Editor

Whether you choose to use HomeSite, BBEdit, or another application as your external code editor, the process of designating it within Dreamweaver is the same. To designate an external code editor:

1. Select Edit | Preferences from the menu bar.

2. Select the File Types/Editors category.

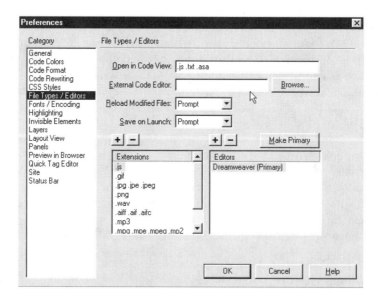

3. Designate your code editor:

- In Windows, enter the path to your preferred editor in the External Code Editor field, or use the browse button to locate it.

- To use BBEdit on the Mac, select Enable BBEdit Integration, and then click OK.

- To use a different code editor on the Mac, deselect the Enable BBEdit Integration option, and then enter the path to your preferred editor in the External Code Editor field.

4. Set your Reload and Save on Launch preferences, as explained in Chapter 3.

5. Click OK.

Accessing an External Code Editor

Once you designate your editor of choice, you have easy access to it. To launch the editor, simply press CTRL-E or select Edit | Edit with [External Editor] on the menu. Both HomeSite and BBEdit have buttons on their toolbars to make the return trip to Dreamweaver.

Find and Replace

As your document becomes filled with tags and content, it becomes harder and harder to find a specific tag. Syntax coloring and line numbering can help you scan your code more quickly, but a lot of manual labor is still involved in locating the tag you seek. The Find and Replace feature can locate that tag in seconds.

Going a step further, the Find and Replace feature can seek out any character or group of characters in any document, folder, file group, or even the entire site. Throughout this book, I discuss the concept of a Web site devoted to relaxation and vacation pursuits. In developing this site, let's say I decide to develop a metaphor around a fictitious island named La Isla del Encanto. After designing 50 pages containing this name, I realize La Isla del Encanto is the nickname of Puerto Rico. A name change is most definitely in order—maybe just a shortened version of the name—La Isla. Find and Replace can make that change.

As you read up on Cascading Style Sheets, you decide to remove all the <font> tags from your site to bring it into compliance with the latest W3C standards. Again, Find and Replace is on the job, this time removing the tag containers without cutting the content within the tags.

Accessing Find and Replace

The Find and Replace feature is available from the Edit | Find and Replace option on the menu or the CTRL-F (CMD-F) keyboard shortcut. The following illustration shows the

Find and Replace dialog box. If you're in Code view or the Code Inspector, you can also RIGHT-CLICK (CTRL-CLICK on the Mac) to bring up the context menu, and choose Find and Replace from the menu.

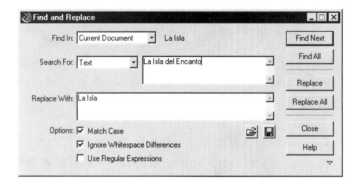

The context of the Find and Replace dialog box is dependent on the window from which you launch the feature. If you're searching an entire site or folder, launch Find and Replace from either the Site window or the Document window. If you're searching only the current document, launch from the Document window, as the Site window won't have the proper context of a "current" document. If you're searching a specific file or group of files, launch from the Site window to select those files, as the Document window only knows the context of the current document, folder, and site.

The process is slightly different if you want to search specific files or folders. If you want to limit your search to specific files or folders within your site:

1. Open the Site window, if it isn't already open.

2. Select the files you want to search. To select a range of files, SHIFT-CLICK on the first and last file in the list. To select individual files, CTRL-CLICK on each file.

3. Choose Edit | Find and Replace.

4. From the Find In drop-down menu, choose Selected Files in Site.

5. Set your find (and replace) criteria and perform your search.

You can also search other folders on your local computer. To do this, launch the Find and Replace tool within the Site window. In the Find In drop-down menu, choose Folders. A text box and browse button appears to the right of the Find In box. Either enter a complete path or use the browse button to locate the folder on your computer.

Find

When you're searching the current document, you can start your search from the position of the cursor using the Find Next button. If the search criteria aren't met by the end of the document, Dreamweaver gives you the option of continuing to search from the beginning of the document. If the search criteria are found, they're highlighted in the document. You can edit the document without closing the Find and Replace dialog box. This makes it possible to switch between the Document window and the Find and Replace dialog box to find and change each iteration individually.

Another way to perform the search is to Find All. When you select this option, all the matches in the entire document (or folder or site) are listed at the bottom of the Find and Replace dialog box. To hone in on a specific match, double-click it, and that match is highlighted in the document.

> **Tip** *Use the Find All feature to tighten up your text. If you tend to overuse certain favorite words or phrases, search for them in your documents. Dreamweaver tells you how many matches it has found. If you find ten occurrences of the same idiomatic expression in your document, it's time for some editing.*

Replace

At times, you'll not only want to find something, but you'll also already have a specific change in mind. In those cases, use the Replace options in combination with your searches. You can enter words, paragraphs, tags, or even entire blocks of code, depending on the type of Find and Replace you're performing.

After setting your replacement criteria, you need to execute the replacement. If you choose to Replace, the first item that matches the search criteria is highlighted. To make the replacement, click the Replace button again. Dreamweaver then automatically continues the search and highlight the next match. You need to click Replace to make each change.

If you're absolutely certain you want to change every occurrence of the search criteria with a specific replacement, you can choose Replace All. This automatically executes the replacement.

> **Caution** *Be certain of your Find and Replace criteria before executing a Replace All.*

Limiting Search Criteria

You can limit your searches to meet specific criteria using the three search options. The best way to explore these options is with an example:

```
Visit the
Island Shop and
enjoy the island sun!
Look at the Island reading list
before embarking on your Isla getaway.
```

- **Match Case**—This limits the search to only exact case matches. If you search on the word island without case matching, you can find three occurrences in the previous text. If you select the Match Case option and search for the word **island**, only one occurrence exists because the capitalized words no longer match the search criteria.

■ **Ignore Whitespace Differences**—HTML code can contain extraneous whitespace because of such things as code indenting and carriage returns in the code. With this option selected, as it is by default, all whitespace is considered a single space. Using the Island example, if the Ignore Whitespace Differences option is selected, a search on the words "the island" finds three occurrences. If you deselect this option, only two occurrences exist, as the first one no longer meets the criteria because of the carriage return between the two words.

■ **Use Regular Expressions**—Sometimes, you might want to search for certain character patterns, rather than a specific word or tag. Regular expressions let you enter descriptions of search terms, rather than a specific term. Let's say you decide to change the island theme to a mountain setting. You need to find every reference to the island and its nickname. You can search for **islan?d?** to find every instance of both island and Isla.

When you use Regular Expressions, it finds every iteration that meets all the criteria of the expression; therefore, you cannot ignore whitespace differences when using them.

Common Regular Expressions

Table 4-2 shows some of the more common special characters that can be used in regular expressions.

If you're using regular expressions and attempt to search for a character that's used in creating these expressions, you'll have disastrous results. To search for one of these special characters while using regular expressions, you need to insert a backslash before the character.

Character	Finds
.	Any one character. **t.e** finds "the" but not "title"
^	A character at the beginning of a line. **^I** finds "Island Life" but not "This is life on the Island."
$	A character at the end of a line. **d$** finds the *d* in "island" but not "dream."
*	The preceding character zero or more times. **ea*** finds the "ea" in "beach" and the *e* in "hotel."
+	The preceding character one or more times. **ea+** finds the "ea" in "beach," but not the *e* in "hotel" because there's no *a*.

Table 4-2. *Regular Expressions Enable You to Search for Patterns of Characters Instead of an Exact Search Item*

Character	Finds
?	The preceding character is optional. **Islan?d?** finds both "**Island**" and "**Isla**."
\s	Any whitespace character. **\sch** finds "**ch**air" but not "beach."
\S	Any non-whitespace character. \Sch matches "bea**ch**" but not "chair."
{n}	Exactly *n* occurrences of the preceding character. **s{2}** finds "de**ss**ert" but not "island."
{n,m}	At least *n,* and at most *m,* instances of the preceding character. **F{2,3}** finds #**FF**0000 but not #**F**FFF00.
x | y	Either *x* or *y*. **sand | beach** finds "**sand**" or "**beach.**"

Table 4-2. *Regular Expressions Enable You to Search for Patterns of Characters Instead of an Exact Search Item* (continued)

Four major types of searches exist, depending on your intent. The terminology in some of these choices is unclear at first glance, so let's look at each one.

Source Code Searches

A source code search is used when you consider the source code as simply a text document. In other words, rather than distinguishing between tags and content, a source code search finds any and all matches to the search criteria.

Let's travel back to our Island. You want to search for every occurrence of the word **island** in this code:

```
<a href="island.html">Visit the
Island Shop!</a>
<img src="island.gif" width="50" height="50"
alt="the island sun">
<p>Look at the Island reading list before
embarking on your Isla getaway.</p>
```

Our search turns up five occurrences of the search word: in the anchor tag filename, the link text for that anchor, the image filename, the alt text for the image, and the paragraph content. If you select Case In a Source Code search, Dreamweaver treats every instance of the search criteria with the same weight, whether it's an attribute value, filename, or text.

You can initiate a Source Code find even in the Design view. If you do so, the Find and Replace tool automatically opens the Code Inspector and proceeds to highlight finds in both windows. If you initiate a Find in Code and Design view, matches are highlighted in both panes.

Note *A quirk exists in the Find and Replace feature performing source code finds across views. If you initiate a source code search in Design view, the Code Inspector opens to highlight the code. If you close the Find and Replace box, change views to Code view, and then perform another search, the Find and Replace feature realizes you're already looking at the code, so it doesn't open the Code Inspector. But the Find and Replace dialog box can only determine the view setting when you first open the dialog box. Try this: perform a source code search in Design view, then close the Code Inspector and switch to Code view—without closing the Find and Replace dialog box. Now change the search criteria and perform another search. The Code Inspector reopens even though you're already viewing the code.*

Text Searches

A Text search ignores HTML tags and attributes. Another trip to the island finds this code:

```
<a href="island.html">Visit the Island Shop!</a>
<img src="island.gif" width="50" height="50"
alt="the island sun">
<p>Look at the <b>Island</b> reading list before
embarking on your island getaway.</p>
```

If you search on the island, a Text search finds two matches: in the link text and the paragraph text. In the case of the paragraph text, it still matches the criteria because the bold tag is ignored. In the case of the link text, even though the link tag surrounds the entire search term, the words themselves are still text content, rather than an attribute of the tag. The alt text of the image file doesn't turn up a match, however, because it's a tag attribute rather than text content.

Text (Advanced) Searches

You might have times when you want to single out occurrences of a search criterion within (or without) a specific tag. Consider this line of code:

```
<a href="island.html">Visit the Island Shop!</a>
<img src="island.gif" width="50" height="50"
alt="the island sun">
<p>Look at the Island reading list before
embarking on your <b>island</b> getaway.</p>
```

You might decide you want to change the text within the bold tags while leaving every other occurrence of the same word as is. The Advanced text option on the Find and Replace dialog box gives you greater control over your search. The next illustration shows the options for the Text-Advanced Search.

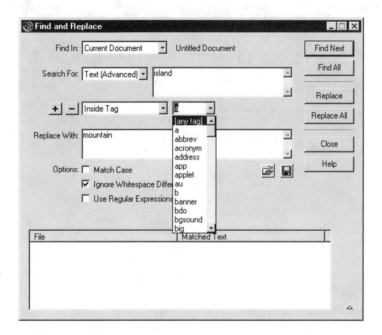

To perform an advanced text search:

1. Open the Find and Replace dialog box.
2. Choose Text (Advanced) from the Search For menu.
3. Enter your search criteria.
4. Enter any replacement text in the Replace With text box.
5. Select your Match Case, Ignore Whitespace Differences, and Use Regular Expressions options.
6. Choose Inside Tag or Not Inside Tag.

   ■ **Inside Tag**—searches for the search criterion only when it's within the specified tags.

   ■ **Not Inside Tag**—searches for all the matches except for those inside the specified tags.

7. Choose the tag from the drop-down menu next to the Inside/Not Inside option.

8. If you want to specify additional filters for the tag, click the plus sign (+) button to enable the filters. You can specify as many filters as you need by repeatedly pressing the plus button.

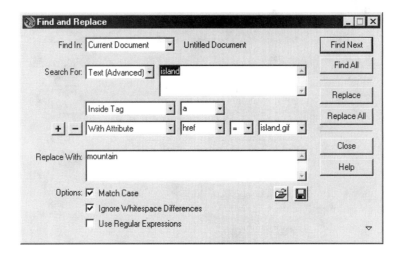

- **With Attribute**—searches for the specified tag with the specified attribute. The attribute can be set as being equal to, greater than, less than, or not equal to the specified value.

- **Without Attribute**—searches for the specified tag only if it doesn't have the specified attribute. This filter has the same options as With Attribute.

- **Containing**—searches for the specified tag if it contains the specified text or tags within it.

- **Not Containing**—searches for the specified tag only if the specified text or tags aren't within it.

- **Inside Tag**—searches for the specified tag only if it's contained within another specified set of tags.

- **Not Inside Tag**—searches for the specified tag only if it's not found within another specified tag set.

9. To remove a filter, press the minus sign (-) button. Unfortunately, you must delete filters in the reverse order of creation, so if you decide you want to remove the filter for the first condition, you must remove all the other filters first.

10. Execute your Find or Replace.

While this type of search makes use of tags as a search criterion, it cannot be used to search for attributes of the tag itself. You can search for text contained within an `<a>` *tag, for example, but you cannot use this type of search to locate alt text in an* `<img>` *tag.*

In the case of the previous example, you set the Inside Tag option and choose the <b> tag. You needn't set any other attributes.

Specific Tag Searches

Specific Tag searches are essentially the opposite of Text (Advanced) searches. Rather than finding and replacing text, the *Specific Tag* option finds and replaces HTML tags and their attributes. This feature is useful for, say, changing all the font color references from #3366FF to #3399CC in every paragraph aligned to the right.

You establish your search criteria similar to that of a Text (Advanced) search, choosing the tags and attributes you require. The difference is the tag and filters you set become the actual search criteria, rather than a string within those settings. Once you create your search criteria, you need to specify an action for Dreamweaver to take on finding matches. The options are

- **Replace Tag and Contents**—replaces the tag and its entire contents, including text and other tags—with your replacement text. You can include HTML in the replacement text box.

- **Replace Contents Only**—replaces the content of the specified tag with what you type in the box. The tag itself remains intact. You can include HTML in the replacement text box.

- **Remove Tag & Contents**—deletes the tag and its contents, including any nested tags.

- **Strip Tag**—the content remains, but the tags are stripped from it. This feature is useful in removing <font> tags if you decide to convert a document to CSS styles.

- **Change Tag**—replaces one tag with another tag, such as if you decide to convert link text to a regular paragraph.

- **Set Attribute**—changes the value of an attribute, adds a new attribute, or adds an attribute and value to a tag. In the example of changing a font color, use this action to accomplish the change.

- **Remove Attribute**—deletes the attribute, but leaves the remainder of the tag intact.

- **Add Before Start Tag**—inserts the contents of the text box before the open tag specified. The text box can contain HTML code.

- **Add After End Tag**—inserts the contents of the text box after the closing tag of the specified tag.

- **Add After Start Tag**—inserts the contents of the text box after the open tag.

- **Add Before End Tag**—inserts the contents of the text box before the closing tag.

While, at first glance, your choices in this type of search may appear as an all-or-nothing deal, this tool is actually quite flexible. Rather than using the Replace All option, you can, instead, choose to Find All tags that meet the specified criteria. Once the list has been generated in the Find and Replace dialog box, you can select each tag in turn and apply a different action to it by changing the Action settings, and then selecting Replace. In changing the font colors, for example, you can find all the font tags that meet your initial criteria, and then change them one-by-one to different colors or styles, or you can remove the `<font>` tag entirely.

Reusing Search Criteria

You'll find you repeat certain searches again and again. Instead of rebuilding the search criteria every time, you can save the criteria for later use.

I prefer to add alt text for my images in the later stages of my design cycle. I like to word my alt text within the context of the surrounding text, so I want my content and layout to be solid first. Because I sometimes do this in Code view—where I cannot see the image in question—I use placeholder alt text as I insert my images to remind me of the nature of the image. At the end of my design process, I want to search for all the alt attributes in the document, so I can finalize the wording. Therefore, I saved a source code search for alt=.

To save a search, set the criteria—and replace criteria, if any—as if you were performing an actual search. Instead of executing the search, however, click the disk icon to save the query, as shown in the following illustration. You are prompted for a name for your query, which is then used to store the query in the Configuration/Queries folder in the Dreamweaver application.

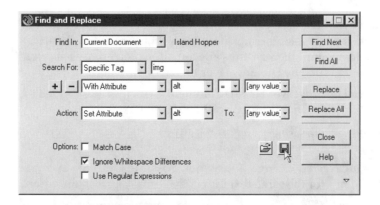

Cleaning Up HTML Code

Even the best of coders don't always write perfectly clean code. Their code may be perfectly valid, but it could still contain a lot of extraneous tags that simply increase the size of the file (and, thus, the page load time) without contributing anything valuable to the document. If you use the Design view to build your pages—as you obviously want to do in a visual editor such as Dreamweaver—you might also find a lot of tag redundancies, particularly in `<font>` tags.

Messy code isn't always your fault. If you inherited a site from another developer or imported your code from another visual editor, you might have inherited quite a mess.

As you learned earlier in this chapter, you can do a lot of cleaning up with judicious use of Find and Replace commands. For a complete cleanup of your code, however, Dreamweaver has a better option, the Clean Up HTML command. The Clean Up HTML command is one example of the power of Dreamweaver's command feature, which is covered in Chapter 30.

The Clean Up HTML command can take care of the following common problems with your code

- **Remove Empty Tags**—such as `<b></b>`, which don't contain any tags or text.
- **Remove Redundant Nested Tags**—such as `<b>The island has <b>seven</b> beaches</b>`, where a bold tag is nested within a bold tag.

■ **Remove non-Dreamweaver HTML Comments**—such as comments you might insert during development. Some coders choose to delete these tags because they pad a document's file size, thus affecting download time. This won't delete any comments added by Dreamweaver to mark Template or Library items.

■ **Remove Dreamweaver HTML Comments**—such as those added by Dreamweaver to mark regions in a Template or Library item code.

■ **Remove Specific Tags**—to remove any specific tag and its attributes. You can enter one tag to remove several tags at once.

■ **Combine Nested <font> Tags when Possible Option**—to combine multiple <font> tags for the same text into one <font> tag with multiple attributes.

■ **Show Log on Completion Option**—to generate a report of all the changes made to the document through the Clean Up HTML command.

To use this command, choose Command | Clean Up HTML from the menu. Choose your options and click OK. If you chose to see a report of the changes made, it displays on execution of the command.

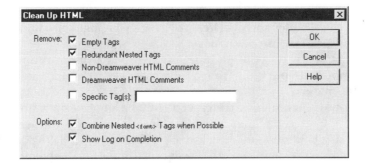

Clean Up Word HTML Documents

When you import an HTML document created by Microsoft Word 97 or later, you inherit a whole other set of problems. Word adds a lot of XML and redundant HTML commands to its code. This type of file requires additional work to make the code more readily usable in Dreamweaver. To clean up a Word HTML document:

1. First save a backup copy of your Word file, just in case. The cleaned-up HTML file may not display properly back in Word.

2. Open the Word HTML file in Dreamweaver. If you use the File | Import | Import Word HTML option from the menu, the Clean Up Word HTML

command automatically executes. If you open the file normally, you need to execute this command manually using Commands | Clean Up Word HTML.

3. If Dreamweaver is unable to determine which version of Word you're using, select your version from the pop-up menu.

4. Choose the basic options you want from the Basic tab.

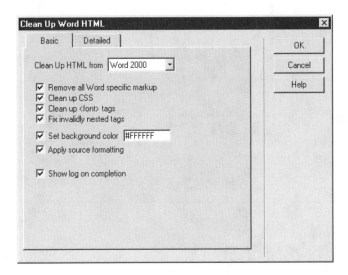

- ■ **Remove all Word specific markup**—removes all Word specific markup. This can be controlled even further on the details tab.

- ■ **Clean up CSS**—removes all Word specific CSS, such as mso style attributes and unused style definitions. This can be further customized using the details tab. See the next section for more information.

- ■ **Clean up <font> tags**—removes the HTML tags and converts the default body text size to size 2.

- ■ **Fix invalidly nested tags**—fixes tags placed in the wrong order, such as <font> tags appearing outside <p> tags.

- ■ **Set background color**—enables you to set the background color. Enter a hexadecimal value for the background color for your document.

- ■ **Apply source formatting**—applies the source formatting options you specified in the Code Format preferences and SourceFormat.txt file.

- ■ **Show log on completion**—generates a log of changes made.

5. Choose the advanced options from the Detailed tab to remove Word specific markup and Clean up CSS.

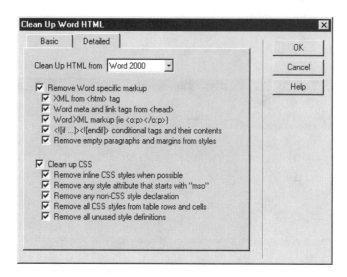

- XML from `<html>`tag
- Word meta and link tags from `<head>`
- Word XML markup (ie`<o:p></o:p>`)
- `<![if...]><![endif]>` conditional tags and their contents
- Remove empty paragraphs and margins from styles
- Remove inline CSS styles when possible
- Remove any style attribute that starts with"mso"
- Remove any non-CSS style declaration
- Remove all CSS styles from table rows and cells
- Remove all unused style definitions

Apply Source Formatting

While you can set many of the Code Rewriting options in the Preferences settings, these are only applied when you open a document. If you make changes to these options while a document is open or if you hand-coded portions of your document without adhering to your own code settings, the document won't be formatted according to your preferences any longer. To bring the document back into compliance with your settings, select Commands | Apply Source Formatting from the menu.

Editing the Source Format File

The Preferences settings offer many options for indenting, coloring, and otherwise formatting your code. In many cases, these Preferences are enough. If you want complete control over your code formatting, though, become familiar with the SourceFormat.txt file. This file is the warehouse for your entire code configuration and it's very customizable.

If you edit the SourceFormat.txt file in Dreamweaver, much of the code is marked as invalid, making it awkward to edit. Instead, exit Dreamweaver and edit the file in Notepad or another text editor. Your changes are then reflected in the code configuration the next time you open Dreamweaver.

The SourceFormat.txt file is divided into three sections: Options, Elements, and Attributes. Each section begins with a comment tag to describe the section and is followed by the settings themselves. The comment tags are helpful because they list the options for each section. To spell things out a bit more, however, here are some additional notes.

Options

The Options section begins with a tag labeled <?options>. Most of the settings in this section relate to those of the Code Format preferences, as you can see from this portion of the file:

```
<?options>
<indention enable indent="2" tabs="4" use="spaces" active="1,2">
<lines autowrap column="76" break="CRLF">
<omit options="0">
<element case="lower" always>
<attribute case="lower" always>
<colors text="0x00000000" tag="0x00000000" unknowntag="0x00000000"
comment="0x00000000" invalid="0x00000000" object="0x00000000">
```

At first glance, these tags are quite straightforward. Your Code view and Code Inspector autowrap settings are in the <lines> tag, and your syntax color settings are in the <colors> tag. You've probably already set these in the Code Format preferences.

Note, a few tags aren't straightforward. The <omit> tag isn't currently used by any function in Dreamweaver, so no corresponding preference choice exists. At first glance, the active="1,2" attribute and value in the <indention> tag is also curious. These numbers relate to *igroups,* special indentation groups for groups of tags such as those used by tables and frames. Tables are assigned to igroup 1, while frames are in igroup 2. You can define up to six additional igroups, numbered 3 through 8. The active attribute in the `<indention>` tag specifies which of these igroups should be considered when formatting your code. In the previous example, both the tables (1) and frames (2) igroups are set as active, so their indentation settings will be used. If you create your own igroups, you can activate them by adding their igroup number to the active attribute.

Consider the case of tables. A table consists of a `<table>` tag, `<tr>` tags to signify table rows, and `<td>` tags to define table cells. Some tables also contain a `<th>` tag to specify the table header. By grouping these tags into an igroup, each nested tag is indented from the position of its parent tag, rather than from the left margin. In other words, if your indentation is set at two spaces, the `<table>` tag is flush left, with the `<tr>` tag set two spaces in from the left. The `<td>` tag is then set two spaces in from the row tag. Nested tables are indented from the starting position of their <table> tag, which is determined by the <td> tag from which they're started. This results in such easily read code as:

```
<table width="75%" border="0">
  <tr>
    <td>Island Hopper</td>
  </tr>
  <tr>
    <td>
      <table width="75%" border="0">
        <tr>
          <td>Hotel</td>
          <td>Rest Area</td>
        </tr>
        <tr>
          <td>Day Spa</td>
          <td>Relaxation</td>
        </tr>
        <tr>
          <td>Rain Forest</td>
          <td>Adventure</td>
        </tr>
      </table>
    </td>
  </tr>
  <tr>
    <td>Shopping</td>
  </tr>
</table>
```

If you turn off the active attribute for this igroup, all the tags are then flush to the left. If you prefer your code to be flush left, you should remove the active attribute.

Elements

The Elements section begins with a `<?elements>` tag. This section of the file lists every HTML tag supported by Dreamweaver. A typical element is listed like this:

```
<p break="1,0,0,1" indent>
```

Each element contains four break values. These determine line breaks in your code in the following order: before the start tag, after the start tag, before the end tag, and after the end tag. If you like to divide your code into logical groups, you can edit the break attributes on your elements to add this whitespace. In the previous example, each paragraph tag in your code starts on a new line directly under the tag above it. If you want to add a line of whitespace before your paragraph tags, you could change the first value to "2," which adds two line breaks: one to separate the tag from its predecessor, and one to create the additional blank line. If the predecessor specified breaks after the end tag, Dreamweaver only uses the larger of the two break settings, rather than adding them.

The indent keyword specifies whether the tag and its contents should be indented after the first line. The first line of a tag always begins in alignment with its container tag. In other words, if a paragraph is entered within the `<body>`, it begins flush left. If a paragraph is entered within a table, however, the tag is indented in alignment with the `<td>` tag in which the paragraph is contained. To make all your paragraphs flush left, regardless of its container tag, remove the indent keyword.

Two other settings can be used in the Elements section. If you add a namecase attribute to a tag, you can specify how the tag appears in the code listing. For example,

```
<ilayer break="1,0,0,1" namecase="iLayer">
```

This element specifies that no matter what case preferences you set, this tag always appears in the code as iLayer.

The other setting is the noformat keyword. The *noformat keyword* is used for tags such as `<pre>`, which is used for preformatted text. Unlike most tags, whitespace is rendered exactly in preformatted text, therefore, any indentation within the tag would set off the formatting.

Note *The Elements section only lists container tags, those with both an open and an end tag. Tags with only a single element are always presented in line with other elements and don't have unique break or indentation settings.*

Attributes

The Attributes section is designated by an `<?attributes>` tag. This section lists tag attributes that require special consideration and provides two possible settings. As in the Elements section, the namecase attribute is used to specify a particular format for the attribute name. JavaScript events, for example, use mixed case names, such as onMouseDown. The other option is the *samecase keyword*, which specifies that an attribute—and its value—use the same case as the tag. This setting should never be changed without careful consideration. If you change the setting of attributes that require filenames or other text as a value, the samecase keyword could render those values improperly, resulting in broken links.

Once you understand how each of the sections of the SourceFormat.txt file is constructed, you can fully customize your code's appearance. Using the Apply Source Formatting command, you can then bring any document you open into compliance with your new settings.

Summary

Understanding how to code in Dreamweaver helps you understand the behind-the-scenes aspects of using Dreamweaver's Design view. The Design view features enable you to focus on the design and structure of your page, but knowing how to access and modify the code puts you in complete control of your development project.

- HTML is a text document with tags and attributes to control the display and structure of a Web page.

- The Code view and Code Inspector enable you to access the code for the entire document in one window, while the Tag Selector and Quick Tag Editor enable you to focus on one tag for quick edits within the Design view.

- The Find and Replace feature is a powerful tool in both Code and Design views, which can be used to search for text and tags.

The next chapter gets into the good stuff—developing a site.

The Complete Reference

Dreamweaver 4

Part II

Building Your Web Site

Chapter 5

Organizing Your Sites and Pages

Newspaper articles, television programs, movies, and music all evoke different emotions. Even an entry in the dictionary has an emotional impact—the readers' relief at finding the word they sought, confusion over an odd spelling, enlightenment at finding a familiar word has additional meanings. And, of course, every conversation you have, whether it be an argument with the telephone company over your bill or a call home to your mother, is fraught with layered emotions.

Just as every form of communication you encounter offline has this effect, so, too, does a Web site. Literally millions of sites are on the Web, and every one of them conveys a message. Some sites strike such a bad note, you don't even wait for the page to finish loading before moving on. Others make you sit in awe at the design or writing style. You study those pages in search of "the trick."

Now think about some of the sites you reject while you're surfing. Yes, some really horrible sites are out there, no matter how you look at them. Some sites, however, are masterpieces of graphic design, but the images don't suit the material. Or, the content is written in a style that jars with the subject matter. The real trick to successful Web design is actually quite simple—design your site and content to evoke the intended emotional response from the site's visitors.

Let's look at what goes into planning a site. Then you learn how to create those sites and pages in Dreamweaver. If you're an experienced Web developer who has had enough of design theory and just wants to get to work, you may want to jump ahead to the section called "Creating Sites."

Site Planning 101

As I mentioned in previous chapters, Dreamweaver takes a site-down approach to Web design. Rather than thinking of your site as a series of interlinked pages, Dreamweaver encourages you to think of your site as a whole. From the very first step in Dreamweaver—defining your site—the application supports this mindset. This approach is further supported in the way Dreamweaver maintains a list of site assets, library items, and templates for your site. Proper planning can help you use all these tools more effectively, as well as improve the consistency and navigation of your site.

Site planning is a combination of far-reaching dreams and knowing the limitations of reality. The keys to this process are

- Determining your site's purpose
- Conceiving a tone or metaphor to convey that message
- Breaking down the message into snippets of information, which then become individual pages
- Developing a navigational structure to enable users to move throughout your site in a logical fashion
- Designing the visual appearance of the site, including the typography, images, and menu structure

Every Web designer has their own approach to this process. You may come up with the navigational system before you have fully mapped out your entire page structure. Or, you may design the visual appearance of the site and allow the tone of the content to follow in suit. As a writer, I tend to do the opposite, creating the visual design around the tone of my text content. As long as you consider each of the previous elements, the order doesn't matter.

Working with Clients

All the tips in this chapter are well and good when you're in control of your project. If you're designing a site for a client, however, all these rules and considerations can quickly become worthless. Working with clients who have no sense of design aesthetic and no writing ability, but tons of ideas on how their sites should be developed, can be incredibly frustrating. Of course, you can also look at this as a challenge to coerce them gently into expanding their vision to something that can actually become a viable plan. Invariably, times will occur when, despite your best efforts, customers are insistent on making poor design choices. In those cases, the best thing you can do is to give clients what they want—and then forget to put that site into your portfolio.

Freelance Web Development Points to Consider

It seems almost everyone is trying to make money on the Web. If you already own Dreamweaver and some good graphics tools, such as Fireworks or Photoshop, you might think it's easy to become a freelance Web developer. Hundreds, if not thousands, of professional Web developers are self-taught, and some are extremely successful. Unless you're well informed and prepared, however, it's also easy to get burned.

Knowing your own strengths and limitations before embarking on a career in Web design is important. Before putting your services on the open market, consider the wisdom in becoming proficient at both the design and development aspects of the business. While the prospect of making upwards of $50 to $100 per hour is enticing, remember, your client expects you to accomplish a lot of work per hour. You'll find yourself responsible for hours of unbillable time if it takes you longer than a reasonable period to accomplish the tasks set before you. This is particularly true if you charge a flat rate for your services. Unless you know your tools and can work efficiently, your dollar-per-hour earnings on a flat-rate project may turn out to be negligible. Being honest with yourself and your client about your skills helps you negotiate a financially satisfactory contract.

Speaking of contracts, *always* use one! No exceptions. I cannot emphasize this strongly enough. Even if you're creating a pro bono (free) site for a friend or a nonprofit agency, a contract sets reasonable terms for the scope of the project and the expectations of both parties. Friendships have been torn apart by arguments over endless design modifications, missing deliverable dates, and simple home pages that turn into 300-page sites. As someone who's been burned, I can say risking a little tension by asking for everything in writing is better than risking an entire relationship over resentment if things get out of hand.

I also urge you to have a lawyer draft a boilerplate contract for you to use, as the legal mumbo-jumbo may vary by state. Consider the following development clauses: some of these may appear in an appendix to the contract, making it easier to use a standard boilerplate, with the specific dates and monetary amounts listed separately.

- **Base Rate**—either an hourly fee or flat rate.

- **Payment Terms**—list deadlines for payment and production of the site. Specify any applicable late fees or redress if payment isn't made on time. Requiring a nonrefundable deposit before work commences is customary. The balance can be made payable in a lump sum on completion of the project or in increments as interim deadlines are reached, such as approval of the design concept. Also, add a clause about cancellation of the agreement, particularly detailing the fate of the deposit and any monies owed to you.

- **Base Package**—the number of Web pages included in this base fee and any limitations on those pages, such as whether the site will use frames or JavaScript or an e-commerce component.

- **Additional Pages**—the cost of pages beyond the maximum specified in the Base Package. This should include pages you created according to the approved design concept, which the client wants to modify significantly.

- **Delivery Dates**—the delivery dates should specify exactly what material you expect from the client to start the project and see it through to completion, and what you'll provide to the client on certain dates. If the client is providing text or graphics, be sure you give yourself some leeway before you're expected to produce pages that use that material.

- **Graphics**—specify whether graphics are to be provided by the client or created by you, and any limitations on the number of graphics. Include any banner ads or buttons you'll create for the client to use as marketing tools on other sites.

- **Text Content**—specify the text required of the client. If you'll be editing the content to increase marketability or readability, set reasonable limits for this work or specify additional fees for these services. Specify the word count per Web page, as longer pages require additional design consideration. Text that doesn't meet your specifications incurs additional editing fees or is returned to the client for revision.

■ **Domain Registration and Hosting**—specify who's responsible for registering the domain name and establishing an account with a host. If you prefer to work with certain hosts, put it in writing. In such instances, allow the client to choose their own host on your approval and if arranged by the client. Additional server requirements such as CGI scripts, a chat server, or any other services should be listed, as they require additional setup by the host. The contract should also be worded to authorize you to access the account.

■ **Training, Customer Support, and Maintenance**—if you'll turn the completed site over to the client, include a clause about training fees, if required. Detail the level of support the client can expect on completion, and fees for further modifications and updates. Any software the client requires to maintain the site is their financial responsibility. Repairs to pages modified by the client are charged at an hourly rate (usually set high enough to discourage abuse of this clause).

■ **Copyrights and Trademarks**—protect against lawsuits by requiring that any material furnished by the client be owned by him or be used with permission. Stock photography or other material you may require during the creation of the site will be dutifully licensed, at the expense of the client.

■ **Design Credit**—if you want to have a credit (usually a line stating, Designed by *X*, with a link to your own site, found at the bottom of the page near the copyright notice) on the site or use it in your portfolio, specify this in the contract. Also stipulate that your by-line cannot be removed from the site unless the site undergoes a complete redesign or at your request.

Deciding Your Site's Purpose

You may be saying to yourself that your site is simply a personal home page, so why worry about site-wide design. Or, you may be designing a huge endeavor for a corporate client and think the corporate identity will provide the cohesion needed for the site. This isn't entirely true in either scenario. While the primary intent of a site might include one of those possibilities, let's dig beneath the surface.

Every site should have a purpose, a reason for being hosted on the Web and visited by—you hope—thousands or even millions of people. Simply putting up a site to "establish an online presence" isn't a valid definition of its purpose. That online presence could be established to provide a way for customers to purchase merchandise from home. Or, it could be simply to provide customers with information about products, so they'll drive to the nearest store and purchase a product. Your site can either provide the news or debate issues in the news.

Whatever your site's purpose, you should be able to summarize it in two sentences. You can think of this as your site's mission statement. If this statement takes more than two sentences, think about whether you're being verbose or if you're trying to cover too much ground with one site.

Personal Home Pages

A personal home page isn't just your own space on the Web; it's also a window into your personality. Understanding this principle gives you the power to control the image you present. If your home page is going to be used as a resume in the hope of leading to professional contacts, this probably isn't a good place to talk about your deep, abiding love for your goldfish. You probably also don't want to use images of your tattoos and piercings—unless they fit into the corporate image of the companies for which you hope to work.

Molly Holzschlag is the author of more than a dozen books on Web design and software, as well as being a Web designer and lecturer. Her site at **http://www.molly.com** (as seen in Figure 5-1) achieves that rare balance between marketing tool and personal insight. The writing is crisp and hip, with a bit of an attitude, much like Molly herself. Her use of *Blogger*, a Weblog package that enables you to keep your site current with regular posts, adds a sense of interaction with the site and its creator. Molly not only uses her site to promote her books in print, but also to generate hype about books in progress. If you read carefully, you can also find a link to Molly's Inner Realm, a place where she shares her creative writing, music, and pictures of friends and family. The Inner Realm doesn't detract from the professional focus of the site—the link isn't even on the navigation bar—but, for those who want to get to know Molly better, it's there.

Of course, not all personal home pages are used for professional purposes. Back to that goldfish, your site may be devoted to your fishy friend. Your choice of subject, as well as the way you approach it, presents yet another aspect of your personality to the world. Consider interjecting a note of humor by making the fish the narrator of your site, describing you from his perspective. Your site's purpose may be to inform people about the care and feeding of goldfish. If your fish has just made that final trip into the sewer system, your site may become an ode to Goldy, complete with original poetry describing your torment. Now, think about the image you project of yourself by choosing each of these possibilities and how each variation serves a different purpose.

Corporate and E-Commerce Sites

Corporate sites present different issues. These sites should reflect the corporate image, not only in the appearance of the company's logo, but also in tone and design. Simply choosing the site's colors from among those in the logo isn't enough. If the company is trendy, such as a record label or teen clothing store, the site design should follow suit. A bank or investment site, however, generally tries to instill a sense of confidence and responsibility, which translates to a more sedate online presence.

The explosion of e-commerce has brought new design considerations. If the purpose of your site is to sell goods online, you want to make your users feel secure about sharing

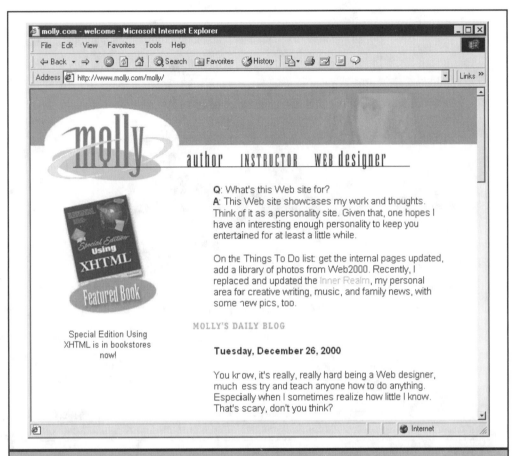

Figure 5-1.   *Molly Holzschlag's site is an excellent marketing tool for her books,
design skills, and lectures, and also gives insight into her personality*

their credit card information, so you want to convey a sense of reliability. You want
visitors to feel your product will look or operate as advertised, and that you'll be
responsible in how you handle their purchase. Reliability and responsibility don't
translate into stodginess, however. Fireside Soaps, at **http://www.firesidesoaps.com,** is a
business that sells hand-made natural soaps and lotions. As you can see in Figure 5-2,
Laura Phillips, the owner of Fireside Soaps and designer of its site, has maintained that
same back-to-basics approach to the site. The text is friendly and approachable, and no
bells and whistles jar you from the calm of the site. Even the choice of green for the navbar
makes you think of nature.

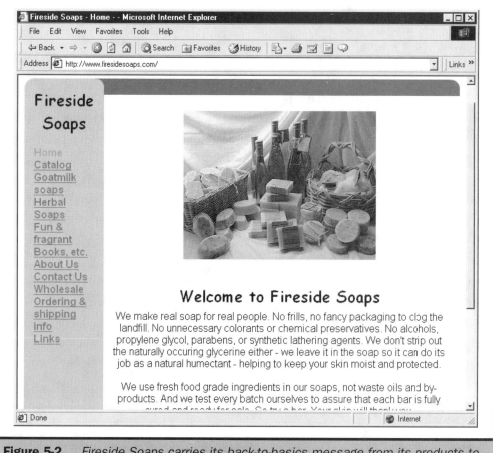

Figure 5-2. *Fireside Soaps carries its back-to-basics message from its products to its site design*

News and Entertainment Sites

Sites that are meant to inform rely on building a steady audience. Because you can't change the salient facts of what's happening in the world from day to day, the information presented is essentially the same from site to site. Therefore, these sites need to find other ways to stand out. Some sites use innovative navigation systems and approaches to organizing the articles. Others use cutting-edge technology to bring the news to life by way of audio and video clips. Some sites even put their own spin on the news of the day by way of commentary or digging deeper into the facts. Other sites create parodies of legitimate news stories.

Entertainment sites have some of the same considerations as news sites. Out of all the movie sites on the Web, for example, there are reasons why the *Internet Movie Database (IMDb)* at **http://www.imdb.com** has become the best movie site on the Web. The IMDb lives up to its simple purpose: to provide the most complete coverage of movies and television on the Web. Using the site's search engine, you can find everything from movie summaries to actor bios to quotes. Even as IMDb has expanded from movies into television, also adding message boards and trivia games, the site hasn't lost sight of its purpose as a warehouse of information. Every feature on IMDb relates to movies or television in some way.

Community Sites

Community sites can be among the most challenging to develop. Community is built by regular interaction between visitors, and this dialogue needs to be guided with diplomacy and discretion. Community sites require daily attention, so ease of use is important for both the site's visitors and the developer. Losing its sense of purpose is also easy for a community site because the needs of its members are constantly changing. If you keep discussion focused tightly on your chosen theme, you risk alienating the members when they find other common interests they want to discuss. Likewise, if the site turns into a free-for-all, then it won't appeal any longer to new visitors who are looking for specific information.

Community sites come in all flavors—from politics to engineering to quilting. Numerous free or low-cost message board and guestbook scripts and services are on the Web, bringing this technology within the reach of even a novice Web developer. One of the most recent exploitations of online community has come from the showbiz industry. Performers and their production houses are using the Web to build communities of fans in the hopes they, in turn, promote the artist on other sites and in their offline communities. Fan clubs, such as Ricky Martin Online at **http://www.rmlac.com** (see Figure 5-3), not only develop a sense of community for the club members—who often find other areas of common interest beyond that of the performer—but also maintain interest in the performer even between movies or CDs.

Dozens of message board and chat solutions are available, with more being added all the time. Yahoo! GeoCities (**http://geocities.yahoo.com**) enables you to add community features to sites hosted on their service, while Bravenet (**http://www.bravenet.com**) and ezboard (**http://www.ezboard.com**) provide interactive features to which you can link from your remotely hosted site. If you want to take the plunge and host your own message board, look at WWWThreads (**http://www.wwwthreads.com**), Snitz (**http://www.snitz.com**), or Ultimate Bulletin Board (**http://www.infopop.com**), among others, but look carefully at their server requirements before investing your time and money.

Chat solutions generally involve a Java client that's embedded into your page, and dozens of them are available. The biggest consideration is finding a chat server, as most Web hosts won't let you host your own because of the considerable bandwidth they use. Bravenet has a Java chat client, which can be embedded into your page, and

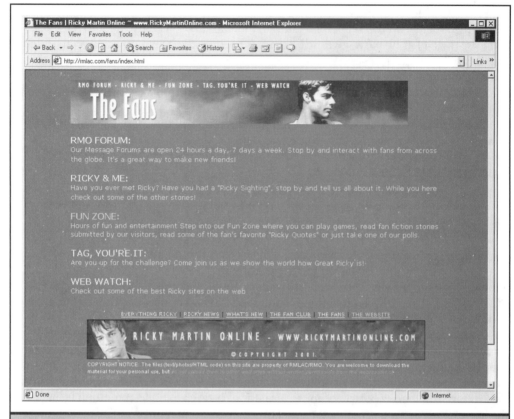

Figure 5-3. *The Ricky Martin Online fan club provides community for its members and information about the performer to promote his latest releases*

automatically connects back to their chat server. You can also establish a channel on an *Internet Relay Chat* (IRC) server. The advantage of this approach is your users then have the option of accessing the chat room either from the chat client on your page or through a third-party application, such as mIRC or Ircle. The disadvantage to using IRC is it's harder to control who has access, so they require more policing to boot out disruptive visitors. Some servers are quieter than others, however, and some even let you establish private or hidden rooms to avoid the worst of these problems. If you want to go this route, consider services like SuperChat (**http://www.superchat.org**). For an applet to allow access to an IRC channel from your page, look at JPilot (**http://www.jpilot.com**).

Developing Your Concept

Once you determine your site's purpose, you need to decide how to present it. Some of this is constrained by the issues described earlier, but you still have a lot of decisions to make.

Theme and Metaphor

As soon as you decided to develop a Web site, for whatever purpose or client, you probably had some initial ideas about how the site should look—maybe even dozens of different ideas. Whether your ideas were as preliminary as a color choice or as advanced as an entire navigation system and Flash animations, those initial ideas can provide a theme or metaphor for your site.

While some designers use theme and metaphor interchangeably, I think of *theme* as being the appearance of the site and the *metaphor* as being the organizational structure on which the theme is developed. You may see your site with a futuristic theme, using chrome effects and flashing buttons, but this relates only to the appearance of the site's elements, not their intent. If your site has a space station metaphor, however, the navigational buttons could represent different decks of the ship or the roles of its inhabitants, all created with those chrome effects and flashing buttons to add that futuristic look. A site metaphor might be subtle or overt, specific or rather abstract. You might use pictures and icons to represent each item, or you could rely solely on description to let visitors paint their own mental images. Theme and metaphor also play a role in your content, as you wouldn't want to use a folksy tone in a futuristic site.

While developing your site's theme and metaphor, think about consistency. The entire site should have a common look and feel. Think about which elements should be repeated on every page, such as a navigational system, and which elements should be unique, such as the content and images. If you have items that appear to break with your theme or metaphor, consider how they can be brought into the fold or if they should be discarded.

Orientation and Navigation

Orientation is more than knowing where you are, it's also knowing where you are in relation to everything else. A book is linear in its construct. You read from page to page, beginning to end. A newspaper, however, follows a nonlinear structure. You might start reading an article on Page one that's continued on Page five. That article may have a sidebar or related article that continues on Page six. Then you might return to the front page to read another article, and so on. No matter where you are in the paper, however, you always know how to get back to the front page.

On the Web, three major constructs exist. A *linear construct* is similar to that of a book. The first page has a link to move forward to the next page. The second page links to both the preceding and following pages, which continues until the last page. This layout is useful if your site tells a story, is a virtual gallery, or contains a series of steps that must be followed in a particular order.

A *hierarchical construct*, as the following illustrates, has both a horizontal and a vertical plane. The top page branches to related pages, which expand on the original in various ways. These pages, in turn, have their own branches. These sites can become quite large, with the lower levels of the hierarchy becoming distant from others on the same level. While jumping from branch to branch can be difficult, however, navigating back through the hierarchy to take a different route is a simple matter. The hierarchical construct is also the basis for a *spoke construct,* whereby the main page is the center of a wheel, with the underlying pages branching out from the center like the spokes of a wheel. Moving from spoke to spoke, just like moving from branch to branch in a classic hierarchy, involves navigating back to the starting point.

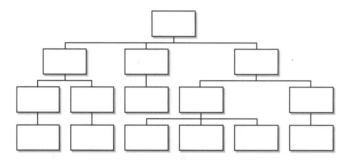

A nonhierarchical construct, which the following illustrates, contains links between branches, giving the site a three-dimensional quality. The trick to pulling off a successful nonlinear site is a good navigational system to help users regain their bearings after they make a jump in logic. These types of sites are becoming more feasible, however, with the advent of drop-down and fly-out menus, which make it easy to navigate directly from the main page of your site to a page several layers down.

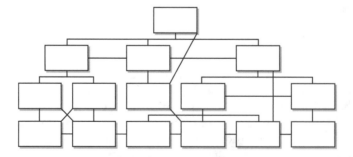

To put this theory into practice, make a list of all the areas you want to cover on your site. As you come up with these ideas, you begin to see logical groups emerge, which then become your main menu items. Now think about how each topic should be presented and how the information should flow from page to page. This can determine your hierarchy. You may find you move pages around, add new ideas, and discard some pages entirely before finding the right structure for your site. The advantage of this approach is you can see at a glance which sections have gaps in material and which pages need further modification to meet the site's purpose and metaphor.

Tip	*This process is referred to as storyboarding. I like to do my brainstorming on the computer using outlining software. For a simple computer solution, try the Outline view in Microsoft Word. Other solutions include ActionOutline (**http://www.greenparrots.com**) or Writer's Blocks (**http://www.writersblocks.com**). You can storyboard the old fashioned way, using index cards or Post-it Notes.*

This planning is essential preparation for designing the navigational elements of your site. You may want to have a horizontal navigation bar across the top of your page. After planning, however, you could find you have too many menu items to fit across the screen while maintaining readability. You might initially want to have each menu item represented by an icon rather than text, and then find some of the items are difficult to conceptualize without some revision.

While these aren't considered part of the navigation system, this is a good time to think about your headers, footers, and copyright information. Like the navigation system, these elements appear on every page of your site and also serve to help your users get their bearings. You want their format to be consistent, as well as in keeping with the theme and metaphor for your site.

Cross-Browser Functionality

Even though browser issues aren't related to the site's purpose or the creative planning of a site, considering them is important before you plan the layout and functionality of a site. A complete discussion of browser compatibility is beyond the scope of this book, but you should be aware of the basic issues. If you want to pursue this topic further, I recommend you visit the Web Standards Project at **http://www.webstandards.org/**.

The current versions of the major browsers are more standards-compliant than ever, but differences still exist in the way each browser handles certain elements. Depending on where you research your Web statistics (I used the Browser News site at **http://www.upsdell.com/BrowserNews/stat_browser.htm**), less than 10 percent of Web surfers are still using older browsers, particularly Netscape Navigator 4.75 or earlier. This may seem an insignificant amount, but these statistics are subject to interpretation.

If you're hosting a gaming site, your visitors are more likely to use the latest computer hardware and software, and they're likely to be early adopters of new browser technology. If you're hosting an educational site, however, you might find your visitors are more likely to use older computers, as many schools rely on donated computer hardware that cannot necessarily use the latest operating systems and browsers. Also, users who rely on a particular application to perform their jobs or pursue their hobbies may be less likely to have the latest hardware/software because they don't want to put those other applications at risk. I know a surprising number of authors who still use Windows 3.1 because they don't want to give up their favorite versions of WordPerfect.

If you're developing an e-commerce site, cross-browser compatibility becomes an issue that can have a financial impact. You (or your client) won't want to risk losing even a small percentage of potential buyers because of something as easily avoided as using features that cannot be rendered in all browsers.

Differences exist in how even the current browsers render Web pages. Some of these are because of differences in computer platform and operating systems. Graphics that appear dark on a PC may be bright on a Mac because of differences in gamma. Text appears larger on a PC than on a Mac.

Other differences are related to browser versions. Users need to have Netscape Navigator 4 or later to see background colors in tables. Neither Navigator 3 nor Microsoft Internet Explorer 3 (or earlier) can correctly position images that use the `texttop`, `absbottom`, `absmiddle`, or baseline values for the `align` attribute. Netscape recently added the capability to view I-frames with its release of Netscape Navigator 6. And, while earlier versions of Navigator used the `<layer>` tag, support for this tag was dropped in favor of the standards-compliant `<div>` tag with version 6 of the browser.

Of course, the problems most maligned by Web designers are those of standards and differences between the browsers. Don't count on Navigator users being able to see your text scrolling across the screen if you use a `<marquee>` tag, because that browser doesn't support it. Changing the color of scrollbars to suit your site's design using Cascading Style Sheets also only works in Internet Explorer.

While keeping these considerations in mind is important, workarounds exist for many of these issues. Netscape 4.75, which at press time is still the most popular version of Netscape, may not position layers properly after the user resizes the browser window, but there's a script that forces the screen to refresh, thereby placing the layers back in position. Some of these other differences are important only from a design standpoint. This isn't meant to diminish design issues, of course. Colored scrollbars aren't visible from Netscape, but the style is simply ignored. Thus, your Internet Explorer users see the colored scrollbars, while Netscape users see the standard scrollbar colors on an otherwise functional page.

The true importance of cross-browser compatibility is solely at your discretion. If you're concerned about reaching every possible user, stay away from the newest bells and whistles, such as DHTML, and avoid complex, nested tables as much as possible. If you're going to push the limits of Web design, do so knowledgeably, and be aware of ways to code your pages to ensure functionality for users with older browsers, even if they cannot experience the full pageantry of your design.

Creating Sites

Asking developers how they approach the design process is akin to asking which came first, the chicken or the egg. By now, you should have some idea of the structure of your site and, at least, a preliminary layout for your pages. Most likely, you've sketched out a few design ideas during your planning and possibly even prototyped your page layout in a graphics package, such as Fireworks or Adobe Photoshop.

From there, however, the process varies widely. Experienced developers often generate the graphics they require for the site before coding the site, as they've already figured out the necessary dimensions and appearance of each element on the page. Other developers prefer to use placeholders or mock-up images until they lay out the page in HTML, preferring to change the dimensions of certain elements as they see how the page is coming together on the screen. There's no right or wrong way to design, even though both factions insist the other is doing it wrong and wasting unnecessary time.

You should complete one more step before opening the Dreamweaver application and getting started. Decide where you want to locate your site on your local computer. Also determine how you'll organize files related to the site. During the course of development, you have source files for your graphics, text content, and raw multimedia files, in addition to the HTML pages, final images, and style sheets that comprise the actual site. If you're a professional Web developer, you may also have production notes and contracts. I have all my projects in one folder, called Web Sites. Each project has its own subfolder, which is further broken down into folders for Content Source, Image Source, Other Sources, Prototypes, and Business. I also have a subfolder for Site, which contains the actual Web site files.

Caution   *Certain file- and folder-naming conventions that are acceptable within a computer's operating system have mixed results on the Web. To play it safe, don't use any spaces or nonalphanumeric characters (other than the underscore character) in your file or folder names.*

Now it's time to move from paper (or your planning tools of choice) to Dreamweaver to define your site and start developing your pages.

Defining Sites

One of Dreamweaver's biggest features is its capability to organize all your site assets—the location of your pages and images, library items, and templates—and to connect with the remote server that is eventually to host your site to transfer this information. When you upload your site, Dreamweaver duplicates the site structure you created locally, including the organization of folders, pages, images, and other necessary files. This is yet another reason that thinking of your site as a whole, rather than as a series of individual pages and images, is so important. To use Dreamweaver to maintain your site, you must first define it.

You need to define two important components in your site: the local information and the remote server info. To define a new site in Dreamweaver, choose Site | New Site from either the Site window (in Windows) or the Document window (in both Windows and the Mac): This opens the Site Definition dialog box, as the following illustrates.

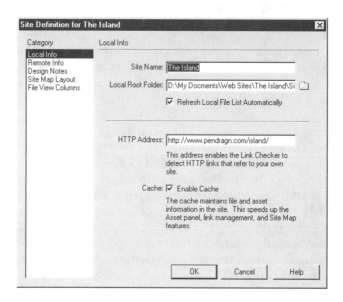

Local Info

The most important category of this dialog box, at least in the early stages of development, is the *Local Info*. This tells Dreamweaver where to find the components of the site, and where to add new pages, templates, and library items.

In the Local Info category, enter the following information:

Site Name   This name appears in the Site List, so you can move from site to site quickly within Dreamweaver if you're working on multiple projects. The name can contain spaces and other special characters, as it's simply an internal reference name.

Local Root Folder   The *Local Root folder* is the folder that serves as the root for your site on your local computer. You can click the folder icon next to this field to access the file browser and navigate to the folder you created, as suggested earlier. Otherwise, you can use the file browser to create a new folder. This folder appears in the Local Folder pane of the Site window.

Refresh Local File List Automatically   Check this box if you want the Site window to refresh the view of the Local Folder automatically when you move files and folders. If you choose not to check this box to improve the speed of Dreamweaver when copying files, you can refresh the entire site view manually by clicking the Refresh icon in the Site window or pressing F5. To refresh only the Local Folder pane, select View | Refresh Local in Windows or Site | Site Files View | Refresh Local on the Mac. You can also use the keyboard shortcut SHIFT-F5 on both platforms. Unless every bit of processing speed is crucial to your system, checking this box is easiest, however, so you always have a current view of your local site root available.

HTTP Address   This is the URL of your completed site once it's uploaded to the remote server. Dreamweaver uses this to verify absolute links—links beginning with http:// and a complete path—to determine if a link is internal (a part of your site) or external (linking to another site). If you aren't yet sure of the URL of your site because you're still shopping for a remote host, you can enter a mock URL at this time. After you contract with a remote host, however, you should update this field and check your links, as explained in Chapter 11.

Cache   If you check the option to Enable Cache, Dreamweaver maintains a list of site assets in the Assets panel. The Assets panel tracks the links, templates, colors, and images you use on your site, making it easy to apply these elements to other pages. In addition, the Assets panel stores library items, which are saved snippets of code you can save to use elsewhere in the site (see Chapter 28 for more information about the Assets panel and library items. The cache also enables the application to accomplish link and site management tasks quickly. If you forget or neglect to enable the cache, you are prompted to do so when you click OK to close the Site Definition dialog box to establish the site. Again, unless you have a good reason not to do so, enabling the cache is worthwhile.

In the early stages of site development, you can define the local info without providing remote info. You might do this if you're still searching for a Web host but don't want to hold up your development process. If this is the case, you can click OK to exit the Site Definition dialog box and define your new site.

Remote Info

If you already have a host, you want to fill out the information requested in the other Site Definition categories, so you can readily upload files to the remote server for testing as you work. If you already closed this box after entering your Local Info, you can edit the site definition by choosing Site | Define Sites, clicking the site name, and then choosing Edit from the Define Sites dialog box. This reopens the Site Definition dialog box. To proceed, click the Remote Info category.

Access

The first choice you need to make is how Dreamweaver should access the remote site. Choose from the following options:

- **None**—This is the default option if you haven't yet established a remote server.

- **FTP**—This stands for File Transfer Protocol and is the most common way to upload files to the Web. If you choose this option, be sure to have the server access information on hand, provided to you by your remote host. The other information required for FTP is detailed in the next section, "FTP Access."

- **Local/Network**—This option is used if you're using your local drive as a Web server or if the Web server is part of your network. If you choose this option, you are then able to select the root folder and tell Dreamweaver to refresh the remote file list automatically. If you choose not to do this, you can do it manually by selecting F5 or the Site window Refresh button to refresh the entire Site window. You also update only the remote pane by selecting View | Refresh Remote from the Site window (ALT-F5) in Windows, or Site | Site Files View | Refresh Remote (OPTION-F5) on the Mac. If you're working as part of a development group, you'll also want to enable File Check In/Check Out to prevent several members of the team from working on the same file at the same time.

- **SourceSafe Database**—Microsoft Visual SourceSafe is a version-control application often used by development groups on large projects. It enables development groups to track changes made to files and revert to earlier versions. If you choose this option, you need to click the Settings button to configure the database. SourceSafe is covered in Chapter 6.

- **WebDAV**—This is a source-control protocol that works on Microsoft *Internet Information Server* (*IIS*) 5.0 and the Apache Web Server. With this protocol enabled on the server side and defined in Dreamweaver, you can use the source control and merging tools made available through it. After choosing this option, you need to select the Settings button to configure the connection. The information you need for these settings should be available through your remote server provider. You are prompted to enter the URL of the folder in which you plan to store your site on the WebDAV server, as well as your username and password for the server.

FTP Access

If you choose to access your remote site using FTP, the context of the Remote Info category changes, as the following illustrates.

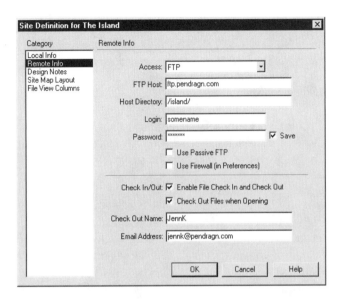

FTP Host   The FTP host is the server location your provider gave you to upload your site. The host is usually something like www.mystuff.com or ftp.mystuff.com, but it can also be an IP address. You needn't preface the host with any protocol information, such as http:// or ftp://.

Host Directory   The *host directory* is the folder on the remote server in which you'll place your site. In many cases, you're automatically connected to the proper directory when you connect to the FTP host from your account, so you can leave the host directory information blank. If you need to use a specific path, you've been provided with this information by your provider.

Tip   *If you're using your server space to develop or test multiple sites, you can give each site its own folder, and use that as the host directory. In this case, enter the folder name in the Host Directory field, such as /island. When providing the URL to site visitors, you need to include the directory information in the URL, such as http://www.pendragn.com/island rather than simply http://www.pendragn.com.*

Login and Password   A login and password combination are required to access the remote server. This information is provided by your remote host and is usually different from the account information you use with your *Internet service provider (ISP)*, even if you're hosting your site through the same provider. Be certain the Save box is checked if you want Dreamweaver to store your account information. Otherwise, you can deselect this box to be prompted for your password whenever you connect to the remote server.

If you use AOL as your remote host, you need to be logged in to the service using the AOL software before you can FTP your site from Dreamweaver. When defining the site in Dreamweaver, set the FTP Host as members.aol.com, and leave the Host Directory field blank. The Login entry should be ftp, and the password is your full AOL address (such as myname@aol.com).

Use Passive FTP and Use Firewall   *Firewalls* are security systems for computers, preventing unauthorized access. Formerly seen only in corporate settings, firewalls have been brought into the home market by the proliferation of home local area networks, high-speed Internet access, and a seemingly endless supply of viruses and malicious hackers. The types of firewalls and the protection they provide vary by product. So, too, do the procedures you must follow to get around these firewalls to communicate with the Internet and, in this case, with remote servers.

If you use a firewall, you may be unable to connect to an FTP server in the usual manner. Normally, a local computer asks a remote server to establish a connection and transfer data back and forth. Some firewalls prevent the local computer from initiating the connection with the server, so no connection is established and transfers cannot be made. Passive FTP allows the local computer to establish the connection, rather than requesting it of the remote server, thereby enabling the transfer.

If you have additional firewall security issues, select the Use Firewall box. Dreamweaver then uses the firewall settings you established in the Site category of the Preferences dialog box (accessible from the Edit | Preferences menu or CTRL-U in Windows, CMD-U on the Mac). The firewall host name and port number are available from your network administrator.

Check In/Out   If you're working in a group, you'll want to access Dreamweaver's collaboration features. These tools keep the group informed as to which member of the team is currently working on a file to prevent files from being inadvertently overwritten by other members of the team and facilitate communication with the group. If you enable this feature, you're prompted for a Check Out Name, which appears in the Site window whenever you check out a file. The E-mail Address information is used for Dreamweaver's Integrated E-mail feature. These are explained in detail in Chapter 6.

Design Notes

When working in a development group, members can easily misunderstand one another's intentions. One member of the group might be using placeholder images while waiting for another to finalize the graphics, while yet another member is wondering why the current images look rather unprofessional. As discussed in greater depth in Chapter 6, Design Notes help the group communicate by allowing notes to be associated with pages. A Design Note could state, for example, the status of the page, whether it's in alpha or beta testing. It could also be used to add a note stating that design is held up while waiting for final artwork from another team member.

As the following shows, two options exist for Design Notes.

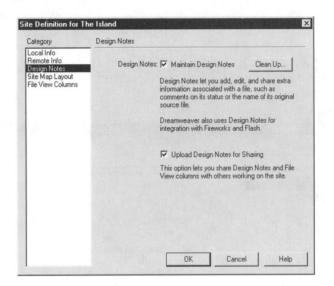

Maintain Design Notes   This option enables the Design Notes feature. *Design Notes* are associated with the pages to which they relate and are stored in a separate folder within the site.

   Design Notes are also a feature of Fireworks and Flash, so notes attached to objects created in those applications can be read in Dreamweaver.

Upload Design Notes for Sharing   Design Notes are only useful in a group setting if the group can access them. If this option is checked, the Design Notes associated with a file move to and from the Remote Server with the file whenever it is checked in or out. This ensures team members always have the most current notes on the file when they access it.

Clean Up...   As I stated earlier, get into the habit of doing all your site maintenance—renaming, moving, and deleting files—from within Dreamweaver. When you delete a file in Dreamweaver, the associated Design Notes are also deleted. If you choose to delete files using another method, however, the associated Design Notes are left behind as orphans. You can remove orphaned Design Notes by selecting the Clean Up button. If you want to remove all the Design Notes for the entire site, such as on the completion of the project, deselect the Maintain Design Notes option, and then press the Clean Up button.

Site Map Layout

A *Site Map* provides a visual orientation for the site. You may have encountered site maps on the Web used to help users navigate through a site. In Dreamweaver terms, however, a Site Map is a developer tool. If you're a visual person, you can use the Site Map view to add and delete pages, change page titles, and check internal links. You can even use the Site Map as a storyboarding tool in planning your site. These features are covered in greater depth in Chapter 6. Before you can use the Site Map, however, you need to define it in the Site Map Layout category of the Site Definition dialog box, as the following shows.

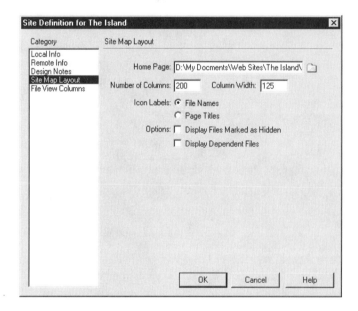

Home Page   The home page of your site is generally the page to which your site defaults when users enter your URL. This is usually called index.html (or index.htm), but sometimes it's also named default.htm. If this page doesn't yet exist in the site—as when you're defining a new site—Dreamweaver asks if it should create an empty file with the name provided in this field.

For existing sites, you can also identify another page as the home page of the site to get a visual representation of the site with the identified file as the top of the hierarchy. This is sometimes helpful in testing or when the site becomes so expansive the file recursion displayed in the Site Map is too cumbersome to comprehend easily.

Number of Columns and Column Width   A Site Map is laid out in a manner similar to an organizational chart, with each block—or file—in a column and row based on its position in the site hierarchy. You can modify the display of the columns by changing the default information in these fields.

The Number of Columns field specifies how many files to display horizontally in each row. If you want to create a vertical site map layout, change this number to 1.

The Column Width field specifies the width of each column. Columns must be 70 to 1,000 pixels wide. The smaller the width, the more truncated the filename and title. The larger the width, the fewer the number of pages that can be represented on the screen in the Site window at one time.

Icon Labels   The Site Map can display either filenames or page titles. The Titles option is useful if you give each of your pages a unique name as you develop your site—and this feature can even serve as a reminder to title your pages immediately. If you use lengthy titles or use the same words to preface each of your page titles, however, this option becomes less feasible. I usually stick with filenames.

Options   The last two options in the Site Map Layout category determine which types of files are displayed on the Site Map. Selecting Display Files Marked as Hidden shows hidden HTML files as part of the Site Map. Selecting Display Dependent Files adds images, multimedia, and external JavaScript files to the display.

File View Columns

The final category in the Site Definition dialog box enables you to configure both the information provided for files in the Site window and the order in which that information is displayed. The following illustration shows the File View Columns category. The built-in file columns are listed here, and they can be reordered or hidden from the file view. You can also add new columns associated with Design Note information.

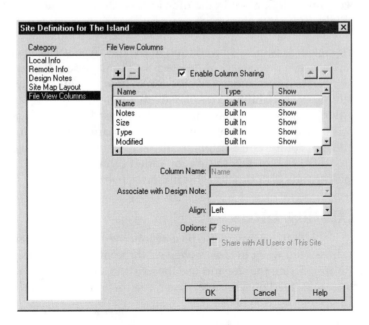

Enable Column Sharing   This option should be checked if you're working in a development group, as it enables you to share custom file view columns with others in the group.

File View Column List   This pane initially displays the default columns—Name, Notes, Size, Type, Modified, and Check Out By. The Name column must always remain the first column in the file view, and it cannot be hidden. The other columns can be moved using the up and down arrow buttons at the top of the pane.

   If you enabled Design Notes, you can add columns to the file view. To add a new column to the list, select the Add (+) button to insert an untitled column to the list. As with the default columns, added columns may be moved up or down in the list. To delete a nondefault column, click the Delete (-) button. The default columns cannot be deleted.

Column Name   When you add a column, give it a unique name in this field. To change the name of a column, highlight it in the file view list, and then type over the name in the Column Name field.

Associate with Design Note   New columns must be associated with a Design Note, which contain the data that populates the column. The options are assigned, due, priority, and status. Once added, these columns remain blank unless the associated information is entered into the Design Notes.

Align   Each column may be aligned according to your preferences. To change the alignment for a column, highlight it in the file view list, and then click the down arrow to choose Left, Right, or Center alignment.

Options   To change the visibility of a column in the file view, select the column name from the file view list, and then select or deselect the Show option. Because the default options cannot be deleted, this setting enables you to hide unwanted columns from the view, while retaining the capability to display them later.

   If you're working in a development group and selected the Enable Column Sharing option at the top of the dialog box, you can set added columns to be shared by others in the group. The default columns are automatically shared by everyone in the development group. To change this setting for added columns, highlight the column in the file view, and then select or deselect this option.

Converting Existing Sites

If you've used other HTML editors in the past or inherited an already developed site, you can convert the site to work in Dreamweaver. If the site is stored on your local drive, you can simply define the site and use the existing site folder as the Local Root Folder. If the files are located on a remote server, use the following steps to copy the site to your local drive:

1. Select Site | New Site to open the Site Definition dialog box.

2. Fill out the Local Info category as previously instructed. You can either establish an empty, existing folder as the Local Site Root or create a new folder in which to store the files.

3. Fill out the Remote Info with the current remote server information.

4. Select Site | Get, use the Get icon on the Site window toolbar, or use the CTRL-SHIFT-D (CMD-SHIFT-D on the Mac) keyboard shortcut to connect to the remote server and copy the files to your local root folder.

If the site is to be hosted on a different server in the future, you can edit the site definition to reflect this new information after you make a copy of the site on your local drive.

Note   *Some HTML editors, particularly Microsoft FrontPage, use extensions and HotBots (bots) to add functionality to sites created in that application. These bots only work on a remote server specially configured to use them, and they can only be edited within FrontPage. If you're converting a FrontPage site to work in Dreamweaver, you'll most likely have to remove any bots contained in the site. This can be done in FrontPage before making the conversion or using the Find & Replace feature of Dreamweaver after converting the site. If you choose to retain these bots, you need to ensure you don't modify them and you continue hosting your site on a remote server with the proper extensions installed. When making this decision, remember, most bot functionality can be re-created in Dreamweaver using more common standards, such as JavaScript.*

The Site Window

After defining a site, the Site window, as shown in Figure 5-4, becomes the primary tool for managing and maintaining the files within the site. The FTP, Site Map, and other tools are to be fully explained in Chapter 6, but familiarizing yourself with the layout of the window first is important.

If you recall, the Site category of the Preferences dialog box enables you to specify which file list appears in which pane of the Site window. I like my local folder to be displayed on the left half of the window, but this is strictly a matter of personal preference.

The first thing to do in a new site is to establish the structure you previously planned. Creating your folders and pages in advance makes linking the pages during development easier and ensures your site is organized from the start.

Adding Folders

When you first define a site in Dreamweaver, your primary concern is creating a local site structure to create your pages. Remember, though, your local site structure is

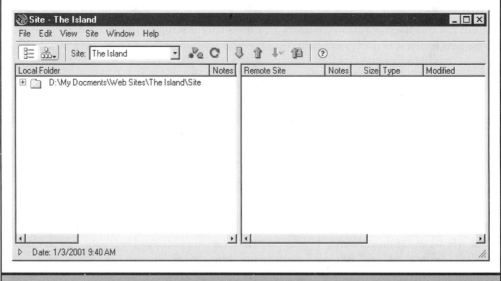

Figure 5-4.   *The initial appearance of the Site window is rather sparse until you add folders and pages to develop the site*

transferred to the remote site when you upload. This is where your site structure planning comes into play.

As mentioned earlier, sites are in a constant state of construction and modification. As you add pages and change images, you can quickly become overwhelmed with files—both active and orphaned—unless you're organized from the start of your project. This is where your site structure planning comes into play. If you're developing a small site with only a handful of pages, you can keep your pages in one directory. If your site consists of dozens of pages, you'll want to create subfolders to organize your site. This can make maintaining the site easier in the future.

The most common approach to page organization is to use folders reflecting the hierarchy of the site's navigation. I like to organize my pages in folders based on the main navigational elements on my index page. For example, if the site's navbar has options for Beach, Gym, and Food, I create folders for each of those areas. Pages accessible from the Beach page then get added to the Beach folder, and so on. If the pages in a subfolder contain images that aren't used anywhere else on the site, sometimes it's helpful to place them in their own images folder within that subfolder.

In almost all cases, you'll want to create a separate folder for your images. Many reasons exist for this:

■ You'll always know where to look for an image file when adding it to a Dreamweaver page.

- Scrolling through a list of pages is easier without image files cluttering up the directory.

- Common image files, such as those used for navigation, can be easily located and shared by multiple pages.

If you're adding Shockwave or other multimedia objects, you'll also want to create directories for those objects, generally in a multimedia folder.

While you can create folders in Windows Explorer (Windows) or MultiFinder (Mac), it's better to get into the habit of always maintaining your site in Dreamweaver. This habit also ensures you only move files and folders inside the application, which is the only way Dreamweaver can maintain link integrity.

To add folders in Dreamweaver, select File | New Folder from the Site window (or CTRL-ALT-SHIFT-N) in Windows, or Site | Site Files View | New Folder (CMD-SHIFT-OPTION-N) on the Mac.

Creating Pages

Once you create the major folders for your site, you can create your first page. This page is your index page and is the keystone of your site. If you followed the instructions for enabling the site map feature in the Site Definition dialog box, you may have already created your index page. Otherwise, create a new page by doing the following:

1. Open the Site window, if it isn't already available.

2. Confirm you're in the local folder of your new site by checking the site name in the Site field of the toolbar. If you're in another site—such as if you have been working through the tutorials that came with the Dreamweaver application—use the drop-down menu in the Site field to select your new site.

3. Choose File | New File from the menu or the keyboard shortcut CTRL-SHIFT-N (CMD-SHIFT-N).

4. A new file appears in the file view of the Local Folder pane. The name of the file is highlighted, so you can change it. If this is the first file you've created for the site, name it either index.html or index.htm, depending on the naming convention you want to use throughout the site and any naming conventions imposed by your provider.

5. Press ENTER (RETURN on the Mac) to establish the new filename.

If you're working in the Document window, you can add a page by choosing File | New (CTRL-N or CMD-N). You can also add pages from the Site Map view in the Site window, as covered in Chapter 6.

To add a page to one of the subfolders in the site, highlight the folder in the Local Folder list, and then follow the previous steps. The unnamed page is then added to the folder you selected, ready to be named.

Keep your naming conventions consistent. If you chose to use the .html extension, use it throughout the site. Also be certain your page names make sense to you (and others on your development team), so you don't waste time down the road scanning multiple pages to find the one you seek.

As shown in Figure 5-5, the Site window quickly fills up with folders and pages, illustrating why good organization is critical.

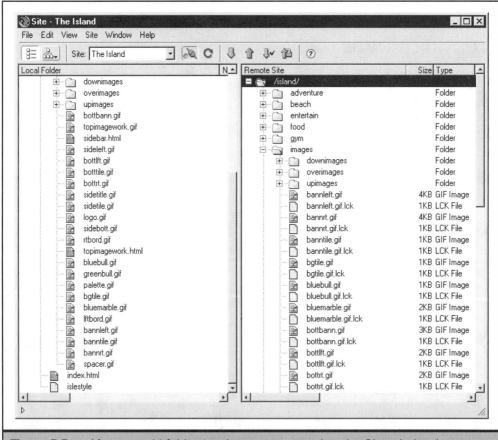

Figure 5-5. *After you add folders and pages to your site, the Site window becomes a useful tool*

Summary

If you've made it this far, you should have a pretty good understanding of how to develop your basic site idea and set up the structure of that site within Dreamweaver. Keep these key points in mind:

- Always remember the mission statement or purpose of your site.

- The site's theme is related to the site's appearance. The site's metaphor is the organizational elements and tone that associate the site with a familiar offline concept or object.

- To enable Dreamweaver's site management tools, you must define the site.

- The Local Root is the folder on the local computer that contains the site.

- Pages can be added to the site from the File menu of either the Site window or the Document window. If you add your key pages to the site from the start, it's easier to establish links to these pages while you develop the site.

- The Remote Server is where the live site is stored for access on the Web. If you're on a development team, the Remote Server might also serve as the central storage system for the site while it's under development, leaving your Local Root as the location only of the files on which you're currently working.

The next chapter explores the other features of the Site window and explains how to move pages to and from a remote server.

BUILDING YOUR
WEB SITE

The
Complete
Reference

Dreamweaver
4

Chapter 6

Site Management

The previous chapter introduced the Site window, so let's learn how to use it to manage your site. This may feel like skipping around a bit, going straight from the planning stage to the uploading stage but, in the end, it'll all make sense. After you plan your site and create some pages, knowing how to get those pages onto the Web to share them with the world is important. Then you'll be ready to learn how to put the window dressing on those pages.

In the early days of the Internet—when the Internet was strictly used to present textual content without any thought to graphic design—you could create a site that presented your information and leave it up indefinitely, as long as the salient facts of your subject didn't change. The Web has certainly changed a lot since those days. Now, not only must you present your content, but you also need to wrap it in a visually pleasing package. As design trends change so, too, must your site. Web surfers also want to interact with your site, by way of guestbooks, forms, e-commerce, and community. This all requires active management of your site.

Using Dreamweaver's FTP Tools

As mentioned in Chapter 5, the File Transfer Protocol (FTP) is the most common method of transferring files from a local computer to the Internet. The reasons for its popularity are because FTP facilitates the transfer of large files and allows transfers to be resumed if the connection is severed. FTP is also an open standard, allowing for the creation of dozens of clients, each with their own feature set and user interface. Dreamweaver's FTP tool is one of these clients.

Note   *This chapter wouldn't be complete with mentioning that many professional Web developers choose to transfer their files using a third-party FTP client, such as WS_FTP (available at **http://www.ipswitch.com**) or Cute FTP (found at **http://www.cuteftp.com**), instead of Dreamweaver. These clients provide greater control over files and directories on the remote server. They also let you work with files other than those maintained within Dreamweaver's defined sites, enabling you to access other directories on the server. If you choose to use one of these clients, you should still define your local site root in Dreamweaver to use the link integrity tools and other features. Instead of uploading the file through the Site window, however, launch your FTP client and transfer from there.*

If you plan to use Dreamweaver's FTP features to transfer your site to the remote server, you should have already configured the remote info in the Site Definition dialog box, as shown in Chapter 5. If you only entered local info at that time, you can edit your site definition to add the necessary server information.

1. Choose Site | Define Sites.

2. From the Define Sites dialog box (illustrated in the following), highlight the name of the site.

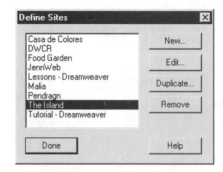

3. Select Edit from the buttons on the right side of the dialog box. This brings up the Site Definition dialog box.

4. Choose Remote Info from the category list.

5. Enter the appropriate remote server information, as explained in Chapter 5.

6. Click the OK box to return to the Define Sites dialog box.

7. Click Done to return to the Site or Document window.

Connecting to the Server

Most file transfer activity takes place in the Site window. If this window isn't already open, you can access the Site window by choosing Window | Site Files (F8). Before connecting to the remote server or transferring files, confirm you're in the correct site by checking the Site field in the toolbar. If you're in the wrong site, use the drop-down menu to change sites.

The Site window is divided into two panes, for the local folder and the remote site. The Remote Site pane remains empty (as seen in Figure 6-1) until you connect to the remote server to update the file view. To connect to the remote server, simply click the Connect button in the Site window toolbar (CTRL-ALT-SHIFT-F5 in Windows or CMD-SHIFT-OPTION-F5 on the Mac). Once connected, the Remote Site pane automatically updates with a file list. To disconnect from the server, click the same button in the toolbar.

Note *Dreamweaver automatically connects to the remote server when you initiate a file transfer, so you needn't manually connect and disconnect when transferring files.*

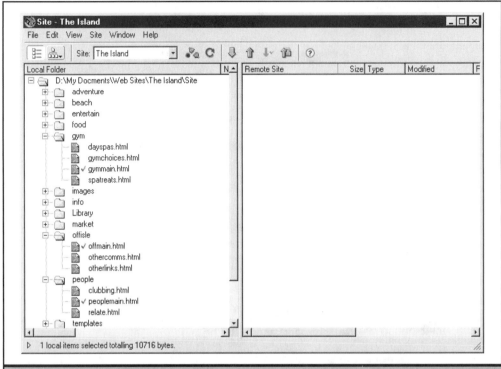

Figure 6-1.   *The Remote Site pane of the Site window remains empty until you connect to the remote server*

Get and Put

Of course, before the Remote Site pane can display a list of files, files must be on the server. Unless you're working in a development group, the commands you use to transfer files are Get and Put. The *Get* command gets files from the remote server and transfers them to the local site. The *Put* command puts files onto the remote server from the local site.

To put files onto the remote server, choose one of the following steps:

1. Highlight the file or files you want to transfer, and then click the Put button on the toolbar.

2. Highlight the file or files and select Site | Put (CTRL-SHIFT-U in Windows or CMD-SHIFT-U on the Mac).

3. Drag files from the Local Folder pane to the Remote Site pane.

If you attempt to transfer a file that hasn't been saved, you'll be prompted to save the file. If you want Dreamweaver to save files automatically before proceeding with a Put command, you can change this setting in the Preferences dialog box (by selecting Edit | Preferences), in the Site category.

If you don't highlight any files before issuing the Put command, the entire site is transferred to the remote server, as shown in Figure 6-2. Dreamweaver asks if you're sure you want to transfer the entire site, because this can be a time-consuming mistake if you only meant to transfer a file or two.

To download files from the remote server onto the local site, choose from the following options:

- Highlight the file or files and click the Get button on the toolbar.

- Highlight the file or files and select Site | Get (CTRL-SHIFT-D in Windows or CMD-SHIFT-D on the Mac).

- Drag files from the Remote Site pane to the Local Folder pane.

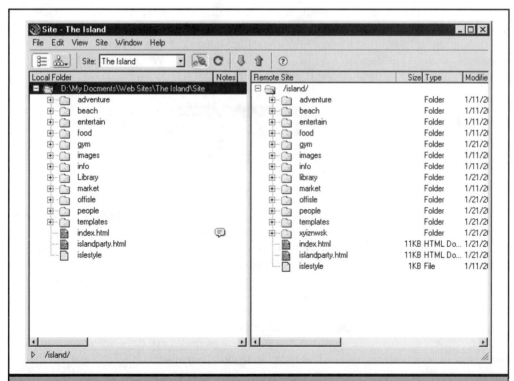

Figure 6-2.   *After transferring the site to the Remote Server, both the local and the remote sites contain the same files*

The Get and Put commands work consistently in the same direction, regardless of which pane is active when you issue the command. A Get command always transfers from the remote server to the local site, even if you're in the Remote Site pane at the time. A Put command always transfers from the local site to the remote server. This can be confusing at first, as you would expect the command to function within the context of the active pane. To avoid this confusion, simply drag the files you want to transfer from one pane to the other, thereby avoiding the Get and Put buttons.

You can also transfer files from the Document window using either the Site menu or the keyboard shortcuts. Site commands issued from the Document window relate only to the open file. Use this feature to upload the current file quickly to the server without having to switch windows.

 If the open document isn't part of the current site, Dreamweaver searches for the site to which the document is related and opens the site before continuing with the command.

Dependent Files

As you know, HTML pages are made up of many files—the HTML document itself, as well as any images, multimedia, scripts, and applets called from the page. These files are dependent on the HTML file, so they're called *dependent files*. Whenever you transfer a file that has dependent files, Dreamweaver asks if you also want to transfer those files at the same time, as the following illustrates.

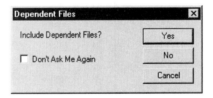

To transfer dependent files automatically, select the Don't Ask Me Again option. If you later want to change this setting, you can do so from the Site category of the Preferences dialog box. The Preferences dialog box also enables you to set automatic dependent file transfers for Get and Put separately. My Preferences are set to prompt me to download dependent files when issuing a Get command, but to transfer the files automatically with the Put command. My reason is this: I generally have the most current versions of image files on my local site, so I want to share them with the remote server when transferring to the server, but I don't want to overwrite them when downloading a file from the server. Your preferences may vary depending on your work style and whether you work at more than one computer.

Synchronizing Folders

You can view the files in the Site window in other ways. To highlight those files that are newer in one or the other pane, choose Edit | Select Newer Local or Edit | Select Newer Remote in Windows. On the Mac, those same commands are available by choosing Site | Site Files View | Select Newer Local or Site | Site Files View | Select Newer Remote. This view verifies which files must be transferred to bring the site into synch by highlighting the newer files.

Caution	*The synchronization features are disabled if Dreamweaver cannot ascertain the time on the remote server. It does this by creating a dummy folder on the remote server, and then verifying the timestamp. Certain versions of the FTP server daemon convert this folder name to lowercase rather than the uppercase required by Dreamweaver. If Dreamweaver cannot find the folder as a result of this naming inconsistency, the time check fails and Dreamweaver then warns you it's unable to get the time from the remote server. If you have this problem, contact your server administrator.*

Another approach to ensuring that only the most recent files get transferred is to synchronize the two file views. To synchronize files:

1. Select the files and folders to be synchronized in the Site window. To synchronize the entire site, select the root folder at the top of the file list.

2. Choose Site | Synchronize.

3. In the Synchronize dialog box, shown in the following illustration, choose Entire Site. To transfer selected files and folders, choose Selected Local Files Only or Selected Remote Files Only, depending on the pane from which you made your file selection.

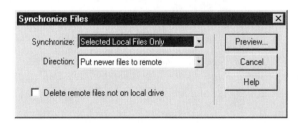

4. Choose the direction of the synchronization from the following:

   ■ **Put Newer Files to Remote**—to transfer local files that are more current than those on the remote server.

   ■ **Get Newer Files from Remote**—to transfer remote files that are more current than those in the local folder.

   ■ **Get and Put Newer Files**—to transfer the most current files in both directions to ensure both copies of the site have all the latest files.

5. Select the Delete Remote Files Not on Local Drive option if you want the remote server to reflect a true mirror image of the local site by deleting any files that don't appear in the Local Folder pane. Of course, this option isn't available if you choose Get and Put Newer Files, as this automatically updates both copies of the site to reflect each other.

Caution *Deletions on the remote server cannot be undone. If you're using the remote server to store extra files for use on the site or as a remote FTP server for other purposes, don't select this option or you'll lose those files.*

6. Select Preview to open the Synchronize Files dialog box, as the following shows, and identify the files to be changed during this process.

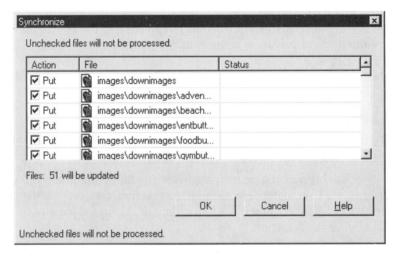

7. Verify the files to delete or transfer. If no files are there to transfer, Dreamweaver states no synchronization is necessary.

8. If you don't want to proceed with a particular action in the list, deselect the check box next to that item.

9. Click OK.

10. To save a log of these actions, click Save Log.

If you're in the habit of regularly uploading your entire site to the remote server, you probably won't require the use of the synchronization tool. If you're working on a large site with extensive modifications and maintenance, however, this tool can be quite powerful. The synchronization tool is also extremely helpful if you're recovering from a hard disk crash that's wiped out your local folder or if you accidentally deleted a file or folder.

 Collaboration

When you're working in a one-man shop or when you design a site for your personal use, it's easy to keep control over the project. The files you need are always available, your deadlines are your sole responsibility, and office communication requires nothing more than a reminder Post-it note taped to your monitor. If you're part of a Web development team, however, communication is crucial. If members of the team aren't kept informed of the project's status, they can't work together to see it through to a timely completion. Fortunately, Dreamweaver has tools to make this communication easier.

Tip   *These collaboration tools also work easily if you run a one-man shop on multiple computers, or in both a home and office situation. Give each computer a unique Check Out name in the Site Definition dialog box, and use the Check In/Out and Design Notes features to track the status of files between computers.*

Checking Files In/Out

When you defined your site, you had the option of enabling file Check In/Check Out in the Remote Info category. If you enabled this feature, you'll use the Check In and Check Out commands to transfer files, instead of the Get and Put commands. The Check Out feature transfers files from the remote server—which is home for the entire project because it's the common directory for all members of the team—to the local folder. The Check In feature transfers files from the local folder to the remote server.

Along with performing the same functions as Get and Put, the *Check In/Out* commands inform the other members of the team that a file is in use. Files checked out to another member of the team appear with a red check mark next to the filename on the remote server. Files you check out appear with a green check mark. Files without a check mark are available to transfer and edit. The Check Out feature also tells the other members of the team exactly which member has locked the file.

Perhaps the best feature of the Check In/Out tools is the way it locks files in use. If a file is checked out, the file is locked on the remote server to prevent changes from being overwritten when that member transfers the file back to the server. Because Dreamweaver cannot actually lock a file on the remote server, it uses a special .lck file to inform the Site window of the file's status.

Caution   *If you're using Dreamweaver's collaboration tools, it's important that every member of the team use these tools consistently. If someone on the team uses a third-party FTP client, files won't appear to be checked in or checked out properly. If members of the team use various FTP clients and tools, consider using a version control system, such as Microsoft Visual SourceSafe or a WebDAV protocol.*

Likewise, once you check a file back into the server, the copy in your local folder becomes read-only to prevent you from making changes without checking out the file again.

Note *If you issue a Get command when working in a collaborative environment with Check In/Out enabled, the Get command copies a read-only version of the file to the local site. The file on the server can still be checked in and out by others in the group, so it's important to remember always to use the Check In and Check Out commands when they're enabled.*

To Check Out files from the remote server, highlight the file or files in the Remote Site pane, and then either click the Check Out button on the toolbar or select Site | Check Out (CTRL-ALT-SHIFT-D in Windows or CMD-OPT-SHIFT-D on the Mac).

To Check In files to the remote server, highlight the file or files in the Local Folder pane, and then either click the Check In button on the toolbar or select Site | Check In (CTRL-ALT-SHIFT-U in Windows or CMD-OPT-SHIFT-U on the Mac).

Caution *If you have a file checked out from the remote server and you then exit Dreamweaver, you won't be prompted to check the file in before closing the application. This could keep other members of the team from being able to access the current version of the file. Unless you're sure no one else will need to use those files in the interim, remember to check your files back into the server before exiting Dreamweaver.*

If you check out a file, and then decide not to modify it, you can free it up for the other members of the team by selecting Site | Undo Check Out.

Design Notes

As mentioned in Chapter 5, Design Notes enable group members to communicate with messages associated with specific pages or objects. Some development groups use comments in the actual HTML pages to note progress or issues for other team members, but these sometimes pose a security or PR risk. Remember, users can view HTML source from their local browsers. You wouldn't want a user to see comments about the subject of a particular image looking dour, especially if the subject in question is the CEO of the company. Comments also increase file size and are generally specific to certain sections of a page rather than the project itself.

Another way to correspond with the group is by e-mail. This keeps comments about the project more secure, but can be overlooked by members of the team because they aren't directly attached to the file in question. Important issues or status reports can also become lost in a sea of e-mail about other details relating to that and other projects, not to mention the latest jokes and chain letters making the rounds.

Design Notes, therefore, are a good solution to project-specific group communication. They provide security because they aren't visible when viewing the source for a page and they're easily accessible within the Dreamweaver environment.

To add a Design Note to a page, you must have enabled them when you defined the site. These settings were explained in Chapter 5. If you didn't do this initially, edit your site definition, as explained earlier, and select the appropriate features from the Design Notes category.

Design Notes may be attached to any file in the site, including HTML documents, images, style sheets, and applets. They can also be attached to ActiveX controls and Shockwave objects. Design Notes for HTML documents are stored as separate files in a _notes folder within the local site root. This folder doesn't appear in the Site window, although you can see it in Windows Explorer and MultiFinder. Design Notes for objects are stored in a _notes folder in the same directory as the source object, which may or may not be within the local site root. Each note is named after its associated file, with a .mno extension. Therefore, a Design Note for the index.html file would be named index.html.mno. If you chose to share Design Notes when you defined the site, the _notes folder would be transferred to the remote server when you upload the site, so the rest of the group can access it.

BUILDING YOUR
WEB SITE

Caution

Fireworks uses Design Notes to track the name of the source .png file when you export an image in a different format. This enables you to edit the source and reexport later. If you add Design Notes to an image within Dreamweaver, they're then added to this original Design Note. Be careful not to delete the source information from the Design Note, or the exported image won't be linked to its source file any longer.

Adding a Design Note

To add a Design Note to a file or object, follow these steps:

1. Open the Design Note dialog box.

   - From the Site window, select a file (either an HTML document or an object), and then choose File | Design Notes, or choose Design Notes from the context menu (available by using RIGHT-CLICK in Windows or CTRL-CLICK on the Mac).

   - From the Document window, select File | Design Notes to attach a Design Note to the open document.

   - For an object within an open HTML document in the Document window, select the object, and then choose Design Notes from the context menu.

2. To note the status of a file, choose from the Status menu in the Basic Info tab (seen in the following illustration).

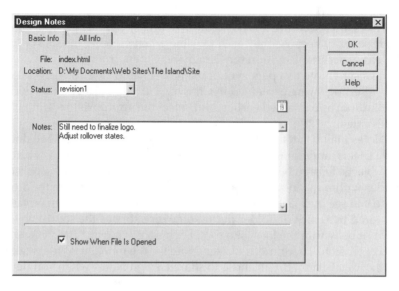

3. To add comments, enter them in the Notes field. You can date stamp your comments by clicking the calendar icon, and then typing the comment.

4. If you're adding Design Notes to an HTML document and want them to open automatically every time you edit the file in Dreamweaver, select the Show When File Is Opened option. This option only works with HTML documents, not other objects.

5. Click the All Info tab (as seen in the following illustration) to add keys and values you want to use consistently in relation to the document.

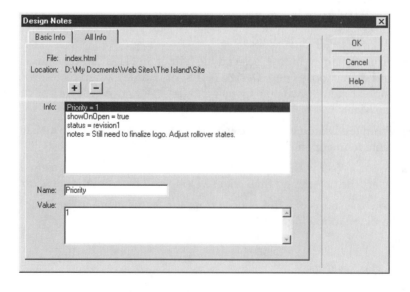

6. Click the Add (+) button to add a new key and value.

7. In the Name field, type a key. This can be anything you want, such as Priority or Last Revised By.

8. In the Value field, provide a value for the key, such as Urgent or Jennifer. Again, this can be any value that makes sense to you and your project.

9. Click outside the value text box to record the addition, which then appears in the Info box.

10. Click OK to save the Design Notes and exit the dialog box.

Once you create a Design Note, you can access it by repeating Step 1 or by double-clicking the yellow Design Notes icon in the Notes column of the Site window. If you attached the note to an HTML document and chose the Show When File Is Opened option, the Design Note dialog box automatically appears whenever you open the file.

To delete an entry in a Design Note, access the note, as shown in the previous steps, and then click the All Info tab. Highlight the line you want to delete, and then click the Delete (-) button.

The Status field offers several default options. If you want to use a different status value, you can do so from the All Info tab. Add a new key and value using the previous steps, and use Status as the name and your desired status option as the value.

Note   *You can only set one new status value per document. This value is only available within that document.*

Aside from their obvious use in a group situation, Design Notes can also be helpful in a solitary production environment. I use them to keep track of drafts and to critique my work in progress. If I don't like the logo for the site, for example, I note it in a Design Note, so I remember to modify that image the next time I work on the project. I find this keeps me better organized than using scraps of paper.

Tip   *Consider adding Design Notes about images and other objects to the HTML document in which the object is applied. If you add a Note to an image file, the only way to access the Note in the future is to select the image (in either the Site window or the Document window) and to choose to view the Design Note by choosing File | Design Notes. With potentially dozens of image files on a page, it's both time-consuming to set specific Design Notes for each file and easy to forget to check them. A Design Note attached to an HTML document, however, can be set to display automatically whenever you open the file within Dreamweaver, serving as a reminder of the status of both the document and its objects. Your comments can also relate to a range of objects within the document, rather than being specific to one object.*

Integrated E-mail

While Design Notes are a good way of adding comments to a page, at times direct communication is the only way to go. Suppose you just completed the copy for a page, but the document has been checked out for the last two days. If your design team uses integrated e-mail, you can see at a glance that John Doe is the person holding up your workflow. You can click John's name next to the file in the Site window and send an e-mail asking him to please finish so you can have the file.

To enable integrated e-mail, you and the other members of the team must have enabled file check in/out and entered an e-mail address and checkout name in the Remote Info category of the Site Definition. Once this is configured, files checked out have a field labeled Checked Out By, which contains the checkout name of the person using the file. This name appears as a clickable link, which sends e-mail using your e-mail application.

Visual SourceSafe (VSS)

Many large development shops use version control software to maintain their projects. *Visual SourceSafe (VSS)* is the most common version control software. The Windows version is from Microsoft, and the Mac version is put out by MetroWerks. As even one-man development shops take on large-scale projects, version control software is becoming an important component of the developer's toolbox.

Version control software tracks and stores file changes. This tracking enables you to review a file's revision history and revert to earlier versions of the file. Version 6 of Microsoft Visual SourceSafe also has file transfer and site map capabilities, but you're unlikely to use those features if you're using Dreamweaver for site management.

Dreamweaver can integrate with VSS if your development team uses that application to maintain version control. Instead of defining your site to use FTP Access, set the access for SourceSafe Database. If you didn't do this when you initially defined your site, as explained in Chapter 5, you can edit the Remote Info category of the Site Definition dialog box.

> **Note**
>
> *This option only works with VSS Client version 6 in Windows. For the Mac, you need to have MetroWerks SourceSafe client 1.1.0 installed, and you can only access version 5.0 SourceSafe databases. Dreamweaver won't integrate with a MetroWerks Visual SourceSafe version 6.0 database.*

The Visual SourceSafe database must be configured separately before it can be integrated with Dreamweaver. The SourceSafe documentation instructs you on how to install and use the client.

While SourceSafe can be a useful tool, it does have certain limitations. Because VSS acts as a barrier between the local folder and the remote server, Dreamweaver cannot obtain a timestamp from the remote server. Therefore, the Synchronize and Select

A Note for Mac Users

Before using Dreamweaver with MetroWerks Visual SourceSafe, you must have ToolServer installed on your system.

ToolServer enables MPW commands to be used in a stand-alone capacity, as required by the Dreamweaver/VSS integration. ToolServer is shipped on the Dreamweaver 4 CD. You might already have a version of ToolServer installed on your system as part of another application. Check your hard disk before reinstalling it because having multiple copies installed can cause conflicts. If Toolserver isn't already installed, you can install it simply by copying the folder from the Dreamweaver 4 CD on to your hard drive.

If you downloaded Dreamweaver from the Macromedia Web site, you can obtain ToolServer from the Apple Developer's Web site (**http://developer.apple.com/tools/mpw-tools/**). From this page, choose FTP Site, and then select the MPW-GM directory. Within this directory is a folder for MPW, which contains the ToolServer file.

After ToolServer is installed, you can proceed with the MetroWerks VSS installation. This installs the *MetroWerks Code Manager* (*MWCM*) tool into the ToolServer/Tools folder.

Once these installations are complete, you can launch Dreamweaver and edit your site definition to use SourceSafe Database integration. If you have questions about this process, see your system administrator.

Newer Files options are unavailable. Balancing out this negative, however, is the fact that VSS itself has tools to synchronize projects.

If you're using VSS in Windows, be aware of one other problem. When you Check Out or Get a file from the remote server, Dreamweaver doesn't actually copy the file from the server and overwrite your local version of the file. Thus, if your local file isn't the most current, once you check the file back into the VSS database for uploading to the server, you overwrite any changes made by other team members. To get around this problem, always delete the file from your local folder before using Check Out or Get. This forces Dreamweaver to retrieve a fresh, current copy of the file from the VSS database.

Site FTP Log

A little-known feature of Dreamweaver is the Site FTP Log, shown in the following illustration. This window, accessible from the Site window by selecting Window | Site FTP Log in Windows (Site | Site FTP Log on the Mac), maintains a log of FTP activity. If you encounter problems transferring a file, this log can help pinpoint the source of the trouble.

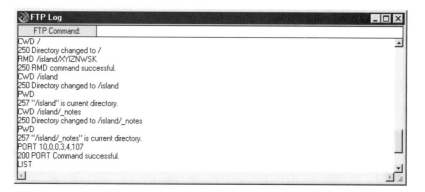

The Site FTP Log can also be used to issue remote server commands. This feature is useful when changing file permissions, such as when you're using CGI/Perl scripts, as discussed in Chapter 22. You can also use the Log window to gain more control over your remote server than is afforded by the standard Dreamweaver FTP tools.

The most common remote FTP commands are the following:

- **LIST**—List the files and folders contained in the directory.

- **MKD**—Make a new directory.

- **CWD**—Change directories, such as CWD /island to change to the island directory.

- **RMD**—Remove (delete) a directory.

- **DELE**—Delete a file.

- **SITE CHMOD**—Sets file permissions.

- **QUIT**—Terminate the connection.

You can get a list of other server commands by typing HELP in the Site FTP Log window while connected to your remote server.

Site Maps

Some people can look at a list of files and folders, and then immediately visualize the flow of the site. I'm not one of those people. Just as I want to see a visual representation of my HTML code using the Design view in Dreamweaver, I also want to see a visual representation of my site structure in the Site window. That's where the Site Map comes in.

Whereas the default Site Files view shows the directory structure of the site, the *Site Map* displays the page hierarchy of the site. This is helpful in checking the logical progression of the site as it would be navigated by a user. As such, the Site Map view can be used for storyboarding, as discussed earlier in this chapter. The Site Map also enables you to add pages to the site, edit filenames and page titles, and link to other pages in the site.

To change your Site window to the Site Map view, select Window | Site Map (ALT-F8 in Windows, OPT-F8 on the Mac) or choose the Site Map button on the toolbar (the second button from the left). The site map appears, as shown in Figure 6-3. If you click and hold on the Site Map button, a drop-down menu lets you choose either a Map Only view, which allows the site map to take up the full Site window, or a Map and Files view, which keeps a standard local folder view in one pane of the window. If you can afford the screen real estate, keeping a file view available is handy even for visual types. Because the site map doesn't display the full path of the pages unless you individually mouse over them, you can become disoriented in terms of where these pages are stored in the local folder. The Site Files view also provides fast access to files not currently visible in the Site Map pane.

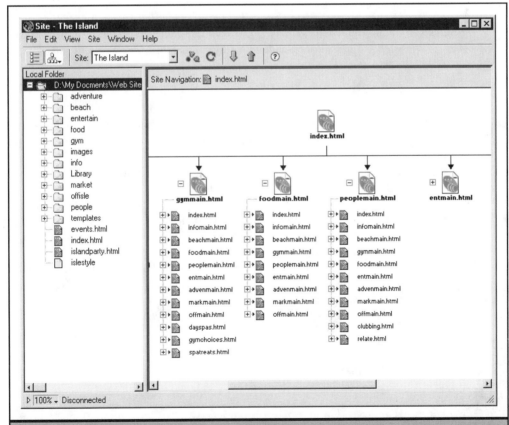

Figure 6-3.   *The Site Map provides a visual representation of the site's structure*

BUILDING YOUR
WEB SITE

Note *Only the local folder is available in the Site Map view. Before using the site map, be sure to synchronize the site to ensure the local folder is current.*

The Site Definition dialog box contains configuration options for the Site Map Layout, as covered in Chapter 5. If you didn't set these options when you originally defined your site, you can edit the site definition to change them now. In particular, you may want to decrease the column width if you want to see more pages on the screen at once. Conversely, you can increase the column width to view the complete filename under each page. If your file naming convention is rather obscure, you can view the pages by title instead. Of course, this assumes you give your pages unique and descriptive titles.

Tip *As you delve deeper into the site hierarchy, the column width becomes too limited to display the filename or title for every page. If even part of the filename or title is displayed, hold your mouse over that text to view a pop-up of the complete name. The pop-up won't work at the deepest levels of the site, where only the icon or a portion thereof is viewable. To view the names or titles of these pages, use the Map and Files view. Then, whenever you click an icon on the Site Map pane, the file is automatically selected in the Site Files file pane.*

The site map presents the site in a visual hierarchy. The index page is at the top of the map. Pages linked from the index are shown on the second row of the map, connected to the index by solid lines, as in an organizational chart. The files in the second row may have a plus (+) sign next to them, indicating they link to other files. Clicking a plus sign expands the site map, displaying the third level of the site's hierarchy and changing the plus sign to a minus (-) sign. The plus and minus signs enable you to expand and contract each additional level of the site map.

Note *The Site Map can become redundant, particularly if you're using navigational elements to link every page to the rest of the site. It's possible to link from the index to a page that, in turn, links to yet another page, which links back to both that page and the index, which can then be expanded to display the links to the second page in the hierarchy, and on to the third page, and so on. Confusing, no? This recursion is one of the drawbacks to Dreamweaver's site map tools.*

A visual display of files isn't very helpful if everything looks exactly the same. This is why Dreamweaver uses the following conventions:

- Standard HTML documents appear in black.
- External and e-mail links are in blue, with a globe to the right of the page icon.
- Broken links are in red, and are accompanied by a broken-link icon.
- If you work in a collaborative environment, files checked in or out appear with a red or green check mark, just as in the Site Files view.

Some files, such as dependent files, are automatically hidden from the site map. This is convenient if you're using the site map to determine the overall structure and hierarchy of the site. Times may occur when you need to see these hidden files, however, such as if you're compiling a chart of all the images used throughout the site. To display these files, choose View | Show Dependent Files (or Site | Site Map View | Show Dependent Files on the Mac). You can also edit the Site Map Layout in the Site Definition dialog box to display these files.

You may also want to hide certain pages while you're working in the Site Map view. To mark a file as hidden, select the file or files, and choose View | Show/Hide Link (or Site | Site Map View | Show/Hide Link on the Mac). To toggle the actual display of these marked files, use View | Show Files Marked as Hidden (Site | Site Map View | Show Files Marked as Hidden). You can unmark the file entirely by repeating the Show/Hide Link command.

Tip *Hide the main navigational pages of the site to see how other pages on the site are linked to each other. Without the distraction and redundancy of these navigation pages, these other links should become clear.*

Because the site map provides such a visual roadmap of the site, you might want to use it offline for notes and to mark the progress of the project. The site map cannot be printed within Dreamweaver, but you can save it as a file by choosing File | Save Site Map. You can then edit and print the image from a graphics package. I use this feature to print color-coded site maps displaying the phases of a complex site launch when some pages are developed and live on the Web before others are added.

The site map can be used to change filenames and titles, depending on which view is set for the site map. To change the filename or title, click the name once, pause, and then click again. The name is then highlighted, so you can type over it. If you're changing a filename, don't forget to add the proper extension (.htm, .html, and so forth).

When you click a page in the first two levels of the hierarchy, a point-to-file icon appears to the right of the page icon. The point-to-file icon is used to link the selected page to others in the site. The site map's link capabilities are its best feature.

Linking in the Site Map

If you're using the site map for storyboarding, it's possible to establish the entire site and its linking structure before you ever open a page in the Document window. As discussed earlier, having a site structure in place—either on paper, in a storyboarding tool (as discussed in Chapter 5), or in Dreamweaver—keeps the project more organized and ensures every page is accounted for. If you choose to use Dreamweaver as your storyboarding tool, you're then one step ahead of the process.

Both advantages and disadvantages exist to using Dreamweaver for storyboarding. If you like to flesh out your storyboards with descriptive text and other important information, you'll want to use a different tool. You can use Design Notes to add this information, but it's not the same as having it readily available on the same page as your storyboard. You may also want to use another tool to give you more flexibility over the layout of the site map because the Site window fills quickly when you add pages and requires a lot of scrolling to see the entire map. The advantage of using the site map is all your pages are created within Dreamweaver, saving you the extra step of executing the site structure you planned elsewhere, right down to the links between pages.

Linking to a New File

The site map enables you to add new pages and immediately link them to others in the site. To link to a new file:

1. Select a page in the site map.

2. Choose Site | Link to New File (CTRL-SHIFT-N) in Windows or Site | Site Map View | Link to New File (CMD-SHIFT-N) on the Mac. This brings up a Link to New File dialog box.

3. Enter a filename and title in the dialog box, as the following illustrates.

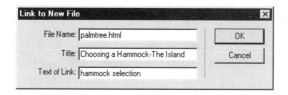

4. In the Text of Link field, provide some text to serve as the linked content in the original site. When you modify the page in Dreamweaver, you see this text in the document and you can view the link in the Property Inspector.

5. Click OK.

The new page appears on the site map in the appropriate position in the hierarchy. By default, the page is created in the same folder as the file you used as the root of the link. If you want to create the page in a different folder, enter a path in the File Name field of the Link to New Files dialog box.

Linking to Existing Pages

You can add links to existing pages in three methods. The easiest is to use the point-to-file icon. Select a file, and then click its point-to-file icon and drag it to the file you want to link, as seen in Figure 6-4. Once the link is established, a page icon is added to the appropriate position in the site hierarchy. As already mentioned, this can become confusing because you see multiple entries of the same file in the site map, depending on where it's linked.

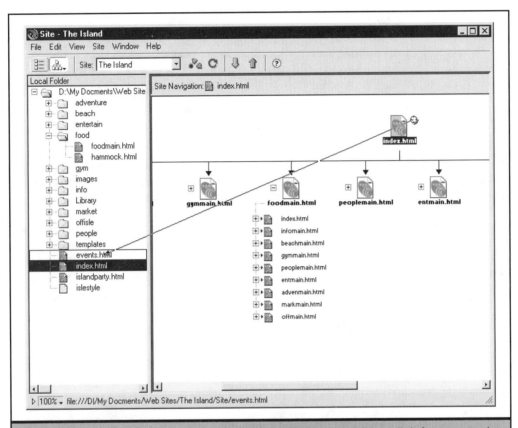

Figure 6-4.   *The Point-to-File icon enables you to click-and-drag a link from pages in the site map to other pages in either the site map or the file view*

Tip   *The point-to-file button is unavailable in the lower levels of the site map. To access the link features from these pages, you must use the Link to Existing File option.*

Another way to link to an existing file is to use the Site | Link to Existing File (CTRL-SHIFT-K) option from the menu (Site | Site Map View | Link to Existing Site or CMD-SHIFT-K on the Mac) or the Link to Existing File option on the context menu. This approach brings up a dialog box that enables you to select a file to link. This method enables you to link to files not included in the local site folder. If you link to a file outside of the site, you are prompted to copy the file to the site.

The third method for linking is simply to drag a file from the file view onto a page in the site map. This adds the page to the site map if it isn't already included.

If you're using Dreamweaver templates, you cannot use the linking features of the site map. The link commands rely on being able to add text links to the bottom of the page from which you're linking. Because templates use editable regions and lock the rest of the page, the link cannot be added and, therefore, the process fails. If you're linking to a new page, the new page is created, but no link is established, thereby creating an orphan page that's added to the file view, but not to the site map.

Changing Links

Particularly if you are using Dreamweaver as a storyboarding tool—when you'll be changing your mind and fine-tuning the site structure—you may want to change or delete links after you establish them. To modify a link, select the linked page's icon, and then choose Site | Change Link (CTRL-L in Windows, CMD-L on the Mac). Use the file selection box, which the following illustrates, to choose a new file or otherwise modify the path of the link, and then choose OK. Depending on your Preference settings, you're either prompted to Update the links on the site or this process occurs automatically. If you set your Preferences to never update links, you need to update your links manually.

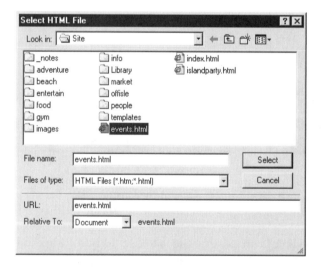

To delete a link, select the page icon, and then press Delete (in Windows) or use the Site | Remove Link (Site | Site Map View | Remove Link on the Mac) option. You can also use the keyboard shortcuts, CTRL-SHIFT-L in Windows and CMD-SHIFT-L on the Mac. Be careful when using this feature because it cannot be undone, although you can easily re-create it if you make a mistake.

Note	*When you delete a link, the* `<href>` *tag is removed from the text that provided the link, but the text itself remains unless you open the page in the Document window and remove it. If you delete a link and later re-create it, new text is then added even if the original text wasn't removed.*

If you use the Change Link Sitewide command, covered in Chapter 11, those changes are reflected in the site map. This is yet another way to control page linking.

Modifying the Site Map Layout

Although the site map defaults to using the site index or home page as the root in the hierarchy, you may need to gain a different perspective on your site. To set a page as the site root temporarily, select the page and choose View | View As Root (CTRL-SHIFT-R). On the Mac, use Site | Site Map View | View as Root (CMD-SHIFT-R). Any pages above the new root in the hierarchy are hidden from view because the site map now relates solely to that root, as shown in Figure 6-5. You can set other pages as roots, as well, and then toggle between them by clicking the filenames in the Site Navigation bar at the top of the Site Map view.

Link Checker

Even with the best of planning, broken links are an inevitable fact of life on the Web. The larger the site, the greater the potential for broken links, as pages are moved into folders to accommodate growth. Old pages are no longer referenced from other pages as their material becomes outdated but, somehow, they never get deleted from the server and become orphan files. And, of course, every link to another site remains intact purely at the whim of the site owner at the other end of the link.

Within a site, the most common form of broken link is missing image files. These are unsightly because they detract from the page design and are immediately visible to the user. Unfortunately, it's easy to make this mistake, either by accidentally deleting an image file from the remote server or by renaming the file during a redesign. Broken links are also caused by deleting an outdated page without realizing other pages still reference it.

The opposite of the latter problem is failing to delete pages from the server after they've lived out their usefulness on the site. If a page is no longer accessible from elsewhere in the site and isn't meant to stand alone, it only serves to take up precious server space if it isn't deleted. Again, however, in a large site, it's easy to overlook these files.

If you've ever used a search engine or a list of links found on another Web site, you've surely seen a representational sample of the number of sites that have disappeared without a trace. While you cannot be held responsible for someone else shutting down their site, your users can get frustrated at clicking a long list of "related links" that go nowhere, particularly if that link promised the answer to a user's pressing question.

BUILDING YOUR WEB SITE

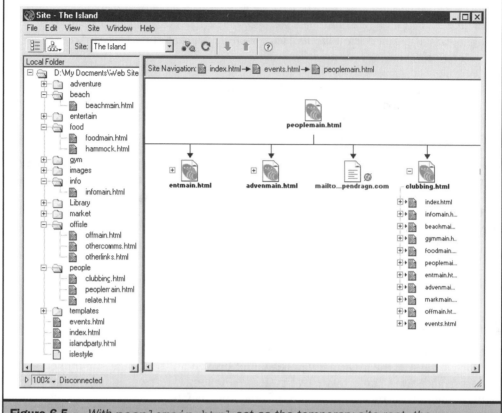

Figure 6-5.   With `peoplemain.html` set as the temporary site root, the `index.html` page disappears and all other pages are displayed in relation to the new root

Perhaps even worse than sites that disappear are those that change the topic. Some domain registration companies are also in the business of reselling domain names that have expired. When the domain name changes hands, so does the content found at that domain. Another thing to watch out for is advertising. Even if the content of a site is acceptable, it might post banner ads for objectionable material; this is a big concern for those who host sites targeted at children.

In short, link maintenance is an important, yet time-consuming, part of site maintenance that shouldn't be ignored. Enter the *Link Checker*, a Dreamweaver tool that can ease the burden of maintaining your site's links. The Link Checker examines every link on a page, selection of pages, folder, or site, and returns a report of any problems. This report can be saved in a file for further review or can be used immediately to repair broken links.

The Link Checker can only be used in the local folder, so confirm the current versions of the files you want to check (or the entire site, if you want to do a sitewide link check) are in the local folder before initiating the process. To use the Link Checker:

1. Select one of the Check Links options:

   ■ To check the current document from the Document window, choose File | Check Links (SHIFT-F8).

   ■ To check selected files and folders from the Site window, highlight the selected files, and then choose File | Check Links (Shift-F8). You can also RIGHT-CLICK (CTRL-CLICK on the Mac) and choose Check Links | Selected Files/Folders from the context menu.

   ■ To check the entire site, choose Site | Check Links Sitewide (CTRL-F8 in Windows, CMD-F8 on the Mac). You can also choose Check Links | Entire Site from the context menu.

2. From the Link Checker dialog box, shown in the following, choose the type of links you want to review from the Show menu:

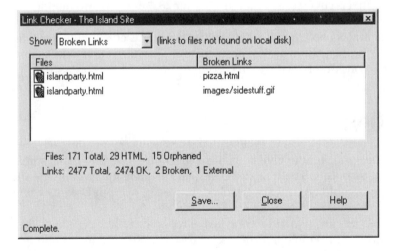

   ■ **Broken Links**—displays broken internal links to other files and pages within the site. You can fix these links within the Link Checker dialog box by clicking the broken link name and either typing the correct path or using the folder icon to navigate to the proper file. If you double-click the name of the file containing the broken link, the file opens in the Document window, so you can change the link path from the Property Inspector.

   ■ **External Links**—displays a list of all external links. Because Dreamweaver cannot check the integrity of these links, you cannot make any changes from this list. You can, however, save the list to a file and use this as a guide to visit every site on the list. I recommend doing this on a monthly basis because sites come and go quickly.

■ **Orphaned Links**—displays a list of all files not linked by any other page in the site. As you would expect, this option is only available when you've checked the entire site, instead of a subset of pages. To open the file, double-click the filename. To delete the file directly from the Link Checker, select the file and press DELETE.

3. To change to a different link report, choose another option from the Show menu.

4. To save the link report, press the Save button.

If you perform a sitewide Link Check anytime you make significant changes to your site, you can save your users the frustration—and save yourself the embarrassment—of broken links.

Assets Panel

The Assets panel is covered in detail in Chapter 28, but it's worth mentioning here. This panel can be extremely useful in site maintenance, as all the URLs, colors, images, and other elements used in the site are stored here. This enables the panel to be used as a style guide for the site—if a color or navigational image is unavailable from the Assets panel, consider if it's the correct color or image for the site.

Reporting

Throughout your development cycle and, particularly, as you approach the completion of your project, you want to give your site a check-up of sorts to make sure everything is proceeding smoothly. The Link Checker helps validate the links on the site. Several other nuisances could be easily overlooked, however, without Dreamweaver's Reports feature.

Dreamweaver runs two different types of reports: reports that check the status of the production by providing information about checked out files and design notes, and reports that validate HTML code. You can run all the reports concurrently or select only the ones you need. The HTML Reports can be used in tandem with the Clean Up HTML command, described in Chapter 4. The Report lists any HTML problems, whereas the Clean Up HTML command actually corrects those problems.

To create a report:

1. Choose Site | Reports.

2. From the Reports dialog box, illustrated in the following, choose which files should be examined:

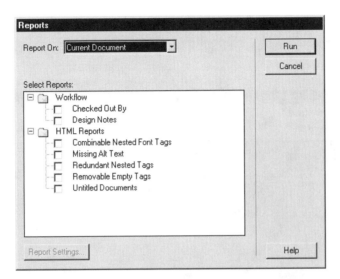

■ **Current Document**—reports on the current file in the Document window.

■ **Entire Local Site**—reports on the entire site. Be sure the site is synchronized before running the report to ensure the local folder is current.

■ **Selected Files in Site**—reports on files selected from the Local Folder pane of the Site window.

■ **Folder**—prompts you to choose a folder.

3. Select the reports you want to run:

■ **Checked Out By**—lists who has the selected files checked out.

■ **Design Notes**—displays the Design Notes for the selected files.

■ **Combinable Nested Font Tags**—lists all nested `<font>` tags that can be combined into one `<font>` tag with multiple attributes.

■ **Missing Alt Text**—lists all `<img>` tags missing an alt attribute.

■ **Redundant Nested Tags**—lists tags unnecessary because they're nested within another tag of the same element, such as `<b>Come <b>visit The Island!</b> It's party time!</b>`

■ **Removable Empty Tags**—removes tag pairs that don't have any content, such as an empty `<b></b>` pair.

■ **Untitled Documents**—lists pages that don't have a unique title.

4. Click the Run button to generate the selected reports. The reports are displayed in the Results window, as the following illustrates. The results can be sorted by clicking one of the column headings.

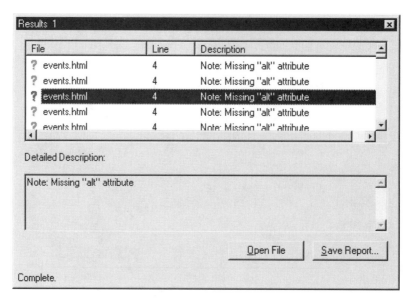

5. For more information about an entry, select it from the list.

6. To save the report as an XML file, press the Save Report button. The XML file can be imported into a database or spreadsheet for tracking.

7. Select Open File or double-click an entry to open the file. If the entry is an image file, double-clicking opens the external graphics editor associated with your image files.

Some of the reports are quite useful in performing a final check of your site before going live. Running these reports and giving your site a thorough review before it goes live can ensure that your users have the experience you intended.

Site Testing Checklist

As you develop your pages, you'll become more proficient with your use of the Dreamweaver tools and Web design, in general. Before turning your site live, however, some critical steps shouldn't be overlooked.

Proofread Content   Read your pages one last time, looking for typos or sentences that may have been cut off while cutting-and-pasting.

Check for Stray Tags   If you haven't yet run any reports to validate your code, you should do so before the site goes live. Some browsers, particularly Internet Explorer, are more forgiving than others when they encounter invalid HTML code. If you primarily use Internet Explorer, be certain to test your pages in at least one other browser, as well.

Link Checking Perform one last check with the Link Checker to ensure all your internal and external links are in working order.

Window Size Selector Your site should be able to accommodate various screen resolutions. Use the window size selector in the Design view to examine the site under a variety of settings. Even if you took this step while designing your site, it's worth another check to ensure your text content didn't throw a table out of whack.

Check Browser Compatibility You should test your site in as many different versions of as many different browsers as possible. While it's unlikely you'll be able to code a page that looks identical in every browser, no page should look truly horrendous in any browser. If your site is on the cutting edge of Web technology, consider adding redirects, so users with earlier browser versions can see an alternate page. If you choose not to accommodate certain browsers, do so understanding the pros and cons of your position, and knowing exactly which group of users you're likely to lose.

One tool that can help make this decision is the Check Target Browsers feature. This check can be performed on the current document, on selected files and folders, or on the entire site. The tool validates the site's code against the various browsers and provides a report of incompatibilities.

Note *Netscape 6 was released shortly before Dreamweaver 4 and, therefore, isn't included in the Check Target Browsers list.*

To access the Check Target Browsers feature:

1. Select the file or files on which you want to run the report: If you use this command from the Document window, the report is run on the current document. If run from the Site window, the report is run on the selected file or files. To run the report on the entire site, select the local root folder at the top of the file list.

2. Choose File | Check Target Browsers.

3. Select a browser from the list.

4. Click the Check button.

The report results are displayed in a browser window, as shown in Figure 6-6. To save the report, choose File | Save As...

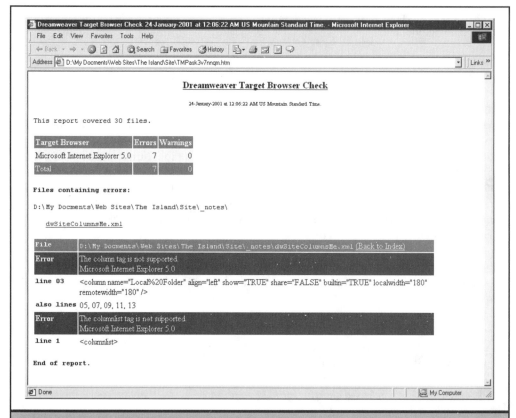

Figure 6-6.   *The Check Target Browsers feature generates reports about browser incompatibilities in a site's code*

Note   *To test the site in various browsers and compare the report results, you must save the report under a different filename each time you use this feature. The results aren't stored by Dreamweaver.*

Although it's useful, the Check Target Browsers tool cannot replace your own eyes. Even sites using standard code that's readable on multiple browsers can look different in each of those browsers.

Check Accessibility   The Web is a melting pot of people from all parts of the globe, all races and backgrounds, and all manner of disability. To ensure accessibility for blind and physically challenged users who may be using tools to facilitate their Web surfing, consider adding text-based navigational elements at the bottom of the page, rather than relying solely on a graphical navbar. This is particularly important if you use an image map for navigation purposes. Be sure to add `alt` attributes to all your image tags and also consider adding captions to your pictures. For more information about accessibility, see the W3C Web Content Accessibility Working Group site at **http://www.w3.org/WAI/GL/**.

Summary

Dreamweaver's site management tools offer everything you need to maintain a site on both the local computer and the remote server.

- Before transferring files or performing other site management tasks, the site must be defined in Dreamweaver, as explained in Chapter 5.

- To transfer files from the local site to the remote server, use the Put or Check In commands.

- To transfer files from the remote server to the local site, use the Get or Check Out commands.

- Design Notes enable development groups to track the progress and status of all the files and objects in the site.

- The Site Map provides a graphic representation of the site's hierarchy. This view can be used to add, move, and title documents.

- Before announcing a new site to the public, conduct a beta test, during which all links, content, images, and browser issues are tested and reviewed.

The next chapter is about choosing a color scheme for the site to maintain consistency and provide a visually pleasing site.

The
Complete
Reference

Chapter 7

Establishing a
Color Scheme

Think about the magazines you read on a regular basis. How does the use of color on the cover, in the titles and callouts, and in the graphics set the tone for the magazine? Now think about how your experiences taint your perception of new publications. If you encountered a magazine with bright orange headlines, would you expect it to contain serious coverage of world events or would you immediately assume the magazine took an off-beat view? When a magazine uses soft pastels, do you think sports or hearth and home?

As you can see, color is a strong visual cue, and, in turn, evokes a response to both the image being viewed and its content. In other words, your choice of colors for your site affects how people view the site itself, the content of the site, and you as its creator. Therefore, understanding color and how to use it effectively is important.

What's in a Color?

Color is a combination of light and pigment. *Pigment* provides the variation in color by refracting light in such a way as to create different colors. An example of this is a rainbow, which refracts white sunlight when it enters a group of raindrops. The angle at which your eye views the refracted light in each raindrop determines which color is visible to your eye.

Color Categories

Most people can distinguish hundreds of colors in nature, but they all come from the same foundation of three colors—red, blue, and yellow. Even black and white are a result of these colors, or the absence thereof.

If you ever took an art class in school, you most likely encountered a color wheel, displaying a spectrum of colors in a circular pattern from shade to shade, as shown in Figure 7-1. The red, blue, yellow palette is referred to as the *primary* colors because they're the colors from which all other colors are created. Combining two of these colors results in a *secondary* color. The three primary colors can be combined in the following ways: red and yellow create orange, red and blue create purple or violet, and yellow and blue create green. When primary colors are mixed with one of the secondary colors, the result is a *tertiary* color. The six possible results are yellow orange, yellow green, blue green, blue violet, red violet, and red orange. Continuing to build combinations of primary colors with tertiary colors, and so on, results in thousands of intermediate colors.

Subtractive and Additive Color

Objects in the real world use a *subtractive* color model. This is sometimes called *natural* color. As the primary colors combine, they approach black, or the absence of color. You can re-create this yourself using pieces of tissue paper or paints in the colors of red, blue, and yellow. Mix all three and you achieve a muddied brown or blackish color. The print media approximates the subtractive model using cyan, magenta, and yellow,

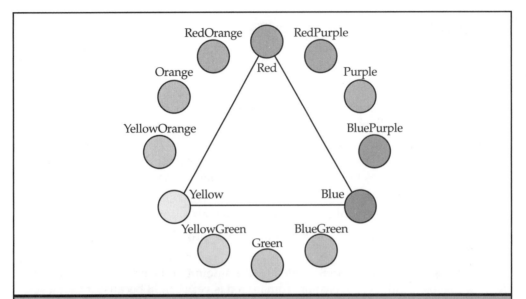

Figure 7-1.   *Although displayed here in grayscale, the basic subtractive color wheel should be a familiar sight. The subtractive color model duplicates how colors are found in nature*

with the addition of a true black to avoid the muddied effect of combining the primary colors. This color model is known as *CMYK,* for the initials of the colors used (*K* comes from the word black).

Whereas paper and other objects in nature absorb light to reflect color back to the eye, computer monitors generate light. The result of this difference is a color model known as *additive* color. In additive color, combining the three primary colors results in light, or white. Computers use an additive color palette known as *RGB,* which comes from the red, green, and blue lights used in a monitor.

If you come from a print background, the difference between color models is critical. Using a CMYK model, red and green result in a brown hue. Using the RGB model, however, the same color mix results in yellow. If you add blue to this mix using the RGB spectrum, you still won't achieve that desired brown color—instead, the resultant color is white.

This capability to create yellow from a mix of green and red is also important. As stated, the lights comprising a computer monitor are red, blue, and green. The primary color palette, however, is red, blue, and yellow, and all other colors in nature result from combinations of those colors. Understanding how the RGB model differs from nature helps you approximate natural colors on the computer screen.

Color Properties

Of course, millions of colors are beyond the primary, secondary, and tertiary colors represented on most color wheels. These colors result from a combination of *color properties*.

- **Hue**—a specific color on the color spectrum or color wheel. Hue differentiates purple from yellow, regardless of the tint or shade of each color.

- **Value**—the lightness or darkness of a particular hue. The degree of separation between two values is known as the *contrast*. The amount of white added to the image is known as the *brightness*. Maroon is darker than tomato red, which is darker than coral.

- **Tint**—the hue plus white. Red plus white equals a tint of pink.

- **Shade**—the hue plus black. Red plus black approaches a shade of brick red.

- **Saturation**—measures the intensity, or the brightness or dullness, of a hue. The saturation of a color is determined by the amount of the original hue that remains identifiable in a color. Tomato red is very bright because it's almost fully saturated, whereas brick red is duller because it's less saturated with the original red color because of the influx of black.

By changing the value and saturation of a hue, you can create thousands of colors. If you want to experience this power for yourself, open an empty document in Dreamweaver to use as a test environment. Try the following:

1. Open the Property Inspector.

2. Click the color swatch icon in the Property Inspector. This opens the Color Picker.

3. From the Color Picker, click the System Color Selector, which is the icon that looks like a pie chart, as the following illustrates. This opens your computer system's Color dialog box.

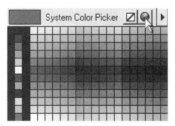

4. The Color dialog box displays the basic colors for your computer system. The Windows Color dialog box is illustrated in the following. On the right side of the dialog box are a color spectrum and a series of fields to enter hue, saturation, luminance, and RGB values. Enter one of the following hue values as a starting

point: 0 for red, 40 for yellow, 80 for green, or 160 for blue. You see the selector in the color spectrum move to the hue you chose.

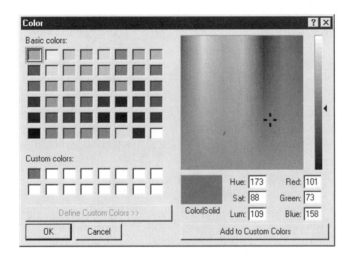

5. Enter a number from 0 to 240 in the saturation box. A setting of 0 results in a gray color, or a total lack of saturation. A setting of 240 results in a pure, fully saturated color.

6. Enter a number from 0 to 240 for the *luminance* setting, which is another term for the value of the color. As you change this number, you'll notice the slider to the right of the color spectrum changes to show the new value of the color. You can also change the luminance setting by moving the arrow on the slider up or down.

7. To save a color for later use, click the Add to Custom Colors button.

8. To exit the dialog box, click OK to apply your final color choice to any object that might be selected in your document. Click Cancel to exit the dialog box without changing the document.

Remember, not all of the thousands of colors you can generate in this method can be viewed consistently on all monitors in all resolutions. Unless you're designing a site for a limited audience, each member having a similar computer configuration, your color choices are most likely going to be limited to those in the Web-safe color palette.

The Web-Safe Color Palette

In the magazine example used to open this chapter, a printed medium was described where every reader of each publication—unless they were color blind or otherwise visually impaired—would see each color as intended. The neon orange of *Wired* magazine looks the same on my copy as it does on yours. The Web isn't nearly as accommodating to designers. Actually, it's not the Web at all but, instead, the wide range of computer configurations that are limiting.

The *Web-safe palette* came about as a solution to the problem of users each having a different combination of operating system and graphics capabilities. The basic color palette for the Mac in 8-bit color is different from that of a PC using the Windows operating system at the same color depth. And, of course, not all computers are set to the same color depth. A high-end computer is capable of 32-bit color, which has millions of colors available. But, you have no way of knowing what your users can handle color-wise unless you're designing for an Intranet site to be viewed only by a controlled audience. And, even then, some users might have lowered the color settings for their displays even if their computers are technologically capable of a higher bit depth.

Enter the Web-safe color palette. The safe palette is comprised of 216 colors common to most platforms and display settings. If you use only the colors of the Web-safe palette, your site has a better chance of displaying properly in all browsers. The downside to this palette is it's limiting. If you have a computer capable of handling 32-bit color, it's frustrating to ignore that beautiful spectrum of choices in favor of only 216 colors. The Web-safe palette can often be doubly frustrating if you want to design your site in reds, oranges, and yellows because the palette is heavier on the cool colors than the warm ones.

> **Caution**   *Although the Web-safe palette does address many of the differences between the Mac and Windows platforms, the gamma settings on each platform are different. Gamma is the proportion of light intensity relative to the input voltage. An understanding of the whys and wherefores of gamma aren't necessary for most developers, but the result of varying levels of gamma control on different computer platforms is important. In short, colors on a Mac often appear lighter because Macs offer better gamma correction and, therefore, better interpretation of color values. The same colors viewed on the Windows platform often appear darker because of the lack of proper gamma correction. Testing your site on both platforms is important, therefore, to ensure the subtlety or vibrancy of your design isn't lost.*

Ignoring the Web-Safe Palette

You can, of course, ignore the Web-safe palette and use the full spectrum of color choices available to you. Do so only with a complete understanding of the downside, however. Your site can look incredible, with the capability to use subtle color variations for text, background, and links. But it only looks that good for those users who have the hardware to view those colors. On an 8-bit display, the browser converts the colors to the Web-safe palette, as those are the only colors it can display. As a result, the subtle colors may shift to the same value, creating red text on a red background that's impossible to read.

Dithering

If you use unsafe colors for images, they will dither at lower monitor settings. *Dithering* simulates a color by creating a pattern of individual pixels of varying colors. When viewed from a distance, these pixels blur together to approximate a different color. Up close, however, dithering looks jagged and splotchy, particularly in text and other detailed images.

Banding

Banding occurs when an image's colors are reduced without dithering. In this case, areas with subtle color changes become the same color, resulting in bands of solid color. This effect is particularly noticeable in images of people and nature, as the subtle gradations in skin tone or shading are lost.

Tempting as it may be to design only for high-end computer users, the benefits of using the Web-safe palette usually outweigh the frustrations.

Converting to Hexadecimal

If you followed the previous color experiment, you may have noticed the Red, Green, and Blue settings changed as you changed the settings in the other fields. These numbers tell the computer how much of each of the three RGB colors is needed to create the color you desire. In a Web setting, these numbers must be converted to hexadecimal before they can be used.

In the Web-safe color palette, the only hexadecimal values used are 00, 33, 66, 99, CC, and FF. As you can see, each of these values is a pair and, in the case of the Web-safe palette, both components of the pair are the same. A color is composed of three pairs: one pair for each of the RGB settings. If a hexadecimal color code contains values other than those six, you can be sure the color isn't part of the Web-safe palette. For the Web-safe palette, these conversions are as seen in Table 1.

RGB	Hex
00	00
51	33
102	66
153	99
204	CC
255	FF

Table 7-1. *Although RGB Numbers Can Range from 0-255, Only Six of These Values Are Used in the Web-Safe Palette*

*Dozens of sites have RGB-to-hex converters. One of my favorites is at
http://www.zoltech.net/colorconvert.html. Another good site is Color Center,
at http://www.hidaho.com/colorcenter/cc.html.*

Named Colors

An alternative to using hexadecimal codes for color settings is to use named colors.
There are 140 colors that have been given a name for reference purposes. While
it's certainly easier to remember a color name than to remember a hex code, support
of color names isn't as widespread. Also, only a handful of the named colors are
Web-safe. If you want to use named colors in Dreamweaver, enter the name of the
color by hand in the color field of the Property Inspector. No option to choose
named colors exists in the Color Picker in Dreamweaver.

*For a list of the named colors, visit the ProjectCool Developer Zone at
http://www.projectcool.com/developer/reference/color-chart.html.*

Choosing a Color Scheme

Once you understand the basics of color theory and how it's applied on the Web
by way of the RGB color spectrum and the Web-safe color palette, you can make
knowledgeable color choices for your site. Aside from background and text colors, you
need to choose colors for the various states of links on the page and any navigational
or decorative images on the site. Remember, the color scheme can help set the tone
for your site, support the metaphor or theme of the site, and provide navigational
cues for the site.

Some people have a knack for creating a color scheme, while others pull their hair
out trying to find the perfect combination of colors or just the right shade of blue for a
visited link. Using one of the following color selection guides should help save at least
a few hairs on your head.

Picture the color spectrum as a wheel again. From this wheel, you can make the
following color choices:

- **Complementary Colors**—also known as contrasting colors, these color schemes
  are created by choosing opposing colors from the color wheel. Blue and orange
  are complementary colors. To vary the scheme a bit, play with the tints and
  shades for each color. These schemes also tend to work well with the addition
  of a neutral color.

- **Contrasting Triad Colors**—similar to a complementary color scheme, this
  option chooses colors that form a triangle in the color wheel. Blue, yellow, and
  red form the most basic of contrasting triads. Orange, purple, and green form a
  contrasting triad of secondary colors.

- **Analogous Colors**—also known as similar color schemes, these are colors chosen from the same section of the color wheel. To create an analogous scheme, choose a color, and then choose the color (or two colors) closest to it on either side. If you choose blue, for example, the analogous colors are green and purple.

- **Monochromatic Colors**—composed of one hue in various values. Usually, black and white are added to the scheme to provide contrast, particularly for text.

- **Graduation Colors**—similar to a monochromatic scheme, this option chooses a range of colors in a graduated pattern of hue, saturation, and value. In this case, choose two or three colors next to each other on the color wheel, and then change the saturation and value of the colors to transition smoothly from one to the next.

Color and Emotion

Color is both visual and emotional. If I say the word "green," you immediately have an impression. You may think of envy, being ill, or a perfect leaf. If I further define the color as lime green, your thoughts could change, maybe to a tropical island or the color of the carpet in your childhood bedroom. Those thoughts, in turn, bring with them a

Accessibility and the Use of Color

Color brings a lot of beauty to the world and to your Web site but, don't forget, for many Web surfers, color is inconsequential or detrimental. Blind users won't see your page at all. Color-blind users might be unable to differentiate between certain colors on the site or might not see certain colors at all. And, many other users could simply be annoyed by the eye strain of reading text that's in low contrast with the background.

If you're relying heavily on a visual, color-based metaphor for your site, consider adding textual cues for visually impaired visitors. If this isn't feasible, go to the other extreme and remove references to your graphics from your text, allowing the textual content itself to entertain and inform the user without relying on visual cues.

Color-blind users do best with high contrast. While this doesn't mean you should necessarily limit yourself to black and white, do consider making your text a contrasting color to your background.

If you're color blind yourself, you may find a tool called WhatColor useful in your design efforts. WhatColor, available at **http://www.hikarun.com/e/**, can be used to select a pixel on the screen and identify the color by hex value and color name. WhatColor also magnifies the area around the selected pixel, making it easier for some visually impaired designers to see the selected area.

different range of emotions, depending on your experiences on tropical islands or during your childhood.

Choosing a color scheme is more than a matter of deciding what type of scheme you want for your site, and then randomly selecting a hue. Rather, it involves consideration of your site's theme and/or metaphor, a visually pleasing design, and the message you want to project. Here are some of the emotional cues evoked by various colors.

Colors are generally divided into two temperatures:

- **Warm Hues**—colors such as orange, yellow, and red are considered warm because they are hot and earthy, such as the sun, the core of the Earth, and the mountains. Warm hues invoke passion and raw emotion.
- **Cool Hues**—colors such as blue, green, and purple are considered cool because they invoke images of cool things, such as ice, the ocean, or a forest. Cool hues are calming and soothing, as they cool or temper passionate emotions.

Individual colors also have meanings. As you'll notice, some of these meanings overlap. All of them are subject to personal interpretation, as each person's own experiences factor into how they respond to different colors.

- **White**—purity, peace, truth.
- **Red**—fire, energy, strength, passion. Red can also mean anger, debt, or danger in a negative setting. Red is generally considered the most dynamic color.
- **Pink**—romantic love, femininity, compassion, nurturing, harmony, friendship.
- **Purple**—royalty, influence, spiritual power, wisdom, self-assurance.
- **Blue**—calm, quiet, good fortune, creativity, healing. Negatively, blue can signify depression. Blue is considered the most soothing color.
- **Green**—success, abundance, fertility, growth, sensitivity, healing. In a negative connotation, green can also mean jealousy or envy.
- **Yellow**—memory, communication, intelligence, clarity. The negative meanings of yellow are cowardice, caution, and betrayal. Yellow, particularly when highly saturated, is considered the most tiring color to the human eye.
- **Orange**—ambition, success, justice, strength, authority, joy.
- **Copper**—money, professional growth, power.
- **Gold**—wealth, winning, masculinity, humor.
- **Silver**—dreams, communication, intuition.
- **Brown**—friendships, masculinity.
- **Black**—negativity, death, evil, funerals, darkness. Although this color has mostly negative interpretations, some people think of black as protection against those negative influences, thereby turning a negative into a positive.

Because the Web has a global reach, your site probably is going to be viewed by users in other countries. In some cultures, colors have different meanings from those previously listed. Yellow, for instance, represents royalty or wealth in Malaysia, but signifies betrayal in Vietnam. If you're designing for a particular audience, you should research the color meanings of that culture or country.

For more ideas about the emotions and images evoked by various colors, visit colorspeak at **http://www.coolstop.com/colorspeak/1/**. This site encourages visitors to choose colors that call to them and share the reason they were drawn to that color. Great links to articles on color theory and color palettes are also there.

Color and Functionality

Along with setting a mood and being visually appealing, color serves a functional purpose. Creating headings in a different color than paragraph text draws the eye to the headings, enabling users to skim your content more readily. Setting certain content in a bright color in contrast to the rest of the page draws the eye to important information. This is why many e-commerce sites use the color red to draw attention to new or sale items.

No matter your exact color scheme, be sure your colors serve their functional purpose. While light blue text might look visually pleasing against a dark blue background, the actual readability of such a page may be minimal, especially when you take various monitor and display settings into consideration. If a page causes users severe eyestrain, don't expect them to stick around long.

Another functionality issue comes into play when users print your pages for their own offline use. Colors with enough contrast on the screen might not have much contrast at all when printed in a draft setting on a low-quality printer. Also, to save on ink cartridges, many users change their browser settings to ignore background colors and images when printing a page. This can be problematic if you're using a light text color.

As a designer, you need to decide if print readiness is important to you. Some of the factors in this decision include how likely is it for users to want to print your content, do you want them to do so easily, and do your pages require a certain amount of consistency on the printed page versus being viewed onscreen? If having your pages printer-friendly is important, consider using a plain white background and dark text for your page design. Some developers create a printer-friendly copy of their pages with a link to those files from the design-rich site. Others even go so far as to create an Acrobat (.pdf) file containing the site's content.

Note *To learn more about Acrobat and .pdf files, visit the Adobe site at http://www.adobe.com.*

Setting Color in Dreamweaver

Dreamweaver has several methods for bringing color to your pages. Chapter 2 explained how to use the Color Picker, which is used to set color in the Property Inspector and the Page Properties dialog box. These selectors enable you to control the color of the page background, table backgrounds, and text elements, as long as you're using solid colors.

Of course, another way to add color is to design images in Fireworks or another graphics package. These images can be anything from a logo to a decorative background image, from a custom bullet image for lists to a navigation bar. To learn more about how to create these images and to put them to use in Dreamweaver, see Chapter 12 and Chapter 13. Images are used to create more sophisticated designs than you can develop using Dreamweaver alone.

Setting Page-Wide Colors

When you create a new page in Dreamweaver, certain colors are used by default for the page background (white) and text (black). In addition, Dreamweaver uses your browser's default color settings for the various link states. You can change these defaults by modifying the page properties for the document. To do this, choose Modify | Page Properties from the menu, or use the CTRL-J (CMD-J on the Mac) keyboard shortcut to open the Page Properties dialog box. You can also right-click the Document window to bring up the context menu and choose Page Properties. The following shows this box. To change a color setting, simply click the color swatch next to the element you want to modify, and then make your selection from the color picker. Or, enter either the hex code or named color directly into the text field to the right of the color swatch.

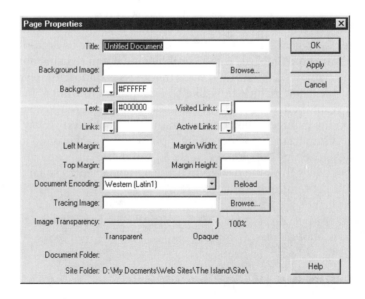

The elements whose colors can be controlled using the Page Properties dialog box are as follows:

- **Background**—the background color for the entire page. Even if you're using a background image, also setting a similar background color is advisable to provide cross-browser functionality and design consistency for those users who turn off images in their browsers.

- **Text**—the font color for text that isn't a link. The text color is also used for borders around images, if you set an image border.

- **Links**—the color used for a link that hasn't yet been clicked. This color is used for both text and image links.

- **Visited Links**—the color used for a link that's been clicked or visited. A sneaky trick some designers play is to make this the same color as the link color, so all links on the page always appear as new.

- **Active Links**—the color used for a link as it's being clicked. This is a temporary link state.

To exit the Page Properties dialog box and register your color selections, click OK. You can also click Apply if you want to register those changes while still using the Page Properties dialog box to change other settings.

Using Dreamweaver's Color Schemes

Even with all the knowledge you've gleaned about color theory at the beginning of this chapter, the actual prospect of choosing colors for your site can be daunting. To guide you on your way, Dreamweaver provides a Set Color Scheme command. This command features color schemes for 11 background colors, with 3–9 possible schemes for each background, for a total of 56 possible choices. The color schemes were developed for Macromedia by Bruce Heavin and Lynda Weinman, one of the best-known experts in Web graphics.

| Tip | *To learn more about Lynda Weinman's color and graphics expertise, visit her site at **http://www.lynda.com**, or look for one of her many books at your favorite online or brick-and-mortar bookstores. Her Designing Web Graphics books are particularly useful.* |

To use the Set Color Scheme command, do the following:

1. Choose Commands | Set Color Scheme from the menu. This opens the Set Color Scheme Command dialog box, as the following shows.

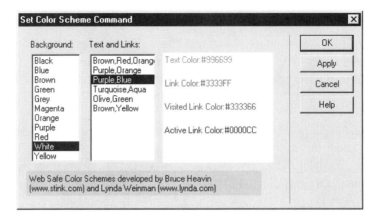

2. In the Background list, choose a background color for your page. Each background color has its own set of text and link color options, which is displayed in the Text and Links list.

3. Choose a color scheme from the Text and Links list.

4. Click OK to exit the dialog box and make the color changes to your document. If you want to see how the various color schemes change the appearance of your site, click Apply rather than OK. This applies the changes to your document without closing the dialog box.

After you choose a color scheme and exit the dialog box, Dreamweaver makes the necessary changes to the Page Properties dialog box and to the <BODY> tag of the page.

Setting Site-Wide Colors

Although the Page Properties dialog box can be used to set colors effectively, it's no longer the most efficient way to control your color settings. The Page Properties dialog box sets its color options as attributes within the <BODY> tag. These attributes have been deprecated by the W3C in favor of Cascading Style Sheets (CSS).

Style sheets enable you to control not only the text on the page, but also the text for individual elements, such as Level 1 headings or blockquotes. Rather than using the same color for text and image borders, you can set a style to use a different color for borders. Using external CSS enables you to set these color (and other) selections on a site-wide basis, which ensures consistency. Site redesigns are also easier with CSS because changing a color setting in the style sheet updates the appearance of every page using that style sheet, which is certainly much more efficient than modifying every page in the site.

Cascading Style Sheets are covered in-depth in Chapter 17. I merely introduced the subject here as a consideration in planning how you can put your color choices to work in Dreamweaver.

Setting Individual Element Colors

At times, you'll want to change only a particular block of text or a specific link without changing the remainder of the page's content or the style for every instance of a particular tag when using CSS. In those cases, you have two options. If you're using <font> tags and color attributes rather than CSS, you can highlight the text or other object and use the Property Inspector to change the color setting. This change then only affects the selected objects.

If you're using CSS, you can create a class definition and apply it to the selection. Again, this is covered in detail in Chapter 17.

Summary

Color is one of the most powerful tools available to the Web designer, so apply it judiciously. Here are some key points to remember:

- A color is a hue on a spectrum or color wheel.
- The value is the amount of black or white added to the hue.
- Saturation is the intensity of the color.
- Hue, value, and saturation combine to form different color variations.
- Colors have different meanings founded in the culture and experiences of the viewer.
- Color can be set in Dreamweaver through the use of page properties, CSS, or the Property Inspector.

In the next chapter, you learn how to give your page a title and set other <HEAD> attributes.

The Complete Reference

Chapter 8

Page Properties

When you create a document in a word processor, parts of the file are visible in the final printout—the words and their formatting. Portions of the file are also intended to help you, as the author, identify the file for your own use—the filename, certainly, and the document title, author, description, and keyword information you can enter optionally.

Just as in a word-processing document, a Web page has two key sections. The obvious section is composed of elements that establish the appearance and content of the page. If you come from an HTML background, you know these elements appear in the <body> of the page. The other section is comprised of information about the page. This information doesn't appear on the page itself, but can be just as important to the success of your site. In HTML code, these elements appear in the <head> of the page.

The blank screen of the Document window enables you to develop a design and content unique to your site. Almost every Web page has certain common elements, however, that establish the overall layout of the page, as well as identify it to the browser and the Web at large.

Setting Page Properties

The Page Properties dialog box in Dreamweaver provides a mix of settings that apply to the look of the page and provide information about the page. To access this dialog box, choose Modify | Page Properties from the menu or press CTRL-J (COMMAND-J on the Mac).

At first glance, this dialog box seems a hodgepodge of unrelated information. If you look more closely, however, you see this dialog box (Figure 8-1) offers the bare minimum settings you need to consider to begin development. You can add more structure to your site throughout the design process, but you're almost certain to begin this process by setting some preliminary colors and margins. And, while you'll almost certainly want to add more information about your site using head content and <meta> tags, you should start your development by giving the page a title, which is included in this dialog box.

Page Titles

The first item in the Page Properties dialog box is the Title field. The page's title is one of those elements that don't appear on the page itself, but is a required piece of information about the page. Every page of your site should have a unique title. For your own purposes, these titles can help you identify pages in the Site Map view of the Site window. For your users, page titles can provide an orientation cue, as they appear in the title bar of the browser window. Finally, search engines use page titles to identify pages in their listings, and some use the contents of the title as an indexing criteria.

Your title should orient users to your site, as well as the page. A good naming convention is to use the name of the site, followed by a dash and the name of the page,

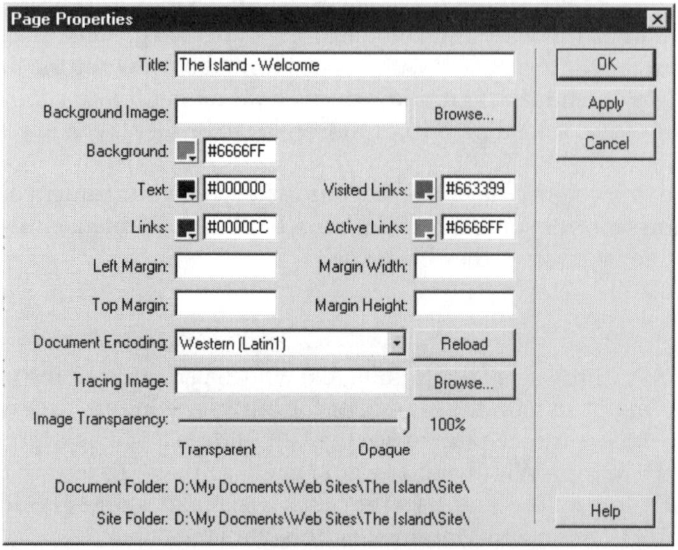

Figure 8-1. *The Page Properties dialog box should be one of your first stops when you design a new page*

such as The Island—Find a Day Spa. Simple is best. While you can make your titles quite long and detailed, most users find long titles a nuisance. Browsers' favorites or bookmarks use page titles for their menu listings, and a long title causes the menu to become ungainly. Save your prose for your site's content, and keep your titles short and direct.

Dreamweaver 4 has another way to title a page. The toolbar in the Document window offers a Title field. Entering a title either here or in the Page Properties dialog box has the same effect.

Background Images and Page Colors

The first elements you're likely to add to a page are the background image—if you're using one—and the overall color settings. Chapter 7 explained how to decide on a color scheme and set the colors for your page. Chapter 12 explains some of the considerations when you're designing or selecting a background image. Once you choose an image, set it in the Page Properties dialog box by entering the path and filename in the Background Image field. You can also use the Browse button to open the File Selection dialog box and choose the file from there.

Even if you set a background image, a good idea is also to set a similar background color. For users with slow modems, the background color displays before the image, making the page readable even as the image is loading. Some users also choose not to display images. If you design your site for a dark background image using light-colored text for contrast, users with images turned off will see the light-colored text against a default white background, which could render it unreadable—unless you thought ahead and set a dark background color to be displayed in place of the background image.

The text and link colors determine the color scheme of your content and link borders. For more information about links, see Chapter 11. Remember, users may override your color settings, if they choose.

Margins

Margins are used by browsers to determine the white space around the page. If your design entails being flush with the top-left of the browser window, you want to set the margins at zero (0). Internet Explorer uses the Left Margin and Top Margin settings. Netscape uses the Margin Width and Margin Height settings. To ensure that your page displays properly in both browsers, set the Left Margin and Margin Width to the same value, and the Top Margin and Margin Height to the same value.

Document Encoding

Document encoding determines the character set to use for your Web page. To learn more about document encoding, see Chapter 3. The encoding you set as the default in your Preferences shows up as the default in the Page Properties dialog box. If you're creating your document in English or another language using a Western character set, keep the encoding at Western (Latin 1). Languages such as Russian, Japanese, and Chinese require a different character set. You also need to have the appropriate fonts installed on your computer to develop and view pages in these languages.

 *A complete discussion of internationalization issues is beyond the scope of this book. If you want to know more about encoding your pages for different character sets, visit the Unicode Consortium site at **http://www.unicode.org**.*

Tracing Images

Like the page title, a *tracing image* is an element that's never seen on the actual page. Unlike the page title, however, a tracing image isn't even an HTML element. Rather, it's a design guide feature unique to Dreamweaver. Tracing images are a graphic prototype of your site's design created in a graphics package and saved in GIF, JPG, or PNG format. The image is positioned as a layer on the page, and you use it as a guide for setting frame and table widths, aligning text and images, and otherwise re-creating the design in Dreamweaver. The tracing image layer only appears in Dreamweaver and doesn't affect the functionality of the finished page.

Tracing images are a convenient design tool for developers who prototype a complete page in Fireworks or Adobe Photoshop (among other applications). When I design sites, I usually create an image of the entire site in Fireworks. This serves as a prototype of my design. I then slice the image into pieces like a puzzle and export the smaller images. Those pieces—individual GIF and JPG images—are reconstructed into a cohesive page in Dreamweaver. A tracing image enables me to view that original image within Dreamweaver to ensure the pieces are put back into the proper positions with the proper dimensions. I simply use the complete prototype as my tracing image and rebuild the site over that image.

Note
A tracing image can help you reconstruct your design in Dreamweaver but, as should be expected, it doesn't account for differences in browsers. It's simply a graphic design guide. You still need to test your pages in various browsers, particularly in Netscape 4.x, which often renders advanced tables incorrectly.

To insert a tracing image into a Dreamweaver document, take the following steps:

1. Access the tracing image file selector:

   - If the Page Properties dialog box is already open, click the Browse button next to the Tracing Image field.

   - Otherwise, choose View | Tracing Image | Load.

2. Select an image file from the File Selection dialog box. If the image isn't already within the site root, you're prompted to put a copy of the file into the site root.

3. After selecting a file, the Page Properties dialog box appears with the filename in the Tracing Image field.

4. Click OK.

Changing the Transparency of Tracing Images

You can change the transparency of the tracing image to facilitate easier design. I like to use a 50 percent transparency because it fades the image enough to differentiate from the actual images and elements you set for the page during the design process, but is still visible enough to serve as a guide. When you add images over the tracing image, it's almost like seeing pieces of the puzzle come into focus, as seen in Figure 8-2.

To change the transparency of the tracing image, use the Image Transparency slider in the Page Properties dialog box. You can set this option when you first add the tracing image. If you want to tweak the transparency until you find one you like, click the Apply button instead of OK. This applies the transparency setting while leaving the Page Properties dialog box open for further adjustment. When you find an appropriate setting, click OK.

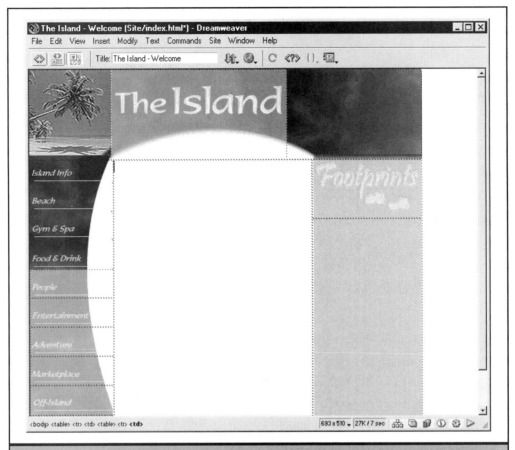

Figure 8-2. *A tracing image makes it easy to insert your images in the proper position on your page*

While you're working, you may want to turn off the tracing image to see your design without any background distraction. To toggle the visibility of the tracing image, choose View | Tracing Image | Show. A check mark next to this menu item indicates the tracing image is visible. Choosing this menu option again toggles the image into hiding, as indicated by the removal of the check mark next to the menu option.

If you forgot whether you set a tracing image for a page, look at the View | Tracing Image menu. If no image is set, the only available menu option is to Load a tracing image. If other options are available, this means you set a tracing image that's either in a hidden state or has its transparency set to 0 percent.

Adjusting a Tracing Image

Because a tracing image isn't an actual page element, it cannot be manipulated with the Property Inspector and other Dreamweaver tools. All adjustments to the tracing image must be made either in the View | Tracing Image menu or—in the case of the transparency of the image—through the Page Properties dialog box.

In some ways, however, a tracing image is similar to a layer. A tracing image can be aligned to specific coordinates or with another object on the page. To change the position of the tracing image, do the following:

1. Choose View | Tracing Image | Adjust Position.

2. Adjust the positioning of the tracing image using one of the following options:

   ■ Enter coordinate values in the X and Y fields of the Adjust Tracing Image Position dialog box, as the following illustrates.

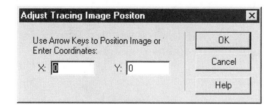

   ■ Use the arrow keys to move the image one pixel at a time. Notice the coordinates change in the Adjust Tracing Image Position dialog box.

   ■ Use the SHIFT-arrow key to move the image five pixels at a time. The coordinates change in the Adjust Tracing Image Position dialog box as you move the image.

3. Press OK to set the new position.

To align the tracing image with an object, select the object in the Document window, and then choose View | Tracing Image | Align with Selection. This aligns the upper-left corner of the tracing image with the upper-left corner of the selected object.

To reset the tracing image to its default position (the upper-left corner of the page, or x-y coordinates 0,0), select View | Tracing Image | Reset Position from the menu.

Head Content

Beyond the title requested by the Page Properties dialog box, you can add a lot of additional behind-the-scenes information to your pages. Tags placed in the <head> of an HTML document—primarily <meta> tags—identify the page by name, description, keywords, and author. They can also refresh a page or load another page in its place.

Meta Tags

By default, Dreamweaver includes a `<meta>` tag in every page it creates. This tag reads

```
<meta http-equiv="Content-Type" content="text/html;
charset=iso-8859-1">
```

and it tells browsers the page is an HTML page using the standard Western character set. Two types of `<meta>` tags exist—those with `http-equiv` and those with `name` attributes. Those with `http-equiv` attributes give the browser information about how to read the page. Those with `name` attributes provide information that doesn't affect the rendering of the page, such as keywords and descriptions used by search engines.

Attributes for `<meta>` tags are structured differently than those of other tags. Rather than grouping attributes within one tag, each different `<meta>` tag attribute is contained within its own `<meta>` tag. Also, each tag has two attributes. One is either http-equiv or name, with a value that describes the content of the attribute. The second is the content attribute itself, with a value containing the actual content. Thus, the `<head>` of your document may resemble something like this:

```
<head>
<title>The Island - Welcome</title>
<meta http-equiv="Content-Type" content="text/html;
charset=iso-8859-1">
<meta name="keywords" content="island, relaxation, rest, retreat,
beach, gym, spa, day spa, food, drink, cuisine, recipes,
adventure">
<meta name="description" content="The Island is a virtual resort.
Share information and ideas on rest, relaxation, relationships,
good food, shopping, and adventure with others in our community.
And find out where and how to bring a taste of the island life into
your real life.">
<meta name="author" content="Pendragn Online">
</head>
```

This `<head>` contains four `<meta>` tags—one to identify the type of document to the server, one to provide keywords for the page, one for a description of the page, and one to identify the author. Each of these tags, as well as the other `<meta>` tags, can use an explanation.

Keywords

The keywords `<meta>` tag contains words that relate to the content of the page. In some search engines, the keywords you set generate hits in search engine listings, so it's important the list is complete. Choosing keywords is an art, so this is worth a bit of study. A good source of information about search engines is Spider Food, at **http://spider-food.net/**. To add a keywords <meta> tag, choose the Insert Keywords object from the Head category of the Objects panel or choose Insert | Head Tags | Keywords from the menu. This brings up the Insert Keywords dialog box, as the following illustrates.

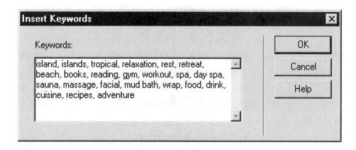

Enter your keywords into the Keywords field, separated by commas. Click OK to save your entries and return to the Document window.

Description

The description of the site is used in some search engines as the content of the search engine listing. As with keywords, powerful descriptions require some planning to yield the best results. The payoff for a good description is a useful search engine entry, as engines like AltaVista use the description along with the page title when displaying results (as well as part of its indexing criteria). In the absence of a description, AltaVista uses the first few words on the page, which may or may not provide any insight into the content of your site.

Add a description by choosing the Insert Description object from the Head category of the Objects panel or choosing Insert | Head Tags | Description from the menu. The Insert Description dialog box appears as the following shows.

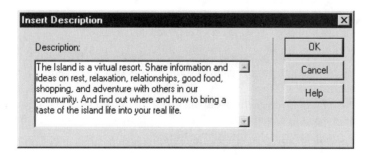

Refresh

The *refresh* <meta> tag is an http-equiv value, which instructs the browser to wait for a set number of seconds before reloading the page. The content attribute of this tag can contain a different URL, as well as the time setting, so it can be used on opening splash screens to load the main page of your site automatically after it displays the splash page for a specified period of time.

A refresh can also be used to redirect users to a new URL for your site. To move a user to the new page immediately, set the delay for zero (0) seconds. This can ease confusion and delay for your users, but some people become frustrated when a page seems to take control of their browser. An alternative solution is to create a brief page for your old domain stating you moved and providing the new URL. Put a refresh <meta> tag on this page, so users are automatically moved to the new page after a delay that gives them enough time to read your message, usually about 10 to 15 seconds. The link on the old page enables users to navigate to the new site manually in case the refresh fails or they don't want to wait out the refresh period.

To add a refresh <meta> tag, choose the Insert Refresh object from the Head category of the Objects panel. You can also access it by choosing Insert | Head Tags | Refresh. The Insert Refresh dialog box appears, as the following illustrates.

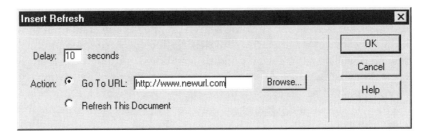

A refresh <meta> tag looks like this in Code view:

```
<meta http-equiv="refresh" content="10,URL=http://www.newurl.com">
```

Base

This tag changes the point of reference for all document-relative links. Rather than being relative to the current page, any links are referenced relative to the filename specified in this tag.

To enter a base <meta> tag, choose Insert Base from the Head category of the Objects panel or choose Insert | Head Tags | Base from the menu. This brings up the Insert Base dialog box, as the following shows.

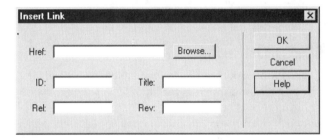

Link

The link `<meta>` tag specifies a relationship between the current document and another file. This is most commonly used with external style sheets. As you can see by the following illustration, you can define the link relationship in four ways beyond identifying the URL of the file you're linking to.

- **Rel**—identifies a relationship between the linked document and the current document. This is commonly used with the `stylesheet` value, but can also be used with the following values. Multiple values can be separated with a space.

  - **home**—identifies the location of the home page for the current site.

  - **up**—indicates the location of the document above the current document in the site hierarchy.

  - **next**—indicates the location of the document that follows the current document in logical order within the site structure.

  - **prev**—indicates the location of the document that preceded the current document in logical order within the site structure.

  - **stylesheet**—indicates the location of an external style sheet to link to the current document.

  - **toc**—identifies the location of the site map or overview.

  - **help**—indicates the location of a help file for the site.

- **glossary**—identifies the location of a glossary file for the site.

- **copyright**—identifies the location of a file containing copyright information.

- **Rev**—indicates a reverse relationship, whereby the linked file is defining the relationship to the current document. This attribute can take the same values as the Rel attribute. This is most commonly used with an e-mail address to establish a relationship between the author of the page with the actual page. Some browsers can use this link to provide feedback to the author.

- **Title**—defines the nature of the relationship. This is used primarily with the rel attribute when describing external style sheets to establish them as being preferred, persistent, or alternate.

- **ID**—specifies a unique identifier.

To build a link `<meta>` tag in the Insert Link dialog box, enter either an absolute or a relative link path in the HREF field, and then enter an appropriate value in one or more of the remaining fields.

Adding Other Meta Objects

Other `<meta>` tags aren't incorporated into Dreamweaver. These attributes can still be easily added to your pages using the generic Meta object. The *Meta* object is useful for controlling search engine robots and setting page expiration dates. To create these tags, use the Insert Meta object from the Head category of the Objects panel or the Insert | Head Tags | Meta option on the menu. Then, use the Insert Meta dialog box to choose the appropriate attribute, and set the proper value and content for that attribute. The following illustrates this.

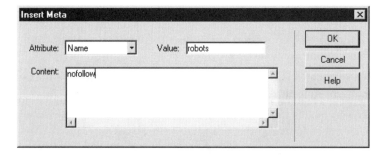

Meta tags can provide and deny search engines access to your site using the name="robots" attribute. If you set the content to `noindex`, the search engine spiders won't index your site. You can also set the tag to index only the main page or to index all the pages on the site. To do this, set the content to `follow` to tell the spider to

follow all the links from your main page and index those pages. Set the content to
`nofollow` to tell the spider to index only the main page of the site.

The Platform for Internet Content Selection (PICS) label is used to rate the
appropriateness of a site's contents for children. The criteria for this rating include
the promotion or discouragement of multiculturalism, sexual content, profanity,
educational information, environmental issues, and even Canadian content. A PICS
`<meta>` tag looks like this:

```
<META http-equiv="PICS-Label" content='(PICS-1.1
"http://vancouver-webpages.com/VWP1.0/" l gen true comment "VWP1.0"
on "2001.02.19T23:501600" r (MC -3 Gam -1 Com 1 SF 0 Edu -1 S 0 Can
-1 V 0 Env -2 P 1 Tol -2 ))'>
```

To add a PICS label to your site, you must first generate a PICS rating. You can do
this at **http://www.vancouver-webpages.com/VWP1.0/VWP1.0.gen.html**. Once you
generate a rating, you can enter it in Dreamweaver, using the Insert Meta object (or the
menu) to establish the attribute (http-equiv), value (PICS-Label), and content (the PICS
rating) in the dialog box.

The Meta object can, in fact, be used to add even the `<meta>` tags that have
dedicated dialog boxes in Dreamweaver, although using the appropriate object is
usually easier.

Tip   *If you want to use the same `<meta>` tags repeatedly across several pages, you can make
this process easier in two ways. If you also want to share design and other elements, you
can use templates for your site. Templates are covered in Chapter 29. Another way to
reuse `<meta>` tags is to change the default.html file in the Dreamweaver application
folder. This file can be found in the Configuration\Templates folder of your application.
If you choose to modify this file, always make a backup of the original first. I like to add
the basic `<meta>` tag structure for keywords and descriptions to my default.html file.
Then I manually type in the unique information for each page in the Code view as I
develop the page.*

Viewing and Editing Head Content

Once you add `<meta>` tags to your page, you have two choices if you need to edit the
information. First, you can switch to one of the Code views and change the information
manually. This is only suggested if you know what you're doing in the code and won't
mess up the structure of the tags.

The second option is to display your head content using the View | Head Content
(CTRL-SHIFT-W in Windows, COMMAND-SHIFT-W on the Mac). This doesn't actually
display the contents of each `<meta>` tag. Instead, it displays icons representing each

<meta> tag you inserted. To edit a tag, click it once to display the tag's contents in the Property Inspector, from where it can be edited.

Summary

The development of every Web page must start somewhere, and the Page Properties and <head> content are good places to begin. These settings give your page its initial structure. Remember these key points:

- The Page Properties dialog box enables you to set the page title, background image and color, text and link colors, margins, and language encoding for the page.
- Every page in your site needs a title, and that title should be unique to help orient the user and increase the search engine score for the page.
- Keywords should be inclusive, but not gratuitous.
- Descriptions should be unique for each page to maximize the search engine score for individual pages.

The next part of the book explains how to develop and design the pages of your site, starting with Chapter 9.

The
Complete
Reference

Part III

Building Your Site's Pages

Chapter 9

Adding Text Content

Words are the way we communicate. They inform and misinform, praise and chastise, entertain and educate. You can develop a great color scheme and smooth navigation, but it's your words and images that bring users to your site. Text on the Web is an intricate dance of content, word choice, writing style, and display. While this book isn't intended as a writing guide, this chapter provides an overview of points to consider when writing for the Web. And once you have the words right, you can learn how to get them into your documents and format them, so the content becomes an integral part of your site design.

Content

This is one of the most important steps in the design of your Web site. The user comes to your site based on your content. The user stays at your site or clicks past based on your content. Well-written, easily accessible content helps draw the user to your pages. Your content should be chosen with the end user in mind. Design the content and layout to make the information easily accessible.

Writing for the Web

Before you write for the Web, you should understand what users read on the Web and how they read it. Reading text on a computer monitor can be tiresome. The user must hold his head up and is usually sitting upright at a desk. Reading colored text puts a strain on the eyes, depending on the color, and the font size can also be a burden. Let's face it, reading on the Web isn't nearly as physically comfortable as relaxing with a book, good or otherwise.

The comfort factor, or lack thereof, coupled with a limited amount of time—whether because of surfing the Web during business hours or needing a specific piece of information to meet a deadline—lend themselves to skimming rather than reading in depth. As a writer, then, long blocks of text are wasted on your audience, and may even be enough of a turn-off to send them to another site. The best Web writing keeps these points in mind:

- Writing should be clear and concise.
- Writing should offer specific pieces of information. Even for an online shopping site—because users cannot put their hands on the product to view it personally—they rely on informative copy, rather than marketing doublespeak to enable them to make buying decisions.
- Use visual cues—such as links or bullet items—to help users find the key points of information.
- Keep paragraphs short to give the eyes a visual white space break and to let users process one point before moving on to the next.

■ Keep pages short, which necessitates writing lean copy. A general guideline is to keep the first page of a site to one screen, scrolling to two at the most. Internal pages can be a bit longer, as the user has demonstrated an interest in the material by clicking deeper into the site. If you have a lot of content to present, break it up into pages with clear navigation to get users from page to page in the proper order.

Making Your Tone Match Your Theme

Chapter 5 discussed planning your Web site and choosing a theme. The tone of your text and the information you present should be in harmony with your theme. If your theme is serious and academic, your writing style and text format should be in keeping with your theme. If you have a professional theme, a whimsical font type and anecdotal stories would be in stark contrast to the tone of the site. If you have a light, comical Web site theme, a corporate writing style would contradict what you're trying to achieve with your theme.

Typography

Both online and off, text is presented in a *font*, also known as a *typeface*. Fonts range from the plain to the elaborate, and from the highly readable to the highly illegible. Fonts are grouped into categories, families, and faces. While you might think this is just another design concept to read and forget, font groupings are actually quite useful when defining style sheets or setting font attributes in your code.

Font categories are the master families of type. They describe the decoration or common features that describe families of fonts. Font families are the font names. Font families can be further broken down into *font faces*, which are the types of appearance a font can take on, such as bold, italic, narrow, or regular/normal. The font categories and some of their families are

■ **Serif**—fonts with serifs, extra strokes at the points of the letters, such as Times, Garamond, and Bookman.

■ **Sans Serif**—fonts without, or sans, serifs. This is the most common category of font on the Web because it's more easily read on a computer screen. This category includes fonts such as Ariel, Helvetica, and Verdana.

■ **Monospaced**—each letter in the font face takes up the same amount of space as every other letter. In other words, an *m* in a monospaced font takes up the same space as an *i*. This category includes Courier and Lucida Sans Typewriter.

■ **Script**—fonts that imitate handwriting, such as Vladimir Script or Riverside.

■ **Decorative**—fonts that are more decorative than functional for reading blocks of text. Examples include Poptics Three and Dragonwick.

Setting Fonts

When deciding how to present your content, one of the first decisions to make is about which font to use. This is often also the first roadblock in formatting your text because of differences between browsers and the lack of control over the fonts users have installed on their computers. You can design a site that looks absolutely beautiful in Niagara Solid font, but if users don't have that font on their machine, the text reverts to the default font setting in the users' browser. There's a world of difference between Niagara Solid and Times New Roman.

Fortunately, you can group fonts in attribute values and Cascading Style Sheets (CSS) definitions. This is where it's important to understand which fonts belong to each category. Rather than choosing one font and taking your chances that all your visitors have that font installed, you can specify a range of fonts, such as `<font face="arial, helvetica, sans serif">`. In this case, the browser first looks to display the text in Arial. If that font isn't available on the user's computer, it looks for Helvetica. If the browser can't find Helvetica, it looks for the default sans serif font installed on the user's computer. While you do lose some control over the specific presentation of your text, you can be reasonably certain everyone has at least one sans serif font on their machine. And adding this font family at least ensures that text you intended to be viewed in sans serif Arial isn't viewed in serif Times Roman.

In Dreamweaver, it's easy to make these font selections according to logical font categories and similar font families. To choose one of the preset groups of font families, choose either Text | Font | your group of choice, or use the drop-down menu in the font field of the Property Inspector to choose from the same list. The default font groups include a few sans serif, two serif, and one monospaced font categories.

 Decorative fonts shouldn't generally be used for content. They're often difficult to read and they aren't common across a wide range of users. Decorative fonts are best used in graphics. If you want to use a decorative font for headings, for example, you can create a graphic of the heading, and use that image in place of an HTML heading.

When choosing a font for text content, sticking with the most common is best. As mentioned earlier, sans serif fonts are most readable on the Web, so consider using Arial and/or Helvetica.

You can add your own font combinations to the font list. If you consistently use Trebuchet MS on your pages—either alone or in combination with other sans serif fonts—you can save time by adding it to the font list. To do this, take the following steps:

1. Select Text | Font | Edit Font List. You can also use the drop-down font menu in the Property Inspector and choose Edit Font List from the bottom of the menu. Either of these bring up the Edit Font List dialog box, as the following illustrates.

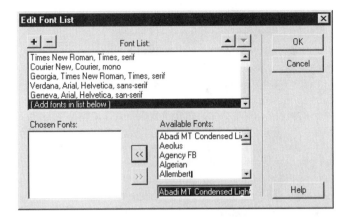

2. If you're adding or removing a font from an existing group, select that group from the Font List. Otherwise, scroll to the bottom of the Font List to select [Add fonts in list below].

3. To add a font, select it from the Available Fonts list. The name of the font appears in the box below the list.

4. Click the arrows pointing to the Chosen Fonts list.

5. To remove a font, select it from the Chosen Fonts list, and then click the arrows pointing away from the Chosen Fonts list.

6. To add a new group of fonts, click the plus (+) symbol atop the Fonts List.

7. To remove a group from the Fonts List, click the minus (–) symbol.

8. To change the order in which the font groups appear in the font menus, select a font group and click the up and down arrows to position the selected group on the list.

9. Click OK to exit the dialog box.

As for the Mac versus PC issue, the standard resolution for text on a Mac is 72 dpi. The standard resolution for text on a PC is 96 dpi. This means text you set up to read correctly on a Mac may appear too large on a Windows machine. If your text displays at a nice size on a PC, it may display too small to read on a Mac. Compound this with the fact that more and more people read Web content on handheld devices, such as the Palm or on Web-enabled cell phones with tiny screens, and you can easily see the font size gets more and more complicated.

This problem has no perfect solution or everyone would be using it. This section gives you some ideas on how to handle these cross-platform problems. You can experiment with your site and decide which solution works best for you. As always, the advice to view your Web site on different browsers, as well as on both a Mac and a PC, can help you decide which approach to use.

Formatting Text

Text is entered into Dreamweaver by either typing directly in the Document window or by cutting-and-pasting from another source. Once the text is entered into the document screen, you have many options for formatting the text.

The text options discussed in this chapter relate to the tools readily available in the Property Inspector and the menus. Remember, though, the W3C has declared CSS as the preferred method for defining the appearance of a site, including text settings. CSS is covered in Chapter 17. Although the W3C has been quite clear about its deprecation of <font> tags and attributes, in point of fact, they are still extremely popular and widely used on the Web. CSS is slowly catching on, however, and will become more prevalent in the coming years.

Using the Property Inspector

The Property Inspector, as the following illustrates, displays the elements and attributes applied to the selected text and enables you to change any attributes.

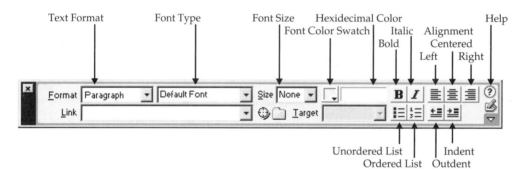

Did you lose the Property Inspector? You can display the Property Inspector by selecting Window | Properties from the menu bar. If your Property Inspector has hidden itself behind other windows, you can click Window | Arrange Panels from the menu bar.

Setting Paragraph Format

A paragraph format displays the block of text according to the defaults of the formatting tag that's applied. Dreamweaver has three basic paragraph styles, as the following illustrates:

- **Paragraph**—the format for most of the text on your page, the paragraph tag is denoted by `<p>` and `</p>` in the HTML code. This format ignores white space and line breaks. Instead, everything within the tag pair is formatted as a single paragraph.

- **Heading**—which includes Heading 1 through Heading 6. *Headings* are used to identify different sections of content on a page. Headings usually range from largest and boldest (`<h1>`) to smallest (`<h6>`), as the following illustrates, although they can be used however you want. Headings are applied to the entire paragraph, so you cannot mix heading styles within the same line of text.

Heading 1

Heading 2

Heading 3

Heading 4

Heading 5

Heading 6

- **Preformatted**—this format enables you to space text exactly as you want, including using white space and line breaks. Also, text doesn't automatically word wrap, so you must press the ENTER key to end a line. When put into practical use, your results with the preformatted format may vary, depending on the fonts used by end users and their screen resolutions.

The default format is Paragraph. There's also an infrequently used None option, which removes all paragraph formatting from the selected text.

Paragraph formats are applied to the paragraphs using the Property Inspector.

1. Go to the document screen and place the insertion point anywhere within the paragraph.
2. On the Property Inspector's Format drop-down list, select an option to apply to the paragraph. Or, select Text | Paragraph Format from the menu, and choose from the options listed.

Font Styles

To change the style of a font, highlight the text you want to change and click the *B* on the Property Inspector to bold the text or click the *I* on the Property Inspector to italicize the text.

You can also choose styles by selecting Text | Style from the menu. These styles may appear slightly different on various browsers. Figure 9-1 shows how the different styles appear in Internet Explorer version 5.0, as well as the HTML code for each style and its intended purpose. Experiment with the different styles to find the one that presents the text the way you like. You can use more than one style on the same text, as when creating a bold, italicized selection.

Style	HTML Code	Used For
Bold	B	
Italic	I	
Underline	U	
~~Strikethrough~~	S or Strikethrough	
Teletype	TT	monospaced font
Emphasis	EM	usually shows as italics
Strong	STRONG	stronger emphasis than just using the emphasis style: usually shows as bold
Code	CODE	text is part of a computer program listing
Variable	VAR	text is a program variable
Sample	SAMP	text is sample output from program
Keyboard	KBD	text is user input
Citation	CITE	source of a quote
Definition	DFN	text is a definition

Figure 9-1.   *The different font styles and their uses*

You can also select the style before you begin typing and it'll affect subsequent text. To turn off the style when you finish, go to Text | Style on the menu bar and deselect the text styles from the submenu. To turn off Bold and Italic, click the *B* or the *I* button on the Property Inspector.

Remember, underlining text is universally used to designate a link on a Web page. Underlining words or groups of words that aren't a link may confuse some end users, so use this option sparingly.

Font Sizes

HTML font sizes are relative rather than a specific point size. When you select 3 or Default in the Property Inspector, in theory, end users will see your text in the default size they have set for their browsers. Sizes 4 through 7 appear larger than the default size, sizes 1 and 2 appear smaller. If users have their browsers set to display fonts at a large size and you pick a large size for your fonts, the output on the end users' screens may be huge.

To change the font size:

1. Select the text to be changed. If no text is selected, the change is applied to subsequent text.

2. On the Property Inspector, click the Size box, as the following shows.

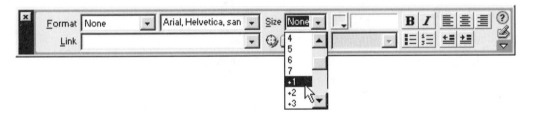

3. Select the size from the drop-down list.

You can see the previous illustration that you can pick a specific HTML size of 1 through 7, or you can choose to increase or decrease relatively from the default size by using the -7 through the +7 options. Browsers have a default size setting, which can be customized by the user. If a user's default size is 3, selecting +2 would make the font size a 5. Selecting -1 would make the font size a 2. Choosing specific size settings gives you more control as a designer, but gives less control to the user.

Font Colors

The default text color is set in the Page Properties, as was discussed in Chapter 7. To change the overall color settings for the page, choose Modify | Page Properties | Text. If no text color is set in Page Properties, the default text color is black.

You can also modify the text color by highlighting your text and choosing Text | Color from the menu bar. The color picker dialog box appears. Pick the color you want and click OK. On the Property Inspector, type in the hexadecimal code or color name in the text box to the right of the Text Color Box

To return text to the default text color, go to the Property Inspector and click the Text Swatch Color box. Click the white square with the red strikethrough button on the Color Picker. This causes the text to return to the default color.

Aligning Text

Dreamweaver makes it easy for you to do simple alignment of your text. You can quickly align text to the left or right, or center the text on your Web page.

To change the alignment of text on a page:

1. Highlight the text you want to align or insert the pointer at the beginning of the text.

2. Click left justify, center, or right justify on the Property Inspector.

3. You can also align text by choosing Text | Alignment on the menu bar and choosing an option from there.

The following are the keyboard shortcuts for alignment:

Alignment	Windows Shortcut	Mac Shortcut
Left	CTRL-ALT-SHIFT-L	OPTION-L
Center	CTRL-ALT-SHIFT-C	OPTION-C
Right	CTRL-ALT-SHIFT-R	OPTION-R

Indenting Text

Text can be indented or outdented in several different ways. Select the desired text and use one of the following methods to indent or outdent the text.

■ Use the Property Inspector and click the Indent or Outdent button as the following shows.

■ From the menu bar select Text | Indent or Text | Outdent

■ If the text you highlight is a list, you can right-click it and choose List from the pop-up menu. Choose Indent or Outdent from the drop-down menu.

Each time you choose Indent by any of these methods, it indents the text. Choose Indent again and it indents the text even more. The same applies to repeatedly choosing Outdent for the same text. While this is easy to do, some browsers don't handle this well. Preview your work on a browser to be sure the desired effect remains intact even when the browser window is resized. Another way to handle this situation is in a fixed percentage table, as discussed in Chapter 14.

Horizontal Rules and Other Text Objects

Horizontal rules and line breaks serve to add much-needed white space to the page, as well as dividing the page into logical sections.

Horizontal rules are good to use to break up sections of text on your page. They're useful for organizing information on your page and dividing sections. The default rule is shaded. On a colored background, this usually shows up like it's etched into the Web page.

To add a horizontal rule:

1. Go to the document window.

2. Place your insertion point where you want the rule.

3. Choose Insert | Horizontal Rule from the menu bar, *or*

4. From the Object panel chose the Horizontal Rule button from the Common category, as the following shows. If the Object Panel isn't visible, choose Window | Objects to open the Object Panel.

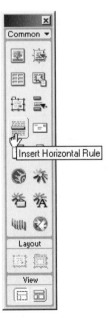

To modify a horizontal rule, select the horizontal rule in the document window. The Property Inspector for the rule gives you the option of changing the width, height, shading, and alignment of the rule. The following illustration shows the Property Inspector for rules.

From the Property Inspector, you can change the width of the rule. The default width is 100 percent of the width of the Web page. The percentage is a proportion of the page's width, no matter what the resolution of the screen. You may want to set the width to a set number of pixels, especially if you're trying to match the width of the horizontal rule to match an object's width.

To change the height of a rule, go to the height box on the Property Inspector. The default height is two pixels on unshaded rules and three pixels on shaded rules. If you give the rule a large number of pixels for height, the rule begins to look more like a box, as the following illustrates.

Text with rule set to two pixel height

Text with a rule set to 10 pixel height

Chose the alignment of the rule from the options in the align box. You can choose left, center, or right align. If you have the width of the line set for 100 percent, the alignment options won't show any difference in the browser. Your rule must be set at less than the full width of the page for the alignment to have any affect.

Dreamweaver defaults to a shaded rule. `<hr>` To make an unshaded rule `<hr noshade>`, simply uncheck the shading box on the Property Inspector.

Nonbreaking Spaces

HTML only allows one space between characters. Browsers collapse all white spaces to a single space. Place your insertion point between two words in a paragraph on your document screen and press the space bar. Nothing happened, did it?

Some exceptions to this rule exist. Text contained in a preformatted text element (<pre>) does allow for space between characters to control the flow of text.

Go to the beginning of a paragraph on your document screen and press the Tab key. Nothing happens. You won't get a five-space indent like your word processor does for you. The way to force more spaces between words or indent a paragraph is to insert nonbreaking spaces into your document ( ). These nonbreaking spaces won't be collapsed to a single white space on the user's browser, so you have more control over the spacing.

To insert nonbreaking spaces:

1. Go to the document screen and place your cursor where you want the nonbreaking space.

2. Select CTRL-SHIFT-SPACEBAR for Windows or OPTION-SPACEBAR for Mac. You can also use the Characters category of the Objects panel, selecting the nonbreaking space icon.

3. A nonbreaking space appears on your screen. You can add as many nonbreaking spaces as you need, for instance, add five nonbreaking spaces at the beginning of a paragraph to simulate the indented paragraphs you're used to seeing in your word processor.

Line Breaks

With most HTML editors, when you press the ENTER key, a new <p> tag is created. Most Web browsers ignore <p> elements that contain no content. So, if you want to create a blank line between bodies of text, you needed to code in a <br> tag.

The Dreamweaver editor handles this a bit differently. When you press ENTER in the Dreamweaver editor, a nonbreaking space is added with the P element: <p> </p>. If you begin to type at that point, the nonbreaking space is overwritten. If you press the ENTER key again, instead of typing in text, the nonbreaking space remains on the line, causing what looks like a blank line on your Web page.

Sometimes you want to start a new line of text without that blank line inserted between the paragraphs. To do this, use a line break. A *line break* inserts a carriage return in the text without closing the paragraph element and, thus, without inserting extra space between the two lines. To add a line break:

1. Go to the document screen and place your cursor where you want to force a line break.

2. Press SHIFT-ENTER for Windows or SHIFT-RETURN for a Mac.

3. This forces the text to a new line.

Special Characters

Many special character entities, such as the copyright symbol or trademark symbol, are used frequently on Web sites. Dreamweaver makes adding these symbols easy for you. These entities can be entered from the Objects Panel under Characters, as the following shows.

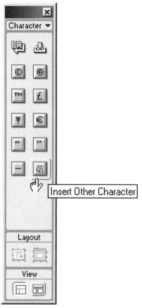

Table 9-1 shows the following special characters available from the Characters panel:

Symbol	Name
©	Copyright
®	Registered Trademark
TM	Trademark
£	Pound
¥	Yen
€	Euro
—	Em Dash
"	Left Quote
"	Right Quote

Table 9-1. *These Characters Require Special Coding to Ensure They Render Correctly in a Browser and Don't Interfere with the HTML Code*

If you press the last button on the menu, you can insert other characters. The Insert Other Character pop-up enables easy access to 99 different symbols, as the following illustrates. Select the character you want to insert, and then select OK. The Character objects insert either a named character or a numbered character. Some browsers don't recognize all the named characters, so Dreamweaver supplies the numbered codes for these special characters to provide greater compatibility with more browsers.

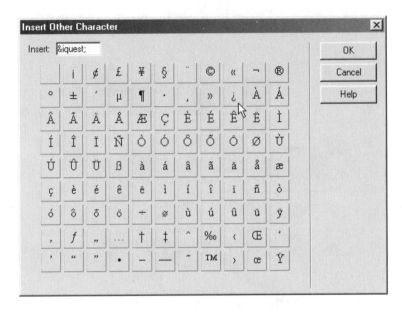

Tip　To enter the copyright symbol on your Web page quickly, use the keyboard shortcut ALT-0169 for Windows or OPTION-G for Macs. These are operating system shortcuts—not Dreamweaver shortcuts—and are fairly standard across applications.

Applying Styles

Dreamweaver gives you many tools to help you achieve consistency across the many pages of your Web site. Using CCS is one way—perhaps the best way—to provide consistency and ease of mass changes to styles across all pages. Unfortunately, older browsers don't handle these CSS, and many Web sites still attract users with older versions of browsers installed on their machines. Cascading Style Sheets are covered fully in Chapter 17.

Another way to apply styles easily and consistently is by the use of HTML styles. These are similar to CCS in letting you define a custom style for characteristics of text, such as size, color, and font type. You can then apply that HTML style to a block of text. Dreamweaver applies the styles using standard HTML tags, instead of CCS declarations. The HTML styles can be saved and used again on subsequent text.

An advantage of using CCS styles is this: when you make a change to a CCS, the change is made wherever the CCS style has been applied. When you change a HTML style, only subsequent applications of that style are changed. CCS styles also offer you some choices that simply aren't available as HTML text tags.

HTML Styles

Dreamweaver 4 has eight preset styles from which you can choose in the HTML Styles panel, as the following illustrates. You can access the HTML Styles panel by any of the following methods:

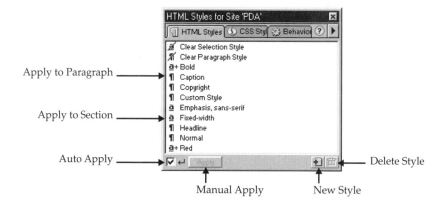

- Select Window | HTML Styles from the menu bar.
- Use the keyboard shortcut CTRL-F11 (Windows) or COMMAND-F11 (Mac).
- Select the HTML Styles button on the Launcher.
- Select the HTML styles button on the bottom-right corner of the document screen. It looks like a yellow paragraph symbol.

The HTML Styles panel has a check box in the lower-left corner. Check this box to have the styles automatically apply. If this box isn't checked, you must press the Apply button to apply the style to the text.

The HTML styles are divided into two types designated with ¶ for paragraph styles and an underlined lowercase *a* for selection styles. A paragraph style is applied to the whole paragraph. A selection style is applied to only the selected text.

The following are the default styles and what they do to the text:

Style	What It Does
Clear Selection Style	Removes all formatting from selected text
Clear Paragraph Style	Removes all formatting from paragraph

Style	What It Does
Bold	Applies bold formatting to selected text
Caption	Changes paragraph to Arial/Helvetica/sans serif, size 2, gray #808080, bold, italic, centered
Copyright	Changes paragraph to Georgia/Times New Roman/Times/serif, size 1, italic, centered
Emphasis, sans serif	Changes selected text to Veranda/Arial/Helvetica/sans serif, bold
Fixed Width	Changes selected text to Courier New/Courier/monospace
Headline	Changes paragraph to Veranda/Arial/Helvetica/sans serif, size +2, bold, left-aligned
Normal	Changes paragraph to Georgia/Times New Roman/Times/serif, size +1
Red	Changes selected text color to red #FF0000

The first two styles are helpful in Web designing. The Clear Selection Style removes all text formatting tags for the selected text, and only for the selected text. It places the appropriate tags before and after the selected text, so the surrounding text remains formatted with whatever style you select for it.

The Clear Paragraph Style removes all tags from the paragraph. This makes trying a new style easy and, if you don't like the effect of something you try, it's easy to remove the style quickly and try another one.

Create Custom Styles

The Dreamweaver default styles are only the beginning of the power of HTML styles. The capability to create custom styles lets you create and save styles to apply to other text or other pages. You can design a new style from scratch. You can create a custom style from existing text you formatted. Or, you can create a custom style by editing an existing style and modifying it. If you duplicate a style first, you can save the old style, as well as your new, modified style.

- To create a new style from scratch, open the HTML Styles panel and press the New Style button.
- To create a custom style from existing text, select the text in the document window. Open the HTML Styles panel. Select New Style by pressing the New Style button in the lower-right corner of the HTML Styles panel.
- To modify an existing style, scroll down the list of available styles from the HTML Styles panel. Right-click the style you want to modify, and then choose

Edit from the context menu. Or, you can double-click, but this has the added result of applying the style to any selected text, which might not be your intention.

- To create a new style based on an existing style, scroll down the list of available styles from the HTML Styles panel. Highlight a style (as opposed to double-clicking it as you did previously). Press the New Style button. This copies the existing style and enables you to create a new style based on the existing one.

Once you open the HTML Styles panel by one of the previous methods, you can define a new custom style.

1. Enter a name for the style if you're creating a new style.

2. Choose whether this style applies to either a selection or a paragraph.

3. Choose whether this style adds to the existing style of the selected text or paragraph or whether it clears the existing style.

4. Choose a font group from the drop-down list, or you can click Edit Font List to add a new font group, as described in the earlier section "Setting Fonts" in this chapter.

5. Choose a font size from the drop-down list.

6. Choose a font color by clicking the color swatch button. The color picker pops up. Choose a color, as described in the earlier section "Font Colors" in this chapter. Remember, the color choices on the Color Picker screen are browser-safe colors.

7. Click *B* for Bold or *I* for Italic. If you click the Other button, you can select from the other font styles also discussed earlier in this chapter, in the "Font Styles" section.

8. If you chose to have this style apply to a paragraph, you can choose the Paragraph attributes, such as Paragraph, Headings 1 through 6, and Preformatted. You can also select to left, right, or center align the paragraph.

9. Click OK to save your custom style.

To apply the custom style:

1. From the document screen, highlight the text you want to change.

2. Open the HTML Styles panel.

3. Scroll down to the style you want to apply and click it. If you have the Auto Apply check box checked, the style applies immediately. If you don't have

the Auto Apply check box selected, press the Apply button to get the style to take effect.

4. Figure 9-2 shows how easy it is to apply your custom styles.

Using HTML styles can give you power and flexibility for designing your Web sites. These styles help with consistency across pages and lead to a professionally designed appearance to your work.

Spell Checking

Were you the fifth grade spelling bee champion, or do you struggle and look at a word, thinking it just doesn't look quite right? Are typos scattered throughout your text? Dreamweaver can't catch all typos and it won't catch the misuse of "by" for "bye" or other such words, but it can help those of us who struggle with spelling and have come to rely on spelling checkers as a way of life.

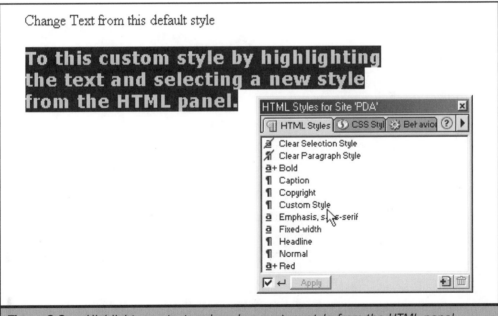

Figure 9-2. *Highlight your text and apply a custom style from the HTML panel*

Before you can spell check, you need to pick which dictionary you want to use. The following illustration shows how to set the Dictionary in the Preferences box.

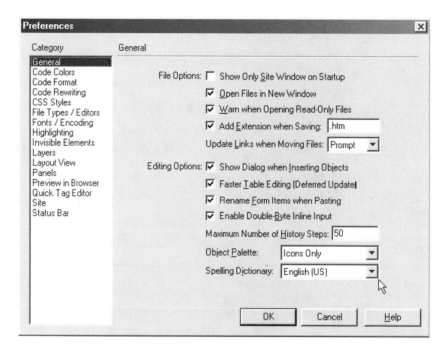

To select which dictionary to use

1. Select Edit | Preferences from the menu bar.
2. Select General from the Category list box.
3. Select the dictionary you want to use from the drop-down list of dictionaries.
4. Click OK.

Now you can run the spelling checker.

1. Open a document.
2. Select Text | Check Spelling from the menu bar or use the keyboard shortcut SHIFT-F7.
3. The spelling checker stops at the first word that isn't in the dictionary.
4. The word is highlighted in the document window and shows in the Check Spelling dialog box, as the following shows.

The spell checker will highlight the ▮mispelled▮ word and offer suggestions to correct the spelling

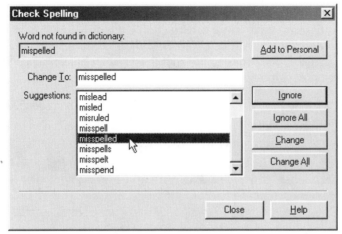

5. If you know the word is spelled correctly, you can press the Add to Personal button to add the word to your dictionary. This adds the word to the Personal.dat file. Your personal dictionary isn't site-specific, so you can access the same entries for all your sites. Both the main dictionary you selected and your personal dictionary are used to spell check your documents.

6. If the word is spelled correctly, but you don't want to add it to your personal dictionary, press the Ignore button. The spelling checker ignores the word this once.

7. You can also press the Ignore All button to have the spelling checker ignore all instances of this word in this document.

8. If the word is misspelled, you can choose from one of the suggested spellings. Highlight the suggestion you want to use and press the Change button.

9. You can also press the Change All button to change every instance of the misspelling.

10. If you don't agree with any of the suggestions, you can type the correct spelling in the Change To box, and then press the Change button.

11. When the spelling check is complete, a dialog box pops up that says Spelling Check Completed.

12. Click OK.

BUILDING YOUR SITE'S PAGES

Summary

Writers spend their whole lives searching for the perfect words to express themselves. Web designers can spend their entire careers perfecting how they integrate typography and content into their sites. If you're a Web developer who's responsible for both the content and the presentation, understand that this chapter has only been the tip of the iceberg. Some key points to remember are the following:

- When writing for the Web, keep it brief, informative, and focused on key points, rather than broad concepts.
- Most Web users skim, rather than read, a site's entire content.
- Fonts are grouped into categories of similar type. Each font also has faces, such as italics and bold, which vary the font's appearance, while it's still recognizable as belonging to that font family.
- Text can be modified from the text menu and the Property Inspector.
- Whenever you set a font's attributes from the Property Inspector or text menu, you use deprecated code, such as <font> tags. Although deprecated by the W3C, these tags remain functional in most browsers and are still widely used.

The next chapter explains how to turn text into lists.

Chapter 10

Creating Lists

When planning your weekend, you don't write a narrative passage about the splendor of the green grass you're planning to mow, the brackish green water of the pool you've been meaning to treat for the last month, and the towering height of the ladder you need to climb to fix the satellite dish on your roof. No, you write a list, breaking each item down into its necessary components—mow lawn, treat pool, fix dish. Lists bring order and structure to your world.

Lists can bring the same order and structure to the online world. Quality content, concisely presented, catches the readers' eye and draws them into your Web site. Web readers want instant gratification. Does your Web site tell them what they want to know? If the answer is yes, they'll stay and read. If it's no, they'll click by. Judicious use of lists can help present your content in a clear, concise manner to help visitors make that instant decision.

Creating Unordered (Bulleted) Lists

An unordered list is commonly used when the sequence of the list items isn't important. Many of you recognize this as a bulleted list from word processing programs. Examples of this would be items on a grocery list—it doesn't matter if you put the milk in the cart first or the chicken, as long as you leave the store with everything you need. On the Web, you could use an unordered list to note the advantages of your product. You want to cover all the key features, but you're not instructing people on how to actually use the product.

Bulleted lists can be easily created from text you already entered or the list can be created as you enter the text manually. To make an unordered list:

1. To configure the list, and then type the list items, position the cursor where you want to start the list.

2. If you're converting existing text into a list, select the text.

3. On the Property Inspector, click the Unordered List button, as the following shows. You can also access this from Text | List | Unordered List on the menu bar.

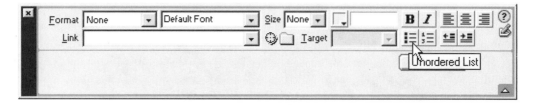

4. Type in the text of your list. Notice the list items are spaced more closely together than paragraphs. Figure 10-1 shows the line spacing between list items versus the spacing between regular paragraphs.

- This is a unordered list
- It uses the standard bullet
- Notice how the lines are more closely spaced than in a regular paragraph. Dreamweaver will also automatically wrap text to the next line without adding a bullet for list items that are longer than one line.

This is the line spacing for text in regular paragraphs. Dreamweaver will automatically wrap the text in regular paragraphs. Notice how the spacing between paragraphs is futher apart than the spacing between list items.

Here is the second regular paragraph. Notice the spacing between paragraphs is greater than the spacing between list items.

Figure 10-1. *Shows an unordered list*

5. To end the list after you enter all the items, press ENTER (RETURN on the Mac) twice or click the Unordered List button again to deselect it.

If you switch to one of the code views, you see how unordered lists are coded in HTML. The list, in its entirety, is created with a `<ul> </ul>` tag pair (*ul* stands for *unordered list*). Each item within the list is enclosed between a *list item* tag pair, `<li> </li>`. In fact, the closing tag isn't required for list items in HTML 4 but, as noted in Chapter 4, getting in the habit of closing your tags is good practice. Dreamweaver uses tags by closing tags by default.

Formatting Unordered Lists

As with every other aspect of Web development, lists are subject to change. To add another item to your list, press ENTER or RETURN to jump to the next line and begin typing. To insert an item in the middle of the list, go to the end of the line above the desired position of the new item. Press ENTER or RETURN, and then type in the new item.

You might decide your list looks a little plain. To dress it up a bit, select your list or portions thereof, and apply text formatting such as bold or italics. You can apply any of the character formatting options on the Text | Style menu.

Be more cautious about adding paragraph formatting. If you apply a paragraph style to the text from the Text | Paragraph Format menu—or by using the Paragraph Format list from the Property Inspector—Dreamweaver inserts extra lines between the list items, just as paragraphs have extra lines between them. If you're only trying to get a larger font size, use the Property Inspector to increase the font size instead of choosing a Heading style. This preserves the spacing of the list.

Notice in Figure 10-1, when text wraps to the next line within one list item, Dreamweaver indents the subsequent lines without adding another bullet. You can also force a line break, as discussed in Chapter 9, by using the SHIFT-ENTER (Windows) or SHIFT-RETURN (Mac). This forces the text to the next line, indents it, but doesn't add another bullet.

You may also decide to remove the list formatting altogether. To do this, select the entire list and click the Unordered List button to deselect it. The text itself remains, but the bullets and formatting of the list are removed.

Editing Bullet Symbols

When you create your unordered lists, you might have noticed the bullet symbol used for each item was a solid circle. Circles are nice and all, but your site's design may be crying out for something more. If your site is designed in a blocky style, for example, you might want to use square bullets. Dreamweaver enables you to change the symbol used for bullets. The options for changing the bullet type are the following:

- **Default**—this defaults to the browser's choice, usually the solid circle

- **Bullet**—the standard solid circle

- **Square**—a solid square

These styles can be applied to the entire list or on an item-by-item basis. To change a bullet symbol:

1. Select an item on the list by placing the insertion point anywhere on the item. Or, you can highlight an item on the list.

2. Select Text | List | Properties from the menu or the List Item button on the Property Inspector. If the List Item box isn't showing, make sure you have only *one* item on the list selected. If you select the entire list or more than one item, the List Item box is grayed out. If you have only one item selected, make sure you have the Property Inspector expanded. Click the down facing triangle on the lower-right corner of the Property Inspector, as shown in Figure 10-2.

Note   *If your list is contained in a table, the List Item button won't display on the Property Inspector. In this case, use the menu instead.*

3. From the List Properties box, click the style you want from the Style drop-down list. The following illustration shows the options on the List Properties box.

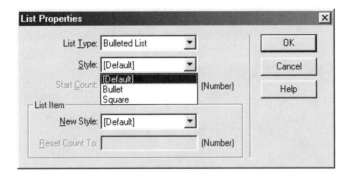

4. Click OK.

5. All the list items have the selected style applied.

To change a bullet for a single list item or a list item and any subsequent items:

1. Select an item on the list by placing the insertion point on the item. Or, you can highlight an item on the list.

2. On the Property Inspector, click the List Item box or select Text | List | Properties from the menu bar.

3. From the List Properties box, select an option from the New Style drop-down list. This changes the one item you selected and any following items. The items

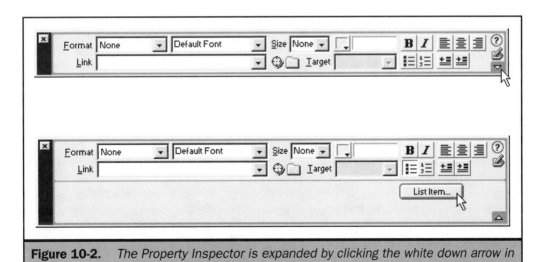

Figure 10-2. *The Property Inspector is expanded by clicking the white down arrow in the lower right-hand corner*

above it on the list still have the symbol you previously selected for them. The following illustrates the options on the New Style drop-down list.

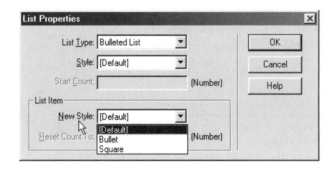

4. Click OK.

The symbol you pick from the New Style drop-down list overrides the setting you select for the whole list in the drop-down list for Styles. Even if you change the Styles for the entire list, the items formatted with the New Styles drop-down list keep the New Style selection unless you change it.

Using Images as Bullets

Maybe even a square bullet isn't enough. If you want to totally customize the appearance of your lists, you can use a graphic image as a bullet, as seen in Figure 10-3. To do this, you need to use CSS to define a list style that uses a bullet image. CSS is covered in Chapter 17. While extra steps are involved in setting up a list style, this option does leave you wide open to creating unique bullets that are integrated with your site design in terms of color, shape, and additional effects. The downside to using CSS for list styles is Netscape 4.0 and earlier browsers won't render the style. Instead, older browsers use the default bullet. Netscape 6 has better CSS support and renders the graphic buttons.

Another solution to create a bulleted list effect doesn't use HTML lists or CSS at all. Rather than using the list formatting, put the text into a two-column table. In the first column, add the bullet image using the Insert Image icon in the Objects panel or Insert | Image from the menu (CTRL-ALT-I in Windows, CMD-OPT-I on the Mac). In the second column, enter the text of the list item. The table provides space between the bullet and the list item, and wraps the text within the second column, so it appears indented.

A third alternative is simply to format the text as a paragraph and add a bullet image before the first word. This is the least favorable option, however, because it doesn't allow for space between the bullet and the text, and it won't wrap attractively if the list item is multiple lines in length. You can manually piece this together using a transparent spacer image after the bullet and manually wrapping the text using the preformatted text style. You need to wrap your text to accommodate low-resolution settings to avoid awkward wrapping, but this can look equally as awkward when

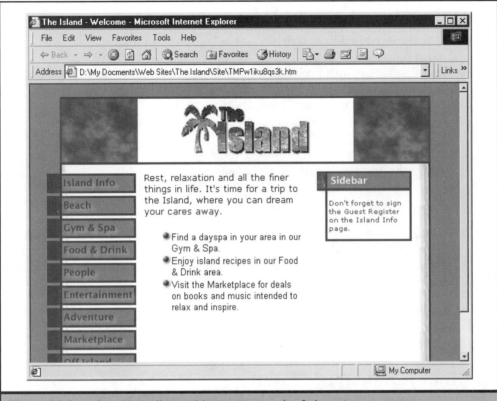

Figure 10-3.   *Graphic bullets add an extra touch of class to your pages*

viewed at higher resolutions because of the extra white space created along the right margin of this text. In short, it's generally not worth the effort to take this approach when faster and better options are available.

You can create your own bullets using a graphics package, such as Fireworks or Photoshop. If you're not the creative type, you can find hundreds of bullet designs on the Web.

> *If you're looking for clipart on the Web, a good starting point is Barry's Clip Art Server, at **http://www.barrysclipart.com**. Along with its own collection, this site has links to dozens of other clipart sites. Another good resource is bellsnwhistles, at **http://www.bellsnwhistles.com**.*

Graphic images are covered in detail in Chapter 12 and Chapter 13.

Creating Numbered Lists

Numbered lists are referred to as ordered lists in HTML terminology. These lists are used when the sequence of the items is important. Examples of this would be instructions on how to do a project or a list of companies ranked by size.

Creating a numbered list follows the same steps as described previously. You simply select the ordered list option instead of the unordered list option.

1. Open the document screen and place the cursor where you want to start the list.

2. On the Property Inspector, click the Ordered List button. You can also access this by selecting Text | List | Ordered List on the menu.

3. Type in the text you want in your list.

4. Apply text formatting, as described earlier.

5. You can also make a list by selecting text you already entered into a document. Highlight the text and press the Ordered List button on the Property Inspector, or select Text | List | Ordered List from the menu. This creates an ordered list from your text.

The HTML code for ordered lists is similar to that of unordered lists. List items are still contained in `<li>  </li>` tag pairs. For ordered lists, however, the list is contained within an ordered list tag pair, `<ol>  </ol>`.

Using Other Numbering Styles

You aren't limited to numbering your ordered list with the standard 1, 2, 3 numbering system. You can choose from the following options on the List Properties dialog box:

- Default (which is 1, 2, 3 unless you change this)
- Number (1, 2, 3, ...)
- Roman Small (i, ii, iii, ...)
- Roman Large (I, II, III, ...)
- Alphabet Small (a, b, c, ...)
- Alphabet Large (A, B, C, ...)

Once again, you can change the numbering style using the same method as you used to change the bullet symbol previously discussed. You can use any of the previous numbering styles, but you can't use alternative styles, such as parentheses around a number or letter or a number followed by a dash. You're limited by the previously shown choices. As always, the end user's browser determines how your list is viewed.

To change a numbering style:

1. Select an item on the list by placing the insertion point anywhere on the item. Or, you can highlight an item on the list.

2. On the Property Inspector, click the List Item dialog box or choose Text | List | Properties. If the list is contained within a table, you can only use the menus.

3. From the List Properties box, click the style you want from the Style drop-down list.

4. Click OK.

All the list items have the selected style applied.

Editing an Ordered List

One of the nicest features of an ordered list is its capability to renumber itself when items are added or deleted. To add an item in the middle of the list, go to the end of the line above the desired position of the new item. Press ENTER or RETURN. Type in the new item. The new item is inserted and Dreamweaver automatically renumbers your list.

To change the order of an item in the list, you can use the drag-and-drop method. Highlight the item to move and drag it to the new position while holding down the left mouse button. Release the mouse button and the item is then inserted in the new location. The list is automatically renumbered.

To change the number or character the list starts with, type a number or character into the text box labeled Start Count. You can also reset the number or character used under New Styles, or start a new numbering scheme in the middle of a list. Type a number or character in the text box labeled Reset Count To on the List Properties box under the List Item section.

Creating Definition Lists

If you're creating a glossary or presenting key points with explanation, you have several presentation choices. An unordered list is one possibility. A definition list is another. *Definition lists* are commonly formatted on multiple lines, with the key term—called the *definition term*—flush left on one line, and the definition itself indented on a line underneath, as shown in Figure 10-4.

Definition lists are formatted differently than the more commonly used ordered and unordered lists. For that reason, they must be entered into Dreamweaver a bit differently. To make a definition list:

1. Place the insertion point on the page where you want to start the definition list.

2. Select Text | List | Definition List from the menu bar.

3. Type the word or term to be defined.

4. Press ENTER or RETURN.

5. Type in the definition.

6. Press ENTER or RETURN.

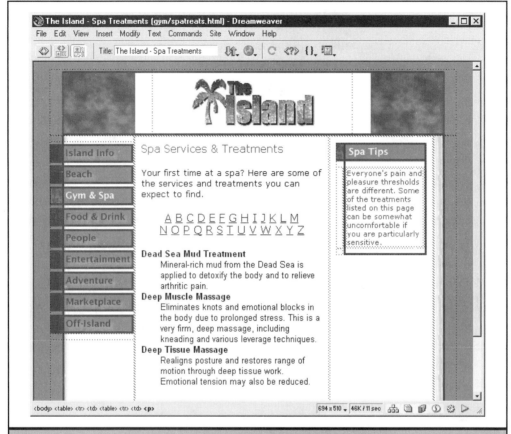

Figure 10-4. *Definition lists aren't used as commonly as ordered and unordered lists, but can be quite useful for glossaries or FAQs*

7. Continue in the same manner to enter all the terms you want to define.

8. To end the list, press ENTER or RETURN twice.

If you look at the code for your definition list, you see it's quite different from that of the other types of lists. As seen in Figure 10-5, the entire list is contained within a definition list tag pair, `<dl>  </dl>`. The term being defined is enclosed within a definition term tag pair, `<dt>  </dt>`. Finally, the definition itself is contained within a definition data tag pair, `<dd>  </dd>`.

Once you create a definition list, you can apply additional text formatting, such as using boldface for the terms.

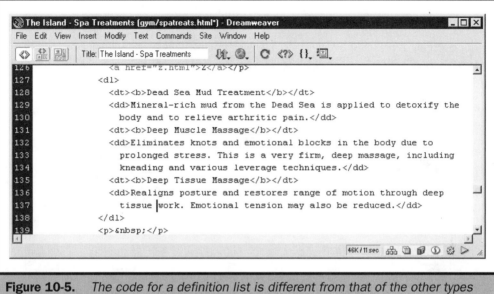

Figure 10-5.   *The code for a definition list is different from that of the other types of lists*

Other Types of Lists

Two other types of lists are available in Dreamweaver. Menu and directory lists were used in earlier versions of HTML, but they never took hold. Current browsers render these as unordered lists, and the tags for menu and directory lists have been deprecated in recent HTML recommendations. To create either of these lists, select Text | List | Properties, and choose your desired list type from the List Properties dialog box.

Creating Nested Lists

Lists aren't always one-level deep. If you're outlining a project or giving step-by-step instructions, you may want to provide additional information that relates to a specific list item, but isn't related to the flow of the list itself. This is where nested lists come in handy. *Nested lists* enable you to insert sublists within lists.

Figure 10-6 provides an example of a nested list. Key points are at the first level of the list. Points relating to those items are nested below them and automatically assume a different bullet style. You can even combine different types of lists and list styles within a nested list. Let's say you're giving a step-by-step list of instructions about how to do something on the computer. If a particular step has different instructions for

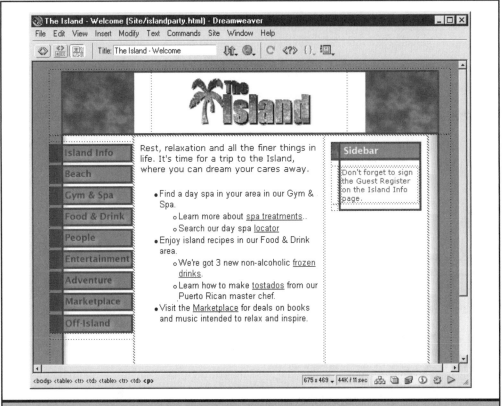

Figure 10-6.   *Nested lists are useful for outlines and to expound further on key points in a list*

different browsers, you could nest an unordered list within an ordered list, so the step-by-step instructions are numbered and the alternate choices are indented and bulleted. Another example is a traditional outline format, where items use Roman numerals (Romance Large) at the top level, uppercase letters (Alphabet Large) at the second level, Arabic numerals at the third, and so on.

To create a nested list:

1. Select text you want to reformat from within an existing list.

2. In the Property Inspector, choose the Indent button or select Text | Indent from the menu.

3. Dreamweaver creates a separate list with the original list's properties.

4. Go to the List Properties box to choose a different list type from the drop-down list.

5. Click OK.

Remember, it's important to indent the selected list items before changing the list type or style. If you forget this step, Dreamweaver breaks the selected items into a separate list that's formatted in line with the original list. If more list items are below the selected items, they are then broken into yet a third separate list.

You can exploit this methodology to add space between list items in a nested list. If you want the effect of more spacing between the lists, but you don't want the third list to start a new numbering sequence, you can change the start number of the third list. To do this, follow these steps:

1. Select the first item on the third list by placing the insertion point anywhere on the item. Or, you can highlight the item.

2. On the Property Inspector, click the List Item button. If the List Item box isn't showing, expand the Property Inspector by clicking the white arrow in the bottom-right corner.

3. Enter the sequential number in the Start Count box to continue the ordering from the first list.

4. Click OK.

If you decide not to nest a list you already nested, you can use the Outdent button on the Property Inspector to remove the indentation and make the selected items part of the main list. Select the nested list and press the Outdent button on the Property Inspector. Or, you can select the nested list and chose Text | Outdent from the menu.

Summary

Experiment with using lists on your Web page. Change the style of the list, preview in your browser, and see which styles convey the effect you want. You can use many combinations of list styles to help present your information clearly and concisely to help the user quickly find the information he seeks on your Web site.

Here are some key points to remember:

■ Lists are used to break text content into manageable snippets, which are easily scanned by the end user.

■ Unordered lists created bulleted lists. You can use CSS to use graphic bullets rather than the default bullets, but these won't be viewable in older versions of Netscape. To work around this shortcoming, you must use tables or paragraph formatting, rather than an unordered list.

■ Ordered lists create numbered lists. You can set the number style and starting value for the list.

■ Definition lists create a unique type of list, which contains a term or key point, with the definition indented beneath.

■ Lists can be nested, with a mix of ordered and unordered lists, and list styles grouped together.

Chapter 11 introduces links, your key to becoming part of the Web chain.

The Complete Reference

Dreamweaver 4

Chapter 11

Links

One of the biggest advantages the Web has over other media is its capability to direct people quickly from place to place. Imagine logging on to the Web to read up on South America. Among other facts, you find an interesting reference to the coffee bean crops in Colombia. This leads to a narrative about the popularity of coffee in the United States, and one of the leading coffee purveyors in the U.S. is Starbucks. You just traveled from Colombia to Seattle in less than five minutes—and you realize you could go for a double latte right about now.

Links are what enable you to move from South America to a discussion of crops in various countries, which leads to a site about coffee beans, and then to another site about coffee exports to the U.S. and Americans' almost patriotic love of a good cup of Joe, which, of course, leads to Starbucks, the purveyor of coffee on almost every street corner in the land. Links are the lifeblood of the World Wide Web. Links are what enable people to surf from site to site, one concept to another, no matter how obscure the path might seem. Links are what make up the click to yet another neat site and even from page to page within your own site.

URLs

An URL (pronounced *Earl*) is a Uniform Resource Locator. URLs are unique addresses on the Web, used to reference every site, page, and even sections within a page, which provide a way to link places on the Web. URLs are made up of different parts in the format of *Protocol://server/path/filename#anchor*, such as **http://www.pendragn.com/ island/islandparty.html#top**

- **Scheme**—The protocol used to access the item. The scheme is always separated from the rest of the URL by a colon. The most common scheme is HyperText Transport Protocol (HTTP), which is used to navigate to sites on the Web. Other schemes include

  - **mailto**—opens the user's e-mail application to send a message to the address identified by the link. A mailto link looks like `mailto:jennk@pendragn.com`. Notice no slashes are between the scheme and the address.

  - **ftp**—File Transfer Protocol, which is used to access a file on an FTP server. This is commonly used to link to a file users can download to their computers.

  - **news**—links to a Usenet newsgroup. A link with this protocol opens the user's news application to read the specified newsgroup.

  - **javascript**—links to and executes an external JavaScript.

  - **gopher**—a server for text documents that contain no graphics or links. All files are presented in a file directory structure. While gopher has been available since the early '90s, it never gained much favor, in part because of the lack of direct linking. Most of the common browsers are able to access a gopher server, however, without launching a separate application.

- **telnet**—a terminal emulation protocol that provides user access to a remote computer system.

■ **Server**—This is the address of the server providing the access. Addresses use an Internet Protocol (IP) address consisting of four sets of numbers, separated by dots, such as 206.117.28.117. IP addresses can be mapped to domain names, which are much easier to remember. This IP address is mapped to my domain, **www.pendragn.com.**

■ **Path**—The path directs the link through the site hierarchy into the proper directory. The path isn't necessary if the page is at the site root.

■ **Filename**—The specific file being sought by the link.

- In the case of a Web page, the filename is usually filename.htm, name.html, or name.asp.

- If the link is to an image file—as might be the case if you're linking a thumbnail image to a larger view of the image—the filename would be name.jpg or name.gif. Links to images display only the destination image in a browser window. It won't display any HTML file in which the image might be contained.

> **Tip**
>
> *If the link is to the main page of a site, the filename may be left off the link. The server will know to call the index.htm or other default page for that server.*

■ **Named Anchor**—A named anchor is only used to point to a specific (named) section of a page. The rest of the page is still available, but the anchor reference in the link causes the page to scroll automatically to the named anchor point.

Absolute URLS

Absolute URLs are used anytime you want to link to another site or access another protocol scheme from your site. Absolute links are the key to the Web because they enable users to move from site to site. You can link to virtually any site or page on the Web using absolute links.

> **Note**
>
> *Most Web developers welcome links to their site from others. Unless you're linking to a large commercial site, however, it's common courtesy to drop a note to other developers, informing them of the link. If the Webmaster asks you to remove your link, you should comply with the request ASAP or risk having a complaint made to your server host.*

An absolute link requires the scheme and server to be specified. An example of an absolute address would be **http://www.pendragn.com/islandparty.html**. As previously stated the path and/or filename are only required if you're linking to a file other than the default page of the site or to a page contained within a directory off the site root.

Absolute URLs are easy to use because they provide a complete path. They also enable you to link to other protocols, such as if you want to allow your users to download a file from your server using FTP or to provide a link to submit feedback via e-mail.

Current browsers don't require you to type the http:// portion of a URL when you're surfing the Web. This doesn't mean you can leave those out of an absolute address when coding in HTML, however. The protocol scheme is a required portion of the link path.

The downside to absolute URLs is their integrity can't be maintained within Dreamweaver. If any part of the URL changes—the domain, the path, or the filename—you must manually edit any page containing a link to that URL. Because the Web is ever-changing, you can count on having to update your absolute links on a regular basis.

To modify all the references on your site to a specific URL, you can use the Find and Replace feature, as explained in Chapter 4.

The lack of link maintenance for absolute links is the primary reason you should only use them to link to external sites or other protocol. For links to other pages within your site, you should use relative URLs.

Relative URLs

Relative URLs are used to link to pages or sections of pages relative to the current site or page. Because these links always refer to another file within the site, the protocol scheme and server aren't required as part of the URL. Two types of relative links exist: document relative and site relative.

Document-Relative URLs

Document-relative URLs provide the location of the linked file relative to the current document. Because the domain is already known, you only need to include the pertinent path information to access the linked file.

For example, if you're at the index page of the Pendragn site, **http://www.pendragn.com/index.html**, and you want to link to the **news.html** file in the same directory, the link reference would be

```
href="news.html"
```

The browser knows to look for the news.html document in the same directory as the current document. If the **news.html** page were in the info directory, however, the reference would be

```
href="/info/news.html"
```

specifying that relative to the directory of the current file—**index.html**—you need to move to the info directory first to find the linked file—**news.html**.

Let's say you want to do the reverse, link from **news.html**, which is contained in the info directory, to **index.html**, which is in the site root. To do this, you use a double dot to move up a folder. The link would look like this

```
href="../index.html"
```

indicating the file is located one directory above the current file. If your starting point were a page deeper into the site, the path would contain a series of dots at each level of the path to move a directory at a time toward the site root. Let's say you're on a page located absolutely at **http://www.pendragn.com/info/books/dreamweaver/tcr.html.** We want to link from that page to the index.html page located at **http://www. pendragn.com/index.html.** Here's the link:

```
href="../../../index.html"
```

Each set of dots takes you up one level in the directory structure from the dreamweaver directory up to the books directory, to the info directory, and, finally, up to the site root.

To use document-relative addresses in Dreamweaver, you first need to define your site, as explained in Chapter 5, and you must save your files within the local site root folder you defined. If you haven't saved your file before you try to link to the current page, Dreamweaver prompts you to save the file first.

Site-Relative Links

Although document-relative links are the most common—and the easiest to understand if you're new to Web development—site-relative links are convenient for extremely large sites. A site-relative link always uses the site root as the starting point for the link path, instead of the location of the current document. To signify this, a site-relative link always begins with a forward slash (/). To use the earlier example, if you want to link from the **news.html** page in the info directory to the **tcr.html** page located at **http://www.pendragn.com/info/books/dreamweaver/tcr.html,** a site-relative link would look like this:

```
href="/info/books/dreamweaver/tcr.html"
```

Now, it might seem that using the document-relative link would be easier, which would eliminate the need to preface the link with the leading slash and the directory name of the current file. If you're operating a large site, however, and you frequently move directories, this form of linking can actually save time. If you move the **news.html** page to another directory, the link to the **tcr.html** page remains the same because the link path starts at the site root, rather than the location of the **news.html** file.

Some definite downsides exist to site-relative linking. Because these links are reliant on the server to establish the directory structure, testing them locally is harder. If you try to open a page with site-relative links directly in your browser, the links are broken because the browser cannot find a site root. Any images you link to your pages in this manner won't appear, and you cannot navigate from page to page. The only way to test your pages is with the Preview in Browser feature within Dreamweaver. Dreamweaver temporarily interprets them as absolute links when using this feature. Here, too, limitations exist because Dreamweaver only translates the links on the current page, not any pages linked from that page. Therefore, if you use the Preview in Browser feature to test a page and click one of the links, any site-relative links within this next page are then broken.

Unless you absolutely need to use site-relative links, you're better off sticking with the common document-relative links.

Creating Links in Dreamweaver

Links are easy to create in Dreamweaver. While it's important to understand the difference between absolute and relative paths, as well as the two types of relative linking, Dreamweaver takes care of the details, such as calculating how many dots are required to represent the directory structure between pages in a link.

Note   *To test a link, you need to view the file in a browser—either outside Dreamweaver or using the Preview in Browser feature—because links aren't active in the Document window.*

Links can be created with either text or an image as the source or "hot" trigger for the link. To create a link in Dreamweaver:

1. Select the text or image for the source of the link.

2. Assign the link destination.

   - Use the Link field of the Property Inspector to assign the link destination.

   - Use Modify | Make Link (CTRL-L in Windows, CMD-L on the Mac) or click the folder icon to the right of the Link field in the Property Inspector to open the File Selection dialog box. For relative links, navigate to the file you want to assign as the destination of the link. For absolute links, type the complete URL of the destination in the URL field.

In a relative link, the file you select must be within the site folder. If you choose a local file outside the site folder, you're prompted to move the file within the site structure.

3. To make a link site relative, use the File Selector dialog box and change the Relative To setting to Site Root.

To use a previously established link path in a new link, click the down arrow in the Links field and scroll through the list of previously used links, as shown in Figure 11-1. This feature is only available for text links.

The URL you use must have fewer than 255 characters. Try to refrain from using spaces in the addresses.

Using the Point to File Button

Dreamweaver provides yet another way to make a link: the point to file button in the Property Inspector. The Link text box is filled in by dragging your mouse to any file in the Site window or to another open Document window. This method is usually quicker than browsing through the folders searching for the file. To use the point to file method:

1. Select the source text or image for the link.

2. Access the Point-to-File feature in one of the following ways:

   ■ In the Property Inspector, click the Point to File icon.

   ■ Hold down the SHIFT key and drag the mouse from the selection to the desired link destination file.

3. While still holding down the mouse button, drag the mouse until it's over the anchor or link, or over a file in the Site window. As you drag the mouse, you see a line extends from the Point to File button to where you're dragging the mouse. Drag to a file to make a link appears in the text box. Figure 11-2 shows the Point to File method of selecting a link.

4. Release the mouse button. The correct link address is automatically entered into the Link text box.

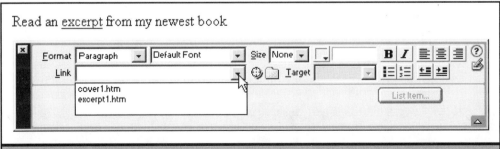

Figure 11-1.   *Enter the URL in the Link text box in the Property Inspector*

BUILDING YOUR SITE'S PAGES

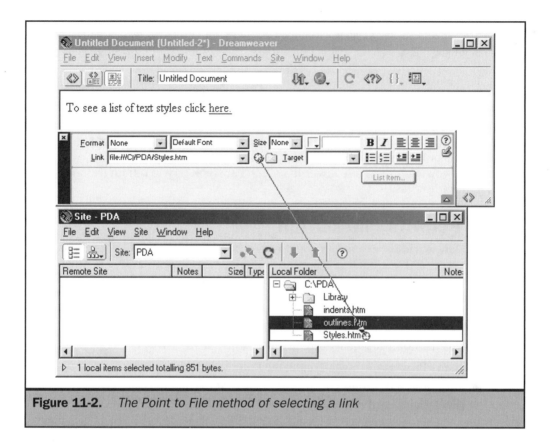

Figure 11-2.   *The Point to File method of selecting a link*

HTML Code for Links

If you switch to one of the code views in Dreamweaver, you can see how a link is coded in HTML. The anchor tag (<a> </a>) anchors the destination file to the source document. An absolute link to the **pendragn.com** site would look like this in HTML code:

```
<a href="http://www.pendragn.com">Pendragn</a>
```

Any text or image that appears between the anchor tag pair becomes the source or "hot" spot for the link. In the case of an image, the code would look like the following:

```
<a href="news.html"><img src=newsbutton.gif></a>
```

Targeting and Formatting Links

Once you establish a link, you can fine-tune it in several ways. The first, of course, is to change the color of the various link states in the Page Properties, as discussed in Chapter 7. Consistent application of color to the links across your pages enables the user to navigate your Web site more easily. If your link colors are inconsistent, you're likely to confuse the user.

You can also change the window or frame in which the linked material appears by changing the link target.

Link Targets

By default, links open in the same window as the current page. At times, however, you might need to target your link to open in a specific location. The target options are

- **_blank**—opens a new browser window containing the linked file.
- **_parent**—used when designing with frames, this loads the linked file into the parent frameset of the source page. Frames are covered in Chapter 15.
- **_self**—loads the linked file into the same window or frame as the source page.
- **_top**—also used with frames, this overrides the frameset to load the linked file into the full browser window.

To add a target attribute to a link in Dreamweaver:

1. Select the text or image you want to use as a link.
2. Establish the link using one of the methods described earlier in this chapter.
3. While the link source is still highlighted, choose a target:
   - From the Property Inspector, select from the Target drop-down menu.
   - From the menu, choose Modify | Link Target, and then select one of the targets.

If you use the menu option, you can also set a target. This feature is used when working with frames. If you assigned names to your frames, you can use that name as a link target to direct linked documents to load in that particular frame. This is covered in Chapter 15.

Formatting Links

As you probably noticed, text links appear underlined by default. This is to provide yet another visual cue—aside from the color—that this text is a link. In the case of image links, the source image has a border around it in the same color as the text link color. While these underlines and borders may be useful in some situations, they can detract from the design of the site.

For images, it's easy to remove the border. In the Property Inspector, click the arrow to expand the Inspector to show all the available options. Then select the image and change the Border setting to zero (0). This removes the link border. This option is so popular, Dreamweaver sets image borders to zero by default. Users still get a visual cue for the link, as the cursor changes to a hand when it moves over the hot image.

Removing the underlining from a text link is a bit trickier because it involves the use of Cascading Style Sheets (CSS). Anytime you use CSS, remember users with older browsers won't necessarily see the resulting page as you intended. That doesn't make this technique any less worthwhile, however, for those users who have recent browsers. To change the link style using CSS:

1. Open the CSS Styles panel by choosing Window | CSS Styles or by pressing SHIFT-F11.

2. Press the New Style icon on the CSS Styles panel, as the following illustrates.

3. In the New Style dialog box, choose Use CSS Selector, and then choose one of the link types from the Selector drop-down menu.

4. In the Style Definition dialog box, which the following illustrates, change the Decoration field to None to remove the underlining from your links.

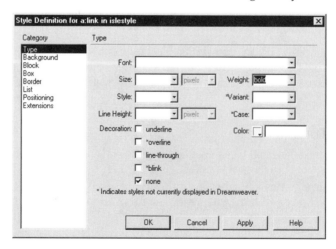

5. If you want to add a different visual cue, such as boldface, for your links, make your changes within the Style Definition dialog box.

6. Click OK to save your style changes.

 Your links still appear underlined in Dreamweaver. To test your style changes, use the Preview in Browser feature.

Figure 11-3 shows a page with the standard underlined links. Figure 11-4 shows the same page with links that were altered using CSS.

As with all CSS styles, this technique may not work properly in all browsers. For more information about CSS, see Chapter 17.

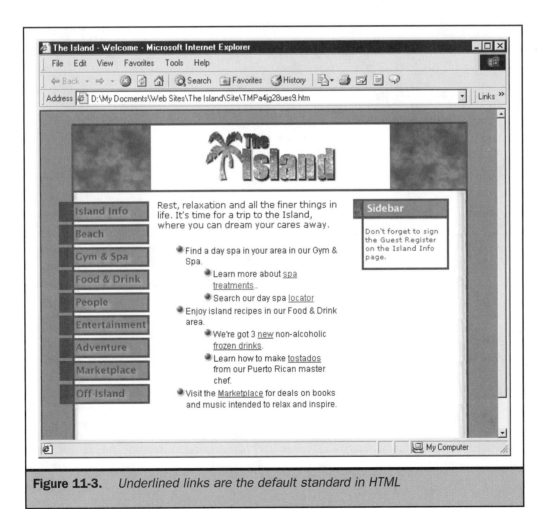

Figure 11-3. *Underlined links are the default standard in HTML*

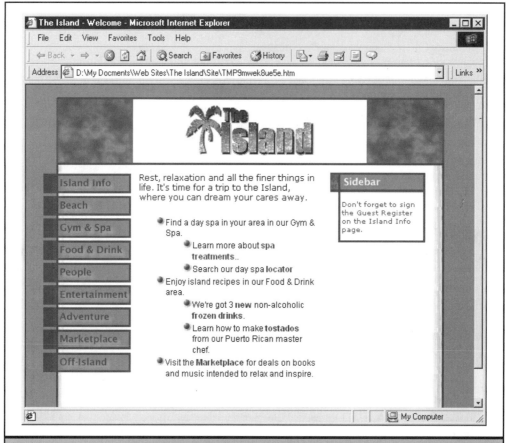

Figure 11-4. *Cascading Style Sheets enable you to change the style of your links*

E-Mail Links

E-mail links enable you to provide support to your users and solicit feedback from them. Rather than expecting users to cut-and-paste an e-mail address into their e-mail application, a mailto link lets them click a link that automatically opens a new e-mail message window from their default mail application. This ease of use facilitates communication.

E-mail links are somewhat unique and can be entered in two ways: using the standard Link field of the Property Inspector or using the E-Mail Link object on the Objects panel. To add an e-mail link using the Objects panel:

1. Place your insertion point where you want the e-mail link to appear.

2. From the Objects panel, choose the Email Link button from the Common category as the following illustrates. If the Object Panel isn't visible, choose Window | Objects to open the Object Panel. Or, you can select Insert | Email Link from the menu bar.

3. The Insert Email Link dialog box then appears, as the following shows.

4. In the Text box, enter the text you want to appear on the page.

5. Enter the e-mail address in the Email text box.

6. Click OK.

Dreamweaver can't verify e-mail addresses, so be sure you type the address properly. If you make a mistake, any e-mail sent using this link will wind up in the Internet version of the dead letter office.

If you already have the text for the e-mail link entered on the page, you can create an e-mail link using the Property Inspector:

1. Select the text for the e-mail link.

2. In the Link field of the Property Inspector enter mailto: followed by the e-mail address, such as `mailto:jennk@pendragn.com`.

You must remember to enter the protocol—mailto—along with a colon before the e-mail address; this isn't added automatically. Unlike other types of protocols, a mailto link doesn't require the forward slashes.

Some e-mail systems use a subject line if you specify one in the mailto link. This not only makes the link fill in the to: field of the e-mail, but also the subject: field. This doesn't work in every mail application, though, so use it with caution. The format of such a mailto link is as follows:

mailto:jennk@pendragn.com?Feedback

Intra-Page Linking

Linking to specific sections of a page enables users to navigate quickly to exactly the content they seek. This type of linking is done with named anchors. An example of using named anchors as links is on a Frequently Asked Questions (FAQ) Web page. All the questions are listed at the top of the page. The answer to each question is given a named anchor, which isn't visible on the page. The questions are linked to the named anchor that corresponds to the proper answer. When a user clicks the link for a question, the page scrolls to the answer. The same effect can be achieved when putting the questions on one page and the answers on another—when the link is clicked, the new page opens and immediately scrolls to the appropriate answer.

An extra touch is to add a link under each answer to take users back to the top of the page, so they can review the list of questions. This is also done using a named answer, in this case, pointing to the top of the page.

To create a named anchor, you must first give the anchor point a name:

1. Place the cursor where you want to insert the named anchor. Placing the named anchor one line above the content to which you're directing the user is usually best. This provides a bit of extra space at the top of the browser screen to help the user's eye find the content.

2. Click the Named Anchor icon in the Invisibles category of the Objects panel. Or, you can select Insert | Invisible Tags | Named Anchor from the menu. The Insert Named Anchor dialog box pops up, as seen in Figure 11-5.

3. Type a name for the anchor in the Anchor Name text box.

4. Click OK.

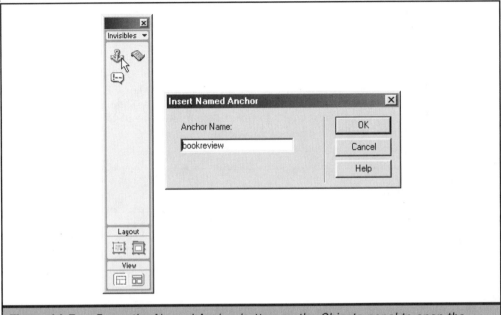

Figure 11-5. *Press the Named Anchor button on the Objects panel to open the Insert Named Anchor dialog box*

If you set your preferences to display invisible tags, you see a yellow anchor icon in your document, representing the named anchor. This icon won't appear in the document when it's viewed in a browser, but only serves as a visual cue for the developer.

Once you set an anchor point, you can link to it from any other page or even another site. To link to a Named Anchor:

1. Select the text or image to serve as a source for the link.

2. In the Property Inspector, type the destination link.

- If you're linking to the named anchor from the same page, type the anchor name preceded by the pound (#) sign, such as #books.

- If you're linking to the named anchor from another page, type the destination link as follows: news.html#books.

- If you're linking to a named anchor from another site, type the destination URL as follows: http://www.pendragn.com/info/news.html#books.

For text links, you can click the down arrow at the end of the Link box to scroll through a list of previously used links and anchors. You can also use the Point to File method by dragging the cursor to the named anchor icon on the page. Dreamweaver automatically scrolls down the page to get to an anchor that isn't visible.

Link Checking

Few things are more aggravating to a Web user than clicking a broken link. Once you design your Web site, you should check your links to make certain they're all valid links. Using the Link Checker is discussed in detail in Chapter 6.

Summary

Links are what connect you to the Web chain. Without them, you're an island in the vast Internet. With them, you become part of the global online community. When creating links on your pages, remember:

- Absolute links are used to link to other sites.
- Relative links are used to link within your site.
- You can target your links to open in other browser windows or in specific frames of a frameset.
- You can change the appearance of links using Cascading Style Sheets.
- Named anchors enable you to point to specific sections of a page.

The next chapter covers images and how to add graphics to your Web site.

The Complete Reference

Chapter 12

Images

The use of images in Web pages, when applied judiciously, can enhance the user experience. Images can add interest and draw the eye to important points on a page, supplying important congruity in a site or maintaining a theme. Images can help the user follow the flow of information in a logical manner.

Images on your Web pages can simply be eye candy or serve a purpose, but they can also be a distraction when used inappropriately. Or, they can drive users away if they're too large and take forever to load. Learning which format to use for an image is a start. The quality of your image can make or break a site, depending on the audience and the needs of the particular Web site.

Choosing an Image Editor

Dreamweaver lets you choose the editor you want to open from within Dreamweaver to edit images. Choose Edit | Preferences and click the File Types | Editors option.

In the bottom section of the dialog window, you see Extensions. Click the extension, and then the plus sign (+) in the Editor section. A window opens, so you can find and select the executable file of the editor of your choice. For PNG files, I have Fireworks as the browser to open. I use Photoshop to edit TIF files (although I wouldn't use a TIF file in a Web page). For illustration purposes, look in the Extension side of the dialog window. There's no option for a TIF file. To add a file format and select an editor, follow these steps:

1. Click the + button in the Extension section of the Preferences dialog window.

2. Type in the format you want to add.

3. Click the + button on the Editor side.

4. Browse for the executable file of the editor you want to use to edit the new format.

5. Click OK when you finish.

Placing Fireworks 4 HTML Code Into a Dreamweaver 4 Web Page

You can get your Fireworks code into a Dreamweaver Web page in two different ways. You can simply use an insert command, or you can copy and paste into the correct areas. To insert Fireworks 4 HTML code into Dreamweaver, follow these steps:

1. Open Dreamweaver 4, choose File | Open, and open the file where you want to use the Fireworks HTML code.

2. Place your cursor where you want the code inserted.

3. Choose Insert | Interactive Images | Fireworks HTML. Or, you can use the Insert Fireworks HTML icon in the Common section of the Object panel.

4. In the window that opens, click the Browse button. Navigate to the folder containing the Fireworks code and click Open.

5. Choose File | Preview in Browser, or click the Globe Icon on the same row as the HTML code icons below the menu bar, and then select the browser you want to view in.

6. Choose File | Save As and save your file.

To copy-and-paste code from a Fireworks HTML page into Dreamweaver takes some knowledge of code. For instance, JavaScript code is placed in the <head> and in the <body> sections. For specifics on how to place Fireworks code containing JavaScript, see Chapter 41.

Optimizing Images from Within Dreamweaver

If you decide you want to change the optimization settings of an image, you can access a version of Fireworks optimization settings from Dreamweaver. To do this, follow these steps:

1. Open a Web page in Dreamweaver that has images on it. Or, make a new document and insert some images. If you make a new page, save it at least once before you try to edit images.

2. Choose Commands | Optimize Image in Fireworks. If a window comes up that says you need to save, it's because you didn't save your document in Step 1.

3. A Find Source dialog box opens asking you if you want to use the source image. You also have the option of selecting Always Use Source PNG, Never Use Source PNG, or Ask When Launching. Dreamweaver tries to find the source file. If it can't find the source file, you can browse to locate the PNG or any other format yourself.

 A good idea is to select Always Use Source PNG when the Find Source dialog box opens. This is particularly important when working with JPEG image. Every time you save a JPEG image, you lose more detail and quality.

4. A version of the Optimize panel opens. When you finish making changes, click the Update button. The changes you made are now updated in Dreamweaver.

Editing Images in Dreamweaver Using Fireworks

You can change anything you want in your image. You can change the Fill, Effect, Style—whatever. To edit an image while in Dreamweaver, follow these steps:

1. Open a page in Dreamweaver, and then click an image to edit.

2. In the Properties Inspector (Window | Properties), click the Edit button. Fireworks opens and you're given the opportunity to locate the image file.

3. Make any changes, as you normally would in Fireworks. You'll notice the top bar of the document you're editing your image in says Editing from Dreamweaver on it. When you finish, click the Done button, located to the right of the Editing from Dreamweaver label.

4. Changes you made in Fireworks are updated in Dreamweaver, except for one. If you changed the physical size of the image, this doesn't get automatically updated in the Dreamweaver code. The image may appear distorted or blurry. In the past, you had to change the size manually, but a great new feature has been added in Dreamweaver 4. The Property Inspector has a button called Reset Size. Click the Reset Size button and the size is changed for you.

Editing Images with Other Editors

You would follow the same steps as you did for editing images with Fireworks. The main difference is this: when you click the Edit button, if you have Photoshop as the editor, Photoshop opens and you edit and save as you normally would. The image isn't in a separate window marked Editing from Dreamweaver. You have no Done button to click. You must save before the change appears in Dreamweaver. If you save with a different name, you need to reinsert the image into Dreamweaver. In other words, you must overwrite the original file you inserted.

Image File Formats

The time it takes for your Web site to load depends a great deal on the amount of images and their size. The two most widely used—and the only two fully supported file formats for the Web—are GIF and JPEG files. Understanding the differences is important, so you know when to use which format.

GIF

GIF stands for Graphic Interchange Format, pronounced *JIF*. The GIF compression algorithm works better for line art than for photographs. Not only is GIF better for line art, but it's better for any image with a lot of flat color. When you have images with 256 colors or less, there isn't a loss in quality when the image is compressed because of the lossless compression scheme. GIF was originally designed specifically for online use, developed for CompuServe in the '80s. The compression used is *LZW*, which is a lossless compression. Some of the advantages of GIF compression are

■ Small files
■ Animation capability

- Transparency
- Interlacing

The disadvantage of GIF compression is you're limited to only 256 colors.

Lossless

Lossless refers to the type of compression used. The GIF format uses a lossless compression, which results in no image degradation if the image is 256 colors or less. An LZW compression looks for patterns of data. When a new color is detected, the file size increases. LZW compression works best on flat color. If you're planning to use the GIF format for your images, you should design your graphics accordingly.

Color Palettes

Color palettes are the colors available when you export your image. Adaptive is the best selection in most cases. Here are a few of the color palette options available for the export of a GIF file:

- Adaptive, 256 of the best color choices based on colors in the image
- MAC System, unrelated to image, looks bad
- 216-Browser Safe palette, unrelated colors, looks worse than system palette

Dithering

Dithering repositions colors to try to simulate colors that don't exist in an image. Dithering gives the illusion of new colors by varying the pattern of dots of color.

Interlacing

Interlacing is an option for GIF files you're exporting for use on the Web. When a file is interlaced, it appears *blocky* or blurry, until it loads, enabling the user to see a blurred copy while the image is loading. The alternative is not to use the interlacing object. In this case, nothing will be seen until the entire image loads. The drawback is they need to load fully before they're clear.

Transparency

Transparency is one of the coolest and most useful benefits of a GIF file. You can make the background transparent, so the background color of the canvas (the rectangle around every image) doesn't show, giving the illusion of a shape cut out (it's still a rectangular image). Not only can the background be transparent, but you can also add colors to the transparency. The following image (from Dynamic Graphics Clipper subscription service

CD for February 2001—**www.dgusa.com**) has a white background. By making the white transparent, the same image can be placed on a colored Web page.

Animation

GIF files have the added benefit of being able to be used as an animation. An animated GIF file contains frames with different images, which are all contained in one GIF animation. You add GIF animations to your Web page just like any other image file. No special treatment is required.

Many reasonably priced animation programs are available from Xara 3D, which is great for text as well as for a program I recently discovered, called EZ Motion by Beatware. The animation program you need depends on your needs. For example, Xara 3D is a wonderful and inexpensive program for animating text, including animate lights, but EZ Motion also offers animation for images. Of course, the price increases as functionality increases. If you develop for Flash or send your animations to someone to incorporate into Flash, then you need a program that can export as a SWF file.

Free and Shareware programs are also available for animation. You'll usually lose features and functionality in a free version, but if you don't need much, it's an option. If you own Fireworks or Photoshop, though, you probably won't get anything extra in a free program. In fact, Fireworks and Photoshop probably have more functionality. You can learn more about Fireworks animation capabilities in Chapter 41.

A big plus to using animation when you require a bit of motion is no plug-ins are required and all the major browsers support GIF animations.

JPEG

JPEG stands for Joint Photographic Expert Group. The JPEG compression algorithms work better for photographs than line art. JPEG is pronounced (*Jay-peg*). JPEG images deal with millions of colors

Lossy Compression

A *lossy compression* removes information from an image. JPEGs are compressed and decompressed when viewed, which can result in a longer loading time. You have control over quality settings in the Optimize panel: the higher the quality, the less the compression.

Progressive JPEG

Similar to GIF interlacing, *progressive JPEG* appears blocky and gradually clear. The drawback is progressive JPEG isn't supported by older browsers (before Netscape 2 and IE 3), and shows a broken image.

Don't JPEG a JPEG image, because it loses information each time and gets considerably worse after the second time. JPEG is good for 24-bit color depth, no less.

The following image shows the original piece of art obtained from the Dynamic Graphics subscription service CD. This particular image uses a lot of gradients and large portions of flat-color areas. Because of the gradients, this piece of art is better suited as a JPEG file.

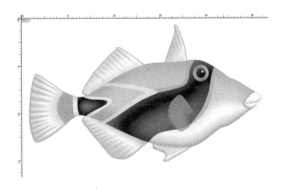

This illustration shows the 4-Up view in Fireworks, showing four different settings. The area, which is being viewed, is the nose part of the fish. Below each of the views, you can see the settings used and the file format. The first view is the original, the second view is GIF using 256 colors without a dither, the third view is the same with 100 percent dither, and the fourth view is a JPEG with a quality setting of 80 percent. Notice the difference in the file sizes. Both GIF files not only look terrible, but the file size is considerably larger than the JPEG. Using the correct file format not only makes an image look better, it also often results in a smaller file size.

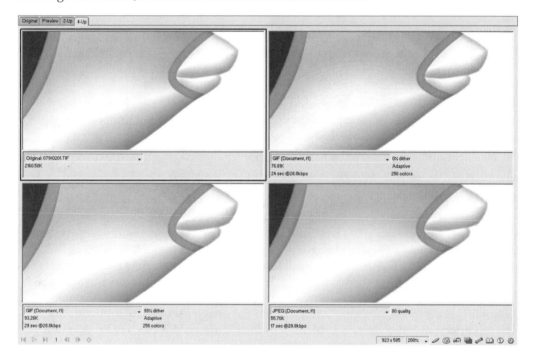

PNG

The World Wide Web Consortium (W3C) has formally endorsed Portable Network Graphics (PNG). The PNG format is the result from developers who wanted an alternative to GIF. The problem was this: the GIF format was free for many years, and then the patent holders starting charging developers for the use of the GIF export technology. PNG is an exciting alternative but, at the present, it's only partially supported by Netscape and IE, which means it isn't a viable option at this point. A PNG file supports full alpha channel and graduated transparency, which the browsers don't support yet.

The PNG format uses a lossless compression and decompresses when viewed. PNG uses many different bit-depths: 8, 24, and 32. It has gamma correction capabilities, which make an image view properly on both Macs and PCs. The PNG format will be a promising technology once it becomes fully accepted.

Choosing Your Images

Because the images used for your site set the mood, the theme, or the purpose of your Web site, it's important to use the right images to convey the message you're trying to deliver or to carry out the theme across the site. Good quality images can be difficult to come by if you aren't a professional photographer or if you aren't an illustrator. Many of us are neither, so good quality sources of art and photography become vital to Web design.

In this section, you're presented with a few of the sources available, but by no means, are the examples exhaustive. Some of the resources for obtaining images I've found useful, easy to find, and reasonably priced are listed here. You can also find recommendations for several plug-ins to enhance the images you use, as well as other useful tools and applications.

Sources for Clip Art

You can visit most computer super stores and find packages containing thousands of pieces of clip art, all of which vary in price. Many of these packages can be a good starting point in developing a logo or adding to a design. As with anything, you get what you pay for. Because many people use the images in these types of packages, they run the risk of their designs looking "packaged." If you need better quality clip art, you may want to check out the following resources.

DGUSA.COM (Dynamic Graphics)

Dynamic Graphics has a clip-art service with illustrations and royalty-free photos. You can get the images on a CD-ROM each month with a print magazine called *Concepts & Designs*, which has tutorials on how to perform techniques using Dynamic Graphics' images to produce a variety of different media pieces. The magazine is both useful and inspirational, and provides a great starting point in the design process for those of us who are layout challenged. The CD contains both color and black-and-white versions of the images. You've already seen some examples in this chapter, which come from the same CD, the February 2001 issue.

As a subscriber, you also have access to images online for only $10 per image. You can get the images from a download or from the mail. Dynamic Graphics can also do a custom image search for you.

Dynamic Graphics has two different services: the Clipper monthly subscription has more images than the Designers Club, and it has photos. The cost for the Clipper subscription is $74.95 a month. The Designers Club subscription is similar to the Clipper, except it has fewer images and no photos. The cost for the Designers Club subscription is $54.95 a month. Both subscriptions include a pictorial index and a print magazine of tutorials and ideas. For more information, check the Web site at **http://www.dgusa.com/**.

Hemera Technologies

The product I particularly like from Hemera Technologies is the Hemera Photo Objects 50,000 Premium Image Collection. This collection contains ready-to-use photos of objects on transparent backgrounds. I've used these images in logos, photo collages, and banners.

The interface for Hemera Photo Objects 50,000 Premium Image Collection is both easy to use and quite impressive. You can search for the items you want. When you locate something of interest and click it, you're told which CD to insert. You can determine the file format and size of image before you open and/or save it. With the Hemera Photo Objects 50,000 Premium Image Collection you get eight CDs and a manual, with 80 categories and the 50,000 premium images for both Windows and the Mac, all for $84.99. For more information and a free demo, go to the Hemera Web site at **www.hemera.com**/.

ArtToday

ArtToday has a free three-day tryout at **www.arttoday.com**. You can access about 870,000 images for $29.95 a year or 1,212,898 images for $99.95 a year. Take advantage of the three days to check the site and see if the quality fits your needs. A lot of the images are just so-so, while others are both bad and good. I found images suitable for icons, background textures, and for use in buttons. Just one of these uses could justify the cost of access. You have no limit to how many images you can use in a year.

Free Clip Art

In the design forums and newsgroups I participate in, people are always looking for free clip-art sites. I've listed a few that aren't free, but they're good. Fred Showker of *DT&G Graphic Design* magazine (**www.graphic-design.com**) wrote an article on the research he did about "free" clip-art sites. In the article, he provides the steps he took when doing his research. You can find the original article at **http://www.60-seconds.com/articles/129.html**. If after reading his article, you still want free clip-art, use some of the links from Fred's note.

As a result of the article, Graphic-Design.com is already getting responses of private illustrators who provide images. Check at **www.graphic-design.com** for updates. Fred is on a crusade for good clip-art resources. So far the best recommendation this author can make is the Hemera Photo objects and the Dynamic Graphics subscription.

Sources for Stock Photography

If you're an active designer or Web developer, you need good sources for stock photography, unless you have an in-house photographer or are one yourself. At times, of course, you need an image and you need it quickly. Here are two resources for stock photography I find useful.

Comstock Images

You can go to Comstock's Web site, **www.comstock.com**, and order a catalog, which comes with a CD containing over 12,000 *comping* images (low-resolution images suitable for layout and presentation to a client). If these images are used in any way, they need to be purchased. And I highly recommend you do that. The CD has a portfolio browser, which makes locating the image you need a snap. Once you find it, a low-resolution sample is included. You can use it in a layout that you need to present to a client, boss, or whoever for approval. If you decide to use the image, all you need to do is order and pay for the high-resolution image. They also have a huge list of CD packages available with royalty-free images, so you can have them at your fingertips. You can see a few from several CD collections in the Plug-in section of this chapter.

EyeWire

Visit EyeWire at **www.eyewire.com**. EyeWire has a lot of resources, if you have the time to search for them. You can access photos, illustrations, audio, type, and more. Photo-Disc CDs are available, art from Art Parts, and Artville, as well as tutorials and tips. You can purchase in different ways—individual images and, in some cases, on a CD.

Digital Cameras

Digital cameras are a great way to obtain the images you need for Web pages. The cameras today are even suitable for print work, but they're even more than suitable for Web design. I've personally used and tested the cameras listed here. They aren't the highest-priced versions because, frankly, you don't need the top of the line for Web work. Of course, if you're going to use the camera for high-end print work or extremely large printed pieces, you'll need a camera with more resolution.

All the digital cameras I've looked at have at least three different quality settings. These setting determine the resolution of the shoot. The *resolution* is the amount of pixels per inch in the image. The larger the final required picture, the more pixels required to obtain an acceptable image.

The settings you choose to use for the digital camera depend largely on the final output required and the lighting required for the shoot.

Images taken with a megapixel digital camera are great for many product catalogs, online stores, and images for use in a Web site.

Kodak DC3400

The Kodak DC3400 is a 2.3 megapixel camera and, besides taking great pictures, it's extremely easy to use. This camera has resolutions of 1,760 × 1,168 (High), 896 × 592 (Standard), and settings of Best, Better, and Good. You can print up to 8" × 10 " prints with the High resolution.

The learning curve for my family was less than a half hour. This is the camera my husband and kids grab when they want to take photos.

Don't let the ease of use fool you, though. This is also a powerful camera. It has a LCD screen to view pictures you've already taken, an auto focus, you can choose different lighting settings and different flash settings, and it even has a 3x digital zoom. The pictures taken don't take a lot of time to set up. If you want to, you can make a few adjustments for the lighting and distance, and then you're ready to shoot. I like the fact that it's easy, but also that I have control over the lighting, flash, and zoom. For the complete specifications go to **www.kodak.com/**.

Nikon CoolPix 800

The first impression of this camera right out of the box was that it felt like and looked like a "real" camera. What I particularly liked about this camera is the control I had over the white balance. I also noticed the background detail was better than some other cameras I've used. This is a 2.11 megapixel camera. The lens is a Nikkor lens, which is a better quality than some of the competing brands.

The learning curve is a bit steeper than cameras like the Kodak because of all the options you have, such as setting the white balance. The LCD is easy to see and I also like the autofocus feature. You can add additional lenses to this camera, which is an attractive selling feature. Go to **www.nikonusa.com/** to see the complete feature list and specifications.

If you primarily do work for the Web, either one of these cameras might be completely satisfactory, depending on the type of client you design for. Because the cameras aren't not meant for print, you don't need extremely high resolutions.

If you're in the market for a digital camera, I recommend reading some of the Digital Camera magazines. If you're looking for a camera that takes print-quality pictures, this is the only way to see an accurate representation of what the camera can do. If you're looking for a camera for Web work, though, then online reviews are fine. Compare the output of the cameras you're interested in.

When you decide on a camera, you can purchase from a company such as Office Depot, which gives you an unconditional 14-day guarantee. If you don't like the camera for any reason, you can return it and get a refund (except on Sony). Or, for a bargain, you can check my favorite resource, which is **www.pricewatch.com**. Note, watch for the various vendors shipping policies at pricewatch, though. They can stick you with outrageous shipping charges.

Scanners

If you have images that aren't digital, then you need to scan them or have them scanned for you. Entire books are written on the subject of scanning images, but only some highlights are mentioned here. One thing to understand is how scanners are rated. The typical term used is DPI, which stands for Dots per inch; the more accurate term is SPI, Sample Points per inch. The various manufacturers use all these resolution numbers, which can be confusing, and terms like interpolated. *Interpolated* means it's a "fake" resolution—the software is guessing what colors to add to make the resolution higher. This isn't the important number to look for when you purchase a scanner. The important number to look for is the *Optical* number. Scanners that range in price from $50 to $200 normally have Optical resolutions of 300, 600, and 1,200: the higher the optical resolution, the better the scanner. The other important specification is the bit depth, or the color quality, of the scanner. In this same price range of $50 to $200, you can find bit depths of 24, 32, and 42.

Here are a few scanning tips:

- Scan at 1½ to 2 times the resolution of the final output.
- If you plan to enlarge the image, scan at the highest Optical resolution your scanner allows.
- Don't use contrast and brightness features on the scanner. This throws out information and you don't want that.
- Try to scan your piece as straight as possible.
- Scan line art at the highest optical resolution you can.

The other categories of scanners are the professional desktop scanners, which can costs thousands of dollars, and Drum scanners, which are even more expensive.

Other Useful Applications

You need some kind of image-editing program to get your images ready for the Web. If you purchased the Dreamweaver Fireworks Studio, then you have what you need. At times, you might need programs for illustrations or for print design. This section gives a brief overview of some of the most popular and useful applications.

Photoshop

Photoshop is a powerful and professional image-editing tool. It's sold with Image Ready, which is great for preparing images for the Web. You can produce rollovers, animations, and slice documents. Photoshop's real power is for print media. If you do a lot of print work, then you're probably already familiar with Photoshop, the number one program for the professional print designer.

Vector Programs

Programs such as Adobe Illustrator—the industry leader—Macromedia's FreeHand, and CorelDRAW are used for sketching and making vector drawings, which are scalable. The program you need largely depends on your budget and the type of illustrations you design. Another vector program rising in popularity is *Xara X,* which is a small, but powerful, illustration program. More and more people are turning to vector graphics for use in programs such as Macromedia's Flash.

Flash

Macromedia Flash is the widely used program for producing special-effect Web sites. Flash can be used for entire Web interfaces, buttons, banners, or just one animation. The flexibility of Flash makes it both a valuable tool and one of the most abused features of the Web.

BUILDING YOUR
SITE'S PAGES

Many Flash-enhanced sites hinder the user experience rather than enhance it. If you use Flash, be sure it's right for your audience and it doesn't drive them away. Nothing is more irritating than when I need to find some quick information and I have to wait for a movie. When people need information and resources, they usually don't want to be entertained. They want to get what they need and move on. If a Flash movie can enhance the information—great—give the option.

Plug-ins

Plug-ins can save you tons of time, add interest to an image, totally change an image, and perform a great number of operations. Some plug-ins are more useful than others. This section gives you a sampling of the ones I found most useful.

With programs such as Fireworks, plug-ins has the added flexibility of being a Live Effect—an effect that remains editable. Most of the plug-ins presented in this section can be used as an effect in Fireworks, see Chapter 38.

Auto FX

Auto FX has been supporting graphic programs for quite a while and has some extremely useful plug-ins that can help you in image manipulation. You can check out the entire product line at **www.autofx.com**.

AutoEye

You can get a demo of AutoEye at **www.autofx.com.** *AutoEye* automatically adjusts the tonal values of an image or, you can do it manually. I tried doing this on a dark photo and was amazed at how much detail was brought out. The automatic feature sometimes adds too much sharpening to the edge, so also try the manual options. With a try-before-you-buy demo, you can't go wrong. This illustration shows an extremely dark and unusable image of a briefcase destined for auction, showing the damage of the top edge. The image was never used. I tried the Automatic, Enhance Very Dark Image filter of AutoEye, and you can see the results in the second image.

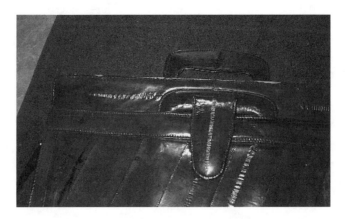

I found the automatic filters work best on objects and the manual features work better on people. Most of the test images I did on people have too much sharpening applied with the automatic feature.

Photo/Graphic Edges 10,000+

A demo of Photo/Graphic Edges 10,000+ can be found at **www.autofx.com**. More edges are in this package than you could ever need. The package comes with a manual, so you can see the different categories and quickly find the edge types you're looking for. They're quick and easy to apply. With Photo/Graphic Edges, there's no reason to have any boring edges on your images. You can make your own edges by using a Mask in Fireworks or in Photoshop, but using this plug-in can save you a lot of time. This is one of my favorite enhancements for an image.

This illustration demonstrates an image found on the Consumer Generation CD from Comstock images, with edge number AF072.AFX applied.

Studio Pro Bundle by Auto FX

Studio Bundle Pro 2.0 contains 11 of Auto FX Software's most popular products in one integrated package for $199.95. This package is worth over $1,250 if sold separately. The effects in this package include Typo/Graphic Edges, Ultimate Texture Collection, Photo/Graphic Patterns, Universal Animator, Universal Rasterizer, Photo/Graphic Frames, Page/Edges, and Web Vise Totality. Check out the Auto FX Web site at **www.autofx.com**. This image uses a picture from the Comstock Diversity Lifestyles CD Collection and has a Photo Frame (AF112.jpg) added to it.

Alien Skin Software

Alien Skin Software has quite a few special effect filters that have won many rave reviews. Check out its informative and useful Web site at **www.alienskin.com**.

Eye Candy 4000

A few filters from Eye Candy 4000 ship with Fireworks 4. If you want a demo, this can be found at Alien Skin's Web site. The demo has some additional plug-ins different from the ones that ship with Fireworks. Alien Skin Software has a great Web site interface, enabling you to see each of the included 23 filters in use. The price is $169.00 or an upgrade price of $69.00. Eye Candy 4000 can be found at **http://www.alienskin.com/ec4k/ec4000_main.html**

Xenofex

A demo of the Xenofex plug-ins can be found at **http://www.alienskin.com/xenofex/xenofex_main.html**. The Xenofex filters from Alien Skin have a collection of 16 filters and 160 presets. Be sure to check out the filters, priced at $129.00, at their Web site. The following image shows a globe found on the Exploring the Universe CD Collection from Comstock Images.

The Crumple filter from the Xenofex plug-in was selected. The following illustration shows you the many options available in the Xenofex interface.

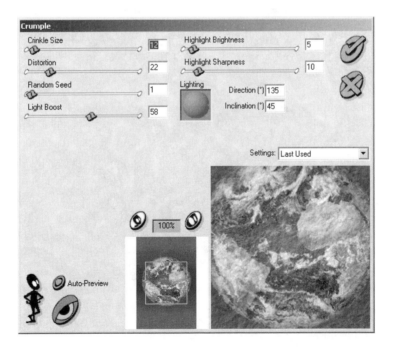

This image is the result of accepting the default settings seen in the previous illustration.

AV Bros. Puzzle Pro

AV Bros. Puzzle Pro is the easiest tool I've found to date for making puzzles quick and easy. All kinds of options exist for puzzle shapes, bevels, and more. The price is $39.95, and you can find out more at **www.avbros.com**. This illustration shows a picture I found on the February 2001 issue of Dynamic Graphics Clipper CD subscription service, which I made into a puzzle using Puzzle Pro.

Flaming Pear

Do yourself a favor and check out the Web site of Flaming Pear (**www.flamingpear.com**), where you'll see a plug-in that's for sale and one that's free. *Flaming Pear* has some free plug-ins, as well as some that are well priced.

SuperBladePro

In September 2000, Flaming Pear released SuperBladePro, adding new effects like dust, moss, water stains, and abrasion, as well as features like undo and a graphical preset browser. Flaming Pear plans to offer more texture packs, presets, and tutorials for SuperBladePro, as well as to continue developing intriguing and useful plug-ins.

SuperBladePro, available via download and online purchase at **www.flamingpear.com**, costs $30. Registered users of the original BladePro can purchase an upgrade for $15.

Primus

The Primus plug-in is free. Just download it and place it into a folder with your other plug-ins. You'll be prompted to register for your free activation code after you use this plug-in for about a minute. The code is sent promptly to your e-mail address, so all you need to do is enter the code and you're all set. This plug-in was so inspiring, I made a Web page with it in less than an hour. Try using one of the textures on a top header with lowered opacity, and then on a button, or fill text with it.

Types of Images

Images come in many forms on Web pages. They can be tiny things used as a bullet, or they can be buttons, backgrounds—the possibilities are almost endless. It's up to us to use images judiciously, though, especially when we start to make them spin and fly all over the page. In this section, you see some of the uses for images.

Page Elements

When used properly, images can help maintain order, establish a hierarchy, and add visual cues. The different uses for images can help the user navigate your site, as well as break up information in readable and usable chunks.

Buttons

I think it's safe to say that buttons are probably the most highly used image on the Internet and this isn't a bad thing. Users are familiar with a button. They've come to expect a button to take them somewhere if they click it. For this reason, using a button image in the manner a user expects is important.

If you begin to use a button simply as a decoration, you can confuse your user. I've seen designers try to be clever or different by using buttons in a nonconventional way. Conventional is good when you're trying to make a Web page user-friendly, especially if the Web site you're designing is going to be used by new Internet users. I can't think of any site that doesn't fall into the category that attracts new users, as well as experienced Web gurus.

Buttons can be a regular static image or a rollover (see later in this section) and they're inserted into the page like any other image. Chapter 13 explains the ins and outs of image insertion.

Flash buttons

Dreamweaver 4 has a new feature. You can now automatically add Flash buttons without writing any code. Dreamweaver 4 ships with some buttons, but you can also use your own. How to insert a Flash button and where to find more is discussed in Chapter 13.

Bullets

Bullets draw your attention to important points and add interest to what could be a boring list. They can be decorative or functional as a link. You can make a bullet using HTML code or by using an image.

Bullets produced using HTML code is a list function in Dreamweaver. An unordered or bulleted list doesn't require a structure to make sense. An ordered list is numbered with numbers or the alphabet and is used for a list, which requires a logical progression of steps. To make a bulleted list, follow these steps:

1. Place the cursor where you want the list to begin.

2. Click the list icon of your choice. Once you click this icon, the List Item button in the Properties Inspector becomes active. You now have several more choices available. The type of list can be a bulleted, numbered, directory, or menu list. The Style drop-down menu gives you options of bullet styles, roman numerals, and large alphabet or small alphabet for the numbered lists.

3. Type your first list item.

4. Press Enter each time you want a new row.

5. Continue until the list is complete.

6. Press Enter to end the list.

7. Then you see one more number or bullet. At this time, click the list icon to deselect and the number or bullet goes away.

When using an image as a button, you need to add a break—`<br>`—or a paragraph—`<p>`—space before and after each bullet image. You might also need to align the text accordingly to line up with the bottom of the button by selecting the text and choosing Baseline or Text Top, or whatever position you want your text to be in relation to the bullet image. If the bullet is also a link, add `<a href> </a>` tags. Be sure to set the border to 0 to eliminate the blue outline, which indicates it's a link. For more information on inserting images, see Chapter 13.

Horizontal Rules

Horizontal rules are often used as page dividers to break information on a Web page in to readable chunks. A horizontal rule can be an image or generated by using HTML code. If you want to use an image, simply insert it like any other image (see Chapter 13). To add a horizontal rule in Dreamweaver, follow these steps:

1. Click the area where you want to add a horizontal rule.

2. Click the Insert Horizontal Rule icon in the Object Inspector.

3. In the Properties Inspector you can set the alignment, name the horizontal rule, and set the height and width.

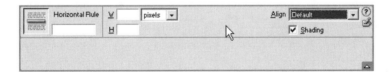

4. You might need to add a break <br> or a <p> break before and after the horizontal rule.

If you look at the code, the horizontal rule uses the <hr> tag. If you don't want the emboss effect, which is automatically applied, then change the code to read: <hr noshade> and you'll have a black line instead. You can make your own custom horizontal rule images using dingbats and small images.

Background Images

Several kinds of background images exist, which you see in this section. Adding background images in Dreamweaver is easy. To add a background to your Web page, follow these steps:

1. Choose Modify | Page Properties.
2. Click the Browse button next to Background Image, select the image to use as the background, and then click Open.
3. Click OK when you finish adding the background image.

You can also add a background image to a table. To add a background to the table:

1. Click the yellow folder next to BG Image in the Properties Inspector.

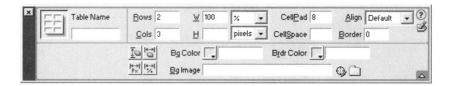

2. Locate the file you want to use as a background and click Open.

To add an image to a table cell:

1. Click inside the cell where you want to add an image.
2. Click the yellow folder next to BG and browse to select the image you want to insert. Click Open when you find the image.

Tiling Background Images

The HTML tag, called `<body background>`, allows a small image to repeat until it fills a Web page, also known as *background tiles*. One image repeats to fill the screen both vertically and horizontally. No restrictions are on the size of the tile; the size is determined by the look you want to achieve. The smaller the tile, the more times it repeats. The larger the tile, the less it repeats. If a border or a distinct pattern is on the tile, it'll be visible when it repeats.

Nontiling Background Images

A *nontiling image* is a large background graphic that fills the user's screen. These types of backgrounds should be used with caution. Another potential problem is guessing what size browser your user is using. You can have a large image fill the browser window but, if the browser is open at a larger size than your image, it will tile. If the browser window is smaller, the image will scroll. With practice, you can get large background images down to an acceptable size. Using two-tone images goes a long way in keeping the size down. Another trick is to use a transparent background with an image in it. Add the background color via HTML code and the image will appear to have a background color. Of course, this technique only works for GIF background images.

Another way to give the illusion of a background image is to place an image in a cell as the cell background. This technique can also be used to achieve a layered look. You can place another image on top of the cell background image, giving the appearance of layered images.

JPEG Background Images

JPEG images are the least desirable format to use as a background image. You can't make large areas of flat color transparent to cut down on file size. Another drawback is a JPEG image has to decompress before it loads, which can cause loading delays in a Web page.

Border Images

Border images, also known as *left-side borders,* are often used as left-side navigation or used on the left and right side of a page to "frame" the page. Borders help break up the white space around the main portions of a Web page and draw the eye in to the main subject. Side borders are made and used the same way as background images, in fact, they are background images. Border images tile like regular tiling images do; the difference is they're short and long. The length should be at least 1,200 pixels wide to accommodate those who browse with larger monitors and window sizes. The height of the image depends on what's in the border, the image, or the pattern. If a distinct pattern occurs, you may not want it to repeat as many times, so the height would be larger.

Nonscrolling Backgrounds

You've probably seen a background that stays put, while only the text and page elements move. It's extremely easy to do, but this is only supported by Internet Explorer. Add the background image, which can be tiling or nontiling—it doesn't matter. Find the <body background="yourimage.gif"> tag and add bgproperties="Fixed". It now looks like this: <body background="yourimage.gif" bgproperties="fixed">.

Window Dressing

Images considered as *window dressing* are nonessential images. The only benefit these images provide is a visual treat or *eye candy*. But, what some consider eye candy can serve several functions, such as carry out a theme, liven a page, or break the monotony of a long page. Images used to illustrate a point or to help make something clear are considered a necessary element of the page, rather than window dressing.

The world would be a boring place without the judicious use of window dressing and eye candy. An image can either draw us in or repel us. The proper use of images can convey a message or a feeling.

Animated GIFS

Animated GIFS give the illusion of motion. They work much like children's flipbooks, where a series of pictures appear to move when fanned by the thumb. Each image in an animation is contained within a frame. Each image varies slightly from the previous image, so the illusion of motion is present when viewed in quick succession.

Many free programs enable you to produce decent GIF animations. Programs such as Fireworks, Photoshop, and Paint Shop Pro also have tools available to make GIF Animations. Here are two new and extremely useful resources:

Wildform SWFX

A demo of SWFX can be found at **www.wildform.com**. This is an easy to use and versatile tool to make quick-text animations for use in Flash. *Wildform SWFX* is a standalone application and comes with 200 different preset text animations to use, as well as to customize. And, all this for only $19.99. This program offers a lot of versatility in making text animations. You can use one of the presets, but you can also customize it. Of course, there's no risk because you can download it and try it out for yourself.

EZ Motion

EZ Motion is made by Beatware. You can download a demo at **www.beatware.com**. Dozens of templates, such as animated banners, buttons, and other graphics, are available. You can use them as is or customize them. A library of graphic objects is also available, including 3-D and 2-D objects, animated objects, designs, gradients, and images. And, you can do more than simple animations, such as movement and fades. You can also animate text on a curve, and change font size, outlines, and fills, as well as shearing and spacing. You can change the size, shape, and opacity, and the elements remain editable. The full version sells for $99.99. You can see a picture of the interface in the following illustration.

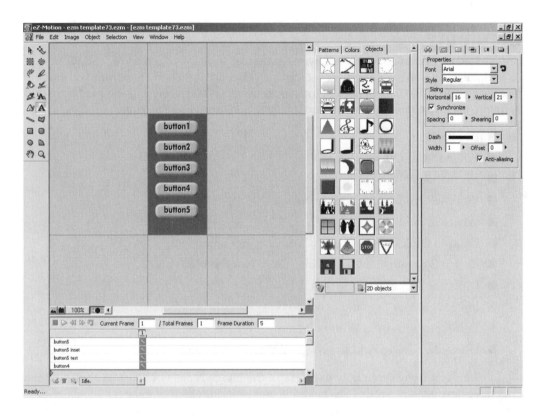

Programs such as Flash and LiveMotion take animation to the next level. Using these types of programs enables you to add additional ActionScript code, so you can actually interact with the animation or motion graphics.

Dreamweaver has limited capability to produce motion graphics. These are graphics that have a starting point and move to an ending point. You can learn more about moving objects across the screen in Dreamweaver in Chapter 20.

GIF animations are added to the HTML document, just as any other image is. No special coding or handling is necessary, making them an easy way to add a little spice to a Web page. But, please use animations with caution; they can drive a user away faster than blinking text when used inappropriately. Animations should serve a specific purpose, exactly as any other image should. Don't add animations simply because you can or because you think they look cool. You should always ask yourself, "How does this image or animation enhance the user's experience?" If you can't answer that question, then use the animation on a personal home page.

Summary

You've had a good overview of the types of images to use on Web pages and where to find them, as well as some places to download good demos to try-before-you-buy. You've also seen the many types of images in use on Web pages, and the hardware and software used to obtain and edit those images. Here are some key points:

- File Formats
- When to Use GIF vs JPEG
- Animations
- Where to Find Good Stock Images
- Where to Find Clip Art
- What to Look for in a Digital Camera or a Scanner
- Useful Programs for Generating Images for the Web
- Different Background Images
- Images Uses as Page Elements
- Editing Images from Within Dreamweaver
- Using Plug-ins to Add Interest or Enhance an Image

In Chapter 13, you learn how to insert all the image types you learned about in this chapter, plus delve into rollovers, navbars, and other interactive images.

The
Complete
Reference

Chapter 13

Using Images in Dreamweaver

Adding Images to Your Pages

Adding images in Dreamweaver is probably one of the easiest tasks you can do. Dreamweaver offers several ways to insert an image, and any one of these can do the job:

■ Click in the document to set the insertion point. Click the Insert image in the Common section of the Objects panel. The cursor in this illustration shows the Insert Image icon.

■ Click in the document to set the insertion point, and then choose Insert | Image.

■ Click in the document to set the insertion point. From the Site panel, you can click an image name and drag it on to your document. You can see the image being dragged in this illustration. You would drag it completely out of the Site panel and drop it into your document.

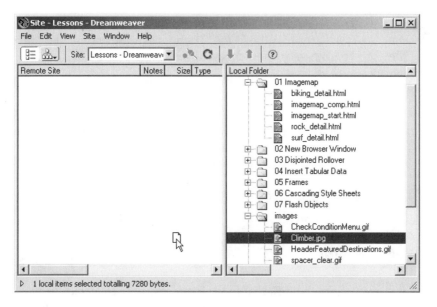

■ Click in the document to set the insertion point, and insert an image using the Assets panel. If you don't see any assets when you open the Assets panel (and you are using a defined site), click the Refresh Site List icon on the bottom of the Asset panel (the first icon to the right of the Insert button). The following illustration shows the cursor pointing to the Image icon. Click the Image icon to view a list of images in your site. Click an image name or the icon representation and drag it onto your document.

■ Click in the document to set the insertion point and use the Keyboard shortcut of ALT-CTRL-I (OPT-CMD-I for the Mac). This opens the Select Image Source window, so you can locate and choose the image you want to insert.

Image Properties

Whenever you insert an image and it's selected, you have access to a number of options you can control in the Property Inspector. This illustration shows the Property Inspector options with an image selected. This view is with the extender arrow in the right corner clicked, showing the entire inspector.

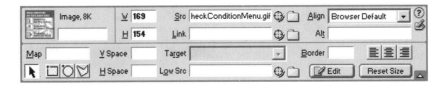

Here's a description of the different fields in the Property Inspector of a selected image.

■ You can see the image icon in the top-left corner. Next to it is the field where you can name your image. Giving your image a unique name is especially important when you design rollovers with a swap image behavior. This isn't the filename, but a separate name you give the image.

■ The H and W are the height and width of the image. The height and width are automatically added when you insert an image, but if you want to resize an image manually, you can change the numbers here.

■ Src field is the name of the image file.

■ To the right of the Src field is the Point to File icon. The yellow folder gives the option to browse for your image.

■ The Align field has quite a few options of how text and other elements align with the image. This is covered in detail in the next section, "Aligning Images," in this chapter.

■ The Alt field is where you type in alternative text, which is discussed in the "Accessibility Considerations" section of this chapter.

■ The three buttons with lines on them are the Left, Center, and Right align buttons,

■ The Border field is where you type in how much of a border you want, if any.

■ The Edit button opens the selected text in an image editor.

■ The Reset Size button resets the image size to the original if you manually entered new height and widths. Or, it resets to the new size if you change the size in an image editor using the Edit button.

- The Target field is where you select a frame to open a linked file.

- Low Src is where you type in or browse to find a file, which is usually a 2-bit version of the final image. This is the image that loads first, while the final image loads.

- V Space and H Space is the vertical and horizontal space in pixels that surrounds the image to keep text or elements from being up against the image.

- The Map field is where you name an image map.

- The three shapes are the Hotspot drawing tools for use in an image map.

Aligning Images

You can choose to insert an image to the Right, Left, or Center of your document, table, or cell, either before you insert it or after. To align before you insert the image, click the icon of your choice. To align after the image is inserted, select the image, and then choose the alignment option of choice. The Align Left, Align Center, and Align Right icons are in the upper-right corner of the Properties Inspector.

After you insert an image, you can also set alignment options, which determine how text or other elements in the same paragraph or line of the image display. The Properties Inspector (shown here) has quite a few options in the Align drop-down list.

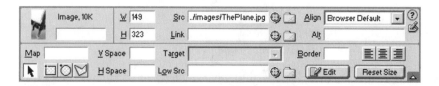

This is the list of alignment options, which specifically deal with how an element that's in the same paragraph or line as the image aligns with the image. The illustrations show the result of each option. The two letter *g*'s were added so you could see the effect of a *descender* (the part of a letter that extends beyond the baseline) and an *ascender* (the part that extends above the other lowercase letters, such as *L* and other capital letters) on some of the alignment options.

- Browser Default—The default is usually the Baseline.

- Baseline—Aligns the text or element to the bottom of an image. This image is a screenshot using Internet Explorer 5. You can see the baseline in this browser is the same as the Browser Default.

- Top—Aligns the text or element to the top of an image.

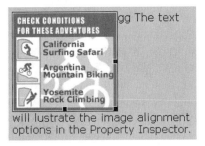

- Middle—Aligns the baseline of the text or element to the middle of the image.

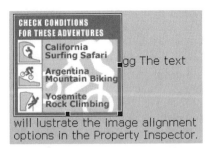

- Bottom—Aligns the text or element to the bottom of an image.

- Text Top—Aligns the tallest character of the text to the top of the image.

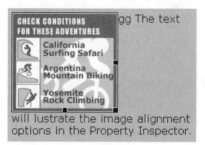

- Absolute Middle—Aligns the middle of the text to the middle of the image.

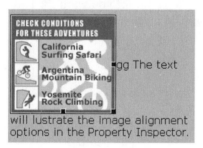

- Absolute Bottom—Aligns the text, including its descenders, to the bottom of the image.

■ Left—Left aligns the image and wraps the text to the right.

■ Right—Right aligns the image and wraps the text to the left.

Notice the last two illustrations, the ones for the Left and Right alignment. You can see the text is right up against the image. You can adjust this spacing in the Properties Inspector for this. Enter the pixel amount you want the text or element from the image vertically in the V Space box and number of pixels you want the text or element from the image horizontally in the H Space box.

Resizing Images

After an image is inserted, you can resize it in Dreamweaver by following these steps:

1. Select the image. The squares you see here on the side, corner, and bottom are the resize handles.

2. Place the mouse cursor over the side handle (a horizontal line with double arrows appears). Click-and-drag the side handle to increase the width of the image.

3. Place the mouse cursor over the bottom handle (a vertical line with double arrows appears). Click-and-drag the bottom handle to increase the height of the image.

4. Place the mouse cursor over the corner handle (an angled line with double arrows appears). Click-and-drag the corner handle to increase the height and width of the image.

5. Place the mouse cursor over the corner handle, press SHIFT-and-drag the corner to increase the height and width proportionately.

You can also change the width in the W box and the height in the H box in the Property Inspector by typing in the desired dimensions.

Why Not Resize Images in Dreamweaver?

Now that you know *how* to change the size, I'll tell you *why* you shouldn't do it. Increasing the size in Dreamweaver visibly distorts your image, unless the increase is only a few pixels. But this isn't the main reason not to do it in Dreamweaver. Many people think by making an image smaller in Dreamweaver, they're reducing the load time of the image—they aren't. The file size of the image is exactly the same, whether you increase it or decrease it in Dreamweaver. The best way to change the size of an image (up or down) is to do it in an image editor. Select the image and click the Edit button in the Property Inspector to open the image in an image editor. Make the changes in the image editor, and then save it. The file size is then updated accordingly. Images edited in image editors are automatically updated in Dreamweaver—except for the size. To update the size, click the Reset Size button in the Property Inspector. This is discussed in more detail in Chapter 36.

Organizing Image Files

How you set up your root directory depends on how you work or what parameters you're given by a client. A good idea is to keep your images in separate folders if you have a lot of assets in a site, so you can easily find them. Many designers use an Images folder or a Graphics folder. You may want to have separate image folders for different parts of the site. Whatever type of convention you follow, organizing your images in folders can help you find them when they're needed.

Image Path Notations

Looking at the code after you insert an image is important to understand how the different paths to an image are coded. This way, if you have a broken image, you can determine why.

The first code we look at is what's generated if the image you insert is in the same folder as the HTML file you're using. The code looks like this (Dreamweaver automatically adds the width and height):

```
<img src="yourimage.gif" width="164" height="150">
```

If you set your site up with an images folder, the code would look like this:

```
<img src="/images/yourimage.gif" width="164" height="150">
```

The forward slash (/) indicates the image is in the folder name that follows the slash. If the HTML file you're using is in a folder other than the root folder, for instance, if you were using one of Dreamweaver's lessons, the HTML files for Biking_Detail.HTML is in the Image map folder. The code for this sort of layout would look like this:

```
<img src=".. /images/yourimage.gif" width="164" height="150">
```

The two dots before the slash indicate the file is in a folder one level up from the HTML file.

Accessibility Considerations

It's important to add alternative text to *every* image on your Web pages, even bullets. This is especially important for users who use text transcribers. Visually impaired users have transcribers that read the text, so labeling every single image is important. And not just a quickie label, either. For example, the following illustration shows where to enter the alternative text. What you can't see is the complete text, which reads: "Conditions for California surfing, Argentina Mountain Biking, and Yosemite Rock Climbing." Use good, descriptive text.

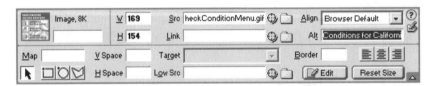

People who browse with images off see the alternative text instead of the image. Even people who browse with images on (the majority), see the alternative text before the image loads. Many people click the link based on the text and don't wait for all the images to load.

Special Images in Dreamweaver

Special images in Dreamweaver are images such as rollovers and Navigation bars. Each of the rollover states occupies the same place on the Web page. A rollover image uses only two images (swap image behavior), which occupy the same space. In other words, one original image shows when you first access the Web page, when the mouse hovers over it, and when the image changes to another image (in the same spot). Each image needs to be the same size. If you want more than two images, you can use a Navigation bar, which has up to four states available.

Other interactive images include Flash text and Flash buttons.

Add Rollovers

If you've made rollovers in Fireworks (see Chapter 41), inserting them into Dreamweaver is extremely easy. Follow these steps:

1. Open Dreamweaver 4, choose File | Open, and open a file you in which you want to use the Fireworks HTML code.

2. Place your cursor where you want the code inserted.

3. Choose Insert | Interactive Images | Fireworks HTML. Or, you can use the Insert Fireworks HTML icon in the Common section of the Object Inspector. Either way, the Insert Fireworks HTML dialog window opens, as seen here.

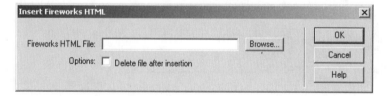

4. In the window that opens, click the Browse button. Navigate to the folder containing the Fireworks code and click Open.

5. Choose File | Preview in Browser or click the Globe Icon on the same row as the HTML code icons below the menu bar. Select the browser you want to view in.

6. Choose File | Save As, and then save your file.

To insert rollovers—you can make the graphics for these in any image editor—follow these steps:

1. Place the cursor in the document and click where you want to set the insertion point.

2. Choose one of these methods to insert the rollover.

■ Click the Insert Rollover Image icon in the Object panel (Common). The cursor is pointing to the correct icon.

■ Or, choose Insert | Interactive Images | Rollover Image. This window opens.

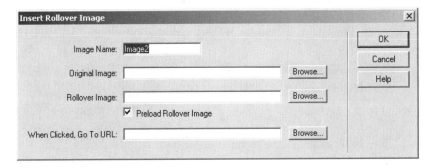

3. In the Insert Rollover Image dialog box, enter a name for your image.

4. In the Insert Rollover Image dialog box, click the Browse button to locate and select the original image (the one that appears when the Web page first loads).

5. In the Insert Rollover Image dialog box, click the Browse button to locate and select the Rollover image (the one that appears when the mouse cursor hovers over the original image).

6. Check the Preload Rollover Image option if you want the rollover loaded prior to the user interacting with the page. In other words, it loads with the rest of the page when the page is opened.

7. Either click the Browse button in the When Clicked, Go To URL field, to locate a HTML file to link to, or type in the URL.

8. Click OK when you finish.

Add Navigation Bars

Use a Navigation bar when you want more than simply a swap image rollover effect. Navigation bars have up to four rollover states. Here is a brief explanation of each of the available rollover states:

- Up—The up state is the default appearance of the button, as first seen by the user.

- Over—the over state is the way the button looks when the user passes the mouse pointer over it. The over state is the one that alerts users this button is "hot" and leads to another page.

- Down—the down state is the appearance when the button has been clicked. It often has a depressed look. In Fireworks, you can set the down state to be active on the page that's being clicked to, to designate the button as the current page.

- Over While Down—the over while down state is the appearance of the down state button when the mouse pointer moves over it.

To place a Navigation bar, which you exported from Fireworks, follow these steps:

1. Open Dreamweaver 4, choose File | Open and open a file in which you want to use the Fireworks HTML code.

2. Place your cursor where you want the code inserted.

3. Choose Insert | Interactive Images | Fireworks HTML. Or, you can use the Insert Fireworks HTML icon in the Common section of the Object Inspector. Either way, the Insert Fireworks HTML dialog window opens.

4. In the window that opens, click the Browse button. Navigate to the folder containing the Fireworks code and click Open.

5. Choose File | Preview in Browser, or click the Globe Icon on the same row as the HTML code icons below the menu bar. Then select the browser where you want to view.

6. Choose File | Save As and save your file.

To insert a Navigation bar, for which you made the graphics in any image editor, follow these steps:

1. Place the cursor in the document and click where you want to set the insertion point.

2. Choose one of these methods to insert the Navigation bar.

■ Click the Insert Navigation Bar icon in the Object panel (Common). The cursor is pointing to the correct icon.

■ Or, choose Insert | Interactive Images | Navigation Bar. This window opens.

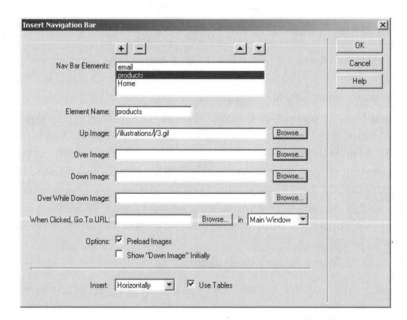

3. In the Insert Navigation Bar dialog box, enter a name for your image in the Element Name field.

4. Click the Browse button in the Up Image field to locate and select the original image (the one that appears when the Web page first loads). The up state is required for all images in the Navigation bar.

5. Click the Browse button in the Over Image field (optional) to locate and select the Rollover image (the one that appears when the mouse cursor hovers over the original image).

6. Click the Browse button in the Down Image field (optional) to locate and select the image that appears when the user clicks the image.

7. Click the Browse button in the Over While Down field (optional) to locate and select the image that appears when the user moves the mouse cursor over the down image.

8. In the When Clicked, Go To URL field, enter the filename you want to open with this link. Or, click the Browse button to locate the file you want to link to.

9. Select the Main Window option if you want the file to open in the same window.

10. If you want the file to open in a frame, select the frame name. If the frame name isn't visible in the drop-down menu (where Main Window is), close the Insert Navigation Bar dialog box and name your frame. The frame name shows when you open the Insert Navigation Bar dialog box again.

11. Check the Preload Rollover Image option if you want the rollover loaded prior to the user interacting with the page. In other words, it loads with the rest of the page when the page is opened.

12. Click to check the Show Down Image Initially option if you want the down image to show on the page when it opens instead of the up state.

13. The Insert field enables you to choose whether you want the Navigation bar to be inserted vertically or horizontally.

14. Click the plus sign (+) in the Nav Bar Elements field (at the top of the dialog window) to add another element to the Navigation bar and repeat Steps 3–13. Repeat again for each element of your Navigation bar.

15. Click OK when you finish.

Inserting Flash Buttons

A selection of Flash buttons ships with Dreamweaver 4. You can also find more at the Macromedia Exchange. To insert a Flash button, follow these steps:

1. Save your document before inserting the Flash button.

2. In Design view, select the Insert Flash Button icon from the Object panel (see the following) or choose Insert | Interactive Images | Flash Button. The Insert Flash Button dialog box opens.

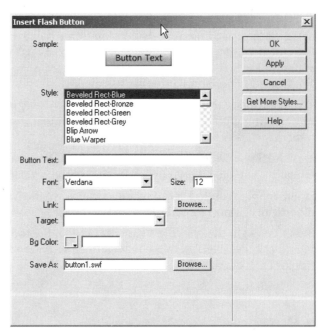

3. A list of the Flash Buttons you have in the Configuration/Flash Objects/Flash Buttons folder appears. Select the button you want to insert. When you make a selection, you can see a preview in the Sample field. If you move your mouse over the button, you can see how the button performs in a browser.

4. Type the text you want on your button in the Text field. This option is only available for buttons with text parameters defined.

5. In the Font field, choose the font you want to use and also select the size.

6. In the link field, either type in a URL, or browse to select the file you want to link to.

For Flash buttons, do not use a site relative link. It won't work. You can only use an absolute link or a document relative link. If you use a document relative link, you need to save the SWF in the same directory as the HTML file that's being linked to. See Chapter 11 for more on linking.

7. If you want the link to open in a frame, select a target from the Target field.

8. Select a Background color in the BG Color field (optional).

9. In the Save As field, name your button.

10. If you click the Apply button, it's inserted into your document. You can see the changes you made and still have the capability to edit in the Insert Flash Button dialog box.

11. Click the OK button when you finish

If you want more Flash buttons, you can click the Get More Styles button, and then you're taken to Macromedia Exchange where you can download additional buttons.

Inserting Flash Text

You can make extremely simple Flash text using the Insert Flash Text option in Dreamweaver. To Insert Flash Text, follow these steps:

1. Save your document before inserting the Flash button.

2. In Design view, select the Insert Flash Text icon from the Object panel (see the following) or choose Insert | Interactive Images | Flash Text. The Insert Flash Button dialog box opens.

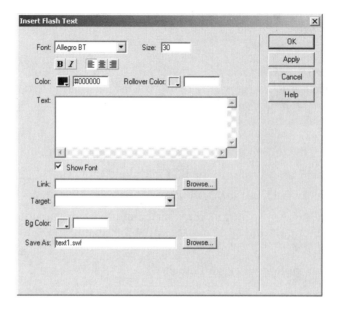

3. In the Font field, select the font you want to use.

4. In the Size field, select the size of the font you want to use.

5. Select any formatting, such as Bold or Italic, and the alignment you want.

6. Select the color of the original text in the Color field.

7. Select the color you want the text for the rollover in the Rollover Color field.

8. In the link field, either type in a URL or browse to select the file you want to link to.

Note *For Flash text, do not use a site relative link; it won't work. You can only use an absolute link or a document relative link. If you use a document relative link, you need to save the SWF in the same directory as the HTML file that's being linked to. See Chapter 11 for more on linking.*

9. If you want the link to open in a frame, select a target from the Target field.

10. Select a Background color in the BG Color field (optional).

11. In the Save As field, name your button.

The options in the Property Inspector are a bit different for Flash buttons and Flash text than for regular images, as you can see here. There's a Play button, and Parameters, Quality, and Scale options, which aren't available for regular images.

Generating a Web Photo Album

You can automatically generate a photo album on a Web page to showcase a folder of images. This command only works if you have Fireworks installed on your system. This is a JavaScript command, which opens Fireworks, and then makes a thumbnail and a larger-sized image of each image in a folder you designate.

To prepare for making a Web photo album, you need to have a folder that contains all the images you want to include in the album. The accepted file formats are GIF, JPEG, JPG, PNG, PSD, TIF, and TIFF. To make the photo album, follow these steps:

1. In Dreamweaver, choose Commands | Create Web Photo Album. The Create Web Photo Album dialog box opens, as the following shows.

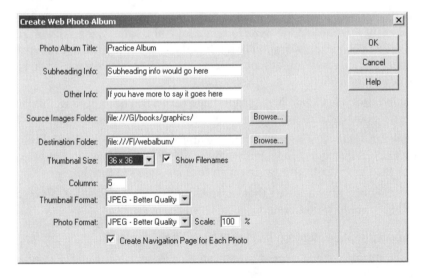

2. In the Photo Album Title field, enter a name for your album. The title you enter is seen at the top of the thumbnail page of the album.

3. If you want a subhead to appear below the title, enter it in the Subheading Info field.

4. If you want to add additional text to the caption of the thumbnail page, add it in the Other Info field.

5. In the Source Images Folder field, click the Browse button to locate the folder where you have images you want to include in the album. When you locate the folder, you won't see the images in it. The folder will be blank because you are simply selecting the folder.

6. The Destination Folder field is where you choose the folder you want the album to be exported to.

7. The Thumbnail Size field is where you designate the size of the thumbnail. Check Show Filenames only if you want the filename of each image to appear below the thumbnail. This is a nice feature if you named your images with meaningful names.

8. In the Columns field, select how many columns you want for your thumbnails.

9. The Thumbnail Format field is where you choose what format to make the thumbnails.

10. The Photo Format field is where you select the format for the larger photos. You can even choose a different format than you did for the thumbnail if you choose.

11. The Scale field is the percentage of the original image in the image folder where you want the photo. One hundred percent is the same size as the original image. If your images aren't all the same size, you may not get the results you expect and, if you want all your images the same size, you must start with the same size images.

12. If you check the Create Navigation Page for Each Photo option, this puts Back, Home, and Next links on each page of the larger images.

13. Click OK when you're ready to make an HTML page with the thumbnails on it. This opens Fireworks, and Fireworks is going to do a batch process on the images. Don't do anything; just wait for Fireworks to finish.

14. A dialog box now appears that says, Album Created. Click OK and wait for the HTML page to be generated.

This is how the Web Photo Album thumbnail page looks:

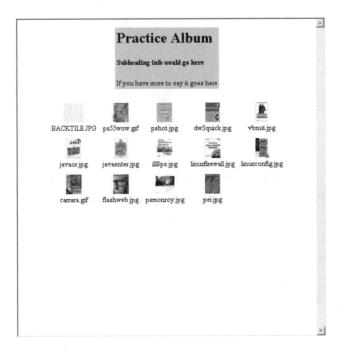

This is the page of the larger image, which includes the Back, Next, and Home links because I checked that option.

Summary

You learned how to place your images and special images in your Web document, and align the text and other elements around the image. You also learned how to insert special images from Fireworks HTML code and from images generated in image editors. Key Features include:

- Adding Images
- Setting Image Properties
- Aligning Text and Elements to the Image
- Resizing Images
- Organizing Images
- Inserting Rollovers
- Inserting Navigation Bars
- Inserting Flash Buttons
- Inserting Flash Text
- Generating a Web Photo Album

In Chapter 14, you learn how to use tables in Dreamweaver, as well as how to set them up, modify, and troubleshoot them.

The Complete Reference

Part IV

Beyond the Basics

The
Complete
Reference

Dreamweaver
4

Chapter 14

Using Tables

J ust like the offline world, the Web is susceptible to trends. These trends affect usage patterns, as users flock to online shopping or chat rooms or parenting sites—and they affect Web designers. Some of these are determined by changing standards and W3C recommendations, as is the case with the current move to XHTML and CSS. Others are started by some creative soul who tries using an HTML element contrary to its original purpose and discovers a truly innovative way to create sophisticated sites. One such trend has been the use of tables as a layout component.

Not too long ago, HTML tables were used strictly to present tabular data on a page. While tables are still used for this purpose, their full potential is in how they can position text and images with much greater flexibility than standard paragraph and image formatting.

Just as with all trends, tables won't remain in favor forever. Layers provide even greater control over layout, and they can be manipulated using timelines and DHTML to be far more interactive—the full possibilities of these tools are still being explored as browser compatibility increases. Also, the W3C has recommended HTML be limited to providing structure for the page's content, leaving layout and display to CSS. Does this mean the use of tables in layout is waning? Not for awhile yet—but you know how trends go.

Tables Basics

At first, you may think of tables as a spreadsheet, a series of columns and rows, with cells at the intersection points. At its most simple, this analogy is correct, but rarely are things this simple. In HTML, tables don't have column definitions. Instead, table rows extend the table horizontally, and table cells are used to extend it vertically. Thus, the only HTML tags required for a table are

- `<table> </table>`—The container tag for the entire table. All tables must be contained within this pair.

- `<tr> </tr>`—The table row tag. Every table row tag adds a new row to the table. Attributes can be added to this tag to specify alignment or color.

- `<td> </td>`—The table data, or cell, tag. These tags are nested within the table row tags to add cells to the row. All content is contained within the cell tag. The cell tag itself can also carry attributes to determine alignment, color, and even background image. As you see in this chapter, the cell tag can also take an attribute that allows the cell to span across other rows and even other cells.

Every time you add a new row, the table becomes vertically longer. Whenever you add a new cell to a row, the table becomes wider. Thus, the final horizontal dimensions of the table aren't defined by a column setting, but rather, by the row containing the most cells.

You can use Dreamweaver's Design view to create and modify tables, and never look at the code. Understanding the underlying code gives you greater control over your tables, however, and allows for quick changes to their structure and attributes.

Using Tables in Standard View

Dreamweaver's Design view has two different views you can use to design documents. The *Layout view* lets you design your page by laying out the various elements where you want them. The Layout view simplifies the normally difficult process of using tables for page layout. Dreamweaver automatically adjusts the underlying tables. However, you cannot manually add a table to your page in Layout view. Instead, you must switch to Standard view.

To switch to Standard view if you're in Layout view, click the Standard View button in the View section of the Objects panel, as this illustration shows.

Inserting a Table

A table can be inserted by using the Table object in the Objects panel or by choosing the Insert menu. To insert a table, follow these steps:

1. Place the insertion point in the document window where you want the table.

2. Click the Table button in the Common category of the Objects panel, or choose Insert | Table from the menu. Or, you can drag the Table button on the Objects panel to the place on the page where you want to insert the object.

3. In the Insert Table dialog box (shown in the following illustration), either accept the current values or input new values. This dialog box enables you to set these table parameters:

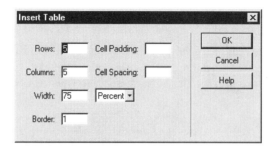

- **Rows**—The number of rows in the table.

- **Columns**—The number of columns in the table.

- **Cell Padding**—Specifies the number of pixels between the cell's content and the cell border. if you leave this field blank, the default value is 1 pixel. You can have no padding by specifying 0 for this field.

- **Cell Spacing**—Specifies the number of pixels between table cells. The default value if you leave this field blank is 2 pixels. Again, you can enter 0 to have no spacing between cells.

- **Width**—Specifies the width of the table. Enter a number and select the units, either pixels or a percentage of the browser width.

- **Border**—The width of the table border. This should be 0 if you don't want the table to have a border.

4. Click OK to create the table.

Figure 14-1 shows the empty table as created, with five rows and columns.

Setting Table Properties

Once a table is inserted into a document, you can modify it using the Property Inspectors for the table, rows, and cells. Some of the properties for individual cells and rows are the same as the properties for the table itself: In these cases, the cell's settings have precedence over the row and table, and the row settings have precedence over the table settings.

Selecting a Table

Selecting a table can be tricky because, just by clicking the table, you might select one of its cells instead. You can select a table in several ways, though, that can ensure the entire table is selected.

To select a table, do one of the following:

- Click the top-left corner of the table, or on the right or bottom edge.

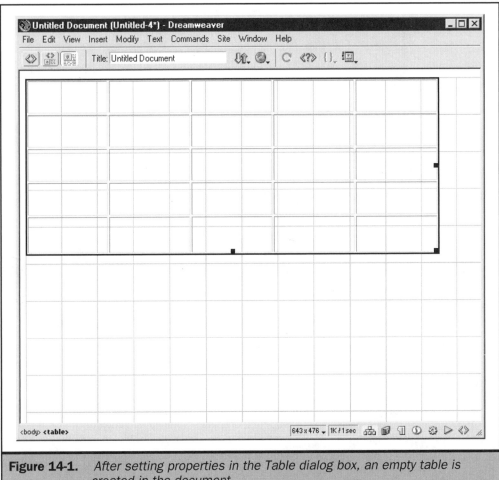

Figure 14-1.   *After setting properties in the Table dialog box, an empty table is created in the document*

- Click inside the table and choose Modify | Table | Select Table from the menu.
- Click inside the table, press and hold the CTRL key, and choose Edit | Select All.
- Click inside the table, and click the `<table>` tag shown in the tag selector at the bottom left-hand corner of the document window, as shown in Figure 14-2.

When the table is selected, it will have a thick border displayed around it, with resize handles. The following illustration shows this.

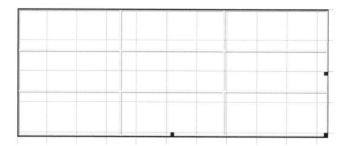

Table Property Inspector

The *Table Property Inspector*, shown in the following illustration, allows most of the overall property settings for a table to be changed.

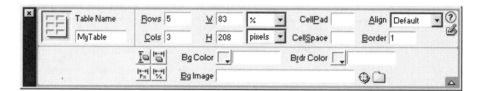

To change table properties using the Property Inspector, select the table as previously described. If the Property Inspector isn't shown, choose Window | Properties to open it. You may also need to open the inspector to show all the options by clicking the expander arrow on the right corner.

The Table Property Inspector lets you change the following properties:

Table Name

The *Table Name property* provides a name for the table, which can be used to identify it in JavaScript.

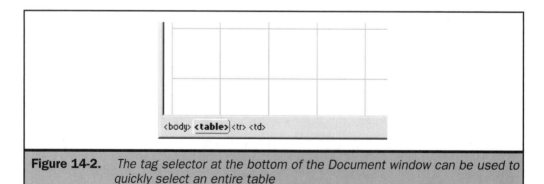

Figure 14-2. *The tag selector at the bottom of the Document window can be used to quickly select an entire table*

Rows and Cols

Rows and Cols enable you to make adjustments to the number of rows and columns in the table. Note, if the table is full of data, reducing the number of rows or columns also causes the data in those cells to be deleted from the page.

Width and Height

The *Width and Height* properties of a table are specified in the *W* and *H* fields. Either setting may use pixels or a percentage of the browser window dimensions.

Cell Padding

The *CellPad* field lets you specify the number of pixels between the cell content and the cell edge. This value defaults to 1 for both Netscape and Internet Explorer.

Cell Spacing

In the CellSpace field, specify the number of pixels between each table cell. This field defaults to 2 in both Netscape and Internet Explorer if they're left blank.

Alignment

The *Align* field specifies the alignment of the table in relation to the other elements at its level. You can choose to align the table to the left, to the right, or to the center. You can also leave this field blank to choose the browser's default.

Borders

The *Border* field lets you specify the width of the table border, in pixels. For tables that are being used for page layout, set the border to 0. For tables being used to present tabular data, set the border to a number greater than 0. Choose View | Visual Aids | Table Borders to continue showing thin lines for table borders in the Design view to help you with your layout placement.

 Table borders can appear differently in IE and Netscape. If you're using table borders, test your pages in both browsers to ensure you're getting the results you expect.

Clear Row Heights and Clear Column Widths

The *Clear Row Heights and Clear Column Widths* buttons in the lower-left of the Table property inspector can remove all height and column values from the table.

Convert Table Widths to Pixels

The *Convert Table Widths to Pixels* button converts the table wi\dth from a percentage of the browser window to its current width in pixels.

Convert Table Widths to Percent

The *Convert Table Widths to Percent* button converts the current table width from pixels to a percentage of the width of the browser window.

Background Color

The *Bg Color* field sets a background color for the table. Choose a color using the Color Picker or enter the RGB values directly on the input line.

Border Color

The *Brdr Color* field sets a border color for the table. Choose a color using the Color Picker or enter the RGB values directly on the input line.

Background Image

The *Bg Image* field lets you specify an image to use for the table's background. Enter the filename directly or browse to it by clicking the folder button. You can also choose an image by dragging the target icon to an image file in your Site Files list.

 You should usually set the background color of a table even if you use a background image. This way, browsers that don't download the image can still see the table elements against a background color that differs from the page background.

Selecting Rows, Columns, and Cells

The other elements of a table—the `<tr>` and `<td>` elements—have their own Property Inspector, which enables you to set properties unique to these elements and also to set properties that override the table's settings. For instance, you might want to give the top row of your table a different background color than the rest of the table to make it stand out as a header.

To select a row, click the leftmost border of the table. To select a column, click the top border of the table. The cursor then changes into a bold arrow pointing in the direction of the available selection as you move around the border of the table.

To select individual cells, click directly on the cell. You can then drag the mouse pointer to select additional cells before releasing the button. Two other methods are to click a cell, and then SHIFT-CLICK another cell to select all cells in the rectangular region, or to CTRL-CLICK (COMMAND-CLICK on the Mac) each cell you want to add.

No matter how many cells you select, the Cell Property Inspector becomes active.

Cell Property Inspector

The *Cell Property Inspector,* as the following illustration shows, allows settings for individual table cells or groups of cells to be changed.

To change the cell properties using the Property Inspector, select a cell, multiple cells, or a row or column as previously described. If the Property Inspector isn't shown, choose Window | Properties to open it. You may also need to open the inspector to show all the options by clicking the expander arrow on the right corner.

The Cell Property Inspector lets you change the following properties:

Horizontal Alignment

The *Horz* pop-up menu is used to set the horizontal alignment of the selected cell or cells contents. Alignment can be left, right, center, or browser default. Browser default is usually left alignment for regular cells and center alignment for header cells.

Vertical Alignment

The *Vert* pop-up menu is used to set the vertical alignment of the selected cell's or cells', contents. Alignment can be to the top, middle, bottom, baseline, or browser default (which is usually middle).

Width and Height

The *W* and *H* fields specify the width and height of selected cells in pixels. To use percentages, follow the value with a percent symbol (%).

Background Image

To set a *background* image for a cell or group of cells, enter the filename in the top Bg field. You can also browse by using the folder button or drag the target icon to the file in the Site Files list. Cell background images don't span cell boundaries: Each cell has its own version of the image. Cell image settings override the parent table's image settings.

Background Color

To set the *background* color for a cell, column, or row, use the color picker with the bottom Bg field. You can also type the RGB values directly into the input line. Cell color settings override the parent table's image settings.

Border Color

The Brdr field is used to set a *border* color. This color must be in place for two adjacent cells; otherwise, the table border color is used.

Merging Cells

The *Merge Cells* button is used to combine the selected cells into one cell. This is discussed in the section "Splitting and Merging Cells," in this chapter.

Splitting Cells

Splitting cells is used to divide a cell into one or more additional cells. This is also discussed in the section "Splitting and Merging Cells."

Click the Split Cell button to divide a cell, creating two cells. See the section "Splitting and Merging Cells."

Text Wrapping

If you select No Wrap, text in the cell won't wrap at the end of the line. As a result, the cells tend to grow wider to handle all the data being displayed in the cell.

Headers

Checking the *Header* field formats the selected cells as table headers, replacing the `<td>` tag with a `<th>` tag instead. Table headers are formatted a little differently to stand out from `<td>` cells. Header cells are usually bold and centered by default.

Adding Content to a Table

Tables aren't much good by themselves. *Tables* are meant to hold content: Whether they are used as a page formatting device or in the more traditional way of displaying columnar data, you still need to get data into a table. Dreamweaver provides two basic ways of filling a table: you can manually enter data into each cell or you can populate an entire table at once from a file.

Adding Content to a Cell

You can nest most HTML tags inside table cells. Most commonly, you see tables with text or images inserted.

To add an HTML element to a cell, click inside the cell to select it, and then insert the HTML objects as you would outside a table.

Importing Tabular Data

Perhaps the quickest way to populate a table is to fill it with data saved in a delimited text file (with tabs, colons, commas, semicolons, or others). To import table data, do this:

1. Choose File | Import | Import Tabular Data, or Insert | Tabular Data. The Import Table Data or Import Tabular Data dialog box appears, as the following illustration shows. These dialog boxes are identical except for the title.

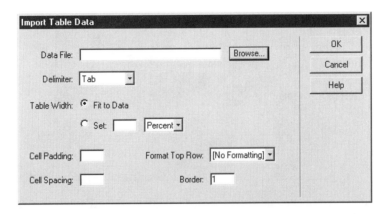

2. Enter the name of the file to import in the Data File field.

3. Specify the delimiter used in the file in the Delimiter menu. If you choose "Other," you can specify the delimiter character in an adjacent input box that appears.

4. In the Table Width field, choose either Fit to Data, in which the table expands to accommodate the largest text string in the data file, or Set, where you can specify the dimensions of the table in pixels or a percentage of the browser window width.

5. In the Cell Padding field, enter a value in pixels to pad each cell. The default is 1.

6. In the Cell Spacing field, enter a value in pixels for separating each cell. The default for this setting is 2.

7. If you want the top row formatted differently, as with a header, select one of the formatting options in the Format Top Row menu. Choices are Bold, Italic, and Bold Italic.

8. Specify a width for the table border in the Border field. To create a table with no border, use 0.

Sorting Data

Dreamweaver has a command that enables you to sort the data in a table based on the data in a single column or to sort based on the values in two columns.

You cannot sort data in a table that has merged cells. This is because the sort requires data to be moved among rows, and the rows must have identical cells.

To sort a table, select it and choose the Commands | Sort Table command. In the dialog box that appears, as this illustration shows, select the column to sort by, whether to sort alphabetically or numerically, and ascending or descending.

BEYOND
THE BASICS

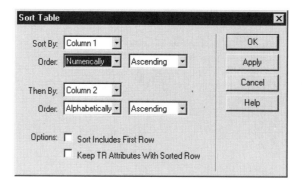

Optionally, you may choose the same options for a second column. Additional options are to include the first row in the sort (because the first row commonly holds header information you don't want to move), and Keep TR attributes with the sorted row. This option is important if your table has some special formatting, such as color coding for certain rows.

Modifying Tables

Table creation used to be quite a chore in the past. Dealing with spans, nested tables, and other strange formatting options isn't much fun when you have to do it by hand. Dreamweaver provides several tools for modifying tables, however, making it easy to format a table exactly the way you want it.

Inserting and Deleting Columns and Rows

Earlier in this chapter, you learned how to change the number of rows and columns in a table by setting the values in the Property Inspector. Dreamweaver provides more than one way of accomplishing many tasks, and this task is no exception. You can also use commands in the Modify | Table menu to do this, and they aren't limited to chopping off the bottommost row and rightmost column: You can insert and delete rows and columns anywhere in a table.

Inserting Rows and Columns

To add rows or columns to a table, do the following:

1. Click a cell in the table where you want the new row or column inserted.

2. Choose Modify | Table | Insert Row or Modify | Table | Insert Column, depending on which you want to add. You can add both rows and columns by choosing Modify | Table | Insert Rows or Columns.

3. If you choose Insert Rows or Columns, a dialog box appears, as this illustration shows. Choose whether to insert rows or columns, and then select the number

to add. For rows, choose whether to put the new rows above or below the currently selected cell. For columns, choose whether to put the new columns to the right or the left of the currently selected cell.

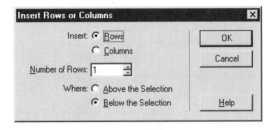

4. Click OK to insert.

Deleting a Row or Column

To delete a row or a column, do the following:

1. Click a cell in the row or column you want to delete.

2. Press DELETE. Or, choose Modify | Table | Delete Row or Modify | Table | Delete Column to delete the row or the column.

Splitting and Merging Cells

The Cell Property Inspector, as described earlier, has the capability of splitting cells into two or more cells, and also merging any number of adjacent cells into one cell. In addition, commands are on the Modify | Table menu to do the same things.

When you split or merge cells, Dreamweaver automatically takes care of the formatting needed to keep the rest of the table consistent, adding any necessary COLSPAN or ROWSPAN attributes.

To split a cell into multiple cells, click the cell and choose Modify | Table | Split Cell. You can also click the Split Cell button in the Property Inspector. The Split Cell dialog box appears, as the following illustration shows.

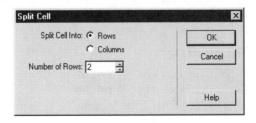

Choose whether to split the cell into rows or columns. Also enter the Number of Rows or Columns to split it into. Click OK.

BEYOND
THE BASICS

To merge multiple cells into a single cell, select the cells you want to merge. The selected cells must all be adjacent and, together, they must form a rectangle, as the following illustration shows.

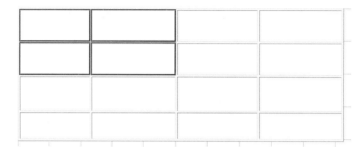

Choose Modify | Table | Merge Cells to merge the selected cells together, or click the Merge Cells button in the Property Inspector. The properties of the first cell selected are applied to the new merged cell.

Resizing Tables, Rows, and Columns

The simplest way of changing table or row/column dimensions is to select them, and then drag their resize borders.

To resize a table, select it and grab one of the resize handles on the sides or bottom-right corner. The bottom and right handles expand the table in that direction; the corner handle resizes it in both directions.

To resize a row or column, simply grab one of the cell borders and drag it to its new position.

Nesting Tables

Nested tables consist of a complete table within another table cell. To insert a nested table, put the selection cursor inside the cell you want to add the table to, and then insert the table using the Table object or the Insert | Table menu item.

Nested tables can be configured just like any other table; the only limit is that its width is limited to the width of the containing cell, as shown in Figure 14-3.

Format Table Command

The *Format Table* command gives you 17 different preset designs you can apply to a table. You can also set additional formatting options.

To use one of the preset designs using the Format Table command, do the following:

1. Select the table where you want to apply the formatting.

2. Select Commands | Format Table.

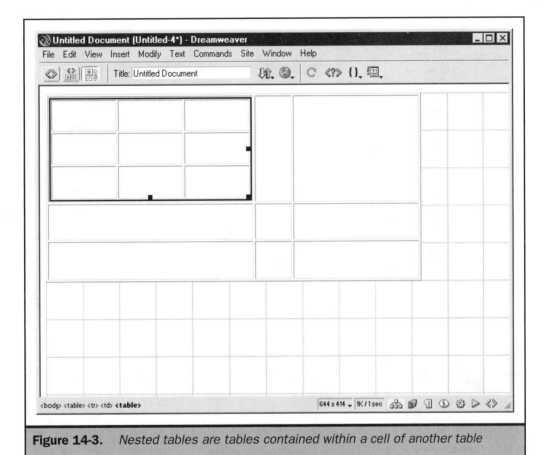

Figure 14-3.   *Nested tables are tables contained within a cell of another table*

3. In the Format Table dialog box, choose a design scheme from the list on the left. The sample table directly to the right updates to show the current table selection. The Format Table dialog box is shown in Figure 14-4.

4. After you choose a design, you can customize the table even more by changing the Row Colors, Top Row, and Left Col options.

5. You can decide whether to add a border and how wide to make it in the Border setting.

6. Choose whether you want the design to be applied to the table rows or to the individual <td> tags. Choosing the rows makes the most sense if most cells in a row will be formatted the same.

7. Click OK when you finish to format the table.

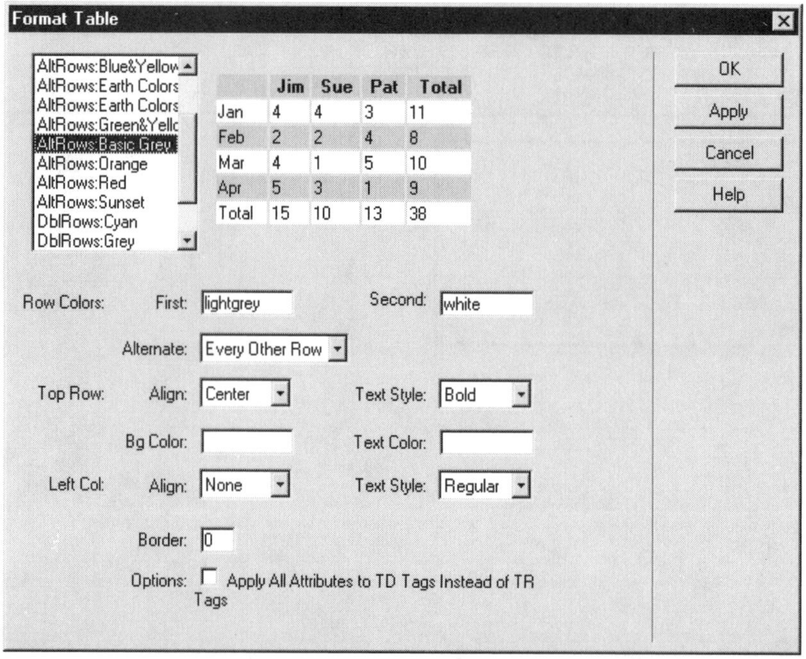

Figure 14-4. The Format Table command allows one of 17 preset table patterns to be used, along with other customization settings

Using Tables for Design

Although tables were first designed to show traditional tabular data, they have since become an important part of advanced Web page design. Tables make segmenting a page into multiple sections easy, without the hassle of frames.

Layout View

Dreamweaver provides the Layout view to simplify the use of tables for design. Layout view uses tables for the underlying structure of the page, but doesn't require you to do any of the traditional table creation steps. Instead, you can simply draw the table and cells in the window.

If you are in Standard view, to switch to Layout view, click the Layout View button in the View section of the Objects panel, as this illustration shows.

The *Layout view* enables you to design your page layout using layout cells. *Layout cells* let you block out parts of your page for the layout. For instance, you could draw a cell along the left side to hold a menu bar, a cell along the bottom of the page for a footer, a cell along the top for a header, and another cell to hold the page content.

When you create layout cells, Dreamweaver automatically adds a layout table if one isn't already created. You can add multiple layout tables to a page and even nest them to achieve the effects you desire.

Laying Out Cells and Tables

In Layout view, you draw layout cells directly on your page. If your page doesn't already contain a layout table, one is created that's the width of your Document window. You can change this to autostretch, if you like.

To draw a layout cell, first make sure you're in Layout view, and then click the Draw Layout Cell button in the Objects panel. The mouse pointer then changes into a plus sign (+), indicating it's ready to draw.

Position the mouse pointer where you want the cell to start on the page and drag to the opposite corner to create the cell. If you hold down the CTRL key (COMMAND on the Mac), you can create multiple cells without having to click the Layout Cell button each time. Figure 14-5 shows the beginning of a page being drawn with layout cells. There's a cell for the topmost header and another one on the left for a future menu bar.

Nested Layout Tables

Layout tables, like all HTML tables, can be nested to create more advanced page formatting. To draw a nested table, click the Draw Layout Table button in the Objects panel, and then click-and-drag the mouse pointer over an existing table to create the table.

Adding Content

Content can be added to layout cells in the same way as with other tables. Click the layout cell, and then insert text or an image as usual.

Formatting Layout Cells and Tables

Layout tables and cells have special Property Inspectors that can be used to set the appearance and format of the layout elements.

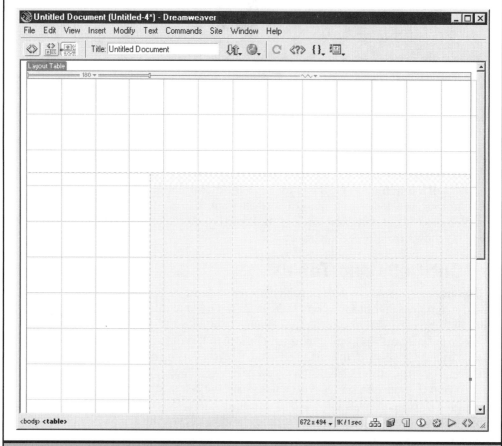

Figure 14-5.   *Layout view lets you design the structure of your page using layout tables and cells*

Layout Table Property Inspector

The *Layout Table Property Inspector* (shown in the following illustration) enables you to specify width and height, cell padding and spacing, as well as other properties. To change the properties of a layout table, click the table tab (at the top) or the edge. The Property Inspector lets you set the following:

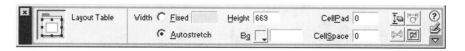

- **Width**—Options for Width include Fixed (with pixel dimensions) and Autostretch.

- **Height**—Height is always specified in pixels.

- **CellPad**—Enables you to set a value for the number of pixels between the cell's content and the cell walls. All cells in the table use this value if you set it above 0.

- **CellSpace**—Specifies the number of pixels between layout cells.

- **Bg**—Specifies a background color for the table. Use the color picker to choose a color or enter it directly in the input line.

- **Clear Row Heights**—Pressing this button causes all cells in the table to lose their height settings.

- **Make Widths Consistent**—This can be used to set fixed width cells, so they all have width consistent with their content.

- **Remove All Spacers**—This button removes all transparent spacer graphics from the table.

- **Remove Nesting**—If this table is nested within another layout table, clicking this button causes the current table to be eliminated and all the cells are made part of the containing table with no loss of information.

Layout Cell Property Inspector

The *Layout Cell Property Inspector* is used to set preferences for individual layout cells. You can set content formatting parameters, width and height, and background colors.

To use the Property Inspector, as this illustration shows, select the layout cell you want to modify by clicking on the edge, or by clicking anywhere in the cell while holding the CTRL key (COMMAND on the Mac). The Property Inspector enables you to set the following properties:

- **Width**—Options for Width include Fixed (with pixel dimensions) and Autostretch.

- **Height**—Height is always specified in pixels.

- **Bg**—Specifies a background color for the table. Use the color picker to choose a color or enter it directly in the input line.

- **Horz**—Specifies the horizontal alignment for layout cell content. Choices are Left, Right, Center, or Default.

- **Vert**—Specifies the vertical alignment for layout cell content. Choices are Top, Middle, Bottom, Baseline, or Default.

BEYOND THE BASICS

■ **No Wrap**—Check this box to prevent text from wrapping inside the layout cell. The cell gets wider to accommodate content that won't fit.

Setting Layout Width

Layout view enables you to specify two options for width: Fixed and Autostretch. You can see the width setting for layout cells by looking at the tabs at the top. Fixed-width layout cells have a pixel value, while autostretch cells have their width indicated by a wavy line. The autostretch column always expands to fill the width of the browser. Only one column in a layout can be autostretch.

You can change whether a particular column has an autostretch width by clicking the tab at the top of the layout cell, as shown in Figure 14-6.

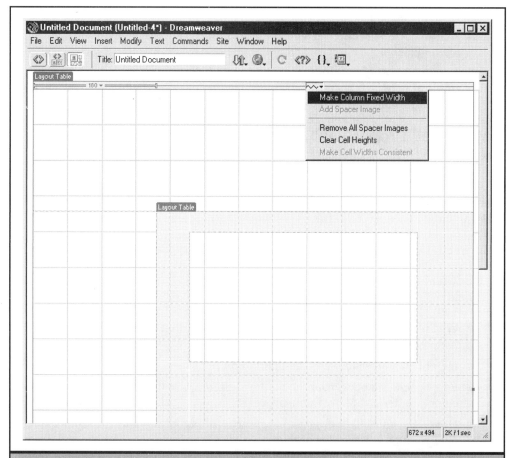

Figure 14-6. *You can change layout cells to have a fixed width or an autostretch width*

Spacer Images

Spacer images are transparent images that don't show in the browser. They're used to control spacing in autostretch tables by columns to maintain their widths. If the spacer files didn't exist, columns would collapse.

Setting Up a Spacer File

If your site doesn't have a spacer file when you add one to a column or specify a column as autostretch, Dreamweaver prompts you with a dialog box asking how to set up the spacer file, as the following illustration shows.

Summary

Tables are one of the most versatile HTML elements, and they have been extended far beyond their original intended use of displaying columnar data. Now, tables are an essential layout tool for advanced Web page design. Dreamweaver makes using tables easy both for displaying data and page layout.

- Traditional tables can be created in Dreamweaver's Standard view.

- Dreamweaver provides a variety of tools to make it easy to create and modify tables to suit your needs.

- The Layout view takes tables to the next level, making them a fundamental tool for designing page layout.

The next chapter discusses frames and framesets, from how to create them to the pros and cons of using them.

The Complete Reference

Dreamweaver 4

Chapter 15

Frames

Frames are a way to compartmentalize a Web page into multiple, mostly independent sections. Each section, or frame, consists of an entire HTML document. All the documents are tied together in yet another HTML document called a frameset.

This chapter explains how to create frames and how framesets can be used to enhance a Web site's design, including the pros and cons of frames, and the problems in using them with older browsers. This chapter then delves into Dreamweaver's features for creating frames.

Frame Basics

A *frame page* has a `<frameset>` tag in place of the `<body>` tag you would find in a normal HTML page. The *frameset* describes how the page is to be divided, and can be defined in terms of either rows (horizontal units) or columns (vertical units), but not both. In addition, the columns or rows can be divided further by nesting additional framesets within them. The following listing shows a frameset consisting of two rows. The first row contains a frame (specified with the `<frame>` tag), but the second row contains yet another frameset. This frameset consists of two columns, both of which contain `<frame>` tags.

```
<frameset rows="80,*" cols="*">
  <frame name="topFrame" scrolling="NO" noresize
src="topframe.html">
  <frameset cols="80,*">
    <frame name="leftFrame" noresize scrolling="NO"
src="leftframe.html">
    <frame name="mainFrame" src="mainframe.html">
</frameset>
```

This creates a page with three frames: one frame at the top of the page going from the left to the right and two more frames running from the bottom of the top frame to the bottom of the page, as shown in Figure 15-1.

The rows and cols attributes of the frameset indicate the number of rows or columns the frameset should have and the size they should be. These attributes use a comma-separated list of sizes that can be specified as either percentages of the window size

```
<frameset rows="%33,%33,%34">
```

or pixel sizes

```
<frameset cols="160,*">
```

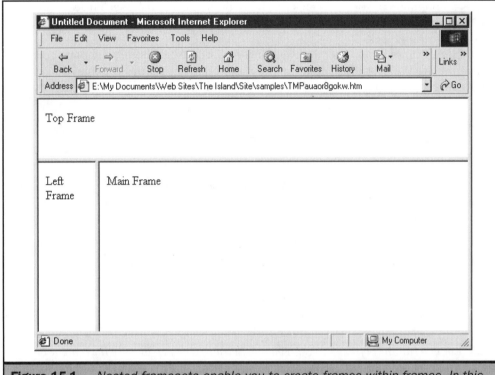

Figure 15-1. *Nested framesets enable you to create frames within frames. In this case, the topmost frameset has two rows, with the bottom frame containing another frameset with two columns*

The "*" value for a size is a wildcard value meaning "use all the rest of the available space." The wildcard can also be prepended by an integer value:

```
<frameset rows="2*,*">
```

In this case, the frameset specifies two frames, with the first one twice as large as the second.

Older Browsers and Frames

Frames were first introduced in Netscape 2.0, and later added to Internet Explorer in version 3.0. While you can be certain the vast majority of Web surfers can handle frames, a few of the older browsers are still in use out there.

When you create a frameset page with Dreamweaver, it automatically adds a `<noframes></noframes>` tag pair after the frameset. Browsers that don't support frames ignore the `<frameset>` tags and display the part of the page enclosed in the `<noframes>` tag. Conversely, frames-capable browsers know to ignore everything in the `<noframes>` block.

In the noframes block, Dreamweaver inserts a `<body></body>` tag pair. You can build an entire Web page here that can only be seen in nonframes-capable browsers. Here's the earlier listing with the `<noframes>` and `<body>` tags added.

```
<frameset rows="80,*" cols="*">
  <frame name="topFrame" scrolling="NO" noresize
src="topframe.html">
  <frameset cols="80,*">
    <frame name="leftFrame" noresize scrolling="NO"
src="leftframe.html">
    <frame name="mainFrame" src="mainframe.html">
</frameset>
<noframes>
<body bgcolor="#FFFFFF" text="#000000">
</body>
</noframes>
```

Tip *Because Dreamweaver displays the frameset and frame content in the Design view, how can you edit the noframes page? You must do an extra step to make the content visible: Checking the Modify | Frameset | Edit NoFrames Content menu item causes the noframes content to be displayed in the Design window. Uncheck this menu item to show the frames again. Another way to show the noframes content is to activate the Code and Design view split window, and then click the `<body>` tag or any subtags in the Code view to activate the noframes view. Click any part of the document outside of the `<noframes>` tag to return to the frames view.*

Planning Frames

Frames require a lot of advance planning. Remember, some visitors could have a lower resolution display than yours when sizing frames. Start with a rough layout of the frames and their relative sizes. That left-side navbar that takes up a modest amount of space on your 1,024 × 768 monitor might occupy half the screen on a browser limited to 640 × 480.

Determine which frames have static, unchanging information and which are to be used for dynamic content. The unchanging frames are typically a navbar or other navigational aids, standard heading or footing frames you want to use on all your pages. Dynamically updated pages are where the main content is displayed on your site.

Decide whether frames should have scrollbars. While scrollbars are sometimes unavoidable, you probably don't want to use them for a frame that contains a small amount of content (say a banner ad image).

Make sure your frames work as one cohesive page. Even though each frame exists in a separate HTML document, your visitors will see them as a single entity. Make sure complementary colors and styles are used for all frames.

Remember, adding frames to a site can significantly affect the initial download time. Make sure that even though your initial download of a frameset includes a different document for each frame, updating the dynamic content should usually only cause a single new page to be downloaded.

Adding Frames and Framesets in Dreamweaver

Dreamweaver provides two methods for creating frames. You can either use the Design view to create frames in a freeform manner or use predefined framesets in the Objects panel's frames category. The choice is yours.

Creating Frames

Before you can create a frameset, you need to make the frame borders visible in the document window. Choose View | Visual Aids | Frame Borders to activate the borders. Initially, because your page doesn't have any frames, the border is visible only around the outside edge of the entire document, as shown in Figure 15-2.

To create a frame, position the cursor over an existing border, and it turns into a double or quad arrow (or a drag hand on the Mac). The quad arrow appears when you position the cursor over a corner. Then, do one of the following:

- Drag the frame border from the outside edge into the Document window. (Figure 15-3 shows a frameset being created in this manner.) Hold down the Alt key (Option on the Mac) when you want to use the drag method to create a new frame from an already existing inner border.

- Select a frame in the document by clicking it in the Design view and choose one of the Modify | Frameset | Split Frames Left/Right/Up or Down menu items to subdivide the frame automatically into two more frames.

Once your frames are created, you can resize them by simply dragging the frame borders. If you want to enter the exact pixel or percentage, you can use the Frameset Property Inspector, described later in this chapter.

Splitting Frames

You can split frames simply by holding down the Alt key (Option on the Mac) and dragging a frame border. Be forewarned, though, this border will go from one side of the frameset to the other. For example, if you have two column frames and you drag from the top of the document in one of the frames to split it, you'll split both the existing frames when you might have only wanted to split one of them. The best way

Figure 15-2. When you activate the Frame Borders visual aid, a box is visible around the edges of the document window

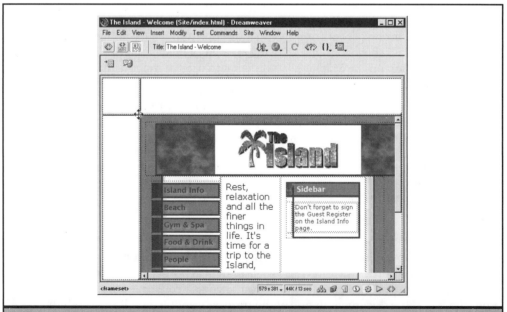

Figure 15-3. You can create frames simply by dragging the frame border from the outside edge of your document in the Design view

to split a frame in this case is to select the frame you want to split and use the Modify |
Frameset | Split Frames menu items. These items create a nested frameset in place of
the existing frame, with the current frame content occupying the side the menu item
specifies. Figure 15-4 shows an example of a split frames operation.

Deleting Frames

Deleting frames is easy to do, but it isn't obvious. You can't simply select a frame and
press Delete.

To delete a frame, drag a border to the edge of a frameset and release it, and the
frame disappears. If your document only contains one frameset, drag it to the
document border. Note, the frame that's shrunk to nothing when you drag the border
is the one that's actually deleted. If any unsaved content is in the frame, Dreamweaver
prompts you to save it first.

Note   *When you delete a frame, you're only deleting the reference to it from the frameset. The
actual content of the frame isn't touched.*

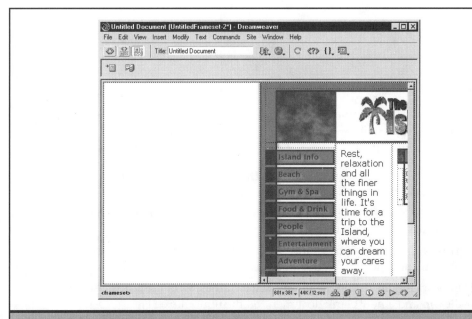

Figure 15-4.   *The result of the Split Frame Right command puts the current
document in the rightmost frame and creates a new blank frame
on the left*

Frame Objects

As easy as Dreamweaver makes it to create frames by hand, an even easier method exists. The Frame objects in the Objects panel provide icons for the eight most common frame layouts to let you automatically set up your frames complete with meaningful names with a single click. The following illustration shows the Frames category of the Objects panel.

The icons representing the predefined framesets each show one frame highlighted. This is the frame that will contain the current document when you add one of these framesets. The eight different frameset choices available on this panel work as follows:

- **Left**—Splits the document into two frames, with the current document on the right and a new blank document on the left. See Figure 15-5.

- **Right**—Splits the document into two frames, with the current document on the left and a new blank document on the right. See Figure 15-6.

- **Top**—Splits the document into two frames, with the current document on the bottom and a new blank document on the top. See Figure 15-7.

- **Bottom**—Splits the document into two frames, with the current document on the top and a new blank document on the bottom. See Figure 15-8.

- **Left and Top**—Splits the document into four frames, with the current document occupying the lower rightmost frame. See Figure 15-9.

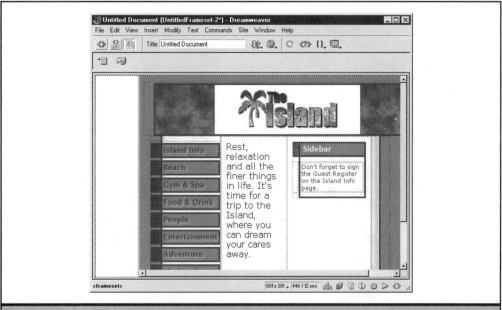

Figure 15-5. *The Left Frame object adds a new blank frame on the left side of the browser window*

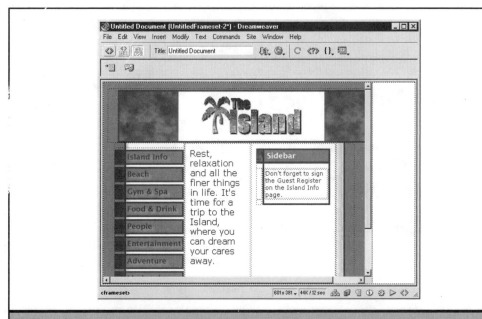

Figure 15-6. *The Right Frame object adds a new blank frame on the right side of the browser window*

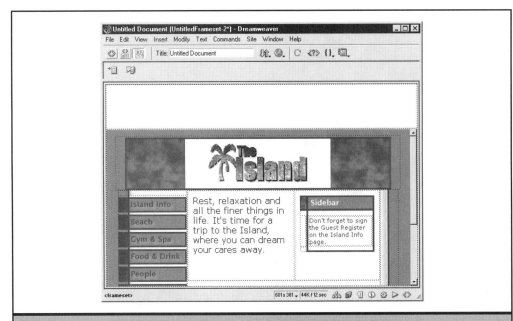

Figure 15-7. *The Top Frame object adds a new blank frame on the top of the browser window*

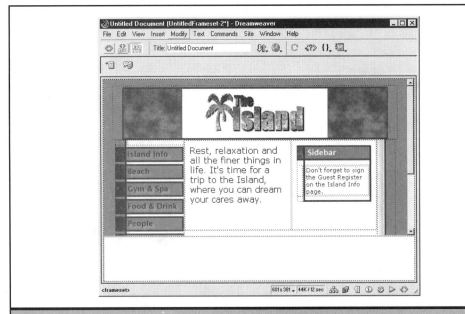

Figure 15-8. *The Bottom Frame object adds a new blank frame on the bottom of the browser window*

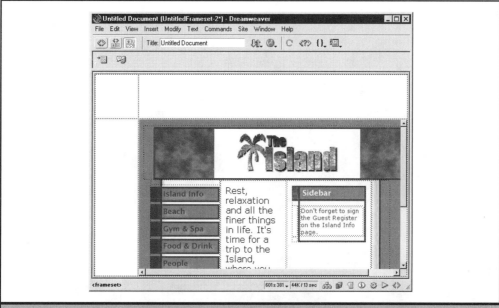

Figure 15-9.   *The Left and Top Frame object adds a new blank frame on the top, left, and upper-left corner of the browser window*

- **Left Top**—Creates a frameset with three frames, with the leftmost frame running from the top to the bottom of the document, and the other two frames splitting the right side using a nested frameset. The current document occupies the lower rightmost frame. See Figure 15-10.

- **Top Left**—Creates a frameset with three frames, with the upper frame running from the left to the right of the document and the other two frames splitting the lower frame using a nested frameset. The current document occupies the lower rightmost frame. See Figure 15-11.

- **Split**—Splits the document into four equal sized frames, with the current document occupying the lower rightmost frame. This differs from the Left and Top frameset only in the row and column sizing. See Figure 15-12.

The Frame objects can also be used to subdivide existing frames. Select a frame in the Design view and click the object icon of your choice. The frame is replaced with a nested frameset using one of the previous formats.

Saving Frames and Framesets

Framesets are saved in a separate HTML file from the frame content files, so be sure to save the frameset and the frames.

BEYOND
THE BASICS

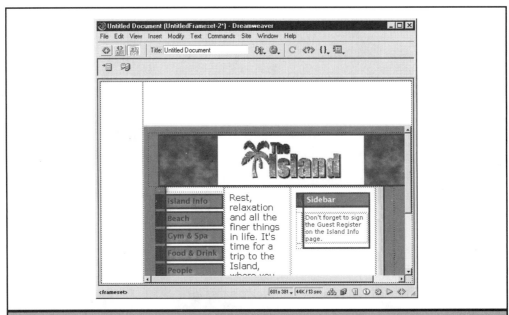

Figure 15-10. The Left Top Frame object adds a frame on the left, and then further subdivides the right side with another frame on the top

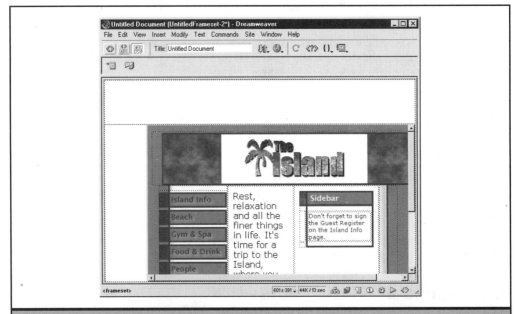

Figure 15-11. The Top Left Frame object adds a frame on the top, and then further subdivides the bottom side with another frame on the left

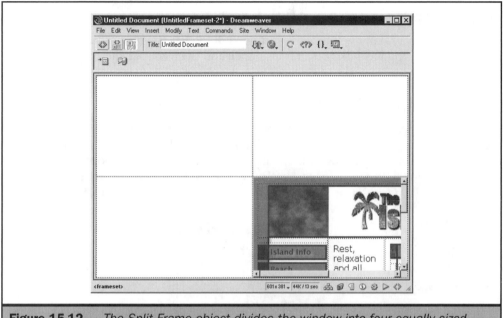

Figure 15-12.   *The Split Frame object divides the window into four equally sized frames*

If you created frames from an existing document, Dreamweaver uses that document's file name in the frameset. Any blank frames created, however, are given generic numbered UntitledFrame names, which are nearly useless. Thus, you want to save each of these files using names that make more sense.

To save a frameset, select it by clicking one of the frame borders. Then choose File | Save Frameset As to be prompted for a filename to use. Once you save the frameset using a name of your choice, the File | Save Frameset menu item can be used to save modifications to the frameset. Another option is to save the frameset as a template using File | Save Frame as Template. See Chapter 29 for more information on how to use templates.

When you select an individual frame in your document as opposed to the frameset, the menu items for saving change to Save Frame and Save Frame As. These work the same way as their frameset counterparts.

Finally, you can save all the frames and the frameset at once by choosing the File | Save All Frames menu item. This prompts you to name any files you haven't saved before in the order they appear in the frameset. If you don't know the order, this can be confusing because the Save As dialog box doesn't say which frame document you're naming.

Modifying Frames and Framesets

Once your frames layout is complete, you can still modify the properties and positions of each frame using tools like the Frames panel, and the frameset and frame Property Inspectors.

Using the Frames Panel

The Frames panel provides a visual representation of the current document's frames. You can use this panel to click a frame or frameset in the Frames panel to select that frame or frameset in the document. Then, you can view or edit the properties of the selected item in the Property inspector. To display the Frames panel, choose Window | Frames from the menu, or press SHIFT-F2.

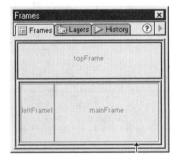

The Frames panel makes seeing the hierarchy of nested framesets easy. Framesets are represented by a thick three-dimensional border, while a thin gray line marks individual frames. Each frame is identified by its frame name. To select a frame, click it in the Frames panel. To select a frameset, click the border surrounding the frames.

You can also select frames and framesets in the Design view. Click a visible frameset border to select that frameset. Select a frame by holding down the ALT key (OPTION-SHIFT on the Mac) while clicking its space.

Setting Frame Properties

The Frame Property Inspector, shown in the following illustration, can be used to modify properties for individual frames. To set frame properties, either select the frame in the Frames panel or ALT-CLICK it (OPTION-SHIFT-CLICK on the Mac). If the Property Inspector isn't visible, choose Window | Properties to activate it.

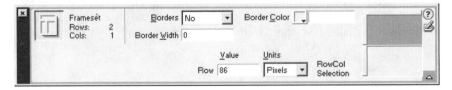

The Frame property inspector lets you set the following frame properties:

- **Frame Name**—Enters a name to use for the frame for scripting and target references. Frame names should be a single word, with the first character being a letter. You may use underscores in the name, but not other special characters. You should also avoid the use of the standard frame names _blank, _parent, _self, and _top.

- **Src**—Specifies the filename of the document to show in the frame. You can either enter the filename directly or click the folder icon to browse to a file. (You can also specify the file to use in a frame by positioning the cursor in the frame and choosing the File | Open in Frame menu item.)

- **Scroll**—Sets the scrollbar properties for the frame. The choices are Auto, Yes, No, and Default. The default for most browsers is Auto, which only shows scrollbars when the frame's content exceeds the dimensions of the frame. A setting of Yes displays scroll bars constantly, regardless of content size, and a setting of No never displays them.

- **No Resize**—Prevents users from resizing a frame in their browsers by dragging its border.

- **Borders**—Sets border properties for this frame. These settings can override the border settings for the frameset. Choices are Yes, No, and Default. If you choose No, any adjacent frames must also be set to No, or set to Default with the parent frameset set to No.

- **Border Color**—Sets a border color for borders adjacent to the frame, overriding the border color in the frameset. Choose a color from the color picker or enter its RGB value in the text box (for example, #FFFFFF).

- **Margin Width**—Adds a margin in pixels between the left and right borders and the frame content. (If you don't see this item, click the expander arrow in the Property Inspector to show the full set of Property Inspector options.)

- **Margin Height**—Adds a margin in pixels between the top and bottom borders and the frame content. (If you don't see this item, click the expander arrow in the Property Inspector.)

Setting Frameset Properties

The Frameset Property Inspector is used to set properties common to all frames. To activate the Frameset Property Inspector, select a frameset by clicking one of its borders in the Design view or in the Frames panel. If the Property Inspector isn't visible, choose Window | Properties to activate it. The following illustration shows the Frameset Property Inspector.

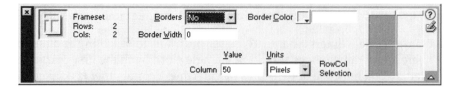

The Frameset Property Inspector enables you to set the following items:

- **Borders**—This property enables you to specify whether the frameset should display borders. Choose Yes to display borders, choose No not to display borders. Default leaves it up to the browser to decide how to display borders.

- **Border Width**—If you choose to display borders, you can specify the width (in pixels) to use for the border. If you aren't displaying borders, leave this set to 0.

- **Border Color**—Use the color picker to specify a color to use for the border, or enter the RGB value directly in the text box.

In addition to these properties, the Frameset Property Inspector enables you to set the precise size to use for each row and column. The grid on the right side is the Row/Column selector. It has tabs to select for each row or column. (If the grid isn't showing, click the expander arrow). Note, this grid only shows frames from the currently selected frameset. If you have nested framesets in your document, they won't be shown in the RowCol selector.

The following steps are used to set the size for a row or column using the RowCol selector:

1. Click the tab on the RowCol Selector for the row or column you want to modify.

2. In the Value field, enter a size value to use. This can be a numeric value or an *.

3. In the Units menu, choose the units to use:

   - **Pixels**—This indicates that the size of the row or column should be set to an absolute pixel value. Use this option if a frame should always be the same size, such as for a header or a navbar.

   - **Percent**—This value specifies the current frame should use a specified percentage of its frameset's space. Frames that have units set to Percent are allocated space after frames with units set to Pixels.

   - **Relative**—This value specifies the frame should use space proportionate to other frames. Frames with Relative units are given space after frames with units set to Pixels and Percent. They use all the remaining space in the frameset to determine their relative sizes.

Setting a Page Title

When a visitor navigates to a frameset page, the title of the frameset page is used for the title in the browser, so any titles on frame pages are ignored. To add a title to a frameset page, use the page properties option.

 It's still a good idea to title your frame pages in case a user opens them in another browser window or you decide to use the same pages for <noframes> content.

1. Select a frameset either by clicking the border in the Frames panel or by clicking the border in the Design view.

2. Choose Modify | Page Properties from the menu.

3. In the Title field, type a name for the document.

Targeting Frames

One of the most useful things to do with frames is to separate a navbar from site content. This way, you can have a frame with your site's navigation controls on one side and have a main frame to display the content as you click links in the first frame. Your main frame can have scrollbars that let a user view long documents without disturbing the navigational frame.

When choosing a target for a link, you can choose to target a frame by name or use one of the standard reserved names to target other aspects of the frameset.

Targeting the Frameset

You learned from the instructions for naming frames that you can't use a few reserved frame names. This is because these can be used to set a target within the current frameset or document. The four reserved targets are _blank, _parent, _self, and _top.

To set a target for a link, select the text or image you want to use for the link. Then do the following:

1. In the Link field of the Property Inspector, enter the target URL to link to. You can enter it directly or browse to a file by clicking the folder icon.

2. In the Target menu, choose a target frame for the linked document to appear. The standard choices for this box are

- **_blank**—Opens the link in a new browser window, leaving the current window alone.

- **_parent**—Opens the link in the parent frameset of the link. This replaces that frameset with the linked document.

- **_self**—Opens the link in place of the current document. This is the default behavior.

- **_top**—The link is opened in the topmost frameset of the current document. All frames are replaced.

Targeting Frames by Name

In addition to the standard targets, you can also choose any frame you have named as a target. Dreamweaver automatically adds any frames in your document to the target list. You can enter this name directly or use the drop-down list to select the name of a frame. Remember, target names are case-sensitive.

Targeting Frames with Behaviors

Several of Dreamweaver's behaviors that deal with navigation enable you to specify a target frame. Among them are Set Text of Frame, Go To URL, Insert Jump Menu, and Insert Navigation Bar. Chapter 23 talks about behaviors and how to use the Behaviors Panel in more detail, so this section only mentions behaviors that use frames.

Set Text of Frame

The Set Text of Frame action enables you to completely replace the content of a frame with new text that you supply. This text can be any valid HTML code, enabling you to dynamically update large portions of your Web pages. You can embed JavaScript statements or function calls to generate the text for the frame by enclosing it in braces:

```
Today's date is {new Date()}.
```

The Set Text of Frame dialog box, shown in the following illustration, enables you to specify the name of the target frame and provides a check box to allow the background color to be preserved. The Get Current HTML button copies the current contents of the target frame.

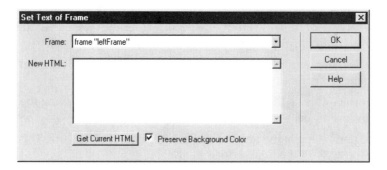

Go To URL

If you want to target multiple frames with a single link, Dreamweaver's Go To URL behavior can be used. Follow these steps to use the Go To URL behavior to update multiple frames:

1. Select the text or image to use as a link.

2. Open the Behavior Inspector by choosing Window | Behaviors.

3. Select the + (Action) button to display a list of actions.

4. Choose the Go To URL action.

5. In the Go To URL dialog box, choose a target frame from the Open In: list. The target can be one of your named frames or one of the standard frames.

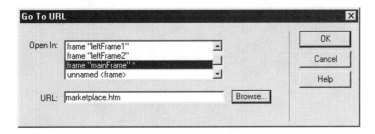

6. Enter the URL to navigate to in the URL field. You see an asterisk appear next to the target frame, as shown in the previous illustration. This indicates the frame has a target.

7. Repeat Steps 5 and 6 for any additional frames you want to target. Dreamweaver chains the Go To URL actions together in the order specified.

8. Click OK when you finish. The default event is the onClick event, which means the actions will be taken whenever the user clicks the link.

Of course, this action isn't limited to the onClick event. You can tie this action to any number of events, including timers, mouseovers, or any other event supported by your target browser.

Insert Jump Menu

Jump menus provide an easy way to navigate around a site. *Jump menus* are drop-down lists that contain entries for every page on your site. When visitors choose an item from the list, they jump to that page.

A Jump Menu action is automatically created when you insert a jump menu into your page. You can also change an existing jump menu by selecting it in the Design view and double-clicking the behavior in the Behaviors panel. To insert a jump menu into a page and target a frame, do the following:

1. Choose Insert | Form Object | Jump Menu from the menu, or click the Jump Menu item in the Forms section of the Objects panel. The Insert Jump Menu dialog box appears, as shown in the following illustration.

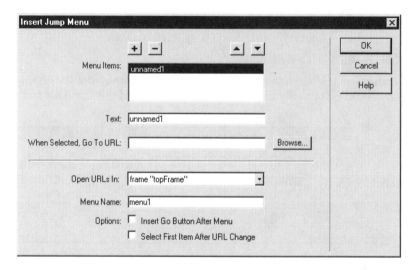

2. If you want the first item in the list to be a selection prompt, enter it now in the Text box. Click the Select First Item After URL box in the Options. Now click the plus sign (+) button to add a new menu item.

3. Enter the name of the next menu item in your list in the Text field.

4. Enter the destination URL in the When Selected, Go to URL field either by typing the path directly or using the Browse button to find a file.

5. Enter the destination frame in the Open URLs In field.

6. To add additional menu items, click the plus sign (+) button to create a new menu item, and then repeat Steps 3 through 5 for each item.

7. You can add a Go button to your jump menu by checking the Insert Go Button After Menu box.

Use the onChange event to trigger the jump whenever a new location is chosen from the jump menu.

Insert Navigation Bar

A *Navigation bar* (navbar) is used to direct a user to specific pages in a Web site. You can attach behaviors to navbar images and set which image displays based on a user's actions. You can, for example, show a button image in its Up or Down state to let a user know which page of a site is being viewed.

In the Navigation Bar dialog box, opened by choosing Insert | Interactive Images | Navigation Bar, the When Clicked, Go To URL field is followed by a target list, where you can select a target frame, as shown in the following illustration. Select one of your frames to use for the target.

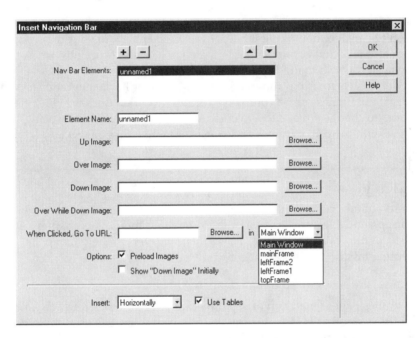

For more information about creating navbars, see Chapter 13. Information about navbars is also in Chapter 23.

The Advantages (and Disadvantages) of Using Frames

Frames have been a topic of heated debate ever since they were introduced. While some people love them, others still think of them as the scourge of the Web and say they should be banished entirely (see **http://www.noframes.org**). The reality is somewhere in the middle. While correctly implemented frames can benefit a site, some drawbacks still exist to using frames, which you should consider.

One advantage framed pages have is scrollbars can be set for individual frames. If you want the menus or ads at the top or side of your page to stay constant while a long document is being scrolled through, frames are the answer. Frames are also nice for aesthetic purposes: Your navbar needn't be redrawn every time a link is clicked if it's done in a frame.

Of course, some disadvantages also exist to using frames. Because at least one frame in a frameset is usually generated dynamically (such as choosing an item from a menu frame causing a new document to be shown in the main frame), it's impossible to bookmark these pages. You can bookmark the frameset, in which case the page loads with all dynamic frames set to default values. In many browsers, you can bookmark a frame individually, but when the visitor returns to that bookmark, all the surrounding frames won't be included, making it harder to navigate back to your main page. Frames can also take away from valuable screen real estate, especially when the site is viewed on systems with limited screen resolution.

Other drawbacks to using frames are because of poor implementations. Web pages with poorly done frames can be confusing because it's often unclear which portion of a page is going to change when a link is clicked. This can be avoided by being conservative with the use of frames and consistent when they're used.

Summary

Although sometimes controversial, there's no doubt that frames are an important tool for Web design and every designer should understand them. This chapter gave an introduction to frames and explained how Dreamweaver can help make the often-daunting task of juggling frames easier.

- Frames are either loved or hated passionately.

- A frames page is made up of separate HTML documents for each frame. In addition, another HTML document, called a frameset, is used to describe the locations and content of each frame.

- Some older browsers can't display frames. The <noframes> tag is used to provide content for these browsers in the frameset page.

- Dreamweaver provides two methods of adding frames to a page. You can create them manually by dragging frame borders to split the frames or by using one of the predefined frame objects in the Objects panel.

- Dreamweaver has a number of behaviors that can target frames, enhancing their utility on a frames-enabled site.

The next chapter discusses forms and how they can be used to add interactivity or solicit feedback from a site's visitors.

The Complete Reference

Chapter 16

Creating Forms

The Web offers unprecedented means of communicating with the people who are partaking of your services, products, or information. The thousands of mailing lists, newsgroups, message boards, and chats prove that a large percentage of Web users want community online. Today's consumers—whether it be of products or information—want to know their opinion means something to those who are delivering those goods.

One of the simplest ways to add interactivity and solicit feedback from a site's visitors is to add a form. Most HTML deals with presentation of information. Forms enable the user to submit information back to you. Forms are used for guest books, surveys, account sign ups, and e-commerce to name a few uses.

Basic Structure of Forms

Forms consist of two parts—the *entry page* that's displayed to the user and the *data collection* portion that disseminates the completed form data to you. All forms have some connection back to a Web server. This is commonly accomplished with a Common Gateway Interface (CGI) script or a mailto, which sends the form values to your e-mail. Of the two options, a *mailto* is the simplest to implement because it requires no additional coding or scripting. *CGI scripts* are the most useful, however because they can be used to parse the data into a useful format and store the data until you're ready to collect it. CGI Scripts are discussed in Chapter 22.

In HTML, forms are composed of a series of tags. The first tag pair defines the form itself and contains attributes to tell the server what to do with the data from the completed form and how to pass the data along. Here is some sample form code:

```
<form name="formdemo" method="post"
action="http://www.pendragn.com/_cgi-bin/inform.pl">
  <p>Last Name:
    <input type="text" name="lastname">
  </p>
  <p>Comments:<br>
    <textarea name="comment" cols="40" rows="4">Enter
comments:</textarea>
  </p>
</form>
```

Notice that paragraph elements—as well as tables, images, and other objects—can be used within the <form> tag pair. These are used to provide structure for the form, so it displays neatly in a browser.

Adding Forms in Dreamweaver

In Dreamweaver, you insert a form similarly to inserting any object into your Web page. You can use the menu bar or the Objects Panel to insert a form.

Points to remember when you use forms on your Web page are the following: you don't expand forms by resizing the form delimiter; forms automatically expand when you add items. And, forms and tables can be used together if the form completely encloses the table or the form is completely enclosed in the table.

Inserting a Form

Do one of the following to insert a form on your Web page:

- Place the cursor on your page where you want the form. Select the Insert Form icon from the Forms category of the Objects panel. Figure 16-1 shows the Forms panel. (If the Objects Panel isn't visible, select Window | Objects or press CTRL-F2.)

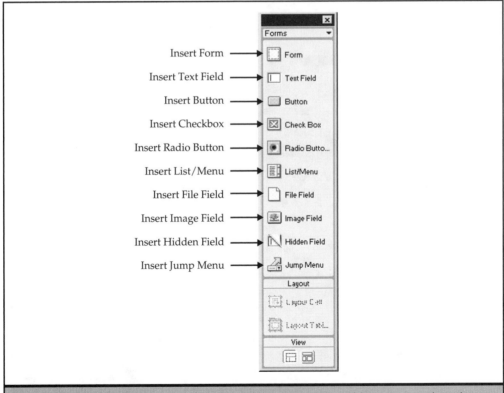

Insert Form	→	Form
Insert Text Field	→	Text Field
Insert Button	→	Button
Insert Checkbox	→	Check Box
Insert Radio Button	→	Radio Butto...
Insert List/Menu	→	List/Menu
Insert File Field	→	File Field
Insert Image Field	→	Image Field
Insert Hidden Field	→	Hidden Field
Insert Jump Menu	→	Jump Menu

Figure 16-1.   *The Forms category of the Objects panel enables you to select the objects to be inserted in the form*

BEYOND THE BASICS

■ You can also drag the Forms icon to the spot on your Web page where you want the form.

■ Or, you can select Insert | Form from the menu bar.

This inserts a dotted red outlined box across the Dreamweaver screen, as depicted in grayscale in Figure 16-2. This is called the *form delimiter*.

If you can't see the red dashed lines, do one of the following:

■ Select Edit | Preferences from the menu bar. Click the Highlight Invisible Elements in the Category list box. Make sure the Form Delimiter check box is checked.

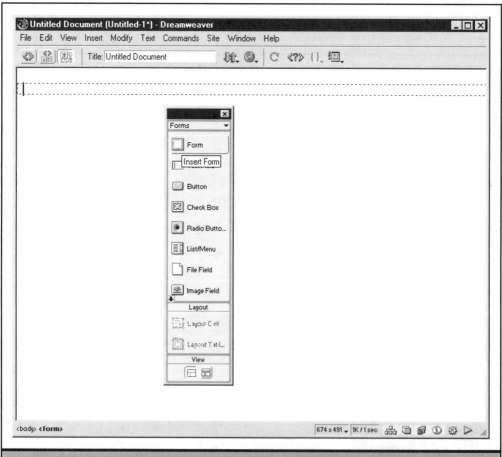

Figure 16-2.   *The forms delimiter shows up as red dashed lines on your document screen*

■ Or, you can select View | Visual Aids | Invisible Elements from the menu bar. Make sure a check mark is next to Invisible Elements. Click Invisible Elements to check mark it.

The form delimiter should now show up with a red dashed line on your document screen. Next, you learn how to set the form properties.

Form Properties

When you place your cursor on the form delimiter on your document screen and look at the Property Inspector for your form, you see three fields for settings for your form. These fields are Form Name, Action, and Method. The following illustration shows the Property Inspector for the form.

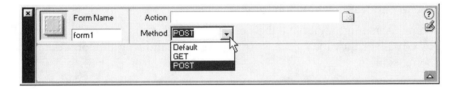

Form Name

Enter the form name in the text box labeled Form Name. Dreamweaver automatically assigns a form name, or you can enter a more descriptive name for the form. This *form name* is used if you're using a scripting language such as JavaScript, which needs to refer to the form.

Action

The *Action* box usually is the URL of a CGI script that processes the form's data. If you enter an URL for a CGI program, that program runs when the form information is submitted. Many CGI programs are available on the Web if you're unfamiliar with writing CGI programs. A program is probably already out there that can do what you need. Search the Web for CGI programs or CGI scripts. One good script archive is Matt's Script Archive at **http://www.worldwidemart.com/scripts/**. Most CGI programs have instructions included on how to adapt them for your Web site. You make the modifications, save the file, and put the file in your CGI directory—usually called cgi-bin. The URL to this program is entered in the Action field on the Property Inspector.

You can also specify a JavaScript program instead of a CGI program. A JavaScript action is entered similar to the following:

```
JavaScript: function()
```

where *function* is the name of your JavaScript function.

BEYOND
THE BASICS

You can also set the action to have the form data sent to you via e-mail. You use a mailto URL to specify that action. A typical mailto URL would be the following:

```
mailto:formdata@pendragn.com
```

The mailto action has a few difficulties.

■ The format of the information isn't easily read. It gets delivered in the same format as the Web server would have received it.

■ The information sent is a long string of field names, ampersands, equal signs, and text. A solution exists for this, however. You can have the submit button call a JavaScript program that parses the information into a readable form and then e-mails it to you. JavaScript programs are available on the Net that you can use to perform this function for you.

■ Some users might not have their e-mail server set so they can submit the form by e-mail, or they may get a warning message and stop the form data from being sent.

Method

Let's make this easy. Three options are available, but in most cases you'll leave the method set to POST. The other options—GET or DEFAULT—leave the method up to the browser.

Adding Text to a Form

Text is added to your form to provide direction to the user on what to enter into the various fields. Text is entered and formatted on your Web page as described in Chapter 9. Enter the text where you want it to appear on the page. Then you insert one of the form objects, as described in the next section.

Form Objects

The *Forms* category of the Objects panel, as previously shown in Figure 16-1, enables you to enter the Forms objects on your Web page. To insert a Forms object, place your cursor in the Form Delimiter on your document screen. On the Forms Panel of the Objects panel, click the icon of the object you want to insert. Continue to insert objects by clicking them. Press ENTER or RETURN to insert the object on the next line. Or, you can choose Insert | Form Objects from the menu bar, and then choose one of the objects from the drop-down menu.

> **Caution** *Each object in a form requires a unique name for reference within the form and within any scripts that may call the form objects. When adding a new object to a form, it's automatically assigned a generic name by Dreamweaver, such as textfield. Additional objects of the same type are given the same name with an incremented number following it, such as* textfield2, textfield3, *and so forth. When you cut-and-paste an object, however, the name is only renamed to a unique entity if you instructed Dreamweaver to do so in the General category of the Preferences dialog box. The setting to select in this dialog box is Rename Form Items When Pasting. If you choose not to have Dreamweaver perform this function for you, be sure to change all your Form object names manually to unique values.*

Text Fields

To insert a text field on your form, do one of the following:

■ Place your cursor on the form where you want the text field inserted. From the Forms Panel on the Objects Panel, press the Insert Text Field icon. The previously shown Figure 16-1 shows this icon.

■ Place your cursor on the form where you want the text field to be inserted. Choose Insert | Form Objects | Text Field from the menu bar.

■ From the Forms Panel on the Objects Panel, drag the Insert Text Field icon to any spot on the form where you want the text field inserted.

The Property Inspector enables you to modify the attributes of the text field, as the following illustrates.

TextField name

Dreamweaver automatically assigns a name to the text field starting with textfield, and then textfield2, textfield3, automatically increasing the number for each field you enter. You can type over this name and use a more descriptive name for your text field if you prefer.

Character Width

Dreamweaver defaults to an approximately 20 character-wide text field, depending on the end user's browser. The Char Width box is the number of characters shown at one time. If no Maximum Character limit has been set, the text scrolls as the user enters it.

Maximum Characters

For Single Line and Password text fields, this field determines the number of characters the user can enter. Again, the Character Width box is the number of characters shown at one time, while the Max Chars box limits how many characters in total the user can enter. For how this field is used for multiline text boxes, see the following discussion of multiline text.

Init Value

The Initial Value box is used to enter a default text string. Users can override this text string if they want. This can be used when the majority of users have the same answer in some field. This can also be used to provide further instructions on how to enter data in this field.

Single Line

Three radio boxes are used to designate what type of text field you're creating. These boxes are Single Line, Multiline, and Password. The Single Line text field can be used for collecting information, such as name or e-mail address.

Multiline

This option is used for collecting more than one line of text. Some examples of this type of text field would be for customer comments or special shipping instructions. When you choose this option for a text field, two more choices appear on the Property Inspector. The Max Chars field now says Num Lines, and the Wrap field is no longer grayed out. Figure 16-3 shows a multiline text field.

The Num Lines field is used to specify how many lines of text display on the user's screen. Scroll bars for vertical and horizontal scrolling are on the multiline text box. Unlike the single-line text field, you cannot limit the number of characters entered into a multiline text box.

The Wrap field is used to determine how word wrapping is handled. The default is set so the text continues with no wrapping until the user presses ENTER or RETURN. The Virtual option wraps the text on the user's screen, but not when the data is transmitted. The Physical option wraps the text both on the screen and when it's submitted.

Password

This field is used to collect sensitive information users may not want to have shown on their screens. When they type in characters, asterisks are displayed on their screens. This is most commonly used for password fields. Only single-line text fields can be made into Password fields.

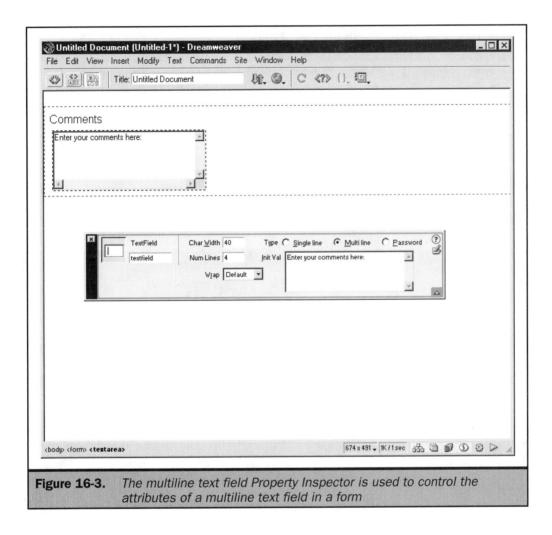

Figure 16-3.   *The multiline text field Property Inspector is used to control the attributes of a multiline text field in a form*

Figure 16-4 shows the three types of text fields on a form.

Buttons

Buttons can be used on your form to allow the user to choose among specific options. *Radio buttons* force a user to select one option from a list of choices. *Check boxes* let the user select more than one option.

Radio Buttons

To insert a radio button on a form, do one of the following:

- Place your cursor on the form where you want the radio button inserted. From the Forms Panel on the Objects Panel, press the Insert Radio Button icon. The previously shown Figure 16-1 shows this icon.

- Place your cursor on the form where you want the radio button inserted. Choose Insert | Form Objects | Radio Button from the menu bar.

- From the Forms Panel on the Objects Panel, drag the Radio Button icon to any spot on the form where you want the radio button inserted.

As previously stated, radio buttons let the user choose only one option. If the user selects a new option, the old option is automatically deselected.

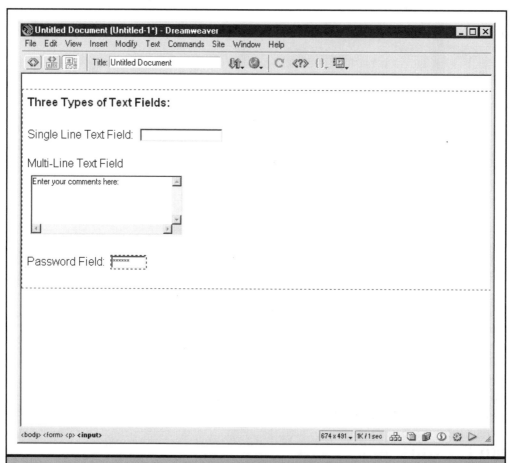

Figure 16-4.   *The three types of text fields are the single-line text field, the multiline text field, and the password field*

The Property Inspector enables you to modify the attributes of the Radio Button field. See Figure 16-5 for the attributes that can be modified with the Property Inspector. Each set of radio buttons on a form is given a name. This allows the form to give one value to the radio button set.

The Checked Value field is the value sent if that specific radio button is selected. Make sure each radio button in a set has the same Radio Button name and a different Checked Value. You needn't have any of the radio buttons set as the default, but if you want to make one of the radio buttons the default choice, select that radio button from the set and select the Checked option by the Initial State field on the Property Inspector.

Check Boxes

Check boxes are used when you want to give the user a choice of selecting more than one option. They give the user the choice of selecting any of the options that apply to them.

To insert a check box on a form, do one of the following:

■ Place your cursor on the form where you want the check box to be inserted. From the Forms Panel on the Objects Panel, press the Insert Check Box icon. The previously shown Figure 16-1 shows this icon.

■ Place your cursor on the form where you want the check box to be inserted. Choose Insert | Form Objects | Check Box from the menu bar.

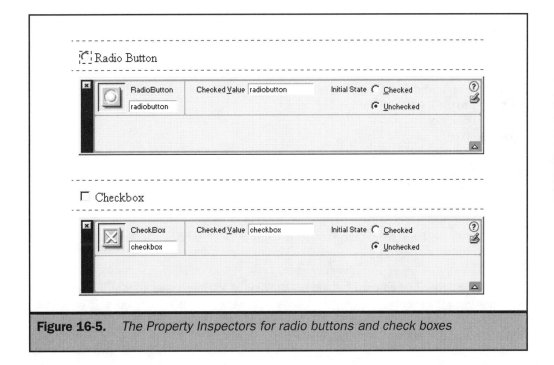

Figure 16-5. *The Property Inspectors for radio buttons and check boxes*

■ From the Forms Panel on the Objects Panel, drag the Check Box icon to any spot on the form where you want the Check Box field to be inserted.

As opposed to each radio button in a set having the *same* name, each check box is given a *unique* name. Dreamweaver automatically assigns a unique name to each check box or you can choose your own more descriptive name. In the Checked Value field, enter the information to be submitted with the form if that particular check box field is checked. The default option for Initial State of check boxes is unchecked, but you can force one to be checked as the default by selecting a check box and clicking the Checked option by the Initial State option on the Property Inspector.

Lists

Lists and menus are used to give your user more options to choose. Both are similar, but lists are usually used to show all the options, while menus are in the form of a drop-down box. Let's discuss how to insert a list or menu, and then see the differences between the two.

To create a list or menu on a form, do one of the following:

■ Place your cursor on the form where you want the list or menu to be inserted. From the Forms Panel on the Objects Panel, press the Insert List/Menu icon.

■ Place your cursor on the form where you want the list or menu inserted. Choose Insert | Form Objects | List/Menu from the menu bar.

■ From the Forms Panel on the Objects Panel, drag the List/Menu icon to any spot on the form where you want the List or Menu field inserted.

Lists, as seen in Figure 16-6, have a scrolling list of options. They are shown on the form with up and down arrows to scroll through the list of options. Use the Property Inspector to define the attributes for the list.

List name

Enter a name for this List, or allow Dreamweaver to name the list automatically. Dreamweaver calls the first list `select`, the next list `select2`, and continues naming the lists automatically.

Type

Select List as the Type by clicking the radio button next to List.

Height

When you choose List as your field type, the height attribute is available. This is usually set to the number of items you have listed for your user to choose. If you set the height to a number less than the total number of items on your list, the user needs to use the scroll bar to scroll through the list.

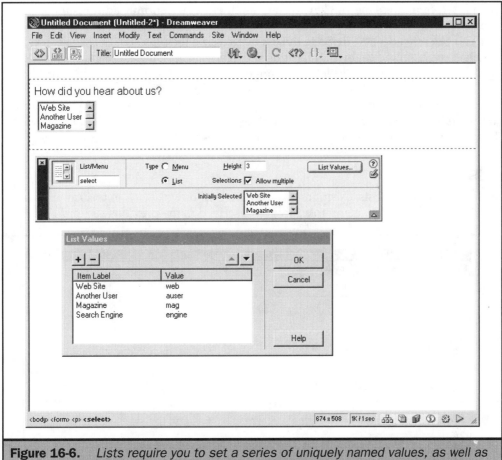

Figure 16-6.   *Lists require you to set a series of uniquely named values, as well as the properties for the List object itself*

Selections

If you select this check box, the user can select more than one option on your list. To enable the user to select multiple options, click the check box marked as Allow multiple.

List Values

When you click the List Values button, the List Values dialog box pops up. The List Values dialog box has two columns: the Item Label is what shows up in the List and the Value is what is submitted with the form, if this item is selected.

To enter items on the list, type in the Item name for the first item and press TAB. This moves the cursor to the Value field. Type in the information you want sent if this item is selected. Press the TAB key to enter another item. Continue adding all the items you want included on your list.

You can also add new items to the list by pressing the plus sign (+) key. You can delete items from the list by highlighting the item and pressing the minus sign (-) key.

The up and down arrows let you change the order of the items that you entered. Highlight an item and click the up or down arrow to move the item up or down the list.

When you're satisfied you've entered all the items and sorted them to the order you want them to appear, press OK. Highlighting one of the items in the Initially Selected box makes it appear as selected when the user accesses the form.

Menus

Menus are similar to lists, except menus have a drop-down selection box rather than a scrolling list. You add a menu to a form as described in the previous section. The

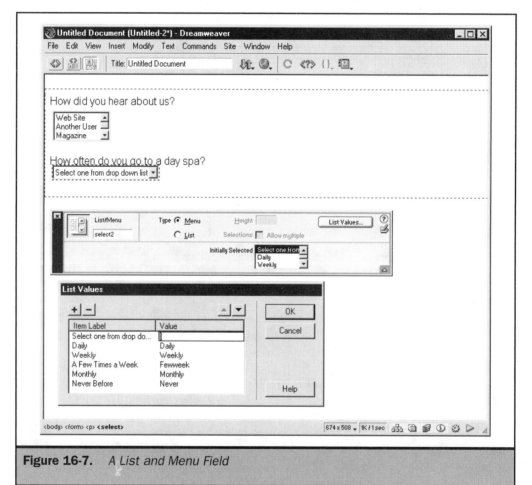

Figure 16-7.   *A List and Menu Field*

menu's attributes are defined with the Property Inspector. You can name your menu or allow Dreamweaver to name it automatically for you. The Height and Selection options are grayed out for Menu fields. Menu values are added by clicking the List Value button and entering the items in the List Value Dialog box, just as you did for List items in the previous section.

Figure 16-7 shows the difference between a List field and a Menu field.

File Fields

The *File field* is used to send a file with the form. The File field is basically a Text field and a browse button. The Browse button lets the user browse the files on his computer and locate a file to include with the form. Figure 16-8 shows a File field.

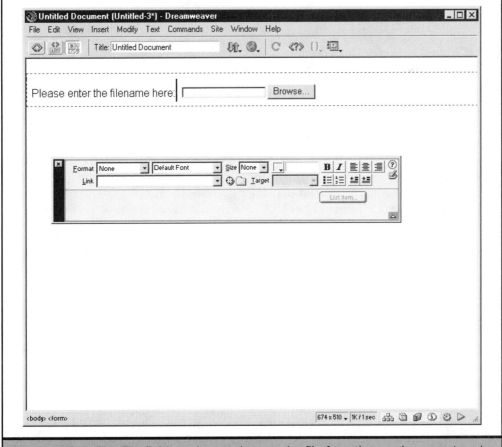

Figure 16-8. *The File field can be used to send a file from the user's computer when she submits the form*

The File field isn't widely used because e-mail allows for the attachment of multiple files along with an explanatory message. File fields also seem to cry out for abuse from users who happen to surf to your page randomly, leaving you open to files that contain viruses or explicit material and to floods of material unrelated to the purpose of your form.

Image Fields

While you can insert an image into a form, just as you inserted an image on your Web page, as discussed in Chapter 13, the image field on a form is also used to create a graphic image to use as a Submit button.

To insert an image field, do one of the following:

■ Place your cursor on the form where you want the image field inserted. From the Forms Panel on the Objects Panel, press the Insert Image Field icon. The previously shown Figure 16-1 shows this icon.

■ Place your cursor on the form where you want the image field inserted. Choose Insert | Form Objects | Image Field from the menu bar.

■ From the Forms Panel on the Objects Panel, drag the Insert Image Field icon to any spot on the form where you want the Image Field inserted.

As seen in Figure 16-9, the Property Inspector displays the image field name, width, and height. The Src field shows the source of the image. You can also use the Browse Folder icon to look for the file on your computer. The Alt field is used for alternate text to show for your image. The Align Field has a drop-down menu with the choice of Browser Default, Top, Middle, Bottom, Left, and Right. The Edit button launches your external editor if you want to edit the image.

You can also use an Image field to make a graphical button that performs other tasks. You can reset the form or attach a sound to the button. Using an image for these types of tasks requires you to attach a behavior to the Form object. Chapter 23 explains how to attach a behavior to an object.

Hidden Fields

Hidden fields cannot be viewed by the end user filling out the form. This field can be used for information that stays the same with all forms, but you want the information transmitted when the form is submitted. This field can be used for such information as the form number or the creation date. Typically, this field is used for information you want submitted with each form, when the user has no need to see or change the value.

To insert a hidden field, do one of the following:

■ Place your cursor on the form where you want the Hidden field inserted. From the Forms Panel on the Objects Panel, press the Insert Hidden Field icon. The previously shown Figure 16-1 shows this icon.

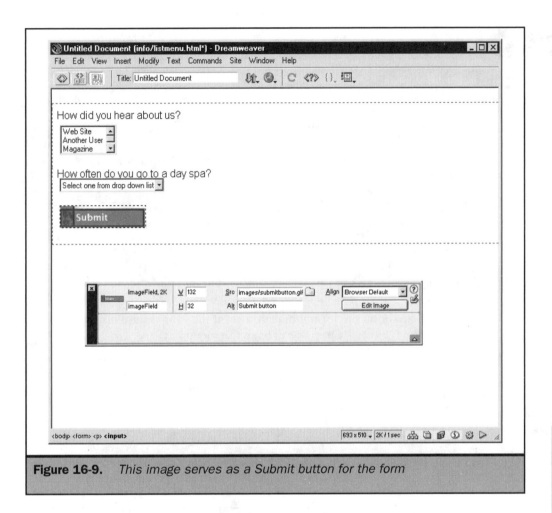

Figure 16-9.   *This image serves as a Submit button for the form*

■ Place your cursor on the form where you want the Hidden field to be inserted. Choose Insert | Form Objects | Hidden Field from the menu bar.

■ From the Forms Panel on the Objects Panel, drag the Insert Hidden Field icon to any spot on the form where you want the Hidden field inserted.

The Property Inspector for a Hidden Field shows the Field Name, which Dreamweaver automatically generates for you, or you can override with any name you want to use. The other field on the Property Inspector for a hidden field is Value. This is simply the value you want sent when the form is submitted. The hidden field doesn't appear on the user's browser but, instead, appears on your document screen as a Hidden Field Invisible Element icon.

If a user views your source code, he'll see you have a hidden field in your table. For that reason, setting the value of the field to something that isn't objectionable to your audience is generally a good idea.

Jump Menus

A *Jump menu* is an alternate means of navigation. Some sites use Jump menus in place of a typical Navigation bar. Other sites use them to navigate throughout subsections of a site, leaving the Navigation bar to move from major section to section. Jump menus can also be used to link to other sites.

Jump menus use the Jump Menu behavior. Behaviors, including use of the Jump Menu and Jump Menu Go behaviors, are covered in Chapter 23. Dreamweaver makes using this behavior especially easy. To insert a Jump menu, do one of the following:

■ Place your cursor on the form where you want the Jump menu inserted. From the Forms Panel on the Objects Panel, press the Insert Jump Menu icon. The previously shown Figure 16-1 shows this icon. If you haven't yet created a form, Dreamweaver can create one for you.

■ Place your cursor on the form where you want the Jump menu inserted. Choose Insert | Form Objects | Jump Menu from the menu bar.

■ From the Forms Panel on the Objects Panel, drag the Insert Jump Menu icon to any spot on the form where you want the Jump menu inserted.

When you do one of the previous options, the Insert Jump Menu dialog box appears, as the following illustrates.

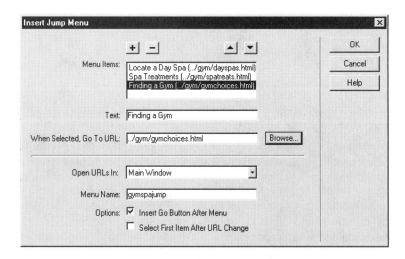

1. In the text field, enter the label for the first item. Use the TAB key to move to the next field. Dreamweaver automatically adds it to the Menu Items field.

2. In the When Selected, Go To URL field, enter the path and filename where you want the user's browser directed when she selects this item. You can also use the Browse Folder icon to search for the file you want on your computer.

3. Use the plus and minus keys to add more items to the list. Follow Steps one and two for each item on your Jump menu.

4. Use the up and down arrows on the Insert Jump Menu dialog box to move the items up or down the list to get them in the order you want them to display.

5. You use the Open URL In field to choose the target destination for the page. The target destination is Main Window, unless this Jump menu is part of a frameset. The main Window option opens the page in the user's browser by replacing his current page. It doesn't open the page in a new window. If you're using a Jump menu in conjunction with a frameset, the list of frames appears in the Open URL in field. Choose a frame from the drop-down list.

6. In the Menu Name field, enter a unique name for your Jump menu or allow Dreamweaver to name it automatically.

7. To insert a button that activates the Jump Menu item when it's chosen, check the Insert Go Button After Menu option.

8. If you want to reset the menu selection to the first item after each jump, check the Select First Item After URL Change option.

9. Click OK.

10. Dreamweaver automatically inserts the Jump menu with the proper linking code.

Many Web designers make the first item on a jump list a text item of instruction to the user, such as "Please Choose One Item from the List." If you decide to use this method, you can set the Go to URL to a pound sign (#). Figure 16-10 shows a Jump menu and the Go button in Internet Explorer.

You can modify the Jump menu by using the List/Menu Property Inspector. Select the Jump menu and choose the List Values button to show the List Values dialog box. The List Values dialog box shows the labels for the items in the left column and the URLs in the right column. You can add, delete, or move these items, as discussed in the "Lists" section of this chapter.

You can also modify the Jump menu by using the Behavior Inspector. Select the Jump menu and double-click the Jump Menu event on the Behavior Inspector.

Sometimes, you might not want to use the generic Go button and you'd rather use an image that ties in with the theme of your Web site.

To use a graphical Go button:

1. Go to your document screen.

2. Insert the image you chose as your graphical Go button next to the Jump menu on your document screen.

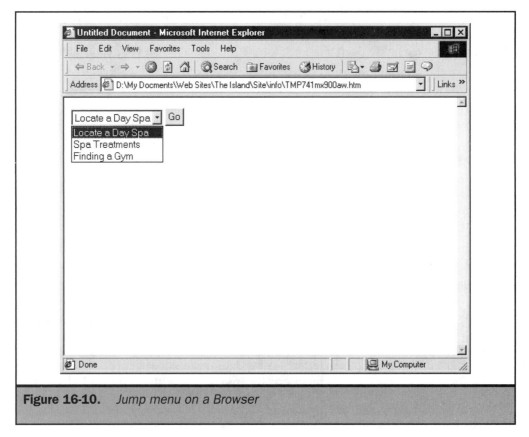

Figure 16-10. *Jump menu on a Browser*

3. Select the image you added and open the Behavior Inspector.

4. From the Add Event drop-down list, choose Jump Menu Go. Dreamweaver automatically lists the available Jump menus.

5. Select the name of the Jump menu from the list on Jump Menu Go dialog box.

6. Click OK.

Generic Fields

You can insert a generic field as a form element. To do this, you need to edit the HTML code for an object and set it to a new parameter. For instance, you could set the `type="checkbox"` to `type="box"`. The Property Inspector, shown in Figure 16-11, enables you to name the Field and give it a value to be submitted with the form. The Parameters button pops up the Parameter dialog box that lets you add the parameter and values from this box.

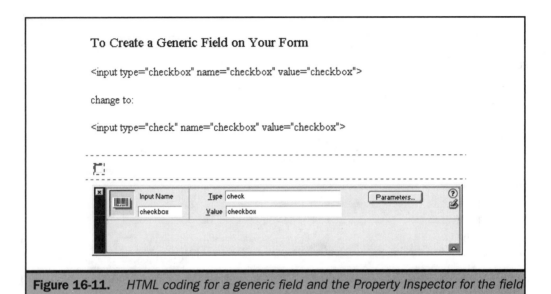

To Create a Generic Field on Your Form

`<input type="checkbox" name="checkbox" value="checkbox">`

change to:

`<input type="check" name="checkbox" value="checkbox">`

Figure 16-11. *HTML coding for a generic field and the Property Inspector for the field*

Submit and Reset Buttons

The Submit button triggers the form to be sent to what was specified in the Action box for this form, as discussed in the "Form Properties" section of this chapter. The Reset button is used to clear all the fields on the form.

To insert a button, do one of the following:

- Place your cursor on the form where you want the button inserted. From the Forms Panel on the Objects Panel, press the Button icon.

- Place your cursor on the form where you want the button inserted. Choose Insert | Form Objects | Button from the menu bar.

- From the Forms Panel on the Objects Panel, drag the Button icon to any spot on the form where you want the button inserted.

Dreamweaver automatically inserts a Submit button on the form. You can change this default by using the Property Inspector, as seen in Figure 16-12.

Enter a label for the button. This text appears on the button on the user's screen. For the Action option, choose Submit or Reset. When the user selects the Submit button, the form is then sent.

You can use a third Action option. Click the None option to make the button trigger a command. You then need to link the button to a specific function. A common use for this is the JavaScript's onClick event. Using JavaScript is discussed in Chapter 21, but be aware you have this option to use a button on your form to invoke a command.

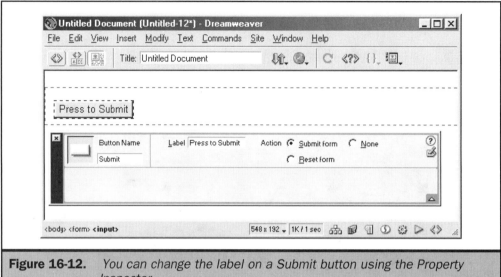

Figure 16-12.   *You can change the label on a Submit button using the Property Inspector*

Formatting the Form

You've seen in this chapter that Dreamweaver gives you many choices for setting up forms, but you may have seen how the forms objects don't line up as you'd like them to in a browser. Lining up form elements is rather hit-and-miss, especially if you're using paragraph style text. Preformatted text gives you more control over wrapping and spacing, but still requires a lot of manual adjustments.

Arguably, the easiest way to control how your form is displayed is to use tables. This gives you greater control over aligning the text labels next to the fields. You can further control the way the Form objects line up by using the table's cell padding and spacing. If you don't want the outline of the table to appear in the browser window, set the table's border width to zero.

To use a table with your form, insert the table as the first object on the form. The Form objects are placed within the cells on the table. The cells are adjusted so the fields line up how you want. Tables are fully discussed in Chapter 14. Figure 16-13 shows using a table with a form. Notice the dotted lines around the cells in the table show the border width set to zero, so the table outline won't show on the user's browser.

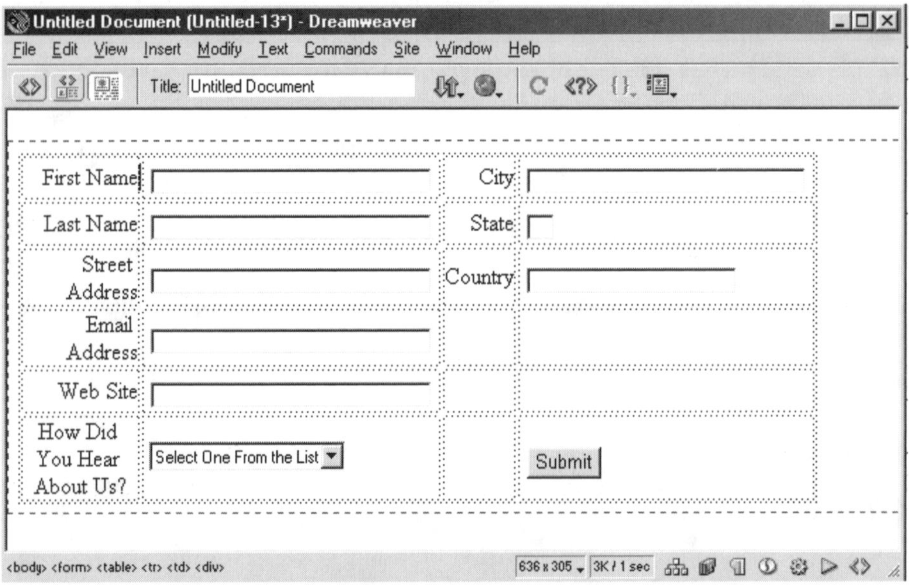

Figure 16-13.   *Tables provide the easiest method for aligning form elements*

Summary

Forms encourage feedback and interaction with your users, and they can provide substantial analytical data to you. Here are some key points to remember when using forms:

- All forms require a basic form definition using the Insert Form object before you can add individual Form objects.

- Forms also require a CGI script or other means, such as a mailto, of disseminating the data. Many CGI scripts parse the data into a usable form, something that cannot be done with a mailto. Many scripts are available for your use if you don't want to create your own.

- Text fields can be a single line, multiple lines of wrapped text, or a password.

- Radio buttons enable the user to choose between multiple options.

BEYOND
THE BASICS

■ Check boxes enable the user to select multiple options. Each of these is a unique form field.

■ Lists and menus scroll or drop down from a predetermined list of options, each with its own value.

■ Jump menus are used to navigate through a predefined list of links, displayed as a drop-down menu. Jump menus use Dreamweaver's behaviors features.

■ Submit buttons may be replaced with a graphic button. Every form requires some type of submission button to send the form to the server or e-mail.

The next chapter introduces cascading style sheets, a powerful tool that enables you to separate the structure of your HTML code from the display of your page.

The
Complete
Reference

Chapter 17

Cascading Style Sheets

In the early days of HTML, tags were merely intended to provide structure for content, specifying that certain content should be contained in a table, for example, or a line of text should be rendered as a heading. The actual display of this structure was left to the browser. Each browser had its own variations on the font size of a heading or whether it should appear in bold or italics. This worked for a while, back when the Web was more about information than entertainment. But it wasn't long before Web designers not only wanted to present their material, but they also wanted it to be visually appealing. In response, new tags were created—usually at the instigation of the various browsers and, later, adopted by the W3C—and the Web became a beautiful, albeit, more complex, thing.

Again, this worked for a while, but this all-encompassing method of HTML coding is problematic. HTML documents have become increasingly cumbersome with <font> tags and color attributes scattered throughout. Also, while these extra tags do provide a means of somewhat controlling the display of various elements in the browser, this control is still limited. The addition of formatting tags has also made for lazier adherence to HTML standards. Many new developers don't see any difference between using a heading <h1> tag and using a paragraph <p> tag with a <font> tag to change the appearance of its contents. While the two may appear the same in a browser, a paragraph doesn't perform the same functional role as a heading. Some search engines use heading content as one of their criteria to determine the ranking of site listings. From a practical standpoint, changing the design of a site coded in this manner is more time-consuming because a standard find-and-replace doesn't differentiate between headings and paragraphs if they're coded with the same tags.

The initial idea of using the HTML file to provide structure and content is sound. HTML documents without formatting information are smaller, easier to modify, and can be readily adapted to numerous design themes. Web designers aren't about to give up their hard-won control over the visual presentation of their material, however, so leaving display totally up to the browser is no longer acceptable. In fact, designers want even more control over their design and the resulting display of their content, not less. Therefore, a component was needed to control the display of the HTML document, to serve as a sort of design buffer between the structure of the material and its display in the browser. Enter the Cascading Style Sheet.

Cascading Style Sheets (CSS) define how the elements of an HTML document are displayed. CSS can be embedded into the HTML document itself or contained in an external document. An external CSS not only gives you control over one HTML document, but can also be linked to dozens or even thousands of documents, providing a consistent design for the entire site. Moreover, a change made to only the external CSS changes the design of every page linked to that CSS. Finally, CSS is one of the three critical elements of Dynamic HTML (DHTML), along with HTML and JavaScript. As you see in Chapter 19, DHTML can make pages come alive using timelines and layer effects, as well as providing interactivity with the user.

This is extremely powerful stuff. And, as with all powerful HTML features, it's limited by certain browser constraints and must be applied judiciously and properly. But as CSS becomes increasingly accepted by the Web development community and supported by newer browsers, its full potential is just coming into view. And, as XHTML and other standards become more than just a theoretical advancement of Web coding, CSS and similar display methodologies are going to become more essential. By mastering CSS now, you can be prepared for these advancements.

CSS Syntax

Cascading Style Sheets enable you to define the display properties of almost every HTML tag. This is done by creating a rule for the display of a particular tag. A *rule* is made up of the following components:

- **Selector**—The element to which you're applying the style. If you want to format the paragraph tag to display text in green, for example, the selector is the <p> tag.

- **Declaration**—The properties and values that describe how to display the selector.

  - **Property**—The property of the selector being modified, such as the color, size, font, margin, or position. For example, to display the green paragraph text, you must modify the color property.

  - **Value**—The setting for the property. For green paragraph text, for example, the value of the color property is green (or the hexadecimal equivalent).

When you put these parts together, the result is a rule that looks like this:

```
p {color: #00FF00;}
```

Notice the declaration is enclosed in curly brackets. A rule can contain multiple declarations within the brackets, each separated with a semicolon. Thus, a rule with many declarations can look like this:

```
p {color: #00FF00; font-size: 14pt; text-align: center;}
```

Tip *The semicolon is important for separating declarations, but it's optional after the last declaration in a rule. If you forget to include a semicolon between declarations, the entire rule may be ignored by a browser. So, get into the habit of always adding a semicolon to the end of declarations, including those at the end of a statement.*

This would result in centered green text in a 14-point size. Declarations can also be used for multiple selectors at the same time, such as:

```
p, h1, h2 {color: green; font-family: Arial;}
```

This rule would define a style for the paragraph, heading 1, and heading 2 tags.

BEYOND THE BASICS

CSS Classes

Applying a rule to a paragraph or other tag is a powerful tool, but what if you don't want every paragraph formatted in the same way? As an example, if you're putting up a script for a play, you might want all the protagonist's dialogue to appear in red text, the antagonist's dialogue in blue, and stage notes in green—however visually unappealing that may sound. You could be clever and code those paragraphs with a different tag, and then set rules for those tags. This changes the structure of your document, however, which can have functional implications, particularly as browsers change their support for various tags. Instead, CSS allows for the creation of a *class*, a custom tag applied to those portions of the document that require customized formatting. Classes can be created either independently of any tag—in essence, becoming a truly customized tag able to be applied to any content—or defined as a subset of a particular element.

Class rules are always preceded by a period before the class name, whether defined independently or in combination with a tag element. Thus, the rules for the play described previously would appear as such:

```
P.protag {color: #FF0000;}
P.antag {color: #0000FF;}
.stagenotes {color: #00FF00;}
```

Notice in the previous example that the protagonist and antagonist classes are defined as being a subset of the paragraph element, whereas the stage notes are defined as a standalone class. This is because blocks of dialogue appear as separate paragraphs, whereas stage directions could be contained in their own paragraphs or as comments within a block of dialogue. Defining the classes this way gives you the flexibility to apply the styles where they're best served. As you can see, defining classes takes advance planning, both in structuring your style sheet and in coding your document.

Defining Nested Tags

Another common use of styles is when you want to specify the style applied to an element depending on the element in which it's contained. For example, you might want to define all paragraph text to be purple, except paragraphs appearing within a table. The style sheet for these rules would appear like this:

```
p {color: #990099;}
td p {color: #0033CC;}
```

Be careful when you apply styles to table elements. The results are often inconsistent across browsers. Also, because so many sophisticated pages rely on tables for layout, styles applied to table elements may affect your entire content.

Applying Style Sheets to HTML Documents

Style sheets can be used by HTML documents in three different ways. Although the use and application of each method varies, they all have the same end result and can all work together in the same HTML document.

External Style Sheets   An *external style sheet* is also called a *linked style sheet* because it's a separate document, which is linked to an HTML document. This type of style sheet offers the greatest amount of flexibility because it can be applied to multiple pages in a site. External style sheets simply contain the rules you defined for your page or site, and they're saved with a .css extension. To apply the style sheet to an HTML document, you add a <link> tag to the head of the HTML document, such as:

```
<link rel=stylesheet href="mystyles.css" type="text/css">
```

This link must be added to every HTML document that uses the style sheet. To modify the display of the HTML document, simply edit the style sheet; the new rules are adopted whenever the page is displayed in a browser.

Embedded Style Sheets   *Embedded style sheets* are used to control a single HTML document. The style rules are placed within the <head> of the document within a <style> tag pair, such as:

```
<head>
<title>The Island</title>
<style>
<!--
h1 {font: 14pt Arial;}
p {color: #00FF00;}
-->
</style>
</head>
```

Notice the actual style rules are contained within a comment tag. This is to prevent them from being displayed in a browser that doesn't support the <style> element. The element itself would be ignored by older browsers—just as older browsers ignore other tags they don't recognize—but the contents of the tag would be rendered as regular text if they weren't enclosed in a comment tag.

Inline Styles   The third type of style, the *inline style sheet*, is an attribute added directly within the body of the HTML document, such as:

```
<p style="color: #00FF00;">The island has beautiful green foliage.</p>
```

This method gives you complete control over that particular instance of that specific element, but doesn't apply the style anywhere else within either the document or the site. Thus, the inline style is most useful for exceptions to either the default display or to an embedded or external style sheet rule.

To apply an inline style to only a portion of an element rather than its entirety, apply a <span> tag to your selection, and then add a style attribute to the span. Simply using the formatting options in the Property Inspector is tempting, but to write strict HTML using the current recommendations, you should resist temptation and use your style sheets consistently. Here's an example of a <span> tag in use:

```
<p>The island has beautiful <span style="color:
#00FF00;">green</span> foliage.</p>
```

In this example, the style is only applied to the word green. You can also apply a style to a wider range of content and elements within a document, using the `<div>` tag. This tag can be used to contain multiple elements and to apply a style to everything within the container.

The `<div>` tag forces a line break after the closing division tag.

Applying Class Styles

Because class styles aren't automatically applied to every instance of a tag, the class must be added as an attribute of any content belonging to that class. The class attribute can be added to <span> and <div> tags, as well as other elements. Here's an example of one of the class tags from the play example applied to a paragraph (with thanks to William Shakespeare):

```
<p class="protag"><span class="role">Beatrice</span> Against my
will I am sent to bid you come in to dinner.</p>
<p class="antag"><span class="role">Benedick</span> Fair Beatrice,
I thank you for your pains.</p>
```

Notice the class attributes were applied to the appropriate paragraph elements to set the style for the dialogue. An additional style was applied to the name of the speaking character to set it apart from the dialogue itself.

Understanding the Cascade

The three types of style sheets aren't mutually exclusive. Quite the contrary: If you look at the level of control each method has over certain portions of your pages and site, you can use them together to gain an incredible amount of control over the presentation of your content.

Back to the earlier example, if you have a site promoting a play, you'd have some pages that discuss the storyline of the play, introduce the actors, and, perhaps, display a small portion of the script. The entire site would be controlled by an external style sheet that ensures consistency among all the site's pages. The class styles for the dialogue to be used on the sample script page can either be included in this external style sheet or embedded only on that particular page. And, if you have a particular paragraph on one of your pages that requires different formatting—perhaps announcing the last-minute replacement of one of the actors—you'd apply an inline style to only that paragraph because it's unlikely to be applied anywhere else in the site.

This exemplifies the cascading nature of CSS. This cascade also applies to the precedence of contrary style rules. While the external style sheet sets the styles for the entire site, it can be overridden by an embedded style for the same element or class placed within a specific document. This embedded style can be overcome with an inline style placed in the body of the document.

One other party is in the cascade parade—the user. Users can set their browsers to ignore style sheets and apply their browser settings to all pages. The CSS standard provides some ways to get around this—most of which aren't yet implemented in the popular browsers—but think long and hard about whether it's worth risking the loss of a user by taking control away from him. When users override CSS rules, they usually have a reason, and that should usually be respected.

Inheritance

Certain HTML tags only exist within other tags. Table rows and cells only appear within `<table>` tags. The superscript (`<sup>`) tag only appears within a paragraph or other text format. Unless you otherwise define those tags with a style, they inherit the style applied to their container, or parent, tag.

Older Browser Considerations

With such a powerful tool at the developer's disposal, you'd think everyone would flock to this standard. In fact, though, CSS has been relatively slow to gain acceptance. Two factors have caused this tepid response. First, the way CSS was introduced initially caused confusion. Just as the current XHTML recommendations have developers wondering how to implement XHTML, developers had a hard time embracing CSS before they understood its full potential. The second factor, which had an impact on the first, was a lack of browser support.

When choosing to use CSS to control your Web site's display, remember, Netscape 3 doesn't use CSS at all, and Internet Explorer 3 has limited CSS support. Both Netscape and IE offer CSS support in their version 4 browsers, but it's limited in many ways and laden with bugs. The current browsers have much better support, but full implementation is definitely still evolving. Because Dreamweaver enables you to set styles that aren't yet implemented in many—if any—browsers, you should check for compatibility before applying the less common styles to your documents. Appendix C provides a list of the most common CSS properties and browser implementation. The Reference panel in Dreamweaver contains the O'Reilly CSS Reference, which also has this information.

> There's much more to Cascading Style Sheets than is presented here. To learn more about CSS, visit W3Schools' CSS Tutorial at **http:// www. w3schools. com/css/ default.asp** or the WebReview.com Style Sheet Reference Guide at **http:// www. webreview.com/style**. One of the best books about CSS is Cascading Style Sheets: The Definitive Guide, by Eric A. Meyer (O'Reilly).

Creating Style Sheets in Dreamweaver

With all the basics out of the way, now it's time to learn how to apply this knowledge in Dreamweaver. The first rule of using CSS in Dreamweaver is to ignore all the text formatting options available in the Property Inspector. Formatting applied that way adds <font> tags to the page, which is what you want to avoid to achieve standards-based code that facilitates easy modification. If you forget and use the Property Inspector to format text, you might want to close the Property Inspector, at least until you grow used to using the CSS Styles panel for adding formatting.

Inline styles are generally coded by hand, as they're infrequently used and are defined and applied on the fly, rather than predefined at the page head or external style sheet level. External and embedded style sheets, however, use the CSS Styles panel, illustrated in the following. This panel facilitates both the creation and application of style rules.

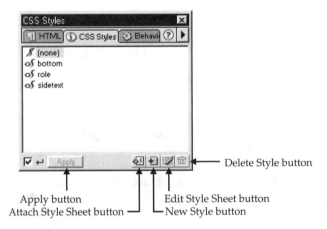

Attaching an External Style Sheet

If you inherited a site from another developer or previously worked on the site in another Web authoring environment, you may have already created a style sheet. To link this style sheet to the current document, do the following:

1. Press the Attach Style Sheet button in the CSS Styles panel.

2. The Style Sheet File selector box opens. Choose a style sheet. If the sheet isn't in your site folder, Dreamweaver offers to move a copy of the file to the local site folder.

3. Press Select to create the link.

Adding New Styles

If you're working on a site from scratch or are adding style sheets to a site previously coded using <font> and other deprecated tags, you need to create a style sheet. The first step in using CSS is to define the styles you need for your site or page. To create a new style, do the following:

Once you create style sheets to cover all the content previously coded with <font> tags, use the Clean Up HTML command to remove those tags. Be sure to double-check your pages in a browser afterward to ensure no stray tags were left behind and your design hasn't been compromised by converting to style sheets.

1. From the CSS Styles panel, press the New Style button or choose New Style from the drop-down menu in the upper-right corner of the panel.

2. The New Style dialog box appears, as the following illustrates. Choose to make the style part of either an external or an embedded style sheet by choosing one of these options from the Define In field:

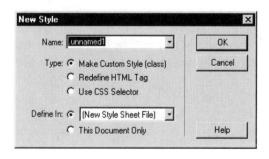

- **New Style Sheet File**—creates an external style sheet. If you haven't yet linked an external style sheet to the current document, you are prompted to name and create this file.

- **Style Sheet File drop-down menu**—if you already created an external style sheet within the current site, you can link to it by pressing the down-arrow button next to the New Style Sheet File option and choosing a style sheet from the drop-down menu.

- **This Document Only**—creates an embedded style sheet within the `<head>` of the current document.

3. Choose a style type from the following. The Select box changes, according to the style type you chose:

   - **Make Custom Style (class)**—creates a class style. If you choose this option, you need to name the class in the Name field above the style type selector. If you don't precede the class name with a period (.), Dreamweaver adds it for you.

   - **Redefine HTML Tag**—applies a style to an HTML element. On choosing this option, select a tag from the Tag field above the style type selector. These styles are automatically applied to the appropriate tags after they're defined. You won't see a difference in the code itself. Rather, the style to be applied to the tag is interpreted from the style sheet—whether external or embedded—and applied to all instances of the tag.

   - **Use CSS Selector**—applies a style to one of the link types listed in the Selector field above the style type selector. These styles enable you to remove the underlining from links and otherwise change the appearance of the various link states. They're automatically applied after they're defined.

Tip   *The Use CSS Selector option can also be used to define styles for nested tags. As explained in the previous section, "Defining Nested Tags," nested tags are used to define the style of a tag only when it's nested within another specific tag, rather than all occurrences of the tag. To do this, type in the tag elements in the Selector field, separated with a space and without the angle brackets. Then proceed with the style definition process, as the following explains.*

4. Choose OK.

5. The Style Definition dialog box opens. Set the style rules by choosing from the various style categories and options. These are explained in the next section of this chapter.

6. Choose OK to complete the style definition and return to the Document window.

Once you create a style, it's easy to apply. Styles defined for an HTML tag are automatically applied, as are styles defined from the CSS Selector option. Class styles are applied by doing the following:

1. In the Document window, select the content to which you want to apply the class style. If the selection is only a small portion of content within a tag, the style is applied using the <span> tag. If the selection extends across multiple paragraphs or tag pairs, the style is applied using a <div> tag. If you don't make a selection, the style is applied to the parent tag of the content surrounding the cursor position.

2. In the CSS Styles panel, choose a style from the list.

3. If you checked the box next to the Apply button, the style is automatically applied when you click the style name. If you deselected this option, the style isn't applied until you click the Apply button.

That's Dreamweaver style definition and application in a nutshell. Of course, the definition of styles is much more detailed than this.

Defining Styles

The Style Definition dialog box contains almost every available option for CSS. Some of these options cannot be rendered in all, if any, browsers. Many of them also cannot be viewed in Dreamweaver's Document window, and these are marked with an asterisk in the Style Definition dialog box. You can apply the style, but you need to test the document in a browser to ensure that the style is effective. One common example of this is using graphic bullets in place of the default bullets in an unordered list. Dreamweaver continues to display the default bullets in the Document window, even though previewing the document in a browser shows the graphic bullets.

The Style Definition dialog box is divided into logical categories to group the style properties. You can choose freely among the categories and properties.

Type Styles

The Type category, shown in Figure 17-1, contains properties pertaining to the appearance of text. If you're removing the underlining from links, one of the most common applications of CSS, you would select None in the Decoration properties. The other properties in this category are

- **Font**—sets the font family, using font combinations established in the Font List settings.

- **Size**—sets the font size. If you specify a numerical value rather than a relative value (small, larger, and so forth), you can also set the unit of measure.

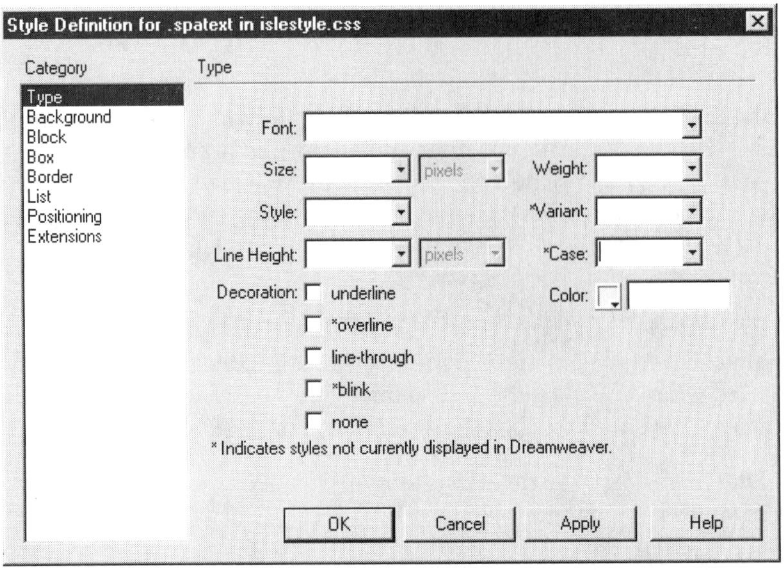

Figure 17-1. *The Type category of CSS styles pertain to text appearance, which replace the deprecated* `<font>` *tag*

Choosing a percentage unit of measure increases or decreases the size of the font relative to the default. The most common unit is points, which is also the default for this option.

- **Weight**—sets the heaviness of the text boldness. Normal text has a weight of approximately 400. Bold text has a weight of 700. A weight below 400 results in lighter text. You can also set the weight as a relative value, such as bold or lighter.

- **Style**—sets the font as normal, italic, or oblique. If you come from a word processing background, you're used to setting bold type in the same manner as normal and italics, but this isn't the case here. Boldness is set by weight, as previously described.

- **Variant**—sets the text to display in small caps. Small caps have the same appearance as capital letters, but are the size of lowercase letters. The keystroke descriptions in this book are set in small caps, such as CTRL-U. This style is only supported by Netscape 6 and Opera, not by Internet Explorer. Dreamweaver cannot display this style in the Document window.

- **Line Height**—sets the leading before a line of text. *Leading* is the space above a letter to separate it from the text above within a paragraph.

- **Case**—sets the text to display in uppercase or lowercase, or with initial caps.

- **Decoration**—sets additional properties for the display of the text, whether it should be underlined, overlined (a line appearing over the text), line-through (giving the text a strikethrough or red-lined effect), or blinking. Blinking text, aside from being one of the most annoying features available to Web designers, isn't supported by Internet Explorer, although it's supported by Netscape and Opera. Overlining and blinking text aren't visible in the Document window.

- **Color**—sets the color for the text using the standard color picker.

Background Styles

The Background category, depicted in Figure 17-2, offers control over background images and colors. Not only do these styles ensure consistency throughout the site, they also offer greater control over the repeat and scrolling of background images. Most background styles aren't supported in Netscape 4, but are fully supported in Netscape 6. The properties in this category are

- **Background Color**—sets the background color for an element. This style can be applied to the `<body>` tag to set a color for the entire page. It can also be applied to `<p>` and other tags to set a background color only for that particular selection. Using this style with link tags makes them stand out on the page.

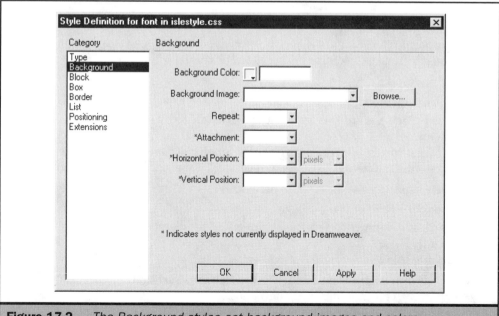

Figure 17-2.   *The Background styles set background images and colors*

- **Background Image**—sets a background image for the page or element. This is most commonly used with the <body> tag or table cells (<td>).

- **Repeat**—sets the repeat tiling for a background image. No Repeat sets the image to display from the upper-left corner of the element to which it's applied, and doesn't repeat at all. Repeat tiles the image horizontally and vertically as needed to fill the entire area used by the element. Repeat-*x* tiles the image horizontally, but not vertically. Repeat-*y* does the opposite.

- **Attachment**—sets the scrolling for the background image. A fixed image remains anchored to its original position, even as the text is scrolled. This creates the effect of the text moving over the background image and also enables you to set a background image to specific dimensions to avoid tiling. A scrolling image scrolls with the text, which is the default. This style isn't viewable in the Document window.

- **Horizontal Position**—sets the initial horizontal position of the background image. The position can be set with numerical coordinates or relative to the positioning of the element to which the style is applied. This style isn't viewable in the Document window.

- **Vertical Position**—sets the initial vertical position of the background image. This also isn't viewable in the Document window.

Block Styles

Block styles, as seen in Figure 17-3, are used to control the alignment and spacing of text blocks. Support for these styles is, at best, spotty and buggy in Netscape 4, but is fully implemented in Netscape 6. Support in Internet Explorer is still rather spotty. The block style properties are

- **Word Spacing**—sets the space between words. The default unit of measure for word spacing is ems, which is the space taken up by the *m* character, although the unit of measure can be changed. Positive values increase the spacing between words, while negative values set words closer together. This style isn't supported in Internet Explorer and cannot be viewed in the Document window.

- **Letter Spacing**—sets the space between letters. This style isn't displayed in the Document window.

- **Vertical Alignment**—sets the alignment of the element relative to the elements near it. These settings are the same as those used to align images, as described in Chapter 12.

- **Text Align**—aligns text relative to the elements surrounding it. Text can have left, right, center, or justified alignment.

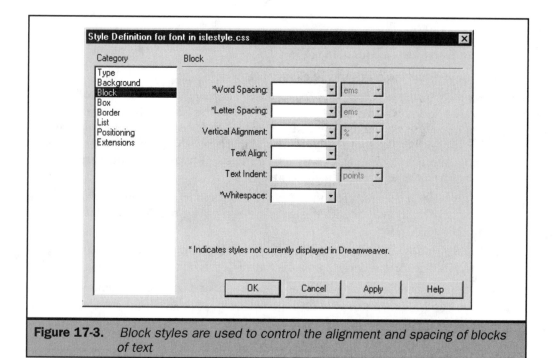

Figure 17-3.   *Block styles are used to control the alignment and spacing of blocks of text*

- **Text Indent**—sets the indentation of the first line of the text block by the specified value. To outdent text, use a negative value.

- **Whitespace**—sets the control of spaces and tabs within an element. Normal causes the text block to be formatted in the same way as a default paragraph tag, where extra whitespace is ignored. The *pre value* preserves whitespace. The *nowrap value* causes text to extend horizontally until a <br> tag is encountered, rather than wrapping to conform to the browser window. Internet Explorer has limited support for this property. This style isn't displayed in the Document window.

Box Styles

Box styles, as seen in Figure 17-4, are used to control the positioning and spacing of elements, much in the same way as tables. With appropriate browser support, which is still somewhat spotty even in the current browsers, you could design your entire site using box and positioning styles rather than tables. A good example of this is the Project VII site at **http://www.projectseven.com/dreamweaver/index.htm**. The main frame on that page has a complex design using boxes and color without using tables.

The properties for the Box styles are

- **Width**—sets the width of the element.

- **Height**—sets the height of the element.

- **Float**—sets the positioning of the element. *Floating elements* are positioned against the margin for which they are set, with the other elements of the page flowing around it. Only floating images can be viewed in the Document window; other floats must be previewed in a browser. Earlier versions of the most popular browsers had problems rendering this style, but the current versions have better implementations.

- **Clear**—clears the area around the box and doesn't let other elements flow around it. Images with this style applied can be previewed in the Document window.

- **Padding**—sets the amount of space between the element and its border or margin. This property cannot be displayed in the Document window.

- **Margin**—sets the spacing between the element and other page elements. The Document window can only display block elements (headings and paragraphs) with this style.

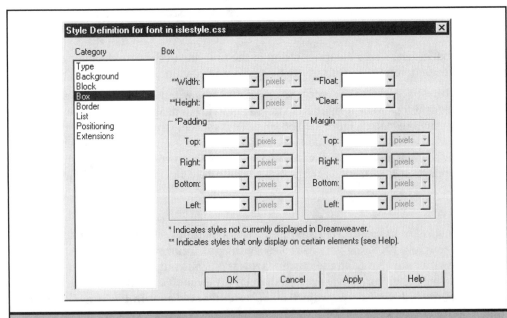

Figure 17-4. *Box styles set the positioning and spacing of elements, similar to the layout of tables*

Border Styles

Border styles, as shown in Figure 17-5, are used to set borders to surround an element. Each side of the rectangular border can have a unique line thickness and color. Borders can also be applied only to select sides of the element, creating text surrounded on top and bottom while the sides remain open, or similar combinations. Eight border styles exist, giving the border an inset, grooved, or dotted-line appearance—unlike the line thickness and color, these styles are applied to all sides of the border. Many of the border properties are buggy in earlier versions of the popular browsers, so they should be applied cautiously and thoroughly tested. The properties of the borders styles are

- **Width**—sets the thickness of the border for each of the sides.
- **Color**—sets the color for the border.
- **Style**—sets the style of the border. The options are dotted, dashed, solid, double, groove, ridge, inset, and outset. Some examples of various border settings are shown in Figure 17-6.

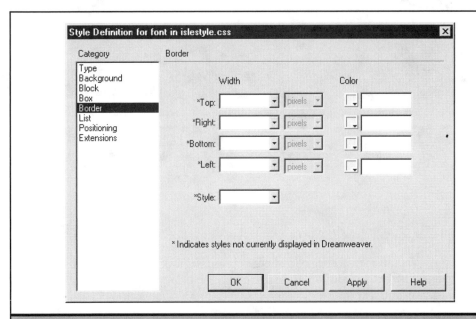

Figure 17-5. *Border styles are used to create borders around an element. Each side of the element can have a unique border style*

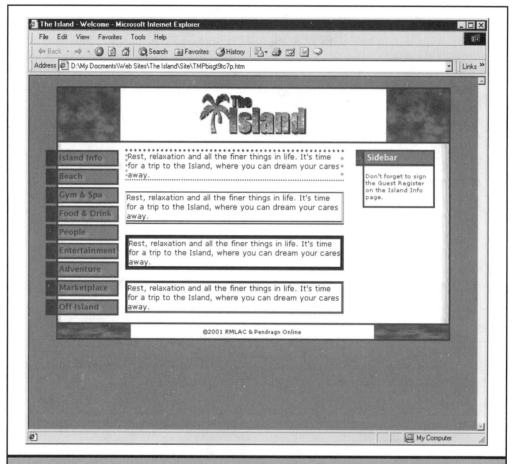

Figure 17-6. *The color and thickness of each side of the border can be set individually. The border style is applied to all sides of the border equally*

List Styles

List styles, as shown in Figure 17-7, offer control over the appearance of lists, as follows:

- **Type**—sets the appearance of bullets in unordered lists from the following options: disc, circle, square, decimal, lowercase roman, uppercase roman, lowercase alpha, and uppercase alpha.

- **Bullet Image**—sets a custom image for unordered list bullets. This image can be any of the common formats, including animated GIF. Bullet images aren't supported by Netscape 4 browsers, but have been implemented in Netscape 6. Bullet images don't appear in the Document window.

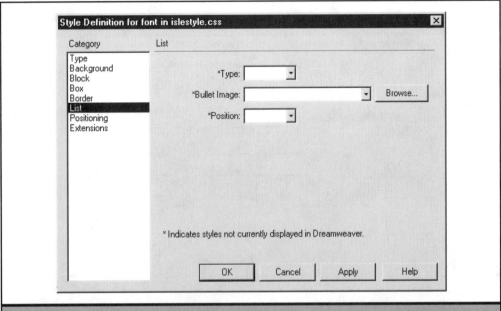

Figure 17-7.   *List properties enable you to control the appearance of bullets and the wrapping of the list contents*

- **Position**—sets the wrapping of the list item. An outside position wraps the text to the indent of the list, while an inside indent wraps the text to the page margin.

Positioning Styles

As noted earlier, Positioning styles, shown in Figure 17-8, control the exact placement of elements on the page. These properties form the basis of layers, which are covered in Chapter 19 and Chapter 20.

- **Type**—sets the positioning format. The types are relative, absolute, and static (at its exact placement within the document flow, rather than independently of the rest of the content).

- **Visibility**—sets the visibility of the layer. Layers can inherit the visibility of their parent tags, or can be set independently of the parent to be either visible or hidden.

- **Z-Index**—sets the stacking order of the layers. A higher Z-index means a layer is closer to the top of the page in depth. A lower value means a layer could be hidden under others.

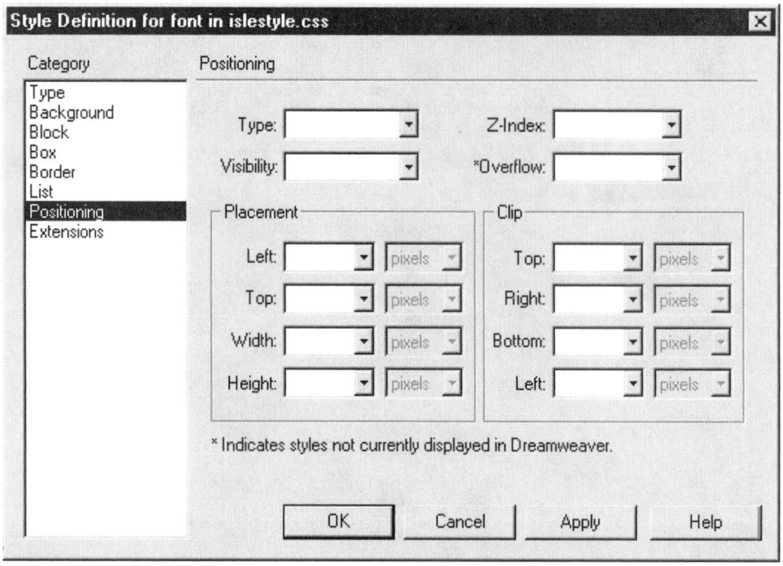

Figure 17-8.   *Positioning styles control the placement of an element*

- **Overflow**—sets the flow of the layer's content when it overflows the dimensions of the layer. The overflowing content can be hidden, scrolled using scroll bars that are added to the element, or auto, which automatically applies the appropriate formatting.

- **Placement**—sets the actual positioning of the layer on the page.

- **Clip**—sets the size of the element, which then determines where the element is clipped.

Extensions Styles

Extensions, shown in Figure 17-9, are specialty properties used only by Internet Explorer. Netscape plans to incorporate support for these style properties in future releases.

- **Pagebreaks**—used to facilitate printing a Web page, this style forces a page break in a long document.

- **Cursor**—sets the style of cursor that appears to the user while she's on your page.

- **Filter**—sets effects independently of Fireworks or other graphics packages. These effects control the opacity, glow, and masking features of the element.

Style Definition for font in islestyle.css

Category: Extensions

Type
Background
Block
Box
Border
List
Positioning
Extensions

Page Break

*Before:

*After:

Visual Effect

*Cursor:

*Filter:

* Indicates styles not currently displayed in Dreamweaver.

OK   Cancel   Apply   Help

Figure 17-9. *Extensions are only supported by Internet Explorer at press time*

Editing Style Sheets

In a perfect world, you'd set your styles once and never need to fix or modify them again. This is far from a perfect world. To edit your style sheets, do the following:

1. Select the Edit Style Sheet button in the CSS Style panel.

2. Select the name of the style sheet in the Edit Style Sheet dialog box, as the following illustrates, and then click Edit.

Edit Style Sheet

islestyle.css (link)

Link...
New...
Edit...
Duplicate...
Remove

File contents
.bottom, .role, .sidetext, a:active, a:hover, a:link,
a:visited, li, p

Done   Help

BEYOND THE BASICS

3. In the style sheet dialog box, as the following shows, select a style, and then choose Edit.

4. This opens the Style Definition dialog box, from which you can change the style.

You can also access this feature by double-clicking the style in the CSS Style panel. If you made a selection in the Document window, the first click of the double-click applies the style to the selection. If you do this inadvertently, you can remove the style by clicking the None option in the CSS Style panel.

Using a Third-Party CSS Application

Although the CSS features have been improved in Dreamweaver 4, many serious developers prefer to use a third-party style sheet application, instead of the CSS Styles panel. The most popular of these applications is TopStyle by Bradbury Software (**http://www.bradsoft.com**), as seen in Figure 17-10. TopStyle Lite ships with HomeSite, which, in turn, is shipped with full versions of Dreamweaver. TopStyle Lite is used primarily for embedded and inline styles. A full version of the software is available from the Bradbury Software site; the Pro version is intended solely for external style sheets.

Because TopStyle is a dedicated CSS application, it includes features beyond the scope of Dreamweaver. TopStyle provides CSS validation to alert you to styles that aren't implemented in target browsers. It also points out styles that are defined in style sheets but aren't used in the site and style sheets that aren't linked from any pages in the site. Another useful feature is the capability to group styles according to the elements to which they're applied or the context of the style.

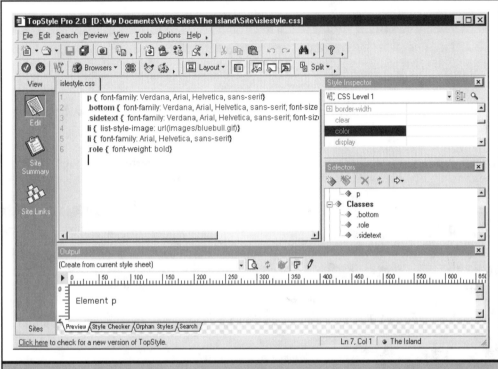

Figure 17-10. *TopStyle is a third-party CSS application that can be fully integrated with Dreamweaver*

Note   *Although not packaged with HomeSite or as tightly integrated with both HomeSite and Dreamweaver, other third-party CSS applications are available. For a list of these applications, visit the W3C Cascading Style Sheets site at* **http:// www. w3 c.org/Style/CSS**. *From there, click Author Tools to scroll down the page to the list of CSS tools.*

Changing the Default CSS Application

As would be expected, Dreamweaver uses its own CSS Styles panel as the default CSS editor. You can change this setting, however, in the Preferences dialog box. To use TopStyle or another third-party application as your CSS editor, do the following:

1. Select Edit | Preferences from the menu, or press CTRL-U (CMD-U on the Mac).

2. Choose the File Types/Editors category from the Preferences dialog box.

3. Press the Add (+) button above the Extensions field.

4. Type .css in the new entry in the Extensions field.

5. Press the Add (+) button above the Editors field.

6. From the File Selector dialog box, navigate to the third-party CSS application you want to use, and then click Open (Select on the Mac).

7. Press OK to exit the Preferences dialog box.

Once you choose a third-party CSS application, you can access it by double-clicking a CSS document in the Site window.

If you're using TopStyle Pro 2.0 as your CSS application, you can integrate it with Dreamweaver by setting the Third-Party Integration option within TopStyle. This has the same end result as the previous steps, but it's much simpler.

Summary

While this chapter provides the theory and technique of using Cascading Style Sheets, it cannot begin to cover the creative freedom offered by this tool. Many Dreamweaver gurus are embracing style sheets, so examples abound. The best way to incorporate style sheets into your sites is to eliminate <font> and other formatting tags from your documents and play with the possibilities of CSS. Here are some key points to remember:

- Three types of styles exist—external style sheets, embedded style sheets, and inline styles. Each has a different sphere of influence, ranging from the broadest sitewide scope with the least power to the smallest inline scope with the highest level of override capability.

- A style rule is created by defining a selector and a declaration. A declaration is a combination of a property and its value.

- Style sheets enable you to maintain consistency throughout your site.

- Dreamweaver uses the CSS Styles panel to define and edit styles.

- Style classes are custom tags that are used to apply a style to a subset of your content.

- Style sheets may eventually replace tables for layout by positioning elements in specific coordinates on the page. This is used for layer positioning, but it's still gaining acceptance within the Web development community and browser implementation.

The next chapter introduces client-side image maps.

The
Complete
Reference

Chapter 18

Client-Side Image Maps

s you learned in Chapters 12 and 13, images add visual appeal to a Web page. When used as elements of Navigation bars and buttons, images can even be used as link anchors to navigate to other pages. Images are limited, however, to a rectangular shape and can only link to one page. Not to devalue the usefulness of links, but they can be rather limiting. To piece together a complex image with multiple links using standard images, you need to slice and carefully reconstruct each piece of the overall image in a table. And, of course, each of those slices is still limited to a rectangular shape.

Image maps take images to a higher level. Instead of being sliced and diced into smaller images, an *image map* is one image that contains hotspots, several clickable areas on one image. The advantages of image maps are numerous. First, using one large image avoids the frustration of using tables to rebuild an image puzzle. Second, hotspots can be oddly shaped, allowing hotspots to take on the exact dimensions of a piece of the image. And, finally, because each hotspot is defined with its own area tag and shape attributes, you can apply alternate text and even behaviors, such as rollovers, to individual hotspots.

Making an effective image map requires a mix of development and design expertise. That said, image maps aren't popular. Whether this is because of the bloated code required to map the hotspots or because image maps are so often associated with cartoonish site mapping metaphors, image maps are generally regarded as a powerful but underused tool.

Still, learning how to use image maps is still worthwhile. Used properly, they can add functionality to your site. And because image maps aren't trendy, they haven't been overdone. Using a well-planned, visually appealing image map can actually make your site appear rather cutting edge.

Image Map Basics

Unless you're incredibly skilled in math and vector calculation, image maps are one of the few objects that cannot readily be hand-coded in HTML. While the formatting of an image map is actually quite simple, defining the area of the hotspots is tricky. Before applications such as Dreamweaver integrated image mapping with their other design tools, many Web developers turned to third-party applications that specialized in creating image maps.

An image map has three components:

- **<img>**—The image tag inserts the image into the HTML document. The *usemap attribute* associates a map element with the image.

- **<map>**—The map tag delineates the map area and names the map. This name is called by the image to create an association between the image and the map coordinates.

■ **<area>**—The area tags define each of the hotspots in the image map. This tag defines the shape of the hotspot and provides specific coordinates for the shape. The complexity of the coordinates depends on the complexity of the shape. A rectangle, for instance, has only four sides, and, thus, the coordinates of a rectangular hotspot require only four coordinates. A polygon, however, can have many irregular sides, each of which must be coordinated when defining the shape. The <area> tag also contains the href attribute to specify a destination for the hotlink and an alt attribute to provide accessibility.

The resulting code of an image map looks something like this:

```
<img src="images/usmap.gif" width="356" height="228" border="0"
alt="Image Map of US" usemap="#usspas">
<map name="usspas">
<area shape="rect" coords="70,83,106,129" href="utah.html"
title="Utah" alt="Utah">
</map>
```

In a map of the United States, for example, the state of Utah has been defined as a hotspot. Clicking this hotspot from a browser takes a user to another page within the site, **utah.html**.

Client-Side versus Server-Side Image Maps

Dreamweaver creates client-side image maps, but you may have also heard of server-side image maps. As the name implies, *server-side image maps* keep all the map data on the server. Server-side image maps are slower than client-side image maps because they need to compare the data received from the user's action—clicking a hotspot—with the data stored on the server—the coordinates of the image map data. Client-side image maps download their data along with the rest of a Web page, to the user's local browser. Because no additional server is hit, the comparison of data from the user action with the data of the image map is much faster.

Creating Image Maps

Image maps are actually quite easy to create. If you have Fireworks, you can create or modify an image, and then set hotspots in your graphic, as shown in Figure 18-1. Fireworks generates the HTML for the resulting image map, which can then be exported as an HTML file. This code can then be cut-and-pasted into an HTML document in Dreamweaver. The advantage of using a tool such as Fireworks is you can magnify the image and use other graphics tools to pinpoint the accuracy of your hotspot selections.

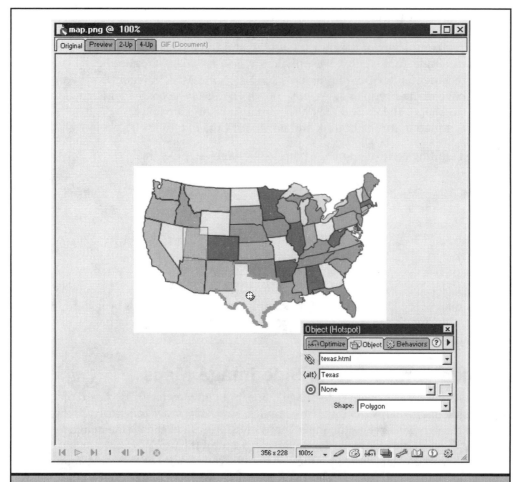

Figure 18-1. Fireworks enables you to create image maps that can be exported into Dreamweaver

Note *Image map coordinates are determined relative to the image itself and not to the document. This enables you to move the image map freely from application to application and page to page.*

If you prefer to create image maps in Dreamweaver, the process is similar. To create an image map, do the following:

1. Insert an image into the HTML document, as covered in Chapter 12. Use the standard image properties to set the vertical and horizontal spacing, alignment, and alt text for the image.

Note *Although you can—and should—set alt text for each of the hotspots, the image itself should also contain an alt tag. This tag is used when the user mouses over a portion of the image that doesn't have a hotspot.*

2. Select the image. The Property Inspector changes context in accordance with the image.

3. In the Property Inspector, name the image map in the Map Name field, as the following shows. Names must be unique.

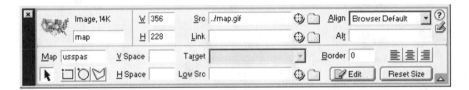

4. Select a drawing tool from the Property Inspector, and then draw the desired shape over a portion of the image.

   ■ **Rectangle**—position the cursor in one of the upper corners of the desired hotspot, and then hold down the mouse button while extending the rectangle to the opposite corner. The four corners of the rectangle become the coordinates for the area of the hotspot.

   ■ **Oval**—position the cursor at one of the upper corners of the desired location, and then hold down the mouse button and drag the circle to the diagonal corner to extend the circle. Although they're referred to as an oval, hotspots created with this tool are always a perfect circle because the coordinates are only the x and y values of the center of the circle and the circle's radius.

   ■ **Polygon**—position the cursor at a starting point, and then click at every point of the shape where it changes direction or angle in some way. The coordinates of a polygon consist of the x and y position of each corner point you set, often resulting in complex coordinate calculations to define the entire shape.

5. Click the hotspot you drew to display the Hotspot Property Inspector, as shown in Figure 18-2, to enter link and alt text for the hotspot. You can also target the link to open in a new browser window or frame.

6. Draw the next hotspot and repeat the process.

Modifying and Aligning Hotspots

Aligning hotspots perfectly when you draw them freehand is difficult. Once you draw a hotspot, you can modify it by clicking the points of the hotspot, and then resizing or reshaping the element.

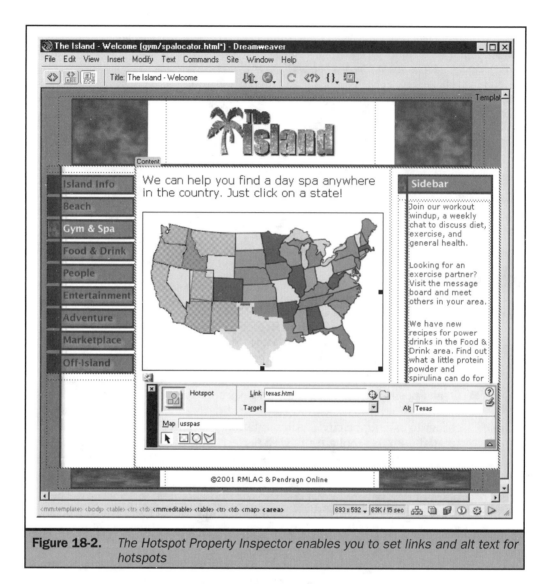

Figure 18-2. The Hotspot Property Inspector enables you to set links and alt text for hotspots

Tip *To nudge a hotspot into position one pixel at a time without changing its shape or size, select the hotspot and use the arrow keys.*

You can also modify the alignment of a group of hotspots using the Modify | Align menu, as the following illustrates. To align hotspots:

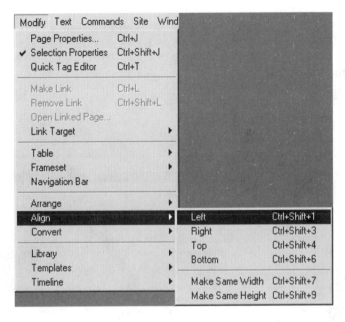

1. Select a hotspot.

2. Holding down the SHIFT key, select the other hotspots you want to align.

3. Choose Modify | Align | and one of the following alignment options:

   ■ **Left**—aligns the selected hotspots to their leftmost point. You can also use the keyboard shortcut CTRL-SHIFT-1 (COMMAND-SHIFT-1 on the Mac).

   ■ **Right**—aligns the selected hotspots to their rightmost point. The keyboard shortcut for this option is CTRL-SHIFT-3 (COMMAND-SHIFT-3 on the Mac).

   ■ **Top**—aligns the selected hotspots to their topmost point. You can also use CTRL-SHIFT-4 (COMMAND-SHIFT-4 on the Mac).

   ■ **Bottom**—aligns the selected hotspots to their bottommost point. The keyboard shortcut is CTRL-SHIFT-6 (COMMAND-SHIFT-6 on the Mac).

   ■ **Make Same Width**—all selected hotspots assume the same width as the last hotspot to be selected in the group. You can also use CTRL-SHIFT-7 (COMMAND-SHIFT-7 on the Mac).

   ■ **Make Same Height**—all selected hotspots assume the same height as the last hotspot to be selected in the group. You can also use CTRL-SHIFT-9 (COMMAND-SHIFT-9 on the Mac).

When hotspots overlap, the one created first takes precedence. To change this order, use the Modify | Arrange options to send some hotspots to the back of the pecking order and bring others to the front.

BEYOND
THE BASICS

After drawing your hotspots and assigning the appropriate links, it's time to test the completed image map. Figure 18-3. As you move your mouse over the image in a browser, notice the alt text changes for each hotspot. If you click one of the hotspots, you move to the linked page.

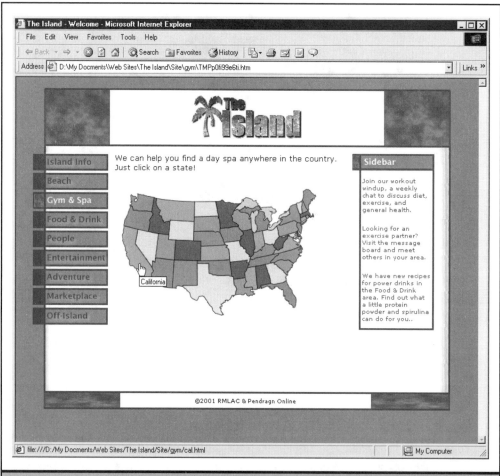

Figure 18-3. *The completed image map as it appears in a browser window*

Summary

Image maps are underused, yet powerful, graphic elements. Here are some key points:

- Client-side image maps download their mapping information to the user's browser, along with the rest of the Web page.

- Server-side image maps store mapping information on the server and compare the data sent by the user after clicking a hotspot with the mapping coordinates on the server. This results in slower image map response.

- Dreamweaver creates client-side image maps.

- Image maps consist of a JPG or GIF image, a map definition, and a series of hotspots.

- Links are applied to hotspots.

- Hotspots may overlap, but the first hotspot drawn takes precedence unless this order has been manually changed.

- You can apply behaviors to image maps and hotspots.

The next chapter introduces Dynamic HTML, a combination of HTML, Cascading Style Sheets, and JavaScript used to increase interactivity and the dynamic presentation of Web pages.

The
Complete
Reference

Dreamweaver
4

Chapter 19

Dynamic HTML

ynamic HTML (DHTML) is designed to offer client-side dynamic content that was undreamed of just a few years ago. DHTML provides for all sorts of, well, dynamic effects to be applied to Web pages. Text and images can appear and disappear, objects can zoom around the screen, and menus can appear as the mouse moves over their title. Best of all, this can all be done directly in the browser without having to use a plug-in or another external program.

DHTML isn't just one specific technology or feature. Instead, it's a lot of different features that can be used separately or together to enable changing the HTML content of a Web page after it's been downloaded and rendered.

This chapter introduces DHTML and layers, and then describes how Dreamweaver can be used to create and control them. The following chapter continues the discussion about layers and discusses how to animate them using Dreamweaver Timelines.

DHTML Basics

So how can HTML content be changed after a page has already been downloaded? Browsers have implemented several innovations in some form or another to make DHTML possible: client-side scripting languages, the Document Object Model and Cascading Style Sheets.

Client-Side Scripting

Client-side scripting languages, in particular JavaScript, have been used to create rudimentary DHTML effects for some time. JavaScript provides the code flexibility and the event model that allows things to change dynamically. An image changing because of a mouse rollover is one example. The image source file referenced by an image can be changed when the mouse pointer moves over it, and then changed back when the mouse moves off it. Unlike many DHTML features that didn't come until later, this capability was first available in version 3.0 browsers.

 Dreamweaver uses image swapping and restoring to good effect for its Navigation Bar feature. See Chapter 13 for more information about creating Navigation bars. Chapter 23 also has information about the Preload Images, Swap Image, and Swap Image Restore behaviors that make Navigation bars work.

The 4.0 and later browsers from both Microsoft and Netscape allow even more of the HTML elements on a page to be accessed from JavaScript, which brings us to the next feature that makes modern DHTML effects possible: the Document Object Model.

Document Object Model

The Document Object Model (DOM) is the heart of DHTML. DOM is what makes it possible for a script to change HTML elements on a page. The DOM provides a hierarchy of objects that represent some or all of the elements contained in an HTML document, as well as objects that can give access to information, such as the browser version, the current URL, or the browser's window dimensions. And, most important, a document object provides access to the individual elements of the current page.

While some dynamically alterable features were in the DOMs of earlier browsers (such as the image swapping capability), not until the version 4.0 browsers did the DOM really started to take shape.

Netscape 4.0 introduced the <layer> tag, which allowed content to be placed in a container that could be manipulated using JavaScript. Attributes such as position, visibility, z-order in relation to other layers, and background color could all be changed on the fly. Unfortunately, Netscape's layer capability preceded the W3C's standards for layers, so much of the implementation was proprietary. This led to all sorts of headaches when Internet Explorer 4.0 was released with support for the W3C's DOM specification.

Internet Explorer 4.0 was a quantum leap over Netscape in terms of the DOM. Its Dynamic HTML Object Model for the first time allowed *any* element of an HTML document to be accessed by any scripting language or even by external programs, such as Java applets or ActiveX controls. It won't just let you show and hide content using layers, the content itself can be modified on the fly. Netscape 6.0 finally addresses this weakness in Netscape by also providing a comprehensive DOM.

 *The W3C has produced several levels of standards for DOM. For current information about the W3C's DOM activities, see **http://www.w3.org/DOM.***

Cascading Style Sheets

Another important component of DHTML is the Cascading Style Sheet (CSS). A CSS can be used to control the style (formatting attributes) for HTML elements and tags, for many documents at once or for an entire site. This is because CSS can be linked to multiple documents at the same time. With styles in HTML documents, on the other hand, you have to update each one by hand.

In addition, CSS enables you to control many properties that you can't control with plain HTML. For example, you can specify font sizes in terms of pixels or points, as opposed to simply using the limited range of sizes the <font> tag typically supports.

 You can find more information about creating and using Cascading Style Sheets in Chapter 17.

Layers

Layers are containers on a Web page that hold HTML elements. By using layers, you gain more control and flexibility regarding positioning content on the screen.

Dreamweaver provides a lot of flexibility when dealing with layers. You can overlap them, hide them, or animate them using a timeline. Dreamweaver's DHTML behaviors let all of this happen in response to events and, if you don't want to, you needn't learn JavaScript at all.

Layers are defined using one of the following HTML tags: `<div>`, `<span>`, `<layer>`, and `<ilayer>`. Note, `<layer>` and `<ilayer>` tags are specific to Netscape version 4.0, so in the interest of cross-platform compatibility, you should stick with the `<div>` or `<span>` tags. The following is an example of a layer created using Dreamweaver using the default settings. These defaults can be changed by setting the layer preferences, as discussed in the next section.

```
<div id="Layer1" style="position:absolute; left:400px; top:100px;
width:100px; height:75px; z-index:3"></div>
```

Setting Layer Preferences

Before you create layers, you should indicate your preferences for the default settings that new layers should use. Choose Edit | Preferences from the menu and select the Layers category, as the following illustrates. You can set these preferences:

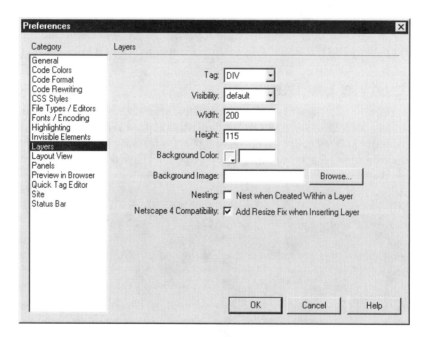

■ **Tag**—This sets the default HTML tag to use when creating layers. The options are DIV, SPAN, LAYER, or ILAYER. Leave this as DIV or SPAN in most cases for the widest browser compatibility.

- **Visibility**—Select from default, inherit, visible, or hidden. Default specifies the browser default should be used. Inherit should be used with nested layers to assume the visibility of the parent. Visible and Hidden are exactly what they describe.

- **Width and Height**—Sets the default width and height for inserted layers (those created by dragging from the Objects panel or by choosing Insert | Layer).

- **Background Color**—Select a color to use for the default layer background color using the color picker, or enter the string value for the color (for example, #FFFFFF).

- **Background Image**—Sets a default background image. Enter the image file to use in the text box or click the Browse button to locate the file.

- **Nesting**—When you draw a layer within the boundaries of another layer, it becomes nested in that layer when this option is checked. Whatever you choose for this setting can be overridden by holding the Alt key (Windows) or the Option key (Macintosh) when drawing a layer.

- **Netscape 4 Compatibility**—Netscape 4.x browsers have a known bug that causes layers to be positioned incorrectly when a user resizes their browser. This option inserts a JavaScript function into the document head that forces the page to reload whenever the browser window is resized. Note, this option can also be toggled on and off using the Commands | Add/Remove Netscape Resize Fix.

Creating Layers

Dreamweaver provides several ways of creating layers on a page. You can insert a layer using the menu, drag it from the Objects panel, or simply draw it on the page.

To create a layer, do one of the following:

- Insert a layer by choosing Insert | Layer from the menu. A layer is created in the document with the default size. The layer is created at the current cursor position in the Document window.

- Drag a layer from the Objects panel by dragging the Draw Layer button (in the Common category) into the Document window. The layer is then created in the document in the closest position possible to where you release the button.

- To draw a layer, click the Draw Layer button in the Common category of the Objects panel. Then click in your document view at the upper left-hand corner where you want the layer to be positioned, and then drag the cursor to the lower right-hand corner, as seen in Figure 19-1. If you hold down the CONTROL key (COMMAND on the Macintosh) while you draw, you can continue drawing layers without having to click the Draw Layer button again.

BEYOND
THE BASICS

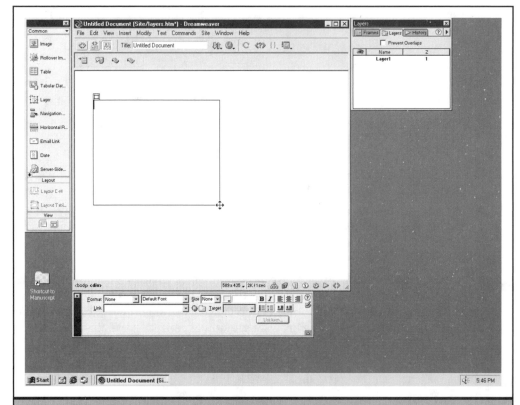

Figure 19-1.   *Draw a layer by clicking the Draw Layer icon in the Objects panel, and then clicking-and-dragging in the Design view to define the size and position.*

Note *If you have Invisible Elements turned on (by choosing View | Visual Aids | Invisible Elements), a layer marker is shown in the Document window for each layer. When Invisible Elements is active, the elements on your page may appear in a shifted position. Turn off this option to see how your page is viewed in a browser.*

Adding Content to Layers

You can insert HTML elements into a layer just as you can with your base document. Before placing elements in a layer, you must first activate the layer by clicking anywhere within the layer border (don't click the layer border itself, though, because that selects it for resizing or moving).

When you activate a layer, the insertion cursor is shown inside the layer, and any objects you insert or text you type is placed inside the layer, as seen in Figure 19-2.

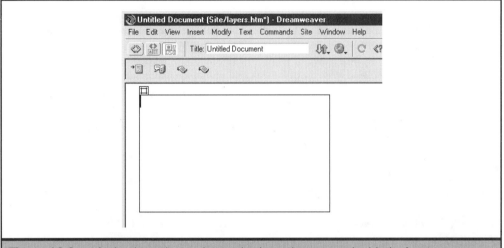

Figure 19-2.   *Activating a layer places the insertion cursor inside it. Any text or objects inserted are placed in the layer*

The Layers Panel

The Layers panel provides a convenient way to view and modify the layout properties for the layers in a page. Choose Window | Layers, or press F2 to activate it. This illustration shows the Layers panel.

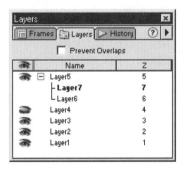

Layers are shown in the list in the reverse order from how they were inserted, from the most recently inserted layers at the top to the earlier inserted layers at the bottom. *Nested* layers (layers contained within other layers) are shown as a tree view descending from the parent layer. From the Layers panel, you can select layers, set their visibility, rename them, change their stacking order, nest them, and set the layer overlap setting.

Layer Visibility

The initial visibility of a layer can be changed from the default value using the Layers panel. The leftmost column (showing an eye at the top) indicates the current visibility state for all layers. If the eye is open, the layer is visible. If the eye is closed, the layer is hidden. If the eye icon does not appear, it indicates the layer is set for the default value for the browser. You can toggle the initial visibility for the layer by clicking its position in this column.

You can also set the visibility for all layers at once: Click the eye icon in the column header to toggle through the visibility states.

Renaming Layers

Although Dreamweaver inserts unique names for layers it creates, you'll frequently want to rename the layers to give them easier to remember names that indicate their purpose. This way, you can easily tell which layer is being targeted by a JavaScript operation.

To rename a layer from the Layers panel, double-click its name. The name then becomes editable, and you can simply type in a new name as the following illustrates.

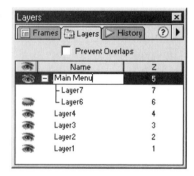

Changing the Stacking Order

The stacking order for layers, otherwise known as the *z-order,* specifies which layer is seen on top when two layers overlap. Layers with a higher value for the z-order are shown on top of layers with a lower number. You can change the stacking order for layers in the Layers panel in two ways:

- Select the layer you want to change and drag it up or down the layer list to the desired position. A line is shown indicating the new layer position. Release the mouse button when the layer is in the correct position. The values in the Z column are then renumbered to accommodate the new order, as the following illustration shows.

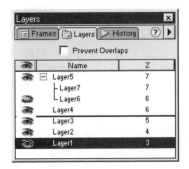

- In the Z column, click the number for the layer you're changing. An edit box appears and you can type a new number. Enter a higher number to move the layer up in the stacking order or click a lower number to move it lower. The numbers you enter needn't be in sequence, which is convenient when moving your layers out of order. Click return and the layer is then moved to its new position in the list.

Nesting Layers

Nested layers are contained within other layers. You can nest layers when creating them or by using the Layers panel.

To nest a layer using the Layers panel, hold down the CONTROL key (COMMAND on the Macintosh) and drag it into another layer, as described in the "Changing the Stacking Order" section.

Layer Overlap

You can indicate whether you want to allow layers to overlap in two different ways:

- In the Layers panel, check the Prevent Overlaps box, as shown in this illustration.

- Check the Modify | Arrange | Prevent Layer Overlaps menu item (as shown in Figure 19-3).

When the Prevent Layer Overlaps option is on, you cannot create a layer in front of another layer. If you try to move or resize a layer, you won't be able to make it overlap other layers.

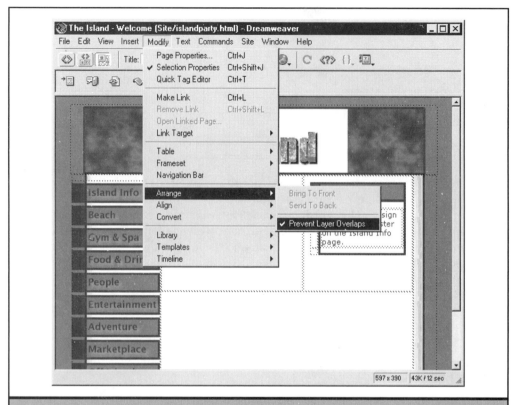

Figure 19-3. *You can keep layers from overlapping when you move them by checking the Prevent Layer Overlaps option*

Dreamweaver won't fix existing overlapping layers when you activate this option after they've already been created. When you move or resize one of the overlapping layers, it is moved away from the other layers.

The Prevent Layer Overlaps option takes precedence over the Snap to Grid option. If both are enabled and you move a layer, it won't snap to the grid if doing so would cause it to overlap another layer.

Even with the Prevent Layer Overlaps option, you can still cause layers to overlap. If you insert a layer from the menu, enter a new position in the layer Property Inspector, or move layers by editing the HTML code in the Code view, or the Code Inspector layers will overlap or nest. In all these cases, if you attempt to drag an overlapped layer, it immediately moves so it doesn't overlap other layers.

Layer Properties

The Property Inspector can be used to set new options for layers after they're created. To see the Property Inspector for a particular layer, select it in the Layers panel or by clicking its border in the Document window. The layer Property Inspector is shown in this illustration. Click the expander button on the right side if you don't see all the options.

This Property Inspector lets you set the following layer options:

- **Layer ID**—Specifies the name of the layer to use for scripting. Every layer must have a unique name, and the name cannot contain any special characters such as spaces, hyphens, or periods.

- **L and T**—Specify the left and top coordinates for the layer. You can change these by entering new values here.

- **W and H**—Specify the width and height of the layer. These are the minimum sizes to use for the layer. If the size of the layer content exceeds these dimensions, the layer can be made larger, depending on the Overflow setting. Size and position options are specified in pixels by default using the px suffix. You can also use the following unit suffixes: picas (pc), points (pt), inches (in), millimeters (mm), centimeters (cm), or percentage of the parent window (%).

- **Z-Index**—Specifies a value to use for stacking layers. Layers with higher values for this option are always shown on top of layers with lower values.

- **Vis**—Specifies the initial visibility for the layer. Choices are default, inherit, visible, and invisible.

- **BG Image**—Specifies an image to use for the layer background. You can enter a filename directly into the text box or locate it by clicking the Browse button.

- **Tag**—Specifies the HTML tag to use for the layer. SPAN or DIV are recommended choices. LAYER and ILAYER are also available choices, but they're Netscape-specific tags.

- **Overflow**—Specifies what happens if the content of a layer exceeds its dimensions. The choices are the following:

  - **Visible**—The layer is resized to show all the content

  - **Hidden**—Any content exceeding the layer size is clipped

- **Scroll**—Scroll bars are visible at all times in the layer
- **Auto**—Scroll bars appear only when the content exceeds the layer dimensions
- **Clip**—Defines the visible area of a layer. This can be used to cut content from the edges of a layer to focus on a specific area. The values represent the distance in pixels from the layer's boundaries, relative to the layer.
- **Use Left, Top,** and **Page** *X,* **Page** *Y*—These settings, specific to `layer` and `ilayer` tags only, specify whether the layer should be positioned relative to the left and top of its parent or relative to the top-left corner of the page.
- **Src**—This `layer` and `ilayer` specific setting lets you specify the filename of an HTML document to display in the layer.
- **A/B**—This `layer` and `ilayer` specific setting lets you specify the layer to place above (*A*) or below (*B*) this layer in the stacking order. Choose the layer from the list on the right.

Setting Properties for Multiple Layers

If you select more than one layer at once (press SHIFT as you select the layer in the Layer panel or the Document view), the Property Inspector changes to the Multiple Layers Inspector, as shown in the following illustration.

The Multiple Layer Property Inspector lets you make changes to a subset of the layer properties, which are L and T, W and H, Vis, Tag, Bg Image, and Bg Color.

Also present are options for setting text properties for the selected layers. You can set font, format, size, and color properties.

Manipulating Layers

When you insert layers, they are seldom where you want them in your document. Fortunately, manipulating layers is easy. You can move, resize, or align layers in Design view.

Moving and Resizing Layers

To move or resize a layer, select it in the Design view by clicking its border, or select it in the Layers panel by clicking it. A resize border is created around the layer and a drag box is shown in the upper-left corner (See Figure 19-4).

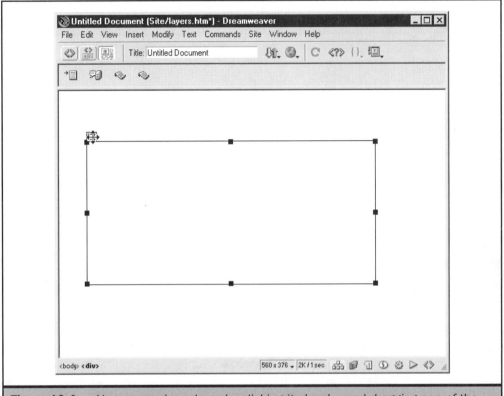

Figure 19-4.   *You can resize a layer by clicking its border and dragging one of the resize points around the edge*

To move a layer, position the cursor over the box shown at the top of the left corner or anywhere over the border except where the resize points are located. A quad arrow cursor is shown, enabling you to drag the layer to a new position.

To resize a layer, position the cursor over one of the eight resize points on the sides and corners. A double arrow cursor appears, indicating the direction you can resize. Click-and-drag to resize the layer.

Layer Alignment

You can align layers by selecting multiple layers (by pressing SHIFT as you select them) and choosing one of the items from the Modify | Align menu. Choices include Align Top, Align Bottom, Align Left, and Align Right. Choose Make Same Width and Make Same Height from this menu to give layers the same dimensions.

All alignment actions are done relative to the last layer selected. The last layer selected is represented by solid resize points on the border, others by hollow resize points, as this illustration shows.

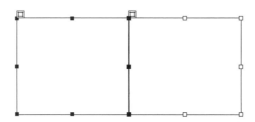

Older Browsers and Layers

One problem with using layers is they aren't supported in Netscape or Internet Explorer versions earlier than 4.0. If you want to provide as close an interface as possible for older browsers, you can convert the layers on a page to tables.

Converting to 3.0 Browser Compatibility

Dreamweaver provides a method for converting a document that contains layers or CSS, which 3.0 version browsers don't support, to one that uses a table and HTML attributes instead. Use the File | Convert | 3.0 Browser Compatible menu item to open the Convert to 3.0 Browser Compatible dialog box. This box gives you the option to convert CSS styles to the equivalent HTML attributes and also lets you convert layers to a table to maintain the position of the layer contents. The following illustration shows this dialog box.

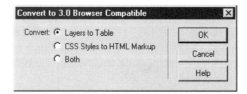

When you click OK, Dreamweaver creates a separate document preserving the original formatting and opens this converted file in a new untitled window. You can then save the file as an alternative version of your page.

Remember, if the layers on your page overlap or if they have negative top or left attributes putting them off the screen, they cannot be converted. Positioning of the content may also change during the conversion, so check the alignment of the new table content with that of the surrounding content.

If you selected Convert CSS Styles to HTML Markup or Both, CSS properties are replaced with HTML character styles wherever possible. Any CSS property that cannot be converted is removed. If your document uses Timelines to animate layers, the timeline is removed when you convert the layers to a table. Timeline code that's unrelated to layers, on the other hand, will still execute. For more information on animating layers and creating time lines, see Chapter 20.

Converting Layers to Tables

If you'd rather not have to maintain two different documents—one using layers and one using tables—you can also convert a single document using layers to one using a table and back again. This enables you to create your page layout using layers, and then convert the final document into one using tables when you finish working with it. If you need to work with the document again later, Dreamweaver enables you to convert your tables back into layers for editing convenience.

To change the layers on your page to a table, do the following:

1. Choose Modify | Convert | Layers to Table from the menu. Your currently selected view must be the Design view or this option will be grayed out. This activates the Convert Layers to Table dialog box, as this illustration shows.

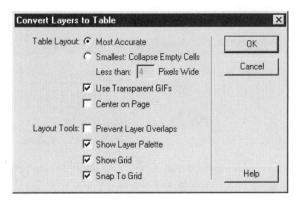

2. In the Convert Layers to Table dialog box, choose your desired layout properties.

   - **Most Accurate**—This creates a table cell `<td>` for every layer, plus placeholder cells necessary to fill the space between layers.

   - **Smallest: Collapse Empty Cells**—This causes layer edges to be realigned if they're currently positioned within the specified number of pixels. This option is designed to create a simpler table at the expense of accurate positioning.

   - **Use Transparent GIFs**—Checking this option causes the table's last row to be filled with transparent GIFs to ensure the table will be displayed with the same column widths in all browsers.

- **Center on Page**—Checking this box causes the table to be centered on the page. Otherwise, it's aligned left.

- **Prevent Layer Overlaps**—Checking this box turns on the Prevent Layer Overlap feature. Any new layers you then create won't be able to overlap existing layers. Whether or not you check this box, if your layers overlap, you won't be able to convert them to table cells.

- **Show Layer Palette**—If checked, this activates the Layers panel. If unchecked, the Layers panel is hidden.

- **Show Grid**—Checking this item causes the grid to be shown when OK is pressed.

- **Snap to Grid**—This item activates the Snap to Grid option when checked.

3. Click OK. Any layout changes you select take effect.

Converting Tables Back to Layers

In addition to converting layers to tables, you can also do the reverse. Do the following steps to convert tables back to layers:

1. Choose Modify | Convert | Tables to Layers from the menu. This activates the Convert Tables to Layers dialog box, as this illustration shows.

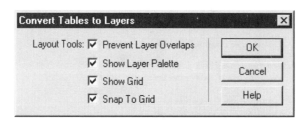

2. Select the layout tools options you want to modify. These are the same options as listed for the Convert Layers to Table dialog box.

3. Click OK. Any layout changes you selected take effect.

You cannot convert a single layer or table independently of all others. You must convert an entire page at one time.

Dynamic Layers

Internet Explorer 4.0 and Dynamic HTML Object Model let you apply many dynamic behaviors to layers. In many cases, these behaviors also work with Netscape 6; however, this browser isn't directly supported by Dreamweaver 4 behaviors. Chapter 23 talks about behaviors and how to use the Behaviors Panel in more detail, so this section only mentions behaviors that apply to layers.

Behaviors that can target layers include Change Property, Set Text of Layer, and Show-Hide Layers and Timelines.

Timelines aren't discussed here. The next chapter is devoted entirely to using timelines to animate layers.

Change Property

The Change Property action can be used to change the value of a layer's attributes. You can use it to set size, position, z-index, and other properties in recent browser versions. Although this action is only available by choosing actions for Internet Explorer 4.0 or 5.0, this behavior also works in Netscape 6. The dialog box for the Change Property action is shown in the following illustration.

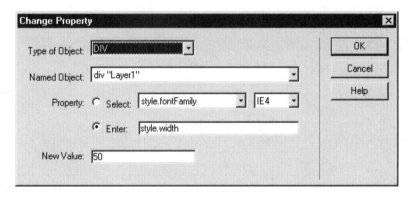

Other properties can be set as well.

- **Type of Object**—Choose the kind of object you want to target. For layers, choose one of the layer tags (LAYER, DIV, or SPAN). This limits the name choices in the Named Object drop-down list.

- **Named Object**—This is a list of the objects in your document that match the type of object you choose.

- **Property**—You can choose a target browser from the drop-down list on the right side, which provides a list of supported properties on the left. As an alternative, you can check Enter and enter the name of any property directly. This enables you to set properties you know about, but that aren't listed as choices.

- **New Value**—Enter the value you want the property to have after the event is fired, for instance, a new color if you're changing a color property.

Here are some of the unlisted properties that can be set for layers manually in the Enter: text box. With Internet Explorer 4.0 and later, and with Netscape 6.0, virtually any tag attribute may be set dynamically:

- **style.width**—Enables you to set a new width for the layer.
- **style.height**—Enables you to set a new height for the layer.
- **style.z-index**—Specifies a new z-index value for the layer.

Set Text of Layer

The Set Text of Layer action enables you to completely replace the content of a layer with new text you supply. This text can be any valid HTML code, letting you dynamically update an entire layer at once. The Set Text of Layer dialog box, shown in the following illustration, provides an input box where you can type or paste the JavaScript code you want to use.

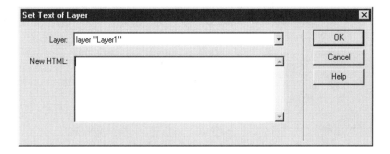

You can embed JavaScript statements or function calls to generate the text for the layer by enclosing it in braces, like this:

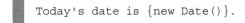

```
Today's date is {new Date()}.
```

The result is shown in Figure 19-5.

Show-Hide Layers

One of the most useful features of layers is the capability to be shown or hidden on demand. A page might have layers that make up drop-down menus, which you might want to make visible when the mouse pointer moves over the navbar buttons. The Show-Hide Layers behavior makes tying this process to a variety of events easy.

The Show-Hide Layers action lets you show, hide, or return to a default state of any and all layers you choose with a single action.

To use the Show-Hide Layers action, first select an object to trigger the action. This object can be anything except a layer, (in every browser with the exception of Internet Explorer 4.0). Then open the Actions menu of the Behaviors panel and choose Show-Hide Layer.

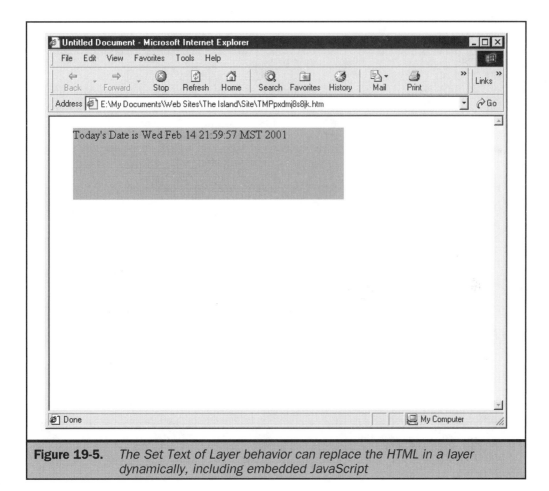

Figure 19-5. *The Set Text of Layer behavior can replace the HTML in a layer dynamically, including embedded JavaScript*

The Show-Hide Layer dialog box, shown in the following illustration, provides a list of all layers in your document. Select each one that you want to affect with this action individually, and then click a new state for it: Show, Hide, or Default. When you finish, click OK.

Summary

DHTML isn't a single technology but, instead, it's the use of several different browser features to enable HTML to be changed dynamically after a page has been downloaded. Browser incompatibilities have kept many from using some of the more advanced DHTML capabilities. Dreamweaver, however, can produce content in layers that can be dynamically controlled using either Netscape or Internet Explorer.

- DHTML typically involves the use of JavaScript to modify HTML components using the Document Object Model.

- DHTML is only supported by 4.0 and later browsers. Extensive DOM support is provided in Internet Explorer 4.0 and later, and in Netscape 6.0.

- Blocks of code, called layers, can be absolutely positioned in 4.0 and later browsers.

- Layers are where Dreamweaver uses the bulk of its DHTML capabilities.

- Dreamweaver provides several behaviors that enable you to modify layers dynamically, including Change Property, Set Text, and Show-Hide Layers.

The next chapter provides even more information about layers and explains how to use Dreamweaver's Timeline feature to animate them.

The Complete Reference

Chapter 20

Layer Animation

he previous chapter introduced Dynamic HTML (DHTML) and layers. Layers can be modified using Dreamweaver behaviors to set dynamic properties such as size, position, and visibility, or even to replace the text in a layer entirely.

Dreamweaver's timelines go one step further: they provide a mechanism for animating layers by changing their properties in a timed, sequential order. Timelines can change the position, size, visibility, and stacking order of a layer by using DHTML at key intervals, or keyframes, along the timeline. Timelines can also change image source files at any point along the animation.

Timelines can also be used to call other Dreamweaver behaviors. For example, you could use the Play Sound behavior to play a wave file when an animated layer reaches some destination. You could use the Swap Image or Set Text behaviors to change the displayed contents of a layer. You could even call a custom JavaScript function to perform some arbitrary action.

While animated layers are certainly not the only way to add multimedia content to a site, they have a few advantages compared to other approaches, such as Java applets, Shockwave, and Flash movies. These approaches require extra content files and, sometimes, even plug-ins to be downloaded before they can be used. Animated GIFs are supported, and used often, in nearly every browser. However, they aren't really controllable, and they can't be moved to a new position on a page by themselves. They must be contained in a layer instead.

The best reason to use animated layers is because layers contain plain old HTML code. This makes creating impressive animated displays possible without needing to use a third-party package or any tools other than Dreamweaver and an image editor. Also possible is to combine other animation types with layers. For example, you could have an animated GIF image in a layer and move it around the browser window using timelines.

The biggest drawback to layers may be they only work on 4.0 versions of Netscape and Internet Explorer or later.

This chapter shows how to create and manage timelines in Dreamweaver, as well as how to use the Timelines panel to animate layers.

The Timelines Panel

Like most other Dreamweaver features, a panel is devoted to creating and editing timelines. To activate the Timelines panel, choose Windows | Timelines from the menu, or use SHIFT-F9. The following illustration shows the Timelines panel.

frame numbers

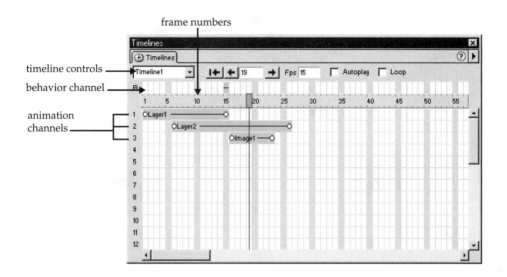

timeline controls

behavior channel

animation channels

The Timelines panel shows a timeline in a grid format, with columns representing animation frames and individual layers shown in the rows called Animation Channels. The elements of the Timelines panel are listed here:

- **Animation channels**—This section displays bars representing the layers and images animated in this timeline. Each layer or image is shown per row, with the bar extending from the first frame that affects it to the last frame. A row can have multiple objects represented as long as their animations don't overlap in time. Similarly, an object cannot be controlled in two different rows at once. Keyframes can be added to an animation channel. *Keyframes* are used to specify an exact position the object should occupy at that frame and positions between keyframes are interpolated. A keyframe is represented on the animation channel by a circle: By default, all channels have keyframes on the first and last frames.

- **Frame numbers**—Above the animation channels are the *frame numbers*—a sequential ruler showing numbered frames. The currently selected frame is shown here by a red marker called the *playback head*. A line extends from this marker through the animation channels to make seeing the current frame easy. The document window shows the position of images and layers in the position they would be at the currently selected frame during an animation.

- **Behavior channel**—Above the frame numbers is a special channel that shows the frames with behaviors attached to them. The *behavior channel*'s action is executed during playback of the timeline when the specified frame is reached. Multiple behaviors can be attached to a single frame.

- **Context menu**—This menu is obtained by right-clicking the Timelines panel or by clicking the Context Menu button at the upper-right side of the panel. Various options on this menu may be grayed out, depending on the applicability to the currently selected object. The Context menu is shown in the following illustration. Many of these options are also available from the Modify | Timeline menu.

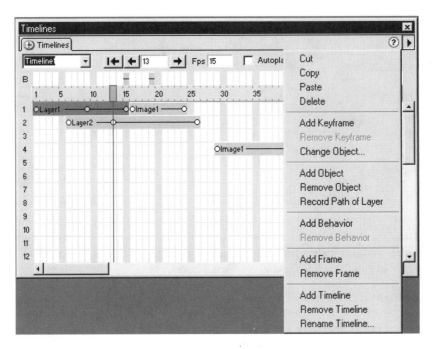

- **Timeline controls**—The *Timeline* control bar is located above the behaviors channel and provides VCR-like controls for stepping through the timeline's frames. The controls on this bar are shown in the following illustration:

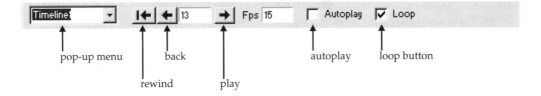

- **Timeline pop-up menu**—This menu is used to select a timeline to display in the panel if your document has more than one timeline.
- **Rewind**—The rewind button moves the playback head to the first frame of the timeline.
- **Back**—The back button steps the playback head backward one frame.

■ **Forward**—The forward button steps the playback head forward one frame.

■ **Fps**—Indicates the playback frame rate the timeline should use, in frames per second. While many browsers can handle a frame rate as high as 15, it usually shouldn't be set higher. This value is the maximum frame rate you desire: The actual frame rate is only as high as the browser is able to render frames.

■ **Autoplay**—Checking this box attaches a Play Timeline behavior to the `onLoad` event for the page. This causes the animation to begin playing immediately after the page loads on a browser.

■ **Loop**—This check box can be used to make the animation start over at the first frame when the animation finishes. Checking this box adds a Go To Timeline Frame behavior, causing the animation to jump the first frame when it reaches the target frame.

Creating Timelines

Creating a timeline is simple once you have a layer on your page (see Chapter 19 for information about creating layers). Once your layer is created, do the following:

1. Open the Timelines panel. Choose Windows | Timelines from the menu, or press SHIFT-F9.

2. Position your layer in the location where you want it at the start of the animation.

3. Make sure the layer is still selected, and then drag the layer to the Timeline panel or choose Modify | Timeline | Add Object to Timeline from the menu. An animation channel bar is created representing this object.

> **Tip** *While you can put both layers and images in a timeline, only layers can have their positions changed. To move an image on a page, put it in a layer and move the layer instead.*

4. Click the keyframe marker at the end of the animation channel (shown as a small circle), and then move the layer to the *x-y* position it should be on the page at the end of the animation.

5. You can make the layer move along a curved path by adding additional keyframes. Do this by CTRL-CLICKING (CMD-CLICK on the Mac) a spot on the animation channel, or choosing Add Keyframe from the context menu.

6. When you add additional keyframes to the timeline, you need to indicate a position for the layer at that point in time. Make the keyframe the current frame by clicking it and drag the layer to an intermediate spot. Steps 5 and 6 can be repeated for as many frames as you like. When the animation is played, the layer moves along a curved path through the keyframed positions, as shown in Figure 20-1.

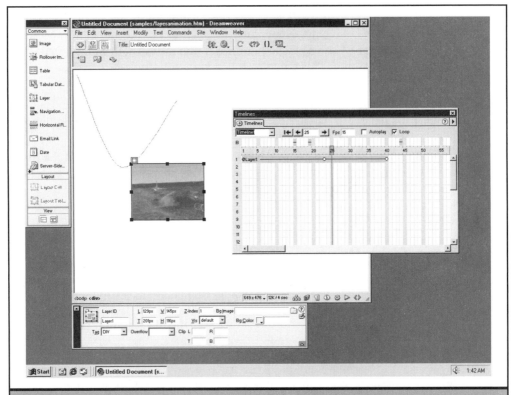

Figure 20-1. Add keyframes for each explicit position you want your layer to occupy during the animation. Dreamweaver plots a curve to move the layer through to transition smoothly from one keyframe to the next

Clicking the Play button advances the Forward button in the Timelines panel, advances the playback head by one frame, and moves all the animated layers on your page to their new positions. You can click-and-hold the mouse button down on this button to move through the frames rapidly. This gives you an idea of how the animation looks in motion on your page.

Recording an Animation Path

Dreamweaver provides another method of creating an animation path: it can record the movement of a layer as you drag it around the window. Individual keyframes are created automatically for you when the recording is used to create an animation channel.

To create a timeline by recording its path, do the following:

1. Select a layer and move it to the position it should be at the start of the animation.

2. Choose Modify | Timeline | Record Path of Layer from the menu. You can also choose Record Path of Layer from the drop-down menu in the timeline panel.

3. Drag the layer around the page along the path you want it to follow, ending on the position you want the layer to be in when the animation stops.

4. Release the mouse when the layer is positioned in the final location.

When you release the mouse, Dreamweaver creates an animation channel for the layer. Figure 20-2 shows an example of a more complicated path, created by dragging the layer and recording its movement.

Changing Image Source and Layer Properties

In addition to moving layers, timelines enable you to perform other common image and layer manipulations. You can change an image's source file, or make a layer visible, change its stacking order, or change its size.

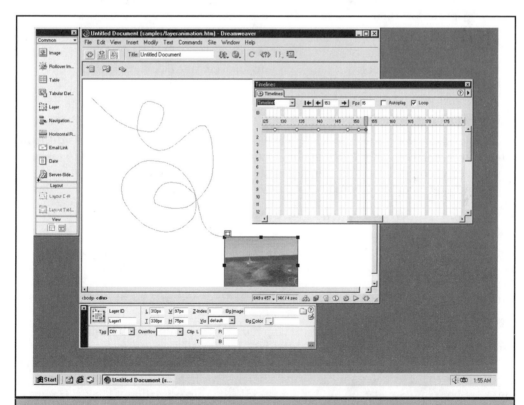

Figure 20-2. *You can define the path for an animation by dragging the layer along the path and recording it. Dreamweaver automatically creates keyframes in the locations needed to animate the object*

Changing an Image Source File

To change the source file for an image in the timeline, either select an existing keyframe or create a new one for the image. In the document window, select the image and choose a new file for it using the image property inspector.

Changing Layer Properties

You can change layer properties as well. Select (or create) the keyframe you want to use to modify the layer, and select the layer in the document window or in the Layers panel (see Chapter 19 for more information on setting layer properties). You can change these properties:

- **Visibility**—Use the layer property inspector to choose hidden, visible, inherit, or default.

- **Z-Index**—Enter a new value to use for the stacking order in the property inspector or use the Layers panel to order the layers.

- **Resize**—Drag a layer's resize box to the new dimensions or enter the new sizes directly in the layer property inspector. Note: The resize capability can only be used with Internet Explorer 4.0 and up, or Netscape 6.0. Netscape 4.75 and under cannot resize layers.

Modifying Animations

Getting your layers to look exactly the way you want them to on the first try is difficult. Once you have layers added to a timeline, though, it's simple to tweak them to make any needed changes. *Tweaks* are usually made by dragging some part of the animation channel to a new position. Here are some ways you can modify a channel animation:

Adjusting Playback Time Length

You can extend or reduce the number of frames an animation takes to complete by resizing its Animation channel bar. To make the animation play longer, drag the end frame marker on the right to the right. To make it shorter, drag it to the left. All of the keyframes shift, so they remain in the same relative position in the new animation. If you'd rather not have the keyframes move—say, you're only trying to add to the end of an animation—hold down the CTRL key (COMMAND on the Mac) while dragging the end frame.

You can increase or decrease the playing length of an animation by using the Modify | Timeline | Add Frame and Modify | Timeline | Remove frame menu items, or Add Frame and Remove Frame items from the Timelines panel's context menu. The animation is changed one frame at a time, allowing for fine adjustments. Add frame and remove frame can also be used in the middle of your animation, to adjust frames between any two keyframes.

Adjusting Keyframes

You can move a keyframe to another position on the animation channel by grabbing it and dragging it with the mouse. This has the effect of causing the animation to reach the keyframe's position either earlier or later, depending on the direction you move it. You cannot drag a keyframe past another keyframe on the channel.

Changing the Starting Frame

You can change the frame an animation starts on by clicking the Animation bar twice (*not* double-clicking) or clicking anywhere there isn't a keyframe to select the entire bar. Then simply drag it left or right to change the frame the animation starts with.

You can select multiple animation channels by holding down the SHIFT key as you click them.

Adding and Removing Timelines

While one timeline might be enough for most needs, if you have a complex set of movements applying to different layers and possibly to different frame rates, you might be better off with two or more timelines. A new timeline is then created, which you can access by selecting it from the Timelines panel's Timeline pop-up menu.

To create a new timeline, use the Modify | Timeline | Add Timeline item from the document window menu or choose Add Timeline from the Timelines panel context menu.

To remove a timeline, choose Modify | Timeline | Remove Timeline, or Remove Timeline from the panel. The current timeline and all its animations are then deleted.

Renaming Timelines

Timelines can be renamed by selecting them in the Timelines panel and either choosing Rename Timeline from the context menu or Modify | Timeline | Rename Timeline from the document window menu. A dialog box appears, prompting for a new timeline name, as shown in this illustration.

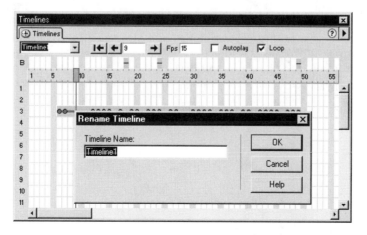

BEYOND
THE BASICS

One thing to remember is any Play Timeline behaviors that target this timeline are *not* automatically updated when a timeline name changes. You need to select the object used to trigger the timeline and edit the behavior to use the new timeline name.

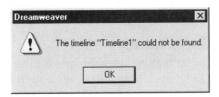

Copying-and-Pasting Animations

If you need to keep reusing key animation sequences, you can simply copy-and-paste them to a new animation channel, a different channel, or even a channel in a different document. To copy-and-paste an animation sequence, do the following:

1. Click an Animation channel bar to select it (or click twice if you click a keyframe). You can select additional channels by holding down SHIFT and clicking additional bars, or select all animations by pressing CTRL-A (CMD-A on the Mac).

2. Copy (or cut) the selection. Cutting the selection, of course, removes it from the current animation.

3. To paste the animation into a new spot in the current timeline, move the playback head to another position. You can also paste the animation to a different timeline in the same document or in a timeline in a different document.

4. Paste the selection into the timeline. Dreamweaver automatically moves the selection to a spot that doesn't overlap if the chosen paste point would overlap the original animation. If the document you paste the selection into contains a layer with the same name, the animation properties of the selection are applied to the existing layer. If the document doesn't have a layer with the same name, the entire layer is pasted from the first document.

You can use the copy-and-paste method of copying animation sequences to apply an existing animation to a new object. Make a selection and copy it as previously described and paste it into the document at a new frame position. Then use the context menu's Change Object item to select a new object to apply the pasted sequence to, as shown in this illustration.

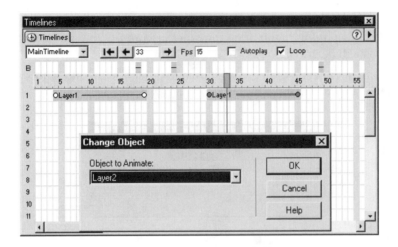

Controlling Timelines with Behaviors

Behaviors are an important Dreamweaver feature that are used to control all dynamic functions. This section discusses the behaviors used to control timeline playback. Chapter 23 talks about behaviors and the Behaviors panel in more detail.

Three behaviors are used to control timelines: Play Timeline, Stop Timeline, and Go To Timeline Frame.

Play Timeline

The *Play Timeline* behavior is used to start playing a timeline in response to an event, such as a mouse click or a mouse rollover. If you select Autoplay in the Timelines panel, this behavior is attached to the onLoad event of the <body> tag, so it occurs as soon as the page is loaded.

To attach a Play Timeline behavior to an event, do the following:

1. Create a timeline as described in this chapter.

2. Select the object you want to use to trigger the timeline, such as an image or a button.

3. Open the Behaviors panel by choosing Window | Behaviors, or by pressing SHIFT-F3.

4. Click the plus (+) button on the Behaviors panel, and choose Play Timeline from the Actions pop-up menu. If no timelines are present in your document, these options will be grayed out.

5. In the Play Timeline dialog box (shown in the following illustration), select a timeline to play from the menu.

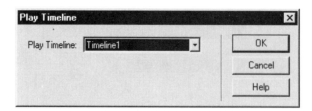

6. Click OK.

7. Check that the default event is the one you want. If it isn't, choose another event from the pop-up menu. If the events you want aren't listed, you can change the target browser in the Show Events For pop-up menu.

Stop Timeline

The *Stop Timeline* behavior is added in much the same way as the Play Timeline behavior. You can attach it to events, such as mouse clicks or even mouseovers.

Along with the option to stop a specific timeline, the Stop Timeline dialog box adds an option to stop all timelines on a page, as shown in the following illustration.

Go To Timeline Frame

One other behavior that targets timelines is *Go To Timeline Frame*. As the name indicates, this behavior lets you jump to any frame in the timeline in response to an event.

The Go To Timeline Frame dialog box, shown in the following illustration, lets you choose the timeline to target, as well as some additional options. The Go to Frame field is used to set the frame to jump to. Set this to 1 if you want to start the animation from the beginning. If you set it to another frame, it jumps to that frame and continues playing from that point. The Loop setting is only valid if you attach the behavior to a frame in the timeline using the Behavior channel of the Timeline window.

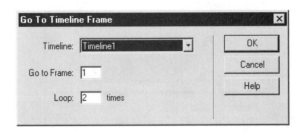

Putting Timelines to Work

As you can see from reading this chapter, timelines are a flexible and powerful tool for animating layers. You can use them for anything ranging from whiz-bang animation effects with items flying onto the screen, to somewhat more mundane, but still quite useful, tasks.

This section shows the steps needed to use timelines and layers to create a pop-up menu that's animated using timelines. The pop-up menu timeline is triggered by a mouse rollover on a main menu item and uses the layer resize feature to zoom from nothingness to full size. Finally, the Show-Hide Layer behavior is used to hide the pop-up layer again when the mouse is no longer on it.

Creating a Pop-up Menu

To create a pop-up menu, you simply need to create a layer on the page in the position where you ultimately want the layer to appear. Figure 20-3 shows the main page with a pop-up menu added for one of the main menu items. The text for the menu is also added here. This pop up could contain any HTML content: text, links, or images. Set the size to the final size you want to use for the menu.

When you create layers, a good idea is always to put the layer content in a table. Tables can help control text flow and help prevent problems, such as layer resizing in Netscape. Tables also make interpreting CSS definitions easier for Netscape because they enable you to apply CSS to the <td> tag, as opposed to the layer.

BEYOND
THE BASICS

Figure 20-3. *Create a pop-up menu for a page by creating a layer and putting the pop-up menu content in it*

The next step is to add this layer to a timeline. Figure 20-4 shows the layer added and sized to the desired duration. The animation lasts for 5 frames, which means, at 15 frames per second, it takes 1/3 of a second for the menu to open fully.

The current size and visibility for the menu are how it should look at the end of the animation, so you can leave the final keyframe alone.

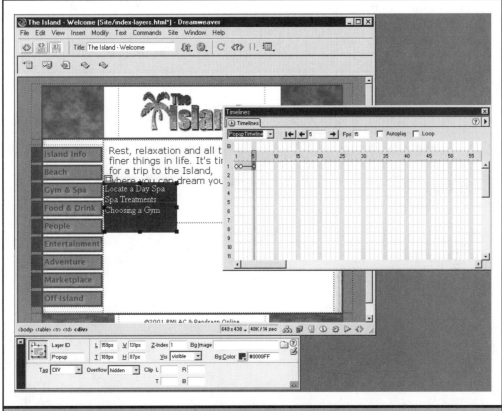

Figure 20-4.   *Add the layer to a timeline, so it can be triggered by an event*

Dreamweaver sets the initial layer visibility to the first value in the timeline, whether or not the timeline has been triggered. Therefore, the first keyframe should have the layer set to hidden, and its size set to a small amount, such as 1px × 1px. Also, set the Overflow parameter to hidden, so content that exceeds the dimensions of the layer will be clipped. Figure 20-5 shows the timeline and the layer property inspector together with these settings. One thing to remember is Dreamweaver doesn't display layers correctly when they're sized smaller than their content in the Document window. They will be sized correctly in the browser, however.

Next, add a keyframe for the second frame of the layer. This is the frame that's used to make the layer visible when the timeline is triggered. Figure 2-6 shows the change in the layer properties: the layer is now visible.

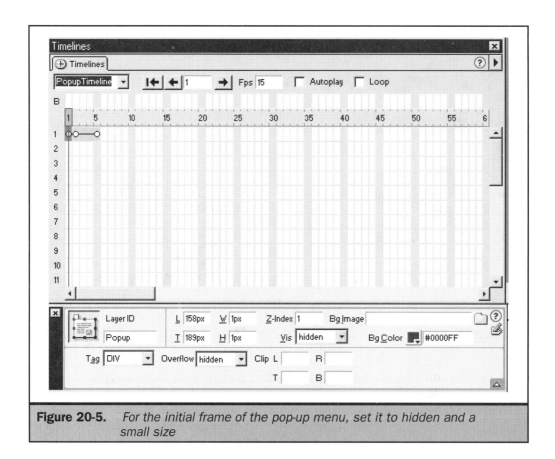

Figure 20-5.   *For the initial frame of the pop-up menu, set it to hidden and a small size*

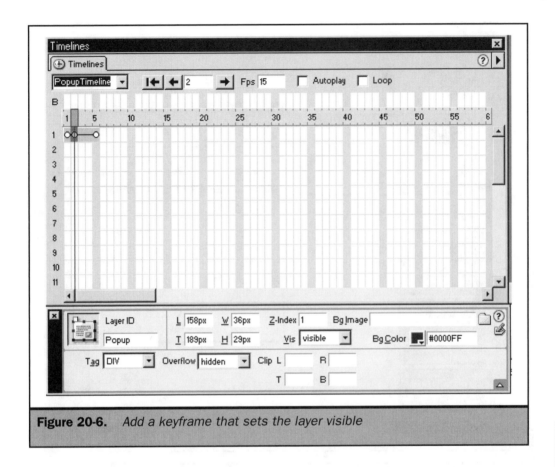

Figure 20-6.   *Add a keyframe that sets the layer visible*

Now the timeline must be triggered. In this example, I want a mouse rollover on the Gym & Spa main menu item to trigger the pop up. Select that button and use the Behaviors panel to add the Play Timeline behavior. Attach it to the onMouseOver event. As Figure 20-7 shows, multiple actions can be triggered by one event, in this case onMouseOver is used for a navbar, as well as for the pop-up menu.

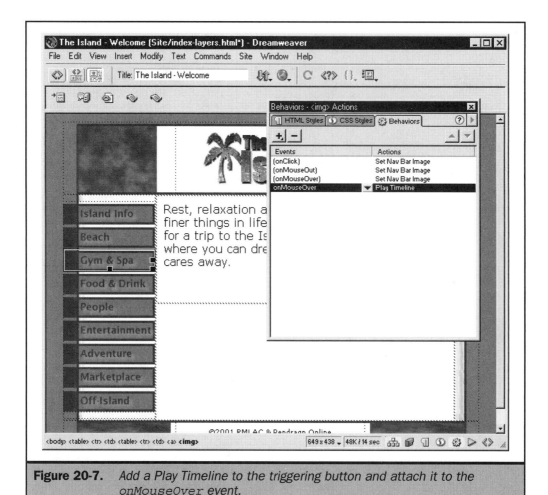

Figure 20-7. Add a Play Timeline to the triggering button and attach it to the onMouseOver event.

Now, when the mouse is moved over the button in the browser, the pop-up menu appears and zooms to its final size. You can add additional behaviors to hide the layer again, such as an onMouseOver event on the layer triggering Stop Timeline and Go To Timeline Frame actions to reset the timeline to frame 1.

Figure 20-8 shows the pop-up menu being triggered in Netscape 6.

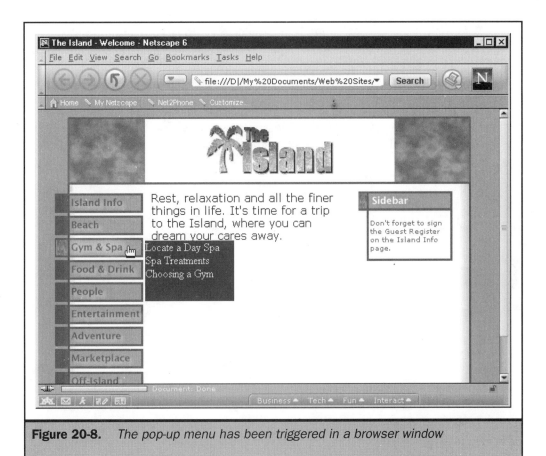

Figure 20-8.   *The pop-up menu has been triggered in a browser window*

Summary

In many cases, being able to include animation on a page without having to learn a new graphics package would be nice. Dreamweaver provides a feature called *timelines* that can accomplish animation using standard HTML and JavaScript to animate layers and images.

- The Timelines panel provides a common place to work with timelines.
- When creating timelines, when you want some change to an object to occur, you mark the frames as *keyframes*.

- You can copy-and-paste animation sequences to apply them later in the same timeline, or on another timeline or document.

- Dreamweaver's timeline behaviors—Play Timeline, Stop Timeline and Go To Timeline Frame—can be tied to most events to give flexible control over timeline playback.

Part V covers the more advanced programming concepts supported by Dreamweaver. The next chapter starts it off with a discussion about JavaScript.

The
Complete
Reference

Part V

Advanced Web Programming

The Complete Reference

Chapter 21

JavaScript

An important part of today's Web development is the use of scripting languages to enhance a page beyond the capabilities afforded by plain HTML. Client-side scripting languages (those that run on the user's browser) were one of the first ways Web pages evolved from simply displaying static pictures to true interactivity. JavaScript, in particular, is a critical component of *Dynamic HTML (DHTML)*, as you saw in Chapter 19. Therefore, scripting languages remain important even in today's Internet Web environment of server-side scripting, ActiveX objects, Java applets, and Flash content.

JavaScript is currently the most widely supported scripting language among browsers. Despite its name, JavaScript doesn't have anything in common with the Java language developed by Sun Microsystems, other than syntactical similarities. Java is a full-featured, standalone programming language that can be used for anything from embedded objects in Web pages to full-blown, standalone applications. JavaScript, on the other hand, is used primarily to add functionality to a Web page and requires a browser to interpret and execute the script.

A scripting language consists of functions and statements embedded directly into a Web page's HTML code. A script can respond to such events as mouse clicks, mouseovers, and form element changes. It can be called periodically to update the page with a timer. Scripts can dynamically adjust the page depending on the capabilities of the browser being used, seamlessly presenting an improved experience to users with up-to-date browsers, while also not alienating those with older software.

While Dreamweaver has many features that make it easy to incorporate JavaScript into your pages, unfortunately, it won't write the code for you. You either need to become familiar with writing JavaScript yourself or to find a source of third-party scripts to incorporate into your pages. Either way, you'll appreciate Dreamweaver's code editing and debugging features.

This chapter gives you an overview of the JavaScript language in its various incarnations and explains the process of adding JavaScript with Dreamweaver. It also walks you through the creation and testing of a useful script, a calendar showing the current month. At the end of the chapter, you can find information on where you can get more information on JavaScript and other scripting languages, as well as where you can go to find some third-party scripts to add to your pages.

Tip

If you're already proficient at writing JavaScript or if you only want to know how to use Dreamweaver to add a JavaScript program you downloaded from another source, skip ahead to the section titled "Adding JavaScript in Dreamweaver" to learn more about the specific features Dreamweaver offers. Even if you have no interest in writing JavaScript code yourself, you can find it's helpful to learn how to insert scripts and use Dreamweaver's new integrated debugger.

Sources for JavaScripts

Dozens of sites have scripts available for the taking if you don't want to reinvent the wheel, or if you have neither the time nor the interest in coding your own scripts. Any of these sites can also give you links to plenty of other JavaScript resources online.

- The JavaScript Source—**http://javascript.internet.com/**
- ScriptSearch—**http://www.scriptsearch.com/**
- JavaScript Search—**http://www.javascriptsearch.com/**

You may not realize the full potential of JavaScript to enhance your site until you visit one of these Web sites. Look at the many scripts offered to generate ideas for your site. You may find exactly what you need—such as a script to fade your text into the page or a simple game—or decide to write your own script based on ideas you get from the listings.

When you find a script you like at these sites, you'll either be given a code listing, which you can copy and paste into your documents, or a .zip file containing the code listing and any additional files required to implement the script. In either case, the recommendation is that you make a copy of the script and/or files before using them.

JavaScript Basics

A full-fledged tutorial covering JavaScript is beyond the scope of this book. If you have a desire to learn more about JavaScript, see the Internet and book resources at the end of this chapter for some good places to start. This section gives you an overview of the language and how it fits into a page.

The `<script>` and `</script>` tags are used to mark the beginning and end of a JavaScript block on a page. You may add as many script blocks to a page as you like but, typically, you'll have one block in the `<head>` that contains your functions and other blocks in the `<body>` of your document for inline scripts.

Scripting languages weren't supported by most browsers until their version 3.*x* release. Older browsers that don't understand the `<script>` tag ignore the tag itself, but the script contents are displayed as if it is document text. To get around this, JavaScript engines allow an HTML comment to encompass the entire block of script text between the `<script>` and `</script>` tags. This allows older browsers that cannot interpret scripting languages to present a reasonable page to the user. If you need to support older browsers on your site, you must add these comment tags manually, as Dreamweaver doesn't add them itself. A script block with the comment tag looks like this:

```
<script language="JavaScript">
<!-- This HTML comment hides your script from ancient browsers

  . . . JavaScript statements . . .

//-->
</script>
```

The `<language>` attribute of the `<script>` tag is used to tell the browser which script engine to use, in this case, JavaScript. Newer versions of JavaScript have version numbers appended to the name (for example, JavaScript1.2) to indicate the script contains code incompatible with older versions of JavaScript. JavaScript, in its various versions, is supported by both Internet Explorer and Netscape. Internet Explorer also supports JScript, Microsoft's proprietary version of JavaScript. Remember, recognition of a particular language version (such as JavaScript1.2) by two browsers doesn't mean those browsers have identical support for the language. Some significant differences still need to be mentioned, particularly in the object models. These differences are covered later in this chapter.

Objects and Variables

Like most programming languages—including HTML—JavaScript code consists of a series of statements executed to perform a task. Unlike HTML, looping and branching statements can be used to alter the flow of execution. JavaScript statements can be organized into functions. Functions can be called repeatedly from the `<head>`—for instance, a mouse click event that's called every time the mouse clicks an element. JavaScript statements can also exist in the `<body>` of the document. These inline statements are only executed once, while the page is loading. For example, you could use inline statements to display content dynamically, based on the browser version of the user.

To understand JavaScript, you must first understand variables and objects.

- **Variables** are the way JavaScript stores information. If you create a variable and assign it the value 2, every time you make use of that variable, it will be as if you are using the number 2. If you assign it the string "Dreamweaver", and use the variable in a write statement, "Dreamweaver" will be output. To use variables, you must declare them. The `var` keyword is used to tell JavaScript you want to declare a variable. Follow it with the variable name you want to use, typically something descriptive about the kind of value the variable will hold. You can also assign an initial value to the variable, but this is optional. Variables can be used to hold simple data types, such as strings or numbers, but they can also be used to hold objects.

- **Objects** are more complex than simple types, such as integers or strings. Objects are collections of related data types and functions that operate with that data called *methods*. For example, JavaScript's built-in Date object holds a value representing the current date or one with which the object was created. JavaScript's Date object also contains methods such as getYear() and getMonth(), which calculate specific useful values based on the Date object's value.

- **Arrays** are variables that contain more than one value, whether simple types or objects. You can access individual elements of an array using an index.

Next, we'll start writing a JavaScript example that makes use of variables, objects, and arrays.

Writing JavaScript: An Example

Let's build a JavaScript, a calendar that displays the current month. We start by creating an empty script block, as described in the previous section. This consists of an empty `<script></script>` tag pair and, as we create JavaScript code, it's placed inside this block. We also add the comment tag to hide the JavaScript code from older browsers:

```
<script language="JavaScript">
<!--
//--></script>
```

Now let's declare some useful global variables, inserting them between the start and end script tags, inside the comment tag:

```
<script language="JavaScript">
<!--
var aDaysOfWeek = new Array("Sun", "Mon", "Tue", "Wed", "Thu", "Fri", "Sat");
var aMonthNames = new Array("January", "February", "March", "April", "May",
 "June", "July", "August", "September", "October", "November", "December");
var curDate = new Date();
var iYear = curDate.getFullYear();
var iMonth = curDate.getMonth();
//-->
</script>
```

This listing shows two arrays being declared: aDaysOfWeek and aMonthNames. An array in JavaScript is an object created by using the "new" operator. A handy shortcut allows the strings for the days of the week and the names of the months to be added to the array at the time its object is created. Because this is a calendar, you'll want to know the date so you can display the calendar for the current month. The Date object is used to provide this information. You can use the curDate object just created to get two values you'll need later: the current year and the current month. These can be obtained by calling the Date object's getFullYear() and getMonth() methods, respectively.

Functions

You're also going to need a few functions for your calendar. To draw a calendar, you need to know how many days are in the month. Unfortunately, the Date object doesn't provide this information, so let's write a function to calculate it. This function also demonstrates the use of variables and objects.

```
<script language="JavaScript">
var aDaysOfWeek = new Array("Sun", "Mon", "Tue", "Wed", "Thu", "Fri", "Sat");
var aMonthNames = new Array("January", "February", "March", "April", "May",
  "June", "July", "August", "September", "October", "November", "December");
var curDate = new Date();

function getDaysInMonth(iYear, iMonth) {
    var dtCurMonth = new Date(iYear, iMonth-1, 1);
    var dtNextMonth = new Date(iYear, iMonth, 1);
    var iMillisInMonth = dtNextMonth.getTime() - dtCurMonth.getTime();
    return iMillisInMonth / 86400000;
}
</script>
```

This function is passed two parameters—iYear and iMonth—representing the current year and month, respectively. Two new Date objects are created, as well as a Milliseconds variable. The dtCurMonth object represents the first day of the current month.

This script actually provides a good example of the potential for mistakes in calculations if the starting value differs. While we commonly think of months as ranging from 1-12, the Date object starts at a base of 0 and, thus, ranges from 0-11. Therefore, we need to subtract one from the month because we expect iMonth to range from one to twelve, whereas the Date object uses zero as its base. The dtNextMonth object represents the first day of the month following iMonth. If the month passed to the dtNextMonth object exceeds the 0-11 range, which would signify January of the following year, the Date object adjusts the year and month values accordingly.

The iMillisInMonth variable is used to calculate the number of milliseconds in the current month. It does this by calling the Date object's getTime method to get the number of milliseconds elapsed since January 1, 1970, for both the current month and the next month. The difference between these values for the two months gives you the number of milliseconds in the current month. Finally, our function returns this value divided by the number of milliseconds in a day to arrive at the number of days in the month.

Before completing this script, let's examine the built-in browser objects.

The Document Object

The browser provides a number of built-in objects you can make use of in JavaScript. The following three are supported on most platforms:

- **Navigator**—This object can be used by JavaScript to learn information about the user's browser. Scripts can use the Navigator object to determine the brand and version of the browser, the platform it's running on, whether cookies are enabled, and many other useful bits of information.

- **Window**—The Window object represents the browser window or current frame. Scripts can get the dimensions of the window, which can be useful for positioning. This object can also be used in frame windows to access the parent (frameset) window and, from there, other frames.

- **Document**—The Base object of the Document Object Model, the Document object is used to access individual elements of an HTML page, to get their values, or to modify them a la DHTML. The Document object also contains methods that allow scripts to generate HTML text on the fly. As you see with the Calendar object, you can use it, for instance, to write the elements of a table dynamically as your page is loading.

To create the dynamic content your calendar requires, use the Document object's write method:

```
document.write("This text will be written as part of our HTML document");
```

The write method adds whatever text it's given to the document stream as it's loaded. Let's add another function to the calendar example to demonstrate how this can be used.

```
<script language="JavaScript">
var aDaysOfWeek = new Array("Sun", "Mon", "Tue", "Wed", "Thu", "Fri", "Sat");
var aMonthNames = new Array("January", "February", "March", "April", "May",
 "June", "July", "August", "September", "October", "November", "December");
var curDate = new Date();
```

```
function getDaysInMonth(iYear, iMonth) {
    var dtCurMonth = new Date(iYear, iMonth-1, 1);
    var dtNextMonth = new Date(iYear, iMonth, 1);
    var iMillisInMonth = dtNextMonth.getTime() - dtCurMonth.getTime();
    return iMillisInMonth / 86400000;
}

function writeDay(iDay) {
    if (iDay == 0) {       // Empty day
        document.write("<td width='40' height='40'></td>");
    } else {
        document.write("<td align='left' valign='top' width='40' height='40'
                    style='CURSOR:Hand'>");
        document.write("<font style='CURSOR:Hand;FONT-FAMILY:Arial;
                    FONT-SIZE:12px;FONT-WEIGHT:bold'>" + iDay + "</font>");
        document.write("</td>");
    }
}
}
</script>
```

As you can see, the function writeDay writes out a `<td>` element that corresponds with a day on the calendar. If the value of the parameter iDay is 0, an empty cell is created to pad out the table. Otherwise, a cell is created with the number of the day as the text in the cell.

This function only writes out one cell of a table. It's apparent that we need to add a function to write the entire calendar table. This function, writeCalendar, calls both of our previous functions—getDaysInMonth and writeDay—and writes out all the rows in the table.

```
<script language="JavaScript">
var aDaysOfWeek = new Array("Sun", "Mon", "Tue", "Wed", "Thu", "Fri", "Sat");
var aMonthNames = new Array("January", "February", "March", "April", "May",
 "June", "July", "August", "September", "October", "November", "December");
var curDate = new Date();

function getDaysInMonth(iYear, iMonth) {
    var dtCurMonth = new Date(iYear, iMonth-1, 1);
    var dtNextMonth = new Date(iYear, iMonth, 1);
    var iMillisInMonth = dtNextMonth.getTime() - dtCurMonth.getTime();
    return iMillisInMonth / 86400000;
}

function writeDay(iDay) {
    if (iDay == 0) {       // Empty day
```

```
                document.write("<td width='40' height='40'></td>");
        } else {
            document.write("<td align='left' valign='top' width='40' height='40'
                        style='CURSOR:Hand'>");
            document.write("<font style='CURSOR:Hand;FONT-FAMILY:Arial;
                        FONT-SIZE:12px;FONT-WEIGHT:bold'>" + iDay + "</font>");
            document.write("</td>");
        }
    }

    function writeCalendar(iYear, iMonth) {
        var iDaysInMonth = getDaysInMonth(iYear, iMonth);
        var dtCurMonth = new Date(iYear, iMonth-1, 1);
        var iDayOfFirst = dtCurMonth.getDay();
        var iVarDate = 1;

        // Write days of week
        document.write("<tr>");
        for (dow = 0; dow < 7; dow++) {
            document.write("<td align='center' style='FONT-FAMILY:Arial;FONT-
                SIZE:12px;FONT-WEIGHT: bold'>" + aDaysOfWeek[dow] + "</td>");
        }
        document.write("</tr>");
        // Write out each row
        for (iWeek = 0; iWeek < 6; iWeek++) {
            document.write("<tr>");

            for (iDay = 0; iDay < 7; iDay++) {
                if (iDay+iWeek*7 >= iDayOfFirst && iVarDate <= iDaysInMonth) {
                    writeDay(iVarDate++);
                } else {
                    writeDay(0);
                }
            }
            document.write("</tr>");
            if (iVarDate > iDaysInMonth)
                break;
        }
    }
}
</script>
```

The only thing left to do for your calendar is to put the call to writeCalendar in the document <body>. First, add a JavaScript block to put the month and year at the top of the calendar. These are acquired from the global variables declared earlier—iYear and iMonth—and the array of month names—aMonthNames. The JavaScript block that makes the writeCalendar call is inserted between the `<table>` and `</table>` tags in the `<body>` of your page.

```
<div align="center">
<script language="JavaScript">
  document.write(aMonthNames[iMonth] + "    " + iYear);
</script>
</div>
<div align="center">
<table border="1" cellspacing="0" align="center" cellpadding="2">
<script language="JavaScript">
  writeCalendar(iYear, iMonth+1);
</script>
</table>
</div>
```

Adding JavaScript in Dreamweaver

So now that you know the basics of JavaScript and have a sample code, how do you apply this knowledge to Dreamweaver? As is common with Dreamweaver, you have several options for adding JavaScript code to your document.

Inserting Scripts

If you have a script you developed yourself or you obtained a script from a third-party source, you can insert it by positioning the cursor where you want the script to go—in either Design or Code view—and choosing Insert | Invisible Tags | Script from the menu. You can also use the Invisibles tab of the Objects panel to select the Script object, as shown in the following illustration.

This brings up the Insert Script dialog box. Choose the language type from the drop-down list, and then cut-and-paste your script from another editor into the Content box, as shown in the following illustration.

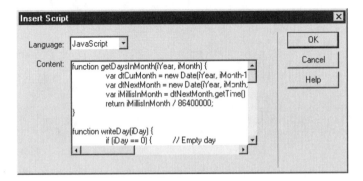

Or, you can use the Script Property Inspector (see the following illustration) to add JavaScript code that exists in an external file. Simply put the filename in the Source field.

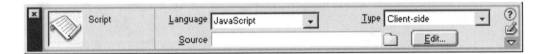

Editing Scripts

In some instances, simply typing or pasting your script directly into the Code view is easier. The Code view (or Code Inspector) lets you precisely place your script code in the document (see Figure 21-1).

Code Navigation

Dreamweaver provides a convenient way to view all the script functions on a page. From the code navigation pop-up menu on to the toolbar, you can move to any function in the code view, or set and clear breakpoints for the debugger (See Figure 21-2).

To navigate to a function, simply select it from the pop-up menu. The cursor in the Code view is repositioned to the function and its name is then highlighted.

You can see your functions listed in alphabetical order if you hold down CTRL (in Windows) or OPTION (on the Macintosh) when you click the Code Navigation button.

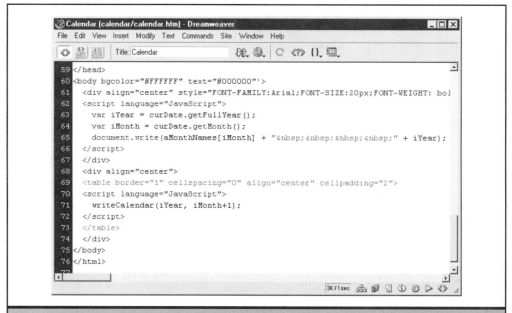

Figure 21-1. *The Code view lets you add or edit JavaScript code directly into your document*

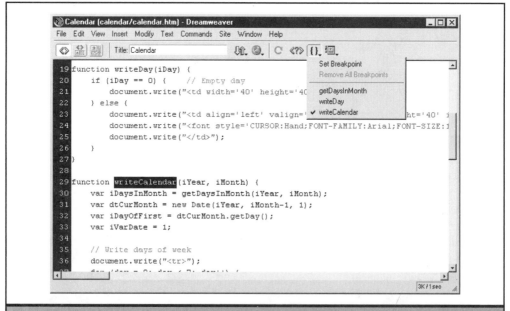

Figure 21-2. *The Code Navigator makes it easy to find your JavaScript functions*

JavaScript Debugger

A powerful feature in Dreamweaver (new to version 4) is the JavaScript Debugger, which works in conjunction with your browser (either Internet Explorer or Netscape in Windows, or Netscape on the Macintosh) to let you step through your JavaScript code to find errors. As anyone who has ever spent hours trying to track down manually what ended up being a trivial bug can attest, a debugger can significantly reduce your coding time.

Running the Debugger

The debugger is started either by choosing File | Debug In Browser from the menu or by clicking the Preview/Debug In Browser button on the toolbar (See Figure 21-3). When the debugger is first run, it checks your code for syntax errors, such as missing semicolons, duplicate global variable declarations, or brace mismatches.

If a syntax error is found, the debugger stops and lists the errors in the JavaScript Syntax Errors window. All your syntax errors are then listed. The Detailed Description area gives you more information on a particular error. Double-clicking an error or clicking Go To Line moves the Code view to the reported line number (See Figure 21-4). Going back to fix any reported syntax errors before you proceed is a good idea.

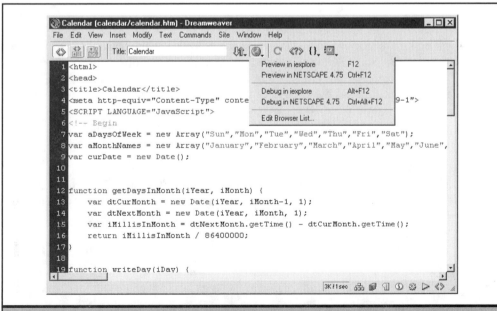

Figure 21-3.   *Click the Preview/Debug In Browser button on the toolbar to start the debugger*

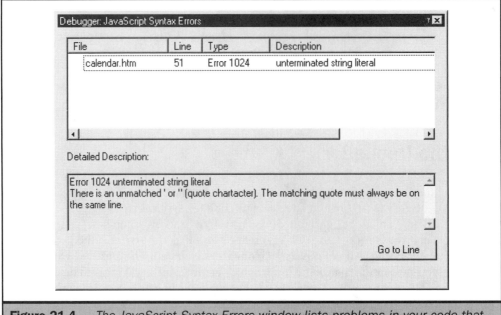

Figure 21-4.   *The JavaScript Syntax Errors window lists problems in your code that are found before it's run in the browser*

When the debugger no longer reports syntax errors (or if you were lucky enough to get everything right the first time!), you are ready to run it in the browser. If you are using Netscape, first click OK in the warning message box that appears, and then click Grant in the Java Security dialog box. If your browser is Internet Explorer, click Yes in the Java Security dialog box, and then click OK in the Debugger Warning message box to bring up the Debugger window.

The Debugger Window

The Debugger window appears along with the browser. Your page doesn't immediately load. Instead, the debugger stops at the first line in your file, giving you the opportunity to set breakpoints, step through your code one line at a time, watch and edit variables, or run until the next breakpoint or until the complete page is loaded (See Figure 21-5). All the debugger functionality is contained in this window and is controlled from the toolbar (seen in the following illustration) or by using keyboard shortcuts.

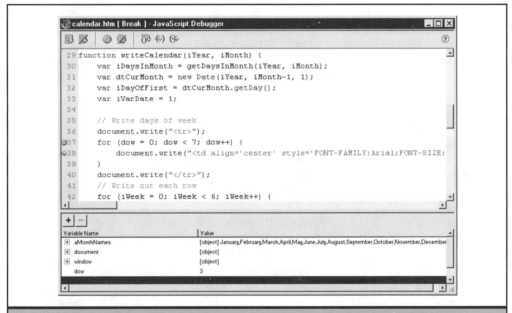

Figure 21-5. *The JavaScript Debugger window lets you step through your code and examine variable values at any point*

Running Your Script

Once the Debugger window is waiting for your input, you can click the Run button to start executing your code. If you have no breakpoints set, your page will be loaded in its entirety, and you won't have a chance to follow the execution flow or inspect your variables. It looks like we'll have to do a little more to make the debugger useful.

Setting Breakpoints

You can set breakpoints in your code to stop the execution of your code at a specific place. Select the line in the code pane and click the Set/Remove Breakpoint button to toggle a breakpoint on or off at that point. Now, when you click Run, your script will only execute up to the first breakpoint it encounters. Then, your script waits for your command. If, for some reason, you want to stop debugging before the page is fully loaded, you can click the Stop Debugging button.

You can use the Remove All Breakpoints button to clear any breakpoints you may have added.

Stepping Through Your Script

The debugger lets you step through your script by using the three buttons on the right side of the toolbar. The *Step Over* button advances to the next JavaScript statement, but it steps over function calls. Although the functions are still executed, they aren't shown in the debugger. The *Step Into* button continues stepping into functions. The *Step Out* button enables you to step immediately to the end of a function you're debugging. If you aren't in a function, this option is grayed out.

You can also debug external JavaScript files. The new file is shown in the code pane.

The Variable Window

As you step through your code, be certain to observe the values of your variables. The variable list is located in the bottom pane of the JavaScript Debugger window. The left column lists variables you're watching and the right column lists their current values. The values are only updated if you're stepping through the code or when you stop at a breakpoint. Remember the scope of your variables. You can only look at values for global variables or those defined in the function in which you are currently stopped.

To add a variable to the list, select it in the code pane, and then click the Plus (+) button above the variable list. A new entry is then created with your variable name, and you can simply press ENTER. Or, you can type the name in a variable directly after clicking Plus (+). If the variable is an object or an array, you'll get a tree view, which you can expand to see the values easily for each object property or array value.

To remove a value, select it in the list, and then click the Minus (-) button above the pane.

If you want, you can change the value of a variable as your code is running to see the effect it has. Simply select it in the variable list and click the value. You can then edit the value (see the following illustration).

+	−	
Variable Name		**Value**
⊞ document		[object]
iYear		2000
iMonth		12
dow		5

Results

When your script has run to completion in the debugger, the result in the browser will be your complete page. Figure 21-6 shows the results of your calendar example. Notice the mangled filename in the address bar? This is because Dreamweaver actually created a temporary version of the file embedded with extra JavaScript code to make the debugger work. Try viewing the source from the browser to see just what's involved in making this magic work.

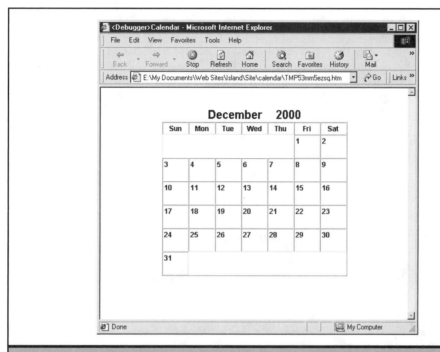

Figure 21-6. *The calendar example has run to completion in the debugger*

VBScript

VBScript, a scripting language similar to JavaScript, is capable of using the same browser and document objects. In fact, you can even call JavaScript functions from VBScript and vice versa—even on the same page. Whereas JavaScript borrows much of its syntax from the Java language, VBScript is based on a subset of Microsoft's Visual Basic language. Although this is an attractive advantage for Visual Basic programmers who are already familiar with the language, the drawbacks of using VBScript shouldn't be overlooked.

Currently, browser support for VBScript is limited to Internet Explorer. With the popularity and standardization of JavaScript, this situation is unlikely to change anytime soon. Although third-party plug-ins are available for Netscape, which add VBScript capability, you can't count on a potential user having one installed just to view your page. Use of VBScript, therefore, should be discouraged for general Internet development. VBScript should be limited to intranet-only development (where the use of Internet Explorer can be mandated) or to server-side scripting via ASP.

VBScript can be added to your pages in the same way as JavaScript (see the following illustration). You can either add your code directly in the Code view or add it to the Design view using the Insert Script dialog box from the Script button on the Objects panel, or by choosing Insert | Invisible Tags | Script. This is pretty much the extent of Dreamweaver's VBScript capabilities. If you want to take advantage of advanced features, such as the debugger, you need to use JavaScript.

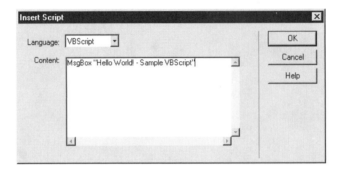

```
<script language="VBScript">
MsgBox "Hello World! - Sample VBScript"
</script>
```

You can see VBScript is used in much the same way as JavaScript. The `<script>` tag simply specifies VBScript as the language. A browser such as Netscape that doesn't support VBScript simply ignores the script.

JavaScript Resources

This chapter barely scratches the surface of what you can do with JavaScript. A wealth of online and print resources is available for learning more.

To start, Dreamweaver itself comes with an extensive O'Reilly JavaScript reference (see the following illustration), along with the HTML and CSS references in the Resource window, and it's always readily available when you are running Dreamweaver.

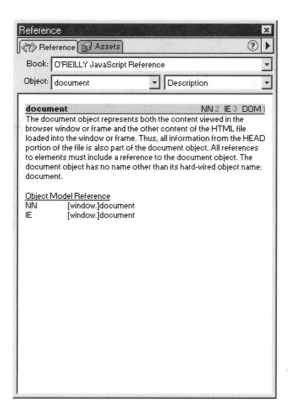

Learning JavaScript

For information on VBScript, JScript, and other Microsoft scripting products, see the comprehensive online documentation for Microsoft Scripting Technologies at **http://msdn.microsoft.com/scripting/**.

Netscape also has a wealth of online information about JavaScript and Netscape browsers. Check out **http://developer.netscape.com** for their developer pages.

JavaScript.com, the Definitive JavaScript Resource at **http://javascript.com**, is another good source of information.

Two of the best reference books available are the *JavaScript Bible,* by Danny Goodman and Brendan Eich (IDG Books), and *JavaScript: The Definitive Guide,* by David Flanagan (O'Reilly & Associates).

Summary

This chapter touched on the power of JavaScript. If you're using DHTML and behaviors, you can see some of these basic concepts put to work in practical ways. Visiting some of the script resources listed in this chapter can also fire your imagination.

In this chapter, you learned about the following:

- The basic structure of JavaScript, includes objects, variables, and functions.
- There are several ways to add scripts to a Web page, including the Script object on the Invisibles tab of the Objects panel and using the Insert | Invisible Tags | Script menu path.
- You can set breakpoints for testing your script with the JavaScript Debugger.

In the next chapter, you learn how to use plug-ins, CGI, and other advanced components.

The Complete Reference

Dreamweaver 4

Chapter 22

Applets, Plug-ins, and Other Embedded Programs

While client-side scripting is one of the most versatile ways of extending Web pages beyond the capabilities of standard HTML, it's by no means the only way. CGI scripts, browser plug-ins, Java applets, and ActiveX controls all have a role in modern Web development.

Java Applets

Java, a programming language developed by Sun Microsystems, was conceived as a "write once, run anywhere" language. With programming languages such as C++, you compile a program into machine code that only runs on a specific processor on a specific operating system. A Java program, on the other hand, is compiled by a Java compiler into an independent intermediate language called *Java bytecode*. An interpreter called a *Java Virtual Machine* (Java VM) running on the target platform interprets the bytecode.

Although it was originally developed for use in TV set-top boxes and other appliances, the development of Java coincided nicely with the emerging popularity of the World Wide Web. Thus, adapting Java's technology for use in Web browsers was a natural for Sun. The platform-independent philosophy made Java an ideal language to use for embedded objects for Web pages, in the form of Java applets.

The applets you download can come in several forms. A file with a .java extension is a Java source file. This is a text file containing Java source code that must be compiled to be useful, using a Java compiler from Sun or another party. A compiled Java file has a .class extension. Larger Java applets consist of more than one class, which are typically bundled into a file with a .zip or a *.jar* extension, for *Java Archive.* Put these files in an Applet folder within your local site root. If the applet requires additional files, such as sounds and images, they typically go in the same folder as the class files.

Remember, Java applets aren't the same as JavaScripts; these two are entirely different animals, sharing only a similar name. If you want to learn more about JavaScript, turn back to Chapter 21.

Inserting Java Applets

You can use Dreamweaver to insert Java Applets into a Web page. To insert an applet, take the following steps:

1. In either the Design or Code views of the Document window, position the cursor to where you want to place the upper-left corner of the applet.

2. Click the Applet button in the Special tab of the Objects panel (it's the button that looks like a steaming cup of coffee). If you prefer, you can drag the Applet icon to your document instead, or choose Insert | Media | Applet from the menu.

3. From the Select File dialog box, either enter your class file in the File Name box or browse to it using the folder list. Be sure the file is selected as being relative to the document and not the site root. A placeholder <applet> tag is created when you choose Select.

4. After the applet has been inserted, you can use the Property Inspector to set its basic attributes. You may need to click the expander button in the lower-right corner to see all the options (see Figure 22-1).

   ■ The **Applet Name** field sets the name attribute of the tag, which identifies the applet when scripting.

   ■ The **W** and **H** fields specify the width and height of the applet in pixels. You can also use unit modifiers to specify the size in alternative units: *pc (picas)*, *pt (points)*, *in (inches)*, *mm (millimeters)*, and *cm (centimeters)*, or % for a percentage of the parent object's width and height.

   ■ The **Code** attribute specifies the class file containing the applet's code. This is the filename that was selected in Select File dialog box during the previous step.

   ■ **Base** specifies the folder containing the applet if it's not in the same folder as your document.

   ■ **Align** sets how the object will be aligned on the page. The various alignment options are covered elsewhere in this book.

   ■ **Alt** lets you provide alternate content to be displayed if the user's browser doesn't support Java applets or has disabled them. You can browse for an image filename or enter text to be displayed in the edit box. If you add an image and you still want to present alt text for a text-only browser, you must manually edit the <img> tag that's created to add its own alt attribute.

   ■ **V** and **H Space** let you specify the amount of blank space to put around the applet. The spacing must be specified in pixels.

Setting Applet Parameters

The Parameters button on the Properties Inspector activates the Parameters dialog box, which enables you to specify custom parameters for the Java applet. Java applets that you download should have documentation describing any special parameters supported by the applet. These are added to the applet as <param> tags. To enter a parameter, click the Plus (+) button. Enter the name of the parameter in the Parameters column and the value of the parameter in the Value column. Use the Minus (-) button to remove a selected parameter. You may also reorder the parameters by selecting one and then by using the up and down buttons.

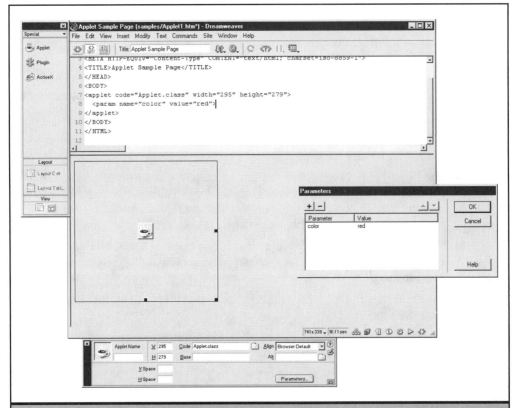

Figure 22-1. When you create a Java applet object, a placeholder is created in your document. You use the Property Inspector to change most of the basic attributes for a applet

---

Note *If an applet you download is contained in an archive (a .jar or a .zip file), you cannot use the Property Inspector to edit your applet tag. If you used the Select File dialog box to choose the archive file, you must go to the Code view and manually change the <code> attribute to the <archive> attribute. Then you can add a new <code> attribute that points to the main class in the archive to use. You can usually find the name of the class to use in the documentation for the applet or in a sample HTML file that came with it. For example, an applet tag using the archive attribute might look something like this:*

```
<applet archive="myapplet.jar" code="myapplet.class"
width="320" height="200">
```

Finding Java Resources Online

Sun's Java site at **http://java.sun.com** is the best place to start if you want to learn everything there is to know about Java and related technologies.

A number of good sources exist for third-party Java applets. One popular site for developers are the Java Technology pages of Earthweb at **http://www.developer.com**. Another source for third-party applets is the Java Boutique at **http://javaboutique. internet.com/**. Here, you can find a wealth of applets, including games, chat applets, visual effects, navigation tools, and more, which you can easily add to your Web pages.

Browser Plug-ins

Although plug-ins are typically used for the playback of media content, such as QuickTime movies, RealPlayer audio and video, or Flash and Shockwave files, this isn't their only use. Dreamweaver can be used to insert files you make with a content creation package such as Macromedia Director.

Much like Java applets, *plug-ins* are small programs designed to extend the capabilities of the browser. Unlike a Java applet, a plug-in is written specifically to run on a particular platform. This means if you want to incorporate content files requiring a plug-in on your Web site, each platform will require a plug-in specifically made for it. Although plug-ins were originally designed for Netscape, Internet Explorer also provides support for them. Some plug-in makers also make ActiveX versions of their controls available to run with Internet Explorer. You learn how to combine the use of Netscape plug-ins and ActiveX controls in the ActiveX section of this chapter.

Inserting Plug-in Content

When you use a plug-in on your Web page, you don't actually embed the plug-in itself into the page. Instead, you embed a reference to a content file with a particular *Multipurpose Internet Mail Extension (MIME)* type. The browser uses that MIME type to decide which plug-in to use to play back the content. When you use Dreamweaver to insert a plug-in, you are really inserting plug-in content. The user will require the appropriate plug-in to view your file. If that plug-in isn't available on the user's computer, that user must download and install it to view your content. You should always give the user information about any required plug-ins, whether by including the icon of the product with a link to download it or by referencing it in your text.

To insert plug-in content into a document using Dreamweaver, do the following steps:

1. In either the Design or Code view of the Document window, position the cursor where you want to place the content.

2. Click the Insert Plug-in button in the Special tab of the Objects panel (see the following illustration). You can also drag-and-drop the Plug-in icon or choose Insert | Media | Plug-in from the menu.

3. As with Java applets, the Select File dialog box appears. Either enter your content file in the File Name box or browse to it using the folder list. When you choose Select, an `<embed>` tag is created that refers to your content.

4. Now that the placeholder object is created, you can configure it by using the Property Inspector (see the next illustration). You might need to click the expander button in the lower-right corner to see all the options.

- The **Name** field sets the name attribute of the tag, which identifies the tag for scripting.

- The **W** and **H** fields specify the width and height of the plug-in content in pixels. You can also use unit modifiers to specify the size in alternative units: pc (picas), pt (points), in (inches), mm (millimeters), and cm (centimeters), or % for a percentage of the parent object's width and height.

- **Src** specifies the source data file. This is the filename selected in Select File dialog box during the previous step. If you want to change this filename, you can click the folder icon.

- **Plg Url** specifies the URL of the site where users can download the plug-in. If the user doesn't have a plug-in installed that can play this content, the browser attempts to download it from this URL. This field's value is put in the `<plug-inspace>` attribute.

- **Align** sets how the object is aligned on the page.

- **V** and **H Space** enable you to specify the amount of blank space to put around the applet. The spacing must be specified in pixels.

- **Border** specifies the width of a border to put around the plug-in.

Setting Plug-in Content Parameters

Many plug-ins can accept additional parameters to control various features. The Parameters button on the Properties Inspector activates the Parameters dialog box, which enables you to specify custom parameters for the plug-in. The Parameters dialog box functions the same way as the one for Java applets. Any special parameters your plug-in can use may be entered here, and they'll be added to the `<embed>` tag as attributes. Some parameters don't take values. In these cases, simply leave the Value column blank for that parameter.

Using Behaviors to Detect Plug-ins

If you're writing a page that supports plug-in content, chances are you'll want to provide a means to detect whether a visitor has the plug-in installed or has a browser capable of running it. Dreamweaver behaviors can be used to accomplish this task. You can attach either the Check Browser or the Check Plug-in behavior to a link or a body tag to provide an alternate page to use if the plug-in cannot be supported. Behaviors are covered in-depth in Chapter 23.

Note

In most instances, the Windows version of Internet Explorer cannot use the Check Plug-in behavior to detect whether a plug-in is installed. Internet Explorer on the Macintosh cannot detect plug-ins at all. This doesn't mean you cannot or should not embed media into your pages. This simply means you cannot count on a script to handle the contingency of a user not having the required plug-in. However, the Dreamweaver Check Plug-in behavior has a setting that will be used if it determines it's being run on one of these browsers. In the Check Plug-in dialog box, check the "Always go to first URL if detection is not possible" check box to set the course of action to take when a browser that can't detect a certain plug-in visits your site.

Problems with Plug-ins

If you run into problems playing content for any particular plug-in in Dreamweaver, you can try a few things:

Plug-ins can be memory-intensive, so make sure you have enough memory to run it. On the Macintosh, make sure you have enough memory allocated to Dreamweaver.

Make sure the content you're trying to play is compatible with the version of the plug-in you have installed and that it's installed properly. Try to play the content in your browser instead of Dreamweaver.

A file in Dreamweaver's configuration/plug-ins folder named UnsupportedPlug-ins.txt is used to keep track of plug-ins that cause problems in Dreamweaver. You can open this file in a text editor to see if the plug-in in question is listed or add it yourself if you're ultimately unable to preview the content in Dreamweaver. Any plug-in listed in this file can still be added to a page using Dreamweaver, but you won't be able to play it in the Design view.

Playing Plug-in Content

One interesting feature Dreamweaver provides is the capability to play plug-in content, such as movies or animation, directly in the Design view of the Document window. This makes it easy to test your content and get a feel for how it integrates with your page design. To do this, the appropriate plug-ins must already be installed on your system. Dreamweaver searches for plug-ins at startup in its own configurations/plug-ins folder, followed by Netscape's plug-ins folder.

To play plug-in content, either click the Play button in the Property Inspector, select View | Plug-ins | Play from the menu, or use CTRL-ALT-P (CMD-OPT-P on the Mac). You can also choose to play all plug-in content on a page by choosing View | Plug-ins | Play All from the menu, or use the CTRL-ALT-SHIFT-P (CMD-OPT-SHIFT-P on the Mac) keyboard shortcut.

To stop content from playing, either click the Stop button in the Property Inspector, or select View | Plug-ins | Stop or View | Plug-ins | Stop All from the menu. The respective keyboard shortcuts are CTRL-ALT-X (CMD-OPT-X) to stop and CTRL-ALT-SHIFT-X (CMD-SHIFT-OPT-X) to stop all plug-ins.

ActiveX Controls

ActiveX controls are a Microsoft-developed technology built on its *Component Object Model (COM)* for Windows. ActiveX controls perform the same sorts of tasks as

Netscape plug-ins, but they're limited to Internet Explorer 3.0 and higher on the Windows platform only and won't work with Netscape without the use of a third-party add-on. ActiveX controls aren't available at all on the Macintosh. Why would you then want to use ActiveX controls given these limitations? Because many times, ActiveX controls will provide more flexibility than other plug-ins. It is definitely worth considering these controls when the target browser is Windows-based Internet Explorer. You can also add equivalent plug-ins for other platforms, thereby providing enhanced functionality for those on Internet Explorer while not sacrificing the Netscape and Mac audience.

ActiveX controls are typically developed using Visual Basic, C++, or even Java, but you needn't learn those languages to use ready-made ActiveX controls on your pages. To add an ActiveX control to your page, follow these steps:

1. In either the Design or Code views of the Document window, position the cursor to where you want to place the control.

2. Click the Insert ActiveX button in the Special tab of the Objects panel (see the following illustration). You can also drag-and-drop the ActiveX icon or choose Insert | Media | ActiveX from the menu. You now have a placeholder `<object>` tag in your document.

3. You can now use the Property Inspector, as seen in the next illustration, to set the parameters and attributes for the ActiveX object.

■ The **Name** field sets the name attribute of the tag, which identifies the tag for scripting.

■ The **W** and **H** fields specify the width and height of the applet in pixels. You can also use unit modifiers to specify the size in alternative units: pc (picas), pt (points), in (inches), mm (millimeters) and cm (centimeters), or % for a percentage of the parent object's width and height.

■ **Class ID** identifies the control to the browser. Class IDs are 32-character unique identifiers generated by the author of the control. These identifiers virtually guarantee that no two ActiveX controls will ever have the same Class ID. A Class ID should be provided with any ActiveX control you download, either in documentation or in a sample HTML file showing how to use it.

■ **Embed** causes Dreamweaver to insert an <embed> tag within your <object> tag. This lets you specify a Netscape plug-in to use instead of the ActiveX control on Navigator browsers. If you check this box, the Src field becomes active and you can enter the name of the plug-in data file there.

■ **Align** sets how the object is aligned on the page. The various alignment options are covered elsewhere in this book.

■ **V** and **H Space** let you specify the amount of a blank space to put around the applet. The spacing must be specified in pixels.

■ **Base** sets the <codebase> attribute, which is a URL from which the ActiveX control can be downloaded if it isn't already installed on a visitor's system.

■ **Alt Img** lets you specify an image to be displayed for browsers that don't support the <object> tag. You cannot use this option and the Embed option at the same time.

■ **ID** is used to set the ID attribute, which is used as a unique object identifier in the document.

■ **Data** specifies a data file to use with the control. Not all ActiveX controls use this field.

Using ActiveX and Netscape Plug-ins at the Same Time

When you use the Embed option of the ActiveX Property Inspector, you insert an
<embed> tag into your <object> tag. This allows Netscape and other browsers that
ignore the <object> tag to still be able to play content using a plug-in. Internet
Explorer also ignores <embed> tags within the <object> tag, so this method gives
you a way to support both browsers without having to use JavaScript to insert special
code for each browser.

The following code listing shows how nesting the <embed> tag works. Notice
that attributes and parameters of the ActiveX object are converted into attributes of the
plug-in. These attributes are automatically inserted by Dreamweaver when you check
the Embed option in the Property Inspector.

```
<!-- Object tag for Internet Explorer -->
<object id="NSPlay1" width=160 height=128
    classid="clsid:2179C5D3-EBFF-11CF-B6FD-00AA00B4E220"
    <param name="FileName" value="netshow/sample.asx">
    <param name="ControlType" Value="1">
    <!-- Embed tag for Netscape Navigator -->
    <embed type="application/asx" width=160 height=128
        src="netshow/sample.asx"
        ControlType=1>
    </embed>
</object>
```

Using CGI Programs

Up until now, this chapter has dealt with embedding external programs on the client
(browser). At times, however, you might want an external program to reside on the
server so the pages you download are generated dynamically. When you navigate
to a Web page, your browser is sending an HTTP request to the Web server behind
the scenes to retrieve an HTML page. An HTML page is traditionally static and
unchanging. What do you do when you want to generate dynamic content on the fly
from the server? You use a *Common Gateway Interface* (*CGI*) program on the server. CGI
is a standard for interfacing external applications with Web servers, receiving requests
from a user, and outputting dynamic HTML pages back to the browser. Because CGI
programs run on the server and generate standard HTML pages, they are compatible
across all browsers and platforms. The only problem you're likely to encounter is users
who don't accept cookies, which are used by several CGI scripts, including message
boards. CGI programs can be written in a wide variety of languages from C++ to shell
scripting languages. Perl is one of the most popular languages for writing CGI programs,
however, mainly because of its text manipulation prowess. Perl is also an interpreted

language, which means the Perl source files needn't be compiled into a binary executable before they're run. Instead, the Perl interpreter reads and executes the source files directly at run time. This makes modifying Perl programs (also called *Perl scripts*) easy, an additional plus for Web developers who might not have access to a compiler on the server's computer.

CGI programs can be used to build community on your sites. For the Island project, for example, you could add a message board system for people to discuss their favorite getaways and relaxation techniques. If you want feedback on the merchandise available in your online store, a message board or guestbook could facilitate communication with your customers. CGI programs also exist for search engines and file libraries.

File Permissions and Security

CGI programs need to be installed on your Web server to run properly. Most of the time, they need to be put into a special directory on the server called *cgi-bin*. While some servers allow Web developers to write to this directory, some don't. Some may also place additional restrictions on running CGI programs for security reasons. If so, you must talk to the system administrators for your site host to arrange for access to the cgi-bin.

If your server is a UNIX host and you're able to upload your CGI programs to a server directly, make sure the file permissions are set correctly to allow the program to be executed. UNIX systems enable you to set a file to be readable, overwritable, or executable for three types of people: the file owner, the administrative group, and outside visitors. In general, you want to allow all classes of users to read and execute the file, but only allow the owner to overwrite the file. File permissions are set using the UNIX `chmod` command.

You can set file permissions in Dreamweaver using the built-in FTP client. From the Site window, select the site you are working with, and follow these steps:

1. Click the Connect button to open an FTP connection to your host (go online first, if necessary).

2. Open the FTP Log window from the Site window by choosing Window | Site FTP Log from the menu (Site | FTP Log on the Mac).

3. Enter the site `chmod` command in the FTP Command box at the top of the FTP Log window, followed by 755 for the permission parameters and your filename (see the following illustration for an example). Each digit of the 755 parameter represents a permission for each class of user, File owner, administrative group, and visitors. You, as the file owner, are giving yourself full permission to read, write and execute with the first 7. Other users are only given read and execute permissions with the 5 settings. The command should look something like this:
   ```
   site chmod 755 myscript.pl.
   ```

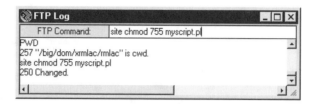

If you're using a Windows NT server, you must get any special requirements concerning how to upload your CGI programs from the server administrator. Dreamweaver's FTP client is covered in-depth in Chapter 6.

Sending Data: The GET and POST Methods

Generally, you can send data to a CGI program in two methods. If your data is obtained from a form, the information is typically sent using the *POST* method, which embeds the data into the HTTP request. Or, the *GET* method attaches the data to be sent to the end of the URL used to make a page request. Both methods have their uses and both can be created using Dreamweaver.

Posting Form Data

Forms are a common way of sending information to a CGI program. Forms created by Dreamweaver default the POST method of sending data, which is the most common way. Dreamweaver's Form Property Inspector enables you to set the method and the action for your form (see the next illustration). Set the method as POST and the action to the URL of your CGI Program. Now, when a visitor fills out the form and clicks the Submit button, the values of all the named elements of the form are posted to the CGI program.

You can find more information on creating forms with Dreamweaver in Chapter 16.

Sending Data Through a URL

Another way to send data to CGI programs is the GET or QUERY_STRING method. This is a standard method of sending data by appending it directly to the URL of the CGI program you are requesting, rather than hiding it in the HTTP request as the POST method does.

The form of the query string consists of a question mark followed by the name of each field and its value:

```
http://www.pendragn.com/cgi-bin/islandscript.pl?request=5+name=Jenn
```

One advantage this method of sending data has is you can embed the data directly into a link without having to use a form. You can do this in Dreamweaver by using the Link Property Inspector, as shown in the following illustration.

Script Resources

As with the other types of programs mentioned in this chapter, you needn't write CGI programs yourself. Many sources for CGI programs are on the Web. The CGI Resource at **http://www.cgi-resources.com** is a great place to find scripts and information. The CGI Directory at **http://www.cgidir.com** is another provider of free scripts.

For information on the CGI specification, visit the NCSA's collection of CGI documentation at **http://hoohoo.ncsa.uiuc.edu/cgi/**.

Summary

This chapter has provided an overview of plug-ins and external applications that can be embedded into your Web pages. Choose wisely to reach the widest possible audience and have the most positive impact on your visitors' experience at your site.

- Plug-in content requires the user to have the related plug-in installed.

- ActiveX components only work on the Windows platform and have limited Netscape support. However, many times the ActiveX control will give you advanced functionality in Internet Explorer. In these instances, you can use an equivalent plug-in for other browsers.

- CGI Scripts are well-suited for interactive applications, such as message boards, guestbooks, and file libraries.

The next chapter covers behaviors. Dreamweaver's behaviors make use of advanced JavaScripts to add Web events to a site with little or no coding knowledge required.

The Complete Reference

Chapter 23

Behaviors

If the previous chapter covering JavaScript has you totally bewildered or if you're just not into coding, but want to add advanced features to your pages, Dreamweaver comes to the rescue with a powerful feature called behaviors. Dreamweaver *behaviors* enable you to insert prewritten JavaScript code into your pages, which can be called as a result of specific viewer actions. These JavaScript functions have been written by Macromedia's experienced developers to ensure maximum cross-browser compatibility, giving you one less thing to worry about when you're trying to handle events.

This chapter explains the various included Dreamweaver behaviors and how to use them in your pages. It shows you where you can find additional behaviors on the Web and how Dreamweaver organizes them. You'll discover that, even if you don't understand a bit of JavaScript code, Dreamweaver makes it simple to add event handlers to your pages and to bring them to life. Finally, for the do-it-yourself minded among you, this chapter explains how you can create your own behaviors or modify existing ones.

Events and Actions

A behavior consists of an action and a corresponding event. *Events* are messages generated by the browser in response to something the visitor does. For example, when a visitor moves the pointer over an element such as a link, an onMouseOver event is generated for that element. When the visitor clicks the link, an onClick event occurs. When these events occur, the browser checks to see if the event has an action associated with it. The *action* is nothing but an inline JavaScript statement or a call to a JavaScript function. Different browsers support different events for various elements.

When an action is assigned to handle a particular event, its JavaScript code is called whenever the event occurs. For example, if you assign the Play Sound action to an onMouseOver event, the associated sound is played any time the user moves the mouse over the element. You can even use a single event to trigger multiple actions in the order you specify.

Dreamweaver includes JavaScript functions for 25 actions and more that can be found on the Macromedia Exchange Web site at **http://www.macromedia.com/ exchange** (or by choosing Get More Behaviors from the Actions (+) menu of the Behaviors panel). Experienced JavaScript developers can even create their own actions, as I demonstrate later in this chapter.

The Behaviors Panel

The *Behaviors panel* is where you attach behaviors (consisting of actions and events) to elements, or tags, on a page. This is also the panel you use to modify various parameters for behaviors (for example, the sound file to use with the Play Sound action). The following illustration shows the Behaviors panel.

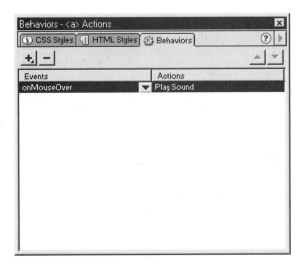

To use the Behaviors panel, open it by choosing Window | Behaviors from the menu, or press SHIFT-F3 (on either Windows or Mac). You can also click the Show Behaviors button at the bottom right of the Document window, and then you can see the currently selected tag from the Document window in the title bar of the panel. The panel shows two columns, for events and actions. If behaviors are already assigned to the tag, they are listed alphabetically by event. If an event has multiple actions, the actions are listed in the order they will be called when the event occurs. If the currently selected tag has no behaviors assigned to it, nothing is shown in the behaviors list.

Note *If you manually change a page using the Code view, you have to refresh the Design view before any behaviors can be seen in the Behaviors panel. Choose View | Refresh Design View, or press F5. You can also click the Refresh button if it's shown in the Property Inspector window.*

The Behaviors panel provides the following options:

- **Actions (+)**—activates a pop-up menu of actions. Any inappropriate actions for the currently selected element are grayed out. Selecting an action from this menu brings up a dialog box where you can specify any parameters this action requires (such as image filenames for the Preload Images action or text to display in the status bar for the Set Text of Status Bar action). Two of Dreamweaver's included actions—Set Text and Timeline—have submenus with more options. Two special items on this menu are the Show Events For submenu, which lets you limit the events to choose from to those available on a particular browser, and the Get More Behaviors... item, which launches a browser window to navigate to the Macromedia Exchange.

- **Delete (-)**—removes a behavior. Select an event and action in the behavior list by clicking it, and then click this button to remove it.

- **Events**—is a pop-up menu you can use to change the event that triggers an action. When you add an action, it has a default event assigned to it, which you may want to change. Select the action in the behavior list and an arrow to activate the Events menu is shown in the event column. A description of all events is provided later in this chapter. Some events may be shown in parentheses. These events may only be used for links—selecting one automatically generates a null link to the specified element and attaches the behavior to that link.

- **Show Events For**—is a submenu available from the Events menu, as well as the Action menu. It enables you to limit the events you can choose to those available on a particular version of IE or Netscape, or to those available on a particular generation of browsers. This submenu is also available from the Action (+) menu. Selecting older browsers limits the number of events available to only those that function properly in those browsers. Selecting specific versions of Netscape or Internet Explorer lists proprietary events for that browser.

- **Arrow Buttons**—are only activated if you have multiple actions assigned to a single event. These buttons enable you to change the order that actions will be executed for an event. Click the up arrow to move a selected action ahead of others in the list, and click the down arrow to specify the action should be executed after other actions.

Attaching Behaviors

A behavior must be attached to an element (HTML tag) on your page. The most common elements to have behaviors attached are <body>, <a>, <area>, <form>, <frameset>, <img>, <input>, <select>, and <textarea> elements. These tags have handled events since version 3.0 browsers, so you can be sure behaviors using these tags and events can give your pages a wide audience.

To attach a behavior to an element, follow these steps:

1. Open the Behaviors panel, as described in the previous section.

2. Select the element (or tag) in the Design or Code view. If you want to attach the behavior to the document, click the <body> tag in the tag selector at the lower left of the Document window, or select the <body> tag in the Code view. The selected tag is shown in the title bar of the Behaviors panel.

3. Click the Action (+) button and choose the action you want from the pop-up menu. If the action is dimmed, you'll be unable to use it for this tag. Actions may be dimmed if they require a specific object, such as a timeline, or a plug-in, such as Flash. All actions are dimmed if there are no supported events for your selected tag. The parameters dialog box now appears.

4. Enter any parameters the action requires, and click OK. The action appears in the Behavior list with a default event.

5. If the default event isn't the one you want to trigger your action, choose another from the Events pop-up menu. See the next section for more information about events.

Events

Modern graphical user interfaces are said to be *event-driven*, which means actions in a program occur in response to some action from the user, such as clicking the mouse, pressing a key, choosing a menu item, or even from a repeating timer. This paradigm has been used in Web browsers since the beginning, but originally event handling was all done internally in the browser.

As browsers have matured, the internal event systems have been exposed little by little to the pages themselves, enabling Web page authors to harness the power of events by writing JavaScript event handlers.

Dreamweaver's Behaviors panel allows many different events to be associated with actions for your page elements. Newer browser versions support more events than older browsers do, so the Behaviors panel enables you to show only events for the browser version you're targeting. You may choose to show events for Netscape 3.0, Netscape 4.0, Internet Explorer 3.0, IE 4.0, IE 5.0, Version 3.0 browsers (events supported by both Netscape 3.0 and IE 3.0), and Version 4.0 browsers (events supported by both Netscape 4.0 and IE 4.0). The list in Table 1 shows the default events Dreamweaver supports for various browsers. To see if an event can be used with a particular element, select the tag in your document and add an action. You can then see supported events in the Events pop-up menu.

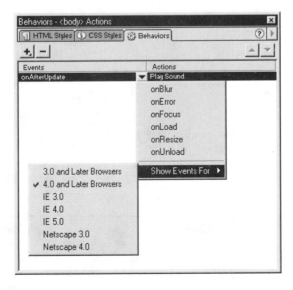

ADVANCED WEB PROGRAMMING

Event	Browser Support	Description
onAbort	Netscape 3.0 or higher, Internet Explorer 4.0 or higher.	An onAbort event is fired when a visitor stops a page from loading completely, for example, when the Stop button is pressed.
onAfterUpdate	Internet Explorer 4.0 or higher.	An Internet Explorer event dealing with elements bound to a *Data Source Object* (*DSO*). This event fires after the transfer of data to the data provider.
onBeforeCopy	Internet Explorer 5.0 or higher.	This event is fired before a copy operation copies the selected item to the clipboard.
onBeforeCut	Internet Explorer 5.0 or higher.	This event is fired before a cut operation deletes the selected item from the document.
onBeforePaste	Internet Explorer 5.0 or higher.	This event fires on the target object before the current selection is pasted from the clipboard to the document.
onBeforeUnload	Internet Explorer 4.0 or higher.	This event fires before a page is unloaded and can override the unloading. It can be used to give the visitor the opportunity to remain on the page.
onBeforeUpdate	Internet Explorer 4.0 or higher.	Like onAfterUpdate, this element deals with elements bound to a Data Source Object (DSO). This event fires when the element has lost the focus and the data in the element has changed. This event can be cancelled, providing the opportunity to fail data validation.
onBlur	Netscape 3.0 or higher, Internet Explorer 3.0 or higher.	This event is fired when the attached element loses focus, whether by clicking another control or the background of the page, switching applications, or opening another browser window.

Table 23-1. *Dreamweaver's Behavior Panel Supports a Wide Range of Events*

Event	Browser Support	Description
onBounce	Internet Explorer 4.0 or higher.	This event only applies to the Internet Explorer `<marquee>` element. It fires when the contents of the marquee reach the side.
onChange	Netscape 3.0 or higher, Internet Explorer 3.0 or higher.	This event is generated when a visitor changes a value on the page, such as by entering data into a text field or choosing an item from a list box.
onClick	Netscape 3.0 or higher, Internet Explorer 3.0 or higher.	This event is generated when the visitor clicks the specified element. This click isn't recognized until the mouse button is released.
onContextMenu	Internet Explorer 5.0 or higher.	This event is fired when the context menu is activated (right mouse click on Windows, mouse hold on the Mac). This can be used to override the default context menu or disable it altogether.
onCopy	Internet Explorer 5.0 or higher.	This event fires on the source element when the user copies the current selection to the clipboard.
onCut	Internet Explorer 5.0 or higher.	This event fires on the source element when the user cuts the current selection to the clipboard.
onDblClick	Netscape 4.0 or higher, Internet Explorer 4.0 or higher.	onDblClick is fired when a visitor double-clicks the specified element.
onDrag	Internet Explorer 5.0 or higher.	This event is fired continuously while the visitor is dragging a selected item.

Table 23-1. *Dreamweaver's Behavior Panel Supports a Wide Range of Events* (continued)

Event	Browser Support	Description
onDragDrop	Netscape 4.0	This event occurs when an object, such as a shortcut or file, is dragged-and-dropped into the browser window. If the event handler returns true, the browser attempts to load the dropped item into its window and, if fals, the drag-and-drop process is cancelled.
onDragEnd	Internet Explorer 5.0 or higher.	This event fires on the source object when the user releases the mouse button after a drag operation.
onDragEnter	Internet Explorer 5.0 or higher.	This event fires when the visitor first drags a selection over a target object.
onDragLeave	Internet Explorer 5.0 or higher.	This event fires when the visitor drags a selection off a drop target without dropping it.
onDragOver	Internet Explorer 5.0 or higher.	This event fires continuously while a visitor is dragging a selection over a valid drop target.
onDragStart	Internet Explorer 5.0 or higher.	This event fires when the visitor starts to drag a text selection or selected object.
onDrop	Internet Explorer 5.0 or higher.	This event fires on the target object when the mouse button is released over it during a drag operation.
onError	Netscape 3.0 or higher, Internet Explorer 4.0 or higher.	onError is fired when a browser error, such as a JavaScript error, occurs while a page loads.
onFinish	Internet Explorer 4.0 or higher.	This event only applies to the Internet Explorer `<marquee>` element. It fires when the contents of the marquee have completed a loop.

Table 23-1. *Dreamweaver's Behavior Panel Supports a Wide Range of Events*
(continued)

Event	Browser Support	Description
onFocus	Netscape 3.0 or higher, Internet Explorer 3.0 or higher.	This event is generated whenever the specified element gains the focus. This occurs when the user clicks the element with the mouse or tabs to it using the tab key.
onHelp	Internet Explorer 4.0 or higher.	This is an Internet Explorer-specific event that's fired when the browser's help button is pressed. This event can be used to provide context-sensitive help for the element that has the focus (is the currently selected element) when help is pressed.
onKeyDown	Netscape 4.0 or higher, Internet Explorer 4.0 or higher.	This event is fired in response to the visitor pressing any key. The browser cannot detect which key was pressed using this behavior.
onKeyPress	Netscape 4.0 or higher, Internet Explorer 4.0 or higher.	This event is fired in response to the visitor pressing and releasing any key. The browser cannot detect which key was pressed using this behavior.
onKeyUp	Netscape 4.0 or higher, Internet Explorer 4.0 or higher.	This event is fired in response to the visitor releasing a key press. The browser cannot detect which key was pressed using this behavior.
onLoad	Netscape 3.0 or higher, Internet Explorer 3.0 or higher.	onLoad fires when the page or the specified element (such as an image, applet, or plug-in) is done loading.
onLoseCapture	Internet Explorer 5.0 or higher.	This event fires when an object that's captured mouse input using the "setCapture" method loses the capture.
onMouseDown	Netscape 4.0 or higher, Internet Explorer 4.0 or higher.	This event is generated when a mouse button is clicked on the specified element. Note, the button needn't be released for this event to be fired.

Table 23-1.   *Dreamweaver's Behavior Panel Supports a Wide Range of Events* (continued)

Event	Browser Support	Description
onMouseMove	Internet Explorer 3.0 or higher. (Note: Although it's not mentioned in Dreamweaver's menu, this event is also supported by Netscape 6.0.)	This event is generated when the mouse pointer is moved while already over the specified element.
onMouseOut	Netscape 3.0 or higher, Internet Explorer 4.0 or higher.	This event is generated when the mouse pointer moves off the specified element.
onMouseOver	Netscape 3.0 or higher, Internet Explorer 3.0 or higher.	This event is generated when the mouse pointer first moves over the specified element.
onMouseUp	Netscape 4.0 or higher, Internet Explorer 4.0 or higher.	This event is generated when a pressed mouse button is released.
onMove	Netscape 4.0 or higher.	This is a Netscape-specific event that fires whenever the window or frame is moved.
onPaste	Internet Explorer 5.0 or higher.	This event is generated when the visitor pastes data from the clipboard into the element.
onPropertyChange	Internet Explorer 5.0 or higher.	A DHTML event that's fired when an element property changes. You can use the event object's propertyName property to determine the name of the changed property.
onReadyStateChange	Internet Explorer 4.0 or higher.	This event is fired by elements that can have different states, such as when an object is loading or initializing.
onReset	Netscape 3.0 or higher, Internet Explorer 3.0 or higher.	onReset is generated when a form is reset to the default values.
onResize	Netscape 4.0 or higher, Internet Explorer 4.0 or higher.	onResize is fired whenever the browser window or the frame is resized.

Table 23-1.   *Dreamweaver's Behavior Panel Supports a Wide Range of Events (continued)*

Event	Browser Support	Description
onRowEnter	Internet Explorer 4.0 or higher.	This is an Internet Explorer-specific event pertaining to elements bound to Data Source Objects. It fires when the row has changed in the data source and new data is available.
onRowExit	Internet Explorer 4.0 or higher.	This is an Internet Explorer-specific event pertaining to elements bound to Data Source Objects. It fires just before the data source changes the current row.
onScroll	Internet Explorer 4.0 or higher.	This is an Internet Explorer-exclusive event and may apply to elements that have scroll bars, namely the <body> and <textarea> elements.
onSelect	Netscape 3.0 or higher, Internet Explorer 3.0 or higher.	This event applies to <input> and <textarea> elements and fires when the selected text is changed.
onStart	Internet Explorer 4.0 or higher.	Applies only to the <marquee> tag of Internet Explorer. This event is fired when the contents of the element begin a loop.
onSubmit	Netscape 3.0 or higher, Internet Explorer 3.0 or higher.	This event is fired when a form is about to be submitted. This event can perform client validation of the data and override the submission of invalid data.
onUnload	Netscape 3.0 or higher, Internet Explorer 3.0 or higher.	This event occurs immediately before a page is unloaded.

Table 23-1.   *Dreamweaver's Behavior Panel Supports a Wide Range of Events* (continued)

If an event is shown in parentheses, it can only be attached to a link. Dreamweaver automatically wraps an <a> tag around an image to create a null link. A *null link* is represented by `'javascript:;'` for the link. You can change this link value to a real link by editing it in the Property Inspector, but you cannot delete the link without removing the behavior.

Using Dreamweaver's Default Behaviors

Dreamweaver comes with 25 actions that have been written to work in version 4.0 and later of Netscape and Internet Explorer. Although Macromedia has made every effort to support as many browsers as possible, not all actions work in version 3.0 browser. At the end of each action, you can find information on how the action works with each of the 3.0 browsers.

Note that some actions, particularly those dealing with layers, fail in Netscape 6. Macromedia is actively working on fixing these known issues. For more information about compatibility and announcements regarding any fixes, please visit Macromedia's Dreamweaver Support Center at **http://www.macromedia.com/support/dreamweaver**.

This section lists all the built-in actions, their behaviors and their browser limitations. These actions are organized according to the kinds of things they do. In each case, some sample code is shown to demonstrate how to use the action.

Text Actions

Several of Dreamweaver's standard actions deal with setting text to display a message to a visitor.

Popup Message

The *Popup Message* action is used to display a JavaScript alert dialog box with a message you specify. The JavaScript alert function only provides a dialog box with an OK button, so use this action to display informational messages to the visitor.

You can embed JavaScript code in the text by enclosing it in braces ({ }). To display a brace in your text, precede it with a backslash (\{). This code can consist of a function call or a single line of code that can access global variables, objects, and their properties. See the next illustration for an example of how to set the message text for this action in the Popup Message dialog box.

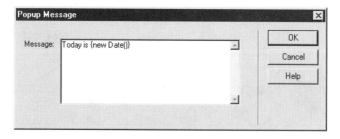

The following behavior attribute is added to the selected element. The MM_popupMsg is a JavaScript function Dreamweaver automatically adds to your document's head.

```
onMouseOver="MM_popupMsg('Today is '+(new Date())+'')"
```

The Popup Message action works correctly on Windows using both Netscape 3.0 and Internet Explorer 3.01 browsers. On the Mac, it works correctly using Netscape 3.0, but fails without error using Internet Explorer 3.0.

Set Text of Frame

Set Text of Frame is a powerful action that lets you completely replace the content of a frame with new text you supply. This text can be any valid HTML code, enabling you to update large portions of your Web pages dynamically. As with the Popup Message, you can embed JavaScript statements or function calls to generate the text for the frame by enclosing it in braces.

Set Text of Frame can only be chosen if your page is in a frameset. The Set Text of Frame dialog box, shown in the next illustration, enables you to specify the name of the target frame and provides a check box to allow the background color to be preserved. The Get Current HTML button copies the current contents of the target frame. If you want more information about creating pages with frames using Dreamweaver, Chapter 15 covers the subject in depth.

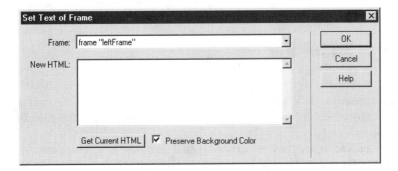

The Set Text of Frame action works correctly on Windows using both Netscape 3.0 and Internet Explorer 3.01 browsers. On the Mac, it works correctly using Netscape 3.0 but fails without error using Internet Explorer 3.0.

Note, at press time, Macromedia stated this action doesn't work in Netscape 6.

Set Text of Layer

Much like the Set Text of Frame action, *Set Text of Layer* lets you completely replace the text of a layer with valid HTML code. This enables you to change the content and formatting of a layer dynamically, while preserving the layer's attributes, such as color, position, and z-order.

The Set Text of Layer dialog box enables you to specify the ID of the target layer and the HTML text to put in the layer.

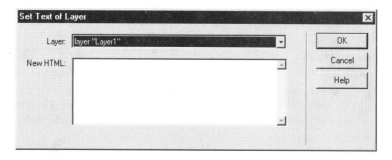

See the section on Layer actions in this chapter for more information on using Behaviors with layers. In addition, see Chapter 19 for more information on using layers in your Web pages.

The Set Text of Layer action fails without error using 3.0 versions of Netscape and Internet Explorer on both Windows and Mac platforms, since these browsers do not support layers.

Note, at press time, Macromedia stated this action doesn't work in Netscape 6.

Set Text of Status Bar

The *Set Text of Status Bar* action enables you to change the message displayed in the status bar at the bottom of the browser window. This action is typically used to set contextual information when the mouse is moved over an object. As with the other text actions, you can embed JavaScript function calls or statements in the message text by enclosing it in braces ({ }).

To use this object to display information as the mouse is moving over an object, you need two Set Text of Status Bar behaviors: Use one behavior fired by the onMouseOver event with the text of your message to set it while the mouse is moving over the element. Use another behavior fired by the onMouseOut event with no text to clear it. The following illustration shows the Set Text of Status Bar dialog box.

The Set Text of Status Bar action works correctly on Windows using both Netscape 3.0 and Internet Explorer 3.01 browsers. On the Mac, it works correctly using Netscape 3.0, but fails without error using Internet Explorer 3.0.

Set Text of Text Field

Set Text of Text Field enables you to set the text for form text input elements, either single line `<input type="text">` or multiline `<textarea>` tags.

A drop-down list (see the following illustration) enables you to choose the target text element. All the text and textarea elements on your page are listed by name. Enter the text you want the behavior to put in the element in the New Text field.

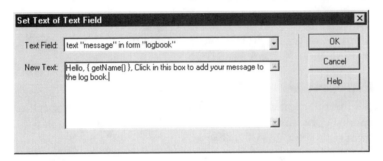

If your text or textarea elements show up in Set Text of Text Field dialog box as "unnamed", they probably aren't inside a `<form>` tag or your form tag is badly formed. Double-check your page.

As with the other text actions, you can embed JavaScript function calls or statements in the message text by enclosing it in braces ({ }).

This action works correctly on Windows using both Netscape 3.0 and Internet Explorer 3.01 browsers. On the Mac, it works correctly using Netscape 3.0 but fails without error using Internet Explorer 3.0.

Page and Navigation Actions

Many of Dreamweaver's actions are used to modify page and element properties, call JavaScript code, check Plugin or Page settings, or navigate to other pages. The following actions deal with these kinds of tasks.

Call JavaScript

The Call JavaScript action lets you specify a custom JavaScript function or a single line of code to be executed when an event occurs. This can be JavaScript code written by you or obtained from a third-party source. See Chapter 21 for more information on finding or creating JavaScript code.

In the Call JavaScript dialog box, enter the name of the JavaScript function you want to call or a single line of JavaScript code.

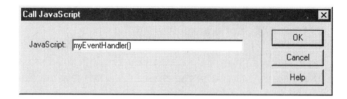

This action works correctly on Windows using both Netscape 3.0 and Internet Explorer 3.01 browsers. On the Mac, it works correctly using Netscape 3.0, but fails without error using Internet Explorer 3.0.

Change Property

The Change Property action can be used to change the value of properties for several different elements. For example, you can use it to change the value of form elements or to set a new font style for a `<div>` or `<span>`.

The Change Property action is dependent on the target browser, and it only allows the choice of Internet Explorer 3.0, Internet Explorer 4.0, Netscape 3.0, or Netscape 4.0. Of those four choices, choosing Internet Explorer 4.0 allows a much larger number of properties for most of the supported tags. The tags supported by this action include `<layer>`, `<div>`, `<span>`, `<img>`, `<form>`, `<input>`, `<textarea>`, and `<select>`, with a varying number of properties supported depending on the browser version chosen. Note, the choice of browser only limits the choice of properties to choose from in the dialog box. No browser type is checking in the behavior itself.

The illustration shows the dialog box for the Change Property action. The following describes the various settings:

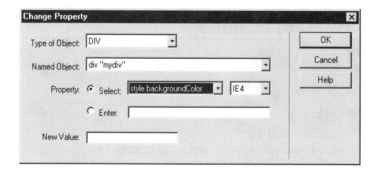

- **Type of Object**—Choose the kind of object you want to target. This limits the name choices in the Named Object drop-down list.

- **Named Object**—This is a list of the objects in your document that match the type of object you choose.

- **Property**—You can choose a target browser from the drop-down list on the right side, which provides a list of supported properties on the left. As an alternative, you can check Enter and enter the name of any property directly. This enables you to set properties you know about, but that aren't listed as choices.

- **New Value**—Enter the value you want the property to have after the event is fired. For instance, a new color if you're changing a color property or a filename if you're changing an image source file.

Tip	*If you're changing a property supported in both Netscape and Internet Explorer, but with a different property name, you can add multiple Change Property behaviors to an action. For example, both browsers enable you to change the background color of a layer in version 4, but Netscape uses the property* `document.bgColor` *and Internet Explorer uses* `style.backgroundColor`*. Add a Change Property behavior for each one to make code work on both browsers.*

This action works correctly on Windows using both Netscape 3.0 and Internet Explorer 3.01 browsers. On the Mac, it works correctly using Netscape 3.0, but fails without error using Internet Explorer 3.0.

Check Browser

These days, customizing a Web site by providing unique browser-specific pages to provide the best possible experience for every visitor isn't uncommon. Dreamweaver's Check Browser behavior makes it easy to add the capability to route users to different pages, depending on the browser type and version they are using.

You can use this action in two ways. You can attach it to the onLoad event of the <body> tag of your main page, and it can automatically route users to a page written explicitly for their browsers. If you do this, you want to make sure the page doing the redirecting remains the default page for visitors who have browsers that don't support JavaScript or who have it disabled.

You can also attach this action to the onClick event for a link to direct your visitors to a different page when the link is clicked. If you do this, the result of the Stay on this Page option for any of the browsers, instead, allows the link to navigate to its own specified URL.

The Check Browser dialog box enables you to specify two alternate routes for the action. Although one is called the URL and the other the Alternate URL, both are usable in the same way—to provide two alternate paths to take.

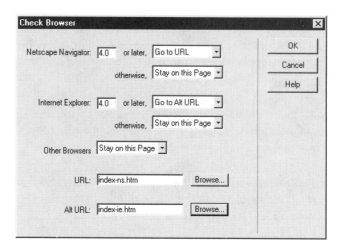

The various options for this dialog box are as follows:

■ **Netscape Navigator**—Enables you to set the version number for which to check. In the two adjacent pop-up menus, you can choose what to do if the visitor's browser version is equal to or greater than the specified version number, and what to do otherwise. In both cases, you can choose from Go to URL, Go to Alt URL, or Stay on this Page. Note, in the case of a link, choose Stay on this Page.

■ **Internet Explorer**—Again, this enables you to set the version number to check for, an action to take if the visitor's browser version is equal to or greater than specified, and an action to take otherwise.

■ **Other Browsers**—Here, you can set an action to take for any other browser, such as the text-based Lynx or Opera. Note, no version checking exists for this field. Generally, if you have this action attached to the <body> tag, you want to leave this set to Stay on this Page. This is because browsers that don't support JavaScript do this anyway.

■ **URL**—This is the URL that's navigated to if you choose Go to URL as any of your routing options.

■ **Alt URL**—This is the URL that's navigated to if you choose Go to Alt URL as one of your routing options.

This action works correctly on Windows using both Netscape 3.0 and Internet Explorer 3.01 browsers. On the Mac, it works correctly using Netscape 3.0, but fails without error using Internet Explorer 3.0

Check Plugin

Web designers can use many popular plug-ins to enhance the content of their pages, including QuickTime, Acrobat, Flash, and Shockwave (among others). All these third-party file formats require the proper plug-in module to be installed before any content can be viewed. The *Check Plugin action* can be attached to the <body> of your document to direct visitors who don't have a particular plug-in to a page with alternate content or to a page where they can download it.

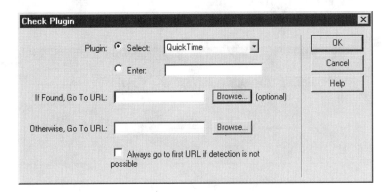

The Check Plugin dialog box gives you the following options:

- **Plugin**—Check either Select, where you can choose a plug-in from a list of known plug-ins, or Enter, where you can specify the plug-in by name. Remember, if you enter the plug-in name by hand, you need to enter the full name as provided by the plug-in documentation.

- **If Found, Go To URL**—This box is where you specify the URL you want to use for those who have the plug-in. Leave this blank if you want it to be the current page.

- **Otherwise, Go to URL**—Specify the URL you want to use for those who don't have the plug-in installed.

- **Always go to the first URL if detection isn't possible**—With the exception of Flash and Shockwave, you cannot detect specific plug-ins in Internet Explorer. For this reason, in most cases it's better to assume the IE user has the plug-in and leave this box checked. You can always use the ALT attribute for the <embed> tag to tell viewers where to get the necessary plug-in or use an equivalent Active X control. See Chapter 22 for more information about embedding plug-ins and ActiveX objects.

This action works correctly on Windows using both Netscape 3.0 and Internet Explorer 3.01 browsers. On the Mac, it works correctly using Netscape 3.0, but fails without error using Internet Explorer 3.0.

Go to URL

The *Go to URL* action is a simple way to turn nearly any event into a link. Two possibilities would be using it to make any element that recognizes the `onClick` event to navigate without having to make it a link or using it in response to an `onHelp` message to go to a help page. Because this action enables you to specify a target frame, you can even use multiple Go to URL actions to load multiple frames with a single click.

In the Go to URL dialog box, select the target frame from the list if you're using frames, and then enter the path to the file to open in the URL text box. You can also click the Browse button to locate the file.

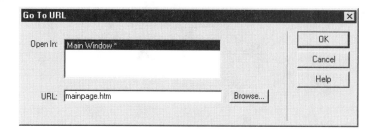

This action works correctly on Windows using both Netscape 3.0 and Internet Explorer 3.01 browsers. On the Mac, it works correctly using Netscape 3.0, but fails without error using Internet Explorer 3.0.

Jump Menu

Jump menus are a handy way to provide an easy way to navigate around a site, and Dreamweaver makes it easy to create them. Jump Menus are drop-down lists that contain entries for every page on your site. When a visitor chooses an item from the list, they then jump to that page.

Unlike most actions, the Jump Menu action is automatically created when you insert a jump menu into your code. Once it's created, though, you can select it in the design view and double-click the behavior in the Behaviors panel to bring up the dialog box again. To insert a jump menu into a page, do the following:

1. Choose Insert | Form Object | Jump Menu from the menu, or click the Jump Menu item in the Forms section of the Objects panel. This opens the Insert Jump Menu dialog box.

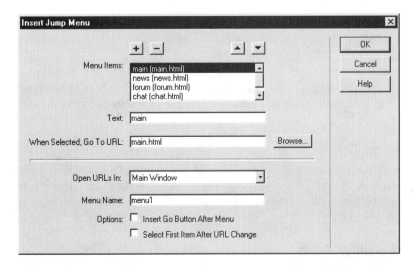

2. If you want the first item in the list to be a selection prompt, enter it now in the Text box. Click the Select First Item After URL box in the Options. Now click Plus (+) to add a new menu item.

3. Enter the name of the next menu item in your list in the Text field.

4. Enter the destination URL in the When Selected, Go to URL field either by typing the path directly or by using the Browse button to find a file.

5. If your site uses frames, enter the destination frame in the Open URLs In field.

6. To add additional menu items, click Plus (+) to create a new menu item, and then repeat Steps 3 through 5 for each item.

7. You can add a Go button to your jump menu by checking the Insert Go Button After Menu box.

Note   *Dreamweaver adds the Jump Menu behavior to your menu when you create it, but it doesn't necessarily add the proper JavaScript functions to your page until you edit the object in the Behaviors panel. You have to select the menu and edit it once in the Behaviors panel to get the* MM_jumpMenuGo() *JavaScript function to appear.*

Another way to create a jump menu is, instead, to use the List/Menu object from the Forms section of the Objects panel, or choose Insert | Form Objects | List/Menu

ADVANCED WEB
PROGRAMMING

from the menu. This creates an empty `<select> </select>` tag pair. You can then select this tag in the Document view or the list in the Design view, and then use the Behaviors panel to add the Jump Menu event to it. This method has one advantage because it automatically adds the proper JavaScript functions to handle the action on your page. Typically, you use the `onChange` event to trigger the Jump Menu action.

This action works correctly in Netscape 3.0, but fails without error in Internet Explorer 3.0.

Jump Menu Go

The Jump Menu Go action is tied to the Jump Menu action. This action is typically assigned to a button that causes the jump menu to navigate to its current selection. Normally, when you make a selection from the jump menu list, navigation occurs automatically. You may, however, prefer to have your visitors click the Go button to navigate instead.

To create a Jump Menu Go button, you must first create a button by choosing Insert | Form Objects | Button from the menu, or clicking the button object in the Forms section of the Objects panel. If you insert the button in the Design view (as opposed to the Code view), and it's not inside a `<form>` tag, Dreamweaver prompts you to add the `<form>` tag. Click NO in this case.

The default button type is a submit button. We don't want the button to perform any automatic action in the form, so change the button type to none in the button's property inspector.

Next, make sure the button is selected in the editor and use the Action (+) to add the Jump Menu Go action to it.

In the Jump Menu Go dialog box, select the target list to use as a jump menu. This list needn't have been inserted as a jump menu. Any named `<select>` tag is shown and can be made into a jump menu.

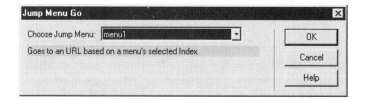

This action works correctly in Netscape 3.0, but fails without error in Internet Explorer 3.0.

Open Browser Window

Many Web sites now use secondary browser windows to display various information without disturbing the main browser window. In many cases, this has been used for evil and loathsome things like pop-up ads the user is forced to close. Such uses might annoy your visitors, even if the ads do pay the bills. Many possible uses for pop-up windows won't chase away your customers, though: You could use them to preview E-Commerce orders, to display help for a page, or to view a video. Visitors appreciate being able to view additional content without having to lose their place on your site in the main browser window.

You can control various aspects of the new browser window you create. You can make it with or without borders, a menu, scroll bars, a status bar, and a toolbar. You can size it so your HTML document fits perfectly. These options give you more control over display of the content than you would have displaying it in your main window.

To create an Open Browser Window action, select an object to use as the trigger and add the Open Browser Window action in the Behaviors panel. This brings up the Open Browser Window dialog box.

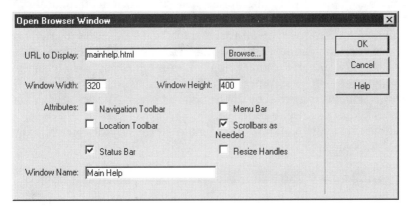

The parameters you can set for the Open Browser Window action are as follows:

- **URL to Display**—Enter the path or browse to the file to use as the source file for the window.

- **Window Width and Window Height**—Enter the size of the window in pixels.

- **Navigation Toolbar**—If this isn't checked, the new browser window won't have a navigation toolbar (the buttons for back, home, reload, and so forth).

- **Location Toolbar**—If not checked, the new browser window won't have a location (address) toolbar.

- **Status Bar**—If not checked, the window won't have a status bar.

- **Menu Bar**—If not checked, the window won't have a menu bar.

- **Scrollbars as Needed**—If the page content size is larger than the window dimensions, you need to set this option explicitly if you want scroll bars to appear.

- **Resize Handles**—If this item isn't checked, visitors won't be able to resize the window by dragging the lower-right corner. This also removes the minimize/maximize controls (Windows) or the size box (Mac).

- **Window Name**—The name to use for the window for scripting purposes.

If you don't specify any attributes for the new window, this is automatically created with the same attributes and dimensions as the current window.

This action works correctly in Windows using both Netscape 3.0 and Internet Explorer 3.01 browsers. On the Mac, it works correctly using Netscape 3.0, but fails without error using Internet Explorer 3.0.

Validate Form

The *Validate Form* action provides a way to check the contents of form text fields to make sure they contain correct information. You can enforce rules that say the data must be numeric or a certain number range, insist a field be filled in, or insist on an e-mail address.

The Validate Form action may be attached to a text field `<input type="text">` element if you want to validate each item one at a time. The other alternative is to attach the action to a submit button `<input type="submit">`, so the entire form can be validated before it's submitted. When assigned to an individual text field, the Validate Form action is triggered by the onChange event. The onClick event is used if the action is tied to a submit button.

The Validate Form dialog box enables you to set up the rules for validating each of the text fields of a form.

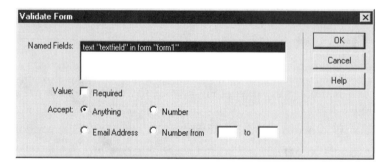

To set up a Validate Form action, follow these steps:

1. Choose a text element or a submit button on your page, and then activate the Behaviors panel.

2. In the Named Fields list, choose the name of the item you want to validate.

3. If you want to require a field to contain something, check the Required box.

4. In the Accept group of radio buttons, choose one of the following validation methods:

   ■ **Anything**—Accepts any entry.

   ■ **Number**—Requires the field to contain numeric info.

- **Email Address**—Requires the field to contain an e-mail address. Actual validation simply consists of looking for an @ sign.

- **Number Range**—Requires the field to contain a number in the specified range. Enter the low and high values in the appropriate boxes.

5. If the action is tied to a submit button, choose another field from the Named Fields list and repeat Steps 3 and 4.

6. When you finish, click the OK button.

This action works correctly on Windows using both Netscape 3.0 and Internet Explorer 3.01 browsers. On the Mac, it works correctly using Netscape 3.0, but fails without error using Internet Explorer 3.0.

Image Actions

Some of Dreamweaver's most powerful features are the behaviors you can add that work with images. You can have images preload with the page, swap images, or even create a full-functioning navigation bar using these behaviors.

Preload Images

Preload Images is a handy action you can tie to the onLoad event for a page. With it, you can specify a number of image files that may not be used the right way to preload into the browser cache. These images may be used for swapping with current images, JavaScript, timelines, or any other use. This action puts all the load time up-front and keeps your visitors from having annoying delays to download images later. In almost all cases, you'll want to leave this action tied to its default event, onLoad. Because this event fires after the page is loaded, the specified images are loaded after everything else on the page.

The dialog box for the Preload Images action is straightforward. Choose the <body> tag of your document and attach the Preload Images action from the Add Action menu in the Behaviors panel. Either enter the path to the filename in the Image Source File field or find it by clicking the Browse button. Then, click the Plus (+) button to add the image to the list. Repeat this until all the images you want to preload are listed.

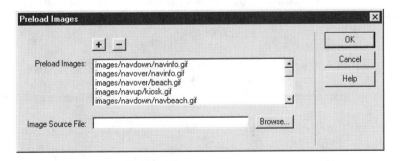

This action works correctly in Netscape 3.0, but fails without error in Internet Explorer 3.0.

Swap Image and Swap Image Restore

One of the most popular effects in Web design today is to have images on the page change as the mouse moves over them. This effect is called a *rollover* and is usually used to highlight a button. Dreamweaver's *Swap Image* action makes it easy to add rollovers for your images. This action lets you specify a new image file to swap for the original in the `src` attribute of an `<img>` tag and is assigned to the `onMouseOver` event by default.

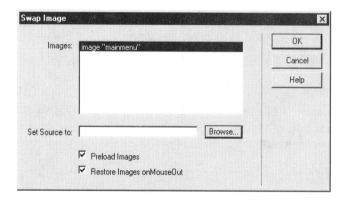

The Swap Image dialog box enables the following options:

■ **Images**—This is a list of all images in your document. Choose the one you want to have swapped.

■ **Set Source To**—Enter the path to the substitute image file. For the best-looking results, this image should have the same dimensions as the original one. Otherwise, the swap image is scaled automatically to fit the dimensions of the original image, with mixed results.

■ **Checking Preload Images**—adds a Preload Images action to your document, so the new images are cached when your page is loading.

■ **Restore Images onMouseOut**—This automatically restores the original image when an `onMouseOut` occurs. Check this if you are doing a rollover effect.

If you don't check Restore Images onMouseOut in the dialog box, you must add a Swap Image Restore action tied to a different event to restore the original image.

This action works correctly in Netscape 3.0, but fails without error in Internet Explorer 3.0.

Note, at press time, Macromedia indicated this action doesn't work across frames in Netscape 6.

Set Nav Bar Image

One of Dreamweaver's most extremely useful objects is the Navigation Bar. A *navigation bar* (or *nav bar*) consists of a sequence of images, arranged either horizontally or vertically, that make up a series of navigational buttons. In addition to the standard images, each button can have up to three additional images—for the mouse over, down, and mouse over while down states.

When you create a nav bar, the actions to control it are automatically added to your page. The main thing you should do from the Set Nav Bar Image action on the Behaviors panel is to customize the nav bar. You can add a lot of functionality to a single event by using the advanced tab. Any named image on your page can be swapped at the same time as the button image, giving you the capability to create disjoint rollovers, such as an informational image that shows what clicking the button can lead to.

The glue that holds a nav bar together is the Set Nav Bar Image action tied to the button events (onClick, onMouseOver, and onMouseOut). You can modify the behavior of an existing nav bar item by selecting it and double-clicking one of the events in the Events list. Remember, all three events edit the same Set Nav Bar action—if you change one, the others will also be changed.

The Set Nav Bar Image dialog box gives you many more powerful options for controlling images than the dialog box used to create the nav bar from the Insert | Interactive Images | Navigation Bar menu. Two tabs exist: Basic and Advanced. The *Basic* tab enables you to change the standard button images. The *Advanced* tab lets you set additional images to create disjoint rollovers. Take these steps to add additional image changes to a nav bar element.

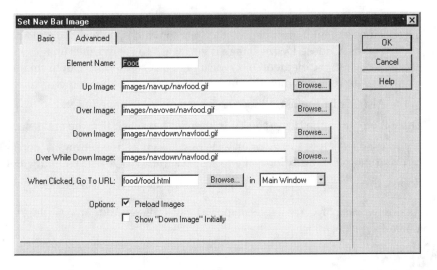

1. Select a nav bar element in your document. This is easiest to do in Design view.

2. In the Behaviors Panel, click one of the events shown in the Events window (onClick, onMouseOut, and onMouseOver). This brings up the Set Nav Bar dialog box.

3. Edit the basic image settings in the Basic tab. You can add images here for states you didn't use when creating the nav bar, or change the element's target page.

4. Click the Advanced tab to bring up the Advanced settings.

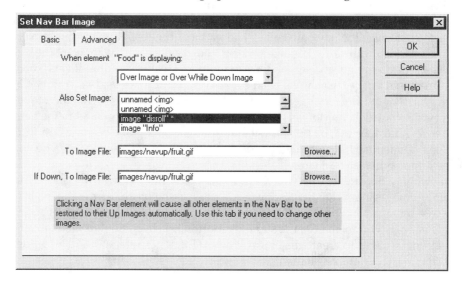

5. In the *When Element "name" is displaying* field (where "name" is substituted by the specific element name), choose the state to which you want to add additional image swaps. Choose Down Image if you want to swap other images after a user has clicked the element, or Over Image or Over While Down Image if you want to swap images when the mouse pointer is over the element.

6. In the Also Set Image list, choose an image on your page to set.

7. Enter the path to the file in the To Image field, or click Browse and select it.

8. If you used the Over Image or Over While Down Image setting in Step 5, you can also choose an additional file to display in the If Down, To Image field.

9. Repeat Steps 6 through 8 for any additional images you want to set.

This action works correctly in Netscape 3.0, but fails without error in Internet Explorer 3.0.

Layer Actions

Layers, as described in Chapter 19 and 20, are small HTML pages that can be dynamically shown and hidden, or moved on a page. Dreamweaver provides two-layer related actions that make it easy to change the visibility of layers or allow them to be dragged across the page.

Drag Layer

With the capability to drag layers, new avenues of interactivity are opened up to a Web designer. *Draggable layers* make it possible to create interactive games and puzzles, custom slider controls, and many other moveable objects that wouldn't be possible otherwise.

Dreamweaver's *Drag Layer* action makes it easy for a designer to implement draggable layers quickly. To make use of this behavior, first insert a layer into your page (the action won't be active in the Behaviors panel until you do so). The Drag Layer action must be called before the layer can be dragged, so you should use an event that triggers the action before any attempt is made to drag the layer. In most cases, you should add it to the <body> tag of your document using the onLoad event.

To make a layer draggable after it has been inserted, follow these steps:

1. Select the <body> tag of the document, open the Behaviors panel, and select Drag Layer from the Actions menu. This brings up the Drag Layer dialog box.

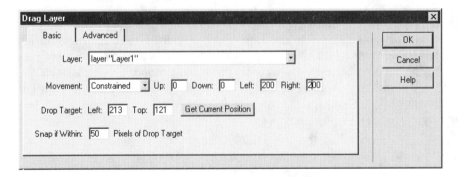

2. Choose the layer you want to target from the Layer drop-down list.

3. From the Movement drop-down list, choose Constrained or Unconstrained. If you choose Constrained, four additional text boxes appear that enable you to specify limits to the layer movement in the up, down, left, and right directions. Enter these values in pixels. Entering 0 for the up and down or left and right values limits movement to only the horizontal or vertical axis, respectively.

4. If you want to specify a target spot for the layer, enter the location in the Drop Target Left and Top fields. Use the Get Current Position button to use the layer's current position in the document.

5. Enter a value in pixels in the Snap if Within field to determine how close the layer must be to the target before it snaps to the target.

In addition to the previous basic options, the Drag Layer dialog box has an Advanced tab that lets you set more options:

1. If you want to limit the grabbable area of the layer, select Area Within Layer from the Drag Handle list. Enter the top Left, Top, Width, and Height values,

relative to the top of the layer itself. For instance, if your layer is 200 × 200 pixels, and you wanted to limit the grabbable area to the upper-right corner, you might assign Left = 0, Top = 0, Width = 100, and Height = 100.

2. If you want the layer to move to the top of the z-order while dragging, check the While Dragging option Bring Layer to Front. Then, choose whether to restore the z-index or leave the layer on top by selecting the option you want from the drop-down list.

3. You can call a custom JavaScript function while the layer is being dragged by specifying a function name to call in the Call JavaScript text box.

4. You can call a custom JavaScript function when the layer is dropped by adding a function name to the When Dropped: Call JavaScript item. If you want this function to be called only if the layer is snapped to its target, check the Only if Snapped box.

If you're going to make use of the custom JavaScript function calls in the Advanced tab, you'll most likely want to get information about the position and state of the layer in question. The Drag Layer action assigns three properties to each draggable layer: MM_LEFTRIGHT, MM_UPDOWN, and MM_SNAPPED. You can use these properties to determine the layer's relative horizontal position, its relative vertical position, and whether it's at the drop target. Use the MM_findObj() function to find your layer object like this:

```
var myLayer = MM_findObj("mylayername");
var curVertPos = myLayer.MM_UPDOWN;
var curHorizPos = myLayer.MM_LEFTRIGHT;
var layerAtHome = myLayer.MM_SNAPPED;
```

This action fails without error using 3.0 versions of Netscape and Internet Explorer on both Windows and Mac platforms.

Note, at press time, Macromedia stated this action doesn't work in Netscape 6.

Show-Hide Layers

One of the most useful features of layers is the capability to be shown or hidden on demand. A page might have layers that make up drop-down menus you may want to make visible when the mouse pointer moves over the nav bar buttons. The Show-Hide Layers behavior makes it easy to tie this process to a variety of events.

The Show-Hide Layers action enables you to show, hide, or return any and all layers you choose with a single action to a default state.

To use the Show-Hide Layers action, first select an object to trigger the action. This object can be anything except a layer for every browser except Internet Explorer 4.0. Then, open the Actions menu of the Behaviors panel and choose Show-Hide Layers.

The Show-Hide Layers dialog box provides a list of all layers in your document. Select each one you want to affect with this action individually and then click a new state for it: Show, Hide, or Default. When you finish, click OK.

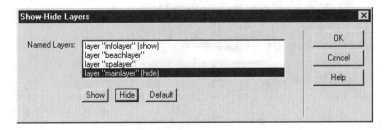

This action fails without error using 3.0 versions of Netscape and Internet Explorer on both Windows and Mac platforms.

Note, at press time, Macromedia indicated this action doesn't work across frames in Netscape 6.

Sound and Multimedia Actions

Play Sound

At times, you'll want to tie a sound to button clicks or informational messages, or have a MIDI song playing in the background when the page loads. The Play Sound action enables you to attach sounds to events.

Typical supported file types are the digital audio formats, including .wav, .aiff, and .au, as well as MIDI files with a .mid extension. Other sound formats may require a plug-in your visitors may or may not have.

To insert a Play Sound action, select the object you want to trigger the sound. If you want the sound to play in the background of your page, you can select the <body> tag. Choose the Play Sound action from the Actions menu and enter the sound filename in the Play Sound dialog box that appears.

The sound file is included in your Web page in an <embed> tag, hidden with a width and height of 0, a hidden=true and autostart=false. The file plays when it's triggered by the event you choose, perhaps an onClick event for a button or the onLoad event for your page.

See Chapter 26 for more information about audio file formats and how to use them on your pages.

This action works correctly in Netscape 3.0, but fails without error in Internet Explorer 3.0.

Control Shockwave or Flash

Many Web pages today use Macromedia's Flash and Shockwave content to liven up the experience for their visitors.

The Control Shockwave or Flash action enables you to take control of shockwave or Flash movies on your pages. This action enables you to play, restart, stop or go to a specific frame in a movie.

To make use of this action, you must already have a Flash or Shockwave movie inserted in your page. Chapter 27 covers the steps necessary to accomplish this. To use the Control Shockwave or Flash action, select the element (such as an image) you want to use to control the movie. The element must have a name attribute set for both the <object> tag and <embed> tag inside it or you won't be able to assign the movie as the target. The easiest way to set the name attribute is to use the Shockwave object's Property Inspector to do it. The name assigned there is used for both tags.

The Control Shockwave or Flash dialog box has the following fields:

- **Movie**—This list shows all the movies in your document in <object> and <embed> tags. Select the one you want to make the target of the action.

- **Action**—Choose Play, Rewind, Stop, or Go To Frame. Play starts the movie, Rewind starts over from the beginning, Stop stops the movie, and Go To Frame can be used to jump to a particular frame in the movie.

This action works correctly in Netscape 3.0, but fails without error in Internet Explorer 3.0.

Timeline Actions

A *timeline* defines a sequence of steps to follow when animating a layer. Timelines can change the size, position, visibility, and z-order of layers, as well as swap out images in a layer. If your page uses Dreamweaver's timeline feature, the actions listed here to control timeline playback can be triggered by events attached to various elements on your page.

Information on how to create a timeline is covered in Chapter 20, "Layer Animation."

Play Timeline, Stop Timeline, and Go To Timeline Frame

Once you have a timeline inserted on a page, you have three behavior choices for controlling it: Play Timeline, Stop Timeline, and Go To Timeline Frame. Select an element, such as the <body> tag, or an image. Open the Behaviors panel and choose one of the three timeline actions from the Timeline submenu of the Actions menu.

The *Play Timeline* and *Stop Timeline* actions enable you to start and stop timelines in response to a mouse click or some other event, such as a rollover. If you want the animation to play when the page is loaded, remember, the Play Timeline action is automatically assigned the onLoad event of the <body> tag when the timeline is set to Autoplay in the Timelines panel.

The Play Timeline dialog box and the Stop Timeline dialog box only have one item to choose: Select the timeline to control from the Timeline list. The Stop Timeline action gives you an additional choice, to stop all timelines.

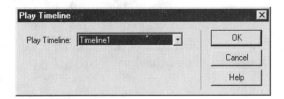

The *Go To Timeline* dialog box enables you to select the timeline to target, as well as some additional options. The Go to Frame field lets you set the frame to jump to. Set this to 1 if you want to start the animation from the beginning. The Loop setting is only valid if you are attaching the behavior to a frame in the timeline using the Behavior channel of the Timeline window. See Chapter 20 for more information about how to do this.

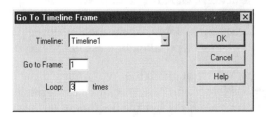

Because timelines depend on layer animation to work, these actions fail using Internet Explorer 3.01 on Windows and Internet Explorer 3.0 on the Mac. For Netscape 3.0 on all platforms, image source animation and invoking behaviors work, but layer animation fails without error.

Creating Behaviors

Although Dreamweaver provides quite a few good standard behaviors, you'll undoubtedly find yourself wanting more. Dreamweaver's extensibility enables you to add your own behaviors or even modify existing ones. The only thing you need to have is proficiency in coding JavaScript.

Of course, you may prefer to use behaviors written and tested by somebody else. You can visit a number of places to find behaviors someone else has sweated the details of creating. You should check some of these sites and the sites they link to, before you try to roll your own complicated behavior. In many cases, you'll find a behavior already exists to suit your needs.

- Dreamweaver Exchange (**http://www.macromedia.com/exchange/ dreamweaver**)—This is the first place you should look for third-party Dreamweaver, including behaviors.

- Massimo's Corner of the Web (**http://www.massimocorner.com**)—This site is a source of many high-quality Dreamweaver tools, including behaviors. An extensive links section connects to other Dreamweaver developers.

- Yaromat (**http://www.yaromat.com**)—The Yaromat is a great resource for free Dreamweaver tools, including behaviors.

Creating Actions

As mentioned before, a behavior consists of two parts: an action and an event. Events are defined by the browser, so when you create a behavior. you are simply creating the action portion of the behavior.

Dreamweaver actions are stored in Action files (stored in Dreamweaver's Configuration/Behaviors/Actions folder). An Action file is an HTML file containing a form used to create the action dialog box, along with JavaScript functions to process the form and to control how the behavior is inserted into a document.

When a developer selects an element, opens the Behaviors panel, and clicks the Action (+) button, the following steps take place behind the scenes:

1. Dreamweaver iterates through all the Action files in the Configuration/ Behaviors/Actions folder and calls its canAcceptBehavior() function to see if the action is appropriate for either the document or the selected element. These actions are used to set valid options in the Actions menu.

2. The canAcceptBehavior() function returns either a Boolean value or a list of events. If events are returned, these are used to populate the Events menu with acceptable events for the action.

3. When the developer chooses the action from the Action menu, Dreamweaver creates the parameters dialog box for the action. If the windowDimensions() function exists for the action, it's called to determine the size of the window. Otherwise, the dimensions are determined automatically.

4. The dialog box is displayed with the form elements in the `<body>` tag of the Action file.

5. If the file has an onLoad handler, Dreamweaver executes it.

6. After the developer fills in the form and clicks OK, Dreamweaver calls the behaviorFunction() and applyBehavior() functions. These functions return the function to include in the document's `<head>` and the event handler code to be added to the element, respectively.

7. If the developer edits the action at a later date by double-clicking it in the Events menu, the parameters dialog box is loaded again and the inspectBehavior() function is called to populate the form with the data previously entered for the action

To create a new action, you have to add a new Action file to the Configuration/ Behaviors/Actions menu. This consists of at least one .htm file, along with an additional .js file to hold helper JavaScript functions, if desired. Starting with one of the existing actions, copying it to a new Action file, and editing it is generally easier than creating a new action from scratch. Use one of the simpler actions—such as Call JavaScript—as a starting point, as some of the more complex behaviors may be hard to follow.

Behavior API

Dreamweaver's *Behavior API* is the set of functions you implement in your action that allow Dreamweaver to use it. Only two functions are required: applyBehavior() and behaviorFunction(). The rest are optional. Here is a brief rundown of some of the Behavior API functions:

- **applyBehavior()**—The applyBehavior() function inserts an event handler into the user's document to call the action function. This function can also modify other aspects of the user's document.

- **behaviorFunction()**—The behaviorFunction() function returns one or more functions to be inserted into the `<head>` of the user's document. This function can either return a function string directly or a function included in the Action file itself.

- **canAcceptBehavior()**—This function can check the user's document to see if certain required objects exist (such as layers if the action applies to layers). It returns true if the action is allowed but has no preferred events, false if it's not allowed, or lists preferred events in descending order.

■ **displayHelp()**—You can use this function to display any help files that explain how to use the action. Defining this function causes a Help button to appear automatically on the parameters dialog box.

■ **deleteBehavior()**—Removes any changes to the user's documents done by applyBehavior(). This function is only necessary if the action modifies the user's code more than normal, for example, adding embedded objects in the code. Dreamweaver automatically removes any added functions and event handlers when an action is deleted.

For more information on adding actions to your documents, see Dreamweaver's Extending Dreamweaver document. You can open it from Dreamweaver's Help menu.

Summary

This chapter covered behaviors and the standard behaviors that come with Dreamweaver. We only just touched upon the power of JavaScript, however. If you're using DHTML and behaviors, you can see some of these basic concepts put to work in practical ways. Visiting some of the sources of third-party behaviors on the Web listed in this chapter may also fire your imagination. The keys to understanding behaviors in Dreamweaver are:

■ The two components of a behavior are the event, which triggers the behavior, and the action, which is the result of the behavior.

■ The 25 behaviors packaged with Dreamweaver contain powerful tools for text, navigation, images, layers, multimedia, and timelines.

■ If you're proficient in JavaScript, you can add your own behaviors or modify the existing ones using the Behaviors API.

■ You can find additional behaviors on the Macromedia Exchange and other Dreamweaver resource sites.

In the next chapter, you learn how to use Dreamweaver's Objects palette and how to add new objects.

The Complete Reference

Dreamweaver 4

Chapter 24

Objects

Whenever you add an element to a page using Dreamweaver, you're inserting an object. An object can be something as simple as a special character object that generates a copyright symbol or foreign currency symbols, on up to complex tables or plug-in and ActiveX object helpers.

This chapter describes the Objects panel and explains how to use it. It also describes Dreamweaver's standard objects. Finally, for advanced users, the last part of this chapter shows you how to modify existing objects or even create your own from scratch.

Dreamweaver Objects

In Dreamweaver, an *object* consists of an HTML tag and its attributes, and possibly some JavaScript code to make certain features work. Some objects are simple—they may consist of a single HTML tag, such as `<hr>`, or special characters. Others are fairly complex, such as the Navigation Bar object, which enables you to insert a nav bar, complete with multiple button state images and complex behaviors.

Using the Objects Panel

The *Objects panel* is a handy tool to ease adding objects to your pages. Each object Dreamweaver supports is represented in the Objects panel by a button that can be used to create it. The standard buttons are organized into seven categories by default: Characters, Common, Forms, Frames, Head, Invisibles, and Specials.

Some of Dreamweaver's General Preferences settings apply to the Objects panel. Choose Edit | Preferences from the menu and select the General category. You can set the Object Panel to display as icons only, icons and text, or text only.

The panel is activated by choosing the Window | Objects menu item or by pressing CTRL-F2 (CMD-F2 on the Mac). If the panel is already visible, these same commands hide it again.

At the bottom of the Objects panel are two sections: View and Layout. View lets you choose between Standard (the default) and Layout view. If Layout view is selected, the Layout section of the Objects panel is activated, giving you two tools: Draw Layout Cell and Draw Layout Table. These table creation tools are covered in more detail in Chapter 14.

To insert an object, click the icon or drag it to the Document window. Some objects have special parameters that need to be set. These objects bring up a parameters dialog box prompting you to add this additional information. In many cases, you can bypass this dialog box and insert a placeholder object by holding down the CTRL key (Windows) or the CMD key (Mac). Placeholders are useful when you know you want to insert a particular object, but don't yet have the final content or configuration of the object. In HTML terms, this is similar to inserting a tag before you know the attributes and values of the element. Placeholders can be edited in the Property Inspector just like any other object, enabling you to configure it when you're ready. This doesn't work for all objects—some cannot be inserted as placeholders and require you to set parameters. This effect can be permanently achieved by unchecking Show Dialog when Inserting Objects in the General Preferences.

A drop-down list at the top of the Objects panel is used to select the category of objects from which you want to choose (shown in the next illustration). Following is a list of the standard objects provided with Dreamweaver.

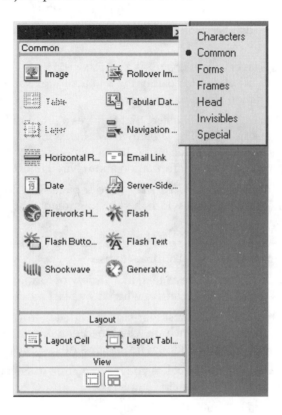

Characters

The Characters category provides a handy way to use 11 common special characters, such as the copyright symbol (©), trademark symbol (™), and currency symbols, such as Yen (¥) and Euro (€). You can insert special HTML characters, such as line breaks (`<br>`) and nonbreaking spaces (` `). An *Other* button even brings up a dialog box, containing 99 special characters from which to choose.

Common

The Common category contains many of the most commonly used HTML elements, as well as objects helpful for integrating Macromedia Flash and Shockwave files. They are

- **Image**—Adds an `<img>` tag, prompting you for the image file to use.
- **Rollover Image**—Adds an `<img>` tag, but also prompts for an additional image to swap in when the mouse moves over it. This object also adds all the necessary JavaScript behaviors to do this.

- **Table**—Inserts a `<table>`. The parameters dialog box prompts for Rows, Columns, Width, Spacing, Padding, and Border values. The rows and columns are added as empty `<tr>` and `<td>` elements in the table. See Chapter 14 for more information about working with tables in Dreamweaver.

- **Tabular Data**—Inserts a table, but fills it with data contained in an external delimited text file.

- **Layer**—Adds a layer to your page, as a `<div></div>` tag pair with a style attribute specifying absolute positioning and a z-index value. See Chapter 19 for more information about using layers.

- **Navigation Bar**—A complex object that features a set of rollover link images used to navigate on a site. The Dreamweaver behavior you can attach to this object enables you to create disjoint rollovers among other effects. See Chapter 12 and Chapter 23 for more information about Navigation bars.

- **Horizontal Rule**—Inserts an `<hr>` tag to your page. The Property Inspector for this object enables you to set width, height, alignment, and shading attributes for this tag.

- **Email Link**—Inserts an `<a href="mailto:...>` tag to your page, prompting for the link text and an e-mail address to use.

- **Date**—Adds the current date as text, in a variety of formats. Useful for date stamping a page, so visitors can see when it was last modified.

- **Server-Side Include**—Adds a server-side include tag in your page, specifying a file that a Web server can include when loading your page. See Chapter 28 for more information about working with server-side includes.

- **Fireworks HTML**—This object lets you insert a Fireworks-generated HTML file. This option is covered in detail in Chapter 40.

- **Flash**—Inserts a Flash file into your page.

- **Flash Button**—Inserts a Flash Button into your page.

- **Flash Text**—Inserts a Flash Text object into your page.

- **Shockwave**—Inserts a Shockwave file into your page.

- **Generator**—Inserts a Flash Generator object. All the Flash and Shockwave objects are covered in detail in Chapter 27.

Forms

The Forms category contains objects used in creating forms, covered in Chapter 16. These include

- **Form**—Inserts a `<form></form>` tag pair to define a form. Sets the attributes `method="post"` and `action=""`.

- **Text Field**—Inserts an `<input type="text">` tag to add a text field.

- **Button**—Inserts an `<input type="submit">` tag to add a Submit button. The Property Inspector can be used to change the button type to Reset or None.

- **Check Box**—Inserts an `<input type="checkbox">` tag to add a check box item. Assigns a default name and value. The Property Inspector for this object can be used to change the name, checked state, and the checked value.

- **Radio Button**—Inserts an `<input type="radio">` tag to add a radio button item. Assigns a default name and value. The Property Inspector for this object can be used to change the name, checked state, and the checked value.

- **ListMenu**—Inserts a `<select></select>` tag pair to add a list to a form. The Property Inspector allows height, whether to render as a list box or a pop-up menu, whether multiple selections are allowed, and an initially selected value. It also lets you specify values for the list, which are then added as nested `<option>` tags.

- **File Field**—Creates an `<input type="file">` tag. This provides a text field and a browse button the user can specify or browse to a file.

- **Image Field**—Inserts an `<input type="image">` tag. This is a graphical button only used to submit the form, with the coordinates clicked in the image.

- **Hidden Field**—Inserts an `<input type="hidden">` tag.

- **Jump Menu**—This is a specialized version of the ListMenu object. Choosing it brings up a dialog box prompting for menu items and their destinations. Jump Menu also adds an event handler to the onChange event that tells the browser to navigate to the selected URL.

Frames

The Frames category contains several common frameset arrangements. Choosing one automatically creates a frameset page with your current page as one of the nested `<frame>` elements. See Chapter 15 for more information about creating frames with Dreamweaver. The standard objects in this category are

- **Left**—Adds a new frame on the left side of the page.

- **Right**—Adds a new frame on the right side of the page.

- **Top**—Adds a new frame to the top of the page.

- **Bottom**—Adds a new frame to the bottom of the page.

- **Left and Top**—Adds small frames on the left, top, and top left of the page.

- **Left Top**—Adds a frame to the top of the page, and then one on the left, extending from the top of the page to the bottom.

- **Top Left**—Adds a frame to the left of the page, and then one on the top, extending across the entire width of the page.

- **Split**—Divides the page into four equal frames, with the current page in the lower-right corner.

Head

The Head category provides a convenient way to add elements inserted in the `<head>` tag of your document. These elements are covered in Chapter 8 and include

- **Meta**—Inserts a `<meta>` tag. You can specify the value and content of the tag, as well as whether it contains descriptive information or HTTP header information (`http-equiv`).

- **Keywords**—Inserts a `<meta>` tag, with a name attribute set to `keywords` and the content set to the searchable keywords you supply.

- **Description**—Inserts a `<meta>` tag with a name attribute set to `description` and the content set to the text you provide.

- **Refresh**—Adds a `<meta>` tag with an `http-equiv` attribute set to `refresh`. This tag is used to force navigation or a page reload after a specified amount of time. This is typically used when forwarding users to a new page or for refreshing a Web cam.

- **Base**—Inserts a `<base>` element, which is used to specify a path for all relative URL references or to specify a default target frame for any links in the document.

- **Link**—Inserts a `<link>` tag, which is used to establish links with external documents, such as style sheet definitions.

Invisibles

The Invisibles category contains objects that aren't visible on a page. These include

- **Named Anchor**—Inserts an `<a name=...>` tag, used as markers for quick navigation to specific points on a page. See Chapter 11.

- **Script**—Inserts a `<script></script>` tag pair. The parameters dialog box lets you choose the scripting language and the script content itself. See Chapter 21 for more information about using JavaScript with Dreamweaver.

- **Comment**—Inserts an HTML comment block (`<!--this is a comment.-->`) after prompting you for the comment text.

Specials

The Specials category provides objects that let you add external content to a page, including Java applets, ActiveX objects, and plug-ins. Find more information about using these objects in Chapter 22.

Modifying the Objects Panel

Dreamweaver's open extensibility features make it easy to add new objects. Any object Dreamweaver provides can also be modified to fit your needs. This can be used to take advantage of new technologies Dreamweaver doesn't yet support, such as XHTML (see Chapter 33 for an example of how to add objects to create XHTML tags in Dreamweaver).

Objects in Dreamweaver consist of a minimum of two files—a GIF file, used for the icon on the Objects Palette, and an HTML file, which contains information that tells Dreamweaver how to add the object to your code. Some of Dreamweaver's objects also have an additional file with a .js extension that contains the JavaScript code necessary to implement the object.

The object files are stored in Dreamweaver's Configuration/Objects folder. This folder contains seven folders (by default) that correspond to each of the Object panel's standard categories (see Figure 24-1), plus an additional Tools folder containing Layout view tools. You can easily add a new category by creating a new folder at the same level as the existing ones. In fact, if you're adding new objects to your Dreamweaver collection, a good idea is to put them in your own object categories, so they're easy to distinguish from the standard objects.

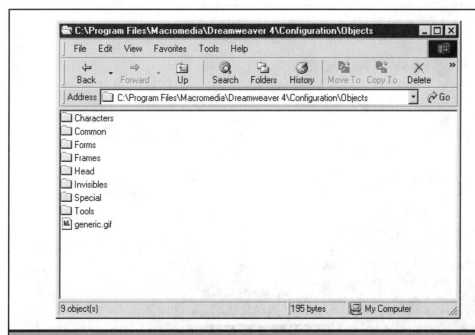

Figure 24-1.   *The Objects panel categories are organized according to the contents of Dreamweaver's Configuration/Objects folder, as this Windows Explorer view shows. The file generic.gif is used as a default icon for any object that doesn't provide its own*

ADVANCED WEB PROGRAMMING

| Note | *Dreamweaver only allows one level of object categories in the Objects panel. You can add a new category folder as a subfolder to one of the existing categories for organizational purposes in managing your application files but, within Dreamweaver, the folder name will be ignored and any objects in this folder will appear as if they belong to the main category in the Objects panel.* |

One possible reason to add a new folder is to reorganize the existing objects. If you use the same tags over and over, you can move their object files into a different category. For example, if you embed Java applets on a regular basis, you may want to move or copy the Applet object's files into the Common folder.

Adding Objects to the Insert Menu

Any object you add to an Objects panel submenu is automatically added to the bottom of the Insert menu. If you want this object to reside in a different position in the Insert menu or on another menu entirely, you need to edit the menu.xml file. This file, located in the Configuration/Menu folder, contains an XML document that provides the entire menu structure for Dreamweaver. For information on how to modify the menu.xml file, see Chapter 30.

Adding New Objects

Dreamweaver's powerful open extensibility certainly applies to objects. If you repeat a task regularly, the possibility is good that someone else has also run into the same problem and created a Dreamweaver object to help.

The Web, of course, is a vast resource for Dreamweaver objects. A list of several popular object resources follows.

- Dreamweaver Exchange (**http://www.macromedia.com/exchange/ dreamweaver**)—The first place you should look for any Dreamweaver object or behavior. Many of these objects are tested and approved by Macromedia engineers to ensure their functionality and compatibility.

- Massimo's Corner of the Web (**http://www.massimocorner.com**)—This site is a source of many high-quality Dreamweaver objects and tips. An extensive links section to other Dreamweaver developers is also here.

- WebMonkey Code Library (**http://hotwired.lycos.com/webmonkey/reference/javascript_code_library**)— The Editor Extensions section of the library focuses primarily on Dreamweaver.

- The Dreamweaver Supply Bin (**http://home.att.net/~JCB.BEI/Dreamweaver**)— Provides a wide variety of Dreamweaver objects and behaviors.

Installing Objects

Most objects that you download are usually packaged as a Dreamweaver extension. These files have a .mxp extension; launching the file automatically installs the object using the Macromedia Extension Manager. In the Extension Manager, you can get helpful information about running extensions. You can also turn extensions on and off, or install or delete extensions. You can find more information about the Extension Manager in Chapter 31.

If an object isn't packaged as an extension, you must install it manually. Follow these steps to install an object manually:

1. If the files are packaged in an archive, such as a ZIP or Stuffit file, you need to extract the object files.

2. If desired, create a new category for the object by creating a new subfolder in the Dreamweaver 4/Configuration/Objects directory. For example, if the object is used to insert audio or video files, you may want to create an object category called media.

3. Transfer the object files to the category of your choice, either an existing category or one you created in step 2. Make sure all the object's files are put there; at a minimum, an HTML file and a GIF file should be in the category.

4. Restart Dreamweaver or Reload Extensions. You can reload extensions by holding down the CTRL key (OPT key on the Mac) at the same time you open the drop-down list of categories at the top of the Objects panel. A new item is added to the category menu to reload the extensions, as shown in the following illustration.

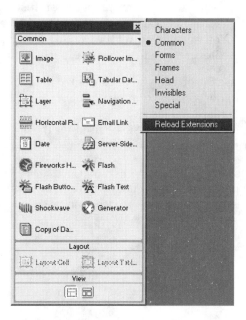

Creating Objects

As you've already seen, Dreamweaver objects can vary quite a bit in complexity. Likewise, when you create custom objects, they can range from simple to complex, taking advantage of the Dreamweaver Objects API and its *Document Object Model* (*DOM*). First, let's explore the basics of how objects work. Second, you create a simple object to gain an understanding of the basic object file format. And, finally, you move on to a more complex example.

Simple Objects

The simplest Dreamweaver objects consist of a file containing only the HTML element(s) you want the object to insert. These objects have no parameter form or JavaScript functions. They aren't even complete HTML files. To have Dreamweaver recognize a simple object, it only has to contain the HTML element or text to insert. It won't have any `<html>`, `<head>`, or `<body>` tags.

For an example, say you frequently use the subscript tag `<sub>` to add mathematical equations to your pages. Instead of typing the tag repeatedly, you want to click an object button and have it inserted. To create an object to do this, take the following steps:

Create the HTML File   This simple subscript object example consists of a single line HTML file, containing only the tag you want it to add:

```
<sub>
```

You can create this file using the Dreamweaver editor. Just remember, when you create a new document in Dreamweaver, it automatically adds the `<html>`, `<head>`, and `<body>` framework. You must delete all the existing text in the document first. You can, of course, use whatever text editor you like, such as Notepad or BBEdit.

Save the Object   To use the object, you need to save the HTML file in the Configuration/Objects folder. Create your own category, MyObjects, to keep created objects away from the standard objects.

The filename of the object is the name to be used for the object on the Objects panel, so save it using a descriptive filename: Subscript.htm.

Add a Button   If you want to add a custom button icon to use in the Objects panel, use your preferred drawing package (such as Photoshop or Fireworks) to create an 18 × 18 GIF file. The only restriction is the dimensions—the icon can use whatever colors you like.

Save the GIF in the MyObjects folder using the same base filename as the HTML file: In this case, Subscript.gif.

For this trivial example, don't bother creating an icon. Instead, note, if the GIF file for the object doesn't exist, the generic.gif file found in the Objects directory is used instead.

Finally, restart Dreamweaver, or choose Reload Extensions as described earlier in this chapter. The new category and object should now be visible in the Objects panel (as the following shows).

Using the Object

Now that the simple object exists, try inserting it into a document. Notice the closing `</sub>` tag wasn't included in the example file. You could have done this, but it isn't strictly necessary because Dreamweaver recognizes the `<sub>` tag when you insert it and automatically adds the ending tag, as seen in Figure 24-2.

Simple objects can be used for more than just inserting a single tag. They are also helpful when you repeatedly add the same elements to your pages, such as page headers or footers, or if you use the same plug-in again and again. You can create a simple object containing only that portion of HTML code.

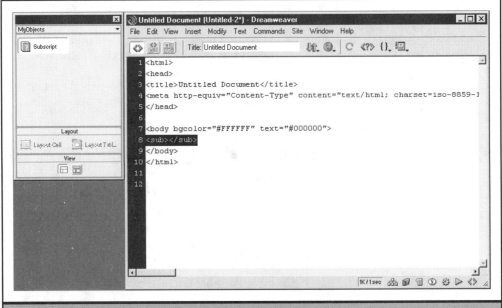

Figure 24-2. *Dreamweaver automatically adds a required end tag if your object doesn't include one*

More Complex Objects

The previous example was admittedly trivial, but no more trivial than the special character objects Dreamweaver provides. Still, you can easily add a little more functionality to the object by using a little JavaScript and a form for the object properties. Let's create another object that does more than the previous one. This object now lets you choose whether to create a subscript or a superscript, and enter the text that goes in the tag.

Create the Object

Unlike the simple object example, you need to make this object a fully formed HTML document. Again, you can use either the Dreamweaver editor or another editor to create the file. Dreamweaver may be the best choice in this case because you need to design a parameters dialog box form. This form is the only element that must be in the body of the document.

In the parameters dialog box, add two radio buttons: one to select Subscript and one to select Superscript. Also, add a text box that lets the user enter the text to subscript or superscript. Figure 24-3 shows the form in the Dreamweaver Document window.

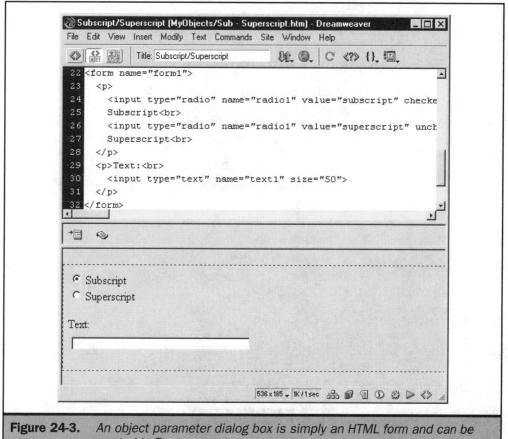

Figure 24-3. *An object parameter dialog box is simply an HTML form and can be created in Dreamweaver*

In addition to the form, you need to add a JavaScript function to the object document's <head>. This function reads the fields of the form and uses them to generate the text to insert for the object. The function to do this must be named objectTag().

```
<script language="JavaScript">
function objectTag()
{
  var szTag = "";
  if (document.form1.radio1[0].checked == true)
    szTag = "<sub>" + document.form1.text1.value + "</sub>";
  else
    szTag = "<sup>" + document.form1.text1.value + "</sup>";
```

```
    return szTag;
}
</script>
```

In this function, check the status of the first radio button (Subscript). If it's checked, a tag pair is returned, with the text from the form's text box inside. Because the radio buttons are grouped, if the first one isn't checked, the second one is. Therefore, the else case is to return a tag pair with the text from the form's text box inside.

After inserting the objectTag() function into your document (you can use the JavaScript object), your object is complete. Here's a complete listing:

```
<html>
<head>
<title>Subscript/Superscript</title>
<script language="JavaScript">
function objectTag()
{
  var szTag = "";
  if (document.form1.radio1[0].checked == true)
    szTag = "<sub>" + document.form1.text1.value + "</sub>";
  else
    szTag = "<sup>" + document.form1.text1.value + "</sup>";
  return szTag;
}
</script>
</head>
<body>
<form name="form1">
  <p>
    <input type="radio" name="radio1" value="subscript" checked>
    Subscript<br>
    <input type="radio" name="radio1" value="superscript" unchecked>
    Superscript<br>
  </p>
  <p>Text:<br>
    <input type="text" name="text1" size="50">
  </p>
</form>
</body>
</html>
```

Save the Object

As with the previous example, save this object to the MyObjects folder and restart Dreamweaver (or reload extensions). The object is now visible in the Objects panel.

Using the Object

When you click the object's button and you haven't turned off the Show Dialog when Inserting Objects in the General Preferences, the parameters dialog box for your custom object is displayed (as the following illustrates). Choose either Subscript or Superscript to generate the tag you want to use.

The Object API

The Object API is the set of JavaScript functions you can create in your object that Dreamweaver recognizes. None of them is required, as the simple object example demonstrates, but they can be used to enhance your objects.

- **displayHelp()**—If you use this function in your object, a Help button is added to the Parameters dialog box. This function is called when the user clicks the Help button. You typically use this to open an HTML file containing help for your object.

```
function displayHelp(){
    dreamweaver.browseDocument('myobjects_hlp.htm');
}
```

- **isDomRequired()**—If this function returns true or if this function isn't defined, Dreamweaver assumes a valid DOM is required. This causes Dreamweaver to synchronize the Code and Design views automatically.
- **objectTag()**—As seen in the example, this function is called to determine the text string to insert into the user's HTML document.

- **windowDimensions()**—This function can return the dimensions to use for the Parameters dialog box window. If this function isn't defined, the dimensions are then computed automatically using the dimensions of the form elements. The dimensions are returned in a string of the form "width_in_pixels,height_in_pixels". This function has a parameter, a string indicating either `windows` or `macintosh` depending on the user's platform.

```
function windowDimensions(platform){
  var szDimensions = ""
  if (platform == "windows"){
    szDims = "640, 400";
  }else{
    szDims = "660, 580";
  }
  return szDims;
}
```

How Dreamweaver Objects Work

When you insert a Dreamweaver object into your page, either by clicking it in the Objects panel or choosing it from the Insert menu, Dreamweaver takes the following steps:

1. The Object file is scanned for a `<form>` tag. The presence of this tag indicates a parameter dialog box should be created. If no form exists, or the Show Dialog When Inserting Objects option is unchecked in the General Preferences, steps 2 and 3 are skipped.

2. The file is scanned for a `windowDimensions()` function. If it exists, it's called to determine the dimensions of the dialog box to be created.

3. The parameters dialog box is displayed, and the user enters the parameters for the object, and then clicks OK.

4. The `objectTag()` function is called and the return value is used as the text to insert in the document.

Summary

One of Dreamweaver's easiest to use features is also one of its most powerful. The Objects panel consists of many standard objects, but if none of them meet your needs, creating custom objects is easy.

- Dreamweaver provides a large number of standard objects to make adding elements to your pages easier, without always having to remember the object's HTML syntax.

- The Objects panel is organized into categories. These categories correspond to subfolders in the Configuration/Objects folder.

- An object consists of an HTML file, along with a GIF file for the Objects Panel button. The HTML document implements functions from Dreamweaver's Object API and provides a form to use for the parameters dialog box.

In Part VI, you learn how you can use Dreamweaver to spruce up your pages by adding multimedia content such as video, sound, and Shockwave and Flash movies. You start with video, and then get instructions on how to insert and use the latest video formats.

The Complete Reference

Part VI

Enhancing Pages With Multimedia

The
Complete
Reference

Dreamweaver
4

Chapter 25

Adding Video

In recent years, video on the Web has finally started to live up to its promise. Now that broadband technologies such as DSL and cable modems are relatively cheap and growing in popularity, providing enough of a customer base to justify it, a significant number of Web sites have now adopted this technology. The number continues to grow.

However, recent studies have shown that people still aren't giving Web video high marks in terms of quality compared to traditional video sources, and for good reason. Much Web-based video, especially streaming video, is low resolution, blocky, and with a low frame rate. It's true: video on the Web still leaves a lot to be desired in comparison to even the cheapest TV set. Web video has one important advantage, however, that makes it worth the current limitations: instant access. You can go to a movie studio site and download and view a trailer for an upcoming film. You can go to your favorite news site and watch the top stories. You can even digitize home movies of the grandkids and put them on a Web site for relatives across the country to see instantly. These factors coupled with advancing technology ensure that Web video is here to stay and it's only going to get better.

Downloadable Video

The original method of putting video clips on the Web is still one of the most popular. Encode your video into one of the popular formats, place the resulting file on your site, and provide a link to it in your page. When visitors click the link, the file can be downloaded to their computers and either played in the browser if the proper plug-in is installed or saved to their hard drive for later viewing with a stand-alone player. If a plug-in is installed, the viewer could still choose to download the clip by right-clicking the link and choosing Save Target As (Internet Explorer) or Save Link As (Netscape Navigator). One reason to allow this is you may want to make it easier for viewers to save the file. Because they will specify the download directory, viewers can view the file again without having to return to your site.

Another option is to embed the file in a page directly as plug-in content. If the proper plug-in is installed, the video is played directly on your page. Depending on the player, the video typically either downloads completely before playing or downloads until enough is buffered to ensure seamless playback while the rest of the clip downloads. Sometimes this doesn't work, though, which causes the video to pause continually when playback reaches the end of the buffered data. When this works, however, it's great, especially on a high-speed connection. You gain many of the benefits of streaming video, combined with the typically higher video quality of downloaded video clips.

Linking or Embedding Video Clips with Dreamweaver

You can use Dreamweaver to ease the creation of either linked or embedded video content. To put a link to a video file in your page, do the following:

1. Place an image or text to serve as the link into your page.

2. Highlight the image or text.

3. Use the Property Inspector (see the following illustration) to browse to the file in the Link box or enter the filename complete with the path directly into the link box. You can also drag the Point to File icon from the Property Inspector to your video clip file in the Site window.

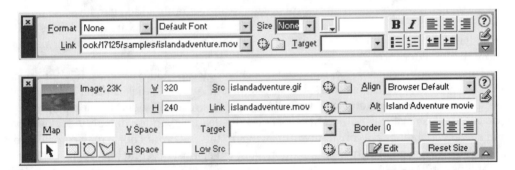

The other option is to embed the video in your page by using Dreamweaver's Plugin object. This gives you some flexibility because many plug-ins enable you to change aspects of playback using custom plug-in parameters. To embed a video clip, do the following:

1. Click the Insert Plugin button in the Special tab of the Objects panel. You can also drag-and-drop the Plugin icon to your document or choose Insert | Media | Plugin from the menu.

2. In the Select File dialog box, either enter the name of your file in the File Name box or browse to it using the folder list. When you choose Select, an <embed> tag is created referring to your content.

Plug-ins are covered in more detail in Chapter 22.

You may want to keep the embedded video from playing when the page loads. To do this, you usually need to specify a parameter for the particular plug-in you're using. For example, setting `autoplay=false` for QuickTime or `autostart=false` for RealPlayer keeps the video from playing until the Play button is pressed.

Note	*Dreamweaver has the capability to load Navigator plug-ins. This gives you the capability to play embedded videos directly in Dreamweaver's Design view to see how a video will look in your document. Simply select the object and click Play in the Property Inspector. You can also select View	Plugins	Play from the menu or use* CTRL-ALT-P *(*CMD-OPTION-P *on the Mac) to play and* CTRL-ALT-X *(*CMD-OPTION-X *on the Mac) to stop. See Chapter 22 for more information on this feature.*

Streaming Video

Streaming video has been gaining in popularity along with broadband Internet connections. With a fat pipe through which to download and video encoded with advanced compression algorithms, surprisingly high-quality video can be achieved. Today's generation of video encoding allows for smart video servers and players that can adjust the playback bit rate if the viewer's bandwidth changes, rather than skip and jerk like older formats.

Three major vendors of streaming video technology exist today. Microsoft's Windows Media Technologies, Real Network's RealSystem, and Apple's QuickTime all compete in the streaming video marketplace. Determining which streaming video vendor is right for you isn't an easy task. Stiff competition between the leading vendors means video quality and server capabilities are constantly improving. In the end, your choice may come down to a subjective image-quality determination weighed against other factors, such as server capabilities and cost.

To create streaming video, you need a video source, a video capture card or a digital input (depending on the capabilities of your source), and one of the video encoding software packages mentioned in the following.

Note	*Other books explore video content creation in much more detail than can be covered here. For example, check out* e-Video: Producing Internet Video as Broadband Technologies Converge, *by H. Peter Alesso (Addison-Wesley Professional), or* The Art of Digital Video, *by John Watkinson (Focal Press).*

Windows Media

Now, in version 7, Microsoft's Windows Media Technologies is a full-featured product that can stream *Active Server Format* (*ASF*) files. Microsoft's home for Media Technologies is **http://www.microsoft.com/windows/windowsmedia/**. A showcase of content available in this format is at **http://www.windowsmedia.com**.

- **Windows Media Player 7** counts a CD player, audio and video player, and an audio CD burner among its many features (see the following illustration). Media

Player 7 also provides a search capability to let you find media content on the Web. And it enables the user to customize its look and feel using skins. Media Player 7 is available on the Windows platform. At press time, a beta version is available for the Mac.

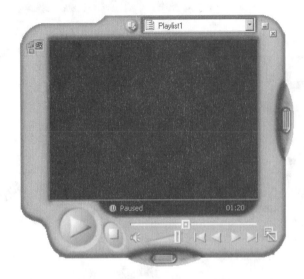

- **Windows Media Encoder 7** is Microsoft's latest content creation package. Media Encoder 7 is only available for the Windows platform (98/Me or NT/2000).

- **Windows Media Server** is a highly available streaming server for the Windows 2000 OS.

RealVideo

RealNetworks is one of the pioneers in streaming audio and video, and it's still going strong. Their RealVideo product is one of the most popular ways to view streaming video on the Web. Like Windows Media, there are three main components to Real's offering.

- **RealPlayer 8** is the player program for RealVideo and RealAudio. RealPlayer 8 Basic is the freely available player. Although the interface is busier than some of its competitors, it's a very functional player. RealPlayer 8 supports full-screen video, motion and still images, and Internet radio tuning, as well as Flash and streaming MP3. Windows and Mac versions of RealPlayer are available.

- **RealProducer 8** is a versatile video-encoding tool. It enables you to preview your content as it looks at various data rates and gives you the option of optimizing audio for voice or music. It supports two encoding formats—HTTP and SureStream—to take full advantage of RealSystemServer's streaming capabilities. RealProducer is available for both Windows and Mac systems.

- **RealSystem Server** is RealNetwork's server product, now in version 8. Available in three flavors, RealSystem Server Basic is free, but it's limited to 25 concurrent streams. This could be enough for many users. If you need more capability, you can purchase RealSystem Server Plus to support up to 60 users at a time. RealSystem Server Pro is also available for large webcasting organizations, with support for up to 400 simultaneous users. RealSystem Server is available for Windows NT/2000 and various UNIX platforms.

You can find more information on RealPlayer at **http://www.real.com,** *and information about the producing and server products at* **http://www.realnetworks.com.**

QuickTime

While Apple's QuickTime isn't as popular a solution as the competition when it comes to streaming video, it's still a potent package and may be ideal if you're in an all-Mac environment.

■ **QuickTime Player** provides support for video, sound, animation, and one of QuickTime's strong points: QuickTime VR. The latest version at press time is a preview release—QuickTime 5—and it's available at **http://www.apple.com/ quicktime/**. The new version improves on the look of QuickTime 4, and provides support for new features, such as skip protection and QuickTime Cubic VR. A 360 degree version of the popular QuickTime VR, Cubic VR enables you to have panoramic images you can view in any direction, as the second illustration shows.

- **QuickTime Pro** is built into QuickTime Player and is unlocked with a key when purchased. Pro gives you content creation and editing capabilities, and works with over 30 audio, video, and image formats, including Macromedia Flash. Versions of QuickTime Pro are available for both the Windows and Mac platforms.

- **QuickTime Server** The latest version of QuickTime Server is available for the Mac OS X platform, as well as for Windows NT/2000 and UNIX platforms. QuickTime Server supports *Real-Time Streaming Protocol* (*RTSP*) for true streaming capabilities, and it's the only one of the major streaming servers available for a Mac operating system. An interesting feature in an upcoming version, QuickTime Server 3, provides source code for the server to allow it to be ported or modified by the end user.

Apple publishes a popular book explaining the ins and outs of QuickTime. QuickTime for the Web: A Hands-On Guide for Webmasters, Site Designers, and HTML Authors, *by Stephen Guiles (Apple Computer, Inc.) even includes QuickTime Pro on the accompanying CD-ROM.*

WebCams

An idea that started with Netscape's Amazing Fish Cam among others in the early '90s, *WebCams* have been intriguing Web surfers ever since. The Amazing Fish Cam, located at **http://www.netscape.com/fishcam/** in all its aquatic splendor, is a WebCam pointed at a fish tank in the Netscape office. Netscape claims it was the second WebCam ever in existence (the first being the Trojan Room Coffee Pot, which even predates the Internet as we know it).

By the way, try CTRL-ALT-F *(Ctrl-Option-F on the Mac) in Netscape Navigator 4.0 through 4.75. There's a Fish Cam Easter egg.*

WebCams can be used to provide anything from a simple still picture updated every few minutes to full-blown live streaming video. Certainly more reasons exist to add a WebCam to your site than to let your visitors watch fish. They can be and have been used to promote restaurants, hotels, amusement parks, and any number of places where potential customers may like to visit virtually before they visit in person.

Setting Up a WebCam

Because of the modest hardware and server bandwidth required, the most common type of WebCam is the still picture variety. Still pictures are relatively easy to set up. The most important thing to have is a computer at the camera site that can maintain a connection to the Internet. A permanent connection such as DSL or a cable modem at the site is preferable. If you only have a dial-up connection available, you can only update the picture when that line is available to make the connection.

Of course, you need some sort of camera, either video or even a digital still camera. You also need to have some means of connecting the camera to your computer. A video capture board can be used to take snapshots from a video camera. Logitech (**http://www.logitech.com**) makes the popular QuickCam series of cameras designed for WebCam use.

A popular and recommended WebCam software package for Windows is Webcam32 from Surveyor Corporation at **http://www.surveyorcorp.com/**. This comprehensive package lets you set up snapshot and even streaming video WebCams.

*One site you may want to visit for information on setting up a WebCam is WebCam Developers at **http://developers.webcamworld.com/**. Check here for information on various WebCam hardware and software products.*

Once you have the hardware and software set up, and you're uploading files to your Web server, it's a simple matter to present the content to a visitor. Using Dreamweaver, add an image object that points to the uploaded file. You'll probably want to set the page to refresh automatically. You can do this by setting the refresh meta tag. Choose Insert | Head Tags | Refresh from the menu or choose Insert | Refresh from the Object panel. Set the Delay field to the same interval that snapshots are uploaded to your server. For the Action, choose Refresh This Document as shown in the next illustration.

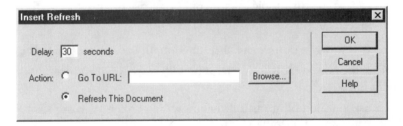

As an alternative to refreshing the entire page, you can use a Java applet, such as JavaCam, provided with the Surveyor Corporation Webcam32 package. This applet scan display the camera image and refresh without having to refresh the entire page. See **http://www.surveyorcorp.com/webcam32help/java.html** for details.

Sure You Can, But Should You?

All this video stuff sounds really neat and you think you want to give it a try. But just because you can, should you do it? It really depends on your site and the type of experience you want to provide for your visitors. Although broadband connections are becoming more commonplace, remember, many people still connect to the Internet with 56K or even 28.8K modems. At those speeds, streaming video becomes postage-stamp size and multimegabyte files take much longer to download than is usually practical. Another thing to remember is this: whether your site is small or large, streaming video quickly eats server bandwidth.

Another issue is context. Will your site truly gain value by including video? If your site is a photo gallery, you would probably be better off limiting yourself to static images. Yes, you can create a 3-D tour of your gallery, but you probably won't get much bang for your buck in terms of an enhanced user experience. Remember, just because something *can* move doesn't mean it *should* move.

A major consideration that's often overlooked on the Internet is copyright. George Lucas won't thank you for putting *Star Wars: Episode I* on your Web site. More likely, his lawyers will send you a harshly worded cease-and-desist letter. Even movie trailers are copyrighted and should only be used with permission. When choosing video content, think about originality. What can you show your visitors that sets your site apart from the others?

If the entire focus of your site is to showcase video technology or to provide tons of Webcast content then, by all means, you should do so. Remember, though, by always staying at the bleeding edge of technology, you're likely to alienate potential visitors who might not have the latest and the greatest. The focus of your site should be on the value it provides your visitors, so keep features in balance.

Summary

You should now understand the basic elements of creating and implementing video on your Web site. To explore this topic in more depth, please be sure to visit the Web sites listed throughout this chapter and obtain a copy of one or more of the books mentioned.

- Video is gaining in popularity and functionality as connect speeds increase.
- The most common tools for generating video are RealProducer 8 and Windows Media Encoder.
- The most common plug-ins for viewing video on the Web are RealPlayer, QuickTime, and Windows Media Player.
- Before adding video to your site, think about context, copyright, and your audience.

In Chapter 26, you learn about adding audio files to your site.

The Complete Reference

Chapter 26

Adding Sound

While adding resource-devouring video to a Web site may still be out of the question for smaller sites, audio files can be used by nearly everyone. In this chapter, you get an introduction to various sound formats for music—both downloadable and streaming—and how to incorporate them into your Web pages using Dreamweaver.

Sound File Formats

Sound files existed long before the Web. They've been around since the first home computers were capable of making sounds. Many sound formats were proprietary and died out when the systems for which they were designed became obsolete. Today, a few surviving formats have emerged victorious and have been adopted for use on the Web.

MIDI

The *Musical Instrument Digital Interface,* or *MIDI* format, was created in 1983 as a standard for electronic devices—such as synthesizers, drum machines, and computers—to interact and work in synchronization with each other. A master device, such as a synthesizer, can play back a MIDI track on every connected device, like a player piano for the digital age. MIDI files can either be generated from a music composition program or recorded from a live performance by linking with a MIDI-capable instrument. MIDI files only contain the information about how to create the music, not a recording of the music itself—much like the difference between sheet music and a recording of a performance. This makes the quality of the playback on a computer dependent on the capabilities of the computer's sound system. Some may produce an excellent synthesized sound from digitized instrument samples, but others, especially older systems, use a fairly low-quality synthesizer.

One reason MIDI files are so popular on the Web is the files are small and, therefore, quickly downloaded over slower dial-up connections. Sources for MIDI files on the Web are plentiful. MIDI.com, at **http://www.midi.com,** provides information on the MIDI standard, message boards, and hardware and software information, as well as a search engine for MIDI files. The files typically have a .mid extension.

 Before you put a MIDI file on your page, remember, compositions of popular songs are copyrighted, preventing their legal use even in MIDI format. Even if you don't have a composer at your beck and call, sources of original songs are on the Web. Many original MIDI files can be purchased or even, in some cases, used free.

Digital Waveform Formats

Digital audio files contain sampled data from an audio stream. They can be monophonic or stereo, generally with 8- or 16-bit resolution, and with sample rates that range from voice to CD quality.

A number of formats exist that provide uncompressed digital audio. The three most popular formats at this time are AU, WAV, and AIFF, corresponding to the top three popular platforms, UNIX, Windows, and Mac, respectively. As all three of these formats preceded their use on the Web, small file size simply wasn't as much of an issue. Users were delighted to be able to record sound snippets from their favorite TV shows and movies. The formats were (and, generally, still are, especially for Web use) unwieldy for anything larger than a few seconds of sound.

One of the advantages digital audio files have over MIDI files is they can be used for much more than music. Speech and any other sounds can be digitized just as easily. For Web use, you might want to provide an audio tutorial discussing your site, sound effects, or audio warnings. If you want to add a personal touch, you could record a voice greeting for your visitors. The possibilities are endless.

AU

One of the first formats used for putting digitized audio on the Internet, the *AU* format is a venerable one now showing its age. Created by Sun Microsystems, it is, not coincidently, a sound format widely used in Java applets.

WAV

Considering that Windows machines are far and away the predominant platform when it comes to Web use, it stands to reason that its audio standard, the *WAV* file, would become one of the most widely used audio formats. While the WAV standard can offer high-quality sound, it comes at a price. For a CD-quality stereo WAV file sampled at 44.1 KHz, at 16-bit resolution, just 30 seconds of audio consumes more than 5MB of disk space.

AIFF

The *Audio Interchange File Format* or (*AIFF*) is a standard created by Apple for the Mac. It's similar to WAV in that it provides an uncompressed bitstream at a variety of bit rates and resolutions. The AIFF-C format adds compression to the format, but isn't widely supported, especially in browser plug-ins.

MP3

Unless you've been living on Pulau Tiga for the past few years, you're well aware of the MP3 format. Few media technologies have been as controversial primarily, because so few have become so useful so quickly, in both legitimate and not-quite-so legitimate ways.

While the legality of much of the MP3 material on the Web may be questionable, the MP3 format is here to stay. As a subset of the MPEG-1 standard, *MP3* is an open standard now supported by all the major media players and plug-ins.

MP3 files, like WAV files, contain high-quality digitized audio. MP3 files, however, are highly compressed using advanced algorithms that attempt to minimize the loss of sound quality: the higher the compression rate, the lower the quality of the file. The usefulness of MP3 compression becomes apparent when compared with the original file. While a CD quality (44.1 KHz) stereo WAV file requires a bit rate of 1411 Kbps per second, an MP3 of similar quality can be transferred at a rate of 128 Kbps, easily within the capabilities of broadband connections. When using an MP3 on a Web page, CD quality isn't usually necessary, so the bit rate can be even lower.

Both Windows and the Mac have a wide variety of MP3 players available. MP3.com, the top MP3 information site on the Web, provides a comprehensive listing of players for Windows, Mac, and Linux at **http://software.mp3.com/software/guide/**. Popular players for Windows include WinAmp and Sonique. Mac users may want to look at MACAST, Audion, or SoundJamMP. The major media players including Windows Media Player, QuickTime, and RealPlayer all now also support the MP3 format.

Streaming Audio

Much as with video (see Chapter 25), one way to keep download times to a minimum for audio files is to use a streaming format such as RealAudio, Windows Media, or streaming MP3. Streaming audio isn't limited to files. A continuous audio source, such as a radio station, can be digitized and streamed over the Internet in real time. Visitors can listen in just as they would to a real radio station, joining and leaving in midstream.

RealAudio

The granddaddy of all streaming formats—RealNetwork's RealAudio—is still one of the most popular. *RealAudio* was originally designed when 28.8K modems were the speed champs, so obviously low bandwidth was one of the main design constraints.

RealAudio can be streamed using the RealSystem Server. In addition, the RealAudio files can be streamed from a Web site using HTTP.

Streaming MP3

A relative newcomer to the streaming audio scene, the *streaming MP3* format is fast becoming popular for high-bandwidth audio transmissions. The latest versions of the big three media plug-ins (Windows Media Player, RealPlayer, and QuickTime) all support the Streaming MP3 format, so expect it to become even more popular, especially for broadband users.

*Nullsoft's SHOUTcast, at **http://www.shoutcast.com**, is a service anyone can use to serve streaming MP3 audio that plays through the popular MP3 players WinAmp on Windows and Audion on the Macintosh. Thousands of streams are served up every day. You can also set up your own SHOUTcast server.*

Windows Media

At press time, Microsoft had just announced its new Windows Media Audio and Video 8 beta. The preliminary results are impressive: The sound quality is comparable to an

MP3 encoded at almost three times the bit rate. You can find more information about this product and other Microsoft Media Technologies at **http://www.microsoft.com/ windows/windowsmedia**.

Audio Players and Plug-ins

The browser decides which plug-in to use for a particular file by the MIME type of the file. Because media players like to assert themselves as the dominant player on a system, they often override a user's previous settings to the point where users don't even know which plug-in is the default for their files. Many of the plug-ins available for audio are the same ones also used for video.

QuickTime Player

The Apple QuickTime plug-in supports QuickTime animation, MIDI, audio, and video, as well as VR panoramas and objects directly in a Web page. The QuickTime plug-in's fast-start feature enables you to see content while it's downloading.

At press time, a preview version of QuickTime Player 5 for Windows and the Mac was available for download at **http://www.apple.com/quicktime**. Version 5 adds support for streaming MP3 and allows custom skins.

RealPlayer 8

While it doesn't have as stylish an interface as some of its competition, RealPlayer's strength is in its versatility. Version 8 now includes support for the ubiquitous streaming MP3 along with improved RealAudio performance. See **http://www.real.com** for more details on RealPlayer 8.

Windows Media Player 7

Microsoft's goal with *Media Player 7* was to provide a one-stop player that does nearly everything the user needs. This latest incarnation of Media Player supports downloadable and streaming content. Media Player 7 also supports playback of Microsoft's proprietary Window*s Media Format* (*WMF*), a compressed digital format that lets you record near CD quality sound at about half the size of an equivalent MP3 file.

The stand-alone player adds audio CD playback and recording, recording a CD to your hard drive, and transfer of media files to portable devices. You can customize the player with a wide variety of available skins that completely change the user interface.

Version 7 is available for Windows and PocketPC hand-held computers. At this time, Macintosh and Solaris versions are also available for beta testing.

WinAmp

NullSoft's *WinAmp* for Windows is a popular player that plays MP3 files, as well as streaming MP3 through SHOUTcast. A Full version is available that also plays

Windows Media audio and M-Juice audio. This was one of the original players to support skins and plug-ins. And one of the best features is all versions are free.

Embedding Music and Sounds

As with video, you can use two basic methods to include audio files on a Web page: providing a link and embedding the file into your page with the help of a plug-in. Here's a description of how to accomplish both with Dreamweaver.

Linking to an Audio File

The simplest way of presenting an audio file on a Web page is simply to provide a link to it. Using Dreamweaver to link to a sound file works the same way as creating other links. Highlight the image or text you want to turn into a link and, in the Property Inspector, either type the path and filename in the Link field or browse to the file using the folder icon. See Figure 26-1 for an example.

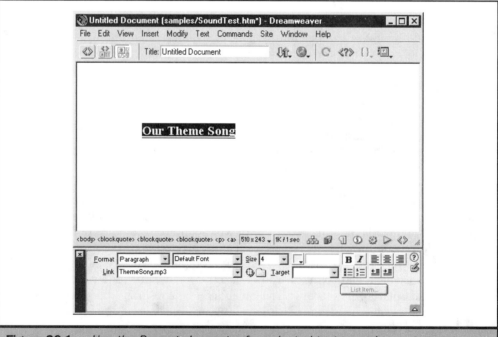

Figure 26-1. *Use the Property Inspector for selected text or an image to create a link to an audio file*

ENHANCING PAGES
WITH MULTIMEDIA

Embedding Audio Files

To play audio files directly in a page without requiring a visitor to click a link, you must *embed* the audio file. The other option is to embed the video in your page by using Dreamweaver's Plugin object. This gives you some flexibility because many plug-ins enable you to change aspects of playback using custom plug-in parameters. To embed an audio clip, do the following:

1. Click the Insert Plugin button in the Special tab of the Objects panel (see Figure 26-2). You can also drag-and-drop the Plugin icon to your document, or choose Insert | Media | Plugin from the menu.

2. In the Select File dialog box, either enter the name of your file in the File Name box or browse to it using the folder list. When you choose Select, an <embed> tag is created, referring to your content.

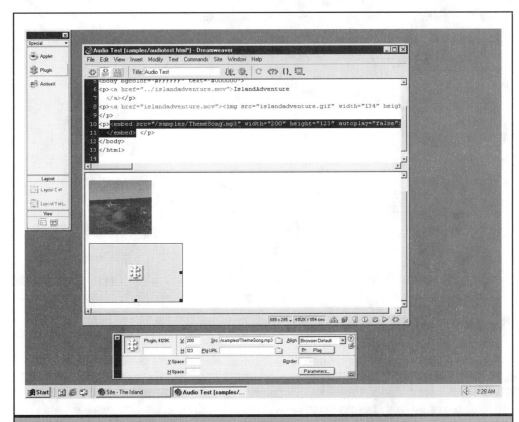

Figure 26-2.   *You can click or drag the Plugin icon from the Objects panel to embed an audio file*

If your plug-in is an ActiveX control—like Windows Media Player—you can add it by inserting the ActiveX object instead.

1. Like the Plugin object, you can click the ActiveX button in the Special tab of the Objects panel, drag-and-drop the ActiveX icon to your document, or choose Insert | Media | ActiveX from the menu. Dreamweaver also automatically creates an <embed> tag nested inside the object to let you add an equivalent Netscape plug-in if one is available.

2. To specify that your ActiveX object is the Media Player, you need to add the Media Player ClassID in the property inspector. Insert this string in its entirety: CLSID:22D6F312-B0F6-11D0-94AB-0080C74C7E95, or choose it from the drop-down arrow in the ClassID box if you've used this ID before.

3. Open the Parameters dialog box by clicking the Parameters button in the Property Inspector. Add the parameter `FileName` with a value indicating the path and filename of your Windows Media file.

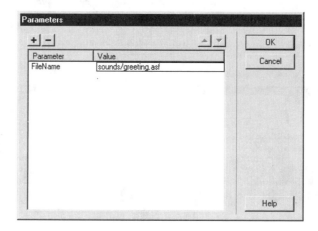

For a more information about plug-ins, ActiveX objects, and setting parameters, see Chapter 22.

Setting Plug-in Parameters

Once an audio plug-in or an ActiveX control is embedded on your Web page, you can use custom parameters to adjust the look and feel of its control panel and presentation. All audio plug-ins allow additional parameters to control various features. The Parameters button on the Properties Inspector activates the Parameters dialog box, which lets you specify these custom parameters. Any special parameters your plug-in can use may be entered here, and they are then added to the <embed> tag as attributes (or to an ActiveX <object> tag as PARAM attributes).

Each plug-in typically has its own parameters for playback. Remember, if you only specify a MIME type attribute for your plug-in object, the browser simply uses whichever application is registered to handle that type. The registered plug-in might not be the one your visitor has installed. This means you can't guarantee a particular parameter will work with the plug-in your visitor happens to be using.

For instance, the Media Player object uses the showcontrols and showdisplay parameters to hide or make the control visible, while QuickTime and RealAudio plug-ins use the hidden parameter. For another example, both Windows Media and RealAudio plug-ins use the autostart parameter to specify whether the file should automatically play when the page is loaded, but QuickTime uses autoplay. To be sure a specific plug-in uses the proper parameter, include them both. The plug-in should ignore parameters it doesn't recognize.

Sound Creation Tools

So, what tools can you use to create amazing sound content for your Web sites? Plenty of popular software tools can help you. Here are a few of the more popular packages:

Sonic Foundry

Sonic Foundry produces a number of professional audio tools for Windows. *Sound Forge* is a powerful sound editing package that lets you cut-and-paste sounds, add special effects, or even apply time compression to a sound clip without the pitch. *ACID Music* is a tool for creating original royalty-free music, which enables you to "paint" music using its library of over 600 loops in a multitude of genres. *Stream Anywhere* lets you create streaming content for either Windows Media or RealSystem Server. You can find more information about Sonic Foundry products at **http://www.sonicfoundry.com**.

Syntrillium Software

Syntrillium Software is the maker of popular, cost-effective tools for Windows. *CoolEdit 2000* (Figure 26-3) lets you record, play, edit, and convert files in many different formats, including MP3 and RealAudio. You can apply special effects or use noise reduction to clean up your files. CoolEdit 2000 even supports plug-ins to enhance its capabilities. CoolEdit Pro adds 64-track mixing capabilities, MIDI time code synchronization, and a host of other features for audio professionals. Demos of these products can be downloaded from Syntrillium's home page at **http://www.syntrillium.com**.

Beatnik

Unlike other plug-ins that merely play files or streaming audio, the *Beatnik* plug-in is designed to add interactive sound to a Web page. The files Beatnik is capable of playing are its own proprietary *Rich Music Format* (*RMF*) files, which consist of digital audio and MIDI data supercompressed for rapid download. The Beatnik Editor

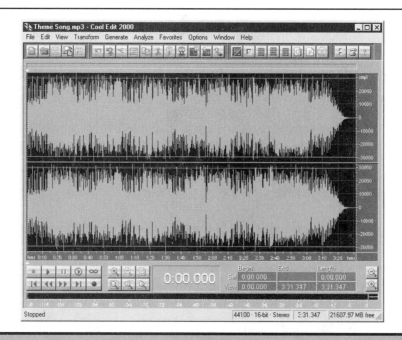

Figure 26-3. *Syntrillium Software's CoolEdit 2000 is an advanced sound file editor that can even work with MP3 files*

(Figure 26-4), available for both the Mac and Windows, lets you combine MP3, WAV, MIDI and other sound formats into RMF files for use in your Web pages. You can control RMF file playback interactively using JavaScript in Web browsers or with Lingo in Shockwave movies. You can add musical cues to smooth transitions between pages or sound effects that react to mouseovers, clicks, or other events. See **http://www.beatnik.com** for more details or to download a trial version.

 Beatnik is especially useful with Dreamweaver. The Beatnik ActionSet Pro *is a collection of 48 Dreamweaver behaviors that make it easy to add interactive sound to your pages or to sonify it, to use Beatnik's terminology.*

Caveats

Once upon a time, in the far distant Internet past (the early '90s), the Web was silent. One day, someone came up with a way to embed a music file into a Web page so it automatically played when the page was loaded. This most likely was an awful amateur MIDI file, and that person's mailbox must have overflowed with complaints from unsuspecting surfers.

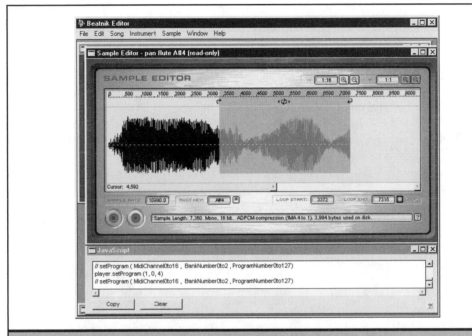

Figure 26-4. *Beatnik's editor enables you to combine digital clips and MIDI files to create impressive Web content*

That totally fictitious anecdote points out something you should seriously consider before adding audio content to your pages. Few things are more annoying than to stumble on to a site that's playing a rather obnoxious, endlessly repeating MIDI file in the background. You don't want to force potential visitors to turn off their sound every time they visit your site. They will simply stop visiting instead. If you simply must have a particular song playing on your site, you should always make it optional by embedding the plug-in's control panel into your page and requiring the visitor to press the Play button, rather than having it start automatically.

Another point to consider is a large number of Web users are simply incapable or unwilling to play sound at all. Corporations don't always give sound cards and speakers to all their employees, some visitors may be hearing impaired, and a vast majority just don't want to use sound on the Web. Personally, I usually have a CD playing in my CD-ROM throughout the day. If an embedded audio file is going to try to take control of my speakers, it better have a good reason. Keep the use of music and sound files judiciously restrained, and never make sound capabilities a required part of your site navigation.

When you make the decision to include audio on your site, consider the context of your pages and choose your music accordingly. Including a snippet of "Only the Good

Die Young" on a mortuary site might be mildly amusing, but your visitors are likely to consider it highly inappropriate. Similarly, if the theme of your site is very Gen-X, with lots of bright color and movement, the mood will be considerably changed by a Gregorian chant in the background.

> **Note** *These issues aren't limited to audio files you may intentionally include on your site. Many popular Web bulletin board systems have an option to let users include HTML tags. All it takes is one person to embed a link to a WAV file in his signature for your site to be flooded with complaints. If you're managing a Web-based message board with these features, consider disabling such options.*

Summary

Adding audio is an easy, inexpensive way to enhance your site. With the wide variety of audio formats, players, and sound creation tools, you can turn your site into an aural as well as a visual experience.

- The most popular file formats for audio are MIDI, MP3, and WAV. Additional formats include AIFF and AU.

- You can link to an audio file, using a standalone player to control the audio experience.

- You can embed a player into your pages, either hiding the controls or allowing the user to control the audio experience from your site.

- As with video, you should consider the context, audience, and copyright issues before adding audio files to your site.

In the next chapter, we discuss Flash and Shockwave.

The Complete Reference

Dreamweaver 4

Incorporating Flash and Shockwave

Flash and Shockwave movies are among the most popular ways to add interactive animated content to Web pages. Both products have been around for several years, gaining a large following among designers and users alike.

Flash provides a vector graphics format that's popular for creating custom animated controls, splash screens, cartoons, and other interactive elements for a page. It's optimized for use on the Web, producing tiny files that can be incorporated into many sites. *Shockwave* is a versatile interactive multimedia format with audio, video, animation, and text, and is used to create everything from custom interfaces to movies and even games.

As you might expect, considering Director and Flash are both Macromedia products, Dreamweaver makes adding Flash and Shockwave content to your pages easy with built-in objects that simplify setting all the basic properties.

Flash Basics

Macromedia Flash creates animated movies for Web sites. Flash movies consist of graphics created with Flash, as well as imported bitmap graphics and sounds. You can use Flash to create "flashy" buttons and text, animated logos, or even complete Web sites. The interactivity Flash provides with its event-driven ActionScript language enables viewers to move objects, jump to different points in the movie, and many other possible scriptable actions.

One advantage Flash movies have over other animated content is they consist mainly of vector graphics. *Vector graphics* consist of images created by specifying the positions of connected line segments and curves, as well as color information. This allows for small files—with the cost being a somewhat sparse, cartoony look.

Flash movie files (those with a .swf extension) are played back with the Flash Player, which is available as a plug-in for Netscape Navigator and an ActiveX component for Internet Explorer for Windows. The .swf extension is included with the latest versions of each browser. The wide browser support and small file size make adding interactive content possible to any Web site with only a little imagination.

Note *If you want to learn how to create Flash movies, there are a number of good books on the subject.* Foundation Flash 5, *by Patrick Rey, Amanda Farr, and Sham Bhangal (Friends of Ed) provides a solid introduction to Flash using a Web site case study.* Flash 5 for Windows and Macintosh: Visual QuickStart Guide, *by Katherine Ulrich (Peachpit Press) is a Flash edition of this popular introductory series.*

Inserting Flash Movies

Flash movie files can be played back on Web pages or in Dreamweaver using its plug-in playback capability. You must, however, have Macromedia Flash to create or edit Flash movies.

To insert a Flash movie into your document using Dreamweaver, do the following:

1. Choose Insert I Media I Flash from the menu. Or, you can click the Insert Flash icon on the Common tab of the Objects panel or drag the icon to your document. This brings up the Select File dialog box.

2. In the Select File dialog box, select a Flash movie file (with a .swf extension). A Flash object is then created in your document.

> **Tip**
>
> *You can preview Flash movies on a page in the same way as with audio and video plug-ins. Select a Flash object and either click Play in the Property Inspector, select View I Plugins I Play from the menu, or use* CTRL-ALT-P *(CMD-OPT-P on the Mac). You can also choose to play all plug-in content on a page including Flash by choosing View I Plugins I Play All from the menu, or use the* CTRL-ALT-SHIFT-P *(CMD-OPT-SHIFT-P on the Mac) keyboard shortcut. To stop Flash movies from playing, either click the Stop button in the Property Inspector or select View I Plugins I Stop or View I Plugins I Stop All from the menu. The respective keyboard shortcuts are* CTRL-ALT-X *(CMD-OPT-X) to stop one plug-in and* CTRL-ALT-SHIFT-X *(CMD-SHIFT-OPT-X) to stop all plug-ins.*

When you insert a Flash movie into your document, Dreamweaver uses both the <object> tag for the Flash Internet Explorer ActiveX control and the <embed> tag for the Netscape Flash plug-in to get the best results in both browsers. Note, Dreamweaver also sets a <codebase> attribute parameter for the ActiveX control that tells Internet Explorer where to download it automatically.

Specifying Properties for Flash Movies

Once you insert a Flash movie into your page, use the Property Inspector to set the most common properties. A list of the properties you can set for Flash movies (including Flash Buttons and Flash Text, discussed later) follows.

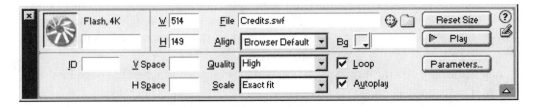

■ The **Name** field specifies a value to use for the HTML name attribute. This enables you to identify the movie to control it from JavaScript. While the Name attribute has been replaced by the ID attribute in the HTML 4.0 specification, some older browsers still require the Name attribute. To ensure cross-browser compatibility, providing both Name and ID attributes is best.

- The **W** and **H** fields specify the width and height of the object in pixels. You can also use unit modifiers to specify the size in alternative units: pc (picas), pt (points), in (inches), mm (millimeters), and cm (centimeters), or % for a percentage of the parent object's width and height.

- **File** specifies a path to the Flash .swf file. You can either enter the path directly or browse to a file using the Browse button.

- **Reset Size** returns the selected movie to its original size.

- **Align** sets how the object is aligned on the page. The various alignment options are covered elsewhere in this book.

- The **Bg** field is where you can set a background color. This is the color that appears when the movie isn't playing. Choose a color from the color picker or enter the hexadecimal RGB values directly.

- **ID** is used to set the ID attribute, which is used as a unique object identifier in the document. This attribute is the preferred way of identifying elements as of HTML 4.0, but, in some cases, some older browsers still require the Name attribute. The easiest solution is to use both and set them to the same value.

- **V** and **H Space** enable you to specify the amount of blank space to put around the object. The spacing must be specified in pixels.

- **Quality** specifies the rendering quality the plug-in uses in playing a movie. Possible values are Low, High, Auto Low, and Auto High. This determines how movies are to be handled on computers with slower processors. Specifying High quality produces the best results, but your visitors need a faster processor to play the movie back correctly. A good choice to use is Auto High, which attempts to produce the best possible playback, but scales back to lower quality rendering if it finds the computer is unable to keep up with the demands of the movie. Low gives the lowest visual quality, while Auto Low starts with a lower quality, but increases the quality if it determines the CPU is capable of handling it.

- **Scale** specifies a scale setting for the plug-in. The possible values relate to how the Flash movie should be displayed in a box with different dimensions than the movie itself. A thorough description of how the various scale settings work is provided later in this chapter.

- **Autoplay** sets the movie to start playing automatically when the page loads.

- **Loop** makes the movie loop indefinitely.

- The **Parameters** button opens the Parameters dialog box for entering additional parameters to pass to the movie. See Chapter 22 for more information on setting parameters for plug-in objects. Note, the movie you create must support these additional parameters.

Resizing and Scaling Flash Movies

Because Flash movies are vector-based, you can resize and scale them without sacrificing image quality. Flash movies have an *aspect ratio*, the ratio of the width to the height. You can get the width and the height of a movie in Flash, using the Movie Properties dialog box.

In most cases, you'll want to keep the aspect ratio of the Flash object the same as that of the movie. If the Flash object in your document has a different aspect ratio than the source movie, however, the player needs to be told how to display the movie. This is done through the Scale field in the Flash Property Inspector. The next illustration shows the effect the various options for the Scale field.

- **Default (show all)** scales the movie so it's as large as possible in the window without altering the aspect ratio. If the aspect ratio of the viewing window is wider or taller than the movie, the background color is then shown in the rest of the box.

- **No Border** specifies the movie should be expanded so it completely fills the window. The movie isn't stretched in any direction, so any part that exceeds the dimensions of the box will be cropped. This means if the aspect ratio of the movie is taller than the aspect ratio of the viewing window, the top and bottom of the movie will be cropped. Likewise, if the aspect ratio of the movie is wider than that of the viewing window, the left and right sides of the movie are then cropped.

- **Exact Fit** specifies the movie should fill the entire window. To do this, the movie is stretched asymmetrically (in different amounts horizontally and vertically).

If you want to resize the movie after the aspect ratio is set, hold the Shift key down while dragging the resize handles in the design view. The aspect ratio of your movie will be retained.

Flash Generator

Macromedia Generator files are templates that enable you to modify or replace information in a Flash movie. Dreamweaver has a built-in version of Generator that can be used to create custom Flash movies using some standard templates. Dreamweaver includes templates for Flash Button and Flash Text objects to enable you to create them as custom Flash movies with your own text or links. You can extend this functionality by using the Generator authoring templates for Flash to create new types of buttons.

Flash Buttons

Dreamweaver provides a quick-and-easy way to create Flash-based buttons using a set of button templates. In addition to the templates provided when you install Dreamweaver, you can find additional buttons at the Macromedia Exchange for Dreamweaver at **http://www.macromedia.com/exchange/dreamweaver/**.

Follow these steps to insert a Flash Button object into your document:

1. Choose Insert | Interactive Images | Flash Button from the menu. Or, you can click the Flash Button icon on the Common tab of the Objects panel or drag the icon to your document. This brings up the Insert Flash Text dialog box.

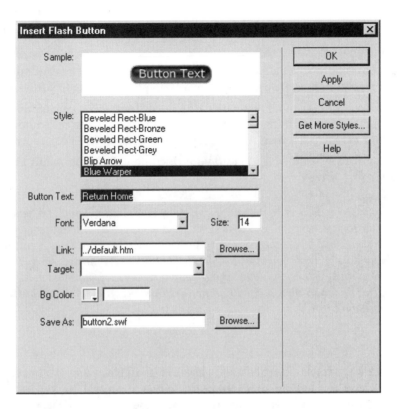

2. Select the button style you want from the Style list. The Sample field shows you what the selected button will look like when you move the mouse over or click the button. But, remember, the button text doesn't update in response to changes in the Button Text field.

3. Enter the text you want to appear on the button in the Button Text field. You can leave this blank if you don't want the button to have text.

4. Choose Font and Size for the font in the respectively labeled fields. If you want to see how the text looks rendered in that font, you can click Apply to see the button in your document.

5. You can make the text a link by entering it in the Link field. You can browse for a document to link to using the Browse button. The Browse dialog box enables you to specify a document relative to the current document or relative to the site root.

6. Select a frame or window as the target for a link by choosing it in the Target drop-down list.

7. Select a color for the background color using the color picker button or by directly entering an RGB value in hexadecimal into the Bg Color field.

8. The Save As field contains the filename to use for the object. You can change this filename to anything you like, but be sure to save it in the same directory as your HTML document to make any document relative links work correctly.

9. Click OK to insert the button into your document. Clicking Apply inserts the button, but leave the dialog box open for further editing.

Tip *Although Dreamweaver comes with a variety of Flash button templates, you might find they don't fit your needs. If you have Flash, you can use it to create your own button styles and export them as Generator templates for use in Dreamweaver. To create custom buttons, you must use the Generator InsertText authoring extension. Download these extensions and find out more information from Macromedia at http://www.macromedia.com/support/dreamweaver/assets/flashbutton/ flashbutton.html.*

Flash Text

Dreamweaver's Flash text object lets you generate small Flash movies that contain nothing but text. These simple text objects enable you to control the font, size, color, and a color to use for a rollover. The biggest benefit these text-only Flash movies provide is the capability to use a nonstandard font without expecting a viewer to have it. As with Flash Buttons, you can reuse the same object on multiple pages—or even on the same page—by simply cutting-and-pasting the object to each page. The text is embedded using the font's vector information rather than using the font itself, so your visitor needn't have the font installed to view the text. You can also resize the text by simply dragging the resize box in the Design view (See Figure 27-1). One possible disadvantage can be that the font style and color cannot be controlled using style sheets. Then you have to edit the Flash Text objects separately.

To insert a Flash text object, follow these steps:

1. Choose Insert | Interactive Images | Flash Text from the menu. Or, you can click the Flash Text icon on the Common tab of the Objects panel, or drag the icon to your document. This brings up the Insert Flash Text dialog box.

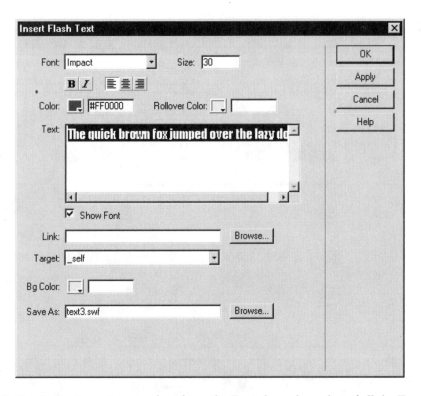

2. In the dialog box, choose a font from the Font drop-down list of all the TrueType fonts on your system.

3. Enter a point size to use in the Size box.

4. Choose the style attributes you want to apply by clicking the Bold or Italic buttons. You can also choose to justify the text to the left (default), center, or right.

5. Select a color using the color picker button or by directly entering an RGB value in hexadecimal into the Color field. In the rollover field, do the same thing to select a color to use when the mouse pointer rolls over the object.

6. Enter your text in the Text field. The text is displayed in your selected font if you have the Show Font box checked.

7. You can make the text a link by entering it in the Link field. You can browse for a document to link to using the Browse button. The Browse dialog enables you to specify a document relative to the current document or relative to the site root.

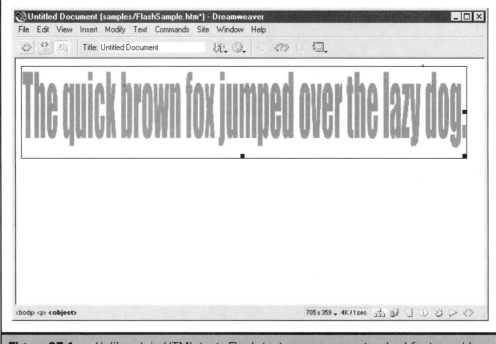

Figure 27-1. *Unlike plain HTML text, Flash text can use nonstandard fonts and be scaled in unusual ways*

8. Select a frame or window as the target for a link by choosing it in the Target drop-down menu.

9. Use the Bg Color field to set the background color in the same way you selected the other colors. Choose from the color picker or enter the RGB hexadecimal values directly.

10. The Save As field contains the filename to use for the object. You can change this filename to anything you like, but be sure to save it in the same directory as your HTML document to make any document relative links work correctly.

11. Click OK to insert the text into your document. Clicking Apply inserts the text, but leave the Insert Flash Text dialog box open.

Once your Flash Text object is created, you can modify it using the Property Inspector in the same manner as other Flash objects.

Tip   *If you use the Flash Text feature with the same font and colors often, you might grow tired of reselecting the same colors and fonts over and over because Dreamweaver doesn't remember your last selection. You can solve this by taking advantage of the fact that Dreamweaver uses HTML templates to create its dialog boxes. Load the file* `Dreamweaver 4\Configuration\Commands\Flash Text.htm` *into Dreamweaver and alter the default value in the color box, as shown in Figure 27-2. Changing the default font is a bit more of a challenge, and you have to understand JavaScript. You need to edit the* `Flash Text.js` *file, which contains the JavaScript behavior for the dialog box. Enter the following lines right after the MENU_FONTS.setAll() call in the initializeUI method, with the font name you want to use as the value of the Font variable.*

```
MENU_FONTS.setAll(fontArray,fontArray);
  var theFont = "Impact";
  if (!MENU_FONTS.pickValue(theFont))
  {
    if (!confirm(errMsg(MSG_FontDoesNotExist,theFont)))
      window.close();
  }
```

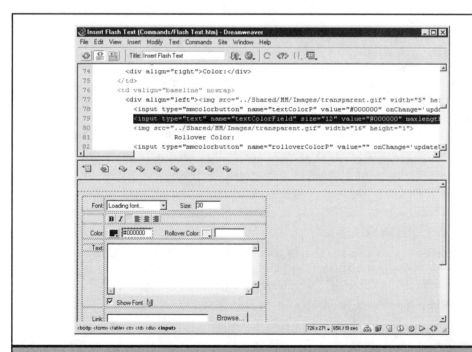

Figure 27-2.   *You can take advantage of Dreamweaver's HTML dialog templates to change default values of the Insert Flash Text dialog box*

DON'T do this if you don't know what you are doing—and always make a backup of any Dreamweaver file before you change it.

Shockwave Basics

Shockwave movies are created by Macromedia Director Studio and are one of the leading ways of creating rich interactive media content for the Web. Now in version 8, Shockwave has been a de facto standard since 1995. The majority of people on the Web today have Shockwave players installed.

 *To see what Shockwave is capable of, visit the Macromedia sponsored Shockwave.com at **http://www.shockwave.com**. You'll find cartoons, music, puzzles, and games here that put Shockwave through its paces.*

Adding Shockwave Movies to Your Pages

Dreamweaver's Shockwave object makes adding a Shockwave movie to your Web site simple. Like Flash movies, Shockwave files can be played back in Dreamweaver using its plug-in playback capability. You must, however, have Macromedia Director to create Shockwave content.

To use Dreamweaver's Shockwave object to insert a Shockwave movie into your document, follow these steps:

1. Choose Insert | Media | Shockwave from the menu. Or, you can click the Insert Shockwave icon on the Common tab of the Objects panel, or drag the icon to your document. This brings up the Select File dialog box.

2. In the Select File dialog box, select a Shockwave movie file (with a .dcr extension). A Shockwave object is then created in your document.

3. Enter the width and height of the movie in the W and H boxes of the Property Inspector.

Shockwave Properties

You don't have as many options to set for the Shockwave object, primarily because Shockwave movies aren't scalable. The height and width must be the actual values of the movie as created in Director. The following illustration shows the Shockwave Property Inspector window.

ENHANCING PAGES
WITH MULTIMEDIA

- The **Name** field specifies a value to use for the HTML name attribute. This enables you to identify the movie from JavaScript.

- The **W** and **H** fields specify the width and height of the object in pixels. You can also use unit modifiers to specify the size in alternative units: pc (picas), pt (points), in (inches), mm (millimeters), and cm (centimeters), or % for a percentage of the parent object's width and height.

- **File** specifies a path to the Shockwave .dcr file. You can either enter the path directly or browse to a file using the Browse button.

- **Align** sets how the object will be aligned on the page. The various alignment options are covered elsewhere in this book.

- **Bg** lets you specify a background color. This is the color that appears when the movie isn't playing. Choose a color from the color picker, or enter the hexadecimal RGB values directly.

- **ID** is used to set the ID attribute, which is used as a unique object identifier in the document.

- **V** and **H Space** let you specify the amount of blank space to put around the object. The spacing must be specified in pixels.

- The **Parameters** button opens the Parameters dialog box for entering additional parameters to pass to the movie. The movie must support these extra parameters.

- **Play** lets you preview the movie, just as with Flash objects.

Summary

This chapter has provided an overview of how to use Dreamweaver to include Flash and Shockwave content on your pages.

- Flash is a compact, fast-loading vector graphics-based format that can be used to include interactive animated content.

■ Shockwave is a versatile format that can be used to create rich multimedia movies, games, and puzzles.

■ Flash Text and Flash Buttons enable you to add Flash elements to your site quickly without any knowledge of—and without owning—Flash.

Part VII covers the tools Dreamweaver provides to simplify redundant tasks and aid in consistency throughout your site. Let's start with a look at the Assets panel.

The Complete Reference

Part VII

Dreamweaver Tools

The
Complete
Reference

Chapter 28

The Assets Panel

hen the Web began, sites were a sea of text on a dull gray background. These days, it's a little more complicated. Web design and development often mean keeping track of large numbers of templates, images, links, color choices, Flash and Shockwave movies, multimedia, and more.

In those early days, keeping all the assets of your site in one folder was easy. Now, large Web sites with many pages of content can have assets in multiple locations, and keeping track of all the assets that make up your site can be difficult. Because you're using Dreamweaver, though, the Site Assets panel can come to the rescue. This panel provides an easy way to access the various assets that make up your site.

The Assets Panel

Dreamweaver's *Assets* panel, new in Version 4, is a tool to simplify the job of finding and using your site's assets. The Assets panel is shown in the following Figure 28-1.

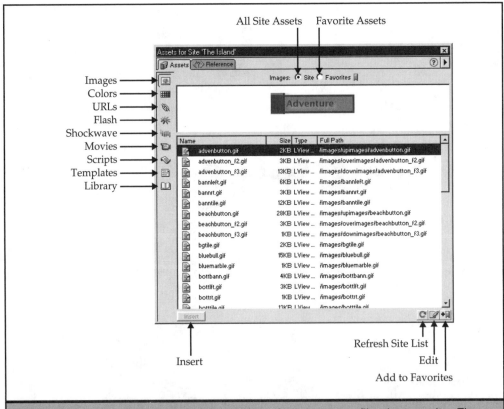

Figure 28-1. *The Assets panel builds a list of all the asset files in your site. The Site view, which lists all files of a particular category, is shown here*

When activated, this panel goes through your site's folders and builds a list of all the asset files. To open the Assets panel, either select the Window | Assets menu item, or press F11.

The Assets panel listing is a complement to the Site window's directory tree that shows all the files on your site at once (see Chapter 6 for more information on using the Site window). Instead, the Assets panel only shows the files for one type of asset at a time and, instead of the Site window's tree view of the directory structure, it shows all the assets in a single list. In addition, the Assets panel lets you see your assets in a preview pane to ensure you choose the right object from the list.

Refreshing and Re-creating the Site List

The first time you open the Assets panel for a site, it scans for assets to build a site assets list. From then on, new assets created outside the Assets panel are not added to the list unless you refresh the Site list. To refresh the Site list, do the following:

1. Make sure the site list is showing by clicking the Site button at the top of the panel.

2. Click the Refresh Site List button at the bottom of the panel (shown in Figure 28-1). Or, you can RIGHT-CLICK (CTRL-CLICK on the Mac) anywhere in the asset list and choose Refresh Site List from the context menu.

| **Note** | *Refreshing the site list doesn't remove any assets that may have been modified from outside Dreamweaver. For instance, if you delete image files using the Windows Explorer, they're still shown in the Assets panel. To make these assets disappear, you need to re-create the site assets list. This is yet another reason why you should only maintain your local site directory within the Dreamweaver application.* |

Re-creating the site list makes Dreamweaver remove all the entries from the Site list, and then scan the site to rebuild the list from scratch. To do this, you must hold the Control key down (Command key on the Mac) when you click the Refresh Site List button. You can also access the context menu by RIGHT-CLICKING (CONTROL-CLICK on the Mac) in the assets list and choosing Re-create Site List.

Site and Favorites Lists

The Assets panel can be used to view assets in two different ways. The site list provides a list of all the assets in your site's folders. The favorites list, on the other hand, only displays the assets you choose to put there. These two lists make finding the assets you commonly use easier, while still providing convenient access to those you may use less frequently. Choose the list you want to view by clicking either the Site or Favorites radio button at the top of the panel.

To add one or more assets to the favorites list, select them in the site list. Click the Add to Favorites button at the bottom right of the panel (shown in Figure 28-1). As an alternative, you can right-click (CTRL-click on the Mac) the selected elements and choose Add to Favorites from the context menu. This context menu item is also available for supported files in the Site window (accessed with Window | Site Files, or F8).

Even when you refresh or re-create the site list, assets aren't removed from the favorites list until you remove them explicitly. To remove an asset from the favorites list, select it, and then click the Remove From Favorites button (shown in Figure 28-2), or press BACKSPACE or DELETE. You may also use the context menu—right-click (CTRL-click on the Mac) on the asset you want to remove from the favorites list to access, and choose Remove From Favorites.

Note   *Removing an asset from the favorites list doesn't delete the asset. It's still accessible from the site list.*

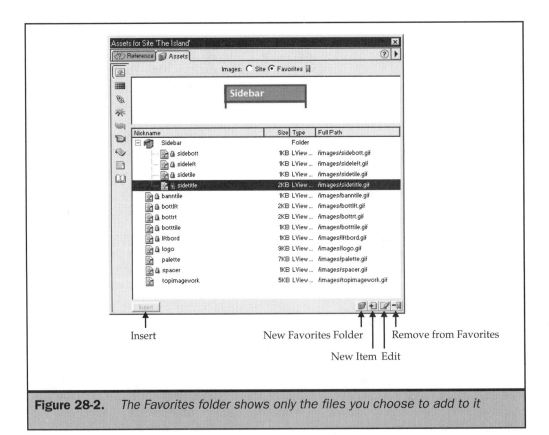

Figure 28-2.   *The Favorites folder shows only the files you choose to add to it*

Nicknames

One of the handy things the favorites menu lets you do is to assign a nickname to an asset. This nickname is displayed instead of the value or filename in the Nickname column of the favorites list. The value or filename is still displayed in the Value or Full Path columns. To add a nickname, do one of the following:

- Right-click (CTRL-click on the Mac) on the asset in the favorites list, and choose Edit Nickname from the context menu. Enter the nickname and press ENTER (RETURN on the Mac).

- Click the asset, pause for a second, and then click it again. Be certain to pause, as you want to click twice rather than double-clicking. Enter the nickname and press ENTER (RETURN on the Mac).

Organizing Assets Using Favorites Folders

An advantage the Favorites list has over the site list is it enables you to organize assets into groups called favorites folders. Favorites folders can be useful for organizing and quickly locating images you want to use together on your pages. For example, Figure 28-2 shows a favorites folder containing a group of images used to create a sidebar.

Note *The capability to group assets into favorites folders is only for convenience when using the favorites list in the Assets panel. The actual location of the files in your site hierarchy doesn't change when you place them in a favorites folder.*

To create a favorites folder, do the following:

1. Open the Assets panel and select the favorites list.
2. Click the New Favorites Folder button, as shown in Figure 28-2.
3. Type in the name for the new folder.
4. Drag assets from the favorites list into the folder.

For organizational overkill, you may even nest favorites folders inside other favorites folders. Either create a new favorites folder directly inside an existing one or drag it there.

Working with Assets

The Assets panel doesn't only give you a convenient way of organizing and previewing your objects. You can also use the panel to insert assets into your documents or to edit them.

Inserting Assets

You can insert most types of assets directly into a document by dragging them to the Design view of the Document window or by using the Insert button at the bottom of the panel. For assets such as URLs and colors, you can also apply them to selected text in the Design view.

Editing Assets

To edit an asset, either double-click it, or select it and click the Edit button. Some assets, such as images, must be edited by an outside application. The application to use is determined by the settings in the Dreamweaver Preferences. If you want to use a different application or if double-clicking the file has no effect, choose Edit | Preferences from the menu, and select the File Types/Editors category. Then add the application you want to use to the asset's file type.

Assets that don't reside in physical files but are, instead, scanned from your documents, such as URLs and colors, cannot be edited in the Site list. Switch to the Favorites list, and then edit it.

The HTML-based assets, templates, and library items are edited in Dreamweaver. Double-clicking one of these opens a new Document window containing the asset.

When you finish editing a file based asset, save it using the external application you used to edit it. If the asset is a color, you finish when you choose a color with the color picker.

Asset Categories

The Assets panel doesn't recognize every asset type, but it does recognize many of the most common ones. The left side of the Assets panel has a column of buttons that let you choose the category of assets to display, as shown in the following illustration. These assets types are Images, Colors, URLs, Flash, Shockwave, Movies, Scripts, Templates, and Library items.

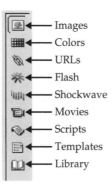

The following discusses the different types of assets managed by the Assets panel.

> **Note**   *Only assets that fit in the previous categories can be viewed in the Assets panel. Other assets, including such items as sound files, Java applets, Adobe Acrobat PDF files, or unsupported media formats like Windows Media or RealVideo, won't be seen in the Assets panel.*

Images

Selecting the Images button shows the image files in your project. These include GIF, JPEG, and PNG (Fireworks) files. See Chapter 12 for more information about image files.

Colors

Dreamweaver scans your HTML documents and your style sheets to find any colors that may be used for backgrounds, text, or links.

You can create a new color directly in the Assets panel by following these steps:

1. Select the Colors category.
2. Click Favorites to show the Favorites list. (Colors can only be added to the Favorites list—the Site list is only for assets already on your site.)
3. Click the New Color button, as shown in Figure 28-2.
4. Use the color picker to choose a new color. See Chapter 2 for information on how to use the color picker.
5. Click the nickname for the color in the Nickname list and give it a more descriptive name, if desired.

URLs

An *URL asset* is a reference to an URL to which a document in your site has a link. When the Site list is created, your documents are scanned for the following types of links: FTP, gopher, HTTP, HTTPS, JavaScript, e-mail (`mailto`), and local file (`file://`).

As with colors, you can create a new URL in the Favorites list. Do the following:

1. Select the URL's category.
2. Click Favorites to show the Favorites list.
3. Click the New URL button (the same button used for New Color, just renamed in this category).
4. Enter an URL and a nickname in the Add URL dialog box, and then click OK.

URLs inserted into a document from the Favorites list can be created with the nickname used as the link text.

Flash

If your site contains *Macromedia Flash movie* (*SWF*) files, they'll be listed in this category. This also includes Flash buttons or text objects that you create. The assets panel lets you preview your Flash content. When one of these assets is selected, a small play button is placed at the upper-right corner of the preview pane. Clicking this button enables you to preview the movie. Most likely, you'll have to resize the preview window to see the entire movie: first resize the Assets panel, and then resize the preview pane by dragging the border between it and the asset list. Double-clicking an asset launches the standalone Flash Player, providing another way to preview the content.

Go to Chapter 27 for more information about creating Flash content.

Shockwave

This category shows any Shockwave movies (with a DCR extension) used in your site. As with Flash movies, Shockwave movies can be previewed directly in the Assets panel preview pane (after manual resizing). They can also be launched in the standalone Flash player by double-clicking the asset.

See Chapter 27 for more information about creating Shockwave movies.

Movies

If your site has any movies in MPEG or QuickTime format, they'll be displayed in this category. As with Flash and Shockwave movies, you can preview these movies in the Assets panel Preview pane or double-click them to launch them in the standalone QuickTime player.

Scripts

Script assets are JavaScript and VBScript files. The list only contains scripts in files with a JS or VBS extension—scripts contained in your HTML files aren't listed. The text of the script file is displayed in the preview pane when you select the asset.

Inserting a script asset into a document creates a `<script src="file://...>` tag, with the `src` attribute containing a link to the script file.

For more information on using JavaScript with Dreamweaver, see Chapter 21.

Templates

This category lists *Dreamweaver Template* (*DWT*) files. A *template* is a document you can use to provide a standardized layout for your pages. Templates enable you to specify which elements can be edited and which ones cannot. A nice feature of templates is this: editing the template automatically updates all pages that use that template with the changes.

Templates are one of the few assets you can create from the Site list. To create a new template, do the following:

1. Click the Templates category button.
2. Click the New Template button.

Information about creating and using templates can be found in Chapter 29.

Library

Library assets are elements you want to use in multiple pages. As with templates, editing a library asset causes Dreamweaver to update each page used automatically.

The following section discusses library assets in more detail, showing how to create, modify, and use them.

The Library

When you create Web pages, reusing the same elements on multiple pages throughout your site is often necessary. You can do this with Dreamweaver. You could create a custom object that makes adding the HTML code for your item easy. This works well, but what if you're still fleshing out the design of your site and making changes to all these objects? Going through each page and finding each object to modify can be tedious, not to mention prone to errors.

A better solution for repeatedly adding the same elements to your pages is to use the Dreamweaver Library, which is where you store sections of HTML code you want to reuse.

The biggest advantage library items have is, when the library item is edited, every instance of the item on your site's pages is updated automatically. Two comment tags are added at the beginning and the end of the library item's HTML code when you insert the item in your page. The comment tag contains a reference to the library file used to create the object. When you make a change to a library file, Dreamweaver scans your pages looking for the library comment tags and replaces all the HTML code between them with the new code from the library.

Library items are stored (with a .lbi extension) in a special folder named Library, which Dreamweaver creates in your site's local root folder. Although you could go into this folder and work with the library files directly, the best place to work with library items is the Assets panel. The Assets panel lets you create new library items, edit them, insert them into objects, and even copy them to another site's library.

Creating Library Items

Library items can be created from any section of HTML code. This includes text, images, tables, forms, navigation bars, or even more complex features of your site. Remember, Dreamweaver only stores the HTML code you select. Note: any images or other external files referenced by the item aren't stored with the library files.

To create a library item, do the following:

1. Activate the Library category of the Assets panel either by clicking the Library button on the panel or by choosing Window | Library from the menu.

2. Select the section of the document you want to save in the Library.

3. Either drag the selection into the Assets panel or click the New Library Item button at the bottom of the Assets panel. Still another alternative is to choose Modify | Library | Add Object to Library from the menu.

4. When you add an item to the Library, you are prompted to create a new name for the item. This name is then used for the library item's filename.

Note   *When copying an HTML element that has a Dreamweaver Behavior attached to it, the element and its event handler attribute are copied, but any associated JavaScript functions aren't copied. However, when you insert the library item into a document, Dreamweaver is smart enough to know to add the appropriate JavaScript functions.*

Figure 28-3 shows an example of the creation of a library item. In this case, I want to create a library item containing a copyright footer to include in all the pages on my site. In this case, the copyright footer is contained in a table, with some images and text in the center. To make this into a library item, select the table in the Design view, or click the `<table>` tag in the Code view. Then either choose Modify | Library | Add Object to Library (or press CTRL-SHIFT-B) or click the New Library Item button on the Assets panel. You can see the original selection turn into the first instance of your object, with the addition of the `#BeginLibraryItem` and `#EndLibraryItem` comment tags.

The Library Item Property Inspector, also shown in Figure 28-3, also enables you to work with a selected library item. This property inspector lets you open the library item for editing, detach the local copy on a particular page from the library item (to prevent it from being updated if the version in the library changes), or re-create the stored library item using the local copy.

Using Library Items

When you insert a library item into a document, the code from the library file is copied into your document, along with comment tags containing a reference to the library file used. Figure 28-4 shows a new page after our copyright library item has been added.

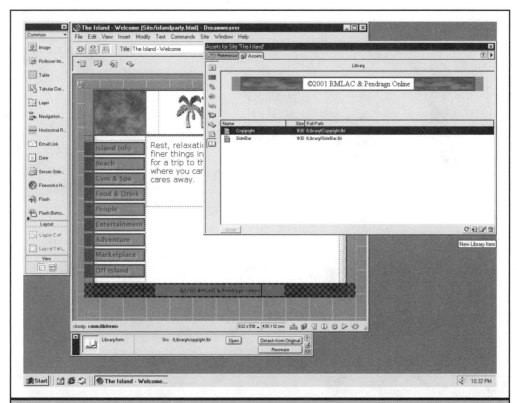

Figure 28-3.   *Create a library item by selecting an element on your page and clicking the New Library Item button on the Assets panel. The element then becomes the first instance of your item. You can also see the Library Item Property Inspector*

To insert a library item, do the following:

1. Activate the Assets panel's Library category, either by clicking the Library button on the panel or by choosing Window | Library.

2. Click the position where you want the library item to be inserted in the Document window, and then click the Insert button in the Assets panel, or simply drag the library item to the Document window.

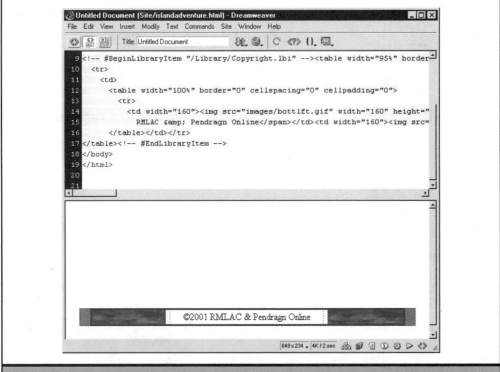

```
 9 <!-- #BeginLibraryItem "/Library/Copyright.lbi" --><table width="95%" border
10  <tr>
11    <td>
12      <table width="100%" border="0" cellspacing="0" cellpadding="0">
13        <tr>
14          <td width="160"><img src="images/bottlft.gif" width="160" height="
15            RMLAC &amp; Pendragn Online</span></td><td width="160"><img src=
16      </table></td></tr>
17 </table><!-- #EndLibraryItem -->
18 </body>
19 </html>
20
21
```

©2001 RMLAC & Pendragn Online

Figure 28-4.   *When you insert a library item, the code is reproduced from the original, along with a comment block referring to the library file*

Inserting a library object without including the reference to the library files is possible. To do this, press the Control key (Windows) or the Option key (Mac) while inserting or dragging an item from the Assets panel. The comment block containing the reference back to the library file won't be added; therefore, any changes made to the library item won't automatically be updated.

Editing Library Items

The advantage you have in using library items is you can change all instances of the item simply by changing the library file. To edit a library item, double-click the item, or select it and click the Edit button. A new Dreamweaver window opens, showing the contents of the library item file.

Note, when editing a library item, you cannot use the CSS Styles panel, the Behaviors panel, or the Timeline panel. This is because these panels insert code into the <head> section of your document. Because the library item is only a code snippet, rather than a fully formed HTML document, this tag isn't used. Note, as well, the Page Properties dialog box is unavailable because it modifies the `<body>` tag, which also isn't included in a library file.

When you finish editing the library item, save it. In the dialog box that appears, as shown in the following illustration, choose whether to update the documents that use the edited library item.

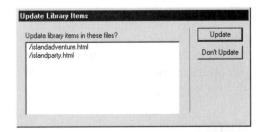

- **Update**—will update all the documents in the local site that use the library item.
- **Don't Update**—won't change any documents. You can update documents later by choosing Modify | Library | Update Current Page or Modify | Library | Update Pages from the menu.

Updating Library Items   If you modify an item and chose not to update your documents when you saved it, you may do so afterward. You can update all the library items on a single page, all of a single library item on all pages, or all the items on all the pages.

To update all the items on a single page, choose Modify | Library | Update Current Page from the menu for that page's Document window.

To update all pages, choose Modify | Library | Update Pages from the menu. The Update Pages dialog box is displayed, as seen in the following illustration.

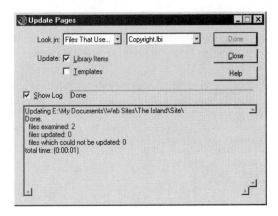

The fields on this dialog box are as follows:

- **Look in**—This field lets you choose to update an entire site or a single library item. Choose which you want to do in this list box. You can then choose either the site you want to update or the library item to update from the adjacent list box.

- **Update**—These check boxes let you choose to update either library items or templates or both.

- **Show Log**—Checking this button causes a running status update to be displayed below while the site is being updated.

- **Start**—Clicking this button starts the update process. When all the documents are updated, this button changes to read Done.

Renaming Library Items

Renaming a library item in the Assets panel is possible. Click the item to select it, pause for a second, and then click it again. The name then becomes editable and you can type in a new name. When you finish, press ENTER (Windows) or RETURN (Mac).

After you rename the library item, you are asked if you want to update the documents that use the item. Click Update to do this. If you don't want to update the documents, click Don't Update. Be aware, though, if you don't update the documents at this time, they will refer to the old library item name, which doesn't exist anymore. Any modifications to the library item won't be applied to these instances with an old reference.

Deleting Library Items

You may decide you no longer need a library item. If so, deleting the library item is the same as deleting other assets. Select the item in the asset list and click the delete button, or press the Delete or Backspace keys. The item is then deleted from the library, but any instances of the item in your documents will be left alone.

The delete process is irreversible, though. If you delete a library item, you won't be able to use the Undo command to bring it back, so use this process with caution.

 If you accidentally delete a library item, you can re-create it if you have an instance of the item in one of your documents. Simply select the instance of the item and create a new library item with it.

Server-Side Includes

Server-Side Includes (*SSI*) are used to incorporate a file on the server into the current document before sending it to the requesting browser. Any document that includes this file contains its contents in place of the include instructions coded in the document. In this sense, server-side includes are similar to Library items.

When you view a local copy of the document, no server is running to process SSI instructions. This can make previewing these documents difficult or impossible. Dreamweaver, however, enables you to preview documents complete with the include instructions. Dreamweaver recognizes server-side include statements in your documents and lets you see the effect of those includes in the Design view or when you preview in a browser.

Placing a server-side include in a document inserts a reference to an external file, rather than the actual file contents. Dreamweaver displays the contents of the external file in the Document window, making it easier to design pages, but you cannot edit the included file directly in a document. To edit the contents of a server-side include, you must directly edit the file you're including. Any changes to the external file are automatically reflected in every document that includes it.

To insert a server-side include, do the following:

1. Choose Insert | Server-Side Include, or click the Server-Side Include button in the Common category of the Objects panel.

2. In the dialog box that appears, browse to and select the file you want to use.

Once your Server-Side Include object is added, you can modify it using the Property Inspector, as seen in the following illustration. This Property Inspector lets you change the included file, whether the include uses the virtual or file attributes, and also provides a button enabling you to edit the file.

Virtual Includes   Virtual includes are of the form:

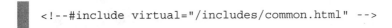

```
<!--#include virtual="/includes/common.html" -->
```

The *Virtual* include is usually used with Apache Web servers. The path specified is a virtual path on the server.

File Includes   File includes use the form:

```
<!--#include file="includes/common.html" -->
```

Th *File* include works best with Microsoft IIS servers. The path specified is relative to the current document.

Troubleshooting Server-Side Includes   If you're having trouble getting server-side include files to work properly after you upload them to a remote server, some of the following tips might help:

- Make sure all files, including the documents and the SSI files, have been uploaded to the server.

- Make sure the server allows server-side includes. You might need to consult your site's system administration to determine any special conditions, such as specific directories or file extensions that server-side include files are required to use on the site.

- Make sure the correct file type (Virtual or File) is being used for your Web server and the path corresponds to that type of file.

Summary

Dreamweaver's Assets panel provides a convenient way to locate, organize, edit, and use many of the assets on which your site depends. The Assets panel is also the main interface for the Dreamweaver Library, allowing library items to be created, edited, and inserted into pages.

- The Assets panel lists several different types of assets: images, colors, URLs, Flash movies, Shockwave movies, QuickTime and MPEG movies, scripts, templates, and library items.

- You can access assets from either the master Site list or from a Favorites list that allows your commonly used assets to be grouped in folders and given convenient nicknames.

- The Dreamweaver Library lets you store commonly used sections of HTML code for reuse.

- Changes made to library items can be automatically applied to all instances of the item in your site.

Chapter 29 explains how to create and use Dreamweaver Template files to provide a consistent layout for all your pages.

The Complete Reference

Dreamweaver 4

Chapter 29

Using Templates

After you design your site, create style sheets, and put all the elements together to form the shell of the site, Web design often turns into a cookie-cutter operation. Unless each page is dramatically different—which would result in a confusing user experience—the finishing work is often a matter of copying the same shell repeatedly and inserting the unique content for each page. Unfortunately, this process is also fraught with problems, as a cut-and-paste in the wrong spot can corrupt the structure of a table or erase a rollover state. The opposite can also happen, such as forgetting to delete all the content from one page before adding the content of the next page and renaming the document. While you personally might not make such a mistake, another member of the development group or a client certainly could.

Dreamweaver's solution to the tedium and delicacy of applying your design across the entire site is templates. Dreamweaver templates protect the elements common throughout the site, while specifying regions to add unique content. Templates eliminate the risk of cut-and-paste duplication of documents by attaching themselves to pages while keeping the original template pure. Perhaps the best feature of templates is the capability to change the design of the template and have those changes apply to every page in the site created from that template. Used in conjunction with CSS, this capability can dramatically cut the time you spend redesigning your site to keep up with new design trends.

Templates aren't to be confused with library items. A *template* is an entire Web page, whereas a library is used for components of a page. As you begin to understand the power—and some of the pitfalls—of using templates, you'll be better able to determine when to use these features.

Template Preparation and Resources

Before jumping into templates, you should do some planning. By now, this is a common refrain. Before creating a template, make sure all the core elements of the Web page are in place. Once you start creating pages from the template, it's easy to modify the design, but impossible to change the overall structure of the template without losing content. Your templates will also be more useful if you do all the design work up-front, so you don't have to add the same elements repeatedly to each document. Remember, the idea of a template is to save you from repetition.

Sources for Templates

Several sources exist for templates. The one closest to home and most widely used by Web designers is, of course, to create your own design from scratch. If you have the design and coding skills—much of which is covered in this book—this is certainly the most rewarding way to develop a site.

If you already created a page or site and you want to continue to use it, you can convert the page into a template. If you're designing a site from scratch and know you'll want to use templates, you're actually a step ahead of the game because you can plan your site development with templates in mind. As you build the first page or even a prototype, think about each element you add. If an element is likely to be repeated on every page throughout the site, it can become part of the template. If the element is an object to be used on some pages, but not on others, make it a library item (see Chapter 28 for more about libraries). If that element's content is unique to a particular page, mark its location as an editable region in the template.

Let's face it, though. Some people simply aren't design-oriented. Maybe they don't have the skill to obtain the graphic results they envision or they simply lack an eye for color. Others don't have the inclination to spend several hours designing graphics and a layout for a personal home page or an intranet site. In those cases, dozens of prepackaged template solutions are available.

Prepackaged Templates

Two different types of templates are available on the Internet: those designed for use with Dreamweaver and those generic templates that can be applied to any Web development environment. Macromedia offers 18 templates on its Web site at **http://www.macromedia.com/software/dreamweaver/download/templates/**. These templates can be modified to suit your needs and even include native Fireworks .png files to enable you to adapt the graphic elements of the site to your own purpose.

Another tremendous resource for Dreamweaver templates is Project VII (**http://www.projectseven.com**). The templates available from this site are not only visually pleasing, but they also serve as tutorials for advanced Web development techniques. Each template has a tutorial focus, whether it be frames or fly-out menus, and the techniques are explained from a Dreamweaver perspective. These templates are a bit pricey for the casual Web developer, but are worth consideration.

You can also use templates that weren't designed specifically for Dreamweaver. Converting the document to a usable Dreamweaver template will take some extra work— in that way, it's similar to converting a standard preexisting Web page to a template—but the graphic elements are already created and a layout is established. For a nondesigner who wants quick, attractive results, this is an option. The types of templates that appeal to you depend on the nature of your site. For an artistic, high-concept site, look at Moyra's Web Jewels at **http://www.moyra.com**. Moyra's templates are linkware for noncommercial sites and at minimal cost for commercial ventures.

Note   *Linkware is a sort of honor system on the Web. In this case, if you use the templates or graphic elements on Moyra's site, you agree to put a link back to her site on every page that uses those elements. In return, the designer grants you royalty-free use of those elements. You can't fool your friends into thinking the graphics are your own creation, which would be a violation of copyright in any case, but you also can't beat the price!*

Locating Common Elements

Unless you're using a prepackaged Dreamweaver template, the next step in planning is to identify the common elements of the page. Templates are divided into two regions: editable and noneditable. The *noneditable* regions contain all the elements your pages have in common, and they're locked to prevent being overwritten as you modify individual pages created from the template.

Some sections of a template are considered noneditable by default. In particular, the `<head>` section of the document is noneditable, other than the `<title>`. Other elements to consider are your Navigation bar and the layout of the page itself. You can set one or more cells to be editable regions for content while locking the rest of the table.

Once you have your plan in place, you're ready to create and apply templates.

Creating Templates

Templates are maintained using the Template category of the Asset panel, as the following illustrates. You can access the Template tools relating to creating and saving the document using the buttons and drop-down menus on this panel. Template tools relating to the structure of the document are found on the Modify menu.

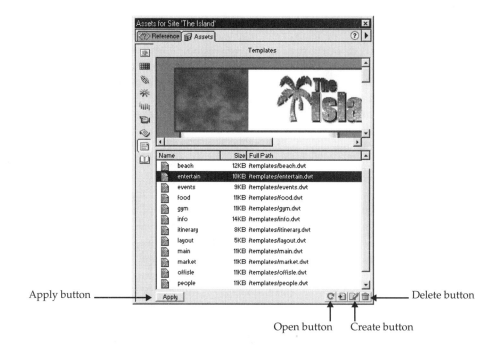

To create a template from an existing Web page:

1. Open the document in the Document window.

2. Select File | Save as Template from the menu.

3. Enter a name for the template in the Save as Template dialog box, as the following shows.

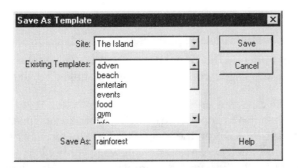

You can use this same approach to create a new file, add elements to it, and then save the file as a template. But you can save a few steps if, instead, you define the empty page as a template before beginning your work. To do this:

1. Click the New Template button in the Template category of the Assets panel. This adds an unnamed template file to the bottom of the templates list, as the following illustration shows.

Note   *The site must contain at least one saved document before the New Template button is available. Also, the New Template button won't be available if the current document is already attached to a template.*

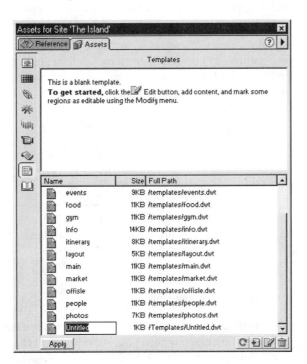

2. Name the new template. You needn't add the file extension; Dreamweaver does that for you.

3. Click the Edit button in the Template category of the Assets panel to open the new blank file and begin work. You can also double-click the filename to open it.

The blank template canvas is used in the same manner as a regular HTML document. Add elements and attributes to lay out the design of your page. To save the document, click File | Save or CTRL-S (CMD-S on the Mac). Because you already defined the page as a template in the Assets panel, Dreamweaver knows to continue saving it as such.

Templates are automatically saved in a templates directory in the local site folder. Templates have a .dwt extension. When you open a template file in Dreamweaver, the word <<Template>> appears before the filename in the title bar of the Document window.

Editable Regions

Once you create a template document, you need to identify which regions of the template are locked and which are editable. By default, all areas of the template are locked, so the only sections that must be defined are the editable regions.

To make a region editable:

1. Select the region you want to mark.

2. Select Modify | Templates | New Editable Region from the menu or the keyboard shortcut CTRL-ALT-V (CMD-OPTION-V on the Mac).

3. In the New Editable Region dialog box, as the following shows, give the region a name. Region names can contain spaces, but cannot contain any characters used to define HTML or JavaScript elements, such as question marks, quotation marks, curly brackets, and angle brackets.

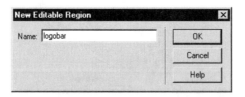

If you're creating various templates to coincide with the various elements on your navbar, consider giving the templates related names. This makes them easier to find and correctly apply later.

4. Click OK to finish naming the region.

You can also create an editable region as you work. To create a new region without making a selection, position the cursor where you want to insert the editable region, and then select Modify | Templates | New Editable Region. Again, you're asked to give the region a name. When you click OK, the new region appears with a highlighted border. The contents of the new region will be the name of the region itself. Simply type over this filler text.

Caution   *If you don't enter and select a paragraph tag when defining a region, you won't be able to add any paragraph breaks in the region. You can add line breaks (<br>), but if you know the region will contain multiple paragraphs, define the region with a paragraph selection already in place.*

Once a region is defined, it becomes outlined in the Document window, so you can see which regions are editable and which are locked, as seen in Figure 29-1. Notice the tabs delineating the editable regions.

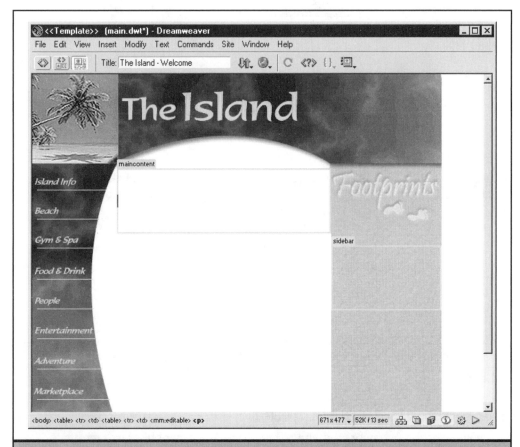

Figure 29-1.   *Editable regions in a template are delineated with a highlighted box surrounding the region and a tab at the top of the region noting its name*

Locking Editable Regions

After creating an editable region, you might change your mind and want to lock the region again. To do this:

1. Select Modify | Templates | Remove Editable Region.

2. Choose the region to lock from the Remove Editable Region dialog box, as the following illustrates. If your cursor was positioned in an editable region before you initiated this command, that region's name is highlighted. You can, of course, choose another region from the list.

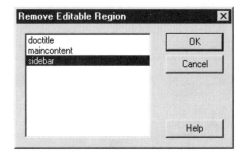

3. Click OK.

Changing Template Highlight Colors

To show the region highlights in grayscale for the previous figure, I changed the highlight colors. The default highlight colors are faint, which can be helpful because they don't detract from your design work. On the other hand, you may want to change the highlight color to blend or contrast with your site's colors. To change the highlight colors:

1. Select Edit | Preferences or press CTRL-U (CMD-U on the Mac).

2. Choose the Highlighting category in the Preferences dialog box.

3. Use the color pickers next to each of the highlight fields to set your colors.

Dreamweaver remembers your latest color settings, even when you work on different sites. Fortunately, this is easy enough to change when you're working on multiple projects if you need to see your editable region boundaries.

Adding Elements to a Template

While you can add behaviors, timelines, links, and any other object to a template, remember these considerations:

Links   When adding any sort of file path, whether it's a link to another page in the site or inserting an image into the document, be sure the path is relative to the document rather than the site root. Templates are saved in a separate folder within the local site folder. If you use *document-relative linking*, Dreamweaver maintains link integrity as you attach your templates to documents in other folders within the site. If you use *site-root linking*, however, Dreamweaver cannot maintain link integrity, and the paths for these links will fail once the template is attached to a page outside the template's folder.

Also, when entering paths by hand, remember the current location of the template is in the template's folder, so you should code the paths accordingly. Dreamweaver automatically modifies the paths as the templates are used.

The easiest way to avoid problems with link integrity when using templates is simply to let Dreamweaver handle all your links. Use the point-to-file and File Selector dialog boxes (accessible from the folder icon in the Property Inspector) to establish links to other pages and images within the site.

Style Sheets   Using and applying style sheets to templates is easy. The link to an external style sheet is maintained by Dreamweaver even as the template is attached to other documents, and styles remain available to use in the editable regions of those pages. Because the style sheet is external to the page and is read by the browser on loading the page for the user, you can modify your style declarations and expect to have them correctly picked up by all your documents.

The only caution in using style sheets is you cannot change the name of either the external style sheet itself or any of the classes you defined within it. If you do so, any styles applied to locked regions of the template won't be modifiable in the attached document, and will continue to search for the old style sheet and/or classes, thus breaking the style sheet.

Behaviors and JavaScript   Remember, the `<head>` of the document will be a locked region once you apply the template. For this reason, applying any behaviors or JavaScript to the template, rather than to the individual pages, is important. In instances where you must add the behavior or script to the final page, you can detach the final page from the template and add your behaviors. This enables you to add behaviors, but precludes the page being updated when you modify the template.

Timelines   Timelines animate even in a locked region. If you need to change the layers or images in the timeline, however, you must set them as editable regions. Also, the Autoplay feature of the timeline won't work in a template because the `<body>` tag is locked, so you cannot add the necessary JavaScript to the tag. A workaround is to use the Play Timeline behavior and use the onLoad event of an image within your document to trigger the action. This applies the behavior to the `<image>` tag, rather than the `<body>` tag. For more information about timelines, see Chapter 20. For more about behaviors, see Chapter 23.

DREAMWEAVER TOOLS

Attaching Templates to Pages

Now you have a template with editable regions and a design you want to apply to pages throughout your site. The next step is to attach the template to HTML documents. To apply a template to a Web page, take one of the following steps:

- Select New from Template from the drop-down menu in the right corner of the Assets panel.

- Select File | New from Template on the Document window menu.

- Open a document, select a template from the Assets panel, and press the Apply button in the Assets panel.

- Drag a template from the Assets panel to an open document, and drop the template on to the document.

- Choose Modify | Templates | Apply Template to Page from the Document window menu.

Each of these options has the same result—applying the template to the current document. If the document already contains content, Dreamweaver attempts to put it into an editable region. If the document is already attached to a template, the new template overrides the old, and existing content is fit as well as possible into the editable regions of the new template. If Dreamweaver can't find a spot for the existing content, it prompts you either to save the extra content in a new region or to delete the material.

 If you're applying a new template to a document that's already attached to a template, create a backup of the document before making the switch. If the conversion doesn't go smoothly, then you haven't lost any content.

Detaching Templates

As stated earlier, situations may occur where you need to detach the document from a template to add behaviors, additional timeline control, and otherwise modify the locked regions of the document. To do this, choose Modify | Templates | Detach from Template. Note, when you choose this option, there's no caution or chance to change your mind. The only way to undo the detachment is to choose Edit | Undo or CTRL-Z (CMD-Z on the Mac). If you took other steps between detaching the template and choosing to reattach it, you must repeat the process to attach the template to the document.

Editing Page Titles in Templates

As soon as you create a template, Dreamweaver automatically creates an editable region for the document title. The region is named doctitle and it contains the <title> tag. To edit the page title, choose any of the normal methods:

- Enter the title in the title field of the Dreamweaver toolbar.

- Choose Modify | Page Properties from the menu, or use the keyboard shortcut CTRL-J (CMD-J on the Mac).

- Chose View | Head Content (CTRL-SHIFT-W in Windows, CMD-SHIFT-W on the Mac), and then click the Title icon and edit the title in the Property Inspector.

- Switch to Code view and edit the <title> tag directly.

Note *If you use the Page Properties dialog box, be aware that none of the other options can be used, including tracing images, because the regions in which those elements are applied are locked. Dreamweaver doesn't warn you of this and you can, in fact, enter data in to the other fields. When you click OK to exit the dialog box, however, none of the settings are applied, other than the title.*

Adding Other Head Content

Before creating a template, you should get your keywords and descriptions settled. If your site is going to use the same <meta> tags throughout, you've made your life a lot easier. If you need to use unique keywords and descriptions for each page, you need to take an extra step to add them.

Because the <head> of a template-created page is locked, you need to exploit the `doctitle` region that enables you to modify the title of the page. To do this, switch to Code view and scroll down until you see the `<title>` tag. Enter your unique `<meta>` tags below the page title, before the end tag for the editable region. Because you'll be coding these by hand, be sure you know the structure of these tags beforehand. See Chapter 8 for reference.

Note *If you're creating unique keyword and description tags for each page, you should avoid adding them ahead of time. Using the workaround to add these elements later is easier than attempting to modify them from within a page attached to a template.*

Modifying Templates

The biggest advantage to using templates is having the capability to modify several pages at once. Style sheets can be modified to change the appearance of content within certain tags, but templates can change the entire structure of the document, including images, layout, and consistent content throughout the site.

Templates are modified in the same way as other HTML documents. Open the template file by double-clicking it in the Assets panel or selecting the template from the list and pressing the Edit icon in the Assets panel. Then simply make your changes, and then save the file. Whenever you save a template file that's been attached to HTML documents, Dreamweaver prompts you to update those documents. If you're planning to make more changes to the template, you can wait to perform this update, particularly if your site is large and the process could take considerable time. At some point, however, you want to apply your template changes to the attached documents.

To update only the current document to reflect template modifications, choose Modify | Templates | Update Current Page. This is a convenient method for testing template modifications to ensure all the editable regions remain correctly positioned and no content is orphaned.

You also have the option of updating all the HTML documents attached to a specific template or updating the entire site at once. The latter is particularly useful when you've made modifications to numerous templates within the site during a major redesign effort. Instead of doing incremental updates while you work, you can wait and do one complete update at the end of the process.

To update a site:

1. Choose Modify | Templates | Update Pages.

2. In the Update Pages dialog box, choose one of the following options:

   ■ To update the entire site, choose Entire Site from the Look in field, and select the site name from the drop-down list of sites, as the following illustration shows.

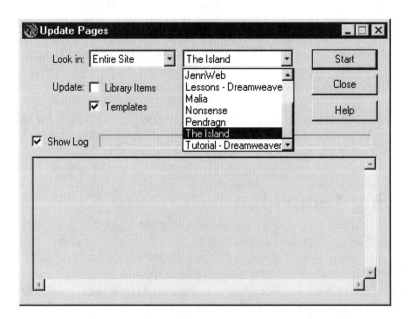

   ■ To update only pages attached to a particular template file, choose Files That Use from the Look in field, and choose the appropriate template from the drop-down list.

3. If you want to see a list of the changes that were made, as the following shows, select the Show Log button.

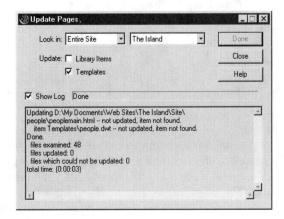

4. Click Start to initiate the update.

The log tracks the number of changes made to the site or pages and reports any problems encountered during the update.

Deleting Templates

After you complete your site and upload it to the Web, you might be tempted to delete your template files. You can certainly do this but, remember, you then have to make any updates to your site to each page individually. If you're deleting templates that are sitting unused on your hard disk, be sure to delete the correct file. Dreamweaver doesn't issue warnings about file deletions, and it won't tell you if you're orphaning HTML documents attached to the template you deleted. An orphaned HTML document is still a fully functional document, but it can no longer be updated using templates.

Exporting XML Using Templates

Templates have one additional purpose that's generally overlooked. When Dreamweaver sets editable regions, it creates name/value pairs for each region. These pairs can be exported into XML files to be used in databases or other applications. Editable regions can also be exported from one template into another.

To export a document containing editable regions to XML:

1. Choose File | Export | Export Editable Regions as XML.

2. From the XML dialog box, shown in the following, choose a tag notation and click OK.

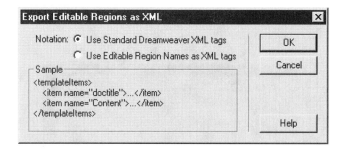

3. Enter a name for the XML file and click Save.

XML can also be imported into a template and used to create new pages. The XML content is inserted into the editable regions of the template. To import XML content into a new document, choose File | Import | Import XML into Template.

To learn more about XML, see Chapter 33.

Summary

Templates make the process of generating large, consistent sites easy. When used in conjunction with library items and style sheets, changing the entire appearance of a site without modifying any individual Web pages is possible. Here are key points to remember:

- Dreamweaver templates are created in the same manner as HTML documents and can contain styles, behaviors, and timelines.

- You can add tables, layers, and other objects to templates. Templates can also use framesets.

- A template consists of editable and locked regions. The editable regions enable you to add content that's unique to a page, while the locked regions protect those elements common to all pages attached to that template.

- To use a template in Dreamweaver, you must first create and save a template file, and then attach the template to an HTML document. The template file remains unchanged while you edit the HTML document.

- If you edit a template file, you must update the attached pages for those pages to reflect the modifications. This can be done automatically by Dreamweaver.

- The template file isn't usually uploaded to the final remote site. Files created using templates are self-contained documents that don't rely on the template file for display in a browser.

- Templates can be used to import and export XML content.

The next chapter explains how to customize your Dreamweaver environment by modifying the menus and creating your own commands.

The
Complete
Reference

Part VIII

Customizing Dreamweaver

The Complete Reference

Chapter 30

Dreamweaver Customization and Additions

One thing is certain in Web development: nothing is certain. Standards and technologies change so often, it's hard for even the most robust development tools, such as Dreamweaver, to keep up with the pace. And, of course, there's the demand of power users who want to wring every last bit of power from a system.

When they developed Dreamweaver, Macromedia's engineers recognized, the ever-changing world of Web design meant Dreamweaver needed to be customizable to support a wide variety of user needs. Macromedia's engineers also recognized that customizability would work best if the end users required the least amount of hand holding possible to be productive.

The way the engineers accomplished this was ingenious: Dreamweaver is extremely customizable by the end user, and the methods they chose to enable customization are the standard technologies Web developers work with every day: HTML, XML, and JavaScript.

Some of Dreamweaver's customizations were already discussed in this book. Here are some of the ways Dreamweaver can be customized that were mentioned in previous chapters.

- You can set the preferences for many of the settings Dreamweaver uses in the Preferences dialog box. This dialog box can be accessed by choosing Edit | Preferences from the menu, or by pressing CTRL-U (CMD-U on the Mac). See Chapter 3 for more information about using the Preferences dialog box.

- You can modify the default keyboard shortcuts as well, using the Keyboard Shortcuts dialog box accessed by choosing Edit | Keyboard Shortcuts from the menu. The default keyboard shortcuts for Dreamweaver are listed in Appendix A.

- Objects can be created and added to the Objects panel or modified from existing objects. The Objects panel allows new categories to be added simply by creating a new directory and copying the object files into it. Chapter 24 shows how to customize features of the Objects panel.

- Extensions can be obtained from a third party, or you can develop your own. Extensions typically use Dreamweaver's JavaScript API, and their use is covered in Chapter 31.

Instead of rehashing any of the previous discussions about objects, this chapter focuses on other ways Dreamweaver can be customized. These include

- **Adding File Extensions**—One of the simplest customizations, you can add additional file types to the Open File dialog box.

- **Source Formatting**—You can modify the source-formatting profile to customize the format of the HTML code produced by Dreamweaver. Source formatting changes are done by modifying the SourceFormat.txt file.

■ **Commands**—You can add custom commands to the nine standard ones by saving steps from the History panel or by creating your own command files.

■ **Menus**—Dreamweaver enables you to change the names of menu items, add new commands to menus, and remove existing commands from menus. You can also create new menus and rearrange existing menu items, all by modifying the Menus.xml file.

I can't stress this enough: whenever you make a change to one of the Dreamweaver files, make a backup of the original file first. This can prevent unnecessary aggravation if you can't get a customization to work and you want to return Dreamweaver to a known working state.

Adding File Extensions

Because Web development is still a rapidly progressing field, new file types for new technologies, such as server-side scripting languages, are being created. Dreamweaver recognizes all the more common file extensions in use today, including HTM, HTML, ASP, CFM, JSP, and PHP, but this doesn't mean new extensions, or some variation of the existing file extensions, won't appear in the future.

Dreamweaver uses a file in the Configuration folder—called Extensions.txt—to determine which type of files it can open. The lines in this file are used to create the different file categories used in the File Open dialog box, as shown in this illustration.

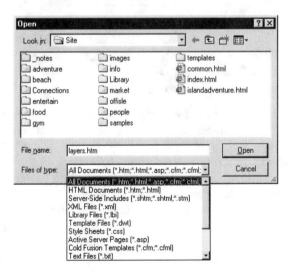

To add a new file extension to this list, do the following:

1. Make a backup of the Configuration/Extensions.txt file.

2. Open the Extensions.txt file in the text editor of your choice (or in Dreamweaver).

3. To add a new file extension (a common one is PHP3), add it to the line for the type of file it is, in this case, a PHP file:

```
PHP,PHP3:PHP Files
```

4. The first line of the Extensions.txt file is "All Documents." This line should show every file format Dreamweaver can open. To add a new file type to the All Documents line, such as the PHP files, simply add them to the file list:

```
PHP,PHP3,HTM,HTML,ASP,CFM,CFML,TXT,SHTM,SHTML,STM,LASSO,XML,WML:A
ll Documents
```

5. Save the file and restart Dreamweaver to see the changes. The new file dialog box is shown in this illustration.

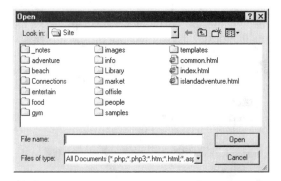

Source Formatting

One of the nice things the Dreamweaver editor provides for you is source formatting. The *source formatting* settings determine how Dreamweaver formats the HTML elements for a document in the Code view.

Dreamweaver allows general format settings to be done in the Preferences dialog box (click the Code Format tab). Also, additional formatting preferences can be set that aren't shown in the Code Format preferences. These preferences must be set by editing the SourceFormat.txt file directly. (This file can be found in the Configuration folder of the Dreamweaver application folder.)

Format preferences set using the Edit | Preferences command aren't saved until you quit Dreamweaver. You should always make sure to quit Dreamweaver before editing the SourceFormat.txt file. Otherwise, the file and all your manual changes may be overwritten when you quit Dreamweaver.

SourceFormat.txt

All source formatting preferences are specified in the SourceFormat.txt file. This file consists of multiple sections, with a special keyword indicating the section, such as `<?keyword>`, `<?options>`, `<?elements>`, or `<?attributes>`. Each section has specific formatting options described in the HTML comment blocks directly above the section.

Tag formatting   Individual tags specified in the SourceFormat.txt file have the following format options:

- **break="before, inside start, inside end, after"**—Specifies line breaks used when formatting the tag and any enclosed text. There are four numbers for the break parameters, which specify the number of line breaks that should be inserted for that portion of the tag. For example, the body tag is formatted like this:

  ```
  <body break="1,1,1,1">
  ```

  These settings mean the body tag must have a line break before the tag, after the tag, before the closing tag, and after the closing tag.

- **indent**—Indicates the contents of the tag should be indented.

- **igroup="group"**—Specifies an indentation group for the element corresponding to the Indent Table Rows and Columns (value of 1), and Indent Framesets and Frames options in the HTML Format preferences (value of 2). Indenting for individual groups can be turned off by removing the number of the group from the active attribute in the `<?options>` section.

- **noformat**—Indicates the tag should never be reformatted once it has been created. The source formatting specified in the SourceFormat.txt file is only used when first creating the element.

Namecase and Samecase   Some of the tag and attribute settings have the term *namecase*: for instance

```
<onMouseDown namecase="onMouseDown">
```

This specifies that the tag or attribute must be capitalized exactly as is specified for the namecase attribute. Therefore, that attribute is always capitalized in this manner when it's inserted into a document by Dreamweaver, no matter what the capitalization preferences specify.

Another keyword used with attributes is *samecase,* which specifies that any attributes of this type created by Dreamweaver have their attribute values with the same capitalization as the attribute's name.

Any attributes not specified in the SourceFormat.txt conform to the default formatting specified in the HTML format preferences.

Command Customization

Dreamweaver commands are entities that can be used to modify a Web page or an object on the page. They can be used to perform almost any kind of edit on the current document, open documents, or even to any other HTML documents in a site. Dreamweaver commands are frequently used to insert tags, clean up unnecessary tags, reformat a document, or do nearly any other edit to an HTML file.

Like objects, which were discussed in Chapter 24, Dreamweaver commands consist of HTML files. The body of a command file may contain a form used to specify parameters for the command, while the head of a Command file contains JavaScript functions that process the form input. The head functions also make any needed edits to the document the command is being applied to.

Commands can perform many of the same tasks as objects and behaviors, except they aren't as limited. Objects are primarily used to insert a single HTML element to the body of a document. Behaviors insert one or more JavaScript functions in to a document head and attach it to an event handler attribute of an element in the body.

Dreamweaver's Standard Commands

Dreamweaver comes with a variety of standard commands that demonstrate the power commands wield. All these commands are available on the Commands menu, though some may be disabled if they don't apply to the current document or selection. Many of these commands are described in more detail in other chapters, so the following is only a brief overview:

- **Apply Source Formatting**—Applies formatting options specified in the Preferences and the SourceFormat.txt file to documents created outside Dreamweaver or those created before the formatting rules were specified. This command is discussed in more detail in Chapter 4.

- **Clean Up HTML**—Activates a dialog box (shown in this illustration) that lets you choose from several clean-up options, including Removing Empty Tags, Redundant Nested Tags, Comments, and Specific Tags. This command is discussed in more detail in Chapter 4.

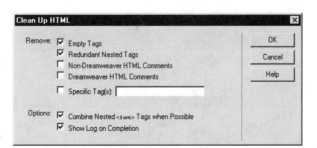

- **Clean Up Word HTML**—Lets you clean up extraneous XML and HTML tags from a Microsoft Word document saved as a Web page. The illustration shows the first pane of the dialog box. This command is discussed in more detail in Chapter 4.

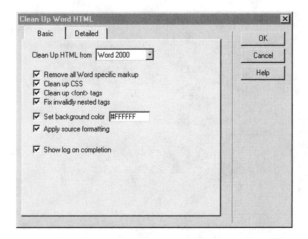

- **Add/Remove Netscape Resize Fix**—Inserts a JavaScript function that's called when the page is resized. In Netscape 4.*x* browsers, resizing a page with layers causes the layers to lose their positioning. This code forces Netscape browsers to reload the page when it's resized to avoid the formatting problem. Using this command again on the same page removes the fix.

- **Optimize Image in Fireworks**—Activates the Fireworks Export Preview dialog box, which allows various optimizations to be performed on an image including color optimizations and format changes. This option requires that Macromedia Fireworks be installed before it works. The Fireworks Export Preview dialog box is shown in Figure 30-1. This command is discussed in more detail Chapter 12.

CUSTOMIZING
DREAMWEAVER

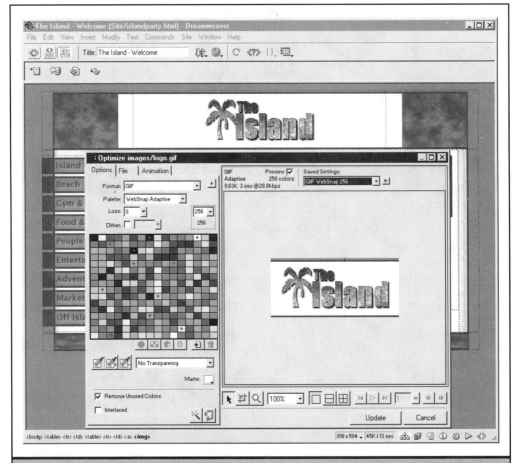

Figure 30-1. *The Optimize image in the Fireworks command launches the Fireworks Export Preview dialog box, enabling you to make changes to an image directly from Dreamweaver*

- **Create Web Photo Album**—Allows the creation of a page of thumbnail images from a directory of images, with the thumbnails linking to the actual image files. The illustration shows the dialog box that's opened when this command is executed. This command is discussed in Chapter 13.

- **Set Color Scheme**—With this command, you can set the color used for the current pages background, text, and link elements, as shown in the illustration. This command is discussed in Chapter 7.

- **Format Table**—This command is used to apply one of 17 preset designs to a table quickly. You can also set options to customize the table further, using the dialog box shown in this illustration. This command is covered in more detail in Chapter 14.

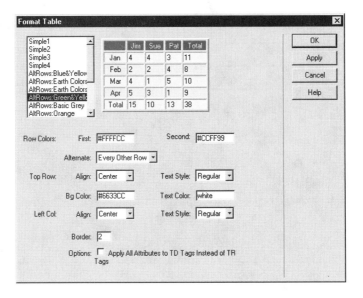

- **Sort Table**—This command enables you to sort a table based on the values in one or two columns. The dialog box, shown in this illustration, lets you choose the columns to sort by, as well as a few other options. See Chapter 14 for more information about this command.

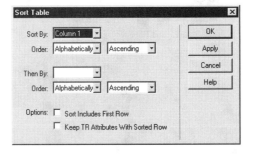

In addition to these standard commands, Dreamweaver enables you to add new commands. The easiest way to add new commands is to obtain them from a source such as the Dreamweaver Exchange (**http://www.macromedia.com/exchange/dreamweaver/**). This should probably be one of the first places you look before you decide to create a new command because one that does what you want might already exist.

If the Exchange doesn't help you, Dreamweaver provides two methods for creating commands. You can record a sequence of actions as a temporary command and save the command from the History panel, or you can create a command from scratch.

Recording Commands

Many times, when you perform a repetitious series of actions, you wish you could automate them in some way. Dreamweaver enables you to do just that with the capability to save your actions from the History panel as a command.

Saving History Steps

The quickest method of creating a new command is to save a set of history steps as a command. You should do this any time you think you might want to repeat the same steps again in the future.

To create a command based on history steps, you first need to execute those steps in your document. Then, follow these steps to save them as a command:

1. Open the History panel (Windows | History from the menu, or press SHIFT-F10). The History panel is shown in this illustration.

2. Select the step or set of steps from the panel. Hold down the CTRL key while clicking the steps to select multiple steps.

3. Click the Save As Command button on the lower-right corner of the panel, or choose Save As Command… from the History panel's context menu. (See the following illustration.)

4. When prompted with the Save As Command dialog box (shown in the following illustration), enter a name for the command and click OK to save it to the Commands menu.

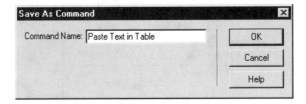

The command is then saved as an HTML file in Dreamweaver's Configuration/ Commands folder. You can repeat the steps at any time by choosing the command from the Commands menu.

Organizing the Commands Menu

If necessary, you can edit the names of commands you placed in the Commands menu or delete them from the menu by selecting Commands | Edit Command List from the menu.

To edit a command name in the Commands menu, do the following:

1. Choose Commands | Edit Command List from the menu.

2. Choose a command to rename by clicking it and enter a new name, as shown in the following illustration.

3. Repeat Step two for any other commands that you want to rename.

4. Click Close to save the command list with the new names.

To delete a command from the Commands menu:

1. Open the Edit Command List by choosing Commands | Edit Command List from the menu.

2. Select the command to delete by clicking it.

3. Click the Delete button.

4. Repeat Step 3 for any other commands you want to delete.

5. Click Close to save the modified command list.

Recording Commands

Instead of saving commands from the History panel, you can also record them as you perform the steps. Recorded commands are only temporary. They disappear if you record a new one or restart Dreamweaver. Saving a recorded command from the History panel is possible, though.

To create a recorded command, do the following:

1. Choose Commands | Start Recording from the menu, or press CTRL-SHIFT-X (CMD-SHIFT-X on the Mac) to start recording steps. The mouse pointer changes to indicate you're recording, as shown in the following illustration.

2. Perform the steps you want to record. When you're in Recording mode, steps that cannot be recorded, such as making a selection with the mouse, aren't permitted.

3. When you finish performing the steps, choose Commands | Stop Recording from the menu, or press CTRL-SHIFT-X (CMD-SHIFT-X on the Mac).

To play back the recorded command, choose Commands | Play Recorded Command from the menu, or press CTRL-P (CMD-P on the Mac).

You can only have one recorded command at a time. To create more, you can save the current one by doing the following:

1. Open the History panel using Windows | History.

2. Play the command back by choosing Commands | Play Recorded Command, or by pressing CTRL-P (CMD-P on the Mac).

3. Select the Run Command step in the History panel, and save it as a command as described earlier.

Command Files

While command recording is an easy way to create custom commands, to leverage the power of commands, you need to create them yourself by writing the command script.

Like behaviors and objects, Commands consist of an HTML file with a form used to create the dialog box to prompt for properties, and some JavaScript functions to apply the parameters. Optionally, the JavaScript functions can be placed in a separate .js file and referenced from the HTML file using the `<script>` tag. One benefit to doing this is JavaScript functions can be shared between different commands that may do almost exactly the same thing, but enable the user to change different parameters by presenting the dialog box differently.

All the command files are located in Dreamweaver's Configuration/ Commands folder.

Command API

Dreamweaver's Command API is the set of functions you implement in a Command file, which allows it to be accessed by Dreamweaver. Only two functions are specific to the Command API, and they're both optional. Other functions are shared with other Dreamweaver entities, such as behaviors and objects. Here's a brief rundown of some of the Command API functions:

- **canAcceptCommand()**—This function may be used in a command to determine whether the menu item should be visible. A command may only apply to certain objects and, therefore, you wouldn't want them accessible if the item wasn't selected. For example, the Optimize Image command in Fireworks is only active when an image is selected. The rest of the time, it's disabled. This function should only be defined for a command if it's needed. Many commands don't depend on a certain item being selected, and forcing Dreamweaver to call unnecessary functions can cause performance to suffer. Here's the canAcceptCommand() function for the Optimize image in Fireworks command. It uses Dreamweaver's DOM to determine if an IMG element is the currently selected element. If it isn't, the command returns false and the menu item is disabled:

```
function canAcceptCommand()
{
  // return TRUE if an image is selected
  //
    var selection = dreamweaver.getSelection();
    var node      = dreamweaver.offsetsToNode( selection[0], selection[1] );

    return ( node != null                 &&
             node.nodeType == Node.ELEMENT &&
             node.tagName  == "IMG" );
}
```

■ **commandButtons()**—This function can be used to add custom buttons to the right side of the Parameter dialog box and define which custom JavaScript functions will be called in the Command file when they're pressed. The buttons typically provided are OK, Cancel, and Help. The following listing is the commandButtons() function from the Clean Up HTML command file:

```
function commandButtons()
{
    return new Array( BTN_OK,      "cleanUpDocument()"  // main entry point
                    , BTN_Cancel, "window.close()"
                    , BTN_Help,   "displayHelp()");
}
```

For more information on the Command API, see Dreamweaver's "Extending Dreamweaver" document. You can open it from Dreamweaver's Help menu.

Creating New Commands

The act of creating commands consists of two steps. First, you have to create the HTML and/or JavaScript files that define how the command works and, second, you have to add it to the menu. This section describes the first step. The command can then be added to the menus by editing the menu.xml file, which is described later in this chapter. You create a command that can comment out the selected HTML element in the document. This command could potentially be useful for developers who inserted some text into a document, but aren't ready to have it shown yet.

Creating the Command

This command needs two files—an HTML file and a JavaScript file—which contain the code that performs the edit. The two files are located in Dreamweaver's Configuration/ Commands folder. They need descriptive names, so let's call them Comment Out.htm and Comment Out.js.

Creating the HTML File   In this example, the HTML file is fairly simple. As described, the command doesn't have any parameter, so the HTML file needn't create a form for the dialog box. The main things this file needs is a title and a `<script>` tag pointing to the other command file, the .js file.

```
<HTML>
<HEAD>
<TITLE>Comment Out</TITLE>
<SCRIPT LANGUAGE="JavaScript" SRC="Toggle Comment.js"></SCRIPT>
</HEAD>
<BODY onLoad="formatSelection()" >
</BODY>
</HTML>
```

Creating the JavaScript File   The JavaScript file for this command consists of the function call made in the HTML file for the onLoad event: formatSelection().

```
// formatSelection()
//
function formatSelection()
{
    var theDOM = dreamweaver.getDocumentDOM("document");
    var offsets = theDOM.getSelection();
    var theSelection = theDOM.offsetsToNode(offsets[0], offsets[1]);

    if (theSelection.nodeType != Node.COMMENT_NODE)
        theSelection.outerHTML = "<!--" + theSelection.outerHTML +
"-->";

    return;
}
```

This function obtains the current selection in the document by first obtaining a reference to the document, and then getting its current selection. The nearest node (that is, the nearest HTML element) is found and a check is made to make sure the node isn't already a comment block. Finally, the node's outer HTML property is modified to add the comment tags.

An exercise in extending this would be to add the capability of removing comments as well. You should be able to determine a comment node and strip off the comment tags. Then you'd need to insert the resulting HTML from inside the comment block in place of the original comment block.

Menu Customization

Dreamweaver creates all its menus from the structure defined in an XML file called menus.xml, which can be found in Dreamweaver's Configuration/Menus subfolder. Making changes to Dreamweaver's menu structure is as simple as editing this file. Although the syntax of this file may seem daunting at first—especially if you aren't familiar with XML—it's not too difficult. If you plan to modify this file, though, you should get an introduction to XML by reading Chapter 33 and by looking at the Web references mentioned in that chapter. This can help you identify XML syntax errors that may be introduced.

While the menus.xml file generally conforms to XML specs, this file is meant to be parsed by Dreamweaver and might not be viewable in another XML editor. Using a standard text editor, such as Notepad or BBEdit, to work with this file is best. Don't edit menus.xml using Dreamweaver.

Menu File Tags and Attributes

Like all XML files, the menus.xml file is a hierarchical collection of tags used to define menu bars, menus, and keyboard shortcuts. Here's a brief look at the tags and their most common attributes.

`<menubar>`

The `<menubar>` tag describes a menu bar used in Dreamweaver. This can either be the menu bar shown in the main window, the menu bar shown in the site window (Windows only), or a context menu. This tag must contain one or more `<menu>` tags.

The attributes used with this tag are as follows:

■ **app**—This optional parameter indicates the application the menu bar is valid for. Valid values are "dreamweaver" and "ultradev." If this attribute is missing, the menu bar is available in both Dreamweaver and UltraDev, if both are installed.

CUSTOMIZING DREAMWEAVER

- **id**—This required attribute is the menu ID for the menu bar. Each menu bar, menu, or menu item in the menus.xml file should have a unique ID value.

- **name**—This is the name of the menu bar. This value is required, but it can have an empty string for a value ("").

- **platform**—This is an optional parameter that indicates the menu bar is only valid for the specified platform. Valid values are "win" and "mac."

The main window menu bar uses the following menu bar tag:

```
<menubar name="Main Window" id="DWMainWindow">
    <!-- menu tags -->
</menubar>
```

<menu>

The <menu> tag is used to specify a menu or a submenu. This tag can contain <menuitem> tags, <separator> tags, or other <menu> tags.

The attributes used with this tag are as follows:

- **app**—This optional parameter indicates the application for which this menu is valid. Valid values are "dreamweaver" and "ultradev." If this attribute is missing, the menu can be seen in both Dreamweaver and UltraDev.

- **id**—This is the menu ID for the menu. Each menu bar, menu, or menu item in the menus.xml file should have a unique ID value.

- **name**—This is the name of the menu as it should be shown in the menu bar. If an underscore is used in the name, the following letter is used for the keyboard mnemonic when the menu is active ("_File"). These underscores are ignored on the Mac.

- **platform**—This optional parameter indicates the menu is only valid for the specified platform. Valid values are "win" and "mac."

Here's an example of the tag used for the Edit menu of the main window.

```
<menu name="_Edit" id="DWMenu_Edit">
    <!—menuitems, submenus here -->
</menu>
```

<menuitem>

The <menuitem> tag specifies a menu item for a Dreamweaver menu. This tag must be contained within a <menu> tag.

The attributes used with this tag are as follows:

- **app**—This optional parameter indicates the application for which this menu item is valid. Valid values are "dreamweaver" and "ultradev." If this attribute is missing, the menu item can be seen in both Dreamweaver and UltraDev.

- **id**—This is the menu ID for the menu. Each menu bar, menu, or menu item in the menus.xml file should have a unique ID value.

- **name**—This is the name of the menu item as it should be shown in the menu. If an underscore is used in the name, the following letter is used for the keyboard mnemonic when the menu is active ("_Open"). These underscores are ignored on the Mac.

- **platform**—This optional parameter indicates the menu is only valid for the specified platform. Valid values are "win" and "mac." The menu item appears on both platforms by default. If you want the same menu item to do different things on Windows and the Mac, add two of them: one with the plaform="win" and the other with platform="mac."

- **key**—This is an optional keyboard shortcut for the command this menu item performs. It can have the following modifiers: to use modifiers, put them before the key they should be used with, joined with a plus (+) symbol. For example, "SHIFT+CTRL+ESC."

  - **Cmd**—Specifies the Control key (Windows) or COMMAND key (Mac).

  - **Alt**—Specifies the ALT key (Windows), or OPTION key (Mac).

  - **Opt**—Specifies the ALT key (Windows) or OPTION key (Mac). OPT and ALT are interchangeable.

  - **Shift**—Specifies the SHIFT key on both platforms.

  - **Ctrl**—Specifies the CONTROL key on both platforms.

  - Some special keys are specified by name: F1 through F12, PgUp, PgDn, End, Del, Tab, Home, Ins, Esc, BkSp, and Space.

- **enabled**—Provides JavaScript code (usually a JavaScript function call) that determines whether the menu item is currently enabled. The menu item is dimmed if the specified function returns false.

- `arguments`—Provides arguments to pass to the JavaScript file used in the file attribute. The arguments value should be enclosed completely in double quotes ("), with the inner arguments enclosed with single quotes (').

- `command`—Specifies the JavaScript expression that's executed when the user selects this item from the menu. You must specify either file or command attributes for each menu item.

- **file**—Specifies the name and path (relative to the Configuration folder) of an HTML file containing JavaScript that controls the menu item. You must specify either file or command for each menu item. This command file can be an existing Dreamweaver one or one you create yourself.

- **checked**—Provides JavaScript code (usually a JavaScript function call) that determines whether the menu item is currently checked. The menu item is checked if the specified function returns true.

- **dynamic**—An optional attribute that indicates the menu item should be created dynamically. The file attribute should contain an HTML element that returns the text and state of the menu item.

- **isdomrequired**—This optional parameter specifies whether the menu item's code uses the Dreamweaver DOM. Valid values are "true" and "false."

Here's an example taken from the menus.xml file, for the Help | Welcome menu item:

```
<menuitem name="_Welcome" enabled="true"
command="dw.toggleFloater('DWWelcomeFloater')" app="dreamweaver"
id="DWMenu_Help_Welcome" />
```

<separator>

This tag indicates a separator should be inserted at this location in the menu and must be enclosed in a <menu> tag.

The separator tag only supports two optional attributes:

- **app**—This parameter specifies the application in which this separator should be seen. Valid values are "dreamweaver" and "ultradev."

- **platform**—This optional parameter indicates the menu is only valid for the specified platform. Valid values are "win" and "mac."

Here's an example of a separator valid only for the Macintosh platform:

```
<separator platform="mac" />
```

Modifying the Menus.xml File

Dreamweaver's various menu bars (including the Main Window, Site Window, and various context menus) are described in the menus.xml file using the <menubar></menubar> tag pair. Individual menus in the menu bar (such as File, Edit, View, Insert, and so forth) are described using the <menu></menu> tag pair. These tags can be nested to create submenus. Finally, the individual menu items are described using the <menuitem /> tag or the <separator /> tag. A simplified version of some of the Dreamweaver main menu structure—showing only a few of the menus and menu items, and not many of the menu attributes for clarity—is structured like this:

```
<menubar name="Main Window">
    <menu name="_File">
        <menuitem name="_New" />
        <menuitem name="_Open..." />
        <menuitem name="_Close" />
        <separator />
        <menuitem name="_Save" />
        <separator />
        <menu name="_Import">
            <menuitem name="Import _XML into Template..." />
            <menuitem name="Import _Word HTML..." />
            <menuitem name="Import _Tabular Data..." />
        </menu>
    </menu>
    <menu name="_Edit">
        <menuitem name="_Undo"  />
        <menuitem name="_Redo"  />
        <separator />
        <menuitem name="Cu_t" />
        <menuitem name="_Copy" />
        <menuitem name="_Paste" />
        <menuitem name="Cle_ar" />
        <separator />
        <menuitem name="Copy HTML" />
        <menuitem name="Paste HTML" />
    </menu>
</menubar>
```

Tip   *While you can also change the keyboard shortcuts used for menu items by editing the menus.xml file, there's an easier way to accomplish this. Instead, use the Keyboard Shortcuts editor by choosing Edit | Keyboard Shortcuts... from the menu.*

Rearranging Menus

One of the easiest modifications to make to the menus.xml file is simply to rearrange the existing menu items. You can move menus and menu items, as well as create submenus easily.

Creating Submenus

A submenu enables you to organize menu items together and access them from one item in the main menu. This lets you group similar items or seldom-used items so the main menus are less cluttered.

To insert a submenu into an existing menu:

1. Open the menus.xml file in a text editor, such as BBEdit or Notepad. (Don't open it in Dreamweaver.)

2. Place the insertion point in the menu tag block you want to add the submenu to, between any <menuitem> tags.

3. Insert a new <menu name="..."></menu> tag pair, with the name attribute set to the name you want the submenu to have. You must also add an ID attribute, such as id="mysubmenu," to have the menu show up.

4. Copy or add new <menuitem> tags in the submenu.

5. Restart Dreamweaver.

Here's an example of moving of all the Select... menu items from the Edit menu into a new submenu (several of the menu item attributes aren't shown for clarity). Locate the Select... menu items from the Main Window's Edit menu and insert the <menu> tags, as shown here:

```
<separator />
<menu name="Select..." id="mySelect">
    <menuitem name="Select A_ll" … />
    <menuitem name="Select Parent Ta_g" … />
    <menuitem name="Select C_hild" … />
</menu>
<separator />
```

Moving Menu Items

To move a menu item, either to put it in a new menu or submenu, or to change the order of an existing menu, do the following:

1. Open the menus.xml file in a text editor, such as BBEdit or Notepad. (Don't open it in Dreamweaver.)

2. Select the entire <menuitem> tag for the item you want to move and cut it.

3. Place the insertion point at the new location, in between <menu> and </menu> tags.

4. Paste the menu item from the clipboard into the new location.

You can add a separator to any menu simply by putting a <separator /> tag where you want it to go.

Rearranging Menus

If you want to rearrange existing menus on a menu bar:

1. Select the entire menu block, between the <menu> and </menu> tags, and cut it to the clipboard.

2. Place the insertion point at the new location, between <menubar> and </menubar> tags.

3. Paste the menu from the clipboard.

Changing Menu and Menu Item Names

Changing the name of a menu or a menu item is possible. To change one of these, locate the appropriate tag (<menu> or <menuitem>) in the menus.xml file and replace the name attribute of the tag with the new value you want to use. Be sure not to change the ID attribute.

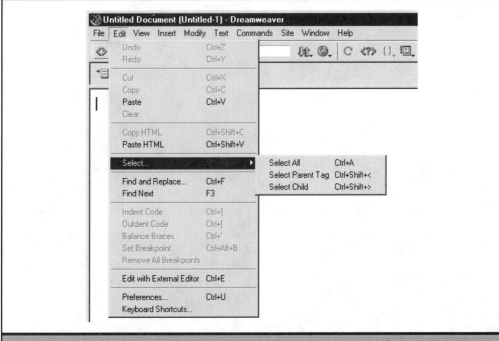

Figure 30-2. *You can create submenus simply by adding a menu tag pair to an existing menu in the menus.xml file*

Summary

In many cases, including animation on a page without having to learn a new graphics package would be nice. Dreamweaver provides a feature called *timelines* that can accomplish animation using standard HTML and JavaScript to animate layers and images.

- File Extensions used in the File Open dialog box are defined in the Extensions.txt file.

- Source formatting is specified in the SourceFormat.txt file.

- Commands can be created by saving history steps or by rolling your own JavaScript functions.

- The menus.xml contains the formatting of all Dreamweaver's menus.

The next chapter talks about how to package up extensions you create using the Extension Manager.

Chapter 31

Extension Manager

As this book has shown, Dreamweaver is an extensible program and has only become more so with each new version. With customizable objects, commands, behaviors, and more, the sky's the limit when it comes to what developers can do with the system. When a popular program such as Dreamweaver enables developers to create custom extensions for it, they'll do it. The problem used to be that keeping track of all the must-have extensions and making sure they didn't clash with each other became too much for the average user to manage.

The *Extension Manager*, Macromedia's solution to the extension management dilemma, is a tool for installing extensible components to its products including Flash, Dreamweaver UltraDev, and, of course, Dreamweaver. The Extension Manager provides a solution to the thorny problem of not only providing extensions for Dreamweaver, but also for making them easy to install and manage. At the same time, the use of the Extension Manager allows for even more complex and powerful extensions to be created because installing them isn't a problem.

Using the Extension Manager

The Extension Manager is a standalone utility, instead of a built-in Dreamweaver function, because other Macromedia products also use it. You can manage extensions for all supported Dreamweaver products at the same time. The Extension Manager used to be optional and installed separately, but now, with Dreamweaver 4, it's bundled with and installed with the program.

About Extensions

Dreamweaver's extensibility is because it uses standard file formats that are easily modified by the end user. To add an object or a command, simply add an HTML file, which contains some JavaScript functions implementing the extension. Menu items may be added without affecting other installed menu items.

More complex extensions may add objects, commands, behaviors, property inspectors, and custom menu items. The Extension Manager provides for packaging up all the disparate files that make up an extension into one file called the Macromedia eXtension Package (MXP). The MXP file contains all the files that need to be installed for an extension, along with information about where the files belong and what the extension does.

Installing Extensions

When you obtain an extension from somewhere, either on a CD or downloaded from the Web, you need to install it using the Extension Manager before it can be used in Dreamweaver. See Figure 31-1.

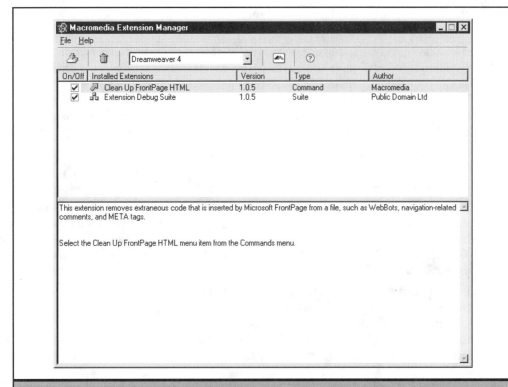

Figure 31-1. *The Macromedia Extension Manager can show which extensions are installed and provide information about what they do and how to use them*

Tip *Keep the original MXP files for any extensions you download. That way, if you have to reinstall them for some reason, locating them will be easy. Macromedia provides a folder called Downloaded Extensions in the Dreamweaver application folder just for this purpose.*

To install an extension file, do the following:

1. Start the Macromedia Extension Manager by using one of these methods:

   ■ Double-click the extension file or open it from Windows Explorer or the Mac Finder.

   ■ In Dreamweaver, choose Help | Manage Extensions to start the Macromedia Extension Manager, and then choose a Macromedia product into which you want to install the extension from the product pop-up menu.

■ Start the Extension Manager by launching it directly from the Start menu (Windows) or the Finder (Mac).

2. If you launched the Extension Manager by double clicking the extension, it automatically installs and you can skip this step. If you started Extension Manager alone, choose File | Install Extension in the Macromedia Extension Manager. You can also use the Install Extension toolbar icon, or press CTRL-I in the Extension Manager. In the File Selection dialog box, browse to the MXP file for the extension and click Install.

3. A disclaimer will be posted for all extensions installed from the Exchange. Select Accept to continue with the installation (provided you agree with the terms, of course.) The Exchange is discussed later in this chapter.

4. Extensions must have unique names. If you have an extension installed with the same name (perhaps an earlier version of the extension), the Extension Manager asks if you want to disable the already installed extension. Selecting Yes replaces the old extension with the new one. Selecting No leaves the old extension installed.

5. Barring any problems with the installation, the Extension Manager then indicates the extension has been successfully installed. If problems occur, you sometimes get information as to why the extension wouldn't install. For example, if your menus.xml file is heavily customized, some extensions may be unable to determine where to install menu items.

Note *If an extension makes changes to the menus.xml file, the Extension Manager creates a backup called menus.xbk. This provides an easy way to restore your previous menus.xml file if the menus.xml file becomes damaged. Simply replace the menus.xml file with the menus.xbk file.*

Managing Extensions

One of the Extension Manager's best uses is for managing extensions. You can enable and disable extensions without uninstalling them, or remove them entirely.

Enabling or Disabling Extensions

While extensions are useful tools to have, sometimes having a lot of extensions installed can bog down application performance. The Extension Manager provides a method for selectively enabling or disabling extensions without having to uninstall and reinstall. This makes disabling your seldom-used extensions easy when they aren't needed.

The On/Off check box on the left column of the extension list controls whether an extension is enabled or disabled. Uncheck the box by clicking it (or by selecting the extension and pressing the Spacebar). You'll be prompted to restart Dreamweaver, as shown in the illustration.

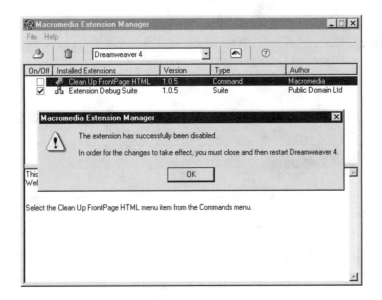

To enable an extension again, simply check the box.

Removing Extensions

Inevitably, you'll download extensions that don't do exactly what you need them to do or you won't use them. You can remove an extension entirely from the Extension Manager by selecting the extension in the list, and then choosing File | Remove Extension. You're prompted to confirm the removal before it actually occurs.

After removal, you would have to reinstall the extension from the original MXP file to use it again.

Importing Extensions

Some extensions are usable from more than one Dreamweaver application. For example, Dreamweaver and Dreamweaver UltraDev can share many of the same extensions because UltraDev is essentially Dreamweaver with added features. Font extensions can be used with any Macromedia application.

Exchange Manager lets you import extensions from other installations of the application, or compatible applications, without having to reinstall the extension for each application.

To import extensions, do the following:

1. Choose the application you want to import an extension to from the Product menu.

2. Choose File | Import. The Select Product to Import From dialog box appears.

3. Choose the application that has the extension installed from the Product menu. If the application isn't listed (it could be on another computer on the network), browse to the application location.

4. Click OK, and the Import dialog box appears (as shown in this illustration).

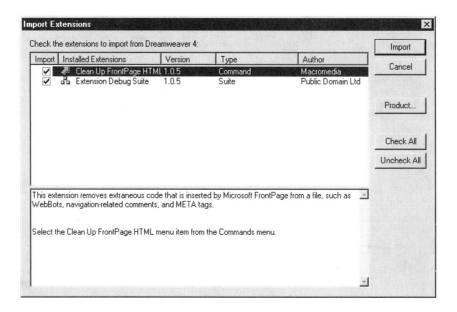

5. Select the extensions you want to import by checking the Import Column check box.

6. Click Import to import the extensions.

Macromedia Exchange

Without a doubt, the first and best place to look for extensions is the Macromedia Exchange at **http://www.macromedia.com/exchange** (as shown in Figure 31–2). Most extension authors submit their extensions to the exchange even if they're available from another source, simply because the Exchange is so well promoted.

To access the Dreamweaver Exchange, you can press the Macromedia button in the Extension Manager's toolbar. Because the Extension Manager navigates to the Exchange for the currently selected product, make sure Dreamweaver is selected if you also have other Extension Manager supported products installed.

 To use the Macromedia Exchange, you must first register. Follow the instructions at the main Exchange page for how to register for an Exchange membership.

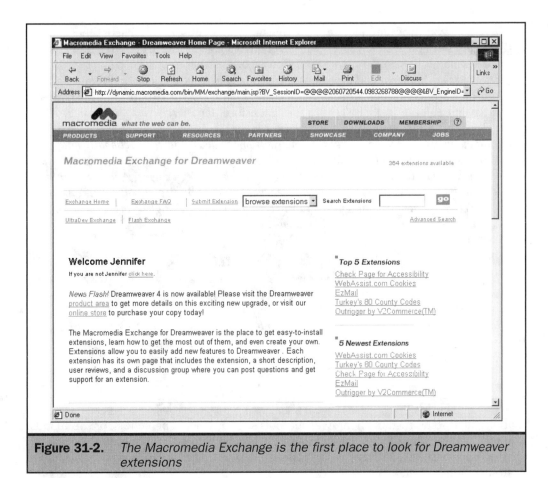

Figure 31-2. The Macromedia Exchange is the first place to look for Dreamweaver extensions

Downloading Extensions

The Dreamweaver Exchange is a repository with hundreds of extensions. To make finding what you want easier, there are both basic and advanced search engines. Use the basic search when you know the name, or part of the name, of an extension. The advanced search lets you specify a category (such as DHTML, eCommerce, Productivity, and so forth) and extension type (Object, Command, Behavior, and so forth). And, you can search based on the rating of the extension by end users, date, or number of downloads if you want to make sure you're getting a well-tested extension.

You can also browse the extensions by choosing a category (or all categories) and perusing the list. This can be helpful for finding those extensions for things you never even thought of.

Dreamweaver provides a forum for extensions so end users can discuss their merits and get help with problems. When you select an extension, you're shown a description of the extension, a link to the forum, and download instructions.

If you decide to download an extension, choose the download option that's right for your platform (Windows or Mac). You can click the Download button directly. The extension automatically installs in the Extension Manager.

In many cases, Macromedia evaluates extensions to determine their reliability and consistency with the Dreamweaver design rules. Downloading the extensions with the Macromedia Approved seal assures you get high-quality extensions. Another useful way to evaluate a potential extension is to see what the users think of it. All extensions can be reviewed by the users and given a rating between 1 and 5. A higher rating means the extension has been well received by its users.

Reviewing and Submitting Bug Reports

One of the nice things about the Dreamweaver Exchange is it's not a one-way source of information. Macromedia encourages Exchange users to submit reviews for extensions, so others can better determine whether to download it.

If you encounter problems or bugs with the extension, go to the forum set up for the extension and see if others are having the same problem. In many cases, the extension author monitors the forum and provides support directly.

Creating and Packaging Extensions

If you created some custom Dreamweaver tools such as objects, behaviors, or commands, you may want to consider packaging them up as extensions. This not only makes sharing your creations with the world possible, it also makes keeping track of your customizations easier.

Creating Extensions

Several of the chapters in this book discuss the process of creating various Dreamweaver extensions. In particular, Chapters 23, 24, and 30 discuss the process of creating various Dreamweaver extensibility objects.

A great source of information about creating extensions is included directly with Dreamweaver. From Dreamweaver, choose Help | Extending Dreamweaver to load the bundled documentation that explains in great detail the extensibility provided by Dreamweaver, as well as a reference for all API functions.

If you want to have your extension become Macromedia Approved or you simply want it to conform to the usability guidelines Macromedia specifies for extensions, two documents are available on the Exchange site: the User Interface Guidelines and the Test plan. To locate these documents, search for Macromedia approved in the site search (not in the Exchange search, which only searches for extensions).

Packaging Extensions

Okay. You created your extension, you followed Macromedia's user interface guidelines, and now you're ready to package the extension up into your own MXP file.

These steps are involved in packaging your own extension:

1. Create a staging folder for your extension and copy all the files that make up the extension to it.

2. Create an extension installation file (.mxi file) for the package (described in the next section).

3. Choose File | Package Extension in the Extension Manager. Browse to your MXI file and click OK.

4. Choose a destination file and location for your extension. Click Save.

5. Using the Extension Manager, test the extension by installing and testing it in Dreamweaver to make sure everything works. Also try disabling and uninstalling the extension.

Extension Installation (MXI) Files

The MXI file format can be somewhat hard to understand without an explanation. The MXI file is an XML-compliant file that describes the extension, its components, and their locations. This listing of a sample MXI file can be used to install the Comment Out sample command from the previous chapter.

```
<macromedia-extension
    name="Comment Out"
    version="1.0"
    type="Command">

    <!-- List the required/compatible products -->

    <products>
        <product name="Dreamweaver" version="4" primary="true" />
    </products>

    <!-- Describe the author -->

    <author name="Jennifer Kettell" />

    <!-- Describe the extension -->

    <description>
```

CUSTOMIZING
DREAMWEAVER

```
<![CDATA[
This is a sample command extension.<br><br>
This command can be used to comment out elements in document.
]]>
</description>

<!-- Describe where the extension shows in the UI of the product -->

<ui-access>
<![CDATA[
Access from the 'Comment Out' entry in the Commands menu.
]]>
</ui-access>
<!-- Describe the files that comprise the extension -->

<files>
    <file name="Comment Out.htm"
destination="$dreamweaver/configuration/commands" />
</files>

<!-- Describe the changes to the configuration -->

<configuration-changes>

    <!-- Add an entry to the commands menu -->

    <menu-insert insertAfter="DWMenu_Commands_SortTable"
skipSeparator="true">
        <menuitem name="Comment Out" file="Commands/Comment Out.htm"
id="Sample_CommentOut" />
        <separator id="Sample_CommentOut_Separator" />
    </menu-insert>

</configuration-changes>
</macromedia-extension>
```

Because this is an XML-compliant file, you might want to read up on XML if you are unfamiliar with it. Chapter 33 gives an introduction to XML and provides resources for learning more. Note, the document has nested tags much like an HTML document. Data to be displayed is contained in CDATA blocks.

An overview of this document may be in order here.

Header

```
<macromedia-extension
    name="Comment Out"
    version="1.0"
    type="Command">
```

The initial header for the document gives the name of the extension, a version number, and the type of extension it is.

Supported extension types are Object, Command, Behavior (or Action), BrowserProfile, Translator, Dictionary, Encoding, Floater, PropertyInspector, jsExtension, Query, Template, ThirdPartyTags, Plugin, Report, and Suite. The type isn't case-sensitive. A *Suite* is an extension that can contain multiple extension types. For instance, a Suite extension could install commands, objects, and behaviors. The extension type is used if the extension is submitted to the Macromedia Exchange, so it can be found in a search for extensions of a certain type.

Supported Products

```
<!-- List the required/compatible products -->

<products>
    <product name="Dreamweaver" version="4" primary="true" />
</products>
```

This section provides a list of the products this object is compatible with. Valid values for the product name are currently Dreamweaver, UltraDev, and Flash. The version attribute specifies the version of the product the extension is designed for. Extension Manager allows an extension to be installed in any version greater than or equal to this version.

Description

```
<!-- Describe the author -->

<author name="Jennifer Kettell" />

<!-- Describe the extension -->

<description>
<![CDATA[
This is a sample command extension.<br><br>
```

CUSTOMIZING
DREAMWEAVER

```
This command can be used to comment out elements in document.
]]>
</description>

<!-- Describe where the extension shows in the UI of the product -->

<ui-access>
<![CDATA[
Access from the 'Comment Out' entry in the Commands menu.
]]>
</ui-access>
```

This section provides the description of the extension shown in the Extension Manager when the extension is selected. This description includes the author name and the extension description. The second section, <ui-access>, describes how the extension is used from the Dreamweaver user interface.

Files

```
<!-- Describe the files that comprise the extension -->

<files>
    <file name="Comment Out.htm"
destination="$dreamweaver/configuration/commands" />
    <file name="Comment Out.js"
destination="$dreamweaver/configuration/commands" />
</files>
```

Files lists all the files that are part of the extension. Provided are the filename and the destination in the Dreamweaver product hierarchy. In this case, both files are going into the Configuration/Commands folder.

Configuration Changes

```
<!-- Describe the changes to the configuration -->

<configuration-changes>

    <!-- Add an entry to the commands menu -->

    <menu-insert insertAfter="DWMenu_Commands_SortTable"
```

```
skipSeparator="true">
            <menuitem name="Comment Out" file="Commands/Comment Out.htm"
id="Sample_CommentOut" />
            <separator id="Sample_CommentOut_Separator" />
        </menu-insert>

    </configuration-changes>
</macromedia-extension>
```

Finally, any needed configuration changes are described. In this case, the command inserts a menu item in the Commands menu right after the Sort Table command.

The configuration changes section can also be used to install shortcuts and ftp extensions.

 *A full description of the .mxi file options can also be found in the Extension File Format Document, found at **http://download.macromedia.com/pub/exchange/ mxi_file_format.pdf**. If you are unable to find it at that URL, search for the file in the Macromedia site search.*

Submitting Extensions to the Exchange

Once an extension is complete and stable, you can submit it to the Macromedia Exchange for other Dreamweaver users. The submission can be started directly from the Extension Manager.

Choose File | Submit Extension from the menu. The Extension Manager then navigates to the Macromedia Exchange extension submission page. Follow the instructions on that page to submit the extension.

Summary

The Macromedia Extension Manager is definitely a boon to extension authors and end users alike. For extension authors, the Macromedia Extension Manager enables them to create increasingly more complex and powerful extensions. For end users, it allows them to manage both simple and complex extensions with the same ease.

- The Macromedia Extension Manager handles the task of installing and managing extensions, so you don't have to keep track of them separately.
- The Dreamweaver Exchange is the first place you should go for Dreamweaver extensions.
- An extension is created from a Macromedia extension installation (MXI) file.

■ Extensions that may be useful to others should be submitted to the
Macromedia Exchange.

Part IX turns the discussion toward Dreamweaver's use with next-generation
technologies. Chapter 32 starts off with a discussion about Dreamweaver and wireless
technologies.

The Complete Reference

Part IX

Dreamweaver into the Next Generation

Chapter 32

Compatibility with the Next Generation

These days, many people find accessing the Web on the go is increasingly necessary. They need and want to access e-mail, stock quotes, and news, as well as their favorite Web sites, all the time and no matter where they are, not just when they're sitting at a desk during office hours.

The explosion of Web-connected *Personal Data Assistants* (*PDAs*) and Wireless Web-capable mobile phones has put the Web within reach for millions of people right now. And no end is in sight—rapidly falling prices because of competition and the arrival of more and more Web-capable devices means supporting these devices in the future is going to become more and more important.

Small devices, such as PDAs and mobile phones, have some rather extreme limitations compared to a personal computer Web browser. Display real estate is miniscule: PDA resolution typically ranges from a high of 240 × 320 pixels on PocketPC devices running the Windows CE operating system to 160 × 160 on the popular Palm Pilot organizer. Mobile phones are even worse. Some models don't display graphics at all; they only display a few lines of text.

Because of these limitations, standard Web pages simply aren't usable. A great deal of work has been focused on producing solutions geared toward wireless users with limited bandwidth and small displays.

This chapter discusses the *Wireless Application Protocol* (*WAP*) standard, which is widely supported by U.S. wireless service providers. Two other popular ways of accessing wireless services are also discussed: AvantGo, a popular content service for PDAs (and, now, for mobile phones), and the i-Mode service, a competitor of WAP, which is popular in Japan.

Wireless, WAP, and WML

With digital cell phones, PDAs, and other miniature electronic gadgetry taking the wired world by storm, the birth of a standard way for all these devices to access the Internet was only natural. The *Wireless Application Protocol Forum,* an industry consortium of over 500 companies with an interest in wireless technologies, has brought forth WAP as that standard.

WAP enables on-the-go users of mobile phones easy access to the Wireless Web, enabling the use of e-mail, news, weather, traffic, electronic commerce, and banking, as well as custom corporate intranet applications. As with the World-Wide Web, the possibilities are endless.

Note   *The browser on a WAP device is sometimes referred to as a user agent. This more generic term could refer to clients that barely resemble browsers, such as voice activated/response systems. User agent is used interchangeably with "browser" in this book.*

To leverage existing Web services and application development resources, WAP uses off-the-shelf HTTP 1.1 Web servers to provide content. This allows WAP content to include server-side technologies used on the Web, such as CGI, ASP, and Java servlets (the server side version of Java applets).

Instead of using HTML, WAP defines a new language, *Wireless Markup Language* (*WML*), which is an application of the *Extensible Markup Language* (*XML*). This means it conforms to XML structure and syntax. Chapter 33 provides more information about XML in general.

You can find more information about WAP and WML at the WAP Forum's site at **http://www.wapforum.org**. *The WAP Forum is an industry association of companies interested in having input in the developing WAP standards.*

One difference between WML and HTML pages is this: while an HTML document contains a single page to be displayed, a WML document, instead, represents a structure called a deck. A *deck* is composed of at least one or more cards, the individually displayable screens in a WML application. The WML page represents a deck, which means an entire deck is downloaded at a time: No need exists for the user to wait for another page to be retrieved if a link simply leads to another card in the deck. In addition to the individual screen cards, a deck may also contain a single template card, which defines information that applies to all cards in the deck.

With this structure in mind, you might imagine how you would structure a hypothetical WAP site. The first card might be the site's main menu. Selecting each item from the menu would bring up a different card, possibly with more menu options or the content the visitor wants.

Because WML is an XML application, it must use XML syntax. The first lines of a WML file include an XML file declaration indicating the version of XML supported by the document. Following that is a DOCTYPE specifier, which points to the WAP forum's document type definition for WML.

Instead of the <head> and <body> sections of an HTML document, a WML document only needs one section. (There's a WML <head> tag, but it's only used to contain access control and metadata, and isn't required.) The rest of the document is enclosed in a <wml></wml> tag pair, with <card></card> tag pairs making up the individual cards. A basic XML document looks like this:

```
<?xml version="1.0" encoding="ISO-8859-1"?>
<!DOCTYPE wml PUBLIC "-//WAPFORUM//DTD WML 1.1//EN"
"http://www.wapforum.org//DTD//wml_1.1.xml">
<wml>
  <card id="card1">
    This is the card1 text
  </card>
</wml>
```

Remember the following three points about WML tags:

- All tags must have close tags. In the case of tags that contain only attributes and no other nested tags or text, a single slash can be used before the closing bracket of the tag. For example, `<br></br>` can also be written as `<br/>`.

- All tags and attributes must be lowercase. For example, `<CARD ID="card1">` isn't allowed. `<card id="card1">` is correct.

- All attribute values must be contained in quotes. You may use single or double quotes. For example, `<card id=card1>` is incorrect. `<card id="card1">` and `<card id='card1'>` are acceptable.

Nokia WML Studio for Dreamweaver

Nokia, a leading mobile phone manufacturer, has created an extension that enables Dreamweaver users to create pages that conform to the WAP standard: the Nokia WML Studio for Dreamweaver. This extension, currently only available for Windows, provides a WML 1.1 parser with visual error feedback from within Dreamweaver's HTML editor. The Nokia WML Studio for Dreamweaver also has a preview feature that runs in your browser and enables you to display your pages as they would look using various Nokia mobile phone interfaces.

*You can download the Nokia WML Studio for Dreamweaver from the Macromedia Exchange at **http://www.macromedia.com/exchange/dreamweaver**. Search for WML using the search extensions box.*

Using the WML Studio

After downloading and installing the Nokia WML Studio, you can see several additions to your Dreamweaver configuration. For starters, a new item is added to the menu bar of the document view window. The WML menu (illustrated in the following) adds several WML-related tasks:

The documentation provided with the Nokia WML Studio goes into much more detail than this book has room to cover. Use the WML | Help menu to view it.

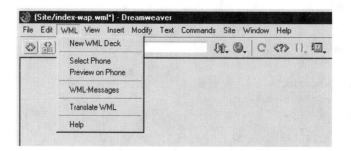

■ **New WML Deck**: Selecting this item opens a new window with the Nokia WML environment. The basic document with the XML header, the DOCTYPE specifier, the <xml> tag pair, and an initial <card> tag pair are created. Figure 32-1 shows the WML Studio operating environment.

■ **Select Phone**: This menu item brings up a dialog box (illustrated in the following), which enables you to select a phone model from a number of Nokia phones. A custom option also enables you to specify your own phone parameters.

■ **Preview on Phone**: Selecting this item launches a browser window containing an applet that simulates the chosen phone. The first time you select this, a Security Warning dialog box is shown, which asks you to verify the installation of the applet. Click Yes.

■ **WML Messages**: This activates the WML Messages window, which validates your WML code and shows you any syntax errors in your deck. The following shows this window. Your deck must be saved and you must have the Design view selected to use the WML Messages window.

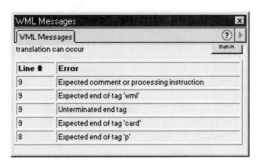

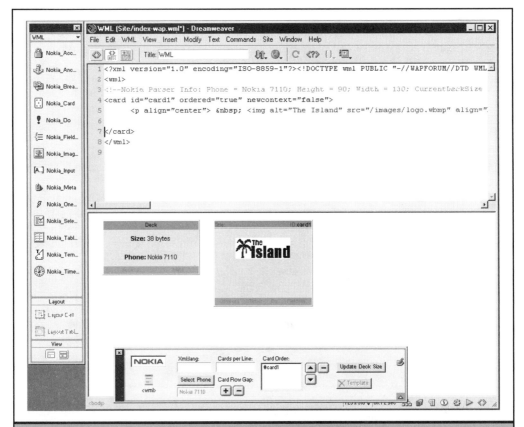

Figure 32-1. *The Nokia WML Studio view cleverly displays WML elements using layers in the Design view*

- **Translate WML**: This item can be used to translate older WML 1.0 pages into WML 1.1 compliant pages. If no DOCTYPE header exists, one is added. The document is also parsed to find any errors.

- **Help**: This menu item launches a browser with local HTML pages containing the WML Studio documentation.

In addition to the WML menu, the WML Studio also adds items to the Objects panel. A new object category, WML, has 14 new objects to assist in creating WML pages. The objects are of six general types: Containers, Presentation, Navigation, User Input, Events, and Invisibles. An explanation of the objects, provided by the WML Studio, follows.

All the objects described in this section can be accessed from the Objects panel by selecting the WML category, a new category created by the WML Studio.

Containers

WML Container objects are those used to create cards and templates. These are the highest-level elements you create in a WML deck.

Template This object is used to insert a `<template>` element. *Templates* enable you to specify event bindings that apply to all cards in the deck. You can set three events in the template object:

- **OnTimer**—Specifies a card the user should navigate to when a timer expires.
- **OnEnterBackward**—Specifies a card the user should navigate to when the user navigates into a card using the `prev` task.
- **OnEnterForward**—Specifies a card the user should navigate to when the user navigates with a go task.

Card This object is used to create a new card. A *card* represents one screen of information and can contain text (including markup), images, and navigation information. Inserting this object by clicking the Nokia_Card object brings up the Insert Card dialog box, which enables you to set the following attributes.

- **Title**—Specifies a title for the card. This can be used at the top of the display, in bookmarks or in other ways, depending on the browser.

■ **ID**—Specifies an ID that can be used to reference the object in an href. This ID must start with a letter (for example, c21).

■ **New Context**—Checking this box tells the browser to delete all in-memory references to other cards, such as variables. They can no longer be accessed afterwards. This is typically used on the first card of a deck.

■ **Ordered**—Tells the user agent (browser) the cards should be referenced in a fixed order.

■ **OnTimer, OnEnterForward, OnEnterBackward**—These event handlers are the same as for Templates, although at the card level they only affect that card. Setting actions for the card event handlers overrides the actions for any template handlers.

Presentation

The presentation objects are used to add formatting hints and tags to a card. The presentation objects provided by the WML studio include images, tables, and breaks.

Image   WAP browsers have a special 1-bit image format used to display graphics, the *Wireless Bitmap* (*WBMP*) format. The Image object is used to insert these files into a card.

Clicking the Nokia_Image object brings up the Insert Image dialog box (shown in the following). This dialog box has the following fields:

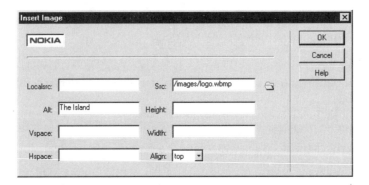

■ **Localsrc**—This attribute specifies an image built-in to the phone. If the localsrc exists, it's used instead of the image file from the server. Development information for specific phones indicates if this field is supported.

■ **Alt**—This specifies alternate text to be displayed if the browser cannot display images. This value is required.

■ **Vspace** and **Hspace**—These attributes specify the amount of white space to show above and below (*Vspace*) or to the left and right (*Hspace*) of an image. The value can be specified in pixels or percentage of screen height. These attributes are only hints; the browser can choose to ignore them if space is at a premium.

- **Src**—This specifies the URL for the image and should specify a path to a WBMP file. For example, `/images/logo.wbmp`. This value is required.

- **Height** and **Width**—These attributes can provide the browser with information indicating the size of the image. The browser can then reserve space for the image while rendering the remainder of the card before the image loads. These values are hints; the browser may choose to ignore them.

- **Align**—Specifies the alignment of the image with respect to the insertion point. Possible values are the following:

  - **bottom**—The bottom of the image is aligned with the current text line.

  - **middle**—The middle of the image is aligned with the middle of the current text line.

  - **top**—The top of the image is aligned with the top of the current text line.

Once an image is inserted, it's displayed in the card in the Design view (as the following shows).

You can also see how the image will look when rendered on a phone by choosing the WML | Preview on Phone menu item, as shown in the following illustration.

*WBMP images can be created with Macromedia Fireworks. Go to **http://www.macromedia.com/support/fireworks** and search for WBMP. You then find a link to the Fireworks WBMP Import/Export Xtra feature. If you don't have Fireworks, a fully functional 30-day trial version can also be downloaded from there. To use the WBMP filter, create a monochromatic (single color) image sized to fit the target phone display. In the Optimize inspector, choose WBMP from the file format drop-down list. Then, you can export the image from the File | Export menu.*

Table   Tables, along with the formatting elements `<td>` and `<tr>`, function in much the same way as they do in HTML pages. A few key differences and limitations do exist, however.

When you create a table object, you're presented with the Insert Table dialog box, which prompts for the rows and columns in the table. After the table is created, you can select it in the card display and edit the following attributes in the Property Inspector, as the following illustrates:

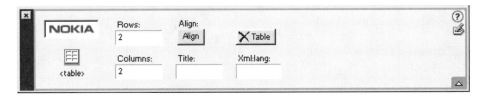

- **Rows** and **Columns**—You can adjust the number of rows and columns in the table. Remember, if you specify a number smaller than the current value, any data in those extra rows or columns is thrown away.

- **Align**—Here you can specify the alignment for each column. Clicking this button activates a pop-up dialog box, which lets you choose a column and an alignment (left, right, or center).

- **X Table**—This button can be used to delete the table.

- **Title**—Specifies a title for the table. This value may be used for presentation by the user agent.

- **Xml:lang**—This attribute specifies the natural or formal language for the element. For example, for U.S. English, the language code is en-US.

WML columns don't contain any formatting information. WML tables have no borders, and the size of the table cells is determined by the browser.

Break   Like the HTML `<br>` element, the WML `<br/>` element (note the use of lowercase and the ending /) is used to force a line break in text.

Navigation

You can create a link in WML in a few ways. The `<a href="link">` method works exactly the same way as in HTML. In WML, however, an `<anchor>` tag provides some benefits over using `<a>`.

Anchor   The `<anchor>` tag can be used to set a hyperlink from one WML card or deck to another. This tag is used with the `<go>` tag to make the link.

Creating an anchor is similar to creating a link in Dreamweaver's HTML editor. Select the text you want to make into a link, and then click the Nokia_Anchor button in the Objects panel. The Property Inspector for anchors is then displayed.

The Property Inspector enables you to set several attributes for an anchor. These are as follows:

- **Title**—This attribute specifies a short text string that labels the link. The user agent can use this to label a button, provide a tool tip, or even ignore it completely. Titles should be limited to six characters or less to work on as wide a range of devices as possible.

- **Xml:lang**—This attribute specifies the natural language of the element. For U.S. English, this should be set to en-US.

- **Task**—This drop-down list enables you to choose from Go, Previous, or Refresh. The Go task specifies navigation to an URL. You can enter the following parameters for this task when you click the Edit button:

  - **Href**—Specifies a destination URL. This can be the ID of another card in the deck or a reference to a local or remote .wml file.

  - **Method**—Specifies the type of HTTP request. This supports both GET and POST methods.

  - **Accept Charset**—This is a comma or space-separated list of character encodings. The server must accept any one of these encodings.

  - **Sendref**—If true, the user agent must provide the URL of the current deck as an identifier to the server. This allows the server to perform access control on the target deck.

  - **List**—This section lists the Setvar and Postfield elements present in the Go task. You can use the plus (+) sign button to add a new variable, along with its name, value, and type (Setvar or Postfield). The minus (-) sign button deletes an element from the list.

  - **Postfield**—These elements specify a field name and value to transmit to the server during an URL request.

  - **Setvar**—Specifies a variable to be set in the current browser context. This variable may be referenced in another card.

- **Previous task**—Used to navigate to the last URL visited. An opportunity occurs to add a *Setvar* variable for reference.

- **Refresh task**—Tells the user agent it must reload the current display context because of changed information in a Setvar variable. Like the Previous task, you have the opportunity to add a Setvar variable in the dialog box.

Do   The *do* element is the basic card-level user interface element. Unlike anchors, which are represented by a link on the screen, the representation of the do element is completely user-agent-specific. As a developer, you should only assume the element will be mapped to a button or some other control on the device.

Do elements can be used at both the card and template levels. Do elements in a template apply to all cards in a deck, unless they're overridden by do elements in the cards themselves.

To insert a do element, click the Nokia_Do button in the Objects panel after positioning the cursor in the card you want to modify. The Insert Do dialog box is shown and enables you to set the following parameters:

- **Label**—This provides a text string the user agent can use to label whichever button is used to activate the link. Labels should be kept to six characters or less to be compatible with the widest range of devices.

- **Name**—This specifies the name of the event binding and can be used to override a do element in a template.

- **Type**—This provides a hint to the user agent about how the element is intended to be used and how it should be mapped to a button or other control. The actual button used depends on the wireless device and how it defines them. For example, if the type is `help`, and the device has a standard button it uses for help, the action is assigned to that button. User agents must be able to accept all types, but may treat those it doesn't recognize as unknown. The supported task types are as follows:

  - **accept**—Positive acknowledgement.
  - **prev**—Backward history navigation.
  - **help**—A request for help.
  - **reset**—A resetting state.
  - **options**—A request for options.
  - **delete**—Delete an item.
  - **unknown**—An unspecified type.

  - **Optional**—This attribute, if checked, tells the user agent it can ignore this element.

When the Do object is inserted, the Property Inspector enables you to set the Task type. The three tasks supported by the Anchor object, Go, Prev, and Refresh are also supported here, and are the same as in the Anchor object. In addition, there's another task: No Operation (sometimes referred to as *No-op*). This task does nothing and can be used when overriding a template do element.

User Input

Like most other Web sites, WML sites must be able to obtain information from the user. WML provides input and select elements, which work similarly to their HTML equivalents.

Input   The *input* element is a text entry device that works similarly to its HTML counterpart. To insert an input element, click the card you want to modify, and then click the Nokia_Input button in the Objects panel. You can then edit the following parameters from the Property Inspector (shown in the following illustration):

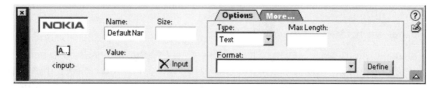

- **Name**—If a variable contains the initial information to load into the input box, this attribute must have the same name as the variable.

- **Value**—This attribute specifies a value to use in the input box. If there's a name attribute, the value of its variable takes precedence.

- **Size**—Specifies the size of the input box in characters.

- **Max Length**—Specifies the maximum number of characters that can be entered into the input box.

- **Type**—Specifies the type of the text input area. The two possible types are text and password. The password method obscures the entry of the text with asterisks so as not to display the actual password.

- **Format**—This specifies an input mask to be applied against the user's input.

- **Xml:lang**—Specifies the language of the input box. The setting for U.S. English is en-us.

- **Tab**—Specifies a tab stop position in the interface.

- **Title**—This element specifies a title for the object. The user agent can decide how or whether to display this information.

- **Empty OK**—Specifies whether empty input is okay. This can be used with optional formatted entry fields.

Select   Like the HTML element of the same name, the select element allows the user to choose items from a list. Each item is specified by an `<option>` tag containing one line of text. Option elements may also be organized into groups using the `<optgroup>` element.

To add a Select object, first click in the card you want to modify, and then click the Nokia_Select button from the Objects panel. After the object is inserted, click it to show the Select object's Property Inspector, as the following illustrates. The parameters you can set for this object are as follows:

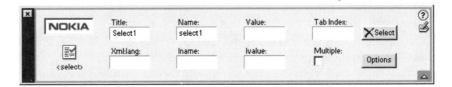

- ■ **Title**—Specifies a title that may be used by the user agent for in the object's presentation.

- ■ **Name**—Indicates a name for the Select object.

- ■ **Value**—Specifies the name of a variable to set with the results of a selection being made. The variable is set to the value of the chosen option. If multiple selections are allowed, this variable is set with a list of all selected values separated by a semicolon.

- ■ **Tab Index**—Specifies a tab stop for the object. This is used to set the order the elements are cycled through when tabbed over.

- ■ **Xml:lang**—Specifies the language of the element's content. The user agent should make every effort to display the data in accordance with this attribute.

- ■ **Iname**—Specifies the name of a variable to set with the index number of the selection. A zero value indicates no items are selected.

- ■ **Ivalue**—Specifies the default option. The `iname` value is assigned to the value of this option when the Select object is first loaded.

- ■ **Multiple**—Indicates whether multiple selections are allowed.

- ■ **X Select**—Enables you to delete a Select object.

- ■ The Options button enables you to add, edit, and delete options and option groups.

The Options and Optiongroups dialog box, illustrated in the following, is used to add and organize option elements. The attributes you can access through this dialog box are as follows:

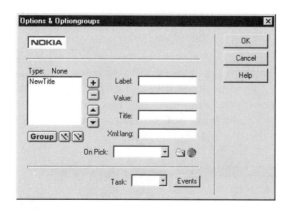

- **Value**—Specifies the value to use when setting the Name variable.

- **Title**—Specifies a title for this option.

- **Xml:lang**—Specifies the language of the element or its attributes.

- **On Pick**—Specifies an action to take when a user selects an item from the list, generating an OnPick event.

- **Label**—This isn't really an attribute. The label is the text that goes between the `<option>` and `</option>` tags. This is the text displayed to the user and it can be used in place of the title attribute if that doesn't exist.

- **Plus (+)** and **Minus (-)**—These buttons can be used to add and remove elements from the list.

- **Up** and **Down** arrows—The arrow buttons can be used to organize the elements in the list.

- **Group**—This is used to create an option group by selecting multiple elements by clicking it.

- If an Optiongroup is in the list, selecting it and choosing the downward slanting arrow on a stairway button shows the elements contained in the group. The button with the upward slanting arrow on a stairway takes you back to the containing optiongroup.

- Deleting an optiongroup means its member elements are moved.

You can assign a task to an element. These are the Go, Previous, Refresh, and No-op tasks described with the Anchor and Do objects.

Events

WML events are used to add some automation to a deck or a card. You can specify new cards to navigate to in response to the events *OnTimer* (fired when a timer element expires), *OnEnterBackward* (fired when a Prev navigates back into a card),

OnEnterForward (fired when a Go navigates into a card), and *OnPick* (fired when the user selects an item from a list).

OnEvent   The *OnEvent* object enables you to attach an event handler to a card. To insert it, click the card you want to modify, and then click the Nokia_OnEvent button in the Objects panel. The Insert OnEvent dialog box appears (see the following illustration), providing you with the opportunity to choose an event and a task to execute in response to the event. The choices are

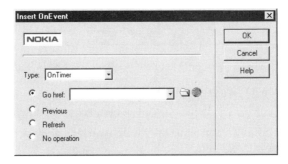

- ■ **Type**—One of OnTimer, OnEnterForward, OnEnterBackward, and OnPick.
- ■ **Go href**—Specify an URL to jump to in response to the event.
- ■ **Previous**—Specify the user agent should return to the previous page.
- ■ **Refresh**—Specify the user agent should reload the current page.
- ■ **No operation**—Specify the user agent should do nothing.

As the following illustrates, the Onevent label is highlighted at the bottom of the card in the Design view when you have an event handler. Clicking this activates the Onevent Property Inspector, which enables you to change any of the Onevent attributes.

Timer   The *Timer* object is used to set an inactivity timer for a card. The timer is set when the card is activated and stopped when the card is exited. If the user hasn't taken an action by the time the timer counts down to zero, the onTimer event is fired. The handler for this event would, in most cases, then navigate to a time out card.

To add a timer to a card, click anywhere inside the card, and then click the Nokia_Timer button in the Objects panel. You then need to set two parameters in the Insert Timer dialog box:

- The **Name** parameter specifies a variable to use for the initial timer value. The variable is then set with the current timer value when the card is exited or when the timer expires.

- The **Value** parameter specifies a default timer value. If the variable specified by Name hasn't been set when the card is loaded, it is set with this value. Otherwise, if the variable already has a value, this parameter is ignored. The timer values is a positive integer representing increments of 1/10 seconds. So, if, for instance, you want to set the timer for 20 seconds, you need to set the Value parameter to 200.

After clicking OK, the Timer indicator at the bottom of the card visualization is highlighted. Clicking this indicator activates the Property Inspector, giving you the opportunity to change any timer values.

Invisibles

The *Invisible* objects are elements that aren't visible to the user, but are useful behind the scenes.

Access   The *Access* object is used to specify access control information for a deck. When an access element is added, access is restricted to the domain and path specified.

To insert an Access object, click the deck element. Then click the Nokia_Access button in the Objects panel. The Insert Access dialog box prompts you for the following parameters:

- **Domain**—This specifies the domain you want to allow access to. Leaving this parameter blank restricts access to the current domain.

- **Path**—This specifies the path you want to allow access to. The default value for the path is / (slash), allowing any URL in the domain to have access.

The referring URL is suffix matched against the Domain parameter (for instance, www.pendragn.com would match pendragn.com) and prefix matched against the Path (if the path specifies /abc, any directory in that tree would be allowed access).

To change these values later, you can click the Access indicator at the bottom of the deck element. This activates the Access Property Inspector.

Fieldset   The *Fieldset* object is used to group related fields or text. This grouping helps the user agent optimize layout and navigation.

To wrap text with a fieldset, select it in a card view and click the Nokia_Fieldset object in the Objects panel. The Insert Fieldset dialog box then prompts you for a Title for the fieldset.

After a fieldset has been added, you can modify it by selecting the highlighted Fieldset indicator at the bottom of the card. This activates the Property Inspector for the Fieldset object.

Meta   *Meta* tags are used to list information about the deck. This information can be used in search engines to bring users to your site, or it can correspond to HTTP headers to specify a refresh value or content type.

The meta object dialog box enables you to set the following attributes:

■ **Attribute**—This can be either name or http-equiv. If it is name, the user agent ignores any metadata named within the attribute. If http-equiv, the content value can be used to generate the following:

■ **Forua**—Specifies the metadata should be sent to the user agent.

■ **Value**—Specifies either name content or the http-equiv value, depending on what you chose for the attribute.

■ **Content**—Enter the values for the http-equiv or name attribute here.

■ **Scheme**—If the metadata requires a specific structure to interpret it, the scheme can be entered here. This value varies depending on the type of metadata.

To edit the metadata later, click the highlighted Meta indicator at the bottom of the deck element. The Property Inspector can then be used to set any of the metadata parameters.

Wireless Bitmaps
The standard for WAP images is the WBMP. These are 1-bit, black-and-white images.

Moving Up to PDAs, or What to Do with All That Space?

A lot of inroads have been made getting Web content onto cell phones. Nevertheless, times still occur when a tiny browser window and monochrome graphics just won't cut it.

In many cases, while PDAs are capable of viewing WAP pages, they're also capable of much more. In some cases, they're capable of full-fledged Web browsing. Although the screen real estate of a PDA is generally much larger than that of a phone, however, most Web pages are still designed with PCs in mind.

A happy medium has been reached in services such as AvantGo, whose sites are tailored for viewing on PDA screens.

AvantGo

AvantGo provides the tools and the infrastructure to deliver PDA-optimized Web sites in the form of channels. An AvantGo channel can be downloaded on a PDA user's docking PC and transferred over the serial link to the PDA. Or, if the PDA user is lucky enough to have a wireless connection to the Web, channels can be updated on the go.

Visit the AvantGo Website at **http://www.avantgo.com** *to get more information about the AvantGo service, subscribe to channels for your PDA, and get developer information for delivering both Internet and Enterprise content.*

AvantGo Extensions for Dreamweaver

At press time, Dreamweaver and AvantGo have announced extensions for Dreamweaver and Dreamweaver UltraDev to enable developers to build AvantGo channels easily. The extensions are designed to make it easy to tag pages as viewable on handheld devices and to provide tools that scan your site looking for potential problems, which could result in less-than-optimal viewing for a user. Once the extensions become available, they can be found on the Macromedia Exchange for Dreamweaver at **http://www.macromedia.com/exchange/dreamweaver**.

i-Mode

In 1999, in Japan, NTT DoCoMo, the national phone company's wireless service provider, introduced an information service for mobile phones called *i-Mode.* Since then, the service has proved popular in Japan, where many people don't own personal computers and depend on their mobile phones as their only link to the Internet. The company is now looking to expand this service to the rest of the world, including the United States. NTT DoCoMo already has a partnership with AOL, and others may be on the way, which would allow the company to leapfrog the established WAP standard in the U.S. Being familiar with the i-Mode service is definitely a good idea for a Web developer that creates content for wireless devices.

Unlike WAP, which uses the XML-based WML, i-Mode uses a subset of HTML. This provides an advantage for developers who can use their existing HTML knowledge and tools such as Dreamweaver. GIF images, including animation, are supported. This capability, along with color displays available on some models, make i-Mode sites appealing for consumers and developers alike.

You can find out more information about developing i-Mode Web sites and supported HTML tags at DoCoMo Net, **http://www.nttdocomo.com**.

At press time, at least one extension is available on the Macromedia Exchange to aid in the creation of i-Mode HTML pages. The i-Mode502i extension adds a browser validator you can use with Dreamweaver's Check Target Browser feature.

Summary

Wireless access to the Web is becoming more and more common, and developers have to keep up with a seemingly endless stream of new technologies and standards to give all visitors the best experience possible. One thing all these technologies have in common is that Dreamweaver can be extended to support them. When embracing a new Web technology, one of the first places you should look for help is the Macromedia Exchange to see if a Dreamweaver extension is available to assist you.

- The Wireless Application Protocol (WAP) and its markup language, WML, are the industry standards for wireless Internet access using mobile phones.

- The Nokia WML Studio for Dreamweaver provides a complete development environment to assist in the creation of WML pages.

- AvantGo is a popular service for creating small Web sites called channels, which are optimized for downloading and reading on PDAs, as well as mobile phones.

- i-Mode is a popular wireless service in Japan, which might make inroads into the U.S. in the future.

The next chapter covers the extensible Markup Language (XML) in more detail and provides a glimpse into the future of XML-compliant Web development.

The Complete Reference

Chapter 33

XML and XHTML

There's a lot of buzz concerning XML. And it's not just in the Internet community, either; XML is fast becoming the standard for information interchange across the computer industry. The reason is, for the first time, XML provides a way of representing any data in a text file in a highly structured way while, at the same time, making the data readable by people. Previously, any program that wanted to import data from another program usually had to understand a proprietary binary format. Now, with XML, programs that can parse XML can, by definition, import from each other, provided they understand the tags used. The result is a cross-platform standard, independent of any particular software or hardware. In the near future, every major application worth its salt will be able to read and write XML-formatted documents.

Many advantages exist to using XML instead of traditional binary or delimited text files. First, because they're simply text files, XML documents are automatically cross-platform compatible with no worries about system concerns, such as byte ordering. In our increasingly Internet-distributed world, having specifications that can work across platforms is important. Although delimited text files (with, say, columns of comma-separated values) can work across platforms and across the Internet as well, they're definitely not structured well. The simple act of adding or removing a column could totally break a parser.

XML is extremely versatile. Both XML and HTML are derived from the Standard Generalized Markup Language (SGML) and both have similar syntax. So much so that creating a version of HTML that conforms to the XML structure isn't that difficult. This, in fact, is what the W3C has done—the XHTML standard is already in place as the future of Web development. This chapter discusses the basics of XML documents and how they're formed. Then, it discusses XHTML and tells you how to make your documents compliant now. Most important for a Dreamweaver book, this chapter also discusses how Dreamweaver deals (or not) with XHTML and some steps you can follow to deal with it.

XML Basics

Just like HTML, XML is a markup language designed to add structure to a document. An XML document consists of elements containing tags, with the capability to nest additional elements between the open and close tags. While HTML was designed to add structure to the display of the data in a document, XML is only concerned with describing the data itself.

While HTML is a language with a predefined set of supported tags and their semantics (how they relate in a document), XML is, instead, a metamarkup language. Instead of defining the elements of the language, it simply provides the rules for creating them. The author of the document defines all the tags used in an XML document. Because no predefined tag set exists, there aren't any preconceived semantics. All the semantics of an XML document are defined by the applications that process them or by Document Type Definition files.

Tip

You can find the complete documentation for XML and related off-shoot technologies at the W3C's site at **http://www.w3c.org**. *Another excellent site to visit to get current information about XML is XML.com at* **http://www.xml.com**. *Popular books to learn about XML include* Inside XML, *by Steven Holzner (New Riders Publishing). Developing XML Solutions, by Jake Sturm (Microsoft Press) provides a lot of information about XML, particularly in how it pertains to Microsoft products.*

The Basics of an XML Document

An XML file may consist of these basic parts:

- An XML file declaration. At the top of every XML document is a line indicating the version of XML the document conforms to. For example, `<?xml version="1.0">` declares the document conforms to the XML 1.0 specification.

- An optional DOCTYPE declaration to specify the Document Type Definition (DTD) to use. A DTD is a file containing a set of rules that define the elements and attributes, and the relationship between objects in the document. The Extensible Hypertext Markup Language (XHTML) is defined in various DTD files. For example, the DOCTYPE specifier for the Transitional XHTML standard would look like this:

```
<!DOCTYPE html PUBLIC "-//W3C//DTD XHTML 1.0 Transitional//EN"
"http://www.w3.org/TR/xhtml1/DTD/xhtml1-transitional.dtd">
```

A DTD is strictly optional. An XML document is referred to as being well formed if it conforms to XML specification without any tag validation. XML documents that conform to a DTD are called *valid* documents.

- Elements, consisting of tags, attributes, and their values. These are like HTML elements, except the XML elements don't have to conform to any set tag definitions. All XML elements must include an end tag. As a shortcut, XML also allows tags without any values or child tags to use a / at the end instead of an end tag. Here are some examples of valid XML tags:

```
<snackfood type="cakes">Devil Dogs</snackfood>
<snackfood type="chips">Doritos</snackfood>
<beverage type="milk"/>
```

- Comments. XML comments are identical to HTML comments. They let you embed descriptive text into your XML documents to make it easier for someone (including yourself) to understand the document later.

```
<!--This is an XML comment-->
```

- CDATA blocks. CDAT Character Data (CDATA) is a way for XML documents to contain text used exactly as it is. The XML parser ignores any information enclosed in CDATA blocks, but they may be used, for example, to enclose example XML content you want displayed, but not parsed, or to enclose JavaScript code.

```
<script type="text/javascript">
<![CDATA[
document.write("Hello, World");
]]>
</script>
```

Exporting and Importing XML from Templates

Dreamweaver uses XML as the data format when exporting data from templates. Each template document enables you to set editable regions. When you export the data to XML, the regions are exported as name/value pairs into an XML file, so you can work with the data outside of Dreamweaver. Conversely, if you have data in an appropriately structured XML file, you can import the data into a document based on a template. For more information about templates and exporting editable regions, see Chapter 29.

XHTML

The future standard for information display on the Web received an official recommendation as a standard by the World Wide Web Consortium (W3C) on January 26, 2000. XHTML 1.0 is the first version of the Extensible Hypertext Markup Language, a language designed to replace HTML. XHTML documents are based on XML standards. Therefore, although based on HTML 4.01, XHTML 1.0 is stricter and enforces some rules that you should adhere to in your document.

- All XHTML elements must be closed. HTML allows some standalone tags, such as `<br>`. In XHTML, you're required to provide an end tag (`</br>`) or the start tag must end with `/>` (`<br />`). This is the biggest syntax deviation between HTML and XHTML. However, existing browsers can interpret this tag if you remember this tip. Note, while strict XML doesn't require a space between the tag name and the ending `/`, it's a good idea to do so in XHTML. The reason is because existing browsers simply ignore tags and attributes they don't understand in the interest of backwards compatibility. They simply ignore the `/`, making most existing browsers able to interpret XHTML pages.

- Attribute values must be quoted and minimization is forbidden. All attribute values must be in quotes:

```
color = "red"
```

- The name attribute has been deprecated in favor of the id attribute.

- A type attribute is required for the script element. The language attribute has been deprecated in favor of the type attribute, which specifies the MIME type of the language:

```
<script type="text/javascript">
```

- XHTML documents have some mandatory elements.

- All tags and their attributes must be lowercase.

- Elements should all be properly nested. In HTML, sometimes you can nest attributes in an improper order, such as this:

```
<i><b>This is the text</i></b>
```

In XHTML, proper nesting is strictly enforced:

```
<i><b>This text is properly formatted</b></i>
```

- Documents must be well formed. In XHMTL, you're required to use the basic HTML root tags for a document, including <html>, <head>, and <body>. The <head> element must contain a <title> subelement, and a DOCTYPE specification at the beginning of the document is required:

```
<!DOCTYPE html
PUBLIC "-//W3C//DTD XHTML 1.0 Strict//EN"
"http://www.w3.org/TR/xhtml1/DTD/strict.dtd">
<html>
<head>
<title>Document Title</title>
</head>
<body>
Body text goes here
</body>
</html>
```

XHTML: What's the Point?

At this point, you may be asking yourself why XHTML is needed. After all, HTML has served just fine for years. The answer is that, in fact, HTML has not always served well. The mere fact that browsers interpret the less strict HTML standard differently has always been a major headache for Web developers, as well as for browser makers who have to code for all sorts of strange permutations of improperly nested tags. This is going to become more and more important in the future, with browsers running not only on desktop PCs, but also on PDAs, wireless phones, and the like. Keeping the parsing engine of the browser simpler can make it less prone to errors and incompatibilities.

DREAMWEAVER INTO
THE NEXT GENERATION

More to the point, XHTML is now the W3C standard, so any new additions to HTML are going to be made using XHTML as a base. Keeping up with the standards now can prevent more problems down the road.

Dreamweaver and XHTML

Unfortunately, Dreamweaver in its current incarnation doesn't generate XHTML 1.0-compliant code. The DOCTYPE specifier is missing, Tags are generated without an end tag, script elements use the language attribute instead of the type attribute, and so on.

Taking advantage of Dreamweaver's massive customizability to make it XHTML aware is possible, however.

Modifying Default.htm

When you create a blank document in Dreamweaver, you either use a template (one you created yourself or obtained from another source) or you create a new document. When you create a new document, Dreamweaver itself uses a template file in the Dreamweaver 4/Configuration/Templates folder called *Default.htm*. You can modify this file to generate an initial HTML document that includes a DOCTYPE tag, as well as properly specified initial tags.

Any time you make a change to one of Dreamweaver's standard files, it's prudent to make a backup copy of the original file first, so you can return to it if the modifications don't go as you planned.

Here's a listing of the original Default.htm file used by Dreamweaver:

```
<HTML>
<HEAD>
<TITLE>Untitled Document</TITLE>
<meta http-equiv="Content-Type" content="text/html; charset=">
</HEAD>

<BODY BGCOLOR="#FFFFFF" TEXT="#000000">

</BODY>
</HTML>
```

Notice the DOCTYPE specifier is missing, the meta tag doesn't have a matching end tag, and the tags are all in uppercase. The uppercase elements aren't necessarily a problem because Dreamweaver automatically converts tags and attributes to lowercase if the code format preference is set to do so (see Chapter 4 for information on setting these preferences). In the interest of conformity, however, we'll change them in this document. Here's a revised Default.htm with the changes necessary to make it conform to XHTML:

```
<!DOCTYPE html PUBLIC "-//W3C//DTD XHTML 1.0 Transitional//EN"
"http://www.w3.org/TR/xhtml1/DTD/xhtml1-transitional.dtd">
<html>
<head>
<title>Untitled Document</title>
<meta http-equiv="Content-Type" content="text/html; charset=" />
</head>

<body bgcolor="#FFFFFF" text="#000000">

</body>
</html>
```

First, notice the DOCTYPE specifier doesn't need to be lowercase. The DOCTYPE specifier is specifying the Transitional XHTML DTD. This form of XHTML allows the use of formatting attributes, such as color and font tags, in the document itself. The intention with the Transitional DTD is to create pages that still contain formatting on browsers that don't support Cascading Style Sheets.

Next, notice the / added to the end of the `<meta>` tag. Remember, this is the XML shorthand method of specifying the end tag directly inside the start tag. We could just as easily have added a `</meta>` end tag.

Now that you've made these changes to Default.htm, every new document you create automatically starts out conforming to XHTML (see Figure 33-1).

Adding Objects

Dreamweaver's Objects panel contains an object for most HTML elements, but most of them aren't XHTML-compliant. Fortunately, Dreamweaver makes extending the Objects panel possible, and you can modify the objects to do whatever you want. Dreamweaver enables you to create a completely new grouping of objects just by creating a subfolder in the Configuration/Objects folder. Create one called MyXHTML to hold the XHTML-compliant objects you want to create.

As an initial example of creating an XHTML-compliant tag, use the Line Break tag (`<br>`). The functionality for the `<br>` tag is defined in the Objects/Characters folder, in the two files, Line Break.gif and Line Break.htm. The gif file contains the icon used to represent this object on the Objects panel, and the HTML file contains an HTML document with two standardized JavaScript functions indicating how the object behaves. Make copies of both of these files in your MyXHTML folder. You can also rename them (to something like "Line Break—XHTML.htm") to ensure you don't get this object confused with the old Line Break object.

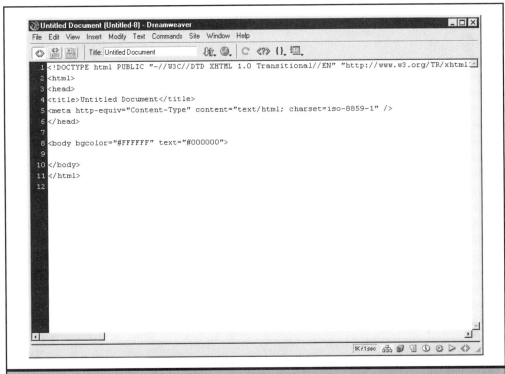

Figure 33-1. *Modifying the Default.htm file enables you to create XHTML-compliant documents automatically*

Bring the new copy of the Line Break.htm file (the one in your MyXHTML folder) into an editor. Dreamweaver's can work, of course, but any changes won't take effect until you exit and reenter the application. The JavaScript function that affects how the tag is created is the objectTag() function. Modify this function to return a line break tag with a / at the end to indicate an XHTML start/end tag.

```
function objectTag() {
// Return the html tag that should be inserted
return "<br />";
}
```

You can also modify the `<title>` tag to indicate the function's new purpose:

```
<title>Insert XHTML Line Break (Shift + Enter)</title>
```

A more complex modification would be to modify the Script object to generate XHTML-compliant script tags. Remember, when you insert a Script object, you're first shown a dialog box with the various script languages in it, so there's a bit more processing to do than simply returning the tag. The Script object files are in the Objects/Invisibles folder. In this case, three files exist: Script.gif, Script.htm, and Script.js. The js file contains JavaScript functions and is referenced by the Script.htm file. If you decide to rename your copies of these files, be sure to update the reference to point to the correct file.

The first thing to modify are the language choices. Because XHTML uses the type attribute, which requires a MIME type, you can modify the select element of the form in the body of the Script.htm file.

```
<select name="Language">
  <option value="JS" selected>text/javascript</option>
  <option value="JS11">text/javascript1.1</option>
  <option value="JS12">text/javascript1.2</option>
  <option value="VB">text/vbscript</option>
</select>
```

Next, in the Script.js file, you must change the objectTag() function to return a type attribute instead of language. The last line in the function should now be the following:

```
return '<script type="' + scriptLang + '">\n' + document.forms[0].script.value + '<\/script>';
```

You can now use these two new objects in Dreamweaver (you must close it before the new objects are available). The Objects panel now has a new group for your XHTML objects, and listed there are the two icons for your modified Line Break and Script objects (see Figure 33-2). These objects may be inserted into your document just like any other objects.

Validating XHTML

The W3C provides a place you can use to check your pages for XHTML (and even HTML) conformity (see Figure 33-3). This service can be found at **http://validator.w3.org**.

A popular package for cleaning up HTML files is HTML Tidy, by Dave Ragget. This command-line utility for a variety of operating systems can clean up common problems and regenerate an HTML document to be XHTML-compliant. See **http://www.w3.org/People/Raggett/tidy/** *for more information.*

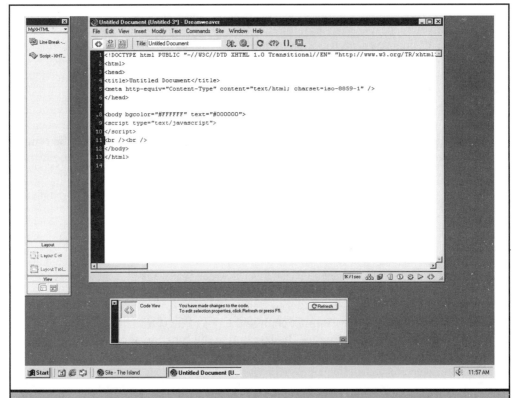

Figure 33-2. Dreamweaver's Objects panel can be extended to provide some degree of XHTML support

Summary

XML is fast becoming the standard document format for exchanging data across platforms and on the Web.

- XML is a metamarkup language that enables a document author to create tags to give structure to data.

- Dreamweaver enables you to import and export data between document templates and XML files.

- XHTML 1.0 is now a W3C standard, replacing HTML 4.01.

- While Dreamweaver doesn't support XHTML natively, you can customize it in a number of ways to help assist in some XHTML tasks.

In Chapter 34, you learn how to integrate Dreamweaver projects with databases.

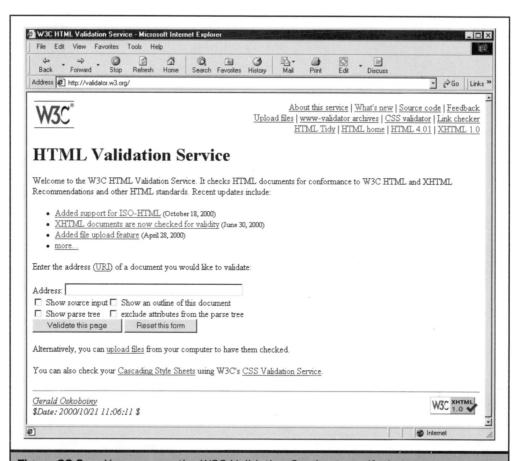

Figure 33-3.   *You can use the W3C Validation Service to verify that your pages conform to XHTML specs*

Chapter 34

Databases

Although scripting languages and plug-ins make doing many things on the browser possible to make a Web site dynamic and interactive, they can't do everything. Server side database connectivity is king when it comes to building data-rich sites with search engines, message boards, and a whole host of other features.

This chapter provides an introduction to databases and the terminology that goes with them, and describes a few of the more common database solutions available. In addition, this chapter provides a basic overview of some of the most popular server-side connectivity tools and standards, and also gives some tips on how these tools can be managed, or at least how they get along with Dreamweaver.

The last part of this chapter discusses Dreamweaver UltraDev, Macromedia's professional Web applications development system that combines the power of Dreamweaver with enhanced capabilities for working with databases.

Database Basics

A *database* is a place where information is stored and organized. Databases were among the first applications for computers when they entered the business world, and they're now more important than ever. Growing right along with the demand for data-centric Web sites is the demand for people knowledgeable about databases and the technologies used to access them.

Introduction to SQL

The most common way to interface with databases today is through the use of the Structured Query Language (SQL). SQL is an American National Standards Institute (ANSI) standard language for accessing databases and is supported by every major database package on the market today. (Although, unfortunately, many database vendors add their own proprietary extensions, which can make writing portable database code difficult—but let's not dwell on such unpleasantness.)

The basic element of storage in a SQL database is the record. A *record* contains related information about a single object represented in the database. For example, a record useful for keeping track of a Web user might contain a name, e-mail address, nickname, and time zone. A record for an item for sale on an e-commerce site might contain the item's name, a description, its price, and the quantity in stock.

The individual fields that make up a record are called *columns* in SQL parlance. This is because of the next highest level object in a SQL database, the table. A *table* is a collection of similar records and is so named because the data is easily displayed in table form. Columns represent the fields of the records in the table, while rows represent individual records. Databases typically contain many tables related by the use of key fields. For example, a table of users might contain an ID number for that user as one of its fields, and that ID might be used in other tables to identify messages the user has left, or orders the user made. This relationship between tables is what is meant by the term *relational database*.

Although a real example would almost certainly have more fields, an example of a list of items for the hypothetical e-commerce table might look something like Table 34-1.

When you retrieve information from the database, you often don't need to know every item a table contains. If you only want to display a list of items and their description, for example, you needn't bother reading the price and quantity columns. Or, you might want to see only items that have a quantity value, indicating they're in stock. For you to check each record to make sure the quantity was greater than 0 would be a waste of time.

SQL enables you to retrieve only the information you want to retrieve using the SELECT command (described in the following). This creates a subset of data from the table called a recordset. A *recordset* is like a minitable that has its own rows and columns. A recordset could contain all the columns from a table or some of them. It could even have columns from more than one table, if the query performed a join operation when doing a SELECT.

SQL databases have four basic commands for accessing and manipulating data. These are the workhorse commands for SQL:

- **SELECT**—Retrieves data from a database. The following SELECT statement retrieves all the records in the items table with a price less than $20 and displays the item, description, and price columns. The parameters directly after the SELECT statement indicate the columns you're interested in. The FROM section specifies a table name to use, while the optional WHERE section specifies a condition that needs to be satisfied to include a particular row—in this case, only retrieve rows where the price field is under $20.00.

```
SELECT item,description,price FROM items WHERE price<20.0
```

To select all columns from a table, you can use the '*' wildcard:

```
SELECT * FROM items WHERE price<20.0
```

- **UPDATE**—Updates an existing record with new information. The following example is used to update the price column of the item named "Ceramic Mug". This command specifies the table to update, the column value to change, and

Item	Description	Price	Quantity
Ceramic Mug	This is a beautiful handcrafted piece that...	20.00	300
Breadbox	This handsomely styled kitchen accessory...	30.00	0
Oven Mitt	This oven mitt is made from the finest...	5.00	150

Table 34-1. *A SQL Table Consists of Records, Represented As Rows and Fields in Those Records, Represented As Columns*

the rows this should apply to—in this case, only rows where the item is a "Ceramic Mug".

```
UPDATE items SET price=25.0 WHERE item="Ceramic Mug"
```

- **DELETE**—Deletes a record from a table. The following example deletes all records that have a quantity of 0.

```
DELETE FROM items WHERE quantity=0
```

- **INSERT**—Inserts a new record into a table. The values to add for the record are in the order of the table's columns. The example shows a new item being added, a tea kettle with a price of $40.00, quantity 100.

```
INSERT INTO items VALUES ("Tea Kettle", "This tea kettle is …", 40.0, 100)
```

In addition to the basic access commands, other commonly used commands define the format of tables and provide constraints. These are typically done by a database administrator when a database is being created:

- **CREATE TABLE**—Creates a new database table
- **ALTER TABLE**—Changes an existing table
- **DROP TABLE**—Removes a table from the database

Note   *This is a basic introduction to SQL commands and data structures. If you want to work with SQL databases and not just learn the basic terminology, further reading is in order. Books to look for include* SQL: The Complete Reference, *by James R. Groff & Paul N. Weinberg (Osborne's Complete Reference Series) and* Instant SQL Programming, *by Joe Celko (Wrox Press).*

Database Connections

To use a database, you first need to know where the database is located and how to access it. The database should already exist on your server before you attempt to connect to it, of course, and you need to know which interface the database uses.

The most common method of connecting to databases is using the Open Database Connectivity (ODBC) interface. Another common method is to use Microsoft's ActiveX Database Objects (ADO). Still another, used with Java language programs, is the Java Database Connectivity (JDBC) interface.

Even if the database you choose doesn't support the native interface of your choice, you can typically use a special bridge interface. If, for example, you're trying to access an ODBC-only database using Java, you could use a JDBC-ODBC bridge to do so (with some possible loss in efficiency compared to a native interface, however). A similar bridge may be used to connect to databases using ADO.

The interface you use to talk to a database is provided through a component called a *driver,* usually written by the database vendor. A Web application must invoke a database driver to establish communications with a database. This is done using a *connection string,* which consists of all the parameters needed to connect to the database. This could be as simple as a connection string specifying just a driver, a database, and its location, along with a userID and a password for security:

```
Driver={SQL Server};Server=Saturn;Database=MessageBoard;
UID=Mars;PWD=jupiter
```

Note, in most cases, you want to define a connection in one place and connect using an alias. This makes changing later easier if your database location or name changes, or if regular password changes must be done. This alias is known as a Data Source Name (DSN).

If your server is running on a Windows NT platform, you or a database administrator can set up a DSN using the ODBC Data Sources Administrator control panel applet. With Windows NT, open the control panel using Start | Settings | Control Panel, and then double-click Data Sources (ODBC). With Windows 2000, you must choose Start | Settings | Control Panel | Administrative Tools | Data Sources instead. The following illustration shows the ODBC Data Source Administrator dialog box. From this dialog box, you can set up DSNs that provide connection information for your database.

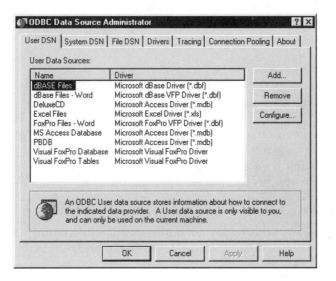

Database Products

Many popular SQL databases are available, but a few have received extra attention either because of the muscle of the companies behind them or because they fulfill a price/performance niche in the market.

Microsoft SQL Server 2000

Microsoft's database product, *SQL Server 2000,* is a powerful server that can scale from a single CPU PC on up to a massive 32 CPUs (at a massive price). Strong points in SQL Server's favor are a wide variety of tools and an easy to use administration interface.

SQL Server is only available for Windows NT or 2000 servers, so if you're looking for a Linux database solution, you need to look elsewhere. SQL Server information can, of course, be found on Microsoft's Web site at **http://www.microsoft.com/sql/**.

For smaller databases, Microsoft provides Microsoft Access, one of the Microsoft Office applications. While Access certainly isn't as full featured or as scalable as SQL Server, it's a popular database format for smaller databases.

Oracle8*i*

The *i* in *Oracle8i* stands for Internet, and Oracle is arguably the best database to use for serving up Web content. Oracle surpasses SQL Server in the capability to stream multimedia content, such as sound clips, pictures, and video. This database also provides a high degree of programmability, with a built-in Java engine to create advanced stored procedures and triggers, as well as the capability to run Enterprise JavaBeans that can make use of the database. Oracle8*i* is available in various feature/price point configurations including Lite, Personal, Standard, and Enterprise versions.

Oracle8*i* is available for a variety of platforms, including Windows NT/2000 and Linux. Visit **http://www.oracle.com** for information.

MySQL

MySQL is a popular database for one important reason: it's available free. More specifically, MySQL is an Open Source product using the GNU Public License (see **http://www.gnu.org**). This means that the complete product including source code is available for download for anyone who wants it. For sites requiring support, however, a licensed version is also available for a fee that is still far less than the price of SQL Server and Oracle.

MySQL is available for a variety of operating systems including NT, Linux, and Solaris. Visit **http://www.mysql.com** for more information.

PostgreSQL

PostgreSQL, from Great Bridge, LLC, is another popular open source database available for the Linux operating system. Visit **http://www.greatbridge.com** for information.

Dynamic Pages

Once you choose and install a database server, how can you access it from your site's pages? A number of popular server-based dynamic-content generation tools can be used, depending on your server platform.

ColdFusion

One popular dynamic-content generation product is Allaire's ColdFusion (**http://www.allaire.com**). When a browser requests a *ColdFusion* page (with a .cfm extension) from a Web server, the server identifies the page and passes it to the ColdFusion Server software. ColdFusion is available for both Windows NT (using IIS or Netscape Enterprise Server) and Sun Solaris (using Apache or Netscape Enterprise Server) servers.

*Allaire has released a set of Dreamweaver objects called, appropriately enough, the Allaire ColdFusion Objects for Dreamweaver. These objects enable you to quickly and easily add ColdFusion markup to your pages. You can find this extension on the Macromedia Exchange at **http://exchange.macromedia.com/dreamweaver**.*

Special tags on a ColdFusion page, called Cold Fusion Markup Language (CFML), are processed by the server to generate a final HTML page to send back to the browser. The browser can never see the ColdFusion tags in the original page, as they could with client-side scripting, so it's safer to include such things as database logins directly in the CFML tags.

CFML provides tags that enable you to connect to and access databases, create dynamic content, and perform conditional processing, among other tasks. CFML talks directly to databases using ODBC, so it can be used with the vast majority of databases available.

Using ColdFusion with Databases

The key to using ColdFusion to access database records is the CFML `<cfquery>` `</cfquery>` tag. This tag is listed before the `<html>` tag in a document and, much like a JavaScript function, isn't executed until it's called from somewhere else. An example might look like this:

```
<cfquery datasource="itemdata" name="itemlist">
    SELECT item,
           description,
           price,
    FROM items
    WHERE price >= #lowprice# AND price <= #highprice#
</cfquery>
```

Notice this query specifies a data source. This field indicates a DSN to use to establish the connection. The `name` parameter is a name for the query used to execute it from inside other ColdFusion tags. The variables in the WHERE clause, #lowprice# and #highprice#, correspond to values passed to the page using the GET or POST methods.

To call this, you can use a tag, such as <cfoutput>:

```
<cfoutput query="itemlist">
   <li>item: #item#, desc: #description#  - price: #price#
</cfoutput>
```

This performs the query and outputs the values from the recordset in place of the #item#, #description#, and #price# values. <cfoutput> does this for every row in the recordset.

At press time, Allaire and Macromedia have announced their merger. Undoubtedly, this means you can look forward to even more integration between Dreamweaver and ColdFusion in the future.

Active Server Pages

Microsoft's Active Server Pages (ASP) is a popular way to implement server-side connectivity, no doubt because of its use of already understood scripting languages—JScript and VBScript—as well as because it's an included feature of Microsoft's Internet Information Server (IIS). ASP pages work nicely with ActiveX objects, giving developers the opportunity to write computationally intensive or complicated tasks in a language of their choosing (such as C++ or Visual Basic). A case in point is the ActiveX Data Objects (ADO) package. This package consists of objects written in C++ to interface with databases as efficiently as possible.

IIS processes ASP pages before they're sent to the viewer. Server-side script blocks are called before the page is generated, giving the page the opportunity to do a database query to customize the output of the page. A new HTML page with none of the server-side code is generated and sent to the browser.

An ASP page (with an .asp extension) contains normal HTML tags and client-side scripts. In addition, it contains server-side scripts inserted between <% %> delimiters:

```
<%
Response.Write("Hello, World!");
%>
```

To establish a connection to a database using ASP, use the ADO Connection object:

```
<%
set conn=Server.CreateObject("ADODB.Connection");
conn.Open("mydatabase");
%>
```

In this case, "mydatabase" refers to an ODBC database. The variable conn is set by calling Server.CreateObject(), which returns an ADO Connection object. This object is then used to pen the database by calling its Open() method. This script should go toward the top of the <body> of your document, so it is executed as the page is being downloaded. You want to open the connection before any dynamic content must be displayed on your page.

The ADO recordset object is used to perform a query on the database:

```
<%
set rset = Server.CreateObject("ADODB.Recordset");
rset.Open("SELECT * from items", conn);
%>
```

In this case, the variable rset is set to an ADO Recordset object. Notice the rset.Open() call specifies the connection object made earlier as a parameter. You can put this script right after the previous one, but it's not important.

The data in the fields can now be accessed and output using the ASP Response object. Finally, to advance to the next row of the recordset, the Recordset.MoveNext() method is called. When the recordset has passed its last row, the EOF property is set to true.

```
<%
while (rset.EOF == false)
{
    for (x=rset.fields[0]; x++; x < rset.Fields.length)
        Response.write(x.name + "=" x.value);
    rset.MoveNext();
}
```

For a more thorough introduction to ASP, visit Microsoft's ASP overview at **http://msdn.microsoft.com/workshop/server/asp/ASPover.asp**.

Java Server Pages

Taking a cue from Microsoft's ASP technology, Sun has developed a similar technology called JavaServer Pages (JSP). JSP provides a Java-based way to serve Web pages dynamically. As with ASP and ColdFusion, an application server (in this case, a JSP application server) running in conjunction with a Web server interprets JSP code embedded in a page and sends the resulting HTML document to the browser. The browser doesn't receive any JSP code at all.

An interesting aspect of JSP is its pages are actually translated into Java code, and then compiled, potentially providing better performance than a JavaScript solution interpreted by the Web server would have. This also allows JSP easy access to external Java classes and *servlets*, the server version of applets, small programs that run on the server.

A block of JSP code begins with <% and ends with %> delimiters. These are the same delimiters used by ASP, and Dreamweaver displays an ASP icon for JSP in the Design view.

A JSP application communicates with a database using a JDBC driver. If a particular database package doesn't have a native JDBC driver, a JDBC-ODBC bridge can be used to translate JDBC requests into ODBC that almost any database can understand.

For more information about JSP, see Sun's JSP page at **http://java.sun.com/products/jsp**.

Editing Server-Side Tags in Dreamweaver

If a document contains ASP or CFML code, then Dreamweaver displays markers in the Design view that identify the scripts whenever it recognizes them, as shown in the following illustration. JSP code uses the same delimiters as ASP; therefore, JSP is indicated in your document using the ASP icon.

To edit a block of code, click its marker in the Design view to bring up the Property Inspector, as shown in the following illustration.

- If you're editing ASP or JSP code, the property inspector has a single button, Edit. Click it to edit the script.

- If you're editing a CFML tag, there are two buttons. Click the Attributes button to edit the attributes of the CFML tag you selected, or click the Content button to edit the content that appears between the opening and closing CFML tags. Some CFML tags have no closing tag: in these cases, the Content button is grayed out.

You can also find the code in the Code view or the Code Inspector, and you can edit it there. The script code is highlighted to stand out from the normal HTML and the client-side scripting tags.

The Code view is also handy for finding problems with your ASP code. Whenever IIS finds an error in your ASP code, it outputs an error message containing the line number in which the error occurred. Dreamweaver's Code view can show line numbers, making it easy to find the point where the error occurred. If line numbers aren't shown, you can turn them on by checking the View | Code View Options | Line Numbers menu item, or by clicking the View Options button on the Code view (or Code Inspector) toolbar, and then checking Line Numbers.

The display of markers is optional. If you don't see markers or highlighted text when it should be there, make sure View | Visual Aids | Invisible Elements is checked in the menu. This is a handy option to remember if you want to see your pages displayed cleanly without the markers.

Dreamweaver UltraDev

Dreamweaver on its own doesn't have much support for technologies, such as ColdFusion and ASP. At best, you can count on Dreamweaver to stay out of your way. This isn't necessarily bad because most of your server-side code will be written by hand (or obtained from a third person) and, hence, wouldn't benefit from Dreamweaver objects or behaviors, which are designed for client-side HTML code.

If you want a package with the power of Dreamweaver along with enhanced connectivity features, Dreamweaver UltraDev is for you. UltraDev is Macromedia's environment for building complete *Web applications,* which are pages that can interact not only with each other on the client, but also with resources, such as databases on the server. While a full-fledged discussion about UltraDev is beyond the scope of this book, it's worth mentioning the package here and giving an overview of some of the additional features it provides.

Dreamweaver UltraDev supports all of Dreamweaver's features for page design and site management, as well as features for connecting to databases, building recordsets, and generating dynamic content.

Specifying an Application Server

UltraDev adds additional site preferences you can set when defining a site. When you activate the Site Definition dialog box (by choosing Site | Define Sites... from the menu, selecting a site, and clicking Edit), you notice an extra category of information you can set. As shown in the following illustration, this category is used to specify the server technology and application server to use for your site. Before you set up this category, you should first make sure you have a local and remote site defined (Chapter 6 shows how to set up the other categories of the Site Definition dialog box).

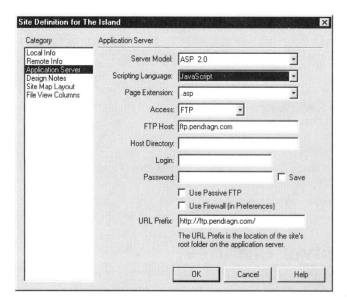

To set the application server preferences for your site, do the following:

1. In the Server Model pop-up menu, choose the server technology you're using. The choices are none, ASP 2.0, JSP 1.0, or ColdFusion 4.0.

2. If you chose ASP, you need to specify a scripting language. Choose either VBScript or JavaScript. If you chose JSP or ColdFusion in Step one, you'll only have the choice of Java or CFML, respectively.

3. In the Page Extension field, choose the extension you want all files to have. All server models allow the use of .htm or .html. ASP allows .asp, JSP allows .jsp, and ColdFusion allows files to have a .cfm extension. If your site is going to have a server model, it's best to use the extension corresponding to the server model.

4. If your application server runs on a different remote system than your Web server, you need to specify the server settings in the Access, FTP Host, Host Directory, login, and Password. By default, these are set to the same values as the corresponding fields in the Remote Info category.

5. In the URL Prefix field, enter the domain and any home directory for your site that you want to use to process Live Data pages. For instance, **http://www.pendragn.com/livedata**.

Live Data Window

The Live Data window in UltraDev can be used to work on your pages in a live data environment. Unlike the Document window, which uses placeholders to represent dynamic content on the page, the Live Data window displays the actual dynamic content.

To accomplish this, a copy of the current document is sent to your server where it's processed by the application server before being returned for display in the Live Data window.

Note *Before you can execute a page using Live Data, all the supporting files it uses, such as server-side includes or image, must already be on the server.*

Choosing Live Data from the View menu can toggle the Document view to show either the Normal or Live views.

The Live Data Settings dialog box, opened by choosing View | Live Data Settings from the menu, is used to set any user data your page might require. This dialog box is shown in the following illustration.

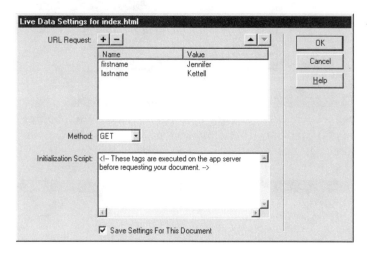

1. In the URL Request list, you can click the plus sign (+) button to enter any variables your page expects to see in the URL. Specify the name and a sample value to test for each variable.

2. In the Method field, choose either POST or GET to specify the HTML form method your page requires.

3. In the Initialize Script area, enter any custom script you want to add to the beginning of your page. You can use this to initialize any session variables that normally would be initialized by the time this page is loaded.

4. Click Save Settings For This Document to have these settings always be the ones used for this page.

5. Click OK to save the Live Data settings.

Creating a Database Connection with UltraDev

The procedure for creating a database connection differs depending on the server model you are using but, in all cases, you're specifying the connection using either a DSN or an ODBC connection string. For example, to set up a DSN connection for ASP, do the following:

1. Make sure the DSN is already configured on your system.

2. Select the Modify | Connections menu item in UltraDev. This brings up the Connections dialog box, the following illustration shows.

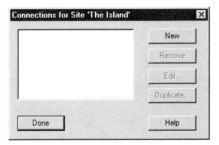

3. If there were any existing connections, they would be listed here. Because this is a new connection, click the New button, and choose Data Source Name (DSN) from the pop-up menu. This activates the DSN dialog box, as shown in the next illustration.

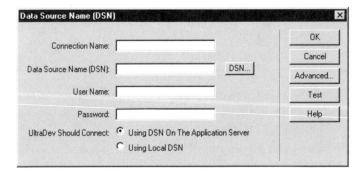

4. Enter a name for this connection in the Connection Name field.

5. Enter a DSN, or click the DSN button to find it on your server.

6. If your database requires a username and password, enter them.

7. Click OK.

Defining a Recordset

If you're unfamiliar with SQL syntax and you don't want to learn it, fear not. UltraDev enables you to set up recordsets for database queries just by filling out a simple dialog box form. All you have to do is specify a connection, a database table to query, and the columns to retrieve.

To define a recordset, make sure the page you'll use this query with is open. Then do the following steps:

1. Activate the Data Bindings panel (Window | Data Bindings), click the plus sign (+) button, and choose Recordset (Query) from the pop-up menu, as the following illustration shows.

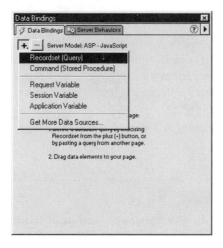

2. This activates the simple Recordset dialog box, as seen in the next illustration.

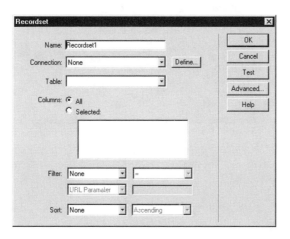

3. In the Name box, enter a name to use for this recordset. You might want to prepend the name with the letters "rs" to identify an object readily as a recordset in your code. For example, "rsUsers" for a recordset used to retrieve user info.

4. Select a connection from the Connection list. If none are defined, click the Define button to do so now.

5. In the Table pop-up, select a database table to use for the query.

6. Choose whether to use all columns or only selected ones. If you choose Select, the columns you can use from this table are listed in the following box. Control-click (Command-click on the Mac) each column you want to use.

7. In the filter section, you can select constraints to place on some or all columns in the table to determine whether they'll be filtered out of the recordset. Select each column you want to compare from the first drop-down list, and then build the expression to compare it with the other fields. The third drop-down list lets you select which type of constraint to apply to the column. You can choose from URL Parameter, Form Variable, Cookie, Session Variable, Application Variable, and Entered Value. In the fourth box, enter the variable name or a static value to use for the filter.

8. In the Sort field, choose a column to sort by and whether to sort in ascending or descending order.

Summary

Whether they'll be used to build a message board or to provide a search engine, the need to marry Web sites with database connectivity is always growing.

- All the modern databases on the market today can use some form of the Structured Query Language (SQL) to access them.

- Popular database products include Microsoft SQL Server, Microsoft Access, Oracle8*i*, MySql, and PostgreSQL.

- Popular server-side dynamic technologies pages include Active Server Pages (ASP), Cold Fusion, and JavaServer Pages (JSP).

- Dreamweaver UltraDev provides database capability, along with all the features of Dreamweaver to make a complete one-stop Web application development tool.

The next chapter discusses e-commerce and how to use Dreamweaver with tools to help sell things on the Web.

Chapter 35

E-Commerce

Almost anything you could ever want to buy—from products to services to stocks—can be found on the Web. From the moment the Web moved into the public eye, people have looked for ways to make money from it. As a matter of fact, the Web wouldn't have reached its current prominence without online services seeking to make money by charging for access to what formerly was the province of those in education and government.

Online shopping began as an offshoot of existing brick-and-mortar or catalog businesses, with these companies promoting goods on their Web sites, while still requiring orders to be placed through traditional means, such as a trip to the mall or a phone order. As the technology for secure encryption and transfer of credit card and order information has developed, consumers have felt increasingly more safe in placing orders online, and a new buying model has been born. Not only have the traditional shopping outlets taken advantage of online shopping, but businesses such as Amazon have built their entire business model on it.

In many cases, the promise of e-commerce has been overhyped, and the industry is still in its infancy. The fields of battle are littered with the corpses of dead e-commerce companies, once hailed as the next best thing. But even with the hype, one thing is certain—e-commerce is here to stay. Online purchasing is not a novelty any longer, but an expectation of thousands of Web users.

Introduction to E-Commerce

Most e-commerce sites work in pretty much the same way: The customer browses or searches through a catalog in a database and clicks a Buy button to add an item to a shopping cart.

When shopping is complete, the customer clicks a link to the checkout page. Here, the items in the shopping cart are presented along with the total cost, including shipping, handling, taxes, and so forth. The customer reviews the order, changing or deleting items if desired. An option to back out of the checkout and shop more is also presented.

After confirming the items in the order, the customer has to provide shipping and billing information. The site should switch to *Secure Socket Layer* (*SSL*) mode for security at this point, ensuring the transfer of information, such as a credit card number, is encrypted to thwart potential eavesdroppers. SSL mode is displayed in the browser status bar as a closed padlock.

Once the customer's form is completed and validated, it's sent to the server. The server system retrieves the information from the form, decrypts the credit card information, and sends it over a secure connection to a credit-card processing service. There, the merchant and the card are authenticated, and the transaction is then forwarded to the bank, where it's either accepted or declined.

The authentication is sent back through the chain to the merchant, and funds are reserved on the user's card until the merchandise is shipped. Once shipped, a final charge can be made to the credit card through the same steps.

Considering all the steps involved, it's no wonder so many products have sprung up to make conducting e-commerce easier.

Preparing for E-Commerce

If you're making your first foray into e-commerce, keep the following issues in mind:

- **Order Fulfillment**—Who fulfills orders? What is the cost of shipping—including packaging supplies? How do you handle an onslaught of orders that require rapid production or acquisition of additional product? How can you handle a lack of orders, resulting in overstocking of product?

- **Customer Feedback**—Who answers product inquiries? Who answers customer order inquiries? What systems do you have in place to track the status of orders?

- **Marketing**—Who are your customers and how can you reach them? Who are your competitors and how is your business the same or different from theirs? How can you promote your site? What should you do to grow your business?

Several considerations are also involved in planning your e-commerce site:

- **Clear Navigation**—Make getting around your site easy for your customers.

- **Search Functionality**—Make finding the products they seek easy for your customers.

- **Useful Information**—Amidst the marketing jargon, include actual information to help customers make a buying decision. Consider adding other articles or features that can give value to your site other than the products for sale.

- **Easy Access**—Don't require potential customers to register with the site until they place an order. And while pop-up surveys and lengthy registration forms may provide you with good demographic information, they might cost you sales. Get the order first, and then ask customers if they're willing to provide additional information. Better still, make quizzes an added—and optional—feature of the site.

- **Easy Ordering**—Make order forms easy to use. If a credit card field requires a specific format, add text next to the field to inform customers. If you're using a third-party order processing firm inform customers, because that name is what will appear on the credit card receipt.

- **Test the Site**—Online shopping involves trust on the part of your customers. If the site is fraught with JavaScript bugs, broken links, and other obvious errors, customers could rightfully feel their credit card information will get the same shoddy treatment.

Shopping Carts

A *shopping cart* is simply a tool to maintain information about what has been ordered as a customer moves from page to page. This can be done by storing a cookie on the client. A cookie is used to track user information, such as the username and password of a user on a message board or, for our purposes here, the contents of a shopping cart. This information is stored on the user's computer, and is accessed whenever he returns to the Web page which passed the cookie. The drawback of cookies is that the customer's browser can be set to reject them, in which case a shopping cart would not work. Using cookies also precludes a customer from checking on an order placed at home from their office computer. Another possibility is to use a server side technology such as *Active Server Pages* (*ASP*) to maintain the cart information in a session variable. Session variables are unique to one visitor's session on a particular site and can be maintained across page navigation boundaries.

Security

The security of electronic transactions is an important issue for e-commerce sites to take into account. Potential customers, especially those new to the Internet and doing transactions online, are wary of hackers intercepting their credit card information as it travels across the Web to a merchant's site.

The most common security system used by e-commerce sites is SSL, mentioned earlier, which is a protocol originally developed by Netscape, but now used by all commercial level Web servers. SSL-enabled servers use a combination of public key and symmetric key encryption to secure both directions of information transfer. The public key is sent by the Web server to the client. The client then generates a session key, which is sent back to the server encrypted with the public key, so only the server can decode it. After a little more negotiating, both client and server start encrypting all data using this session key.

The customer knows a secure page has been entered when the padlock icon on the status bar is displayed and the URL in the address line starts with `https://` instead of `http://`. Depending on the customer's browser settings, a dialog box may also be displayed when entering or leaving a secure area.

To activate a Web server's SSL capability, the merchant must first obtain a valid certificate. These are typically obtained from a third-party certification authority. Before issuing a certificate, the authority verifies the identity of the requester. The certificate issued is a unique identification that the authority guarantees belongs to the issuer, and customers can feel safer knowing you are who you say you are.

Customers see a lot of a number of certification authorities, but none quite so much as (http://www.verisign.com). Obtaining a certificate from VeriSign can help boost the credibility of your online store.

E-Commerce Providers

As you might expect, a huge number of e-commerce solution providers are just waiting for you to give them your business. Solutions range from shopping cart code all the way to site hosting, complete with credit card validation. The one-stop, provide-it-all solutions are usually aimed at small businesses looking to make their first foray into e-commerce. This section lists two e-commerce providers targeted at small businesses that provide extensions for Dreamweaver.

NetStores

NetStores (**http://www.netstores.com**) is one of the companies providing a complete e-commerce solution aimed at smaller businesses. They provide site hosting with domain registration—shopping cart software that provides nearly everything you need to put up a storefront on the Web and credit card verification services for those with a merchant account (which can also be obtained through NetStores).

NetStores has recognized the popularity of Dreamweaver and has created an extension for use with its shopping cart product that makes adding shopping cart and search capabilities to your site a snap. This extension can be downloaded from the Macromedia Exchange for Dreamweaver at **http://www.macromedia.com/exchange/ dreamweaver**.

To make use of the NetStores extension, you must sign up with NetStores as your e-commerce provider. Go to **http://www.netstores.com/open.html**, and then review the terms of service and pricing for the type of account you want.

Installing the Extensions

At press time, the current version of the NetStores extension doesn't use the Dreamweaver Extension Manager for installation. The installation procedure consists of running an executable file that extracts all the extension files and adds them to the proper location in your Dreamweaver folders. The installation prompts you for the correct path to where Dreamweaver is installed. Be sure this points to your correct folder.

Once the files are copied, run Dreamweaver. You now need to run another installation task from inside Dreamweaver to finish setting up the files and menus. From the Command menu, choose Install NetStores. This brings up the dialog box shown in the following illustration. Click the Install button to finish the installation, and then restart Dreamweaver.

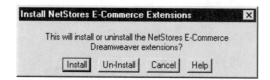

The next step in using the NetStores extension is to configure your store. Use the Commands | NetStores E-Commerce | Configure Your Store menu item. The NetStores Store Properties dialog box is opened (as the following illustration shows). This dialog box has the following fields:

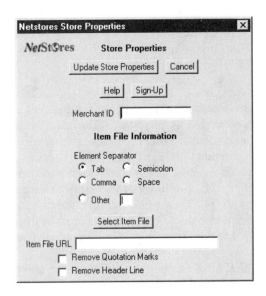

- **Merchant ID**—Enter the merchant ID you chose when you signed up for NetStores. This ties the objects you add to your pages with your Web store.

- The other important item you need to enter in this dialog box is an item file. The *item* file is a tab-delimited file you export from your product database and upload to the NetStores server. Make sure to keep your local item file setting current with your settings on your NetStores store.

The store properties are contained in a file in the root directory or your site called NetStores Properties.nts. This enables you to use separate configurations for multiple sites.

NetStores objects

The NetStores extension adds a new object category to the Objects panel, as shown in the following illustration.

Add to Cart   The Add to Cart object puts a button on your page that adds a particular item to a cart. To allow this, you must enter the product code of an item in your inventory. The first way to enter the product code is to type it in directly in the text box at the top of the dialog box. Or, if your store has been properly configured, you can select the appropriate product code from the Product Code pull-down menu.

The Product Code pull-down menu contains a list of 30 items from your item file. If your inventory has more than 30 items and you want to see the others, use the –30 items and +30 items buttons to change the list to the next group of product codes in your inventory.

Finally, enter the text or select an image to use for the button, and then click OK to add the order button.

View Cart   Every page on an e-commerce site should have a button to allow customers to view their carts. The View Cart object provides this button. This dialog box only gives you the option of viewing the cart and specifying images to use for the up, rollover, and click states of the button.

Search In addition to the cart-ordering buttons, the NetStores extension provides objects to add a search capability easily to your site.

Like the previous objects, the Search button dialog box allows settings for link text, as well as images to use for the button. In this case, you can provide images for the up, rollover, and click states or simply enter text and leave the image fields blank to create a text button.

Quick Search Unlike the Search button, which only provides a link to the NetStores site to do searches, the Quick Search object provides a text input box to enable customers to enter search text directly on the page. You can enter a default search string to be used, if the customer doesn't change it, and provide an image to use for the search button.

Driven Search The Driven Search object lets you predefine the search string and the database fields by which to search and sort results. Use this to provide a link to a list of items.

Quick Form If your site has a small number of products, the Quick Form can be used to list all your products on a single page. After the form is entered on your page, you can build the list of items using standard form controls, such as text entry boxes and check boxes.

NetStores Reporting

Once your online store is operational, you'll want to access customer lists, track orders against inventory, and, of course, track profits. NetStores enables you to access reports either from its Web site or via e-mail. You can integrate its reports with your own database. You can also integrate their accounting reports into Intuit Quicken or Microsoft Money, if you use those packages in your business.

PDG Software

PDG Software, Inc. (**http://www.pdgsoft.com**) offers a wide range of e-commerce products ranging from shopping carts to mall software providing multiple storefronts. They even have an auction package to let you conduct auctions from your online store.

Like NetStores, PDG provides an extension for Dreamweaver that works with its e-commerce products. And, it's also available on the Dreamweaver Exchange. This extension installs easily using the Extension Manager. Once this extension is installed, a new category, containing the five PDG objects, is added to the Objects panel. The following illustration shows this:

PreAdd   The *PreAdd object* is used to create a button for adding an item to a shopping cart. Double-clicking this object activates the PDG PreAdd Action dialog box, which the following illustration shows. This dialog box has the following parameters:

- **Sku**—Enter the SKU of the product you want this object to add to the cart.

- **Link Type**—Specify either a text or image link.

- **Additional CGI Parameters**—Used to specify additional parameters to append to the link's URL. For example, if you're using PDG Mall, you would specify the Store ID here.

- **URL of the Executable**—URL of the application used to run the PDG shopping cart. For example, if you're using PDG Shopping Cart on a Windows NT server, this is typically */cgi-bin/Shopper.exe*, where cgi-bin is the designation of the directory where the shopping cart executables reside.

Display   The *Display* object enables customers to display the current contents of their shopping carts. In addition, customers can modify the contents of a cart by removing some or all items, or by submitting the items for purchase. The Link Type and other parameters work the same way as with the PreAdd object.

CheckOut   When customers finish shopping and are ready to make a purchase, the *Checkout* object is used to navigate to the checkout page, where shipping and billing information are obtained.

HardSearch and SoftSearch   The Search objects are used to search the product database for an item. As with NetStores, two search objects exist: HardSearch and SoftSearch. *HardSearch* is linked to a fixed keyword list always to return a list of the same items. *SoftSearch* provides an input line that enables the customer to specify search terms.

Summary

E-commerce is an essential part of business life. Companies large and small, from tiny retail outlets to large business-to-business providers, all need an online presence to compete.

- E-commerce demands the cooperation of several entities at once to complete a transaction—from the merchant to the authentication server to the credit card processor.

- Customers demand online retailers use secure connections to protect credit card information.

- Many e-commerce packages are on the market. Two that integrate especially well with Dreamweaver are the products from NetStores and PDG Software, Inc.

Part X covers using Macromedia Fireworks with Dreamweaver and how to use Fireworks to its best advantage when generating images for use in Dreamweaver pages. Chapter 36 starts off Part X with an introduction to Fireworks.

The Complete Reference

Part X

Dreamweaver and Fireworks

Chapter 36

Fireworks Basics

ireworks 4 is a full-featured and powerful program that holds its own in the world of Web design. If you understand what Fireworks does and does well, you can appreciate its power and flexibility. Fireworks is designed as a tool to get your images, buttons, and objects prepared and optimized for delivery on the Internet. Fireworks isn't for the print professional—although it does contain a wide range of bitmap tools—but it's for anyone interested in delivering content to the Web. The integration between Dreamweaver 4, Dreamweaver UltraDev 4, and Fireworks 4 is quite good. You can edit images using Fireworks without ever leaving Dreamweaver, and most of the Fireworks code is editable in Dreamweaver, with the exception of the new pop-up menus produced in Fireworks.

The Fireworks Environment

This chapter introduces you to the Fireworks 4 interface, the various tools and panels that make up the Fireworks environment. The look and feel is probably quite familiar because it closely resembles Dreamweaver. Fireworks has panels instead of inspectors that can be moved and altered to customize your work environment. Even if you've used Fireworks before, you may want to take a quick look at this chapter to see where some of the tools and commands have moved, as well as where the new tools and commands are located.

Vectors and Bitmaps

Vectors and bitmaps are the two image types you work with in Fireworks. Because vectors and bitmaps are different in their function and usability, a short description of each follows.

Vector Objects

Vector objects are the backbone of Fireworks. A *vector object* consists of paths that are two points connected by a line. A vector graphic is generated using a mathematical process that basically says, "start a line here at X, Y, and draw it to A, B." Of course, you don't see the calculations being made—they're all done behind the scenes. It's the mathematical part that gives vectors their power.

A vector object retains its image quality no matter how large you stretch it because it simply recalculates and redraws itself. It's this scalability that makes vectors valuable Web objects. Vectors are also the type of graphic that gives programs such as Flash and LiveMotion their flexibility in resizing images on the fly. In Fireworks, vectors remain totally editable. You can add fills, effects, text, and strokes, save and open at a later date, and still be able to make changes to the object. Most of the vector tools in Fireworks can also be used on bitmap images. See Chapter 37 for information on using the vector tools.

Bitmap Objects

Images obtained from a digital camera or a scanner also have an important place in Web design. Images are perfect for demonstrating products and for simply adding a dramatic or elegant touch to a design. These types of images are called *bitmaps* or *rasterized images*. Bitmaps are based on pixels, a certain amount of dots of color per inch that makes a picture. For use on a Web page, 72 dots per inch are sufficient (72 dpi). The difference between a vector and a bitmap image is this: to draw a vector line, you simply need two points and to draw a bitmap line, you need a line full of pixels. To manipulate a vector, you simply click a point and move or alter it. To manipulate a bitmap, you have to draw or redraw each pixel that makes up an image. Chapter 39 discusses how to use the bitmap tools.

The Document Window

The primary work environment for Fireworks is the Document Window, shown in Figure 36-1. This is where you design and edit all your images and objects. The canvas you work on is contained in the Document window; you can have multiple Document windows open simultaneously. Or, you can have multiple Document windows for the same document by choosing Window | New Window or CTRL-ALT-N (CMD-OPTION-N for the Mac).

Original and Preview Tabs

When you open a document or start with a new document, the default is the Original view. The *Original* view is the view where you do all your design work, and interact with the images and objects of your document. If you want to preview your work as it will look in a browser, simply click the Preview tab. You can preview rollovers— except for the new pop-up menus—in the Preview view. To preview the pop-up menus, choose File | Preview in Browser.

The 2-Up and 4-Up Tabs

The 2-Up and the 4-Up tabs are used for optimizing your images or objects. The *2-Up tab* shows you the original image and another one alongside it with optimization settings. You

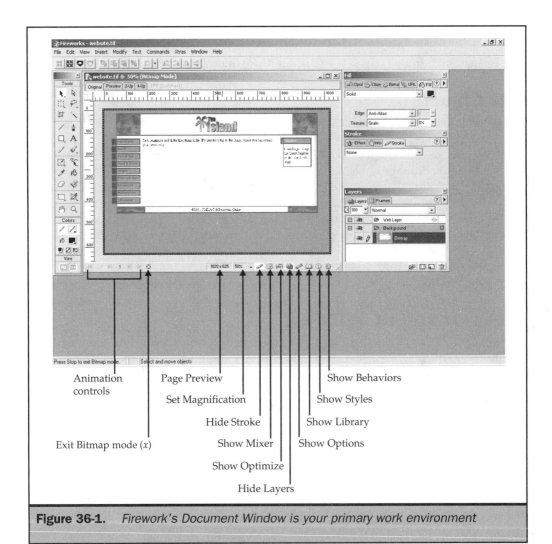

Figure 36-1.   *Firework's Document Window is your primary work environment*

can view the optimization settings by opening the Optimize panel (Window | Optimize). The most useful tab is the 4-Up tab. With the *4-Up tab*, you can view the original and three additional optimization settings at the same time. To change the optimization, select the pane you want to change and, in the Optimize panel, change the setting. Do this for each of the three views. You can see the results on each view. If you look at the bottom of each view, you can see the file type, quality (or dither and colors for GIF), file size, and approximate time required to load the image in a browser. You can view both GIF and JPEG if you desire. The 4-Up tab is shown in the following illustration.

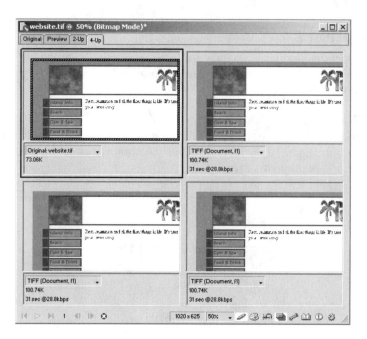

The Fireworks Menu Bar and Toolbars

When you first open a new document or you open an existing one, you notice the name Fireworks is at the top of the Fireworks workspace, and then the title of your document. If it's a new document, the default title is Untitled-1.png. Note, Fireworks doesn't have an asterisk by the title to signify the document hasn't been saved as Dreamweaver does. Below this title bar is the menu. The menu bar contains all the panels, commands, and Xtras of Fireworks. Most of these tools are also accessible from panels, as well as context menus obtained by double-clicking the tool icons.

How you use Fireworks is strictly a matter of personal preference. If you usually use menus, you'll find the panels in Fireworks arranged in a logical manner by default. But, if you want to rearrange the groupings, all you do is drag one tab to another group. Many people prefer to work using keyboard shortcuts. You can find a list of the Fireworks keyboards shortcuts in Appendix D. What's great about Fireworks shortcuts is you can customize them. You can add to the current shortcuts or use Fireworks 4 shortcuts, or you can use Photoshop, Illustrator, or Freehand shortcuts. Basically, whatever you're comfortable with, you can have. What's particularly nice about being able to customize the shortcuts is if Fireworks has no keyboard shortcut for something like File | Save, you can assign one to it or use Photoshop shortcuts that include it.

Menu Bar Options

The *menu bar* contains many commands and Xtras that aren't available through panels, toolbars, or keyboard shortcuts (unless you customize the shortcuts). Every panel is also accessible through the menu bar.

File Menu

The *File* menu controls the generation and saving of documents, as well as previewing and testing of your pages. Table 36-1 describes the commands on the File menu. Commands for a Mac may vary slightly.

Command	Function	Notes
New	Opens a new document in the Document Window.	
Open	Opens the File Selection dialog box to open an existing document.	
Scan	Dialog box for a Twain source, such as a scanner if it's been installed.	If a Twain source hasn't been installed into Fireworks, the Twain Source option lets you point Fireworks to a Twain driver, perhaps in Photoshop or another application.
Close	Closes an open document.	
Save	Saves an open document. This prompts you for a filename the first time you save a new document.	
Save As	Opens the File Save dialog box to save an open document under a new name.	
Save a Copy	Saves a copy of an open document.	

Table 36-1. *The File Menu Lets You Set Up New or Open Existing documents, Export, and Preview*

Command	Function	Notes
Update HTML	Updates or adds either Fireworks-generated HTML and images or images only to an exiting file.	
Revert	Reverts to the last saved copy.	
Import	Select a file from the Import dialog box to place into any open document.	
Export	The Export dialog box opens before exporting a document or images in the format specified in the Optimize panel.	Exporting is discussed in Chapter 40.
Export Preview	The Export Preview dialog box opens before exporting a document.	This dialog box has all the optimization settings available before exporting.
Export Wizard	The Export Wizard dialog box opens for you to select the format and destination of your image, resulting in an analysis and the Export Preview dialog box.	
Batch Process	Opens the Batch dialog box where you choose files for the batch, and then continues on to the commands to perform.	
Run Script	Opens the Open dialog box to locate the script (.jsf) file you want to run.	

Table 36-1. *The File Menu Lets You Set Up New or Open Existing documents, Export, and Preview* (continued)

DREAMWEAVER AND FIREWORKS

Command	Function	Notes
Preview in Browser	Opens the Locate Browser dialog box the first time to select primary and secondary browsers. Thereafter, you select the browser you want to preview in.	
Page Setup	Displays a setup page for printing.	
Print	Opens the Print dialog box prior to printing.	
HTML Setup	The dialog box opens to set the General settings, Table settings, and Document specific settings.	
Exit	Exit Fireworks	

Table 36-1. *The File Menu Lets You Set Up New or Open Existing documents, Export, and Preview* (continued)

Edit Menu

The *Edit* menu offers standard commands, such as cut, copy, and paste. Firework's edit menu also provides other commands that let you select preferences and customizing keyboard shortcuts. Table 36-2 lists the commands available from the Edit menu.

Command	Function	Notes
Undo	Removes the last change you made and reverts to the state of the document just prior to that change.	

Table 36-2. *The Edit Menu Lets You Copy, Paste, Set Preferences, and Customize Keyboard Shortcuts*

Command	Function	Notes
Repeat	Repeats the last change you made to the document.	
Cut	Removes the selection from the document and places it in the clipboard.	
Copy	Copies the selected image or object to the clipboard.	
Copy as Vectors	Copies only Fireworks paths to paste into other applications, such as Freehand, Illustrator, and others.	
Copy HTML Code	Opens the Copy HTML Editor to guide you through exporting images and copying HTML code into the clipboard for pasting in to an HTML editor.	Your images are copied to the folder you choose and the HTML only is copied to the clipboard.
Paste	Pastes the contents of the clipboard to the cursor position.	
Clear	Clears the selection from the file.	
Paste as Mask	Uses the clipboard contents as a mask.	
Paste Inside	Pastes the clipboard contents into a closed and selected path.	

Table 36-2.   *The Edit Menu Lets You Copy, Paste, Set Preferences, and Customize Keyboard Shortcuts* (continued)

Command	Function	Notes
Paste Attributes	Copies the Fireworks-specific attributes (such as effects, strokes, and so forth) of the clipboard contents to a selected object.	
Select All	Selects all objects or all pixels in a document.	
Select Similar	Selects a range of similar colors in a marquee selection based on the tolerance settings.	
Superselect	Selects the entire group of the Subselection.	
Subselect	Selects an individual object within a group.	
Deselect	All objects or pixels are deselected.	
Duplicate	Makes a copy of the selected object or image and offsets it slightly.	
Clone	Makes a copy of the selected object or image and places it directly on top of the original.	
Find and Replace	Opens the Find and Replace dialog box.	You can even search for non-Web safe colors.
Crop Selected Bitmap	Crop handles appear around the image.	
Crop Document	The document is cropped to the selected object.	
Preferences	The Preference dialog box opens.	

Table 36-2. *The Edit Menu Lets You Copy, Paste, Set Preferences, and Customize Keyboard Shortcuts* (continued)

Command	Function	Notes
Keyboard Shortcuts	Keyboard Shortcuts dialog box opens, letting you choose which shortcuts to use and/or customize.	You can use Photoshop, Illustrator, Freehand, and Fireworks 3 shortcuts and customize each.

Table 36-2. *The Edit Menu Lets You Copy, Paste, Set Preferences, and Customize Keyboard Shortcuts* (continued)

View Menu

The *View* menu changes the way you look at Fireworks. This menu lets you adjust the size of the view, and use rulers, guides, and grids. The View menu is also where you decide what edge selections you want to view. Table 36-3 lists the options contained in the View menu.

Command	Function	Notes
Zoom In	Increase the magnification of a document.	
Zoom Out	Decreases the magnification of a document.	
Magnification	Increases the magnification by the percentage selected.	
Fit Selection	Sets the magnification to a percentage that makes everything in the selection visible.	
Fit All	Sets the magnification to a percentage that shows everything in the entire document.	

Table 36-3. *The View Menu Controls the Workspace Appearance*

Command	Function	Notes
Full Display	If selected, you see the object or image as designed. If unselected, you see an outline.	
Macintosh Gamma (or Windows on a Mac)	Simulates a Macintosh Gamma (or Windows on a Macintosh).	
Hide Selection	Hides the selected object.	
Show All	Shows all hidden objects.	
Rulers	Makes rulers visible or invisible, depending on whether it's selected.	Rulers must be visible to drag guides on to the page.
Grid	The grid display is visible or not, depending on selection.	
Guides	Guide options to show, snap to, and edit.	
Slice Guides	Toggles the view of the Slice Guides.	
Slice Overlay	Use to differentiate the area of the document currently being optimized from the rest of the document.	
Hide Edges	Hides the selection border of the Marquee tools.	Hides only if the marquee is still active.
Hide Panels	Toggles the visibility of all the open panels.	
Status Bar (Windows only)	Toggles the display of the Status bar.	

Table 36-3. *The View Menu Controls the Workspace Appearance* (continued)

Insert

The Insert Menu enables you to quickly create buttons, symbols, and pop-up menus. This menu also offers access to the slice and hotspot tools, which are used to divide a large image into smaller segments and to add a link to portions of an image. Finally, this menu contains options for adding layers and frames to a document. Table 36-4 lists the commands available from the Insert menu.

Command	Function	Notes
New Button	Opens the Button Editor.	
New Symbol	Opens the Symbols Properties dialog box.	Converts an existing object into a symbol.
Convert to Symbol	Opens the Symbols Properties dialog box to convert an object to a symbol.	
Libraries	Opens a variety of different libraries you saved in different folders. An Import dialog box opens.	
Hotspot	Inserts a hotspot to the selection object.	
Slice	Inserts a slice object to the selected object.	
Pop-Up-Menu	Opens the Set Pop-Up Menu dialog box.	A slice must be added before this function works.
Image	Opens the Import dialog box.	
Empty Bitmap	Inserts an empty bitmap image object.	
Layer	Inserts a layer.	
Frame	Inserts a new frame.	

Table 36-4.   *The Insert Menu Lets You Insert Numerous Items into Your Document*

Modify Menu

The *Modify* menu contains all the options to change the elements of your document, as well as the individual objects and images. The animation settings, control of marquee selections, and adding masks are all done from the Modify menu. Table 36-5 describes the features of the Modify menu.

Command	Function	Notes
Image Size	Opens the Image Size dialog box.	
Canvas Size	Opens the Canvas Size dialog box.	
Canvas Color	Opens the Canvas Color dialog box.	
Trim Canvas	Eliminates all excess canvas around all objects.	
Fit Canvas	Lets you expand the canvas to enclose objects larger than the canvas, as well as trim away excess canvas.	
Rotate Canvas	Rotates the canvas according to the choices made.	
Animate	Opens the Animate dialog box to set animation settings.	Animations are discussed in Chapter 41.
Symbol	Choose to edit a symbol, tween it, or break it apart.	
Edit Bitmap	Switches to bitmap mode.	
Exit Bitmap Mode	Switches to vector mode.	
Marquee	Various options to modify the edges of a marquee selection.	Marquee selections are discussed in Chapter 39.
Mask	Various options to group as a mask, edit, disable and reveal, or hide.	Using masks is discussed in Chapter 39.
Selective JPEG	Selective JPEG settings.	Selective JPEG is discussed in Chapter 40.

Table 36-5.   *The Modify Menu Lets You Adjust and Alter Elements of Your Document*

Command	Function	Notes
Convert to Bitmap	Converts a vector object into a pixel-based bitmap image.	
Flatten Layers	Flattens all layers into one.	
Transform	Various options to skew, distort, scale, numeric, and flip an image or object.	
Arrange	Various options to arrange the position of objects—front, back, and so forth.	
Align	Various options to align selected object or objects.	Used to center or to distribute heights and widths to line up objects equally.
Join	Joins two or more selected paths or points.	
Split	Splits a joined path or points.	
Combine	Combines selected paths, with the options of intersect, crop, punch, and union.	
Alter Path	Alters a path by simplifying (eliminating points), expanding the border, or altering the fill attributes.	
Group	Groups one or more selected objects.	
Ungroup	Ungroups a group of objects.	

Table 36-5.   *The Modify Menu Lets You Adjust and Alter Elements of Your Document* (continued)

Text Menu

Text is used in Fireworks for buttons, menus and logos, and special effects. Text is a popular feature of Fireworks, especially because it remains fully editable even if it's distorted, transformed, and has effects, fills, and strokes added. Table 36-6 lists the options on the Text menu.

Commands	Functions	Notes
Fonts	Displays the fonts you have installed and available to Fireworks.	
Size	Displays a list of font sizes.	
Styles	A list of styles, such as Bold, Italic, and so forth.	
Align	A variety of alignment options.	The Distribute to Heights and the Distribute to Widths is a great help in aligning buttons.
Editor	Opens the Text editor.	
Attach to Path	Attaches selected text to the selected path.	Discussed in Chapter 39.
Detach from Path	Detaches text from a path.	
Orientation	Options of how text is place on a path—whether it's rotated, skewed, horizontal, and so forth.	
Reverse Direction	Reverses the direction text attaches to a path.	
Convert to Paths	Converts text objects into vector objects, which can be edited as individual objects.	

Table 36-6. *The Text Menu Gives You Control over the Appearance of Your Text and Positioning on a Path*

Commands Menu

Commands are similar to Actions in Photoshop, and a few ship with Dreamweaver. This is where you access any command you add to the Fireworks Command folder (inside the Configuration folder in Windows). Table 36-7 lists the menu items found in the Commands menu.

Xtras Menu

The *Xtras* menu contains color adjustment filters, special bitmap filters, and plug-ins. This is where any plug-in you have in a Photoshop plug-in folder or any plug-in folder you point to (Preferences) is accessed. Table 36-8 shows the options available in the Xtras menu.

Commands	Functions	Notes
Creative	Convert an image to Grayscale or Sepia. Add a Picture Frame to an image.	The only option available for the picture frame is the pixel width of the frame. A wood grain frame is applied.
Document	Center, Hide/Lock Layers, Reverse all Frames, and Reverse Frame Range.	
Panel Layout Sets	Presets for screen sizes of 1024 × 768, 1,280 × 1,024, and 800 × 600.	Panel layouts are optimized for different screen sizes.
Panel Layout	Opens a dialog box, so you can name and save the current locations of your panels.	A saved set appears in the Panel Layout Sets category.
Web	Create Shared Palette, Select blank Alt tags, and Select Alt tags.	

Table 36-7. *The Commands Menu Gives You Control Over the Look of Your Workspace and Document, and Gives Access to Custom Commands*

Commands	Functions	Notes
Adjust Color	Auto levels, Brightness/Contrast, Curves, Hue/Saturation, and Invert and Levels.	All the tools needed for tonal adjustments and color alterations.
Blur	Blur, Blur More, and Gaussian Blur—the selected image is blurred.	Gaussian Blur is the only one that gives you control over how much blur to add.
Other	Convert to Alpha and Find Edges.	There's not much use for these two tools.
Sharpen	Sharpen, Sharpen More, and Unsharp Mask. Adds sharpness to an image by adjusting the edges.	The Unsharp Mask is the most useful and offers control over the amount of sharpness.
Eye Candy 4000 LE	Third-party plug-in that ships with Fireworks.	This is a demo version with three working plug-ins.

Table 36-8.   *The Xtras Menu Contains Filters That Alter the Way a Bitmap Image Looks*

Window Menu

The *Window* menu gives you control over your screen real estate by providing the options you need to open and hide panels. The menu displays a check mark next to open panels. To display a panel, simply select the panel from the Window menu.

By default, many panels are docked within the same window. When you choose an option from the Window menu, therefore, another panel toggles to an inactive setting to bring the chosen panel to the forefront. A panel can also be separated into its own floating panel by clicking-and-dragging the panel to the workspace. You can move the panels and group them anyway you want. The Windows menu lists the panels by the groups they're in and separates each group by the inset line. Table 37-9 shows the options available in the Window menu.

Any open document windows are listed at the bottom of the Window menu. You can use this list to move quickly between pages.

Commands	Function	Notes
Toolbars	Select the Main or the Modify Toolbar.	A selection opens a floating toolbar. You can drag this floating toolbar below the menus, if you like.
Tools	The floating tool palette.	A good idea is to have this open at all times.
Stroke	Opens the Stroke panel.	Sets your stroke type and characteristics.
Fill	Opens the Fill panel.	Chooses the type of fill and color.
Effect	Opens the Effect panel.	Bevels and shadows.
Info	Opens the Info panel.	Great for changing the size of an object numerically.
Optimize	Opens the Optimize panel.	All the setting options needed to make your file sizes smaller.
Object	Opens the Object panel.	
Behaviors	Opens the Behavior panel.	
Color Mixer	Opens the Color Mixer panel.	
Swatches	Opens the Swatches panel.	
Color Table	Opens the Color Table.	

Table 36-9. *The Windows Menu Gives You Control Over What Panels Are Open and Visible in Your Workspace*

Commands	Function	Notes
Tool Options	Opens the Tool Options panel.	If a tool has additional options, they can be accessed by double-clicking the tool icon. Then, this Tool Option panel opens with options for that particular tool.
Layers	Opens the Layers panel.	
Frames	Opens the Frames panel.	The Frames panel is used primarily for making animations and rollover effects.
History	Opens the History panel.	A recording of the actions you performed. You can also save the history as a recording. Perform the same steps to automatically command.
Styles	Opens the Styles panel.	A number of styles ship with Dreamweaver. You can make your own styles and access them from the Styles panel.
Library	Opens the Library panel.	Stores symbols.
URL	Opens the URL panel.	You can save a list of frequently used URLs.
Find and Replace	Opens the Find and Replace panel.	
Project Key	Opens the Project Key.	

Table 36-9.   *The Windows Menu Gives You Control Over What Panels Are Open and Visible in Your Workspace* (continued)

Help

The *Help* menu is where you access the Fireworks documentation, support, and forums. Fireworks also ships with some lessons that can be accessed from the Help menu. If you haven't registered Fireworks 4 yet, you can do so from the Help menu. Table 36-10 lists the menu items available in the Help menu.

Commands	Functions	Notes
Welcome	Displays a Welcome screen with links to help you get started with Dreamweaver.	What's New, Tutorial, and Lessons.
Using Fireworks	The Fireworks manual opens.	The manual has an index, but you can also search.
What's New	Opens a What's New list.	The What's New section of the manual opens.
Lessons	Opens the Lesson menu.	Six lessons.
Fireworks Support Center	If you're online, this link takes you to the Online Support Center.	Latest technotes are here. This is also a great place to look if you have a question. You can enter topics into the search box and see if there's a technote on the subject.
Macromedia Online Forums	If you're online, you're taken to a Macromedia Web page containing links to all of their forums.	The Fireworks forum is a great place to get help. What a great bunch of helpful individuals!
Register Fireworks	You're taken to an online registration page.	
About Fireworks	Displays the copyright and version information for Fireworks.	

Table 36-10.   *The Help Menu Gives You Access to Support and Registration*

Toolbars

Two toolbars are in Fireworks: the Main toolbar and the Modify toolbar These toolbars provide instant access to numerous functions and can be docked under the menu bar.

Main Toolbar

The *Main* toolbar displays the most commonly accessed menu functions. To open the Main toolbar, choose Window | Toolbars | Main. When the toolbar opens, you can drag it to below the main menus for easy access. The following illustration shows the Main toolbar. The options are—from left to right—New, Open, Save, Import, Export, Print, Undo, Redo, Cut, Copy, and Paste.

Modify Toolbar

The *Modify* toolbar gives quick access to grouping, arranging, aligning, and rotating of objects. To open the Modify toolbar, choose Window | Toolbars | Modify. When the toolbar opens, you can drag it to below the main menus for easy access. The following illustration shows the Modify toolbar. The options are—from left to right—Group, Ungroup, Join, Split, Bring to Front, Bring Forward, Send Backward, Send to Back, Align Left, Rotate 90 degrees CCW, Rotate 90 degrees CW, Align Left with a drop-down menu (this menu contains icons for other alignment options, as you can see in the illustration), Flip Horizontal, and Flip Vertical.

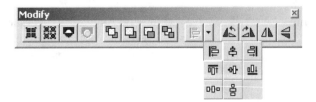

Tools Panel

All the drawing and editing tools of Fireworks can be accessed from the *Tools* panel. Most of the tools work with both vector and bitmap, but a few exceptions exist. The

Marquee tools work only in Bitmap mode and the Knife tool turns into an Eraser tool in Bitmap mode.

Tools that are similar to each other are grouped together, such as the shape tools. You can tell where a group of tools is located by the little triangle in the lower-right corner of the icon. You access the additional tools by clicking-and-holding on the triangle. A flyout opens, you move your cursor over the tool you want, and then you release the mouse button. The following illustration is a representation of the Tools panel with the flyouts open. The list begins with the Pointer tool in the top-left corner of the Tools panel and lists each tool in each set before continuing to the next tool or tool set. Table 36-11 shows the tools, their shortcut keys, and their descriptions, as found in the Tools panel.

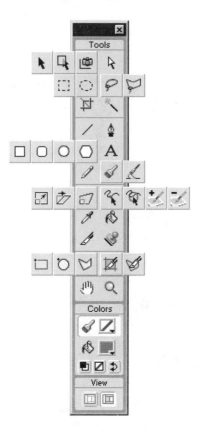

Tool Name	Shortcut Key	Description
Pointer	V, 0	Selects and moves objects.
Select Behind	V, 0	Selects objects behind other objects.
Export Area	J	Exports only a selected area of a document.
Subselection	A, 1	Selects an object contained in a group of objects or points on a path.
Marquee	M	Selects a rectangular shaped part of a bitmap image.
Oval Marquee	M	Selects an elliptical part of a bitmap image.
Lasso	L	Selects a freely drawn portion of an image. Click-and-drag to use.
Polygon Lasso	L	Makes a selection by clicking points around a shape you want to select.
Crop	C	Decreases the size of the canvas and can also increase.
Magic Wand	W	Selects colors that are similar in a bitmap image.
Line	N	Draws straight lines.
Pen	P	Adds points to a path.
Rectangle	R	Draws a vector rectangular shape.

Table 36-11.   *The Tools Panel Is the Control Center in Fireworks, Containing the Entire Vector and Bitmap Drawing and Editing Tools*

Tool Name	Shortcut Key	Description
Rounded Rectangle	R	Draws a vector rectangle with rounded corners.
Ellipse	R	Draws an ellipse vector shape.
Polygon	G	Draws vector polygon shapes.
Text	T	Inserts text.
Pencil	Y	Draws freeform lines.
Brush	B	Draws freeform strokes that can be adjusted using the Stroke panel.
Redraw Path	B	Redraws parts of a path.
Scale	Q	Resizes and scales objects.
Skew	Q	Modifies the perspective of an object by rotating and slanting.
Distort	Q	Reshapes and rotates an object.
Freeform	F	Pulls or pushes a path to alter the shape.
Reshape Area	F	Pulls or pushes all selected paths. An inner circle determines the strength of the pull or push.
Path Scrubber Additive	U	Increases a stroke. Affected by cursor speed or a tablet's pressure.

Table 36-11.   *The Tools Panel Is the Control Center in Fireworks, Containing the Entire Vector and Bitmap Drawing and Editing Tools* (continued)

Tool Name	Shortcut Key	Description
Path Scrubber Subtractive	*U*	Increases a stroke. Affected by cursor speed or a tablet's pressure. The amount of the decrease depends on the pressure and speed.
Eyedropper	*I*	Samples colors from anywhere onscreen and sets it as the active fill or stroke color.
Paint Bucket	*K*	Fills a selected area with a fill selection type found in the Fill panel.
Eraser	*E*	Deletes pixels from a bitmap image.
Knife	*E*	The Eraser turns into a Knife in Vector mode and is used to cut paths.
Rubber Stamp	*S*	Copies portions of a bitmap image.
Rectangle Hotspot		Draws a rectangular image-map hotspot area
Circle Hotspot		Draws an elliptical image-map hotspot area.
Polygon Hotspot		Draws a freeform image-map hotspot area.
Slice		Draws a rectangular-shaped slice area.
Polygon Slice		Draws a freeform polygonal slice area.

Table 36-11.   *The Tools Panel Is the Control Center in Fireworks, Containing the Entire Vector and Bitmap Drawing and Editing Tools* (continued)

Tool Name	Shortcut Key	Description
Hand	*H*	View by clicking-and-dragging to pan the document view.
Zoom	*Z*	Increases or decreases magnification.
Hide/Show Slices Tool	2	Toggles the Document view.
Set Default Brush/Fill Colors	*D*	Sets the default color for fills and strokes.
Swap Brush/Fill Colors	*X*	Reverses the default colors (black, white to white, black).
No Stroke or Fill		No stroke or fill is added.

Table 36-11.   *The Tools Panel Is the Control Center in Fireworks, Containing the Entire Vector and Bitmap Drawing and Editing Tools* (continued)

Panels

Fireworks functionality is accessed not only through the menus, but also through floating panels. The panels are grouped in logical sets. When you open the Window menu, you see the panels listed. They're arranged in the Window menu by the set that Fireworks has placed in each panel. If you want to move a panel, simply click-and-drag it to another group or to the workspace to be a free-floating panel. A good example of when you might want to do this is when you're using the Frames panel while making animations or rollovers. Seeing the Frames and the Layers panels side-by-side is helpful. You can drag the Frames panel out of the Layers panel set and, when you finish using the panels side-by-side, you can drag the Frames panel back again.

How you arrange your panels and which ones you have available on your desktop depends on your work habits and type of projects. If you use certain panels more than others, you may want to leave them open for easy access. You can also save your panel arrangement by choosing Commands | Panel Layouts. A JavaScript window opens, you name the panel configuration, and then you click OK. Your panel configuration is now available in the Commands menu.

All panels have a few common functions:

- A right-pointing arrow opens a pop-up menu with additional options.
- Option lists are accessed by clicking and holding the down arrow.
- Slider controls. When a number is required for a percentage or a size, you can use the slider to select the number or you can type in the amount. If you choose to type in a number, press ENTER (RETURN for the Mac) to accept the setting.
- Color Well. When you see a color well and you want to change a color, simply click the color and choose one from the Swatches panel with the eyedropper tool, select a color from anywhere in the workspace, or type in a Hexadecimal number. If you type in the number, you need to press the ENTER key (RETURN for the Mac).
- Check boxes. If you see a check box and you want to select it, simply click it. When you see a check mark, it's selected. To deselect, click again.
- Edge options. Some of the panels give you the option to select an edge. A Hard edge is a crisp, sharp edge, which appears jagged if the object has any curves in it. Anti-Aliased is a softer edge, which combines some of the pixels in the surrounding area with the edge to give it a softer effect. This option is used when you don't want jagged edges. Feather is the last option. You choose how many pixels around the object's edge you want to feather.

Fill Panel

The *Fill* panel contains all the control you need to add a fill to an object. The Fill Category has a drop-down menu to choose a solid fill, a gradient, or a pattern fill. At the bottom of the Fill panel, you have the option of adding a texture to your fill and the percentage of texture you want.

The following image shows the Fill panel in the center, the Fill options to the right, and a view of the Fill panel when a gradient is selected. When a gradient is selected, you have an Edit button available. You can explore this panel further in Chapter 38.

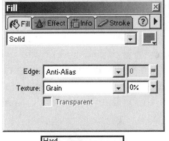
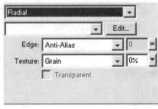

Stroke Panel

When you draw with a shape tool, a Pen tool, a Brush tool, or a Line tool, you have a *path*. Paths have a *stroke*, which can be as simple as a 1-pixel stroke or it can be elaborate. Strokes can be added or altered on vector paths only. This includes Text.

You can see the Stroke panel in the following illustration. The top white area is the Stroke category; to the left are the options you can find in the Stroke category. After you choose a category, options for that category are available in the second boxed area by clicking the down arrow. You can change the color, the tip size, and texture if you choose, all from this one panel. If you have a stroke you like a lot, which you customized, you can save it as a new stroke. See Chapter 38 for more details.

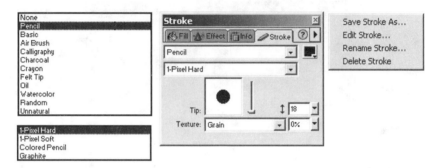

Effect Panel

The top part of the drop-down list in the Effect panel contains everything in the Xtras menu, plus it has a Bevel and Emboss category, and a Shadow and Glow category. The bottom section contains any third-party plug-ins, also listed in the Xtras menu. The following illustration shows some of the options available from within the Effect panel. You can see more details about using the Effect panel in Chapter 38.

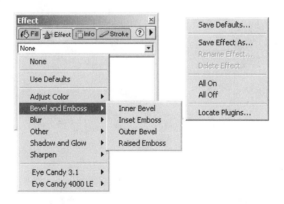

DREAMWEAVER AND FIREWORKS

Info Panel

The *Info* panel is one you'll probably use every time you open Fireworks. You can numerically set the size of an object by typing in Height and Width in pixels. After you type in the size, you must press the ENTER (RETURN for a Mac) key. You can see the X and Y coordinates by passing your cursor over the area where you want to see the coordinates. By passing the cursor over a particular color, you can see the color code in the RGB section (this changes if you change the color space). Choosing another option from the pop-up window can change the color space and the measurement system.

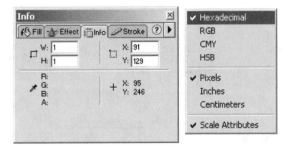

Optimize Panel

The *Optimize* panel gives you the control you need over how your images export. Settings exist for JPEG, GIF, Animations, and more. One of the useful features is the Preview tab in the document window. When you make your settings in the Optimize panel, click the Preview tab to see if the result is acceptable. If not, go back to the Optimize panel and make adjustments. The Optimize panel shown here also shows many of the drop-down lists. You see how to use the Optimize panel in Chapter 40.

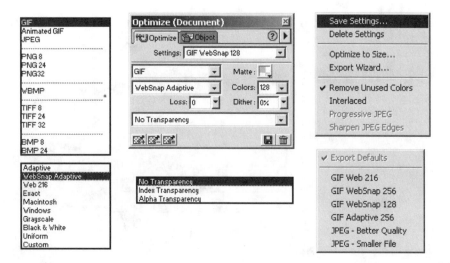

Object Panel

The *Object* panel changes according to the type of object selected. The choices in the Object panel control how the object interacts with the canvas and/or other objects. At the top of the Object panel, the type of object selected is identified, as seen here.

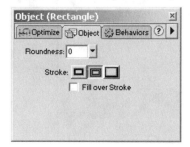

Behaviors Panel

Behaviors are what "give life" to your Fireworks images or objects. With the addition of behaviors, a boring button can become an interesting and visually pleasing interactive image.

Behaviors are JavaScripts that act when triggered by an event. An example is an image swapped with another image when a user clicks the original. This is the Swap Image action

DREAMWEAVER
AND FIREWORKS

triggered by an onClick event. The Behaviors panel is shown here You learn how to use it in Chapter 41.

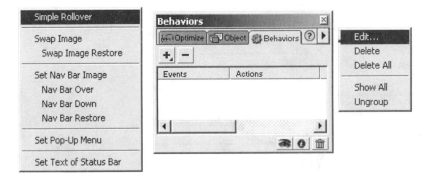

Color Mixer Panel

In the *Color Mixer* panel, you can change the color space you're working in by clicking the right-pointing arrow to access the pop-up list. You can mix your own custom colors and add them to the Swatches panel. This illustration shows the Color Mixer panel.

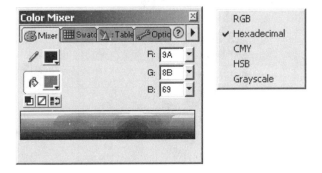

Swatches Panel

The *Swatches* panel shows all the available colors in the color space you have in use, as seen in the following illustration. You can change the swatches available by loading a different set (including Photoshop .aco files). The changes are automatically available in the color wells throughout Fireworks.

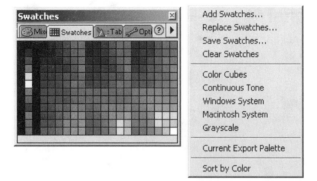

Color Table Panel

The *Color Table* panel shows all the colors currently in use in the current 8-bit or less image in the Preview mode. You would use this table when you optimize an image to see what colors are in use. You can add colors to the Color Table if you like and save the palette for use in the Swatches panel. If you have multiple slices selected or aren't using GIF, the colors won't show up at all. While you're in Preview mode, the Color Table updates automatically. This illustration shows the Color Table panel.

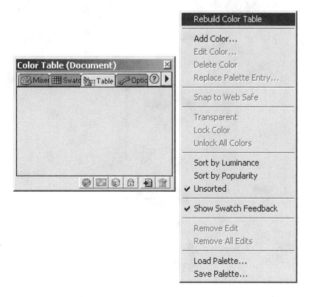

Tool Options Panel

The *Tool Options* panel shows options available to specific tools. Shown here is the Tool Options for the Pen tool.

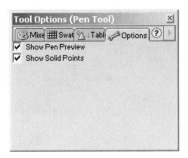

Layers Panel

The *Layers* panel is a powerful tool. This is where you organize your images and objects. You can group them in layer sets. It's also quite helpful to have icon representations to each image/object. You can see the Layers panel here and learn more about it in Chapter 37.

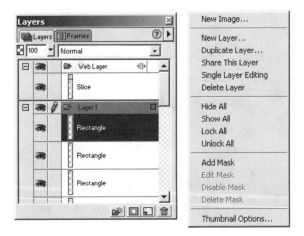

Frames Panel

The *Frames* panel is where you manage your frames for animations and rollovers. You can use Onion Skinning and set the timing delay, all from this panel, as shown in the following illustration. More details can be found in Chapter 41.

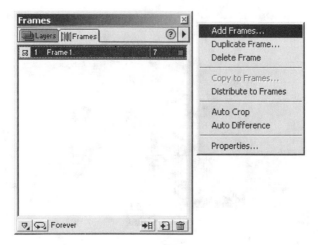

History Panel

The *History* panel is where you can see any actions you performed on your current canvas. You can also record these steps and make them into a command. And, you can undo or repeat actions you've taken. The following illustration shows the History panel.

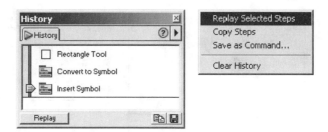

Styles Panel

Fireworks 4 ships with quite a few Styles ready for you to apply to your objects with a click of the mouse. You can also add your own customized styles. The *Styles* panel and some of its options are shown here. The Styles panel is explored more in depth in Chapter 38.

Library Panel

The *Library* panel is where your button, graphic, and animation symbols are stored and accessed. Symbols in your current document automatically show up in the Library panel. If you want to use other symbols you saved, you can load them as you can see from the pop-up list shown here with the Library panel. You learn more about the Library panel in Chapter 41.

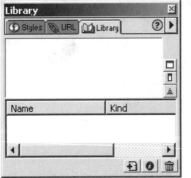

URL Panel

The URL panel stores your frequently used URLs. You add them to the URL panel and they're available for all Fireworks documents, and then are saved when you close Fireworks. In Chapter 41 you see how useful the URL panel can be when you work with the new pop-up menus. For instance, the pop-up menu has a limit to how long a URL address can be. But if you have the pop-up menu in your URL panel, you can use as long an address as you want. The URL panel is shown here.

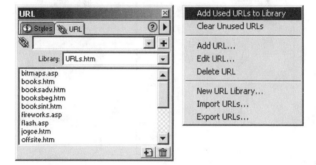

Find and Replace Panel

Using the *Find and Replace* panel, you can find elements in a document, such as text, URLs, fonts, and colors, and then replace them. You can also find non-Web-safe colors and URLs and replace them. You can see some of the options in this illustration. The Find and Replace panel is discussed further in Chapter 40.

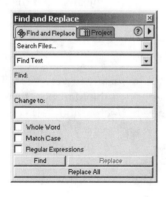

Project Log Panel

The Project Log panel, and the Find and Replace panel interact with each other to perform powerful searches and batch processes. The Project log records every changed document. You can navigate through files, export files, or select files to be batch processed. The following illustration shows the Project Log panel.

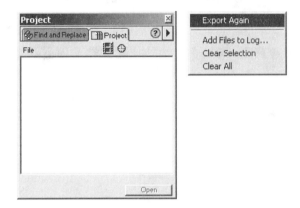

Fireworks Editing Modes

You can work with two types of images and objects within Fireworks: a *path-based image*, which is a vector, and a *pixel-based image*, which is a bitmap or rasterized image. Because both types of images are completely different from one another, Fireworks has two different modes to work in: the Vector mode (formerly called the Object mode) and the Bitmap mode.

Vector Mode

When you open a new document, you are automatically in *Vector* mode. Most of the tools all work in Vector mode, with the exception of the Marquee, Lasso, and Rubber Stamp tools and the Eraser (which is the Knife in Vector mode). If you try to use a Bitmap-only tool in Vector mode, an error message pops up and tells you the tool can only be used on a floating image object.

Vector mode is a path-based work environment. A path is any line with at least two points, which includes all the drawing tools. You can add Effects, Strokes, and Fills to a path object and they remain fully editable. This is known as *Live Effects.* Text is also a vector object, so the same effects can be added to it. You can even distort and transform objects and text, and they still remain editable. If you want to convert your vector into a bitmap, choose Modify | Convert to Bitmap. Changing modes can usually be done effortlessly because the modes are tool-driven. If you choose a bitmap tool and start to use it, the mode changes to bitmap and vice versa.

Bitmap Mode

Bitmap mode is used for pixel-based images. *Pixels* are little dots of color that make up an image. Where vectors draw shapes with points and lines that connect the points, bitmap drawing contains a line of pixels to draw the same line. So, instead of one line, you have multiple pixels.

The Marquee selection tools, Lasso tools, Rubber Stamp, and the Eraser tool all work in the Bitmap mode only. In addition to these tools, many of the vector tools work in the Bitmap mode as well. You can also apply plug-in filters, such as those from Alien Skin's Eye Candy 4000, Xenofex. These are some of the most popular plug-ins in the market today, along with plug-ins from Auto FX, which has a huge selection of filters to alter the edges of your photographs, add textures, light, and much more. The Sharpening and Blur filters, as well as the Adjust Color options found in the Xtras menu, work on bitmap images. The one thing you can't do is apply Live Effects to a bitmap image.

Summary

In this chapter, you explored all the tools, menus, and panels within the Fireworks environment. You should now be quite comfortable with the interface and ready to start designing some great images. Here are some key points:

- Understanding the difference between vectors and bitmaps
- Getting familiar with the document window
- Exploring the multitude of menu options
- Getting familiar with the function of each tool in the Tools panel
- Getting a look at all the Panels in Fireworks

Chapter 37 discusses how to set up your document and make changes to the canvas, as well as how to use the basic Fireworks tools.

The Complete Reference

Chapter 37

Using Fireworks

f you've used other image editing or vector programs, you'll find Fireworks extremely easy to learn. Even if Fireworks is your first image editing and vector program, you can produce stunning effects in no time. You'll be immediately comfortable with the Fireworks work environment because it closely resembles that of Dreamweaver. Also, version 4 of Fireworks has integrated many of the same icons you're already familiar with in Dreamweaver 4.

Working with Canvases

To begin a project in Fireworks, you need to open a new document. A document contains a canvas, which holds all your images and objects. Before you open a new document, you may want to decide whether you want to work on a whole Web page or just an element for a page. This will determine the parameters you set up. You can modify your canvas size while you work, of course, but planning ahead is easier.

Set Up a Canvas

To set up a new canvas, you have to open a new document. Select File | New, and the New Document window opens as the following shows. In the area titled Canvas Size, type in the width and height you want your canvas to be. The drop-down menus to the right give you the choice of using pixels, inches, or centimeters.

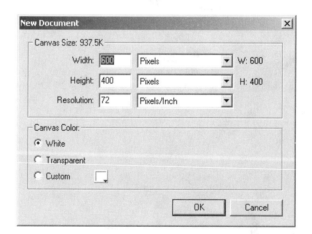

In the Resolution box, type in the amount of pixels per inch/centimeter you want. The default is 72, which is the most common setting for Web graphic design. Some designers prefer to use 96 pixels per inch.

The second portion of the New Document dialog box enables you to set the color of your canvas or to make it transparent. If you choose the custom option, click the color well and use the Eyedropper tool to select a color, or you can type in a Hexadecimal number. If you choose to type in a number, you must press the Enter key (Return for the Mac) to accept the setting.

When you finish selecting all the options for the new document, click OK. The new document and canvas are now in your workspace, as seen in the following illustration.

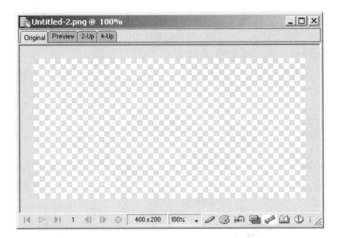

Modifying a Canvas

If you decide your canvas either isn't big enough or it's too big, Fireworks makes it easy to change your mind about the parameters of your canvas. Not only can you change the size, but you also can change it three different ways. Color and rotation can be altered as well.

Changing the Canvas Size

If you find you need more room on your canvas to add an object, increase text size, and add effects, or for whatever reason, Fireworks provides three different ways to adjust the size of the canvas.

Change the Canvas Size Numerically   If you need a bit more room on the canvas to add a special effect or another object, you can adjust the size of the canvas by a specific amount of pixels. Not only can you determine how many pixels to add, but also how they are distributed. In the following illustration, you can see the Canvas Size dialog box. In the center of the dialog box are anchors, the center anchor is the default. If you want to increase the size of the canvas by 200 pixels (add 200 pixels to the Height and the Width) and the center anchor is chosen, 100 pixels would be distributed to all four sides. If you choose the top left anchor, then 100 pixels would be added to the top and side only. To adjust the canvas size numerically, follow these steps:

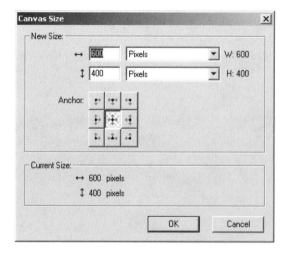

1. Choose Modify | Canvas Size to open the Canvas Size dialog window.

2. To change only horizontal dimensions, enter a new size. Do the same for the vertical size.

3. If you want to change both the horizontal and the vertical dimensions, change them both. The canvas resizes according to the dimensions you enter, not proportionately.

4. If you want to use inches or centimeters, click the drop-down list and choose it. Pixels is the default so, regardless of how you set up your canvas in the New Document dialog box, it always appear as pixels in this dialog box.

5. If you want the added pixels to be distributed other than evenly on all four sides, choose another anchor position. Click OK when you finish.

Change the Canvas Size Using the Crop Tool   When you need to cut away excess canvas quickly around a button or an image, the Crop tool is the ticket. Despite its name, the *Crop tool* can quickly add to the canvas as easily as it can cut it. To access the Crop tool, click the Crop tool icon in the toolbar, shown in the margin. Drag a selection around the area you want to crop. Eight handles appear on the selection. Move your cursor over the handles, and click-and-drag to resize. If you want to extend the canvas a bit, the selection automatically snaps to the canvas edge but, by pulling out on the handles, you can actually make the canvas bigger. When the selection is where you want it, press ENTER (RETURN on the Mac).

Change the Canvas Size Using Trim   The Trim Canvas command is a useful command. If you have a button, a navbar or any other image or object, you can cut away excess canvas by choosing Modify | Trim Canvas. The *Trim Canvas* command takes into account any shadows, glows, or other special effects, and trims away all excess completely and automatically.

Changing the Canvas Color

Even though you set the canvas color when you open a new document, this isn't sealed in stone. You can change the color at any time by choosing Modify | Canvas Color. The same color options are available that you saw when you originally set up the canvas. When you click the custom option, and then click the color well, a 216-color Web-safe palette is the default. If, for any special reason, you need a different color space, you can change the palette by clicking the right-pointing arrow and choosing any palette available. By default the OS palettes are available.

Adding Color Palettes

If you want additional color palettes to be available from the color wells, you need to load them. If you have a custom color palette or one you're used to using and you want it added to the list of palettes, this is an easy thing to do. The Fireworks manual states that the color palettes, cubes, and so forth are supposed to be a GIF file or an ACT file. This is true, but what isn't apparent is that you can also use Photoshop ACO files. You can also select "any" GIF image, and its colors are then added to the Swatches panel.

To add a GIF or ACT file as a color palette, open the Swatches panel (Window | Swatches), and then click the right-pointing arrow and choose Add Swatches. Select the appropriate file and click OK. Adding swatches extends the existing palette. If you want to use only a saved palette, choose Replace Swatches.

To add a Photoshop ACO file, click the right-pointing arrow in the Swatches panel and choose Add or Replace Swatches. When the dialog box opens, locate your file; go to the folder on your hard drive where you know a Photoshop .aco file resides. In the find box, type ***.aco** and press the ENTER (RETURN for Mac) key. You can now see your ACO files. Choose the one you want and click Open.

Rotating the Canvas

If you want your entire canvas rotated, perhaps an image is upside down, or you want everything at an angle for a composition, whatever the reason, it's easy to do. Choose Modify | Rotate Canvas; the submenu is shown here.

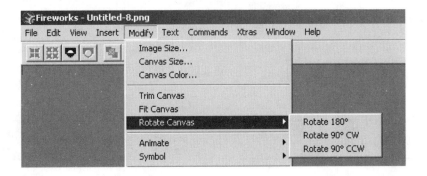

Working with Layers

If you used Fireworks 3 prior to version 4, you'll be pleasantly surprised with the new Layers panel. Icon representations of objects, paths, and images are in the Layers panel, as well as added functionality such as grouping objects and layers into layer sets. If you've worked with layers in other applications, you'll discover that Fireworks handles layers differently. Whereas other applications put each individual object on its own layer, in Fireworks, multiple objects can be placed on one layer and edited individually. This is a timesaver because you needn't scroll through a multitude of layers searching for the item you want to edit. You can work in the same layer with related items and simply click an object if you want to select it. Figure 37-1 illustrates the amount of visual clues to help identify individual elements of your document.

The Web Layer

The *Web layer* is a special layer in Fireworks and always remains on top. You can't delete or move the Web layer. It has a unique function—this layer *only* stores information about slices and hotspots. *Slices* and *hotspots* are Web objects, which are

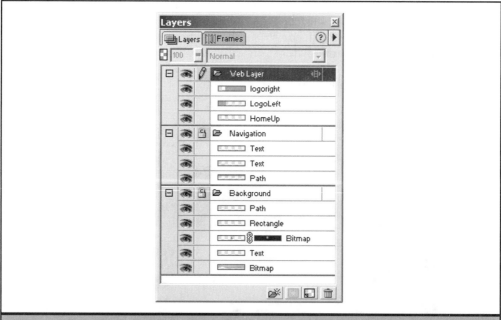

Figure 37-1.   *The Layers panel demonstrates the visual clues as to what's on each layer*

used to attach a behavior, which, in turn, triggers an action or event, such as a rollover, a pop-up menu, or a pop-up window. Slices are also used to define the cutting areas where Fireworks needs to cut an image for exporting.

Adding Layers

You can add new layers in several ways. The easiest method by far is the *New/Duplicate Layer icon,* which is a yellow folder located at the bottom of the Layers panel, as seen in Figure 37-1. All you do is click the yellow folder to add a new layer. A new layer is then added above the currently selected layer. You can also add a layer by choosing Insert | Layer, or by clicking the right-pointing arrow in the Layers panel and selecting New Layer.

Duplicate Layers

Duplicating layers couldn't be easier: with the layer selected you want to duplicate, simply click the right-pointing arrow and select Duplicate layer. A window opens, as the following shows, giving you options of where to add the duplicate layer: to the top, the bottom, before or after the current selection, as well as how many duplicates you want to add.

Delete a Layer

Deleting layers can be done three different ways. Highlight the layer you want to delete and use the delete key on the keyboard, or click-and-drag the layer on top of the trash can icon in the Layers panel. I find the easiest way is to select the layer and click the trash can icon.

Opacity Settings

In Figure 37-1, near the top-left corner is a gray-and-white checked icon with the number 100 next to it. This is the opacity setting. You can adjust the opacity not only for each individual layer, but also for each individual object or image on a layer independently. To change the opacity, select the layer (or object), and either type in the opacity number you want or use the slider to adjust the opacity amount.

Showing/Hiding Layers

To show or hide whole layers (or objects) click the eye icon (Figure 37-1) of any layer or object. If the eye is on, the layer or object is visible in your document; if you click the eye icon again, it toggles the visibility off.

Lock Layers

To lock a layer, click the box to the left of the layers name. Look at Figure 37-1—the padlock indicates the layer is locked. Once a layer is locked, you can't alter anything in that layer, you can't even select it. To lock or unlock all the layers, click the right-pointing arrow in the Layers panel and choose the appropriate action.

Name a Layer

To name a layer or an object, double-click the layer or object name and rename it in the dialog box that pops up.

Single Layer Editing

If you want to work on one layer only in Fireworks, you need to lock all the layers or choose Single Layer Editing. To use Single Layer Editing mode, click the right-pointing arrow in the Layers panel, and then select Single Layer Editing. Now you can only select or edit objects on the current layer. Even though the other layers are visible, you can't alter them.

Share a Selected Layer

Share a Selected Layer comes in handy when you produce animations. If you have repeating elements on a layer that you want on all layers, then all you have to do is to select the layer, click the right-pointing arrow, and choose Share This Layer.

Strokes

Strokes are what make paths visible, and they also give each path its own special character. Adding a stroke is more than just adding a color: you can add a special stroke shape, alter the width and softness of the stroke, and even alter the Tip size and shape. If you use a pressure-sensitive tablet, even the speed, direction, and pressure you draw with alters the appearance of the stroke. With control and versatility like this, you can design whatever you dream up.

The Stroke Panel

The *Stroke panel* is one you'll return to again and again. Figure 37-2 shows the Stroke panel, Figure 37-3 shows the options in the drop-down menu of the Stroke Category, and Figure 37-4 shows the Stroke Name drop-down menu. The Stroke Names vary for each stroke selected in the Stroke Category.

The Stroke panel has 48 built-in strokes, but you can produce an infinite number of variations. Options such as color, strokes, patterns, textures, width, edge, softness, and so on can change the text effect slightly or drastically, to produce a unique new look. To apply a stroke, you select your object and choose a stroke selection from the Stroke panel.

When you choose settings in the Stroke panel, they remain as you set them for the Brush tool, the Pen tool, and the shape tools. The Pencil tool defaults after each use back to Pencil, 1-Pixel Hard.

Adding a Stroke

You can add strokes to newly drawn paths or to existing paths. A wonderful feature of the Stroke panel is you can see in real-time what each stroke looks like before you commit to it. If you type in Hex numbers, percentage numbers, or tip size numbers, you need to press the ENTER (RETURN for the Mac) key to activate a change. If you use the eyedropper to select a color or the sliders for the texture amount and tip size, the change is automatically visible on your canvas. The Stroke panel contains all the controls you need to add a stroke. Follow these easy steps:

1. Open the Stroke panel if it isn't already open, Window | Stroke. Or, you can press CTRL-ALT-F4 (CMD-OPTION-B on the Mac).

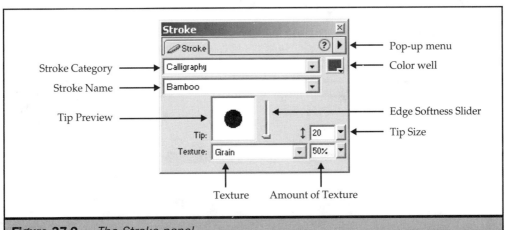

Figure 37-2. *The Stroke panel*

DREAMWEAVER AND FIREWORKS

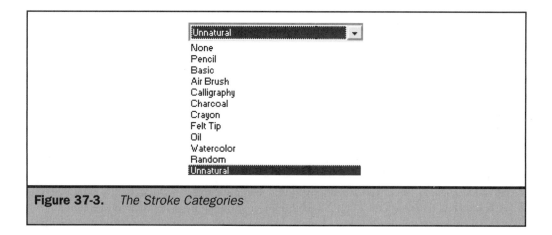

Figure 37-3. *The Stroke Categories*

2. Select a stroke from the Stroke Category (see Figure 37-3) or select None if you want no stroke at all.

3. Each stroke in the Stroke category has variations available in the Stroke name area. Click the arrow next to the Stroke name box and make a selection.

4. To alter how the stroke blends, adjust the Tip Softness using the slider control.

5. Select the color you want to use.

6. Adjust the Tip size using the slider or type in a number. Remember, if you type in a number, press the ENTER (RETURN for the Mac) key to accept the change.

Using the Preset Strokes

As mentioned before, Fireworks ships with 48 preset strokes. Each stroke is preset with a size and texture (if it contains one), and the texture amount. Technically, when you

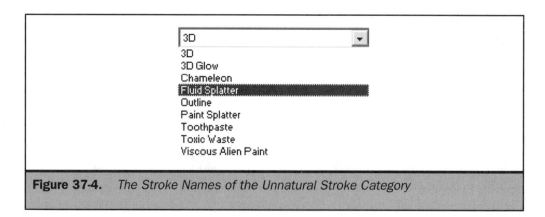

Figure 37-4. *The Stroke Names of the Unnatural Stroke Category*

use one of these preset strokes, you can see the settings used in the Stroke panel. Unfortunately, this is hit or miss. For example, select the Brush tool and draw a line. From the Stroke panel, select Crayon from the Stroke category and Basic for the Stroke name. You see a tip size of 13 and a Texture of Grain at 65 percent. Now change the Stroke name to Rake, and then to Thick. Each time, watch the size change on the canvas, but the Tip size doesn't change. If you select the Pencil option in the Stroke category, it automatically defaults to 1-Pixel Hard as it should. Now, if you select another category, the Tip size changes for the first selection only. The Texture works fine and changes according to each selection—it's the Tip size you can't rely on.

Look at a few samples of the different strokes to get an idea of how the presets work and some of their differences. In the following illustration, you see the Basic stroke. The Hard line is a good one to use when you want a sharp, crisp edge. If you use it on a rounded or curved edge, though, it appears jagged. The next one is the same Hard line, only with the Hatch 1 Texture added at 100 percent. This changes the appearance by adding a texture. The Hard rounded rounds the ends, but it's still jaggy on a curved line. The Soft line has an Anti-Alias edge, so the edge won't appear jagged, and the Soft rounded is the same with the ends rounded. Notice the circles next to the Soft line and the Soft rounded line. The Soft Rounded circle has a smaller stroke added than the Soft line does.

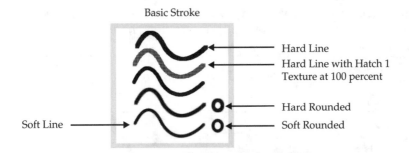

This next illustration shows a sampling of some of the other strokes. The Unnatural category has some interesting effects. Because you can see what the stroke looks like in the workspace, it's easy to experiment until you get the look you want.

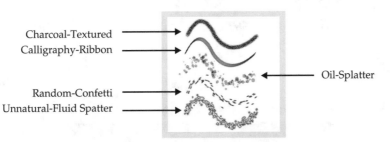

Strokes can also produce some interesting effects. This example shows text with the Unnatural category and using Outline. You can't tell the colors, but the lines are multicolored. The second example is the same stroke, but has a larger stroke size, producing an interesting appearance.

Adding Texture to Strokes

Adding a texture to a stroke can make an object pop out from the page. Figure 37-5 shows some of the textures that ship with Fireworks 4. In the previous section, you saw some textures that were used in the preset strokes, but you can add different textures to strokes, even if they already have a default texture. The one you apply overrides any preset texture. To apply a texture, follow these steps:

1. Select the object you want to add a stroke to. From the Stroke panel, select a stroke from the Stroke category.

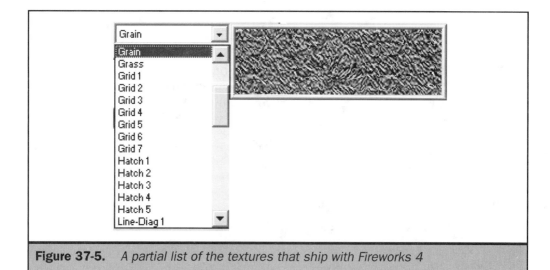

Figure 37-5.   *A partial list of the textures that ship with Fireworks 4*

2. From the Stroke name, choose one of the options available with the category you chose.

3. Adjust the tip size to make it larger. A larger stroke yields a better texture effect—size 20 or larger should work nicely. Adjust the size by typing in a new number or using the slider.

4. From the Texture pop-up menu, choose one of the textures listed, and then set the opacity of the texture by typing in a percentage or choosing with the slider. If you type in a percentage, press the ENTER key (RETURN for the Mac).

You can also add your own textures that will appear in the texture list. These same textures are used for the Fill panel, and adding textures is discussed in the "Filling with Patterns and Textures" section later in this chapter.

Modifying a Stroke

You can modify strokes even after they've been applied. Even a file that's been saved can be reopened and modified. To practice modifying a stroke, follow these steps:

1. If the Stroke panel isn't open, select Window | Stroke or CTRL-ALT-F4 (COMMAND-OPTION-B for the Mac).

2. Be sure the object you want to modify is selected.

3. To modify the stroke color, select the color change you want from the color well.

4. The Edge Softness slider changes how the stroke blends. Change this if you want a softer edge.

5. To change the stroke's thickness, simply click the down arrow next to the thickness number or type in a number.

The Stroke panel is one of the tools you'll use over and over. It adds depth and detail to objects, making them pop out or seem to sink deeper into the page. You can achieve some amazing effects using the Stroke panel.

The Fill Panel

The *Fill panel* works much like the Stroke panel. You select the type of fill you want, the color, the type of edge, and a texture, if you want one. Figure 37-6 shows the Fill panel when you first access it.

Figure 37-7 shows a list of the available Fill options in the Fill panel. To fill an object, text, or path, follow these simple steps:

1. Select a shape tool or a drawing tool and draw something that needs a fill. Whatever the current fill color is will be applied to your selection.

2. Click the drop-down menu in the Fill panel and select Solid.

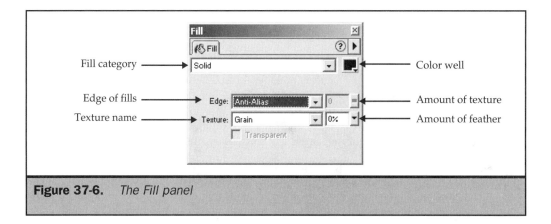

Figure 37-6.   *The Fill panel*

3. From the Edge area, click the drop-down menu and make a selection. Anti-Alias is the default, which helps smooth the edges. A Hard edge gives a sharp edge, but is jagged on any curves. The Feather option can soften the edges a great deal, depending on the amount of feather you use. When the Feather option is selected, the Amount of Feather option becomes available.

4. If you want a texture, click the drop-down menu and choose a texture from the list. Notice the Other option, which is discussed in the next section. If you select a texture, you have to increase the opacity, so you can see the texture. As soon as you increase the texture amount, a Transparent option becomes available. If you click Transparent to select it, the objects or image below (assuming something is below your object) shows through.

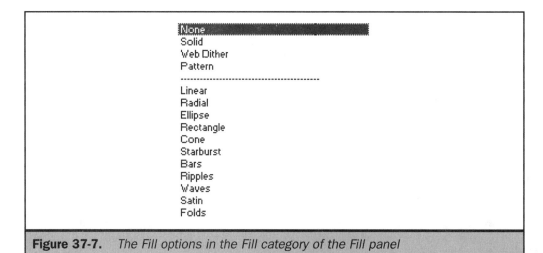

Figure 37-7.   *The Fill options in the Fill category of the Fill panel*

Filling with Patterns and Textures

Using patterns and textures is a commonly used technique to add depth and interest to objects. Fireworks 4 ships with some preset patterns and textures, but the real diversity comes from the capability to use almost any pattern or texture you have available.

Adding Textures

Textures can be added to any fill, and you can use your own textures, in addition to the ones that ship with Fireworks 4. Texture files use the grayscale value of an image. You can use any PNG, GIF, JPEG, BMP, TIF, or PICT file as a texture. To add your own texture files, simply place them in the Fireworks 4\Settings\Textures folder. To add texture to a fill, follow these steps:

1. Select any object containing any fill.
2. From the Fill panel, click the arrow for the Texture Name drop-down and choose one of the included texture files.
3. Adjust the percentage of opacity, which determines the amount of the texture seen.

Filling with Patterns

The use of a pattern in a path object increases your designing flexibility. Fireworks 4 ships with a small selection of 14 patterns. The *Other* option in the Fill panel opens the door to limitless patterns. You're limited only to what you can hold on your hard drive or on CD-ROMs. As long as an image is a 32-bit image in a file format of BMP, PNG, GIF, JPEG, TIFF, or PICT (for the Macintosh), you can have an instant pattern. To use a pattern follow these steps:

1. Select the object you want to fill.
2. From the Fill panel, choose Pattern from the Fill category.
3. From the Pattern name box, choose Other. Browse to an image file, select it, and click Open.

Patterns can be altered in the same way as gradients (more on gradients in the following sections) by moving the handles and the rotation symbol. Another similarity is that pattern alterations cannot be saved for use in another document. If you like the adjustments you made to a pattern and think you want to have it available for another use, then save it as a style (see Chapter 38).

Using Gradient Fills

A *gradient* is a blend of two or more colors. Gradients are often used to produce lighting effects to give the illusion of depth. They are also used as terrific backgrounds and as a fill for transparency masks when working with bitmaps (see Chapter 38).

Filling with Gradients

You can add unique colorization to a graphic with the use of a gradient fill. Fireworks 4 ships with 11 gradient patterns and 13 preset gradient color sets. The best way to describe the 11 types of gradients is to show you a small sample of each. Figure 37-8 shows a representation of each.

To fill using a gradient, follow these steps:

1. Select an object you want to apply a gradient to.

2. From the Fill panel, choose one of the gradient options from the Fill category drop-down list.

3. Choose the color combination you like from the Preset gradient color sets or use the default gradient. The default is a combination of whatever color your brush is and the current color of the Fill tool.

4. You can adjust the Edge attributes in the Fill panel: the choices are Anti-Alias, Hard, or Feather. If you choose Feather, you have the option to type in how many pixels you want the edge of your gradient to be feathered.

If your object is selected, it's automatically filled with the gradient.

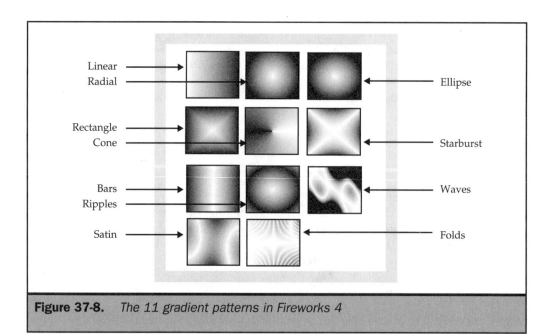

Figure 37-8. *The 11 gradient patterns in Fireworks 4*

Altering Gradients

Altering gradients is where the real power of the Gradient tool becomes evident. Gradients can be customized by adjusting the pattern's center, width, and skew. To alter a gradients position, follow these steps:

1. Follow the preceding steps for filling with a gradient. To alter the gradient's position, select the Pointer tool and click the object to make it active. The gradient handles then appear.

2. To change the position of the gradient, drag the circular handle to adjust the gradient's starting point.

3. Move the cursor over the control handles until you see the rotate cursor. You can now drag the handles to a new location.

4. By dragging the square handle, you change the size of the gradient.

 A gradient's control handles needn't be constrained within the object. You can drag the round or square handles outside the object area to achieve the desired effect. In fact, you can drag both handles completely off the object.

Editing Gradient Colors

Existing colors in a gradient can be changed, deleted, or moved around, or new colors can be added with ease. To change the color settings, follow these steps:

1. Draw a rectangle to fill with a gradient style you like.

2. Click the Edit button in the Fill panel. You see color swatches below the gradient representation. A swatch for each color is in the gradient and at the position where each color begins, as shown here.

3. To change any of the colors, simply click the swatch and choose another color.

4. To add another color, place your cursor anywhere in the row containing the current color markers, where you want another color added. You see a plus

sign (+) next to your cursor; click. Select the color by clicking the color swatch and choosing a color.

5. To move the position of any of the colors, click-and-drag the swatch to the new location.

6. To delete a color, click-and-drag the swatch toward the bottom of the panel.

You have a lot of control when it comes to gradient colors. You can sample colors from other images with the Eyedropper tool to produce some interesting color combinations. If you have an image you like the color composition of, you can make a custom gradient from it. Draw a rectangle to fill with your gradient, and choose a gradient style and any color preset. Following the previous instructions, change the colors in each color swatch by using the eyedropper to get color samples from areas in your image. If you need more colors, add more color swatches.

Using Vector Shape Tools

The Vector Shape tools are some of the easiest to use. Every object drawn with a *Vector Shape tool* always contains a starting point and an ending point, which plot the path of a line. With the Vector Shape tools, those points are automatically placed, although you can control how the points are placed by editing them.

You can constrain the shape of the entire vector by pressing the ALT-SHIFT keys (OPTION-SHIFT for Macs) and drag to draw. If you want to draw from the center out, press the ALT key (OPTION for a Mac) and drag to draw. Many of the drawing tools have tool options. To access any available tool options, double-click the tool icon. If no options appear, then none exist for that particular tool.

Rectangle Tool

The *Rectangle tool* can be used for both Vectors and Bitmaps. To draw a rectangle, follow these steps:

1. Select the Rectangle tool from the toolbar.

2. Click-and-drag a rectangle on your canvas.

3. If you want to set a specific size for your rectangle, open the Info panel (Window | Info) and enter the specific Height and Width measurements you want.

4. If you want to edit the shape, notice the four points automatically added to the rectangle you just drew. The following illustration shows a rectangle with the four points. Select the Subselection tool (white arrow) from the toolbar. Click-and-drag out the point in the lower-right corner. An error dialog box opens, stating, "To edit a rectangle's points, it must first be ungrouped. Click OK to ungroup the rectangle and turn it into a vector?" Click OK.

 A rectangle in Fireworks is a group of four points, which is why the dialog box opens—the rectangle must be ungrouped to be recognized as a path object. Once it's ungrouped, you can manipulate each point. The second half of the error message may lead you to think you aren't in Vector mode, but you are.

5. Now you can use the Subselection tool to click-and-drag any of the points to alter the shape of the rectangle.

Rounded Rectangle Tool

If you tried setting the roundness of a Rounded rectangle, you might have been baffled if you read Fireworks' manual or help guide. The instructions are incorrect. The manual states you should set the Roundness setting in the Tool Options panel before you draw the rounded rectangle. This isn't accurate. The Rounded Rectangle tool doesn't have any options available until *after* you draw the object. Then, the options aren't in a Tool options box; they're in the Object panel. Using the Rounded Rectangle tool is actually quite easy to do. Follow these steps:

1. Select the Rounded Rectangle tool.

2. Drag a shape on the canvas. You can set the size, height, and width in the Info panel (Window | Info).

3. To set the roundness, open the Object panel (Window | Object) and type in the amount of roundness you want or use the slider to choose a roundness amount.

Editing points and making alterations to a Rounded rectangle shape is the same as it is for the rectangle. It needs to be ungrouped before its points can be edited.

Ellipse Tool

The *Ellipse tool* can be used for both Vector and Bitmaps. To draw an ellipse, follow these steps:

1. Select the Ellipse tool from the toolbar.

2. Click-and-drag an ellipse on your canvas.

3. If you want to set a specific size for your ellipse, open the Info panel (Window | Info) and enter the specific Height and Width measurements you want.

4. Add any strokes, fills, or effects you want.

An ellipse has four points added to it automatically, like the rectangle tools do. The difference is, when you want to edit the points, they aren't grouped, so you won't have to ungroup them. If you use the Subselection tool to alter a point, you'll notice handles, which are Bézier control handles. To learn more about using these handles, see the section "Pen Tool" in this chapter.

Polygon Tool

In Fireworks, you can draw an equilateral polygon from a triangle with three sides to a polygon with 360 sides. The Polygon tool also works for both Vectors and Bitmaps. To make a polygon, follow these steps:

1. Double-click the Polygon tool to access the Tool Options panel, as the following illustration shows.

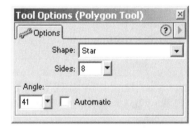

2. The Tool Options panel is where you select the shape you want: Polygon or Star. If the Star shape is selected, an Angle option is also available. If you choose the Automatic option, the Angle varies according to how many sides you have. The closer to 0 the Angle is, the thinner the point is. The closer to 100 the Angle is, the thicker the point is. Choose the settings you want to use.

3. Drag-and-draw a star on your canvas.

4. Double-click the Polygon tool again to have access to the Tool Options panel, and then change the Angle to 90.

5. Drag-and-draw a star on your canvas. Changing the settings doesn't change the current shape. You have to draw a new one to use the new setting.

6. The Polygon tool always draws from the center out. If you want to constrain the shape to a 45-degree angle, hold down the SHIFT key and drag the shape.

Line Tool

The *Line tool* only draws a straight line with two points. If you want to constrain the line to a 45-degree angle, hold down the SHIFT key and drag the shape. The Line tool doesn't have any tool options. If you draw a series of lines that seem to connect into one with the Line tool, this is still a series of *paths*. Every time you drag a line, it's a separate path. If you want a series of lines to become one path, they need to be joined. Joining paths is discussed in Chapter 39. The Line tool can also be used for both Vectors and Bitmaps. To use the Line tool, follow these steps:

1. Select the Line tool from the toolbar.

2. Drag a line on the canvas by holding down the SHIFT key and dragging to draw a line at 45 degrees.

3. To change the size of the line, open the Info panel (Window | Info), enter the Height and Width you want, and press ENTER (RETURN on a Mac).

Vector Path Freeform Drawing Tools

The freeform drawing tools enable you to draw any shape you want. If you have a digital drawing tablet, now would be the time to use it. Drawing freeform lines with a drawing pen is much easier than drawing with a mouse. Of course, you can still draw quite well even with a mouse in Fireworks. Tools such as the *Pen tool*, which uses Bézier curves, make it easy to draw shapes suitable for navigational GUIs.

Pencil Tool

The *Pencil tool* has a default stroke of 1-Pixel Hard. Unlike some of the tools that retain the last setting used, the Pencil tool must be reset each time you use it if you want something different than the default stroke of 1-Pixel Hard. The Pencil tool can be used for both Vectors and Bitmaps. The Pencil tool is often used for freeform drawing with a pressure sensitive tablet. Anything you can draw with your tablet or with a mouse can be done with the Pencil tool. Double-click the Pencil tool icon and you see the Pencil tool Options, which are

- **Anti-Aliased**—Puts a smooth edge on the lines you draw, which is particularly important if the lines are curved. Transitional colors are used along the edge of the object, blending the background color with the stroke color.

- **Auto Erase**—Macromedia describes this function as drawing the fill color over the stroke. It does, but only if you draw over the stroke after you've drawn it. This is a strange feature. It works the same way as drawing a new path and applying a stroke.

■ **Preserve Transparency**—Works only in Bitmap mode. It enables you to draw only in areas containing pixels, not in transparent areas with no pixels (pixels are explained in Chapter 39).

To draw with the Pencil tool, follow these steps:

1. Select the Pencil tool from the toolbar.

2. Click-and-drag to draw with the Pencil tool.

3. If you want an open path (one that doesn't close), release the mouse when you finish drawing.

4. If you want a closed path, draw to the beginning of the line you drew and release the mouse.

Brush Tool

The *Brush tool* looks like paint or ink, but the result is still a path containing points. The Brush tool has the same feature as the Pencil tool in that it can draw anything you can draw with a tablet or a mouse. There are no limitations to points and connecting paths or some of the limitations the other drawing tools have. The lines you draw with the Brush tool can be edited like any other path and you can use strokes, fills, and effects. The Brush tool can be used for both Vectors and Bitmaps. No Brush tool options (when you double-click the brush icon) are available in Vector mode, other than Preserve Transparency. To draw with the Brush tool, follow these steps:

1. Select the Brush tool from the toolbar.

2. Click-and-drag to draw with the Brush tool.

3. If you want an open path, release the mouse when you finish drawing.

4. If you want a closed path, draw to the beginning of the line you drew and release the mouse.

Pen Tool

With the *Pen tool,* you don't actually draw the line, you just define the points, which make up the line—plot out the points, if you will. This is similar to drawing a dot-to-dot picture. Each time you click, you put down a point (dot), and the next place you click adds another point. The line is automatically added between the points, thereby completing a line segment. The Pen tool is a vector tool only. If you're in Bitmap mode and choose the Pen tool, the mode is automatically changed to Vector mode.

The Pen tool has two kinds of points: a *Corner point*, which has at least one straight segment, and a *Curve point*, which has at least one curved segment. To see first-hand the difference between these two types of points, follow these steps:

1. Open a new document (File | New) and use a size of 300 pixels × 300 pixels. Check to be sure you have a stroke color set. In the toolbar near the bottom in the Color section, click the color well next to the pencil icon and choose a color. Be sure the color you choose isn't the same as the canvas or you won't see the line.

2. Select the Pen tool and click somewhere on the left side of the canvas. Go straight across the page a few inches and click again. A line connects the two points you added. Continue clicking anywhere on the canvas. No matter where you click, the lines keep connecting the "dots."

3. Close your first practice document and open a new one (File | New). Any size is fine, but 200 pixels × 200 pixels gives you a little room to practice. Select the Pen tool and click the left side of the canvas. Now click again a few inches away, and then go down the page a bit and click-and-drag. See what happens as you drag? The line is curved (see the following illustration). Getting used to working with a curved line takes practice, but it gives you a lot of flexibility in producing custom shapes.

When you draw with the Pen tool and drag, a curve is formed and Bézier control handles are added to the path. Control handles control the shape of the object. The next section discusses manipulating the Bézier controls handles.

Using The Control Handles of a Bézier Curve

After you draw a Bézier curve, you may want to make adjustments to it. Working with the control handles is done by using the Subselection tool and clicking a point on the path. When the cursor is near a point, it changes to a white arrowhead, which indicates the point can be selected. When you click a point, the solid square turns into a hollow square. Bézier handles are usually visible when you select a point that's a Bézier curve. To practice manipulating Bézier curves by using Bézier control handles, follow these steps:

1. Select the Pen tool and click three points in a row; double-click the ending point of the path.

2. Select the Subselection tool. Click any point. No handles appear because this is a straight line. Press and hold the ALT key (OPTION for the Mac) and drag the middle point down. When you release the mouse button, a control handle is visible, as the following shows.

3. Now press the ALT key (OPTION for the Mac) on the same point (not the handle—the point) and drag straight up. You can see what happens in the following illustration. Another curve has been added and another Bézier control handle is also added.

4. Practice pulling the Bézier control handles by clicking-and-dragging to the right and down. You can move the handles up, down, and all around. The more you practice, the better feel you get for how the curves function.

Converting a Straight Line into a Curved Line

You made a straight line and a curved line in Steps 1 and 2 of the preceding section by clicking points with the Pen tool to make a straight line, and then holding the ALT key (OPTION for the Mac) while you dragged a curved point. You did this while still using the Pen tool.

The technique is the same for adding a curve to a straight-lined shape that's already been drawn. You hold the ALT key (OPTION for a Mac) and drag on the point where you want to add a curve. You can use the Subselection tool or the Pen tool to change a straight line into a curve. I prefer the Subselection tool because you don't have the line "clinging" to the tool, as you do with the Pen tool. If you're adding a curve to a rectangle, you need to ungroup it, and then choose the Subselection or Pen tool to drag on a point.

Text

You'll probably use the *Text tool* frequently in Fireworks, especially for adding text to buttons, as well as making logos and banners. The Text tool is one of the easiest tools to use, and it has a lot of flexibility to boot. The great thing about text in Fireworks is it remains editable. Even after you add strokes, fills, styles, patterns, effects, and whatever else—it's still fully editable! If someone shares a native Fireworks file or even a Photoshop PSD file with effects added, you can open it and deconstruct quite easily. To test a Photoshop file, I typed in a word, added a quick Chrome style to it, and saved it. I opened the file in Fireworks and the following image shows you what happened. The color was lost, but the effects added were visible and editable within Fireworks.

If you double-click the effect name, the dialog box with the settings for that effect open. Then, you can edit the options and click outside the dialog box to accept the changes.

Entering Text

To enter text, simply select the Text tool and click anywhere on the canvas. The Text Editor opens, as seen in Figure 37-9.

If you've used any image-editing program before, nothing in this editor should look foreign. The top row is the area where you select the font you want to use and set the size, color, and attributes, such as Bold, Italic, or Underlined.

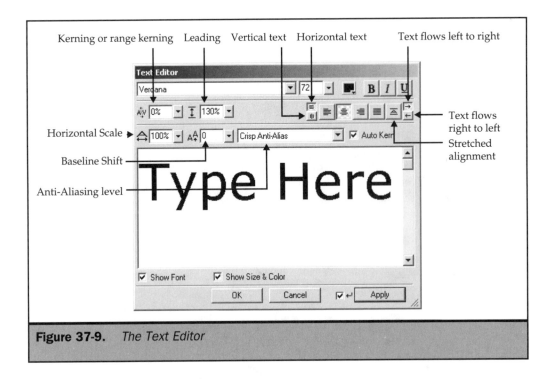

Figure 37-9.   *The Text Editor*

The next row is where you set the *kerning* (how much space is between two characters), the *leading* (how much space is between lines), and the alignment settings. The Left alignment, Right, Center, and so on are familiar, I'm sure. But a few more controls in this area are quite useful. Figure 37-9 shows the names of each option, so you can easily locate it. The Horizontal Text and the Vertical Text options are handy. In some programs, you must to rotate the text to get the special alignments. At the far right, notice you can set the direction the text will flow.

The third line of options is where you set the Horizontal Scale, the Baseline Shift, and the *Anti-Aliasing* (smoothing out jagged edges) Levels. The choices for Anti-Aliasing are the following: No Anti-Aliasing, Crisp Anti-Aliasing, Strong Anti-Aliasing, and Smooth Anti-Aliasing. The rest of the Text Editor is self-explanatory.

Importing Text

You can import text from other applications, such as Rich Text Format (RTF) and ASCII format, into Fireworks by choosing File | Import. Locate the file you want to open and click Open. The cursor changes into a little corner. Place it on the canvas and click.

To open Photoshop PSD files, you can Import if you want to, but you can also open them normally.

Editing Text

Editing text is quite easily done in Fireworks. All you do is double-click the text you want to edit, and the Text Editor opens. Make any changes you want and click Apply. If you want to edit any fills, strokes, or effects, click the text to select it, open the respective panels, and then make any changes you'd like.

Summary

This chapter covered a lot of the basic tools in Fireworks, including setting up a canvas, working with layers, and the basic drawing tools.

- Setting up a canvas for your objects and image objects, as well as how to modify it.

- Organizing and viewing the elements on your canvas, using the many layer features, and getting to know the Layers panel.

- Learning how to use the Stroke panel and trying out many of the options.

- Using the Fill panel, containing many textures, patterns, and gradient fills.

- Using the Drawing tools and understanding how each tool is different, what each tool does, and how to use it.

- Entering, importing, and editing text.

In the next chapter, you learn how to apply effects and special effects, as well as customizing styles and saving them for reuse. You also learn how to mask an object to add transparency.

The Complete Reference

Chapter 38

Applying Effects

The Effect panel and the Xtras menu add a lot of functionality to Fireworks. Using the Effect panel, you can add shadows, bevels, adjust color, and many other things, and they all remain totally editable and change as the image or object changes.

In the Xtras menu, you have many of the same options as you have in the Effect panel, except they're applied to bitmap images and aren't editable, and they aren't Live Effects.

The Commands menu offers quick solutions to many tasks. You'll discover how to use all these tools in this chapter.

The Effect Panel

The *Effect panel* is where you add Live Effects, such as Bevel and Embosses, and Shadow and Glows, as well as some third-party plug-in filters. You may notice many of the options in the Effect panel also appear in the Xtras menu. The difference is this: those in the Effect panel are applied as Live Effects and are totally editable. The effects applied through the Xtras menu convert an object to a bitmap (if it's a vector object) before applying. The Effect panel is shown here.

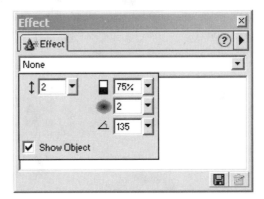

The third-party plug-ins that show in the Effect panel may or may not work as a Live Effect. Try them. If they apply and show up in the Effect list, they work. I tried several from Eye Candy 3.1, Eye Candy 4000, Xenofex, and Av Bros. Puzzler Pro, and they all worked. The Blur filters and the Sharpen filters work as Live Effects as well. See more about these options in the Xtras section.

Adding Effects

For ease of use, you may want to give the group of panels that contains the Effect panel, Strokes panel, and Fill panel a permanent home in your workspace. To open the group of panels, choose Window | Effect.

To add an effect, follow these easy steps:

1. Select the object you want to add an effect to.

2. Click the Effect tab. From the drop-down menu, choose the effect you want applied.

3. Once you make a selection of, say, Shadows and Glows | Drop Shadow, you're presented with a dialog box to set the distance of the shadow, the softness amount, the angle, and the opacity. The settings are similar for most effects.

4. After you press the Return key (Enter for the Mac) or click anywhere, the changes are applied.

Editing Effects

If you ever want to edit a file containing an effect, all you do is open your PNG file and follow these steps:

1. Click the object that contains the effect you want to view or alter.

2. Once the object is selected, click the Effects tab. You see a list of effects added with a check mark next to it. To view what the object would look like without a certain effect, uncheck it. If you decide you don't want a particular effect, select it and click the trash can icon in the lower right-hand corner to delete it.

3. To view the specific settings of any effect, double-click the effect name. You now have access to the settings, and you can make any alterations here.

The capability to see the effects applied to any object can be a timesaver, especially if you have forgotten how you produced an effect. Not only can you edit via the Effect panel, but you can also deconstruct.

Adding Shadows and Glows

Shadows and Glows are Live Effects. Once they're applied, they can be edited. The Shadow and Glow effect also changes as the object changes. For instance, if you have an interface that you drew with a Drop Shadow applied and you punch a hole in it, the hole automatically obtains the same shadow. Live Effects can only be applied to a vector object or image. The Shadow and Glow options are shown here with an example of a Drop Shadow and the settings used.

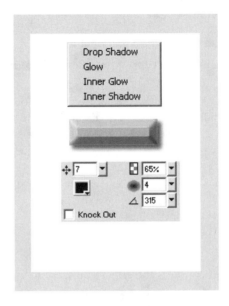

To add a Shadow or a Glow, follows these steps:

1. Select the object you want to add the effect to.
2. Open the Effect panel or click the Effect tab, and then click the down arrow and choose Shadow and Glow. Select the type you want.
3. In the little dialog window that opens, select the settings you want to add to your Shadow or your Glow. Depending on which effect you're applying, some of the choices are distance, size, color softness, opacity, and more.
4. Click anywhere on the screen to accept the settings.

Adding Bevel and Emboss

The Bevel and Emboss options have several choices; they are also Live Effects and editable. They can only be applied to vector images or objects. The Bevel and Emboss options are shown here, as well as an example of an Inner Bevel and its settings.

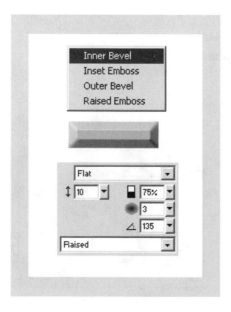

The steps required to apply a Bevel or an Emboss are the same as for applying Shadow and Glow.

Applying Blurs

The *Blur filters* in the Effect panel can be applied to vector objects, and are Live Effects and editable. The Blur filter adds a bit of blur; the More blur adds a bit more. The problem with both these filters is they offer no control—they're automatic filters. The most useful one is the Gaussian Blur filter. To add a Gaussian Blur, follow these steps:

1. Select the object you want to add a blur to.

2. Open the Effect panel, click the down arrow, and choose Blur | Gaussian Blur. This window opens:

3. If you use the slider to adjust the amount of blur, you can see the results in real time on the canvas. You need to click OK to view the results if you type in the amount.

The Styles Panel

Fireworks ships with a number of styles. *Styles* are presets you can apply to an object with the click of a button. The preset styles can be edited, and you can make your own. The Style panel is shown here.

To apply a style to an object, follow these steps:

1. Select the object to receive the style.
2. Open the Style Panel (Window | Styles).
3. Scroll the list of styles and click one.

That's all there is to it!

Modifying Styles

After you apply a style, you may want to change it. Or, if you open a previously saved object with a style applied, you can still change it. To modify or edit a style, follow these steps:

1. Select the object with a style attached.
2. Open the Effect panel. If any Live Effects are applied, they'll show up here. If so, double-click any effect and alter the settings to your liking. If you want to see what the object would look like without a particular effect, you can turn off the view by clicking the eye icon next to the effect. Only the view is turned off; the effect is still there. To turn it on again, click the eye icon again. If you want to delete an effect, click it, and then click the trash can icon.
3. Open the Fill panel. If any fills are applied, they'll show up here. Edit the fills as you would any other fill. See Chapter 37 for more information on editing fills.

4. Open the Stroke panel. If there are any strokes they will show up here.
Edit them just like any other stroke. See Chapter 37 for more on editing
or modifying strokes.

Saving Styles

If you have an object you applied to a custom fill and special effects to that you want to
keep, and maybe use again on another object, then you can save it as a style. The styles
you save, as well as those in the Style panel, can also be used for the Pop-Up menus
that Fireworks can now make. See Chapter 41 for more on making instant Pop-Up
menus. To save a style, follow these steps:

1. Select the object for which you want to save the effects as a style.

2. Click the right-pointing arrow and choose New Style, or click the New Style
icon next to the trash can. This dialog box opens.

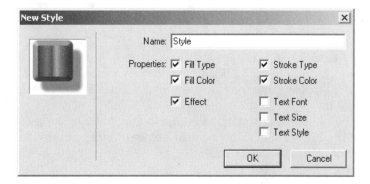

3. Name the style.

4. Select the options you want to save as a style. Remember, if the style is
attached to a font, you don't have to choose font. If you do choose font, then
the same font is applied when you apply the style. If you don't choose font,
then the style effects are added to whatever text you are adding the style.

5. Click OK.

Importing and Exporting Styles

When you make new styles, you can export only one or make several and export them
as a set. Fireworks also ships with a couple different sets of styles. To Import or Export
styles, follow these steps:

1. Open the Styles panel (Window I Styles).

2. Click the right-pointing arrow and choose either Import Styles or Export Styles.

3. A window opens where you can either locate and choose the file to import or choose where to save the export.

4. Click Open or Save.

Xtras

The options in the *Xtras* menu are applied to bitmap images. You learn more about bitmap images in Chapter 39. The Other options won't be detailed here, primarily because the Convert to Alpha is a holdover from Fireworks before the new masking techniques (Chapter 39) were available, making this option obsolete. The Find Edges doesn't offer any apparent benefits except for possibly the rare special effect.

The other options in the Xtras menu are the Adjust Color options, which you learn about in this section, as well as the Blur and Sharpen filters. Some third-party plug-in filters are also discussed in this section.

Using the Blur Filters

The *Blur filters* are helpful in many retouching situations. Blurring can be applied to an image that looks scratchy, speckled, or a bit dirty. Before you start blurring an image that you're repairing, make a duplicate layer. You can always delete it later if you don't need it.

To apply a blur, see the information about applying blurring earlier in this chapter, in the section "The Effect Panel." The only difference is, when applied from the Xtras menu, they're not Live Effects or editable.

Using the Sharpen Filters

The *Sharpen* and the *Sharpen More filters* are automatic adjustments with no choices available. What the sharpening filters do, especially the *Unsharp Mask filter*, is to increase the sharpness of an image by working with contrast. The contrast is emphasized in an image based on the selections you make in the Unsharp Mask dialog box. You can enter three selections, which are

- Sharpen Amount—Specifies the intensity, how much effect neighboring pixels have on one another. The Sharpen Amount is affected by the Radius and Threshold amount as well, so you may have to adjust this setting. The best settings for the Sharpen Amount are between 50 percent and 100 percent.

- Pixel Radius—Is similar to a feather, determines how many pixels are evaluated. The larger the number you select, the more pronounced the contrast. The Pixel Radius settings range should be .5 percent to 1.5 percent of the dpi of the image. So, for a 72 dpi image, the Pixel Radius should be in the range of .35 pixels to 1 pixel. If your image is busy and has low contrast, use the high end of the Pixel Radius settings. If the image isn't so busy and has high contrast, use the low end of the settings range.

■ Threshold—Determines which pixels are affected. Which pixels are affected is based on the number of levels of difference in the surrounding pixels. If the number of levels is greater than the threshold, sharpening is applied based on the settings for Radius and the Sharpen Amount. The higher the Threshold number, the fewer pixels affected. The Threshold is based on how the pixels work against each other, which is based on their differences. For instance a Threshold of 0 allows neighboring pixels to affect one another; a high threshold of 255 prevents pixels from affecting each other.

The Threshold setting is normally 0 to 5 but, most often, 0 is the best choice. If you have an image with a lot of noise, a Threshold of 1 or 2 is the better choice because it prevents the noise from being sharpened. The noisier the image, the higher the Threshold setting should be. Settings above 5 are used only when you want to emphasize contrast of image elements.

To use the Unsharp Mask, follow these steps:

1. Select an image or make a selection of a portion of an image.

2. Choose Xtras | Sharpen | Unsharp Mask. If your image or object isn't a bitmap, this window opens telling you it will be converted to a bitmap. Click OK.

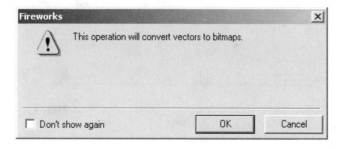

3. This window opens. Enter the settings for the Sharpen Amount, Pixel Radius, and the Threshold, and then click OK.

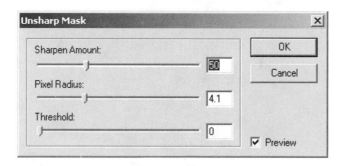

Adjust Color

Many of the Adjust Color options are more advanced and beyond the scope of this book. You get a brief look at each option, and instructions are given for some of the easier and more useful options.

Auto Levels

Levels can adjust the tonal range of an image. If detail isn't visible, levels can often bring it out by automatically adjusting the shadow, midtones, and highlights of the image. *Auto Levels* is like most automatic tools; you have no control. But, if you don't know how to make adjustments to the levels manually, you may want to try this filter to see if the correction is acceptable.

To use Auto Levels, simply select your image and choose Xtras | Adjust Color | Auto Levels.

Brightness and Contrast

The *Brightness and Contrast* option is a quick way to adjust an image's appearance. To use Brightness and Contrast, select an image, and then choose Xtras | Adjust Color | Brightness and Contrast. This window opens

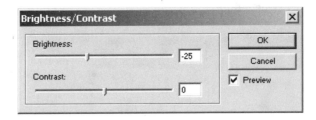

Move the sliders to the left or to the right. You can view in real time on the canvas. When you get it the way you want, click OK.

Curves

Curves is another advanced feature of Fireworks. The Curves option is used to adjust color, brightness, and contrast. This is the Curves dialog window.

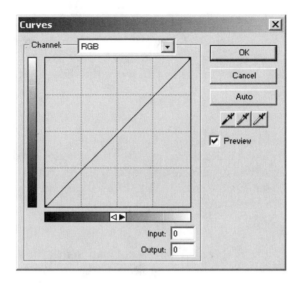

In the Curves dialog window, you can make color adjustments to the entire image or to separate channels. For instance, if you want to change the contrast of only the red channel, you can select the red channel and make alterations.

Hue and Saturation

The *Hue and Saturation* option is a great way to change the color of an image. Let's say you have a button you like and you want to use it, but it's red and you need blue. All you need to do is select the object, choose Xtras I Adjust Color I Hue and Saturation. This dialog window opens.

As you move the sliders, you see the color change. You can add Hue, Saturation, lightness, or color. If you click the Colorize option, you can change an RGB image to a two-tone image or add color to a grayscale image. Be sure to check the Preview option, so you can see the effect on the canvas as you move the sliders. When you get the color you want, click OK.

Invert

The *Invert filter* option can add a funky look to an image or, if you use it on a button with a gradient fill, it can be quite stunning. What the Invert filter does is change each color in an object or image to its inverse on the color wheel. For example, applying Invert to a red image changes the color to light blue. To use the Invert filter, select an object, and then choose Xtras | Adjust Color | Invert.

Levels

Levels is one of the options that require more explanation than this book can cover. For good books on using levels in real-world projects, check out *Fireworks 4 f/x & Design*, by Joyce Evans (The Coriolis Group) or the *Fireworks 4 Bible*, by Joseph W. Lowery (Hungry Minds, Inc.). Levels are used to make tonal corrections in images. The Auto Levels option isn't a bad one to try until you learn how to use the eyedroppers to change the shadow points and Histogram of levels. You can see the Levels dialog window here.

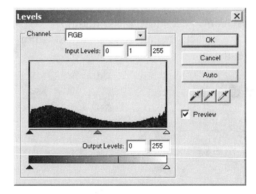

Plug-ins

Plug-ins comes in handy for special effects and quick fixes. Fireworks 4 is compatible with most third-party Photoshop-compatible plug-ins, but not with Photoshop 6 native plug-ins.

Adding Photoshop Compatible Plug-ins

To use Photoshop plug-ins, choose Edit | Preferences and click the Folders tab. The following illustration shows the dialog window that opens. Check the Photoshop Plug-ins option and Browse to locate a Photoshop Plug-in folder. Click Open when you find the correct folder.

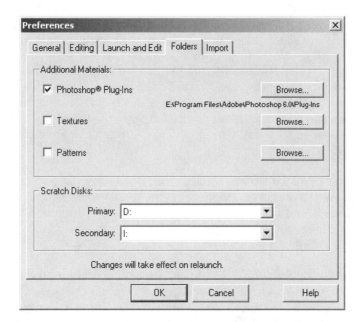

You don't need to have Photoshop to use this option. You can put all your Photoshop-compatible plug-ins in to one folder and use this method to tell Fireworks where to find them. Or, if Fireworks is the only program where you plan to use the plug-ins, you can directly install new plug-ins into Fireworks. When you're asked where to install the plug-ins, find Fireworks4/Configuration/Xtras.

Fireworks 4 ships with Eye Candy 4000 LE (Alienskin) containing three filters. To use any of the plug-ins, choose Xtras | Plug-in name and make your choices in the various dialog boxes.

Third-Party Plug-ins

Quite a few third-party, Photoshop-compatible plug-ins are available. If you search any of the major search engines for free Photoshop plug-ins or simply for Photoshop plug-ins, you'll come up with a wide array of choices. There's a caveat with using free plug-ins, though. It's at your own risk. Most work great, but there may be a time or two when a plug-in might cause your system to freeze. This is the worst that's ever happened to me, but you never know.

Some top-notch, third-party plug-ins are available for sale, which are listed next. If you go to each company's Web site, you can find demo versions to try before you buy.

Puzzle pro   The *Puzzle pro* plug-in is the easiest tool I've found to date for making puzzles quick and easy. All kinds of options are available for puzzle shapes, bevels, and more. The price is $39.95. You can find out more at **www.avbros.com**.

AutoEye   You can get a demo of the *AutoEye* plug-in at **www.autofx.com**. This plug-in automatically adjusts the tonal values of an image or you can do it manually. I tried it on a dark photo and was amazed at how much detail was brought out. The automatic feature sometimes adds too much sharpening to the edge, so also try the manual options. With a try-before-you-buy demo, you can't go wrong. If you decide to purchase it is $99.00.

Photo/Graphic Edges 10,000+   A demo of *Photo/Graphic Edges 10,000 +* plug-in can be found at **www.autofx.com**. More edges are in this package than you'll ever need. The package comes with a manual so you can see the different categories and quickly find the edge types you are looking for; they are quick and easy to apply. The purchase price is $199.00.

Studio Pro Bundle by Auto FX   The *Studio Bundle Pro 2.0* plug-in contains 11 of Auto FX Software's most popular products in one integrated package for $199.95. This package is worth over $1,250 if it's sold separately. The effects in this package include Typo/Graphic Edges, Ultimate Texture Collection, Photo/Graphic Patterns, Universal Animator, Universal Rasterizer, Photo/Graphic Frames, Page/Edges, and Web Vise Totality. You can see it at **www.autofx.com**.

Eye Candy 4000   A few filters from the *Eye Candy 4000* plug-in ship with Fireworks 4. If you want a demo, it can be found at Alienskins Web site. The demo has some additional plug-ins that are different from those that ship with Fireworks. Alienskin software has a great Web site interface, enabling you to see each of the included 23 filters in use. The price is $169.00 or an upgrade price of $69.00. Visit **http://www.alienskin.com/ec4k/ec4000_main.html** for a demo.

Xenofex   A demo of the *Xenofex* plug-in can be found at **http://www.alienskin.com/ xenofex/xenofex_main.html**. The Xenofex filters from Alienskin have a collection of 16 filters and 160 presets. Be sure to check out the filters at Alienskin's Web site. The price is $129.00.

SuperBladePro   In September 2000, Flaming Pear released the *SuperBladePro* plug-in, adding new effects like dust, moss, water stains, and abrasion, as well as features like

Undo and a Graphical Preset browser. Flaming Pear plans to offer more texture packs, presets, and tutorials for it, and to continue developing intriguing and useful plug-ins.

SuperBladePro, available via download and online purchase at **www.flamingpear.com**, costs $30. Registered users of the original BladePro can purchase an upgrade for $15.

Using the Commands Menu

In this section, you use the Creative options part of the Command menu, as well as using Commands. Options in the Commands menu can automate a repetitive task or perform tedious tasks for you. Many commands are freely available on the Internet, and the list for Fireworks is steadily growing.

Using Free Commands

Before you can use commands you either have to find them or make them. A few good places to check for commands made by others are listed here. Making your own commands is also discussed in this section.

Fireworks FAQ   This is the Fireworks FAQ site, but it also has commands at **http://comharsa.com/firefaq/command.php3.**

Project Fireworks   An archive of downloadable commands, patterns, textures, and symbols is at **www.projectfireworks.com/.**

Fireworks 4 f/x and Design Companion Web Site   Tutorials, reviews, and commands are at **http://www.je-ideadeign.com/fireworksbook.htm.**

Massimo Foti   Fireworks Commands, as well as Dreamweaver and UltraDev, are at **www.massimocorner.com.**

Installing Commands

Once you find commands you think sound useful, you need to place them in your Fireworks 4/Configurations/Commands folder. Once the commands are placed in the Commands folder, they're available for use without restarting Fireworks. If the maker of the command has the file zipped, you need to unzip it before it's available for use.

Any command you make yourself and save in Fireworks is automatically saved to the correct folder and immediately made available in the Commands menu.

Creative Options

You have three choices in the Creative menu: the Convert to Grayscale, Convert to Sepia Tone, and Create Picture Frame.

Convert to Grayscale

When you want to eliminate all color and you have a grayscale image, this option is quick and easy. To convert an image or object to grayscale, simply select it and choose Commands | Creative | Convert to Grayscale.

Convert to Sepia

Sepia gives the appearance of an old-fashioned image. The tones are brownish, not gray. To convert an image or object to sepia, choose Commands | Creative | Convert to Sepia.

If you want an image to be two colors similar to sepia, but a different color, you can also choose Xtras | Adjust Color | Hue and Saturation. Check the Colorize box and choose the color you want.

Create Picture Frame

You can add a wood grain frame instantly to any image by opening an image. Choose Commands | Creative | Create Picture Frame and enter the number of pixels you want your frame size to be, and then click OK.

Making Your Own Commands

Commands are similar to actions in other applications. To make your own commands, follow these steps:

1. Perform the steps involved in a task you think you might want to repeat again in another document or to another object.

2. Open the History panel. From the menu bar, choose Window | History or SHIFT+F10.

3. Click the right-pointing arrow, choose Save as Command, and name it.

That's all there is to making a simple command in Fireworks. The History panel shows the steps or actions you've taken. If anything is below the line in the History panel, it probably won't record properly. You may need to repeat some steps or do an action in a different way to record and save it as a command.

You can also make commands by writing your own JavaScript. The major functions in Fireworks are JavaScript-based; therefore, if you can write JavaScript code, commands can be changed according to the way you work. This topic is beyond the scope of this book, but you can find out more about writing your own JavaScript commands at the Macromedia Web site.

Summary

In this chapter, you explored the Effect panel and saw the difference between Live Effects and the Xtras panel, which applies the same effects to bitmap images. You also had the opportunity to check out some third-party plug-ins or maybe you made a command of your own.

Key Points:

- Using the Effects panel and editing the effects used.
- Adding Bevel and Emboss options, and Shadow and Glow options.
- Using the Styles panel, editing and saving new styles.
- Exploring the Xtras panel with special effects and plug-ins.
- Exploring the Adjust Color menu options, such as Hue and Saturation, Levels, Curves and Brightness, and Contrast.
- Exploring of the Sharpen filters and how to use them.
- Using the Blur filters and learning about the difference between them.
- Looking at third-party plug-ins.
- Using, finding, and making commands.

In Chapter 39, you earn how to use the vector editing tools, as well as work with bitmap images, including transparency masks.

The Complete Reference

Dreamweaver 4

Chapter 39

Editing Vectors and Bitmaps

Vector mode offers many editing tools for use on vector objects, which you explore in this chapter. Then you move into working with bitmapped images. You learn what bitmaps are and how work with them, including using gradient masks, which are extremely useful, especially for image compositions.

Vector Editing Tools

Fireworks offers an array of tools for editing vector objects. The Bézier control handles baffle many beginners but, with a bit of practice, you'll wonder what you ever did without them. Then there are the vector mode editing tools, as well as special editing features of the Pen tool.

Drawing a Bézier Curve

A *Bézier* curve (pronounced *Bezz-ey-aye*) is based on mathematical calculations. The name comes from Pierre Bézier, who, in the 1970s, formulated the principles on which most vector objects are now based. The theory is that all shapes are composed of segments and points. A segment can be straight, curved, or a combination of both—straight and curved. When you have a combination of two or more points, which are joined by a line or a curve, it's referred to as a *path*.

A *straight line* is a line that joins two points using the shortest possible distance. A *curved line* is controlled by the position of the points and the control handles, which manipulate them.

When you used the vector drawing tools, you've probably noticed a handle on some of your curves. These are *Bézier control handles*. You see how to manipulate them later in this chapter. To draw a Bézier curve, follow these steps:

1. Open a new document, File | New. A size of 300 pixels × 300 pixels should give you plenty of room to practice.

2. Select the Pen tool and click anywhere on your canvas to set the beginning point of the path.

3. Move your cursor and click somewhere else on the canvas to set the second point of the path. Notice how a straight line automatically connects the points.

4. Move the cursor again and click to set another point but, this time, hold the mouse button down and drag a bit in any direction. As you drag, a curve forms. You can click anywhere to place another point.

5. Double-click to end the path. You can see here that where the click-and-dragged point was added, there's a curve, and a control handle is attached.

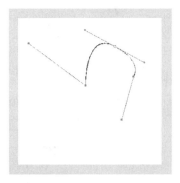

Straight and Curved Segments

If you have straight-line segments and you want to make one or more into a curved segment, follow these steps:

1. Select the Pen tool, click three points in a row, and then double-click the ending point of the path.

2. Select the Subselection tool. Click any point (the point as seen on the middle line in the following illustration turns hollow), press the ALT (OPTION for the Mac) key, and drag the middle point down. When you release the mouse button, a control handle is visible.

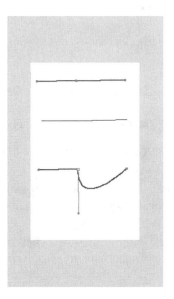

3. To change a Bézier curve back into a straight line, select the Pen tool and click the point of the curve you want to be a straight segment. The curve segment of that point is straight.

Using the Control Handles of a Bézier Curve

Making adjustments to your Bézier curve by manipulating the control handles is easy. Working with the control handles is done by using the Subselection tool and clicking a point on the path. When the cursor is near a point, it changes to a white arrowhead, which indicates the point can be selected. The control handles then become visible. To practice manipulating Bézier curves using Bézier control handles, follow these steps:

1. Draw a path with a curved segment.

2. Select the Subselection tool and click a point you know has a curved segment. The control handles appear.

3. All you do now is click-and-drag one of the ends of the control handle. You can pull up, down, to the side, and so forth. Also, try pulling on the second end of the handle.

Working with Bézier curves takes practice to get a feel for what direction to pull and turn to get the desired shape.

Editing with the Pen Tool

If you have several separate paths you want to join together, break apart, or to continue drawing, this is all done using the *Pen tool.*

Closing a Path

If you try to fill a path object and nothing happens, or if the fill doesn't go just inside the path, producing strange results, your path probably isn't closed. If this happens, you need to join the path or to join multiple paths. To close a path, follow these steps:

1. With the Pointer tool, select the path you want to close.

2. Select the Pen tool, move your cursor over one of the end points of the path (when you're near the end point, a little x appears in the lower-right corner of the cursor), and click the end point once. Now, a little arrow in the corner of the cursor indicates you can select a closing point.

3. Move your cursor to the ending point and click it once. The path is now closed. If you need additional points before you reach the end you want to connect to, you can add points before you click the ending point.

Continue Path

Adding to a previously drawn path is easy. The technique is similar to closing a path, except you needn't close a path to add on to it. If you want to add on to a previous path, follow these steps:

1. With the Pointer tool, select the path you want to add on to.

2. Select the pen tool, move your cursor over one of the end points of the path, and click the end point once.

3. Move your cursor to the next location where you want to add a point and click once. Continuing clicking to add points until you have the path you want.

Joining Paths

Joining paths may sound similar to closing paths. While it's almost the same, the difference is you needn't close the paths. To join paths together, follow these steps:

1. With the Pointer tool, select the path you want to join.

2. Select the Pen tool, move your cursor over one of the end points of the path, and then click the end point once.

3. Move your cursor to the end point of the path you're connecting to and click once.

Add and Delete Points

You need to add points to a path when you want it to turn the direction without adding a curve to do so. To add points to an existing path, follow these steps:

1. With the Pointer tool, select the path you want to add points to.

2. Select the Pen tool, click once on the line of the path to add one point. If you want a curved point with Bézier control handles, click-and-drag.

3. Repeat for as many points as you need. When you finish, select any other tool to end adding points.

If your path has more points than necessary to maintain the design's shape or you want to delete points to alter the shape, follow these steps:

1. With the Pointer tool, select the path you want to delete points from.

2. Select the Pen tool. As your cursor passes over the point, you see a minus sign (-) on the right corner of the cursor. Select the point you want to delete by clicking it one time.

3. Another way to remove unwanted points is to choose Modify | Alter Path | Simplify. You have to type in how many points you want removed. While this option doesn't give you precise control, it's a fast way to make simple changes.

Editing Paths with Vector Mode Editing Tools

The *Vector mode editing tools* enable you to push and pull points visually without editing separate points.

Freeform Tool

The *Freeform tool* enables you to push or pull points to adjust the shape of a path. The Freeform tool automatically adds points as you push or pull a new shape. You can see the Freeform tool options here.

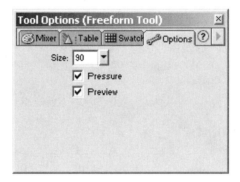

To use the Freeform tool, follow these steps:

1. Open a new document, File | New. Choose 300 pixels × 300 pixels and a white canvas.

2. Select the Rectangle tool and draw a rectangle.

3. Select the Freeform tool and move the cursor toward the bottom of the rectangle to push in on it. Try to click-and-drag up on the rectangle's edge. You then get an error message saying the tool can only be used on paths. (The Rectangle tool was used here to show you this error.)

Note   *Because a rectangle in Fireworks is a path, this might seem like a strange message. The reason this message opens is because, in Fireworks, a rectangle has its four points automatically grouped and must be ungrouped to use the Freeform tools on it. To overcome this minor obstacle, select the Subselection tool and try to move a point. The dialog box asking if you want to ungroup comes up. Click OK. Or, you could choose Modify | Ungroup, whichever is easier for you, and then select the Freeform tool again.*

4. Click anywhere on the bottom line and push up. Click-and drag-down to get a feel for how it works.

5. You can also push and pull from inside the rectangle. Push it toward an edge and see what it does. It takes some practice to get used to how this tool works. Just practice pushing and pulling until you get a feel for how it performs.

6. Double-click the Freeform tool to access the Freeform tool options, which is shown here. This is where you change the size of the circle you push with inside the path or over or above an open path.

Redraw Path

Clicking the little arrow in the corner of the Brush tool accesses the Redraw Path tool. To use the Redraw Path tool, follow these steps:

1. Draw a path or use a rectangle shape and ungroup it (Modify | Ungroup).

2. Select the Redraw Path tool from the Brush tool flyout.

3. Select the path you want to alter. Place the cursor (a circle) over the path's line, and click-and-drag to reshape it.

Reshape Tool

The *Reshape tool* works much like the Freeform tool (access it by clicking the arrow on the Freeform tool's icon). What separates the Reshape tool from the Freeform tool is its capability to warp an entire image. There are Extra options also available, as you can see here.

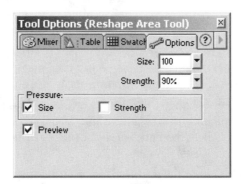

An additional circle is in the Reshape tool cursor. The Strength setting determines how strong the pull is for the path between these two circles. The Pressure settings are for use with a pressure-sensitive tablet. To use the Reshape tool, follow these steps:

1. Draw a path and select it.

2. Double-click the Reshape tool icon to access the Reshape tool options. Set the size and the strength you want for the cursor.

3. Push on a path to reshape it.

Path Scrubber

The *Path Scrubber tool* alters a path after it's drawn. The state of a path can be altered by the settings in the Path Scrubber tool options, as shown in the following illustration. The best way to understand how this tool works is to use it and experiment with the settings.

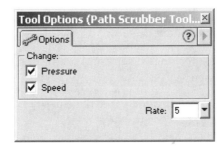

To use the Path Scrubber tool, follow these steps:

1. Open a new document. Choose File | New, a size of 300 pixels × 300 pixels, click Custom, and then choose white for the background.

2. Select the Line tool and draw a line on the canvas. Open the Stroke panel and choose Air Brush | Basic, a color of black, and a large tip size of 60 for easy viewing.

3. Double-click the Path Scrubber tool—subtractive—to open the Path Scrubber tool options. Don't change the Pressure and the Speed (leave them checked) and set the Rate at 50. Place your cursor outside the end of the stroke.

4. Repeat Step 3, except change the rate to 100 and see the difference. This can help you determine how to set the rate and where to place the cursor to achieve the desired result. Select the Path Scrubber tool—additive. Click alongside the path to see what happens.

5. For practice, select either the additive or the subtractive Path Scrubber tools (try both) and click at the end of a point, the center, or off to the side. You begin to see the benefits of this tool.

The Path Scrubber tools are great for making a line with tapered ends. You can achieve a tapered end by using the settings found by double-clicking the tip icon in the Stroke panel as well. The taper you get with the Path Scrubber tool has softer edges than the taper you get by using the Shape settings of the brush.

Knife Tool

The *Knife tool* is in the same location as the Eraser tool. In Bitmap mode, it's the Eraser tool; in Vector mode, it's the Knife tool. The Knife tool is used to cut a path—open or closed. To use the Knife tool, follow these steps:

1. Open a new document. Choose File | New with a size of 300 pixels × 300 pixels and a white canvas.

2. Select the Rectangle tool and draw a rectangle. Fill the rectangle with any color you want.

3. Select the Knife tool. Click-and-drag it through the rectangle. Start at the top and drag all the way through. The slice won't be apparent when you finish.

4. Select the Pointer tool, and then click anywhere other than the rectangle to deselect the rectangle.

5. Click one side of the rectangle and drag. This separates the piece you just cut.

Reshaping Paths Using Path Options

Combining, joining, intersecting, and punching holes in paths are all functions you'll probably use often. The Combine options can be found by choosing Modify | Combine. These options are Union, Join, Intersect, Crop, and Punch.

Union

The *Union option* is used when you want to merge two or more objects. This option combines all the shapes into the outline of them all and removes any overlapping areas. The illustration shown here has no fill applied to the rectangles, so you can see the result better.

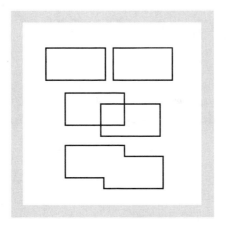

To use the Union option, follow these steps:

1. With the Pointer tool, SHIFT-select each shape you want to merge.
2. Choose Modify | Combine | Union.

Join

This example shows overlapping areas being joined, but you can select multiple shapes and join into one path. A fill was added to this example to illustrate the result of the Join option better.

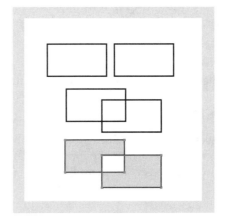

To join paths together, follow these steps:

1. With the Pointer tool, SHIFT-select all the objects you want to join.
2. Choose Modify | Join.
3. If you don't like the result or if you want to split the join apart at a later time, choose Modify | Split.

Intersect

The *Intersect option* works the opposite of the Union option. Where Union throws away the overlapping area, intersect keeps it and throws away the rest. The illustration shown here is only the little center you saw in the Join illustration.

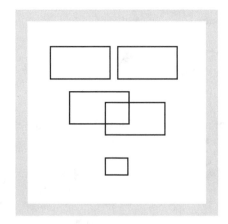

To intersect paths, follow these steps:

1. With the Pointer tool, SHIFT-select all the objects you want to intersect.
2. Choose Modify | Combine | Intersect.

Crop

The *Crop option* yields the same result as the Intersection option, so you can use either one. I tested the two commands on different shaped objects, selecting each object in a different order, and each time the end result was exactly the same.

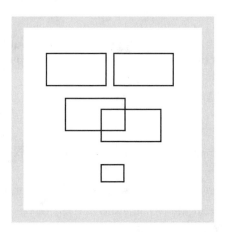

To Crop, follow these steps:

1. With the Pointer tool, SHIFT-select all the objects you want to intersect.

2. Choose Modify | Combine | Crop

Punch

The *Punch* option is one of my favorites. I love to punch holes you can see through, and you can punch objects or text. The example here shows the same two rectangles.

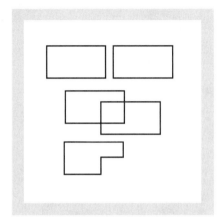

To use the Punch option, follow these steps:

1. With the Pointer tool, SHIFT-select the object you want to punch and the object you're punching it out of. The object on top will be punched out of the object on the bottom, regardless of the order they're selected.

2. Choose Modify |Combine | Punch.

To Punch using text, follow these steps:

1. Open a new document. Choose File | New with a size of 300 × pixels 300 pixels and a white canvas.

2. Draw a large rectangle and fill it with a solid color or, perhaps, a gradient.

3. Select the Text tool and type something on top of your image.

4. Select the text and, from the menu bar, choose Text |Convert to Paths.

5. Select the Subselection tool and SHIFT-click each letter.

6. To use this text as a Punch, you need to ungroup the letters. To do this, select the text path and, from the menu bar, choose Modify | Ungroup.

7. Now you need to make all the letters into one shape by joining them. Choose Modify | Join.

8. SHIFT-select the text and the rectangle. From the menu bar, choose Modify | Combine | Punch.

Bitmap Mode

If you're coming from a vector-only world, here's a quick course in pixel-based images. Photographs are comprised of *pixels,* the smallest component part of a bitmapped image. *Bitmapped images* are also known as *raster images*. In Fireworks, a *bitmap* is referred to as an *image object*. Pixels are many little squares of color, which appear as an image, which looks similar to a mosaic design. Editing pixels involves adding, removing, or coloring individual pixels.

Pixels are what distinguish a bitmapped image from a vector image, which consists of paths. Pixel-based objects can't be scaled up like a vector object can without losing detail and clarity. When you resize a pixel-based image upward, you're actually telling Fireworks it must guess which pixels need to be resampled to "fake" the detail in the increased space. This stretching of pixels results in what is known as a *pixilated image.* Pixilated images can be identified by the obvious squares that can be seen. On the other hand, if you have a bitmapped image that's larger than needed, you can scale it down, which resamples the pixels into a smaller area, producing a sharper image with more detail.

"Resolution" is a word that comes up often when working with bitmap images. The *resolution* is what determines how many pixels are in every inch. The higher the resolution, the more pixels per inch, and the bigger the image can be without degradation. Because Fireworks specializes in producing graphics for the Web, the resolution of 72 dpi is sufficient because that's the resolution of monitor screens.

If you plan on making an image larger in Fireworks, start with the highest resolution you can. For instance, in a photograph, scan at the highest Optical setting your scanner is capable of. Or, if you're using a digital camera, shoot using the highest resolution available. Once you get the higher resolution image, you can then scale up to an acceptable size.

Note, though, Fireworks isn't suitable for high-quality printing. You cannot do separations or CMYK. Fireworks is designed as a Web tool and it does its job well. If you do a lot of printing work, you may want to consider getting a tool suited for the job, such as Photoshop, Corel Photo-Paint, or Paint Shop Pro.

In Chapter 36, you read how to tell when you were in Bitmap mode. As a quick refresher, a blue-striped border is around the canvas or object when it's in Bitmap mode, and you can exit by clicking the red circle with a white *X* at the bottom of the document window. In Chapter 38, you explored the Xtras menu, which includes many filters for bitmapped images. In this section, you primarily look at the bitmap editing tools and masking.

Working with Selection Tools

The Selection tools are only available when editing bitmap images. *The Bitmap Selection tools* include the Rectangular Marquee, Oval Marquee, Polygon Lasso, Lasso Tool, and the Magic Wand.

The Selection tools are used to make selections, whether you want to isolate problem areas, or to select a specific portion to edit or add effects to. Selections can also be copied-and-pasted elsewhere on the same document or to a separate file. Selections also assure you that any changes made while a selection is active occur only to the selected portion, thereby protecting other portions of an image.

Rectangle and Oval Marquee Tools

The *Rectangle and Oval Marquee tools* make selections according to their respective shapes. Click the tool of your choice and drag over an area of the image. To constrain the shape of the marquee to a square or a circle, hold the ALT /OPTION key and drag. To draw from the center out, hold the SHIFT key and draw.

The Oval and Rectangle Marquee tools have tool options you obtain by double-clicking the icon in the Tools panel. You can see some of the options here.

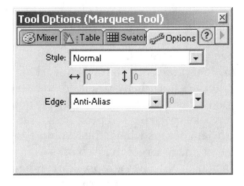

What can be most helpful are the Style options, which are Normal, Fixed Size, or Fixed Ratio. These help in making a specific selection. For instance, I was writing a tutorial that required a 2-pixel wide × 50-pixel high selection. There's no easy way to draw a selection so precisely or this narrow. By choosing a Fixed Size and entering in the dimensions it was a snap.

Once you make a selection, it's surrounded by a moving dotted line, referred to as *marching ants*. Any changes you make occur in this area. You can do a number of things, such as add Blur, plug-in filters, change color, adjust Hue and Saturation, use the Stamp tool, and the list goes on.

Changing the Shape of a Selection by Adding   Once you make your selection, you might decide you want to add additional areas to the selection. No problem. To add to the selection, put your cursor just inside the selected area and press the SHIFT key. Now, drag with the Rectangle, Oval, or the Lasso tool to enclose the new area, ending inside the current selection. To add a totally new selection, press the SHIFT key and make the selections.

Changing the Shape of a Selection by Subtracting   Subtracting from a selection works the same way as adding, except you press the ALT (OPTION for a Mac) key to subtract.

Magic Wand

The *Magic Wand tool* works differently than all the other selection tools. The Magic Wand tool makes selections based on color. You determine the range of color in the selection by setting the tolerance. You can see how to set the tolerance of the Magic Wand tool in the options in the following illustration. The higher you set the tolerance, the more colors are added to the selection.

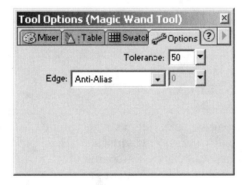

Polygon

The *Polygon Lasso tool* is used for making precise selections of irregular shaped areas. To use the Polygon Lasso tool, select it and click where you want to begin the selection. Keep adding points until the selection is complete. Double-click at the starting point to close the selection. You see blue lines as you click another point. If the line isn't conforming to your shape, add another point (click) a bit closer to the last point.

Add a Feathered Edge to a Photo

To practice using a Marquee tool (the Oval Marquee, in this case) and the Tool options, try this little, but useful, exercise:

1. Open any photo.

2. Select the Oval Marquee tool and draw an ellipse over the part of the photo you want to cut out.

3. Double-click the Oval Marquee tool. In the Marquee Tool options panel, select feather and enter 30 pixels. Use a smaller amount if your image is small.

4. You can now copy (CTRL+C/CMD+C) and paste (CTRL+V/CMD+V) into a new document.

Wasn't that easy? If you want more of a feathered edge, repeat the steps and add a higher number for the feathered edge. If the feather is too large, lower the number of pixels feathered on the edge.

Inverting Selections

Inverting Selections is an often-used tool. If you want to select an object in a photo, sometimes the background is easier to select. So, you could select the background, invert the selection to get the part you want, and edit from there. To invert a selection, choose, Modify | Marquee | Select Inverse.

In the feathering example of the oval picture you made in the previous section, you could add another step:

■ Choose Modify | Select Inverse and press the DEL key to clear the background of the image.

Using the Rubber Stamp

The *Rubber Stamp tool* works by copying one area on to another area. This tool is particularly handy for repairing small blemishes on an image or removing small areas. For instance, you may have a wonderful landscape photo, but the power lines detract from the overall look. You could use the Rubber Stamp tool to stamp out the offending parts. To use the Rubber Stamp tool, follow these steps:

1. Open any image.

2. Select the Rubber Stamp tool from the Tool panel.

3. You need to set the size of the area you're sampling from. To do this, double-click the Rubber Stamp tool. The Rubber Stamp tool options then open. You can see the options in the following illustration. Leave the Source set on Aligned (the options are Aligned or Fixed) and set the Stamp size to 18.

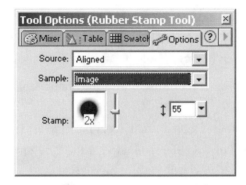

 The Aligned option *means the sampling spot is aligned with the Rubber Stamp tool. As the Rubber Stamp tool moves, so does the sampling point. The* Fixed option *has a sampling point that never changes.*

To set a sampling point, (the area you're copying pixels from), do the following:

1. Press the ALT (OPTION on a Mac) key and click the area you want to sample.

2. Click the area you want to cover with the sampling area.

Masking Images

Masks are often used on images when you want to blend one image into another seamlessly. When you mask an image, the mask allows parts of the underlying image to show through. What shows through is dependent on the varying degrees of black in the mask.

In Fireworks, you apply a mask to a mask object. The mask object resides above the image you want to mask—a mask isn't applied directly to the image. You'll understand that statement better when you follow the steps in the next section, "Using a Mask."

A mask object contains a fill, which affects the pixels of the image or object being masked. The fill color or texture determines how much of an image shows through the mask. In the areas of a mask that are white, the underlying area is totally invisible. Where there's solid black, the image is totally visible. The varying degrees of gray determine the amount of transparency.

Using a Mask

You can draw a bitmap mask using the bitmap tools, such as the Brush tool, Pen tool, and the Rectangle, Oval, or Polygon tools. To apply a mask, follow these steps:

1. Draw any shape you want or use one of the Shape tools, maybe a star.

2. Open any image.

3. Click the yellow folder icon in the Layers panel to add a new layer.

4. Double-click the Polygon Shape tool to get the Polygon tool options. Choose Star and 8 points. Drag a star on the canvas.

5. SHIFT-select the star and the image. The easiest way to select multiple objects is by selecting them in the Layers Panel, especially when they're on separate layers. You can see the progress so far in this illustration.

6. Choose Modify | Masks | Group as Mask. The final result is shown here. This is an easy way to get an image inside a shape, and this technique works with any vector or bitmap shape.

Adding Transparency to a Mask

Adding transparency to a mask is the technique used for blending images into a
background or blending them with each other. Transparency is achieved by using a
black-and-white gradient fill in the masking object or image. Wherever black is used,
the underlying image is visible. Where white is used, the image is invisible. The shades
of gray render the transparency according to the lightness or darkness of the gray. The
following exercise is heavily illustrated because this is an extremely important skill to
have. You'll use this technique often. To add transparency, follow these steps:

1. Open any image. This one is shown so you can see the results in the
   following steps.

2. In the Layer panel, click the yellow icon to add a new layer.
3. Select the Rectangle tool and drag a rectangle over about half your image.
4. Open the Fill panel (Window | Fill) and select Linear from the Fill Category
   and Choose Black, White from the Gradient Presets. This illustration shows
   what the image looks like up to this point.

5. The gradient is going in the wrong direction, so it needs editing. If the rectangle is selected, the gradient handles are visible. Drag the circle handle to the top and the square to the bottom, as seen here.

6. SHIFT-select the rectangle and the image, and then choose Modify | Mask | Group as Mask. This image is the result.

Editing a Masked Group

In the previous example, say you wanted more of the waterfall to show. You'd need to alter the gradient and have less white and more gray in it. To edit the masked group, choose Edit | Select All. See the following image. The Layers panel has an icon with the gradient next to the image icon. A little Pen icon is in it. Click the icon and the gradient handles are then visible. Adjust them as you please. In this example, the circle was pulled down a bit, making the top totally visible, and the square handle was pulled down a little, which produced more gray and less white in the gradient.

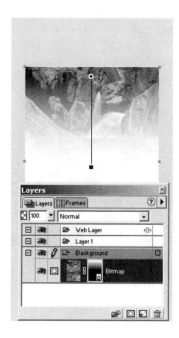

Summary

In this chapter, you became more comfortable using the vector and the bitmap editing tools. You learned the basic difference between bitmap images and vector objects, and you also learned how to mask an image.

Key Features:

- Manipulating Bézier curves
- Editing with the Pen tool
- Joining paths
- Adding and deleting points
- Using the Freeform shape tools
- Using the Combine commands
- Understanding Bitmaps
- Using the Selection tools
- Using Masks
- Adding transparency to masks and editing them

In Chapter 40, you learn how to slice your images and optimize them, as well as how to use the new Selective JPEG option and to export.

DREAMWEAVER
AND FIREWORKS

The Complete Reference

Chapter 40

Importing and Exporting Images

ireworks is compatible with many other applications and, in this chapter, you see how to import files from other applications. Once your images are complete, sliced when necessary, and then optimized, you learn how to export them to use in Web pages.

Importing

Fireworks is compatible with a variety of formats. Some of the most used formats are shown here.

Photoshop PSD Files

Fireworks can open Photoshop PSD files, including Photoshop 6, maintaining edit capability. If you want to open your Fireworks PNG files in Photoshop or someone you send your file to wants to use Photoshop, you can export a Fireworks file as a PSD file. When you export as a PSD, you have the option of exporting with better edit capability over appearance or better appearance over edit capability. To open and use a PSD file, choose File | Open and open like any other file. Or, you can choose File | Import to import them.

  Photoshop 6 PSD files only open in Fireworks 4, not in earlier versions.

Using Illustrator, Freehand, and CorelDRAW Files

Fireworks can open Illustrator, Freehand, and CorelDRAW files with some exceptions. Illustrator files are limited to Illustrator 7 and 8. Illustrator 9 files won't open or import into Fireworks.

You can open and edit Freehand files, including Freehand 9 files.

CorelDRAW 7 or 8 files can be opened in Fireworks and edited. Many of the blends and effects applied in CorelDRAW will be lost.

Other Formats

Other file types Fireworks can open include BMP, TIF, EPS, TAR, and WBMP.

The Web Layer

The *Web layer* is the special layer, which contains all the hotspot coordinates, other information—such as behaviors—and slices you made in your document. This is all the Web layer is used for. The Web layer is shared across all frames, and you can't delete this layer. Every document you open automatically has a Web layer in the Layers panel as seen here.

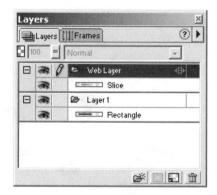

Slicing

Slicing a document is one of the most important things you do in Fireworks. *Slicing* a document, or slicing an image, is when you "cut up" the document or image into smaller pieces. Slicing or not slicing determines how your Web page is viewed or perceived. Many people believe slicing an image makes your Web page load faster, but this just isn't so. In many cases, a sliced image can actually make the page load slower because each image slice is making a separate request to the server.

What slicing does, however, is give the perception that the page is loading faster because parts of the image can be seen as it loads. This is an important perception, and it certainly beats having your user look at a blank screen for an extended period of time. Face it, Internet users are an impatient lot. If it takes longer than a few seconds to see something, it's too long.

So when should you slice? A good rule of thumb is to slice an image if it's over 20K or if you want different formats in the same slice. For instance, if your image is a JPEG, but you want to include an animation as part of the image, then slicing is the only way to accomplish this. Another reason to slice is if you want to add a JavaScript rollover behavior to a button or an image. Behaviors can only be added to a slice or a hotspot. Rollovers and image maps (which deal with hotspots) are discussed in Chapter 41.

Another advantage of slicing an image is you can update one section of the image instead of the whole image. For instance, if you have a Navigational bar and one of the links changes, you can change only one of the links instead of the entire image.

Slicing Tools

The slicing tools are the Slice tool (which is rectangular) and the Polygon Slice tool (icons shown here). The *Slice tool* works the same way as the other rectangle tools: click-and-drag over the area you want to define. The *Polygon Slice tool* also works like it does in other areas of Fireworks: click a starting point and click to add points to define a shape. Note, you can define a polygonal shape with the Polygon Shape tool, but it cannot be exported as a polygonal shape. All slices are rectangular—period.

What happens is this: rectangular slices are automatically generated cutting up the polygonal shape you defined.

Using Slicing Guides

Setting up guides to assist you in making your slice selection is helpful. Using guides is an efficient way of defining your slices. If you choose the Snap to Guides option, it can help you draw a more precise slice. To set up guidelines, follow these steps:

- To enable the guides, the rulers must be visible. From the menu bar, choose View | Rulers.
- Choose View | Guides | Snap to Guides.

 You can set your own preference to how the Snap to Guides responds. Choose Edit | Preferences and click the Editing tab. In the Snap Distance box, enter the distance in pixels, before your object will be snapped into position on the guide.

- To place guides, click a horizontal or a vertical ruler and drag a guide into your document.
- The guide won't be visible until you begin to pull it on to the canvas area. Then you see a green line, which is the default color.

One of Firework's Exporting options is to slice along the guides. You could simply export your whole image right now after placing guides, and Fireworks would automatically slice it for you. Wherever you see a guide, it would become a slice. To do this, go to the menu bar and choose File | Export. Under the Slices option, choose Slice along Guides.

Define the Slices

Although Slice along Guides is quick and easy, it isn't very efficient. You usually end up with far too many slices. Another downside exists to using guides as a slicing method: you can't attach behaviors to a slice made this way. To attach a behavior to the slice, you must define it. To define slices, follow these steps:

1. Select the Slice tool (to the right of the Hotspot tool) from the tool bar.
2. Following the guides, drag a rectangular selection around the area you want as a slice.

Note   *A green overlay appears when a slice is drawn. You can toggle this view on and off using the icons in the Tool panel at the bottom under view.*

3. Repeat Step two for the rest of the slices you want to define in your image.

Note   *Red lines appear after you define your first slice. These show you where Fireworks automatically slices on Export if you choose to have Fireworks slice the remainder of the image. If you want to define more slices, continue. The red lines adjust after each slice is defined, as seen here.*

4. Once the slicing is complete, save your file (File | Save As).

Naming Slices

You can name the slices in the Object panel (Windows | Object). Autonaming of slices is the default setting. *Autonaming* uses the root name of your document, plus the row number and column number. Locating specific slices for editing and for use in rollovers is much easier if you name your slices, so you can identify them easily. To name your own slices, follow these steps:

■   After you make a slice, open the Object panel ALT-F2 (OPTION-F2 for the Mac) if it isn't already open.

■ You can see in this illustration some of the options available for your slice. For now, uncheck the autonaming and type in a descriptive name. Don't type in the file extension, only the name.

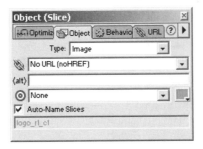

■ If you want to customize the autonaming feature, go to the menu bar and select File | HTML Setup, and then click the Document Specific tab shown here. You can see the options with the current default settings. You can change the default for autonaming from this dialog window. When you finish choosing new defaults (if that's what you chose to do), click the Set Defaults button to save.

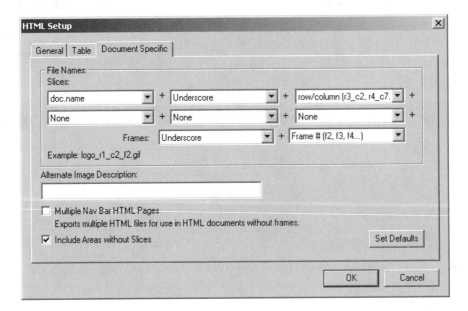

Adding URLs and Alternative Tags

Alternative (Alt) tags are what you see in a browser before an image completely loads. These are quite useful for people who browse without images. They're read by the readers. Another benefit is, a user can click the image if it's a link, without waiting for the image to load.

URLs are simply Web addresses, which you attach to the image to make it a hyperlink, taking the user to another page or area of a page. To add Alternative text and/or a URL, follow these steps:

■ Click the slice you want to add a URL and/or Alt text to. If the Object panel isn't open, go to the menu bar and select Window | Object.

■ In the URL box, type in the link.

■ Type in a target, if you have one.

■ Add the Alternate text in the Alt box.

Text Slices

Use text slices instead of image slices when you want to enter HTML text into a specific area. You can either type in this text from within Fireworks or in Dreamweaver. To define a text slice, follow these steps:

■ Select the slice you want to be a text area.

■ In the Object panel, click the down arrow next to the image and choose Text, as shown in the following illustration.

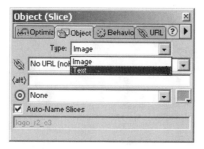

Optimization

Optimization is the most important factor because it determines how fast your images on a Web page load. By slicing an image, you can now not only export with GIF, JPEG, or PNG in the same document, but you can also actually apply different settings to specific areas of a JPEG image. The files currently available for the Web include the PNG format, but all browsers don't yet support this format, so you might want to wait before you use that one.

Optimize Panel for GIF Compression

You can optimize quite a few different formats in the Optimize panel. The ones you'll most likely use are GIF, JPEG, and GIF Animation. This panel is where you set the optimization choices of the entire document, unless you have a specific slice selected, and then the settings are for that slice only. You set your optimization settings before you export. Let's look at the Optimize panel with a Gif setting in Figure 40–1.

GIF stands for Graphic Interchange Format (pronounced *JIF*). The GIF compression algorithm works better for line art than for photographs. Not only is GIF better for line art, but it's also better for any image with a lot of flat color. When you have images with 256 colors or less, quality isn't lost when the image is compressed because of the Lossless compression scheme. *Lossless* refers to the type of compression used. The GIF format uses a lossless compression, which results in no image degradation if the image is 256 colors or less. An LZW compression looks for patterns of data and works best on flat color. When a new color is detected, the file size increases. Some of the advantages of GIF compression are:

- Small files
- Animation capability
- Transparency
- Interlacing

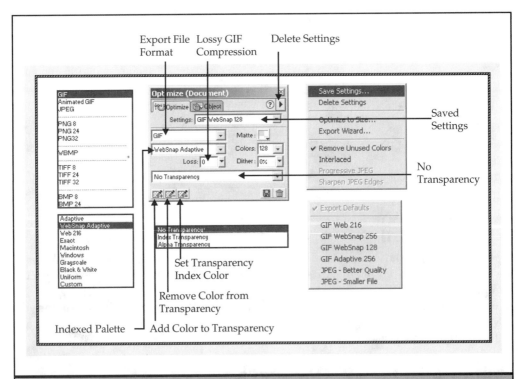

Figure 40-1. *The Optimize panel with representations of the various menus*

Disadvantages are:

- Only 256 colors

As you can see, a lot is going on in the Optimize panel. The little boxes you see around the panel are representations of the various pop-up and drop-down menus. This next section applies not only to GIF optimization, but also to GIF Animation and PNG 8. You see both some of the most important and the most confusing areas in the Optimize panel.

The first white-boxed area is the Saved Settings area. When you select GIF from the Export File Format (just below the Saved Settings area), the saved setting of GIF WebSnap128 is the default in the Saved Settings area.

Avoiding Halos

The Optimize panel gives you many choices. The next area is a little box with gray and white checks, marked Matte. You can probably tell it's a color box: the gray and white checks indicate it's set to transparent by default. Matte lets you export with a background color of your choice—without changing the canvas background color. This option is most often used because of the halo effect you can get with GIFs, which were designed with one color background and placed on another.

When you apply effects, such as drop shadows, and export the image, you get a *halo,* which is a bit of the background color surrounding the image. By setting the Matte color to the color of the destination background, the halo is the color of the background and unnoticeable. To choose a Matte color, simply click the color box and select a color, or type in a Hexadecimal number. Remember if you type in a number to press the ENTER (RETURN for a Mac) key.

Transparency

As you can see in Figure 40–1, you have three choices for transparency: No Transparency, Index Transparency, and Alpha Transparency. No Transparency is self-explanatory. When you choose Index Transparency, the background color is transparent, as well as anything else in your image that's the same color. For instance, if you have a white background and white text, both the background and the text will be transparent.

Alpha Transparency makes only the background color transparent. Test both options for yourself by using these steps:

1. Open a new document 200 pixels × 200 pixels and a white background.
2. Select the Rectangle tool and draw a rectangle.
3. Click the Color box in the Tool panel in the Color section, or use the Fill panel to fill the rectangle with black.
4. Draw another smaller rectangle in the center of the black rectangle and fill it with white.

5. Click the Preview tab in the document window.

6. In the Optimize panel, choose Index Transparency. Notice the background of white and the white square are both transparent.

7. Now, while still in the Preview tab, select Alpha Transparency. See the white square come back?

You have even more control in the Transparency section. Notice the little eyedropper icons below the Transparency options. Figure 40–1 lists each name of the icons. By clicking the Add Color icon, you can choose to add colors, in addition to having the background color be transparent. By choosing the Remove Color icon, you can remove colors you chose. The last choice is the Set Transparent Index color, which lets you choose a color other than the background color to be transparent.

The Indexed Palette

Nine preset color palettes are in the Indexed Palette drop-down menu, plus custom. Each palette makes available a different palette of colors. With each palette, you can customize and save it with a unique name. Here are a few of the most used palettes.

■ *WebSnap Adaptive* palette is the default palette for indexed color in Fireworks. Any color that isn't Web safe is automatically evaluated and snapped to the closed Web-safe color, plus or minus seven values. This doesn't guarantee all the colors will be Web safe, but it's close.

If all Web safe colors are important to you, you can use the Find and Replace feature to locate any color that isn't Web safe and change it.

■ *Adaptive* palette finds a maximum of 256 colors. This isn't a preset color set but, instead, it's the best 256 colors for your image. This technique may contain a mixture of Web-safe and non-Web-safe colors.

■ *Web 216* converts all colors in the image to the nearest Web-safe color.

JPEG Compression

JPEG (pronounced *Jay-peg*) stands for Joint Photographic Expert Group. The JPEG compression algorithms work better for photographs than for line art. A JPEG image deals with millions of colors. JPEG uses a Lossy compression, which removes information from the image. JPEGs are compressed and decompressed when viewed, which results in a slightly longer loading time.

Don't JPEG a JPEG image because it loses information each time and gets considerably worse after the second time.

Fewer options are in the JPEG option in the Optimize panel, which you can see in the following illustration.

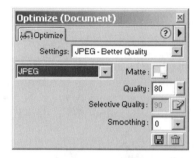

JPEGs are made smaller by lowering the quality setting, which eliminates pixels in the image. With JPEG compression, you can display millions of colors, but no transparency options exist. To compress an image using JPEG compression, follow these steps:

1. Select the image or slice you want to optimize.

2. In the Optimize panel, choose JPEG from the Export File Format area. JPEG Better quality is the default, but you can change the quality setting yourself.

3. If you want to see the image gradually load in a browser instead of waiting for the whole image to load, click the right-pointing arrow and choose Progressive JPEG. This is similar in function to the GIF's counterpart, Interlace.

4. From the same menu (right-pointing arrow), choose Sharpen JPEG Edges if you have text on an image background or, perhaps, a gradient background.

5. To view the different settings and options to decide which choices are best for your image, click the 4-Up tab in the document window. You can view four different optimization settings at once. You can try the sharpen edges, smoothing (coming next), or different quality settings to compare the differences.

6. Select a Smoothing amount from the slider to help soften edges that may be *blockie,* blocks of color where too many pixels were thrown out. The drawback with smoothing is it applies a slight blur. This option may or may not be suitable. The new Selective JPEG compression does a similar job without blurring.

Selective JPEG Compression

Now that you know how to optimize your images, it's time to look at one of the newest features of Fireworks, the *Selective JPEG Compression.* As you know, you can export images for the Web in GIF and in JPEG. Say you have an image with a gradient background, which is best exported as a JPEG image. Because it's an image background, you want to keep the file size down, so you export at maybe 70 percent to 80 percent, using the lowest possible setting and still having an acceptable look. If you have text on this gradient, it

DREAMWEAVER
AND FIREWORKS

may appear blockie or blurred. This occurs when too much JPEG compression is applied. You can now apply higher quality compression to specific areas, such as the text.

Selective JPEG Compression works in Fireworks by using a mask, but there can only be one per document. So, if you are slicing up a large image, you can apply Selective JPEG Compression to separate areas of the document, regardless of which slice it's in. To try this out for yourself, follow these steps:

1. Open a new document, and choose File | New. Use a size of about 300 pixels × 300 pixels, any background colors.

2. In the Layers panel, click the yellow folder icon to add a new layer.

3. Select the Rectangle tool and draw a rectangle to cover the entire canvas.

4. Open the Fill panel (Window | Fill) and, from the Fill category, choose Linear. In the Preset Gradient color sets drop-down menu, choose emerald green (or any color you like).

5. Select the Text tool and type a word—any font you like—in a size large enough to see well on your canvas. If you used the emerald gradient, try red for the text.

6. From the drop-down menu in the Effect panel, choose Shadow and Glow | Drop Shadow and accept the defaults.

7. In the Optimize panel, choose JPEG and a quality setting of 65 percent. You can see the panel so far here.

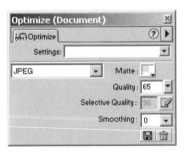

8. Click the Preview tab, zoom in on the text, and then notice the blockie areas (this is with the Sharpen JPEG Edges already selected—it's selected by default). Try turning off that option and you can see how blockie it is.

9. Click the background layer to make it active and be sure it isn't locked. You want the background, not the rectangle, with the gradient fill.

10. Click the Lasso selection tool and draw around the area you want compressed at a higher quality setting. If more than one area exists, shift and make your next selection. You'll probably get a warning that an empty area has been selected. Click OK.

If you have more than one area to use selective compression on, they must all be selected now or you'll have edit them again. These selections are going to become a JPEG mask, and only one can exist per document.

11. Now, go to the menu bar and select Modify | Selective JPEG | Save Selection as JPEG Mask.

12. You can set the selective settings from the menu bar by choosing Modify | Selective JPEG | Settings, but the quicker way is to do it in the Optimize panel. Near Selective Quality is grayed out. Click the icon, and check enable Selective Quality, and then type in the quality number you want. You can change the overlay color, if you like. The settings are shown here: first the Settings dialog box, and then the Optimize panel with Selective Quality activated.

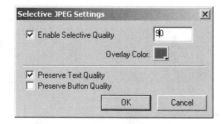

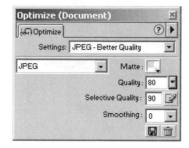

13. Time to preview and see if your setting works. Click the 4-Up tab and experiment with the quality amount you need for the JPEG Selective Mask.

14. If you need to try another quality setting, simply change the number in the Selective quality area in the Optimize panel.

15. To edit the JPEG mask, you can either delete and start over by choosing Modify | Selective JPEG | Remove JPEG Mask or, if you want simply to add to or subtract from the current mask, go to Modify | Selective JPEG | Restore JPEG Mask as Selection. With the Selection active, you can use the SHIFT key and draw another area or add on. If you want to delete a portion, then hold the Alt/Option key and draw around the area to remove.

16. To save the mask, choose Modify | Selective JPEG | Save Selection as JPEG Mask.

Exporting

Before you begin exporting, it's important to have your site structure set up. If you set up your folders locally the same way they'll be uploaded, this can save you many headaches. Most likely, you've already created your local and remote site folders this way in Dreamweaver.

When you export a Fireworks document, the image is sliced into smaller image files, and an accompanying HTML file is created with a table structure to piece the images back together. This file must be saved in the same folder as the file you plan to insert the Fireworks code into. Otherwise, all the links to your images will be broken.

Export Options

You have the option of using the Export Wizard, but the regular Export option gives you greater flexibility and isn't hard to use, so let's review the regular Export option in this section. Look at the export options and export by following these steps:

1. From the menu bar, choose File | Export. The Export panel with the drop-down menu open can be seen in Figure 40–2. Figure 40–3 shows the Export window without the drop-down menu open.

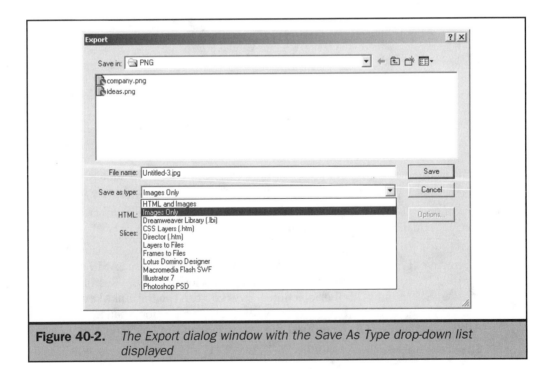

Figure 40-2.   *The Export dialog window with the Save As Type drop-down list displayed*

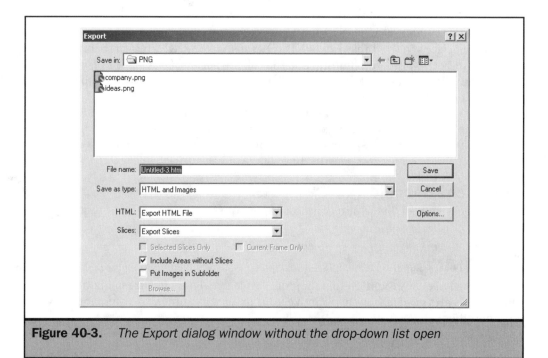

Figure 40-3.   *The Export dialog window without the drop-down list open*

2. The first thing to do is name your file and select the folder to save it in. Remember to save in the same folder as the Web page that will contain the Fireworks code.

3. Select the type of file you're saving. For the entire document with HTML code and slices, choose HTML and Images.

4. Under Slices, you can choose to export no slices, the slices you defined, or have Fireworks slice along the guidelines you placed.

5. The next three options are Selected slices only, Include areas without slices, and Put Images in subfolder. When checked, the Put Images in subfolder enables you to specify where to put your images. If you use an asset, image, or whatever name for images, set it here. On export, your HTML is placed where you have selected and the images are put in a separate folder, if you choose.

6. When you finish choosing your export options, click Save.

Options Button-General Tab

An Options button with more options is within the Export panel; click it. The General tab is where you choose the application where you'll be using the code, the extension of your choice, whether to add comments, and if you want everything in lowercase.

Table Tab

One of the options in the Table Tab is 1-Pixel Transparency, which is probably the most used. When you export, you'll notice one file called spacer.gif. This is a 1 pixel × 1 pixel transparent file used as a spacer to keep a table's integrity. Or, you could also choose to use a Nonbreaking Space instead of the Spacer Image.

You can also choose to export using a Nested table, which places one table into another table. This sort of table layout doesn't require spacers. Or, you can choose to export only a table with no spacers at all. If your table has an image in every cell, then Single table with no spacers can work fine.

Document Specific Tab

This is where you set the default of autonaming your slices.

Summary

You covered a lot of ground in this chapter. You learned how to slice using the slicing tools and guides, how to optimize your images in numerous ways, and how to export them.

Key Features:

- Using files from other applications
- Slicing an image
- Using the Slicing tools
- Naming, plus adding URLs and Alt tags to slices
- Optimizing GIF images
- Optimizing JPEG images
- Using JPEG Selective Compression
- Exporting

The
Complete
Reference

Chapter 41

Advanced Techniques

A vital part, or perhaps the most important part, of a Web page is the navigational controls. You learn to make rollovers suitable for navigation, as well as the popular pop-up menus. You also discover how easy designing *Disjoint rollovers* (sometimes called *arrays*) can be using Fireworks' new drag-and-drop feature. To wrap up the advanced techniques, you discover how to produce animations in Fireworks. When animations are used properly, they can provide visually stimulating and useful Web page elements, including banner ads.

Symbols, Instances, and Libraries

Whenever you can use the same piece of artwork or the same object multiple, this helps cut your production time, not to mention the download time for a Web page. The technique Fireworks uses to let you use the same object multiple times is *symbols*. The symbols you generate are stored in Libraries, and instances are present in the document.

Symbols

Symbols are frequently used when you design navigation systems and when you make animations. You can convert any object into a symbol. If you designed a custom button, you can make it a symbol, which can then be used over and over again. Buttons can also be made in the Button editor, which will automatically be made into a symbol, as you see later in this chapter. But any button or object you make or have already produced can also become a symbol.

Three types of symbols are in Fireworks.

- **Graphic Symbols**—basically any object you want to use multiple times. It can be moved around and edited on your canvas.

- **Button Symbols**—usually contain multiple frames, which contain the different states of a button or a simple swap image. Button symbols are generated in the Button editor, which also automatically applies a slice, to which you can attach a behavior. A Button symbol retains the slice and any URLs or behaviors attached to it.

- **Animation Symbols**—contain all the frames and timing of your animation. A completed animation, including links, is contained in the symbol.

To make any existing object or even an animation into a symbol, follow these steps:

1. Open or draw any object you want. You can even open an existing animation or a piece of clip art.

2. Select the Pointer tool and select an object. Choose Insert | Convert to Symbol from the menu bar. The Symbol Properties dialog box opens, as seen here.

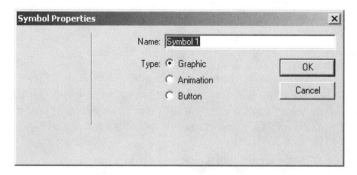

3. Choose the type of symbol you want—a graphic, a button or an animation—by clicking the appropriate option.

4. Give your symbol a name in the name box and click OK when you finish.

Symbols are also editable. The master symbol is stored in a Library and an instance is placed on the canvas. By double-clicking the instance or the symbol, a dialog box opens. Which dialog box opens depends on the type of symbol you're editing. A Graphic symbol opens the Symbol Properties dialog box, while a Button symbol opens the Button editor, and an Animation symbol opens the Animate dialog box. When you edit the master symbol, the changes are made globally to all instances of that symbol.

Instances

When you want to use a symbol, you can convert a current object into a symbol or you can drag one from the library (Window | Library) on to your canvas—but it's not the symbol you see, it's an instance of the symbol—a copy. An instance maintains a link to the parent symbol. You can always tell when an instance is on the canvas because a dotted box and an arrow in the corner surround it, as the following illustration shows. Instances are extremely beneficial for making animations because Fireworks can produce intermediate steps in using only two instances.

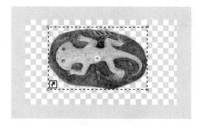

As you know, editing a symbol opens the appropriate dialog window, and changes are made globally to all instances, but you can make two modifications to an individual instance that won't affect all the others. You can use the transform tools and you can alter the opacity on individual instances.

Libraries

Symbols are the master copies and are stored in a library. Symbols are never present on your canvas. You can see the Library panel here with two symbols added. When you make a symbol, you needn't put it into the Library. The symbol is automatically added to the current documents library and it's saved with the document.

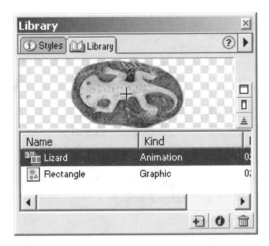

If you have symbols you think you may want to use in another document, you can export them. To export symbols follow these easy steps:

1. Open the Library panel, and then choose Window | Library.
2. Click the right-pointing arrow and, from the pop-up menu, choose Export Symbols.
3. Select the symbols you want to export. If you want them all, choose Select All. If you want several in a row, press SHIFT-CLICK. If you want to pick and choose, press CTRL-CLICK (OPTION-CLICK on the Mac) on the desired symbols. When you finish, click Export.
4. Name your library, choose where you want to save it, and then click Save.

For libraries you think you may use often, save them or move them to the Fireworks Library folder, which is in Macromedia\Fireworks 4\Configurations\Libraries. By placing your file here, it can be accessed by choosing Insert | Libraries submenu. Any new libraries you export into the libraries folder will be available the next time you start Fireworks.

If you want to use a library you currently saved, you need to import it. To import a saved library, follow these steps:

1. Open the Library panel, if it isn't already open. Choose Window | Library.

2. Click the right-pointing arrow. From the pop-up menu, choose Import Symbols.

3. Locate your saved library and choose open.

4. The Import Symbols dialog box opens with the list of symbols in the library you selected to save. Choose the symbols you want and click Import.

Using the Button Editor

The *Button editor* enables you to make multiple rollover states. Using the Button editor helps to streamline your workflow by enabling you to apply up to four different states for the same button, as well as adding links and a slice. Figure 41-1 shows the Button editor.

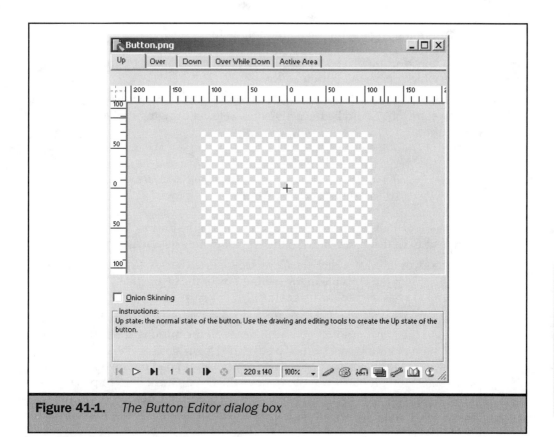

Figure 41-1. *The Button Editor dialog box*

Web Navigation buttons frequently have a rollover effect attached to them. When a mouse hovers over a button, the appearance changes. This is accomplished by a behavior, which uses JavaScript code. Fireworks generates all the necessary JavaScript code for you, so you don't need to know any JavaScript at all. The code Fireworks produces is ready to use in any HTML page or editor.

The four states available in the Button editor are:

- **Up**—The *Up* state is the default appearance of the button, as first seen by the user.

- **Over**—the *Over* state is the way the button looks when the user passes the mouse pointer over it. The over state is the one that alerts users this button is "hot," and it leads to another page.

- **Down**—the *Down* state is the appearance when the button has been clicked; it often has a depressed look. In Fireworks, you can set the down state to be active on the page that's being clicked to, to designate the button as the current page.

- **Over While Down**—the *Over While Down* state is the appearance of the down state button when the mouse pointer moves over it.

To make a button using the Button editor, follow these steps:

1. Open a new document, choose File | New, and then choose Insert | New Button, which opens the Button editor.

2. Now that the Button editor is open, take note of the different tabs (see Figure 41-1). The Up state tab should be the active one. Select a drawing tool and draw your button.

Note   *The Info panel (Window | Info) can be used while you're in the Button editor. To get an exact-sized button, type the dimensions in the Height and Width boxes in the Info panel and press the* ENTER *key (*RETURN *for the Mac).*

3. Select the Text tool and type the text you want on the button. Use the center text alignment from the Text editor, so the text maintains its centered position.

4. Click the Over tab. Then click the Copy Up Graphic button (in the right corner) to put a copy of the Up state in the editing box of the Over state. Add any fill, stroke, or a Live Effect to the Over state.

5. Click the Down tab, click the Copy Over Graphic button, and make any changes to the appearance. If you want to see all the buttons at one time, click in the Onion Skinning check box. To have the Down state active on the page that it's linked to, check the Show Down State Upon Load option box. For the Down state, you probably want to remove the Over state. For example, if you added a glow in the Over state, and then pressed the Copy Over Graphic button while in the Down state, you would want to set the stroke to None in the Down state.

Note *For any of the button states, you can import a button, draw a unique button, or drag a button from another document instead of using the Copy Graphic Up/Down button.*

6. If you want the Over While Down state, click its tab and click the Copy Down Graphic button and make any changes you desire.

7. Click the Active Area button. You see a slice added to your document automatically. The Active Area is set to automatic by default and generates a slice large enough to cover all the button states. You can drag the blue handles on the slice to alter the slice size.

8. Click the Link Wizard (Figure 41-2). The Link Wizard contains tabs for Export settings where you can open the Export preview window by clicking the Edit button. The next tab is Link, which is seen in Figure 41-2. The third tab is Target, where you set a target window or frame for the link to open in. The last tab is the Filename. This is where you either use Fireworks' Auto-Name feature or you name your button yourself.

9. Close the Button editor. An instance of the button is automatically placed in your document and a symbol is added to the library.

10. To add more buttons to your document, drag them from the library.

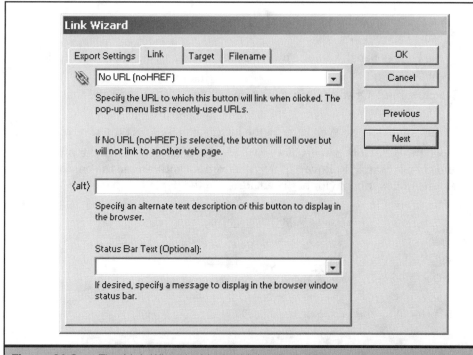

Figure 41-2. *The Link Wizard with the Link tab visible*

Rollovers

Rollovers are popular in Web pages because they add interactivity and are quite easy to implement. JavaScript rollovers all work the same way: when a cursor passes over one graphic, it triggers the display of another graphic or display. The *trigger* is always a hotspot or a slice, which triggers events and performs actions.

Making Simple Rollovers

A *simple rollover* has only two states: an Up and an Over state, or a swapped image. When a mouse cursor passes over the *trigger image* (the slice containing rollover behaviors), an image from Frame 2 is swapped, giving the appearance that the original image is changing.

Both images must be the same size in simple rollovers. For instance, if you add a stroke to the Over state to add a glow, the image is a bit larger. The first image needs its canvas size expanded to match the size of the second image. Things go quicker if you have your images prepared and sized before you start implementing the rollovers.

To make a simple two-state rollover, follow these steps:

1. Select, draw, or import the image you want as the trigger image.

2. Place the image or button where you want it. Choose Insert | Slice, or draw the slice by using the Slice tool.

3. In the Frames panel, add one more frame by clicking the New/Duplicate Frame icon.

4. Select Frame 2. Open or draw the second image. Place it over the first image in your document.

5. In the canvas (or the Web layer in the Layers panel), select the slice you added.

6. Open the Behaviors panel. Choose Window | Behaviors. Click the plus sign (+) and choose Simple Rollover. In this illustration, you can see the onMouseOver Simple Rollover behavior has been added in the Behaviors panel.

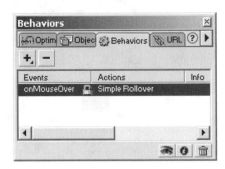

Making a Disjoint Rollover

A *disjoint rollover* is frequently called an *array.* This is when you hover the mouse cursor over an image and an image or text is displayed in a different location on the Web page. You see this technique used quite often on buttons where the trigger area is a button and the target area displays a text description. To produce a disjoint rollover using Fireworks 4's new drag-and-drop functionality, follow these steps:

1. First, select the object to be your trigger, the object that gets the behavior attached to it.

2. Select the button/object, and then choose Insert | Slice. In the Object panel (Window | Object), name your button. The following illustration shows the result so far.

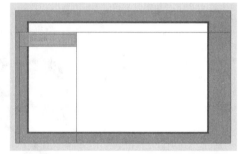

3. In the Frames panel (Window | Frames), click the right-pointing arrow. From the pop-up menu, choose Duplicate Frame.

4. Open the image you want displayed when the mouse hovers over the target image. With Frame 2 selected, place this image where you want it to appear on your canvas.

5. Select the rollover image and choose Insert | Slice, as seen here.

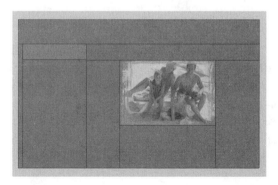

6. The next stage is to set up a Swap Image behavior for a disjoint rollover. Select the slice over the button (the one placed in Step 1). In the center of the button is a white circle, and the pointer turns into a hand as you get near. Click-and-hold the mouse button down. The pointer turns into a fist. Drag to the slice, covering the image you want to change. You can see how it looks here. When you release the mouse button, a dialog box comes up, asking you which frame to swap the image from. Your image is on Frame 2, so that's what you type in, although it probably says Frame 2 already.

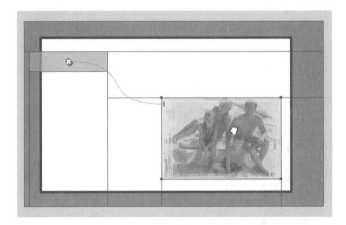

7. Choose File | Preview in Browser to see your new disjointed rollover. As you move your mouse over it, you see the beach scene. When you move your mouse away, you won't.

Pop-Up Menus

Pop-up menus can save on Web page real estate, as well as provide a great deal of navigational flexibility. You can design your menus to coordinate with your Web page design. The pop-up menus are similar to tables, with each cell containing a different link. The Pop-Up Menu Wizard makes building pop-up menus a breeze. To build a pop-up menu, follow these steps:

1. Open a new document. Choose File | New with a size of 300 pixels wide × 300 pixel high.

2. Draw a rectangle. Choose Insert | Slice. With the slice selected, choose Insert | Pop-up Menu.

3. The Set Pop-Up Menu Wizard opens. In the Text box, type the name of a menu entry and, if you want a link, type one in the Link box. Click the + sign next to Menu to add the menu item. Figure 41-3 shows the menu entry; the first entry used in this example is Swimming.

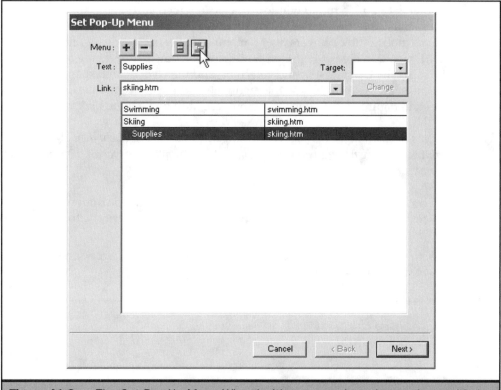

Figure 41-3. *The Set Pop-Up Menu Wizard with menu and a submenu item added*

4. Highlight the menu item in the Text box and type in the next entry (Skiing is used in this example). If you want a link, type it in. Click the + sign next to Menu.

5. Repeat Step 3 and add another item to the list (Supplies is used in this example). This entry is a submenu of Supplies, but it's currently lined up to the left with the other menu items. Select Supplies and click the Indent icon. The Indent icon is the one the arrow is pointing to in Figure 41-3.

6. Continue adding menu and submenu entries. Now click the Next button.

Note   *Menu items aren't indented. When you want a submenu, click the Indent icon, which denotes an entry as a submenu. When you want an item that appears indented to be a menu item, click the Outdent icon. Submenu items should be placed under the menu they're attached to.*

7. Another Set Pop-Up menu window opens, in which you set the appearance of your menus. The choices are HTML or Image: HTML style menu is the default. When a mouse cursor hovers over a menu link, the browser generates an HTML menu. In the Set Pop-Up Menu window, you can select the font, the point size, the Up state text and cell color, and the Over state text and cell color. You can see a preview of how the menu looks at the bottom of the dialog box, as seen in Figure 41-4. Experiment a bit here until you get the look you like.

Note   *The fonts included in the Set Pop-Up Wizard are the ones most likely to be on everyone's computer. If you're using the Image option, only the graphic is exported, not the text. The browser renders the HTML text.*

8. Or, you can use an image for the menu by clicking the Image option. Instead of only text and cell color options, you have a list of styles to choose from. Select a style and experiment.

9. Click the Finish button. To preview, you must preview in a browser. Choose File | Preview in Browser.

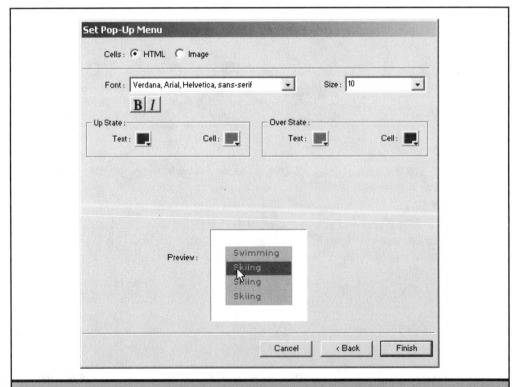

Figure 41-4.   *The Set Pop-Up Menu's second dialog box showing the menu options*

Exporting the Pop-Up Menu

Once this menu is done, it's time to export. Export as you would any other document. Make your slices and optimize. When the document is ready for export, choose File | Export and export as HTML and Images.

The difference with the files exported with the pop-up menus is Fireworks generates all the JavaScript for the menu in a file called fw_menu.js, which is placed in the same folder as the HTML file. If you place the fw_menu.js file in a folder other than the folder the HTML file is in, you'll need to change all the links that reference the fw_menu.js file.

Be sure to upload the fw_menu.js file to your server or your menus won't work. Only one fw_menu.js file exists, no matter how many menus are included. If you have submenus, then an Arrow.gif image file is also produced.

Editing a Pop-Up Menu

You can edit the menu appearance and the menus themselves by double-clicking the blue outline of the menu. The Set Pop-Up Menu Wizard opens. Make any changes you desire.

You can't view the Pop-Up menu in Fireworks (all that shows up is the blue outline). To view the menu, use the Edit | Preview in Browser option.

If the menu doesn't line up the way you want it to—say the menus are higher or lower than you want them—then click-and-drag the blue outline of the menu and drag it wherever you want it to appear.

You can make changes to the menu, but they require opening the fw_menu.js file and editing the JavaScript. If you're interested in editing the JavaScript, you can find details at Fireworks tech support on how to edit settings, such as the bevel color and the timing of the menu.

Limitations of the Pop-Up Menus

A few of the problems you may encounter using Fireworks 4 pop-up menus include the following:

- Pop-up menus don't span frames. If you have a menu in a top or side frame, the only part of the menu that'll show up is whatever fits in the current frame.

- Customization of any serious nature involves knowing how to hand-code JavaScript.

- The Absolute Positioning of the pop-up menus causes several problems when placing the code into other WYSIWYG HTML editors. Editors that don't handle layers can't place the pop-up menus without hand-coding.

- Pop-up menus cannot be used in a centered table in your layout.

Regardless of the few limitations, the Pop-Up Menu Wizard is a fantastic timesaver. It produces a nice menu in a fraction of the time it takes to make a menu in Dreamweaver using the hide-and-show layer techniques.

Design Image Maps

An *image map* is a single image with multiple links. You can make an image map either in Dreamweaver or in Fireworks, whichever is more comfortable for you, but Dreamweaver has a better selection of behaviors than Fireworks. Making an image map in Fireworks is a bit different than making one in Dreamweaver.

Adding Hotspots

You can draw hotspots in Fireworks, using one of the three hotspot tools: the Rectangle, the Circle, or the Polygon Hotspot tools. To add hotspots to an image, follow these steps:

1. Select the Hotspot tool of your choice from the Tools panel. If you want a tool other than the Rectangle tool, click-and-hold the little triangle and release the mouse over the selection you want. Whenever you see a little triangle, this signifies a submenu is with the icon.

2. To draw the hotspot, click-and-drag the Rectangle or the Circle Hotspot tool until the area is covered. To draw with the Polygon Hotspot tool, click points around the area you want to cover with the polygonal shape.

3. Open the Object panel, choose Window | Object, and enter a URL address in the Link box. If you have the URL added to the URL panel, you can select it from the drop-down menu.

4. Enter alternative text in the next area, labeled <alt>.

5. If you're designing a framed site and you want to add a target, add it where you see the little target icon.

Modifying Hotspot Shapes

Fireworks gives you the capability to change a previously assigned hotspot shape without altering the link or other information attached to the hotspot.

Exporting Image Maps

To export your image map, optimize it (Chapter 40) and choose File | Export. Choose the Type of HTML and Images: for HTML, choose Export HTML file; for Slices, choose None. Select the folder you want to export into, and then click Save to export the image map. Fireworks only exports client-side image maps.

The Frames Panel

The next section of this chapter covers how to make animations in Fireworks. The Frames panel is where most of the action is when you produce animations: what is on each frame determines how the animation plays. By default, the Frames panel is in the same panel set as the Layers panel. To work with animations, clicking the Frames panel tab and dragging it out to your workspace is easier. This way, you can see the Layers panel and the Frames panel simultaneously. When you finish using the Frames panel, you can always return it to the Layer panel group simply by dragging it back.

From the Frames panel, you can add, delete, move, duplicate, use Onion Skinning, and set the looping options. Figure 41-5 shows the Frames panel and the menu options you see when you click the right-pointing arrow.

Adding and Deleting Frames

You can add frames one at time or enter a specified number of frames.

To add one frame, click the New/Duplicate Frame icon, which is the icon near the trash can icon, as seen in Figure 41-5.

Note   *The name of this icon is misleading. You won't get a duplicate of the previous layer with this option. Instead, a new blank frame is added.*

Figure 41-5.   *The Frames panel and the pop-up menu options*

To add multiple layers, click the right-pointing arrow to access the pop-up menu. When you delete a frame, you delete all its content. To delete a frame or frames, click the frame or SHIFT-CLICK to select multiple frames and use any of the following options:

- After the selection is made, click the trash can icon to delete.
- Click-and-drag the frame/frames on top of the trash can icon.
- Choose Delete Frame from the pop-up menu by clicking the right-pointing arrow in the Frames panel.

Distribute to Frames

The Distribute to Frames option is used when you have multiple objects on one layer, which you want in individual frames. To distribute objects to individual frames, SHIFT-SELECT each object and click the Distribute to Frames icon (the icon that looks like a ladder). Each object is automatically placed in its own frame. If blank frames are present, they will be placed within those frames. Otherwise, it will generate new frames for each object.

Onion Skinning

When you want to align objects in different frames, being able to see the objects on other layers can help you. This is where the Onion Skinning option comes in handy. Using this feature is like placing tracing paper over the individual frames; you can see through to the other frames. One advantage of using the Onion Skinning feature is you can select the faded objects on frames other than the selected one and edit them. To use this option, click the Onion Skinning icon. In Figure 41–5, you can see its icon on the far-left bottom. The following illustration shows the Onion Skinning options.

Looping

Looping sets the amount of times your animation repeats. You can have it play over and over again indefinitely, choose a specific number of times to loop, or choose not to loop at all. No looping simply means the animation plays one time, and then stops. To set the Looping options, click the GIF animation looping icon, which is next to the Onion Skinning icon. No Looping is the default.

Frame Delay

The *frame delay* determines how long each frame is visible before the next frame appears. The delay settings are specified in hundredths of a second. A setting of 10 would be 10 one hundredths of a second, a setting of 100 would be a one-second delay before the next frame appears. To set the delay settings, double-click the last column in the Frames panel where you see a number. Enter the delay time you want and click outside the dialog box to close. If you want to hide the frame from playback, deselect the Include While Exporting option. If you exclude the option, it won't be present in the playback and it won't be exported. The purpose of adding this feature escapes me. If I didn't want it to be included, I'd simply delete the frame.

GIF Animations

GIF animations can add interest and function to your Web site, as well as detract from it. Many people think the abusive use of animation in many Web sites gives movement a bad name. When an animation moves too fast, blinks excessively, or if numerous animations are on the same page—they tend to irritate more than enhance. But when an animation is used correctly, it can draw positive attention to an important point or feature.

Animated Symbols

If you decide to make GIF animations, the animated symbol will most likely be the most used option. An animated GIF symbol plays independently, enabling you to produce GIF animations, which have more than one symbol interacting together. To make a new animated symbol, follow these steps:

1. Choose Insert | New Symbol.

2. The Symbol Properties dialog box comes up. Type in a name for your symbol, as seen here.

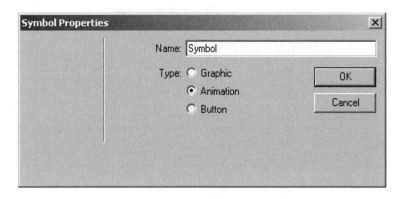

3. Choose the Animation option under the Type choices, and then click OK.

4. The Symbol Editor window opens. This is where you can draw an object or drag an object into the editor. Close the Symbol Editor when you finish. An instance of the symbol is on the canvas.

5. You can now add frames to your symbol in the Object panel (Window | Object) (see The Frames panel section for more information on adding frames). The following Object panel shows some of the options available for your animation.

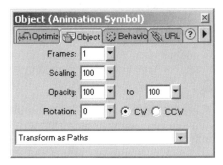

6. Figure 41–6 shows another menu with the addition of a Move and a Direction setting. This dialog box is accessed by selecting the animated symbol and choosing Modify | Animate | Settings.

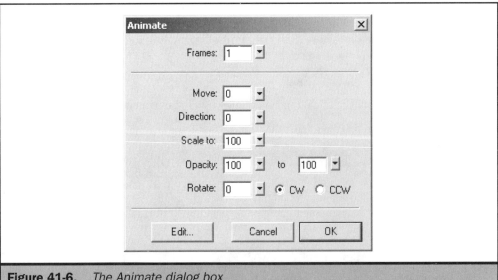

Figure 41-6.   *The Animate dialog box*

Add a Motion Path

To animate a symbol, follow the previous Steps 1–4, and then follow these steps:

1. Choose Modify | Animate | Settings.

2. In the Frames area, type in **5**; in the Move area, type in **52**; In the Direction area, type in **57**. Change Scale to 200, Leave Opacity at 100 to 100, Rotate 0, and choose CW (clockwise).

3. Click OK. A dialog box opens saying, "This animation of this symbol extends beyond the frame of the document. Automatically add new frames?" Click OK. You can see the result of these settings here.

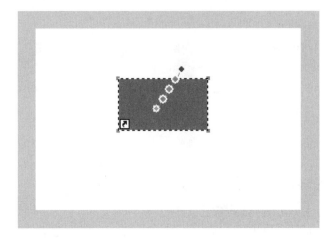

4. To preview the animation you just made, click the Preview tab in the document window, and then click the Play/Stop control (white, right-pointing arrow at the bottom of the document window).

An animated symbol with a motion path attached, when selected, shows a bounding box and the motion path. This path indicates the direction in which the symbol will move. The green dot indicates the starting point, while the red dot indicates the ending point. The blue dots in between represent the frames within the path.

The Move and Direction values can be changed by dragging the handles in the bounding box in your document. You can move the green handle to change the beginning point and the red one to change the ending point. To constrain the movement to 45-degree increments, hold down the SHIFT key as you drag. As you drag the points of the motion path, the setting automatically changes to the position you moved it to.

Exporting Animated GIFs

To export your animation with motion, you must be sure you selected GIF Animation in the Optimize panel. To export as a GIF Animation, follow these steps:

1. Choose Animated GIF in the Optimize panel.
2. Choose File | Export.
3. In the Export dialog box, name the animation, choose where you want to export, and then click Save.

Your animation can be used in Flash and edited further there. To export as a Flash SWF file, follow these steps:

1. Choose File | Export.
2. Choose where you want to save the file.
3. Type in the name of your animation.
4. Click the down arrow under Save As Type and select Macromedia Flash SWF.
5. Click the Options button, choose the options you want, and click OK.
6. Click Save.

Using Fireworks HTML and Images in Dreamweaver

Fireworks uses a generic code for exporting your finished images to use in Web pages. When you choose to Export using the HTML and Images option, the images and the HTML code are generated. The HTML code includes the table that puts the image slices back together, as well as any JavaScript code used for features such as rollovers and Navigation bars.

Placing Fireworks 4 HTML Code into a Dreamweaver 4 Web Page

You can get your Fireworks code in to a Dreamweaver Web page in two ways. You can simply use an insert command or you can copy-and-paste into the correct areas. To insert Fireworks 4 HTML code into Dreamweaver, follow these steps:

1. Open Dreamweaver 4, choose File | Open and open a file where you want to use the Fireworks HTML code.
2. Place your cursor where you want the code inserted. For instance, if you want to add a menu made in Fireworks, place your cursor and click the spot where you want the menu to appear.

3. Choose Insert | Interactive Images | Fireworks HTML. Or, you can use the Insert Fireworks HTML icon in the Common section of the Object Inspector.

4. In the window that opens, click the Browse button. Navigate to the folder containing the Fireworks code and open it.

5. Choose File | Preview in Browser or the Globe Icon on the same row as the HTML code icons below the menu bar. Now select the browser you want to view in.

6. Choose File | Save As and save your file.

Use the Fireworks 4 HTML File

If you think inserting the Fireworks 4 HTML code was easy, you'll find this technique even easier. If you don't yet have a current Web page you want to insert into, then you can simply open the HTML file Fireworks generated when you exported. You can use the Fireworks 4 HTML file as a Dreamweaver template.

Using Exported Dreamweaver Library Items

A *library item* is a portion of an HTML file located in a folder named library at your root site. Library items appear in the Dreamweaver Library palette. Dreamweaver library items simplify the process of editing and updating a frequently used Web site component, such as a Navigation bar. You can drag a copy of the library item from the Library panel to any page in your Web site. To place a library item, follow these steps:

1. Open the Web Page in Dreamweaver where you want to place a library item. When you exported as a library item from Fireworks, you placed the exported library item in the library folder of the same root you're opening a file from now.

2. If the Library panel isn't open, choose Window | Library or Window | Assets. Drag either the image or the text—it doesn't matter—on to the document you just opened. That's all there is to it!

You cannot edit a library item directly in the Dreamweaver document; you can only edit the master library item. Then, you can have Dreamweaver update every copy of that item as it's placed throughout your Web site.

Positioning Fireworks 4 Pop-Up Menus in Dreamweaver

Placing the pop-up menus generated by Fireworks 4 uses the same methods as inserting regular Fireworks HTML code. Special attention will be devoted here to placing the pop-up menus—not because the placement is any different, but because of some of the problems you may encounter.

Centering the pop-up menus on the page is a common problem. Some of the options of how to get them centered are discussed in this section. But, just in case you decide to skip portions of the introductory explanations, before you start experimenting, you should know you cannot center the image containing pop-up menus or the table you place them into.

Absolute Positioning

The first thing to understand about the Fireworks 4 pop-up menus is they use absolute positioning. Fireworks 4 generates a JavaScript file, which generates CSS layers. The JavaScript code assigns absolute positioning of each pop-up menu CSS layer. This is done to keep the menus and the submenus in the same location in relation to the buttons they're linked to. When the button is moved to another location, the menus stay where they were designed. The coordinates written into the HTML code of the pop-up menus is in relation to the position of 0px (zero pixels) from the top-left corner of the browser. If this isn't the same position in the Web page, then the menus won't be positioned correctly. Several options exist to solve some of these problems. Choose which works best for your situation.

Changing the Coordinates

You can change the coordinates of the menu's positioning via the HTML Inspector in Dreamweaver. To change the coordinates, follow these steps:

1. Insert the pop-up menu code in to your document.

2. To change the coordinates in Dreamweaver, open the HTML Inspector. Click the Show Code and Design Views icon. Locate the following line of code. You can find it in the<body> part of the code, not the <head> part. The code you're looking for is

   ```
   onMouseOver="window.FW_showMenu(window.fw_menu_0,145,82);
   ```

3. The second two sets of numbers in the previous code listing (145, 82) represent the X, Y coordinates of the menu. You can change them according to where you want the menus positioned.

4. Open the file you designed in Fireworks. Open the Info panel (Window | Info) and you can see the coordinates of the menu by placing your cursor in the top-left corner of a menu. Look in the Info panel and you can see the X, Y coordinates.

Designing in Fireworks

Another option is to place the menus in Fireworks in the location you want them to appear in the Web page. When the menu is exported and placed in Dreamweaver, the menus are then positioned properly. This technique works well for centering a top navigation.

Using Layers

Because layers are in an absolute position, the pop-up menus work well in a layer. Follow these steps to use a layer for your pop-up menu:

1. In the document where you want to place the pop-up menu, choose Insert | Layer. When the layer is placed, click-and-drag it into the position where you want your menu to be.

2. If you're using Dreamweaver, place your cursor in the layer, click it, and then choose Insert Interactive Images. Locate the file where you want to insert your layer, and then click OK.

 You can also place a top Navigation bar in a layer in a fixed center cell (not a centered table) to center a header.

Working with Images in Dreamweaver

The integration between Dreamweaver and Fireworks is quite good. You can edit and optimize images without ever leaving Dreamweaver.

Optimizing Images from Within Dreamweaver

If you decide you want to change the optimization settings of an image, you can access a version of Fireworks optimization settings from Dreamweaver. To do this, follow these steps:

1. Open a Web page in Dreamweaver that has images on it. Or, make a new document and insert some images. If you make a new page, save it at least once before you try to edit images.

2. Choose Commands | Optimize Image in Fireworks. If a window comes up saying you need to save it, this is because you didn't save your document in Step 1.

3. A Find Source dialog box opens, asking if you want to use the source image. You also have the option of selecting Always Use Source PNG, Never Use Source PNG, or Ask When Launching. Dreamweaver tries to find the source file and, if it can't, you can browse to locate the PNG or any other format yourself.

 A good idea is to select Always Use Source PNG when the Find Source dialog box opens. This is particularly important when you work with a JPEG image. Every time you save a JPEG image, you lose more detail and quality.

4. A version of the Optimize panel opens. When you finish making changes, click the Update button. The changes you made are now updated in Dreamweaver.

Editing Images in Dreamweaver

You can change anything you want in your image. You can change the Fill, Effect, and Style, whatever. To edit an image while in Dreamweaver, follow these steps:

1. Open a page in Dreamweaver, and then click an image to edit.

2. In the Properties Inspector (Window | Properties), click the Edit button. Fireworks opens and you're given the opportunity to locate the image file.

3. Make any changes, as you normally would in Fireworks. Notice the top bar of the document where you're editing your image. It says Editing from Dreamweaver. When you finish, click the Done button, which is located to the right of the Editing from Dreamweaver label.

4. Changes you've made in Fireworks are updated in Dreamweaver, except for one. If you changed the physical size of the image, this doesn't get automatically updated in the Dreamweaver code. The image may appear distorted or blurry. In the past, you had to change the size manually, but a great new feature has been added in Dreamweaver 4. In the Property Inspector, now there's a button called Reset Size. Click it and the size is changed for you.

Summary

You really covered a lot of ground in this chapter, starting with making symbols. Then you learned how to make various rollovers, including the new pop-up menus and how to position them in Dreamweaver.

Key Points:

- Making, saving, and editing symbols.

- Using the Button editor to produce buttons with up to four different states.

- Making simple rollovers using the Swap Image method and learning how to export.

- Making disjoint rollovers using the new drag-and-drop feature of Fireworks 4.

- Using the new Pop-Up Menu Wizard to produce great-looking menus and exporting them.

- Designing image maps and exporting them.

- Gaining an in-depth understanding of the Frames panel.

- Making animations and setting the timing, looping, and motion paths.

- Using Fireworks HTML code in Dreamweaver and overcoming positioning problems of the new pop-up menus.

- Editing and optimizing images from within Dreamweaver.

The
Complete
Reference

Part XI

Appendixes

The Complete Reference

Dreamweaver 4

Appendix A

Dreamweaver Keyboard Shortcuts

This appendix lists keyboard shortcuts that can be used instead of menu items or buttons in Dreamweaver. Keyboard shortcuts are organized into categories of related commands, so you can see where a particular command applies. Some shortcuts fall into more than one category and appear multiple times.

These keyboard shortcuts are Dreamweaver's default settings. You can change the shortcut keys and add shortcuts to commands not listed here by choosing the Edit | Keyboard Shortcuts menu.

Site Management and FTP

Action	Windows	Macintosh
View site files	F8	F8
View site map	ALT-F8	OPTION-F8
Create new file	CTRL-SHIFT-N	COMMAND-SHIFT-N
Create new folder	CTRL-ALT-SHIFT-N	COMMAND-SHIFT-OPTION-N
Open	CTRL-O	COMMAND-O
Open selection	CTRL-ALT-SHIFT-O	COMMAND-OPTION-SHIFT-O
Close	CTRL-W	COMMAND-W
Rename file	F2	N/A
Check Links	SHIFT-F8	SHIFT-F8
Connect to remote site	CTRL-ALT-SHIFT-F5	COMMAND-OPTION-SHIFT-F5
Get selected files from remote FTP site	CTRL-SHIFT-D (or drag files from Remote to Local pane in Site window)	COMMAND-SHIFT-D (or drag files from Remote to Local pane in Site window)
Check out	CTRL-ALT-SHIFT-D (File Check In and Check Out must be enabled in the site definition)	COMMAND-SHIFT-OPTION-D
Put selected files on remote FTP site	CTRL-SHIFT-U (or drag files from Local to Remote pane in Site window)	COMMAND-SHIFT-U (or drag files from Local to Remote pane in Site window)
Check in	CTRL-SHIFT-ALT-U	COMMAND-SHIFT-OPTION-U

Action	Windows	Macintosh
Check links sitewide	CTRL-F8	COMMAND-F8
Refresh	F5	F5
Refresh local site	SHIFT-F5	SHIFT-F5
Refresh remote site	ALT-F5	OPTION-F5
Make root (Site map)	CTRL-SHIFT-R	COMMAND-SHIFT-R
Link to existing file (Site map)	CTRL-SHIFT-K	COMMAND-SHIFT-K
Change link (Site map)	CTRL-L	COMMAND-L
Remove link (Site map)	DELETE	DELETE
Show/Hide link (Site map)	CTRL-SHIFT-Y	COMMAND-SHIFT-Y
Show page titles in site map	CTRL-SHIFT-T	COMMAND-SHIFT-T
Zoom in site map	CTRL- + (Plus)	COMMAND- + (PLUS)
Zoom out site map	CTRL- – (Hyphen)	COMMAND- – (HYPHEN)

File Commands (File Menu)

Action	Windows	Macintosh
New document	CTRL-N	COMMAND-N
Open a document	CTRL-O	COMMAND-O
Open in frame	CTRL-SHIFT-O	COMMAND-SHIFT-O
Close	CTRL-W	COMMAND-W
Save	CTRL-S	COMMAND-S
Save as	CTRL-SHIFT-S	COMMAND-SHIFT-S
Check links	SHIFT-F8	COMMAND-F8
Exit (Quit)	CTRL-Q	COMMAND-Q

Editing Commands (Edit Menu)

Action	Windows	Macintosh
Undo	CTRL-Z	COMMAND-Z
Redo	CTRL-Y or CTRL-SHIFT-Z	COMMAND-Y or COMMAND-SHIFT-Z
Cut	CTRL-X or SHIFT-DEL	COMMAND-X or SHIFT-DEL
Copy	CTRL-C or CTRL-INS	COMMAND-C or COMMAND-INS
Paste	CTRL-V or SHIFT-INS	COMMAND-V or SHIFT-INS
Clear	DELETE	DELETE
Select All	CTRL-A	COMMAND-A
Select parent tag	CTRL-SHIFT-<	COMMAND-SHIFT-<
Select child	CTRL-SHIFT->	COMMAND-SHIFT->
Find and Replace	CTRL-F	COMMAND-F
Find next	F3	COMMAND-G
Indent Code	CTRL-]	COMMAND-]
Outdent Code	CTRL-[	CTRL-[
Balance Braces	CTRL-'	COMMAND-'
Set breakpoint	CTRL-ALT-B	COMMAND-OPTION-B
Edit with external editor	CTRL-E	COMMAND-E
Preferences	CTRL-U	COMMAND-U

Viewing Page Tools

Action	Windows	Macintosh
Toggle visual aids	CTRL-SHIFT-I	COMMAND-SHIFT-I
Toggle rulers	CTRL-ALT-R	COMMAND-OPTION-R

Action	Windows	Macintosh
Toggle grid	CTRL-ALT-G	COMMAND-OPTION-G
Toggle snap to grid	CTRL-ALT-SHIFT-G	COMMAND-OPTION-SHIFT-G
Toggle head content	CTRL-SHIFT-W	COMMAND-SHIFT-W
Toolbar	CTRL-SHIFT-T	COMMAND-SHIFT-T

Code Editor

Action	Windows	Macintosh
Indent code	CTRL-]	COMMAND-]
Outdent code	CTRL-[	COMMAND-[
Toggle between Code view and Design view	CTRL-TAB	OPTION-TAB
Refresh Design view	F5	F5
Select All	CTRL-A	COMMAND-A
Select parent tag	CTRL-SHIFT-<	COMMAND-SHIFT-<
Balance braces	CTRL-'	COMMAND-'
Copy	CTRL-C	COMMAND-C
Find and Replace	CTRL-F	COMMAND-F
Find Next	F3	COMMAND-G
Replace	CTRL-H	COMMAND-H
Paste	CTRL-V	COMMAND-V
Cut	CTRL-X	COMMAND-X
Redo	CTRL-Y	COMMAND-Y
Undo	CTRL-Z	COMMAND-Z
Toggle breakpoint	CTRL-ALT-B	COMMAND-OPTION-B
Select line up	SHIFT-UP	SHIFT-UP
Select line down	SHIFT-DOWN	SHIFT-DOWN

Action	Windows	Macintosh
Character select left	SHIFT-LEFT	SHIFT-LEFT
Character select right	SHIFT-RIGHT	SHIFT-RIGHT
Move to page up	PAGE UP	PAGE UP
Move to page down	PAGE DOWN	PAGE DOWN
Select to page up	SHIFT-PAGE UP	SHIFT-PAGE UP
Select to page down	SHIFT-PAGE DOWN	SHIFT-PAGE DOWN
Select word left	CTRL-SHIFT-LEFT	COMMAND-SHIFT-LEFT
Select word right	CTRL-SHIFT-RIGHT	COMMAND-SHIFT-RIGHT
Move to start of line	HOME	HOME
Move to end of line	END	END
Move to top of code	CTRL-HOME	COMMAND-HOME
Move to end of code	CTRL-END	COMMAND-END
Select to top of code	CTRL-SHIFT-HOME	COMMAND-SHIFT-HOME
Select to end of code	CTRL-SHIFT-END	COMMAND-SHIFT-END

Text Formatting (Design View)

Action	Windows	Macintosh
Indent text (add <blockquote>)	CTRL-ALT-]	COMMAND-OPTION-]
Outdent text (remove <blockquote>)	CTRL-ALT-[	COMMAND-OPTION-[
Remove formatting	CTRL-0 (ZERO)	COMMAND-0 (ZERO)
Format as paragraph	CTRL-SHIFT-P	COMMAND-SHIFT-P
Apply Heading 1 through 6 to a paragraph	CTRL-1 through 6	COMMAND-1 through 6

Action	Windows	Macintosh
Left alignment for selected text	CTRL-SHIFT-ALT-L	COMMAND-SHIFT-OPTION-L
Center alignment for selected text	CTRL-SHIFT-ALT-C	COMMAND-SHIFT-OPTION-C
Right alignment for selected text	CTRL-SHIFT-ALT-R	COMMAND-SHIFT-OPTION-R
Make selected text bold	CTRL-B	COMMAND-B
Make selected text italic	CTRL-I	COMMAND-I
Edit style sheet	CTRL-SHIFT-E	COMMAND-SHIFT-E
Create a new paragraph	ENTER	RETURN
Insert a line break (` `)	SHIFT-ENTER	SHIFT-RETURN
Insert a nonbreaking space ( )	CTRL-SHIFT-SPACEBAR	OPTION-SPACEBAR
Move text or object to another place in the page	Drag selected item	Drag selected item
Copy text or object to another place in the page	CTRL-DRAG selected	OPTION-DRAG selected
Select a word	DOUBLE-CLICK	DOUBLE-CLICK
Add selected items to library	CTRL-SHIFT-B	COMMAND-SHIFT-B
Switch between Design and Code views	CTRL-TAB	OPTION-TAB
Toggle Property Inspector	CTRL-SHIFT-J	COMMAND-SHIFT-J
Check spelling	SHIFT-F7	SHIFT-F7

History Panel

Action	Windows	Macintosh
Open the History panel	SHIFT-F10	SHIFT-F10
Start/stop recording command	CTRL-SHIFT-X	COMMAND-SHIFT-X
Play recorded command	CTRL-P	COMMAND-P

Using Frames

Action	Windows	Macintosh
Select a frame	ALT-CLICK IN FRAME	SHIFT-OPTION-CLICK IN FRAME
Select next frame or frameset	ALT-RIGHT ARROW	COMMAND-RIGHT ARROW
Select previous frame or frameset	ALT-LEFT ARROW	COMMAND-LEFT ARROW
Select parent frameset	ALT-UP ARROW	COMMAND-UP ARROW
Select first child frame or frameset	ALT-DOWN ARROW	COMMAND-DOWN ARROW
Add a new frame to frameset	ALT-DRAG frame border	OPTION-DRAG frame border
Add a new frame to frameset using push method	ALT-CTRL-DRAG frame border	COMMAND-OPTION-DRAG frame border

Using Images

Action	Windows	Macintosh
Change image source attribute	DOUBLE-CLICK image	DOUBLE-CLICK image
Edit image in external editor	CTRL-DOUBLE-CLICK image	COMMAND-DOUBLE-CLICK image

Managing Hyperlinks

Action	Windows	Macintosh
Make selected text a hyperlink (Design view)	CTRL-L	COMMAND-L
Remove hyperlink	CTRL-SHIFT-L	COMMAND-SHIFT-L
Open the document referenced by the hyperlink	CTRL-DOUBLE-CLICK link	COMMAND-DOUBLE-CLICK link
Check links selected	SHIFT-F8	SHIFT-F8
Check all links in the site	CTRL-F8	COMMAND-F8

Using Tables

Action	Windows	Macintosh
Standard view	CTRL-SHIFT-F6	COMMAND-SHIFT-F6
Layout view	CTRL-F6	COMMAND-F6
Select cell	CTRL-A	COMMAND-A or COMMAND-SHIFT-CLICK
Move to the next cell	TAB	TAB

Action	Windows	Macintosh
Move to the previous cell	SHIFT-TAB	SHIFT-TAB
Merge cells	CTRL-ALT-M	COMMAND-OPTION-M
Split cell	CTRL-ALT-S	COMMAND-OPTION-S
Insert a row	CTRL-M	COMMAND-M
Insert a column	CTRL-SHIFT-A	COMMAND-SHIFT-A
Add a new row	TAB in the last cell	TAB in the last cell
Delete current row	CTRL-SHIFT-M	COMMAND-SHIFT-M
Delete a column	CTRL-SHIFT- – (hyphen) (column must be selected first)	COMMAND-SHIFT- – (hyphen)
Increase column span	CTRL-SHIFT-]	COMMAND-SHIFT-]
Decrease column span	CTRL-SHIFT-[	COMMAND-SHIFT-[

Using Layers

Action	Windows	Macintosh
Activate Layers panel	F2	F2
Select a layer	CTRL-SHIFT-CLICK	COMMAND-SHIFT-CLICK
Select and move a layer	CTRL-SHIFT-DRAG	COMMAND-SHIFT-DRAG
Add or remove a layer from selection	SHIFT-CLICK LAYER	SHIFT-CLICK layer
Move selected layer in pixel increment	ARROW KEYS	ARROW KEYS
Move selected layer in snap increment	SHIFT-ARROW KEYS	SHIFT-ARROW KEYS
Resize selected layer by pixel increment	CTRL-ARROW KEYS	OPTION-ARROW KEYS
Resize selected layer by snapping increment	CTRL-SHIFT-ARROW KEYS	OPTION-SHIFT-ARROW KEYS

Action	Windows	Macintosh
Align all selected layers to the last selected layer	CTRL-ARROW KEY (with the arrow direction specifying the side to align to)	COMMAND-ARROW KEY (with the arrow direction specifying the side to align to)
Make all selected layers the same width as last selected layer	CTRL-SHIFT-[	COMMAND-SHIFT-[
Make all selected layers the same height as last selected layer	CTRL-SHIFT-]	COMMAND-SHIFT-]
Toggle grid	CTRL-ALT-G	COMMAND-OPTION-G
Toggle snap to grid	CTRL-ALT-SHIFT-G	COMMAND-OPTION-SHIFT-G

Using Timelines

Action	Windows	Macintosh
Activate Timeline panel	SHIFT-F9	SHIFT-F9
Add object to timeline	CTRL-ALT-SHIFT-T	COMMAND-OPTION-SHIFT-T
Add a keyframe	F6	F6
Remove a keyframe	SHIFT-F6	SHIFT-F6

Playing Plug-ins

Action	Windows	Macintosh
Play selected plug-in	CTRL-ALT-P	COMMAND-OPTION-P
Stop selected plug-in	CTRL-ALT-X	COMMAND-OPTION-X

Action	Windows	Macintosh
Play all plug-ins on page	CTRL-SHIFT-ALT-P	COMMAND-SHIFT-OPTION-P
Stop all plug-ins on page	CTRL-SHIFT-ALT-X	COMMAND-SHIFT-OPTION-X

Using Templates

Action	Windows	Macintosh
Create a new editable region	CTRL-ALT-V	COMMAND-OPTION-V

Preview and Debugging

Action	Windows	Macintosh
Preview in primary browser	F12	F12
Debug in primary browser	ALT-F12	OPTION-F12
Preview in secondary browser	CTRL-F12	COMMAND-F12
Debug in secondary browser	CTRL-ALT-F12	COMMAND-OPTION-F12

JavaScript Debugger

 JavaScript Debugger shortcuts cannot be changed in the Keyboard Shortcuts dialog box (Edit | Keyboard Shortcuts)

Action	Windows	Macintosh
Run	F8	F8
Set/Remove Breakpoint	F7	F7
Step Over	F9	F9
Step Into	F10	F10
Step Out Of	F11	F11

Showing and Hiding Panels

Action	Windows	Macintosh
Toggle Objects	CTRL-F2	COMMAND-F2
Toggle Properties	CTRL-F3	COMMAND-F3
Toggle Site Files	F8	F8
Toggle Site Map	ALT-F8	OPTION-F8
Toggle Assets	F11	F11
Toggle Behaviors	SHIFT-F3	SHIFT-F3
Toggle Code Inspector	F10	F10
Toggle CSS Styles	SHIFT-F11	SHIFT-F11
Toggle Frames	SHIFT-F2	SHIFT-F2
Toggle History	SHIFT-F10	SHIFT-F10
Toggle HTML Styles	CTRL-F11	COMMAND-F11
Toggle Layers	F2	F2
Toggle Reference	CTRL-SHIFT-F1	COMMAND-SHIFT-F1
Toggle Timelines	SHIFT-F9	SHIFT-F9
Show or hide panels	F4	F4
Minimize all	SHIFT-F4	N/A
Restore all	ALT-SHIFT-F4	N/A

Inserting Objects

Action	Windows	Macintosh
Insert an image	CTRL-ALT-I	COMMAND-OPTION-I
Insert a table	CTRL-ALT-T	COMMAND-OPTION-T
Insert a Flash movie	CTRL-ALT-F	COMMAND-OPTION-F
Insert a Shockwave (Director) movie	CTRL-ALT-D	COMMAND-OPTION-D
Insert a named anchor	CTRL-ALT-A	COMMAND-OPTION-A

Help

Action	Windows	Macintosh
Using Dreamweaver help	F1	F1
Open Reference panel	SHIFT-F1 or CTRL-SHIFT-F1	SHIFT-F1 or COMMAND-SHIFT-F1

The Complete Reference

Dreamweaver 4

Appendix B

HTML Elements

Thus appendix is a compilation of information from several sources and personal testing. These sources include the following:

- HTML 4.01 Specification W3C Recommendation (**http://www.w3.org/TR/html4/**)
- Web Monkey Browser Chart (**http://hotwired.lycos.com/webmonkey/reference/browser_chart/**)
- NCD HTML Design Guide (**http://www.ncdesign.org/html/list.htm**)

Note *The World Wide Web Consortium (W3C) has recently elevated XHTML 1.0 to recommended status. Dreamweaver 4, however, still uses HTML 4.0 as the basis for its code and cannot readily generate XHTML code. Therefore, this appendix contains the HTML 4.0 recommendation.*

This appendix isn't meant to replace a complete HTML guide. Rather, it's an overview of each of the HTML 4 tags and their common use.

All elements are listed alphabetically and provide the following information:

- **Tag**—the tag notation and a description of its use.

- **Attributes**—the most commonly used attributes and values for the tag.

- **Dreamweaver Usage**—whether the tag can be viewed in the Design view of the Document window and how the tag is accessed within the application.

- **End Tag**—specifies if an end tag is required in HTML 4. As previously noted, this appendix refers to HTML 4 and not to the current XHTML 1.0 recommendation. The use and notation of end tags varies with certain tags. To be compliant with the new recommendation, please consult an XHTML reference if you are coding.

- **Deprecated**—if a tag is deprecated, it's noted here. A tag is deprecated when the W3C determines it has outlived its usefulness in HTML code. Although such tags remain functional in most browsers and available in Dreamweaver, they should be avoided in favor of other tags or the use of style sheets, unless you are coding for earlier browser compatibility.

- **Browsers**—Which versions of Netscape and/or IE (IE) support the tag. Only version 3.0 and higher browsers are referenced here because the vast majority of Web surfers are now using at least a 3.0 version browser.

Note *As discussed throughout this book, differences exist in how each browser renders particular tags. Using only tags recognized by all browsers still doesn't ensure your page will be rendered identically in each browser and on every platform.*

Standard Attributes

Most, but not all, tags can accept the same set of common attributes and events, in addition to those that are unique for certain tags. These standard attributes and events are divided into three groups—core attributes, internationalization attributes, and scripting events.

Core Attributes

Core attributes are used to identify a tag for reference by other tags, to provide accessibility, and to assign style sheet rules.

- `class="class"`—applies a style to the contents of a tag, as defined in a style sheet.

- `id="id"`—assigns a unique name to the tag for use as a reference from other tags or scripts.

- `style="style"`—applies an inline style to the contents of a tag, as defined in a style sheet.

- `title="text"`—provides descriptive information about a tag. The title text usually appears as a tool tip when the page is displayed in a browser and is considered an accessibility tool. It can also be used with the `<abbr>` and `<acronym>` tags to provide a full definition of the abbreviation or acronym.

Internationalization Attributes

Internationalization attributes are used to notify the browser of the language and character set being used in portions of the page.

- **lang="language-code"**—specifies the language of the tag's content. This can be used to define a different style for each language on a multilanguage page. Pages with language attributes may also be more readily interpreted by search engines as being bilingual. The language attribute can be used as a pronunciation guide for speech synthesizers used for accessibility, although this isn't widely supported as yet. The most common language codes are the following:
  - **en**—English
  - **en-US**—English as spoken in the U.S.
  - **fr**—French
  - **sp**—Spanish
  - **de**—German
  - **it**—Italian
  - **ru**—Russian

- **ja**—Japanese
- **zh**—Chinese
- **he**—Hebrew
- **ar**—Arabic
- **dir="ltr"** or **dir="rtl"**— this specifies the direction of the content, either from left-to-right or from right-to-left. This is primarily used with Unicode characters (such as Chinese, Japanese, and Hebrew) contained within a page that also uses a Western character set. This should be used cautiously because some Unicode character sets automatically change the directional flow of text.

Scripting Events

Scripting events are JavaScripts triggered by the actions of users when they are viewing a Web page. In Dreamweaver, many of these events are added using the Behaviors panel. They can also be coded by hand. For each of the following attributes listed, an appropriate JavaScript must be referenced as a value of the attribute. Only the most common events are listed here; others can be found at the W3C site at **http://www.w3.org/TR/html4/interact/scripts.html#h-18.2.3**.

- **onclick="script"**—activated when the mouse is clicked and released, such as over a link.
- **ondblclick="script"**—the mouse was double-clicked and released.
- **onmousedown="script"**—the mouse was clicked and held down.
- **onmouseup="script"**—the mouse was clicked, held down, and then released after a pause.
- **onmouseover="script"**—the mouse moved over an object without being clicked. This is commonly used in rollovers.
- **onmousemove="script"**—the mouse was moved within an object.
- **onmouseout="script"**—the mouse was moved off an object.
- **onkeypress="script"**—a key was pressed and released.
- **onkeydown="script"**—a key was pressed and held down.
- **onkeyup="script"**—a key was pressed, held down, and then released after a pause.

Tags that accept common attributes are identified as such in the alphabetical listing of HTML 4 tags, as shown in the following. Most tags can also accept other attributes and values, as specified for each tag.

Alphabetical Listing of HTML 4.01 Tags

`<a>` Defines link source and destination anchors.
Attributes:

- Standard attributes

    `href= "URL"` | `"mailto:address"` | `"URL#keyword"` Identifies destination of link.

    `name= "name"` Names anchor to define it as a source for links.
    `target="_blank"` | `"_self"` | `"_parent"` | `"_top"` Identifies window in which to open the destination.

- Dreamweaver Usage: Link field of Property Inspector; E-mail Link object; Named Anchor object, Modify menu

End Tag	Deprecated?	Browser Compatibility
Required	No	Netscape 3+, IE 3+

`<abbr>` Abbreviated form (AZ, NYC, and so forth). When used with the `<title>` attribute, it allows speech applications to read the full form of the word, while the abbreviated form is displayed on the screen.
Attributes:

- Standard attributes

- Dreamweaver Usage: Must be hand-coded.

End Tag	Deprecated?	Browser Compatibility
Required	No	None

`<acronym>` Similar to `<abbr>`. For acronyms such as WWW, ISP, and so forth.
Attributes:

- Standard attributes

- Dreamweaver Usage: Must be hand-coded.

End Tag	Deprecated?	Browser Compatibility
Required	No	IE 4+

`<address>` For contact information. Contents are displayed in italics by default, but can be overridden with a style sheet.
Attributes:

- Standard attributes

- Dreamweaver Usage: Must be hand-coded.

End Tag	Deprecated?	Browser Compatibility
Required	No	Netscape 3+, IE 3+

`<applet>` Adds a Java applet.
Attributes:

- Standard attributes

  `codebase="URL"` Sets the location of the applet.
  `code="filename"` Identifies the compiled applet file.

- Dreamweaver Usage: Insert I Media I Applet.

End Tag	Deprecated?	Browser Compatibility
Required	Yes, in favor of the `<object>` tag	Netscape 3+, IE 3+

`<area>` Defines clickable areas of a client-side image map.
Attributes:

- Standard attributes

  `shape="rect"` | `"circle"` | `"poly"` | `"default"` Defines a region by shape.
  `cords="coordinates"` Defines the position of the shape attribute.

href= *"URL"* Specifies the destination of the link for the defined area.

target="_blank" | **"_self"** | **"_parent"** | **"_top"** Specifies the frame or window in which to open the link destination.

nohref States the defined area has no link associated with it.

■ Dreamweaver Usage: Image map tools in the Property Inspector.

End Tag	Deprecated?	Browser Compatibility
Never	No	Netscape 3+, IE 3+

<b> **Displays contents in bold typeface.**
Attributes:

■ Standard attributes, although they aren't generally used with this tag.

■ Dreamweaver Usage: Property Inspector.

End Tag	Deprecated?	Browser Compatibility
Required	No, but style sheets offer more control over type.	Netscape 3+, IE 3+

<base> **Sets the base URL for the page. All links within the page use this URL as the basis for the path cited in the href attribute.**
Attributes:

href= *"URL"* Sets the path of the base document relative to the current page.

target="_blank" | **"_self"** | **"_parent"** | **"_top"** Sets the frame or window in which the linked document opens.

■ Dreamweaver Usage: Insert | Head Tags | Base.

End Tag	Deprecated?	Browser Compatibility
Never	No	Netscape 3+, IE 3+

<basefont>   Sets the base font attributes.

Attributes:

size= "*number*" | "*+number*" | "*-number*" Sets the font size in either absolute or relative terms from the default size.

color= "*color*" Sets the font color in either hexadecimal format or using one of the predefined color values.

face="*font*" | "*font1, font2, font3*" Sets the font face. The chosen font face is only displayed if users have that font installed on their computers. A range of font face choices may be entered as one value (that is, within the same set of quotation marks), separated by commas.

■ Dreamweaver Usage: Must be hand-coded.

End Tag	Deprecated?	Browser Compatibility
Never	Yes, in favor of style sheets	Netscape 3+, IE 3+

<bdo>   Bidirectional override is used to change the direction of the text flow using the internationalization attributes.

Attributes:

■ Standard core and internationalization attributes.

■ Dreamweaver Usage: Must be hand-coded.

End Tag	Deprecated?	Browser Compatibility
Required	No	IE 5

<bgsound>   Plays background music. Inserted into the **<head>** content of the document.

Attributes:

■ Standard core and internationalization attributes.

src= "*URL*" specifies location of sound file.

loop=*number*" Specifies number of times to play back the sound file in a loop.

■ Dreamweaver Usage: Must be hand-coded.

End Tag	Deprecated?	Browser Compatibility
Never	No, but other methods have better browser support and are more efficient. See Chapter 26.	IE 3+

<big> Displays contents in a larger font size than the surrounding text.
Attributes:

- Standard attributes

- Dreamweaver Usage: Must be hand-coded.

End Tag	Deprecated?	Browser Compatibility
Required. Tags can be nested, with the content of each pair increasing in size relative to the surrounding pair.	No, but style sheets provide more control over text presentation.	Netscape 3+, IE 3+

<blink> Contained text blinks on the user's screen.
Attributes:

- Standard attributes

- Dreamweaver Usage: Must be hand-coded.

End Tag	Deprecated?	Browser Compatibility
Required	No, but it's one of the most annoying tags ever created.	Netscape 3+. IE 4+ won't ignore the tag, so styles can be applied to it, but IE won't blink the text as intended.

<blockquote> Contained text is designated as a quotation, and is usually indented and/or displayed in italics.
Attributes:

- Core attributes and scripting events.

  cite= "URL" Provides the source of the information. This isn't rendered on the page, however, so this attribute isn't used often.

- Dreamweaver Usage: Indent button in the Property Inspector.

End Tag	Deprecated?	Browser Compatibility
Required	No	Netscape 3+, IE 3+

<body> Contains the content of the entire page.
Attributes:

- Standard attributes

  onload="script" Scripting event triggered when the page loads.

  onunload="script" Scripting event triggered when the page unloads.

  background= "URL" Sets a background image for the page. Deprecated in favor of style sheets. In IE, can be used in conjunction with the bgproperties="fixed" attribute to set a fixed background that won't scroll with the content of the page.

  bgcolor= "color" Sets a background color for the page. Deprecated in favor of style sheets.

  text= "color" Sets the text color for the page. Deprecated in favor of style sheets.

  link= "color" Sets the link color. Deprecated in favor of style sheets.

  vlink= "color" Sets the color for visited links. Deprecated in favor of style sheets.

  alink= "color" Sets the color for active links. Deprecated in favor of style sheets.

  bottommargin= "number" Sets the bottom margin space in pixels. Only used by IE.

  leftmargin= "number" Sets the left margin space in pixels. Only used by IE.

  rightmargin= "number" Sets the right margin space in pixels. Only used by IE.

topmargin= *"number"* Sets the top margin space in pixels. Only used by IE.

marginheight= *"number"* Sets the top and bottom margin space in pixels. Only used by Netscape.

marginwidth= *"number"* Sets the left and right margin space in pixels. Only used by Netscape.

■ Dreamweaver Usage: Automatically created in every new document.

End Tag	Deprecated?	Browser Compatibility
Required	No, although some of the attributes of the tag have been deprecated, as previously noted.	All browsers

**
    Forced line break.**
Attributes:

■ Core and internationalization attributes.

clear="left" | "right" | "all" Primarily used to wrap text around images, this breaks the line until the next line with a clear margin matching the value of this attribute. For example, if the value is set to left, the line breaks until the next possible line where no image is at the left margin. This attribute is deprecated in favor of style sheets.

■ Dreamweaver Usage: SHIFT-ENTER (SHIFT-RETURN on the Mac) or the Line Break object in the Characters category of the Objects panel.

End Tag	Deprecated?	Browser Compatibility
Never	No, but the clear attribute is deprecated.	Netscape 3+, IE 3+

<button>   Creates a form button.
Attributes:

■ Standard attributes

name= *"name"* Sets a name for the element for reference by other tags.

type="submit" | "reset" | "button" Specifies the function of the button in the form, whether it's to submit the form contents, to reset (clear) the form, or to trigger a script.

value="*data*" Sets an initial value for the button.

tabindex="*number*" Sets the tab order of the button within the form for users who use the tab key rather than a mouse to navigate through the form. The tab order is set from the lowest to the highest number.

accesskey="character" Sets a single, alphanumeric character as a keyboard shortcut to activate the button.

An alternative button graphic can be specified by nesting an <img> tag within the <button> tag.

■ Dreamweaver Usage: Form category of the Objects panel or Insert | Form Objects | Button.

End Tag	Deprecated?	Browser Compatibility
Required	No	IE 4+

<caption> **Displays a caption for a table.**
Attributes:

■ Standard attributes

align="top" | "bottom" | "left" | "right" | "center" Aligns the caption relative to the table it's describing. The left, right, and center values are only used by IE. This attribute has been deprecated in favor of style sheets.

valign="top" | "bottom" Sets the vertical alignment for the caption, either on top of the table or below it. Used only by IE.

■ Dreamweaver Usage: Must be hand-coded.

End Tag	Deprecated?	Browser Compatibility
Required	No	Netscape 3+, IE 3+

<center> **Centers content.**
Attributes:

■ Standard attributes

■ Dreamweaver Usage: Align Center button on the Property Inspector, but only if the `<center>` tag preference has been set in the Code Format category of the Preferences dialog box.

End Tag	Deprecated?	Browser Compatibility
Required	Yes, in favor of the `<div>` tag and/or style sheets.	Netscape 3+, IE 3+

`<cite>` **Used for citations and references. Usually renders the contents in italics.**
Attributes:

■ Standard attributes

■ Dreamweaver Usage: Text | Style | Citation from the menu.

End Tag	Deprecated?	Browser Compatibility
Required	No	Netscape 3+, IE 3+

`<code>` **Used for code listings. Usually renders contents in monospaced font.**
Attributes:

■ Standard attributes

■ Dreamweaver Usage: Text | Style | Code from the menu.

End Tag	Deprecated?	Browser Compatibility
Required	No	Netscape 3+, IE 3+

`<col>` **Defines table columns as an alternative to the traditional table row (`<tr>`) and table cell (`<td>`) structure.**
Attributes:

■ Standard attributes

span= "number" Specifies how many columns are spanned by the current column definition. Setting the span to zero (0) sets the column to span all the remaining columns in the row.

`align="left"` | `"right"` | `"center"` | `"justify"` Sets the horizontal alignment of the column content.

`valign="top"` | `"middle"` | `"bottom"` Sets the vertical alignment of the column content.

`width= "number"` Specifies the width of the column.

■ Dreamweaver Usage: Must be hand-coded.

End Tag	Deprecated?	Browser Compatibility
Never	No	IE 3+

`<colgroup>` **Serves as a container for `<col>` elements.**
Attributes:

■ Standard attributes

`align="left"` | `"right"` | `"center"` | `"justify"` Sets the horizontal alignment of the column content.

`valign="top"` | `"middle"` | `"bottom"` Sets the vertical alignment of the column content.

`width= "number"` Specifies the width of the columns.

■ Dreamweaver Usage: Must be hand-coded.

End Tag	Deprecated?	Browser Compatibility
Never	No	IE 3+

`<dd>` **Definition description. Used in definition lists.**
Attributes:

■ Standard attributes

■ Dreamweaver Usage: Text | List | Definition List.

End Tag	Deprecated?	Browser Compatibility
Optional	No	Netscape 3+, IE 3+

`<del>` Marks text that's been deleted from view, but remains in the HTML document.
Attributes:

■ Standard attributes

`cite="URL"` Points to a document that explains the rationale for the deletion.

`datetime="time"` Sets the date and time of the deletion.

■ Dreamweaver Usage: Must be hand-coded.

End Tag	Deprecated?	Browser Compatibility
Required	No	IE 4+

`<dfn>` Indicates a defining instance of a term, usually the first time a new term appears in the content. Usually rendered in italics.
Attributes:

■ Standard attributes

■ Dreamweaver Usage: Text | Style | Definition.

End Tag	Deprecated?	Browser Compatibility
Required	No	IE 3+

`<dir>` Defines a directory list, which displays either as an unordered list or as a multicolumn directory across the page.
Attributes:

■ Standard attributes

■ Dreamweaver Usage: Must be hand-coded.

End Tag	Deprecated?	Browser Compatibility
Required	Yes, in favor of unordered lists	Netscape 3+, IE 3+

`<div>`   **Generic container with the capability to be defined by the developer.**
Attributes:

- Standard attributes

  `align="left" | "right" | "center" | "justify"` Sets the horizontal alignment. This has been deprecated in favor of style sheets.

- Dreamweaver Usage: Applied when setting alignment in the Property Inspector or using the Align options on the Modify and Text menus.

End Tag	Deprecated?	Browser Compatibility
Required	No	Netscape 3+, IE 3+

`<dl>`   **Defines a Definition List.**
Attributes:

- Standard attributes

- Dreamweaver Usage: Text | List | Definition List.

End Tag	Deprecated?	Browser Compatibility
Required	No	Netscape 3+, IE 3+

`<dt>`   **The definition term. Used in definition lists in combination with the definition description (`<dd>`).**
Attributes:

- Standard attributes

- Dreamweaver Usage: Text | Lists | Definition List.

End Tag	Deprecated?	Browser Compatibility
Required	No	Netscape 3+, IE 3+

<em> Emphasizes text in relation to normal text, and is usually displayed in boldface.
Attributes:

- Standard attributes

- Dreamweaver Usage: Text | Style | Emphasis.

End Tag	Deprecated?	Browser Compatibility
Required	No	Netscape 3+, IE 3+

<fieldset> Used to group related form controls and labels.
Attributes:

- Standard attributes

- Dreamweaver Usage: Must be hand-coded.

End Tag	Deprecated?	Browser Compatibility
Required	No	IE 4+

<font> Local change to the font.
Attributes:

- Standard attributes

  size="size" Sets the font size in absolute or relative terms.

  color="color" Sets the font color.

  face="font-face" Sets the font face. Can contain multiple font faces in the order of preference, separated by commas.

- Dreamweaver Usage: Any of the font settings in the Property Inspector; The Font, Size, Size Change, and Color options on the Text menu.

End Tag	Deprecated?	Browser Compatibility
Required	Yes, in favor of style sheets	Netscape 3+, IE 3+

`<form>`   **Defines a form.**
Attributes:

- Standard attributes

    `action="URL"` Sets the destination of the form data once it's submitted. Can be either the location of a CGI script or an e-mail address.

    `method="get" | "post"` Sets the method for accessing the URL specified in the action attribute.

- Dreamweaver Usage: Form Property Inspector.

End Tag	Deprecated?	Browser Compatibility
Required	No	Netscape 3+, IE 3+

`<frame>`   **Defines a frame within a frameset.**
Attributes:

- Standard attributes

    `name="frame name"` Sets a name for the frame, allowing it to be referenced elsewhere.

    `src="URL"` Specifies the location of the frame contents.

    `frameborder="1" | "0"` Toggles the border on the frame.

    `bordercolor="color"` Specifies the color of the frame border, if such a border is toggled on.

    `marginheight="height"` Sets the margin between the contents of the frame and the top and bottom frame borders, in pixels.

    `marginwidth="width"` Sets the margin between the contents of the frame and the left and right frame borders, in pixels.

    `noresize` Prohibits the user from resizing the frame.

    `scrolling="auto" | "yes" | "no"` Determines whether a scrollbar appears in the frame when content exceeds the viewable screen area.

    `longdesc="URL"` Links to a destination source that contains a long description of the frame contents.

- Dreamweaver Usage: Insert | Frames; Frames category of the Objects panel.

End Tag	Deprecated?	Browser Compatibility
Never	No	Netscape 3+, IE 3+

`<frameset>` **Defines the frame layout of the window. Replaces the `<body>` tag to define the page content.**
Attributes:

■ Standard attributes

    `border= "number"` Sets the borders for the entire frameset (although individual frames can override this setting with their `frameborder` attribute). A setting of zero (0) removes all frame borders.

    `bordercolor= "color"` Sets the color of all the frame borders.

    `cols= "number"` Sets the vertical layout of the frameset.

    `rows= "number"` Sets the horizontal layout of the frameset.

■ Dreamweaver Usage: Insert | Frames; Frames category of the Objects panel.

End Tag	Deprecated?	Browser Compatibility
Required	No	Netscape 3+, IE 3+

`<h1>` through `<h6>` **Defines contents as a heading. H1 is the highest heading in the hierarchy, H6 is the lowest, and each is usually displayed differently in the browser to distinguish them.**
Attributes:

■ Standard attributes

■ Dreamweaver Usage: Text | Paragraph Format; Format field in the Property Inspector.

End Tag	Deprecated?	Browser Compatibility
Required	No	Netscape 3+, IE 3+

<head> Defines head content of document, containing information about the document, as opposed to the content of the document.
Attributes:

- Internationalization attributes

  profile= "URL" Specifies the source of full metadata profile.

- Dreamweaver Usage: Automatically created in every new document.

End Tag	Deprecated?	Browser Compatibility
Required	No	Netscape 3+, IE 3+

<hr> Horizontal rule used to separate portions of a document visually.
Attributes:

- Standard attributes

  align="left" | **"right"** | **"center"** | **"justify"** Sets the horizontal alignment of the rule when it doesn't stretch across the full width of the container element or page.

  size= "number" Sets the length of the rule in pixels.

  width= "number" Sets the thickness of the rule in pixels.

  color= "color" Sets the color of the rule.

  noshade Sets the rule as a solid color without any shading effects.

- Dreamweaver Usage: Insert | Horizontal Rule; Horizontal Rule object in the Common category of the Objects panel.

End Tag	Deprecated?	Browser Compatibility
Never	No, but its attributes have been deprecated in favor of style sheets	Netscape 3+, IE 3+

<html> Defines the entire document as an HTML document. Required for all HTML pages.
Attributes:

- Internationalization attributes

version= *"data"* Sets the Formal Public Identifier (FPI), which specifies the HTML document type that governs the document. Deprecated in favor of the `<!doctype>` declaration.

■ Dreamweaver Usage: Automatically created in every new document.

End Tag	Deprecated?	Browser Compatibility
Required	No	Netscape 3+, IE 3+

<i> Displays text in italics.
Attributes:

■ Standard attributes

■ Dreamweaver Usage: Italics icon on Property Inspector; Text | Style | Italic.

End Tag	Deprecated?	Browser Compatibility
Required	No, but style sheets offer greater control over text formatting	Netscape 3+, IE 3+

<iframe> Creates an inline frame in the document. Sometimes called a *floating frame.*
Attributes:

■ Standard attributes

name= *"name"* Names the inline frame for reference by other elements.

src= *"URL"* Links to the source of the contents of the frame. Any text added to the `<iframe>` element itself is only displayed in browsers that don't support them. Otherwise, all content for the frame comes from the external source provided in this attribute.

frameborder= `"1"` | `"0"` Toggles the appearance of a border around the frame.

align= `"left"` | `"right"` | `"center"` | `"justify"` Sets the horizontal alignment of the frame.

marginwidth= *"number"* Sets the margin between the content and the left and right borders of the frame.

marginheight= *"number"* Sets the margin between the content and the top and bottom borders of the frame.

hspace= *"number"* Sets the horizontal space between the frame and surrounding content.

vspace= *"number"* Sets the vertical space between the frame and surrounding content.

scrolling= *"auto"* | *"yes"* | *"no"* Sets the appearance of a scrollbar when the content of the frame exceeds the viewable area of the frame.

noresize Prohibits the browser from resizing the frame.

■ Dreamweaver Usage: Must be hand-coded.

End Tag	Deprecated?	Browser Compatibility
Required	No	IE 3+

<img> **Embeds and image into the document.**
Attributes:

■ Standard attributes

src= *"URL"* Specifies the location of the image file.

alt= *"text"* Displays alternate descriptive text if the browser cannot display the image or if the user mouses over the image (in the form of a tool tip).

height= *"number"* Sets the height of the image in pixels.

width= *"number"* Sets the width of the image in pixels.

align= *"left"* | *"right"* | *"top"* | *"bottom"* | *"middle"* Sets the alignment of the image in relation to surrounding content.

border= *"number"* Sets the border width around the image. A setting of zero (0) removes any border from the image.

hspace= *"number"* Sets the horizontal space between the image and surrounding content.

vspace= *"number"* Sets the vertical space between the image and surrounding content.

■ Dreamweaver Usage: Insert | Image; Image object in the Objects panel.

End Tag	Deprecated?	Browser Compatibility
Never	No, but many of its attributes have been deprecated in favor of style sheets	Netscape 3+, IE 3+

`<input>`   **Defines controls in forms.**
Attributes:

■ Standard attributes

`type="text"` | `"password"` | `"checkbox"` | `" radio"` | `"image"` | `"button"` | `"submit"` | `"reset"` | `"file"` | `"hidden"` Defines the type of control to create.

`name= "name"` Sets a control name.

`value="checked"` | `"readonly"` | `"disabled:` | `"user-defined value"` Sets the initial value of the control.

`size= "number"` Sets the initial size of the control.

`src= "URL"` Identifies the image file when the control type has been set to image.

`tabindex= "number"` Sets the tab order between controls in the form to enable users to navigate using the TAB key.

■ Dreamweaver Usage: Forms category of Objects panel; Insert | Form Objects.

End Tag	Deprecated?	Browser Compatibility
Never	No	Netscape 3+, IE 3+

`<ins>`   **Used in revision control to identify text as having been inserted into the document in relation to an earlier version.**
Attributes:

■ Standard attributes

`cite= "URL"` Links to a document that provides a rationale for the change.

`datetime= "time"` Sets the date and time of the change.

■ Dreamweaver Usage: Must be hand-coded.

End Tag	Deprecated?	Browser Compatibility
Required	No	IE 4+

`<isindex>` Added to the `<head>` of the document. Creates an input control to enable the user to enter a keyword and search the document.
Attributes:

■ Core and Internationalization attributes

`prompt="text"` Displays a text prompt for the input control.

■ Dreamweaver Usage: Must be hand-coded.

End Tag	Deprecated?	Browser Compatibility
Never	Yes, in favor of forms	Netscape 3+, IE 3+

`<kbd>` Identifies user-entered text, such as in a how-to description. Usually displayed in a monospaced font in the browser.
Attributes:

■ Standard attributes

■ Dreamweaver Usage: Text | Style | Keyboard.

End Tag	Deprecated?	Browser Compatibility
Required	No	Netscape 3+, IE 3+

`<label>` Labels or describes a form control.
Attributes:

■ Standard attributes

`for="control name"` Associates the label with a specific form control.

■ Dreamweaver Usage: Form Property Inspector.

End Tag	Deprecated?	Browser Compatibility
Required	No	IE 4+

`<legend>`   Sets a caption for a fieldset.
Attributes:

- Standard attributes

  `align="left"` | `"right"` | `"top"` | `"bottom"` Sets the alignment of the legend relative to the fieldset.

- Dreamweaver Usage: Must be hand-coded.

End Tag	Deprecated?	Browser Compatibility
Required	No	IE 4+

`<li>`   Specifies a list item within a list element.
Attributes:

- Standard attributes

  `type="1"` | `"a"` | `"A"` | `"i"` | `"I"` | `"disc"` | `"square"` | `"circle"`
  Specifies the type of bullet or ordering scheme—Arabic numbers, lowercase, uppercase, lowercase Roman numerals; uppercase Roman numerals, solid circle, square outline, or a circle outline.

  `value= "number"` Sets a number or value other than the incremented value for the list item.

- Dreamweaver Usage: Text | List; List options on Property Inspector.

End Tag	Deprecated?	Browser Compatibility
Optional	No, but attributes have been deprecated in favor of style sheets	Netscape 3+, IE 3+

<link>   Defines a link in the **<head>** of a document to indicate a relationship between the current document and another object, such as a style sheet.
Attributes:

- Standard attributes

    charset= *"character-set"* Indicates the character encoding of the linked resource.

    href= *"URL"* Specifies the location of the linked resource.

    type= *"content-type"* Specifies the type of content, such as text/html or text/css, of the linked resource.

    rel= *"link-type"* Defines the relationship of the current document to the linked resource.

    rev= *"link-type"* Defines the relationship of the linked resource to the current document.

- Dreamweaver Usage: Insert | Head Tags | Link; Link object in the Head category of the Objects panel; also added automatically when creating an external style sheet.

End Tag	Deprecated?	Browser Compatibility
Never	No	Netscape 4+, IE 3+

<map>   Defines a client-side image map.
Attributes:

- Standard attributes

    name= *"name"* Specifies a name for the image map.

- Dreamweaver Usage: Image Property Inspector.

End Tag	Deprecated?	Browser Compatibility
Required	No	Netscape 3+, IE 3+

<marquee>   Creates a scrolling marquee.
Attributes:

- Standard attributes

`behavior="scroll"` | `"slide"` | `"alternate"` Determines the movement of the marquee text. Scroll cycles the text endlessly across the screen. Slide moves the text across the screen once and stops on the opposite side. Alternate bounces the text from side-to-side.

`bgcolor= "color"` Sets a background color for the marquee.

`direction="left"` | `"right"` | `"down"` | `"up"` Sets the direction in which the text moves.

`loop= "number"` Specifies how many times the text should cycle.

■ Dreamweaver Usage: Must be hand-coded.

End Tag	Deprecated?	Browser Compatibility
Required	No	IE 3+

`<menu>` **Defines a single-column menu list.**
Attributes:

■ Standard attributes

■ Dreamweaver Usage: Must be hand-coded.

End Tag	Deprecated?	Browser Compatibility
Required	Yes, in favor of unordered lists	Netscape 3+, IE 3+

`<meta>` **Generic metainformation.**
Attributes:

■ Internationalization attributes

`name= "name"` Identifies a name with the meta information.

`http-equiv= "name"` Identifies a name with the meta information used by HTTP servers.
`content= "data"` Contains the content of the meta information.

■ Dreamweaver Usage: Insert | Head Tags; Head category of the Objects panel.

End Tag	**Deprecated?**	**Browser Compatibility**
Never	No	Netscape 3+, IE 3+

`<multicol>` **Sets text to be displayed in multicolumn format.**
Attributes:

- ■ Standard attributes

  `cols="number"` Sets the number of columns into which to split the content.
  `gutter="number"` Sets the width of the gutter between columns in pixels.

- ■ Dreamweaver Usage: Must be hand-coded.

End Tag	**Deprecated?**	**Browser Compatibility**
Required	No	Netscape 3+

`<noframes>` **Defines content to display when frames aren't supported by a browser.**
Attributes:

- ■ Standard attributes

- ■ Dreamweaver Usage: Modify | Frameset | Edit NoFrames Content (must have already created a frameset).

End Tag	**Deprecated?**	**Browser Compatibility**
Required	No	Netscape 3+, IE 3+

`<noscript>` **Defines alternate content for browsers that can't execute a script.**
Attributes:

- ■ Standard attributes

- ■ Dreamweaver Usage: Must be hand-coded.

End Tag	Deprecated?	Browser Compatibility
Required	No	Netscape 3+, IE 3+

<object> Defines an external object or application, such as a Java applet or audio/video file.
Attributes:

- Standard attributes

  align="left" | **"right"** | **"top"** | **"bottom"** | **"baseline"** Sets the alignment of the object relative to the surrounding content.

  classid= "URL" Sets the location of the object's implementation.

  codebase= "URL" Sets the base URL for the object.

  data= "URL" Sets the location of the data for the object.

  type= "content-type" Defines the object's content type.

  codetype= "content-type" Defines the type of content of the data downloaded by the object.

  standby= "text" Displays a message while loading the object.

  height= "number" Sets the display height of the object.

  width= "number" Sets the display width of the object.

- Dreamweaver Usage: Insert | Media; objects in the Special category of the Objects panel.

End Tag	Deprecated?	Browser Compatibility
Required	No	IE 3+

<ol> Defines an ordered list.
Attributes:

- Standard attributes

  type="1" | **"a"** | **"A"** | **"i"** | **"I"** Specifies the type of ordering scheme—Arabic numbers, lowercase, uppercase, lowercase Roman numerals; or uppercase Roman numerals.

  start= "number" Sets the starting number for the list.

■ Dreamweaver Usage: Ordered list button in Property Inspector; Text | List | Ordered List.

End Tag	Deprecated?	Browser Compatibility
Required	No, although its attributes have been deprecated in favor of style sheets	Netscape 3+, IE 3+

`<optgroup>`   Groups `<option>` elements in a `<select>` element.
Attributes:

■ Standard attributes

`label= "text"` Labels the option group

■ Dreamweaver Usage: Must be hand-coded.

End Tag	Deprecated?	Browser Compatibility
Required	No	None

`<option>`   Defines choices in a `<select>` element.
Attributes:

■ Standard attributes

`value= "text"` Sets the initial value of the control.

■ Dreamweaver Usage: Must be hand-coded.

End Tag	Deprecated?	Browser Compatibility
Optional	No	Netscape 3+, IE 3+

`<p>`   Sets content in a paragraph format.
Attributes:

■ Standard attributes

align="left" | **"right"** | **"center"** | **"justify"** Sets the alignment of the paragraph text.

■ Dreamweaver Usage: Default paragraph format; Paragraph option of Format field in Property Inspector; Text | Paragraph Format | Paragraph.

End Tag	Deprecated?	Browser Compatibility
Optional	No, but alignment attribute has been deprecated in favor of style sheets	Netscape 3+, IE 3+

<param> **Passes values to an embedded object.**
Attributes:

■ Standard attributes

id="*id*" Unique identifier for the element.

name="*data*" Names the parameter so it can be called by an object.

value="*data*" Sets the value required by the parameter.

valuetype="data" | **"ref"** | **"object"** Identifies the type of parameter used in the **value** attribute.

type="*content-type*" Specifies the object's content type when the **valuetype** attribute is set to **ref**.

■ Dreamweaver Usage: Property Inspector for embedded object.

End Tag	Deprecated?	Browser Compatibility
Never	No	Netscape 3+, IE 3+

<pre> **Defines preformatted text, which enables the developer to add white space and line breaks within the text block.**
Attributes:

■ Standard attributes

■ Dreamweaver Usage: Format field of the Property Inspector; Text | Paragraph Format | Preformatted.

End Tag	Deprecated?	Browser Compatibility
Required	No	Netscape 3+, IE 3+

<q>   Designates text as a short, inline quotation.
Attributes:

- ■ Standard attributes

    cite= *"URL"* Links to a document containing information about the quotation.

- ■ Dreamweaver Usage: Must be hand-coded.

End Tag	Deprecated?	Browser Compatibility
Required	No	Netscape 3+, IE 3+

<s>   Strikethrough text style. Shows text was deleted.
Attributes:

- ■ Standard attributes

- ■ Dreamweaver Usage: Text | Style | Strikethrough.

End Tag	Deprecated?	Browser Compatibility
Required	Yes, in favor of style sheets	Netscape 3+, IE 3+

<samp>   Identifies sample output from a computer program or script. Used when providing instructions and how-tos, and displayed in monospace font.
Attributes:

- ■ Standard attributes

- ■ Dreamweaver Usage: Text | Style | Sample.

End Tag	Deprecated?	Browser Compatibility
Required	No	Netscape 3+, IE 3+

`<script>` **Inserts a script.**
Attributes:

> `charset="character-set"` Specifies the character encoding of the linked script.
>
> `type="content-type"` Specifies the content type of the script.
>
> `language="data"` Specifies the scripting language of the script. This has been deprecated.
>
> `src="URL"` Specifies the source of the external script.

- Dreamweaver Usage: Insert | Invisible Tags | Script; Script object from Invisibles category of the Objects panel.

End Tag	Deprecated?	Browser Compatibility
Required	No	Netscape 3+, IE 3+

`<select>` **Defines a list of values to be used for lists in forms.**
Attributes:

- Standard attributes

> `name="name"` Specifies a name for the control.
>
> `size="number"` Sets the number of choices to display in the list box.
>
> `multiple` Allows multiple selections from the list.
>
> `tabindex="number"` Sets the tabbing order for the list in relation to other form elements.

- Dreamweaver Usage: Insert | Form Objects | List/Menu; List/Menu object in Forms category of the Objects panel.

End Tag	Deprecated?	Browser Compatibility
Required	No	Netscape 3+, IE 3+

`<small>` **Displays smaller text style than surrounding text.**
Attributes:

- Standard attributes

- Dreamweaver Usage: Must be hand-coded.

End Tag	Deprecated?	Browser Compatibility
Required	No, but style sheets offer greater control	Netscape 3+, IE 3+

`<span>` **Creates a user-defined inline structure. Used primarily with the `class` attribute to apply styles to a selection.**
Attributes:

- Standard attributes

- Dreamweaver Usage: Make a selection in the Document window, and then apply a style from the CSS Styles panel.

End Tag	Deprecated?	Browser Compatibility
Required	No	Netscape 4+, IE 3+

`<strike>` **Displays text as strikethrough.**
Attributes:

- Standard attributes

- Dreamweaver Usage: Text | Style | Strikethrough.

End Tag	Deprecated?	Browser Compatibility
Required	Yes, in favor of style sheets	Netscape 3+, IE 3+

`<strong>` **Displays text with strong emphasis in relation to other text. Usually rendered in boldface.**
Attributes:

- Standard attributes

- Dreamweaver Usage: Text | Style | Strong.

End Tag	Deprecated?	Browser Compatibility
Required	No	Netscape 3+, IE 3+

`<style>` **Creates an embedded style sheet.**
Attributes:

- Internationalization attributes

  `type="content-type"` Specifies the type of the style language, such as text/css.

- Dreamweaver Usage: Added when creating embedded styles in the CSS Styles panel.

End Tag	Deprecated?	Browser Compatibility
Required	No	Netscape 4+, IE 3+

`<sub>` **Displays subscript text slightly lower than the baseline.**
Attributes:

- Standard attributes

- Dreamweaver Usage: Must be hand-coded.

End Tag	Deprecated?	Browser Compatibility
Required	No	Netscape 3+, IE 3+

`<sup>` **Displays superscript text slightly above the baseline.**
Attributes:

- Standard attributes

- Dreamweaver Usage: Must be hand-coded.

End Tag	Deprecated?	Browser Compatibility
Required	No	Netscape 3+, IE 3+

`<table>` **Inserts a table.**
Attributes:

- Standard attributes

  `width= "number"` Sets the width of the entire table, either as an absolute or as a percentage of the screen width.

  `border= "number"` Sets the width of the table border. A value of zero (0) removes all table borders.

  `cellspacing= "number"` Sets the spacing between cells.

  `cellpadding= "number"` Sets the spacing between the cell content and cell borders within the table.

- Dreamweaver Usage: Insert | Table; Table object in Objects panel.

End Tag	Deprecated?	Browser Compatibility
Required	No	Netscape 3+, IE 3+

`<tbody>` **Groups table rows.**
Attributes:

- Standard attributes

  `align="left"` | **`"right"`** | **`"center"`** | **`"justify"`** Sets the alignment of the cell contents.

  `valign="top"` | **`"bottom"`** | **`"middle"`** | **`"baseline"`** Sets the vertical alignment of the cell contents.

- Dreamweaver Usage: Must be hand-coded.

End Tag	Deprecated?	Browser Compatibility
Optional	No	IE 4+

`<td>` **Defines a table's data cell.**
Attributes:

- Standard attributes

  `align="left"` | **`"right"`** | **`"center"`** | **`"justify"`** Sets the alignment of the cell contents.

`valign="top"` | `"bottom"` | `"middle"` | `"baseline"` Sets the vertical alignment of the cell contents.

`rowspan= "number"` Sets the number of rows spanned by the current cell. The default is 1.

`colspan= "number"` Sets the number of columns spanned by the current cell. The default is 1.

`width= "number"` Sets the cell width.

`height= "number"` Sets the cell height.

- Dreamweaver Usage: Modify | Table; initial cells are created when inserting table.

End Tag	Deprecated?	Browser Compatibility
Optional	No	Netscape 3+, IE 3+

`<textarea>` **Creates a text input area in a form.**
Attributes:

- Standard attributes

`name= "name"` Sets a name for the control.

`tabindex= "number"` Sets the tabbing order for the control relative to other controls in the form.

`rows= "number"` Sets the number of visible rows in the text input box.

- Dreamweaver Usage: Insert | Form Objects; Text Field object in Forms category of the Objects panel.

End Tag	Deprecated?	Browser Compatibility
Required	No	Netscape 3+, IE 3+

`<tfoot>` **Groups table rows into a table footer.**
Attributes:

- Standard attributes

`align="left"` | `"right"` | `"center"` | `"justify"` Sets the alignment of the cell contents.

`valign="top"` | `"bottom"` | `"middle"` | `"baseline"` Sets the vertical alignment of the cell contents.

■ Dreamweaver Usage: Must be hand-coded.

End Tag	Deprecated?	Browser Compatibility
Optional	No	Netscape 3+, IE 3+

`<th>` Defines a table cell as serving the role of a header for a column or row.
Attributes:

■ Standard attributes

`align="left"` | `"right"` | `"center"` | `"justify"` Sets the alignment of the cell contents.

`valign="top"` | `"bottom"` | `"middle"` | `"baseline"` Sets the vertical alignment of the cell contents.

`scope=" row"` | `"col"` | `"rowgroup"` | `"colgroup"` Specifies the group of cells which is defined by the header cell.

`nowrap` Disables text-wrapping in the cell. This has been deprecated.

`bgcolor= "color"` Sets the background color for the cell.

`width= "number"` Sets the width of the cell.

`height= "number"` Sets the height of the cell.

■ Dreamweaver Usage: Must be hand-coded.

End Tag	Deprecated?	Browser Compatibility
Optional	No	Netscape 3+, IE 3+

`<thead>` Groups a table row or rows into a table header.
Attributes:

■ Standard attributes

`align="left"` | `"right"` | `"center"` | `"justify"` Sets the alignment of the cell contents.

`valign="top"` | `"bottom"` | `"middle"` | `"baseline"` Sets the vertical alignment of the cell contents.

■ Dreamweaver Usage: Must be hand-coded.

End Tag	Deprecated?	Browser Compatibility
Optional	No	IE 3+

`<title>` **Titles the document. Title appears in the title bar of the browser window and is used by search engines.**
Attributes:

■ Internationalization attributes

■ Dreamweaver Usage: Title field in Document window toolbar; Modify | Page Properties.

End Tag	Deprecated?	Browser Compatibility
Required	No	Netscape 3+, IE 3+

`<tr>` **Defines a table row.**
Attributes:

■ Standard attributes

`align="left"` | `"right"` | `"center"` | `"justify"` Sets the alignment of the cell contents.

`valign="top"` | `"bottom"` | `"middle"` | `"baseline"` Sets the vertical alignment of the cell contents.

■ Dreamweaver Usage: Modify | Table; initial settings determined when inserting table.

End Tag	Deprecated?	Browser Compatibility
Optional	No	Netscape 3+, IE 3+

<tt> **Displays text in teletype or monospaced style.**
Attributes:

- Standard attributes

- Dreamweaver Usage: Text | Style | Teletype.

End Tag	Deprecated?	Browser Compatibility
Required	No, but style sheets provide greater control	Netscape 3+, IE 3+

<u> **Underlined text style.**
Attributes:

- Standard attributes

- Dreamweaver Usage: Underline button in Property Inspector; Text | Style | Underline.

End Tag	Deprecated?	Browser Compatibility
Required	Yes, in favor of style sheets	Netscape 3+, IE 3+

<ul> **Unordered list.**
Attributes:

- Standard attributes

   type="disc" | **"square"** | **"circle"** Sets the bullet style for the list.

■ Dreamweaver Usage: Unordered list button in Property Inspector; Text | List | Unordered List.

End Tag	Deprecated?	Browser Compatibility
Required	No	Netscape 3+, IE 3+

<var> **Instance of a variable or program argument. Distinguishes the variable from other programming code.**
Attributes:

■ Standard attributes

■ Dreamweaver Usage: Must be hand-coded.

End Tag	Deprecated?	Browser Compatibility
Required	No	Netscape 3+, IE 3+

The
Complete
Reference

Appendix C

Cascading Style
Sheet Properties

947

The CSS Properties listed here have been loosely grouped to correspond with the Style Definition dialog box in Dreamweaver. These tables also contain related styles that aren't included in Dreamweaver's options, but can be hand-coded or added using a third-party CSS application. For more information about CSS, see Chapter 17.

Along with the values listed in these tables, all these properties can use the inherit value, which assigns the same values to the element as the parent element.

> **Note**   *Although browser support is listed here, it's subject to change as Netscape and Internet Explorer follow the increased demand for CSS support.*

Text Properties

Property	Description	Values	Browser Support
color	Sets the color of text	color	Netscape 4 IE 3
direction	Sets the text direction	ltr rtl	IE 5
font	A shorthand property for setting all the font properties in one declaration	font style font variant font weight font size font family caption	Netscape 4 IE 4
font-family	A list of font families and categories to apply to the text	family name font category	Netscape 4 IE 3
font-size	Sets the font size	xx-small x-small small medium large x-large xx-large smaller larger specific measurement	Netscape 4 IE 3

Property	Description	Values	Browser Support
font-style	Sets the font style	normal italic oblique	Netscape 4 IE 4
font-variant	Displays text in sm all-caps or normally	normal small-caps	Netscape 6 IE 4
font-weight	Sets the boldness of the text	normal bold bolder lighter 100 200 300 400 500 600 700 800 900	Netscape 4 IE 3
line-height	Sets the distance between lines	normal number length percentage	Netscape 4 IE 3
text-decoration	Sets additional text decoration	none underline overline line-through blink	Netscape 4 IE 3
text-transform	Controls the letters in an element	none capitalize uppercase lowercase	Netscape 4 IE 4

Background Properties

Property	Description	Values	Browser Support
background	A shorthand property to set all background properties with one declaration	background color background image background repeat background attachment background position	Netscape 6 IE 3
background-attachment	Sets whether a background image is fixed or scrolls	scroll fixed	Netscape 6 IE 4
background-color	Sets the element's background color	color	Netscape 4 IE 4
background-image	Sets a background image	URL none	Netscape 4 IE 4
background-position	Sets the background image's position	top left top center top right center left center center right bottom left bottom center bottom right specific coordinates	Netscape 6 IE 4
background-repeat	Sets the background tiling	repeat repeat-x repeat-y no-repeat	Netscape 4 IE 4

Block Properties

Property	Description	Values	Browser Support
letter-spacing	Sets the spacing between characters	normal length	Netscape 6 IE 4
text-align	Aligns the text in an element	left right center justify	Netscape 4 IE 3
text-indent	Indents the first line of text	length percentage	Netscape 4 IE 3
vertical-align	Sets the vertical alignment	baseline sub super top text-top middle bottom text-bottom percentage relative to baseline	Netscape 4 IE 4
white-space	Specifies how to treat white space within the element	normal pre nowrap	Netscape 4 IE 5.5
word-spacing	Sets the spacing between words	normal length	Netscape 6

Box Properties

Property	Description	Values	Browser Support
clear	Sets the sides of an element where other floating elements aren't allowed	left right both none	Netscape 4 IE 4

Property	Description	Values	Browser Support
float	Sets where an image or a text appears in another element	left right none	Netscape 4 IE 4
height	Sets the height of an element	auto length percentage	Netscape 6 IE 4
margin	A shorthand property to set all the element's margin properties in one declaration	top margin bottom margin left margin right margin	Netscape 4 IE 4
margin-bottom	Sets the element's bottom margin	auto length percentage	Netscape 4 IE 4
margin-left	Sets the element's left margin	auto length percentage	Netscape 4 IE 3
margin-right	Sets the element's right margin	auto length percentage	Netscape 4 IE 3
margin-top	Sets the element's top margin of an element	auto length percentage	Netscape 4 IE 3
width	Sets the width of an element	auto percentage length	Netscape 4 IE 4

Border Properties

Property	Description	Values	Browser Support
border	A shorthand property to set all the border properties in one declaration	border width border style border color	Netscape 4 IE 4

Property	Description	Values	Browser Support
border-bottom	A shorthand property to set all the bottom border properties in one declaration	border width border style border color	Netscape 6 IE 4
border-bottom-color	Sets the color of the bottom border	border color	Netscape 6 IE 4
border-bottom-style	Sets the style of the bottom border	border style	Netscape 6 IE 4
border-bottom-width	Sets the width of the bottom border	thin medium thick length	Netscape 4 IE 4
border-color	Sets border colors	color	Netscape 6 IE 4
border-left	A shorthand property to set all the left border properties in one declaration	border width border style border color	Netscape 6 IE 4
border-left-color	Sets the color of the left border	border color	Netscape 6 IE 4
border-left-style	Sets the style of the left border	border style	Netscape 6 IE 4
border-left-width	Sets the left border width	thin medium thick length	Netscape 4 IE 4
border-right	A shorthand property to set all the right border properties in one declaration	border width border style border color	Netscape 6 IE 4
border-right-color	Sets the color of the right border	border color	Netscape 6 IE 4

Property	Description	Values	Browser Support
border-right-style	Sets the style of the right border	border style	Netscape 6 IE 4
border-right-width	Sets the width of the right border	thin medium thick length	Netscape 4 IE 4
border-style	Sets the style of the borders	none hidden dotted dashed solid double groove ridge inset outset	Netscape 6 IE 4
border-top	A shorthand property to set all the top border properties in one declaration	border width border style border color	Netscape 6 IE 4
border-top-color	Sets the color of the top border	border color	Netscape 6 IE 4
border-top-style	Sets the style of the top border	border style	Netscape 6 IE 4
border-top-width	Sets the width of the top border	thin medium thick length	Netscape 4 IE 4
border-width	A shorthand property to set all the border widths in one declaration	thin medium thick length	Netscape 4 IE 4
padding	A shorthand property to set all the padding properties in one declaration	top padding bottom padding left padding right padding	Netscape 4 IE 4

Property	Description	Values	Browser Support
padding-bottom	Sets the element's bottom padding	length percentage	Netscape 4 IE 4
padding-left	Sets the element's left padding	length percentage	Netscape 4 IE 4
padding-right	Sets the element's right padding	length percentage	Netscape 4 IE 4
padding-top	Sets the element's top padding	length percentage	Netscape 4 IE 4

List Properties

Property	Description	Values	Browser Support
list-style	A shorthand property to set the list properties in one declaration	bullet type position bullet image	Netscape 6 IE 4
list-style-image	Sets an image as the list-item marker	none URL	Netscape 6 IE 4
list-style-position	Sets where the list-item marker is placed in the list	inside outside	Netscape 6 IE 4
list-style-type	Sets the type of the list-item marker	none disc circle square decimal lower-roman upper-roman lower-alpha upper-alpha	Netscape 4 IE 4

▣ Positioning Properties

Property	Description	Values	Browser Support
bottom	Sets the bottom position of the layer	auto percentage length	IE 5
clip	Sets the clipping area for overflowed sections	auto rect inherit	Netscape 6 IE 4
display	Sets how/if an element is displayed	none inline block list-item run-in compact marker table inline-table table-row-group table-header-group table-footer-group table-row table-column-group table-column table-cell table-caption	Netscape 4 IE 4
left	Sets the offset width from the left edge of the parent element	auto percentage length	Netscape 4 IE 4

Property	Description	Values	Browser Support
overflow	Sets what happens if the content overflows its area	visible hidden scroll auto	Netscape 6 IE 4
position	Sets the method for positioning	static relative absolute fixed	Netscape 4 IE 4
right	Sets the offset width from the right edge of the parent element	auto percentage length	IE 5
top	Sets the offset width from the top edge of the parent element	auto percentage length	Netscape 4 IE 4
visibility	Sets the visibility of an element	visible hidden collapse	Netscape 6 IE 4
z-index	Sets the stack order of an element in relation to other elements in the stack	auto number	Netscape 6 IE 4

Extensions Properties

Property	Description	Values	Browser Support
text-shadow		none color length	None
cursor	Defines the appearance of the cursor when it's moused over an element	URL auto crosshair default pointer move e-resize ne-resize nw-resize n-resize se-resize sw-resize s-resize w-resize text wait help	Netscape 6 IE 4

The Complete Reference

Dreamweaver 4

Appendix D

Fireworks Keyboard Shortcuts

This appendix lists the keyboard shortcuts that can be used instead of menu items or buttons in Fireworks. These keyboard shortcuts are Firework's default settings. You can change the shortcut keys and add shortcuts to commands not listed here by choosing the Edit | Keyboard Shortcuts menu in Fireworks.

File Menu

Action	Windows	Macintosh
New image	CTRL-N	COMMAND-N
Open image file	CTRL-O	COMMAND-O
Close file	CTRL-W	COMMAND-W
Save	CTRL-S	COMMAND-S
Save as	CTRL-SHIFT-S	COMMAND-SHIFT-S
Import	CTRL-R	COMMAND-R
Export	CTRL-SHIFT-R	COMMAND-SHIFT-R
Export Preview	CTRL-SHIFT-X	COMMAND-SHIFT-X
Preview in Browser	F12	F12
Preview in Secondary Browser	SHIFT-F12	SHIFT-F12
Print	CTRL-P	COMMAND-P
Exit (Quit)	CTRL-Q	COMMAND-Q

Edit Menu

Action	Windows	Macintosh
Undo	CTRL-Z	COMMAND-Z
Redo	CTRL-Y or CTRL-SHIFT-Z	COMMAND-Y or COMMAND-SHIFT-Z
Cut	CTRL-X or SHIFT-DEL	COMMAND-X or SHIFT-DEL

Action	Windows	Macintosh
Copy	CTRL-C or CTRL-INS	COMMAND-C or COMMAND-INS
Paste	CTRL-V or SHIFT-INS	COMMAND-V or SHIFT-INS
Clear	DELETE	DELETE
Paste Inside	CTRL-SHIFT-V	COMMAND-SHIFT-V
Paste Attributes	CTRL-ALT-SHIFT-V	COMMAND-OPTION-SHIFT-V
Select All	CTRL-A	COMMAND-A
Deselect	CTRL-D	COMMAND-D
Duplicate	CTRL-ALT-D	COMMAND-OPTION-D
Clone	CTRL-SHIFT-D	COMMAND-SHIFT-D
Find and Replace	CTRL-F	COMMAND-F
Preferences	CTRL-U	COMMAND-U

View Menu

Action	Windows	Macintosh
Zoom In	CTRL-+ (Plus)	COMMAND-+ (Plus)
Zoom Out	CTRL- – (Hyphen)	COMMAND- – (Hyphen)
Magnification	CTRL-(number 1–8, with the exception of 7)	COMMAND-(number 1–8)
Fit Selection	CTRL-ALT-0	COMMAND-OPTION-O
Fit All	CTRL-0	COMMAND-O
Full Display	CTRL-K	COMMAND-K
Hide Selection	CTRL-L	COMMAND-L
Show All	CTRL-SHIFT-L	COMMAND-SHIFT-L
Toggle Ruler	CTRL-ALT-R	COMMAND-OPTION-R
Show Grid	CTRL-ALT-G	COMMAND-OPTION-G

Action	Windows	Macintosh
Snap To Grid	CTRL-ALT-SHIFT-G	COMMAND-OPTION-SHIFT-G
Toggle Show Guides	CTRL-;	COMMAND-;
Lock Guides	CTRL-ALT-;	COMMAND-OPTION-;
Snap to Guides	CTRL-SHIFT-;	COMMAND-SHIFT-;
Slice Guides	CTRL-ALT-SHIFT-;	COMMAND-OPTION-SHIFT-;
Hide Edges	F9	F9
Toggle Hide Panels	F4, TAB	F4, TAB

Insert Menu

Action	Windows	Macintosh
New Symbol	CTRL-F8	COMMAND-F8
Convert to Symbol	F8	F8
Hotspot	CTRL-SHIFT-U	COMMAND-SHIFT-U
Slice	ALT-SHIFT-U	OPTION-SHIFT-U

Modify Menu

Action	Windows	Macintosh
Trim Canvas	CTRL-ALT-T	COMMAND-OPTION-T
Fit Canvas	CTRL-ALT-F	COMMAND-OPTION-F
Animate Selection	ALT-SHIFT-F8	OPTION-SHIFT-F8

Action	Windows	Macintosh
Tween Instances	CTRL-ALT-SHIFT-T	COMMAND-OPTION-SHIFT-T
Edit Bitmap	CTRL-E	COMMAND-E
Exit Bitmap Mode	CTRL-SHIFT-E	COMMAND-SHIFT-E
Marquee: Select Inverse	CTRL-SHIFT-I	COMMAND-SHIFT-I
Convert to Bitmap	CTRL-ALT-SHIFT-Z	COMMAND-OPTION-SHIFT-Z
Numeric Transform	CTRL-SHIFT-T	COMMAND-SHIFT-T
Rotate 90 degrees Clockwise	CTRL-9	COMMAND-9
Rotate 90 degrees Counter-clockwise	CTRL-7	COMMAND-7
Bring to Front	CTRL-SHIFT-UP	COMMAND-SHIFT-UP
Bring Forward	CTRL-UP	COMMAND-UP
Send Backward	CTRL-DOWN	COMMAND-DOWN
Send to Back	CTRL-SHIFT-DOWN	COMMAND-SHIFT-DOWN
Align Left	CTRL-ALT-1	COMMAND-OPTION-1
Center Vertically	CTRL-ALT-2	COMMAND-OPTION-2
Align Right	CTRL-ALT-3	COMMAND-OPTION-3
Align Top	CTRL-ALT-4	COMMAND-OPTION-4
Center Horizontally	CTRL-ALT-5	COMMAND-OPTION-5
Align Bottom	CTRL-ALT-6	COMMAND-OPTION-6
Distribute Widths	CTRL-ALT-7	COMMAND-OPTION-7
Distribute Heights	CTRL-ALT-8	COMMAND-OPTION-8
Join	CTRL-J	COMMAND-J
Split	CTRL-SHIFT-J	COMMAND-SHIFT-J
Group	CTRL-G	COMMAND-G
Ungroup	CTRL-SHIFT-G	COMMAND-SHIFT-G

Text Menu

Action	Windows	Macintosh
Bold Style	CTRL-B	COMMAND-B
Italics Style	CTRL-I	COMMAND-I
Align Left	CTRL-ALT-SHIFT-L	COMMAND-OPTION-SHIFT-L
Center Horizontally	CTRL-ALT-SHIFT-C	COMMAND-OPTION-SHIFT-C
Align Right	CTRL-ALT-SHIFT-R	COMMAND-OPTION-SHIFT-R
Justified	CTRL-ALT-SHIFT-J	COMMAND-OPTION-SHIFT-J
Stretched	CTRL-ALT-SHIFT-S	COMMAND-OPTION-SHIFT-S
Attach to Path	CTRL-SHIFT-Y	COMMAND-SHIFT-Y
Convert to Paths	CTRL-SHIFT-P	COMMAND-SHIFT-P

Window Menu

Action	Windows	Macintosh
New Window	CTRL-ALT-N	COMMAND-OPTION-N
Toggle Stroke Panel	CTRL-ALT-F4	COMMAND-OPTION-F4
Toggle Fill Panel	SHIFT-F7	SHIFT-F7
Toggle Effect Panel	ALT-F7	OPTION-F7
Toggle Info Panel	ALT-SHIFT-F12	OPTION-SHIFT-F12
Toggle Object Panel	ALT-F2	OPTION-F2
Toggle Behaviors Panel	SHIFT-F3	SHIFT-F3
Toggle Color Mixer	SHIFT-F9	SHIFT-F9
Toggle Swatches	CTRL-F9	COMMAND-F9
Toggle Tool Options	CTRL-ALT-O	COMMAND-OPTION-O
Toggle Layers Panel	F2	F2
Toggle Frames Panel	SHIFT-F2	SHIFT-F2

Action	Windows	Macintosh
Toggle History Panel	SHIFT-F10	SHIFT-F10
Toggle Styles Panel	SHIFT-F11	SHIFT-F11
Toggle Library	F11	F11
Toggle URL Panel	ALT-SHIFT-F10	OPTION-SHIFT-F10
Find and Replace	CTRL-F	COMMAND-F

Help Menu

Action	Windows	Macintosh
Using Fireworks	F1	F1

Tool Selection

Action	Windows	Macintosh
Pointer Tool	*V* or 0 (zero)	*V* or 0 (zero)
Select Behind Tool	*V* or 0 (zero)	*V* or 0 (zero)
Export Area	*J*	*J*
Subselection Tool	*A* or 1	*A* or 1
Marquee Tool	*M*	*M*
Oval Marquee Tool	*M*	*M*
Lasso Tool	*L*	*L*
Polygon Lasso Tool	*L*	*L*
Crop Tool	*C*	*C*
Magic Wand Tool	*W*	*W*
Line Tool	*N*	*N*

Action	Windows	Macintosh
Pen Tool	P	P
Rectangle Tool	R	R
Rounded Rectangle Tool	R	R
Ellipse Tool	R	R
Polygon Tool	G	G
Text Tool	T	T
Pencil Tool	Y	Y
Brush Tool	B	B
Redraw Path Tool	B	B
Scale Tool	Q	Q
Skew Tool	Q	Q
Distort Tool	Q	Q
Freeform Tool	F	F
Reshape Area Tool	F	F
Path Scrubber Tool (additive)	U	U
Path Scrubber Tool (subtractive)	U	U
Eyedropper Tool	I	I
Paint Bucket Tool	K	K
Eraser Tool	E	E
Rubber Stamp Tool	S	S
Hand Tool	H	H
Zoom Tool	Z	Z
Hide/Show Slices	2	2
Set Default Brush/Fill Colors	D	D
Swap Brush/Fill Colors	X	X

Miscellaneous

Action	Windows	Macintosh
Clone and Nudge Down	ALT-DOWN	OPTION-DOWN
Clone and Nudge Down Large	ALT-SHIFT-DOWN	OPTION-SHIFT-DOWN
Clone and Nudge Left	ALT-LEFT	OPTION-LEFT
Clone and Nudge Left Large	ALT-SHIFT-LEFT	OPTION-SHIFT-LEFT
Clone and Nudge Right	ALT-RIGHT	OPTION-RIGHT
Clone and Nudge Right Large	ALT-SHIFT-RIGHT	OPTION-SHIFT-RIGHT
Clone and Nudge Up	ALT-UP	OPTION-UP
Clone and Nudge Up Large	ALT-SHIFT-UP	OPTION-SHIFT-UP
Fill Pixel Selection	ALT-BACKSPACE	OPTION-BACKSPACE
Next Frame	PAGE DOWN/CTRL-PAGE DOWN	PAGE DOWN/CONTROL-PAGE DOWN
Nudge Down	DOWN	DOWN
Nudge Down Large	SHIFT-DOWN	SHIFT-DOWN
Nudge Left	LEFT	LEFT
Nudge Left Large	SHIFT-LEFT	SHIFT-LEFT
Nudge Right	RIGHT	RIGHT
Nudge Right Large	SHIFT-RIGHT	SHIFT-RIGHT
Nudge Up	UP	UP
Nudge Up Large	SHIFT-UP	SHIFT-UP
Paste Inside	CTRL-SHIFT-V	COMMAND-SHIFT-V
Play Animation	CTRL-ALT-P	COMMAND-OPTION-P
Previous Frame	PAGE UP/CTRL-PAGE UP	PAGE UP/CONTROL-PAGE UP

Index

D

Q

X

Y

Z

INTERNATIONAL CONTACT INFORMATION

AUSTRALIA
McGraw-Hill Book Company Australia Pty. Ltd.
TEL +61-2-9417-9899
FAX +61-2-9417-5687
http://www.mcgraw-hill.com.au
books-it_sydney@mcgraw-hill.com

CANADA
McGraw-Hill Ryerson Ltd.
TEL +905-430-5000
FAX +905-430-5020
http://www.mcgrawhill.ca

GREECE, MIDDLE EAST,
NORTHERN AFRICA
McGraw-Hill Hellas
TEL +30-1-656-0990-3-4
FAX +30-1-654-5525

MEXICO (Also serving Latin America)
McGraw-Hill Interamericana Editores S.A. de C.V.
TEL +525-117-1583
FAX +525-117-1589
http://www.mcgraw-hill.com.mx
fernando_castellanos@mcgraw-hill.com

SINGAPORE (Serving Asia)
McGraw-Hill Book Company
TEL +65-863-1580
FAX +65-862-3354
http://www.mcgraw-hill.com.sg
mghasia@mcgraw-hill.com

SOUTH AFRICA
McGraw-Hill South Africa
TEL +27-11-622-7512
FAX +27-11-622-9045
robyn_swanepoel@mcgraw-hill.com

UNITED KINGDOM & EUROPE
(Excluding Southern Europe)
McGraw-Hill Education Europe
TEL +44-1-628-502500
FAX +44-1-628-770224
http://www.mcgraw-hill.co.uk
computing_neurope@mcgraw-hill.com

ALL OTHER INQUIRIES Contact:
Osborne/McGraw-Hill
TEL +1-510-549-6600
FAX +1-510-883-7600
http://www.osborne.com
omg_international@mcgraw-hill.com